FUNDAMENTALS OF
OPERATIONS MANAGEMENT

THE IRWIN/MCGRAW-HILL SERIES

Operations and Decision Sciences

OPERATIONS MANAGEMENT

Bowersox and Closs
Logistical Management: The Integrated Supply Chain Process
First Edition

Chase, Aquilano, and Jacobs
Production and Operations Management
Eighth Edition

Chu, Hottenstein, and Greenlaw
PROSIM for Windows
Third Edition

Cohen and Apte
Manufacturing Automation
First Edition

Davis, Aquilano, and Chase
Fundamentals of Operations Management
Third Edition

Dilworth
Operations Management
Second Edition

Dobler
Purchasing and Supply Management
Sixth Edition

Flaherty
Global Operations Management
First Edition

Fitzsimmons and Fitzsimmons
Service Management: Operations, Strategy, Information Technology
Second Edition

Hill
Manufacturing Strategy: Text & Cases
Second Edition

Hopp and Spearman
Factory Physics
First Edition

Lambert and Stock
Strategic Logistics Management
Third Edition

Leenders and Fearon
Purchasing and Supply Chain Management
Eleventh Edition

Lotfi and Pegels
Decision Support Systems for Operations & Management Science
Third Edition

Melnyk and Denzler
Operations Management
First Edition

Moses and Seshadri
HOM Operations Management Software for Windows
First Edition

Nahmias
Production and Operations Analysis
Third Edition

Nicholas
Competitive Manufacturing Management
First Edition

Pinedo and Chao
Operations Scheduling
First Edition

Sanderson and Uzumeri
Managing Product Families
First Edition

Schroeder
Operations Management
Fourth Edition

Schonberger and Knod
Operations Management: Customer-Focused Principles
Sixth Edition

Stevenson
Production/Operations Management
Sixth Edition

Vollmann, Berry, and Whybark
Manufacturing Planning & Control Systems
Fourth Edition

Zipkin
Foundations of Inventory Management
First Edition

QUANTITATIVE METHODS AND MANAGEMENT SCIENCE

Bodily, Carraway, Frey, and Pfeifer
Quantitative Business Analysis: Casebook
First Edition

Bodily, Carraway, Frey, and Pfeifer
Quantitative Business Analysis: Text and Cases
First Edition

Bonini, Hausman, and Bierman
Quantitative Analysis for Business Decisions
Ninth Edition

Hesse
Managerial Spreadsheet Modeling and Analysis
First Edition

Lotfi and Pegels
Decision Support Systems for Operations and Management Science
Third Edition

Stevenson
Introduction to Management Science
Second Edition

Third Edition

FUNDAMENTALS OF
OPERATIONS MANAGEMENT

MARK M. DAVIS
Bentley College

NICHOLAS J. AQUILANO
The University of Arizona

RICHARD B. CHASE
University of Southern California

Boston   Burr Ridge, IL   Dubuque, IA   Madison, WI   New York   San Francisco   St. Louis
Bangkok   Bogotá   Caracas   Lisbon   London   Madrid
Mexico City   Milan   New Delhi   Seoul   Singapore   Sydney   Taipei   Toronto

Irwin/McGraw-Hill

A Division of The **McGraw·Hill** *Companies*

Domestic: 1 2 3 4 5 6 7 8 9 0 VNH/VNH 9 3 2 1 0 9 8
International: 1 2 3 4 5 6 7 8 9 0 VNH/VNH 9 3 2 1 0 9 8

ISBN 0-256-22557-5

Vice president/Editorial director: *Michael W. Junior*
Publisher: *Jeffrey J. Shelstad*
Senior sponsoring editor: *Scott Isenberg*
Senior developmental editor: *Gail Korosa*
Senior marketing manager: *Colleen J. Suljic*
Senior project manager: *Susan Trentacosti*
Senior production supervisor: *Heather D. Burbridge*
Freelance design coordinator: *Laurie J. Entringer*
Cover illustrator: *Andy Davis*
Senior photo research coordinator: *Keri Johnson*
Photo research: *Connie Gardner*
Supplement coordinator: *Becky Szura*
Compositor: *Interactive Composition Corporation*
Typeface: *10/12 Times Roman*
Printer: *Von Hoffmann Press, Inc.*

Library of Congress Cataloging-in-Publication Data

Davis, Mark M. (date)
    Fundamentals of operations management / Mark M. Davis, Nicholas J. Aquilano, Richard B. Chase. -- 3rd ed.
      p. cm. -- (Irwin/McGraw-Hill series in operations and decision sciences)
    Includes index.
    ISBN 0-256-22557-5
    1. Production management. I. Aquilano, Nicholas J. II. Chase Richard B. III. Title. IV. Series.
TS155.D248   1999
    658.5--dc21   98-40391

INTERNATIONAL EDITION
Copyright © 1999. Exclusive rights by The McGraw-Hill Companies, Inc. For manufacture and export. This book cannot be re-exported from the country to which it is consigned by McGraw-Hill. The International Edition is not available in North America.

When ordering this title, use ISBN 0-07-115694-1

http://www.mhhe.com

To our wives
Cookie, Nina, and Harriet

And to our children
Andy and Alex
Don, Kara, and Mark
Laurie, Andy, Glenn, and Rob

Preface

As we enter the 21st century, we must recognize the need for compatibility between the constantly changing environment in which we operate and how we will produce goods and services for our customers. Barriers to trade across national borders continue to be lowered with the creation of regional free trade zones such as the European Union (EU) and the establishment of the North American Free Trade Agreement (NAFTA); this trend is expected to continue into the foreseeable future. As a result, the world is quickly shrinking to a single *global village* or *global landscape*—facilitated in large part by the rapid advances in information technology. Similarly, the field of operations management must change to address these global issues while simultaneously incorporating this new technology.

Goals

Our goals in preparing this third edition were to:

- Introduce new and relevant concepts in operations management that are now recognized as important factors in businesses that are successful. These include yield management (Chapters 13 and 14), which focuses on maximizing capacity utilization and profits in service operations, and supply chain management (Chapter 11), which addresses both the changing role of the supplier and the fact that supply chains are becoming longer as firms now look to the four corners of the world for suppliers.
- Recognize that the operations function in every organization involves individuals and that their role is changing as are the organizations themselves. As part of these changes, there is an increasing emphasis on teamwork (Chapters 9 and 10).
- Demonstrate how operations management needs to be integrally related and aligned with the other functional areas within an organization, and that many of the operations management tools are being applied in these other functional areas, such as marketing, engineering, and finance. For example, business process analysis can show engineering managers how to accelerate the development and introduction of new products (Chapters 3 and 4), and just-in-time (JIT) concepts (Chapter 12) are used to market mass-customized products that can be delivered to customers with minimal delays. These tools and techniques from operations management are also now used in a wide variety of new applications that go far beyond the walls of the traditional factory. As an illustration, quality management tools such as statistical process control (SPC) are now used to predict impending medical problems for patients with asthma or congestive heart failure.

We tried to do this in a brief and interesting way, focusing on core concepts and utilizing quantitative techniques only where necessary and to make the mathematics intuitive and less formal.

Special Features of the Book

In an attempt to facilitate the learning process, we incorporated several pedagogical features including:

- *Chapter objectives.* At the beginning of each chapter a list of objectives is presented to highlight the important concepts on which the chapter focuses.

- *Vignettes.* Each chapter opens with a short vignette that sets the stage and piques student interest for the chapter material.
- *Application of OM concepts.* Examples of how many of the OM concepts presented in this text are applied in actual business situations are provided throughout the text. The use of real-world examples reinforces the critical role of operations management, showing how it contributes to the overall success of an organization. These applications take several forms, including the opening vignette to each chapter and Operations Management in Practice boxes, as well as in the numerous examples that are included throughout the text itself.

- *Internet exercises.* The Internet has become a powerful tool for obtaining and disseminating information, and this information is constantly changing. Where appropriate, an Internet exercise titled Internet Update is provided at the end of a chapter to encourage students to obtain the latest information on a particular topic.
- *The application of Excel® spreadsheets.* Again, where appropriate, examples are provided using Excel® spreadsheets that encourage the student to explore alternative solutions.

- *Highlighting links with other functional areas.* Ideas and processes flow easily across traditional functional boundaries in successful organizations, often to the point where it is practically impossible to determine where one function leaves off and another begins. To emphasize this integration within organizations, icons are used throughout the text to highlight examples of how OM is linked to other functional areas.

- *Service industry integration.* We have continued our emphasis on balancing both manufacturing and service operations in the text. Specific icons are used to highlight service examples and applications.

- *Global perspective.* Another emphasis of the book is a stress on the global impact of operations today; where appropriate, we show how the concepts apply in a global context. Special icons are used in the book to highlight this area.
- *Margin definitions.* Key terms are in boldface when first defined and definitions added in the margin. At the end of the chapter these key terms are listed with page numbers for quick student reference.
- *Full-color art.* This third edition includes photos and exhibits to enhance the visual appeal and interest of students, to clarify and extend the text discussions, and to help students see operations in action.
- *Examples with solutions.* Examples follow quantitative topics and demonstrate specific procedures and techniques. These are clearly set off from the text and help students understand the computations.
- *Formula review.* Key formulas and equations are numbered within each of the more quantitative chapters and are repeated in summary form at the end of those chapters for easy student review.
- *Solved problems.* Representative example problems are included at the end of appropriate chapters. Each includes a detailed, worked-out solution and provides another level of support for students before they try homework problems on their own.
- *Review and discussion questions.* These questions allow students to review the chapter concepts before attempting the problems and provide a basis for classroom discussion. Suggested responses are included in the Instructor's Manual.
- *Problems.* A wide range of problem material follows each chapter asking students to solve realistic, interesting problems.

- *Cases.* Located at the end of most chapters, short cases allow students to think critically about issues discussed in the chapter. These can also provide good classroom discussions or provide a capstone problem for the chapter. We've included both long and short cases such as Kristen's Cookie Company from Harvard.

Ancillary Materials

- *Student CD-ROM,* packaged with each copy of the text, contains Excel® spreadsheets, PowerPoint® slides, video glossary with over 50 short video clips illustrating key operations topics, and chapter quizzes.
- *Study Guide,* prepared by Marilyn Helms of the University of Tennessee at Chattanooga, provides students with a summary of each chapter, glossary of key terms, chapter exams, and solved problems that parallel text problems.
- *Instructor's Manual,* prepared by Ross Fink of Bradley University, includes answers to discussion and review questions and solutions to text problems. There is a useful reference grid showing which problems correspond to specific topics in the chapters for ease in assignment.
- *Test Bank,* prepared by Steve DeLurgio of the University of Missouri—Kansas City, provides true/false, multiple/choice, and narrative problems for each chapter. Along with the manual, a separate computerized testing package is available allowing instructors to generate, add, and edit questions; save and reload tests; and select questions based on type or level of difficulty.
- *PowerPoint Presentation Slides,* prepared by Mark M. Davis, provides lecture outlines plus graphic material from the text to complement and customize lectures.
- *Videos.* **The Irwin Operations Management Video Series** consists of 21 segments (each about 12 minutes long) on five volumes covering quality, inventory, lean production, computer-integrated manufacturing, production processes and services, and global supply chains. They show students chapter concepts at work and how critical operations management is to organizations such as Motorola, Toyota, Hewlett-Packard, and United Airlines.
- *Operations Management Center Web site* (*http://www.mhhe.com/pom/*). This site supports students and faculty in search of resources related to all aspects of operations management. There are sites with company tours, organizations, on-line publications, resources by topic, and textbook support.
- *Instructor's Presentation CD-ROM* is an interactive lecture aid, putting over 50 video clips, PowerPoint slides, all text exhibits, and print supplements at your fingertips. The presentation manager allows instructors to create customized multimedia lectures easily.

We have also tried to practice what we preach. In applying the quality concept of continuous improvement, we have attempted to incorporate many of the suggestions made by our reviewers.

There is an old Chinese proverb that states, "May you live in interesting times." Like it or not, from an operations management perspective, those "times" are now and we should take full advantage of the opportunity—and enjoy it while doing so!

Acknowledgments

Although only three names appear on the cover of this book, a project of this magnitude could not be successfully completed without the assistance and cooperation of many individuals. Specifically, we would like to thank the reviewers for their evaluation of the second edition text and for their manuscript reviews. We thank them for their suggestions and comments. They include:

Stephen Chapman, *North Carolina State University*

Joe Felan, *Baylor University*

Rhonda Lummus, *Central Missouri State University*

Kamran Moinzadeh, *University of Washington*

Jaideep Motwani, *Grand Valley State University*

Philip Musa, *Texas Tech University*

Nada Sanders, *Wright State University*

Paul Schikora, *Indiana University*

Madeline Thimmes, *Utah State University*

Constantin Vaitsos, *University of Southern California*

Joel Wisner, *University of Nevada—Las Vegas*

Several chapters were rewritten with the assistance of colleagues. Specifically we would like to acknowledge the following individuals for their contributions to this third edition:

Vicki LaFarge, *Bentley College* (Chapter 9 on Human Resource Issues in Operations Management)

Janelle Heineke, *Boston University* (Chapter 5 on Quality Management and Supplement 5 on Statistical Quality Control Methods)

Hans Thamhain, *Bentley College* (Chapter 10 on Project Management)

Dave Carhart, *Bentley College* (Chapter 16 on Scheduling)

In addition, we would like to thank Janelle Heineke and Dave Carhart for their overall review of the text and their constant feedback.

We once again thank those individuals whose input over past editions helped the book evolve to its present form: Timothy Bergquist, *University of Oregon;* Dave Carhart, *Bentley College;* Gayla Delong, *Northwestern Oklahoma State University;* Lissa Galbraith, *Florida State University;* John Haehl, *Lewis-Clark State College;* Marilyn Jones, *Winthrop College;* Birsen Karpak, *Youngstown State University;* Dennis Krumwiede, *Kansas State University;* Rich Luebbe, *Miami University (Ohio);* Mary Jo Maffei, *Miami University (Ohio);* Robert Mefford, *University of San Francisco;* and Rao Tatikonda, *University of Wisconsin—Oshkosh.*

Special thanks to Philip Musa of Texas Tech University, and Madeline Thimmes of Utah State University who solved all of the examples and problems and checked our answers for accuracy. Marilyn Helms of The University of Tennessee at Chattanooga prepared the Study Guide and Ross Fink of Bradley University prepared the Instructor's Manual. Steve DeLurgio prepared the Test Bank. These supplements take a great deal of time and effort to write and we appreciate their efforts.

We especially want to thank Gail Korosa, Senior Developmental Editor at Irwin/McGraw-Hill, for both her patience and perseverance in "keeping our feet to the fire" through the various stages of the process.

Finally, we wish to thank the staff at Irwin/McGraw-Hill for their support, encouragement, and assistance: Scott Isenberg, Senior Sponsoring Editor; Colleen Suljic, Senior Marketing Manager; Susan Trentacosti, Senior Project Manager; Heather Burbridge, Senior Production Supervisor; and Laurie Entringer, Designer.

Mark M. Davis
Nicholas J. Aquilano
Richard B. Chase

Brief Contents

Contents

Chapter 3

PROCESSES IN MANUFACTURING AND SERVICES   42

Supplement 3

FINANCIAL ANALYSIS IN OPERATIONS MANAGEMENT   76

Chapter 4

PROCESS MEASUREMENT AND ANALYSIS 104

Chapter 5

QUALITY MANAGEMENT 132

"We Are
Ladies and
Gentlemen
Serving
Ladies and
Gentlemen"

THE RITZ-CARLTON
CREDO
The Ritz-Carlton Hotel is a
place where the genuine care
and comfort of our guests is our
highest mission.
We pledge to provide the finest
personal service and facilities for
our guests who will always enjoy
a warm, relaxed yet refined
ambience.
The Ritz-Carlton experience
enlivens the senses, instills well-
being, and fulfills even the
unexpressed wishes and
needs of our guests.

Chapter 10

PROJECT MANAGEMENT 348

Chapter 11

SUPPLY CHAIN MANAGEMENT 380

Chapter 12

JUST-IN-TIME SYSTEMS 396

Chapter 16

SCHEDULING   532

APPENDIXES   561

PHOTO CREDITS   581

NAME INDEX   583

SUBJECT INDEX   589

FUNDAMENTALS OF
OPERATIONS MANAGEMENT

1

INTRODUCTION

Chapter Objectives

- Demonstrate that operations management addresses issues in both manufacturing and service organizations, and that manufacturing and services are becoming integrated within an organization rather than being treated as two separate and distinct entities.

- Introduce the application of OM tools to other functional areas within an organization such as marketing and human resources.

- Present an overview of the book.

- Show the impact of a changing and increasingly complex environment on business decision making and on the operations management function and the organization.

- Demonstrate that the operations management function takes a broader global perspective as a company increases its international activities.

- Define the operations management (OM) function and understand how it adds value to the goods and services provided by an organization.

- Present an historical perspective of operations management and how it has evolved to its current role in an organization.

"**D**irect marketing? You want me to manage a direct marketing operation?" Mark Longa, the operations manager at Bose Corporation's stereo speaker manufacturing facility in Westboro, Massachusetts (shown here talking to a worker on an assembly line), stared in disbelief at the telephone, trying to comprehend why this conversation was even taking place. "But I've spent my entire career in manufacturing and have absolutely no experience in direct marketing," Mark continued. "We know that," said the voice at the other end of the line, "but we've finally recognized that the key to our success depends on our ability to develop a smooth running operation that can be responsive to the needs of our customers, and you were recommended as just the person to accomplish this for us." ■

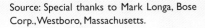

Source: Special thanks to Mark Longa, Bose Corp., Westboro, Massachusetts.

Introduction

 MARKETING While Mark Longa didn't take the job as operations manager for the direct marketing firm, the fact that he was asked is important. Ten years ago, it would never have occurred to a direct marketing firm's top management that they might need an operations manager on its senior management team. Today, however, there is growing recognition that the various elements that typically comprise the operations management function aren't limited solely to the production line, but have applications in the other functional areas within an organization.

Mark Longa's experience isn't an isolated incident; similar conversations with operations managers are becoming very common. Senior managers in manufacturing and services, in for-profit organizations, and not-for-profit organizations and in both the public and private sectors are now recognizing the important contribution of operations management. This renaissance in operations management has created a growing need for highly skilled operations managers like Mark Longa.

Specific Objectives of This Book

Most students do not major in operations management. In fact, many schools and colleges do not even offer a major in operations management. Nevertheless, it is important for you to understand how the operations management function contributes to the overall success of an organization. The reasons are twofold. First, understanding how the different elements within the OM function fit into the overall organizational structure will provide you with a broader perspective which, in turn, will allow you to do your own job better. In addition, as we stated above, the concepts developed initially within the OM function have application in all of the other functional areas within an organization. Understanding and applying these tools and concepts can improve your ability to be both effective and efficient in the way you do your work.

Many students don't appreciate the importance of operations management until after they graduate and begin work (see the OM in Practice box: Excerpts from Two Letters from Former Students). For example, consider the "hot" employment area of information technology (IT). Specialists in IT should really have a working knowledge of the best practices in process management, forecasting, quality control, and project planning to correctly apply many of the software tools that they will encounter on the job.

For these reasons, the specific objectives of this book are to:

1. Introduce the various elements that comprise the field of operations management, and some of the new and evolving concepts within OM.
2. Identify some of the OM tools and concepts that can be applied to a wide variety of situations, including non-OM related areas.
3. Develop an appreciation of the need for interaction between operations management and the other management functions within an organization.
4. Explain the role of technology in operations management and its impact on the different OM elements.
5. Describe the growing trend toward globalization among firms and how it affects operations management.
6. Demonstrate that manufacturing and services are becoming more integrated within companies.
7. Provide an integrated framework for understanding the field of OM as a whole and its role in an organization.

Operations Management in Practice

EXCERPTS FROM TWO LETTERS FROM FORMER STUDENTS

". . . part of an audit for a CPA firm includes learning about the systems of a client. A by-product of the audit is a management letter which suggests how the client might improve their systems. By systems I am referring to the accounting information systems, the inventory control systems, as well as the production process.

In evaluating these systems, one must first understand the generalities underlying all systems. OM explains these generalities as they apply to production processes. The better one understands how processes work, the easier it is to apply this understanding to different systems and provide your client with good suggestions for improving the efficiency of their operations . . .

The course you teach in Operations Management is invaluable, and any student of accounting would be a fool to blow it off and try to just get by without learning anything. . . ."

Gary S. Fortier
B.S.B.A., C.P.A.
Atlanta, GA

". . . if I were to call you on the phone and tell you what I do for work, I think I would hear some of the following from you:
   'I told you so.'
   'You should have paid more attention the second time you took the course.'
   'Maybe if you even went to class . . .'

Well, I have been busy working for the Gillette Company as a production analyst. Basically, it's OM all over again, making sure that the production is running smoothly and keeping management pleased. It's unreal how much of your class takes place in my everyday work.

Scrap rates, net average hours of production, efficiency, sample sizes, shifts, the number of hours a machine can run with a certain product. I tell you I'd take your course a third time if I could squeeze it into my schedule. Putting in 60–70 hours a week and learning OM all over again just kills me, because if I had given some effort in your class, . . . who knows?

I am sure that you are giggling to yourself and saying ha ha, that ought to teach him not to have missed any of my classes. I thought that maybe some of your students that are like me could benefit from this e-mail. . . ."

Erik Geagan
B.S.B.A.
Boston, MA

With respect to the last objective, our goal is to demonstrate that operations management is not just a loosely knit aggregation of tools but rather a *synthesis* of concepts and techniques that relate directly to operating systems and enhance their management. This point is important because OM is frequently confused with operations research (OR), management science (MS), and industrial engineering (IE). The critical difference between OM and these fields is this: OM is a field of management, whereas OR and MS are branches of applied mathematics and IE is an engineering discipline. Thus, while operations managers use the tools of OR and MS in decision making, and are concerned with many of the same issues as IE, OM has a distinct business management role that differentiates it from OR, MS, and IE.

WHAT IS OPERATIONS MANAGEMENT?

A Corporate Perspective

operations management
Management of the conversion process which transforms inputs such as raw material and labor into outputs in the form of finished goods and services.

MARKETING
FINANCE

From a corporate perspective, **operations management** may be defined as the management of the direct resources that are required to provide an organization's goods and services.

The marketplace—the firm's customers for its goods and services—shapes the corporate strategy of the firm. This strategy is based on the corporate mission, and in essence reflects how the firm plans to use all of its resources and functions (marketing, finance, and operations) to gain a competitive advantage. The operations strategy specifies how the firm will employ its production capabilities to support its corporate strategy. (Similarly, the marketing strategy addresses how the firm will sell and distribute its goods and services,

5

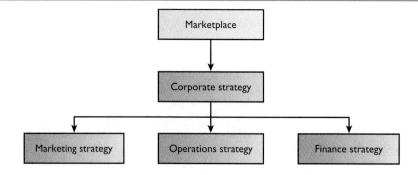

and the finance strategy identifies how best to utilize the financial resources of the firm, as shown in Exhibit 1.1.)

Within the operations function, management decisions can be divided into three broad areas:

- Strategic (long-range) decisions.
- Tactical (medium-range) decisions.
- Operational planning and control (short-range) decisions.

The hierarchical relationship between these three planning functions is shown in Exhibit 1.2.

The strategic issues are usually very broad in nature, addressing such questions as:

- How will we make the product?
- Where do we locate the facility or facilities?
- How much capacity do we need?
- When should we add more capacity?

Consequently, by necessity, the time frame for strategic decisions is typically very long, usually several years or more, depending on the specific industry.

Operations management decisions at the strategic level impact the long-range effectiveness of the company in terms of how well it can address the needs of its customers. Thus, for the firm to succeed, these decisions must be aligned with the corporate strategy. Decisions made at the strategic level then define the fixed conditions or constraints under which the firm must operate in both the intermediate and short term.

At the next level in the decision-making process, tactical planning primarily addresses the issue of how to efficiently schedule material and labor within the constraints of the strategic decisions that were previously made. Thus, some of the issues on which OM concentrates at this level are:

- How many workers do we need?
- When do we need them?
- Should we work overtime or put on a second shift?
- When should we have material delivered?
- Should we have a finished goods inventory?

These tactical decisions, in turn, define the operating constraints under which the operational planning and control decisions are made.

The management decisions with respect to operational planning and control are very narrow and short term, by comparison. For example, issues at this level include:

- What jobs do we work on today or this week?
- To whom do we assign what tasks?
- What jobs have priority?

An Operational Perspective

transformation process
Actual conversion of inputs into outputs.

From an operational perspective, operations management can be viewed as a set of components whose function is concerned with converting a set of inputs into some desired output. This conversion is called the **transformation process** (as seen in Exhibit 1.3), which is often referred to as the *technical core* especially in manufacturing organizations. A component may be a machine, a person, a tool, or a management system. An input may be a raw material, a person, or a finished product from another process. Some transformations are:

- Physical, as in manufacturing.
- Locational, as in transportation.
- Exchange, as in retailing.
- Storage, as in warehousing.
- Physiological, as in health care.
- Informational, as in telecommunications.

These transformations, of course, are not mutually exclusive. For example, a department store can (a) allow shoppers to compare prices and quality (informational), (b) hold items in inventory until needed (storage), and (c) sell goods (exchange). Exhibit 1.4

EXHIBIT 1.3
The Transformation Process

EXHIBIT 1.4
Input-Transformation-Output Relationships for Typical Systems

System	Inputs	Components	Primary Transformation Function(s)	Typical Desired Output
Hospital	Patients, medical supplies	MDs, nurses, equipment	Health care (physiological)	Healthy individuals
Restaurant	Hungry customers, food	Chef, waitress, environment	Well-prepared food, well served; agreeable environment (physical and exchange)	Satisfied customers
Automobile factory	Sheet steel, engine parts	Tools, equipment, workers	Fabrication and assembly of cars (physical)	High-quality cars
College or university	High school graduates, books	Teachers, classrooms	Imparting knowledge and skills (informational)	Educated individuals
Department store	Shoppers, stock of goods	Displays, sales clerks	Attract shoppers, promote products, fill orders (exchange)	Sales to satisfied customers
Distribution center	Stockkeeping units (SKU)	Storage bins, stockpickers	Storage and redistribution	Fast delivery, availability of SKUs

presents sample input-transformation-output relationships for a wide variety of processes. Note that only the direct components are listed; a more complete system description would, of course, also include managerial and support functions.

THE EMERGENCE OF OPERATIONS MANAGEMENT

Operations management has been gaining increased recognition in recent years for several reasons including: (a) the application of OM concepts in service operations, (b) an expanded definition of quality, (c) the introduction of OM concepts to other functional areas such as marketing and human resources, and (d) realization that the OM function can add value to the end product. However, while these distinctions are generally true, contemporary views of OM suggest that they are far too limiting.

 ### Application of OM to Service Operations

There are several characteristics that distinguish goods from services as seen in Exhibit 1.5. As a result of these differences, managers, in the past, often viewed providing services as being totally different from producing goods.

To elaborate, Theodore Levitt of Harvard Business School, in his article entitled "Production-Line Approach to Service,"[1] was one of the first to recognize that many of the concepts that had been previously developed for manufacturing can actually be applied to service operations. He observed that operations concepts can be seen readily at McDonald's fast food outlets (where hamburgers are cooked in batches of 12 at a time) or at Benihana's of Tokyo restaurants (where customers are batched into groups of eight to increase efficiency). More recently, an article entitled "JIT in Services: A Review of Current Practices and Future Directions for Research," by Duclos, Siha and Lummus, showed that Just-in-Time (JIT) concepts are also being applied to a wide variety of service operations such as the Customer Service Center at Northern Telecom, Inc., and the automatic replenishment system at Wal-Mart's retail operations which is actually a pull-type system.[2] (JIT is often described as a pull system for moving material. In this example, the selling of an item "pulls" a replacement order from stock or a supplier.)

In addition, it is becoming more difficult to differentiate between services and manufacturing. Consequently, instead of looking at operations from two perspectives (that is, manufacturing and services), today's approach suggests that the vast majority of products consist of both a goods component and a service component, as suggested in Exhibit 1.6, and that both elements need to be addressed together in order for a firm to be successful. (Throughout this book, *product* will refer the combination or "bundle" of goods and services being provided, whereas *goods* will refer to the tangible output and *services* will refer to the intangible output.)

An Expanded Definition of Quality

Another key component in operations management is quality. Successful firms now recognize that quality is no longer limited to the operations management function, but is important in all functional areas throughout the entire organization. Within marketing, for example, the customer's order must be accurate in terms of: (a) the product ordered, (b) the specified

---

[1] Theodore Levitt, "Production-Line Approach to Service," *Harvard Business Review* 50, no. 5 September–October 1972, pp. 41–52.

[2] L. Duclos, S. Siha, and R. Lummus, "JIT in Services: A Review of Current Practices and Future Directions," *International Journal of Service Industry Management* 6, no. 5, 1995.

EXHIBIT 1.5

Differences between Goods and Services

Goods	Services
Tangible	Intangible
Can be inventoried	Cannot be inventoried
No interaction between customer and process	Direct interaction between customer and process

EXHIBIT 1.6

Most Products Are a "Bundle" of Goods and Services

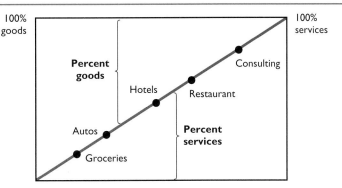

price, and (c) the proper location for delivery. Quality emphasis is also important in accounting: The bill for the items purchased must be properly prepared to reflect any special terms of payment and then sent to the customer at the correct address.

The integration of manufacturing and services has also expanded the definition of quality. Quality is no longer limited to the technical requirements of the goods being produced on the manufacturing floor. Service quality (that is, how we deal with our customers on a wide variety of issues) is equally important. How companies integrate product quality and service quality to properly meet the needs of their customers is a major challenge to today's managers. The customer service department of a car dealership, for example, must know how to resolve customer complaints so that they will continue to do business with the dealership in the future. For these reasons, today's managers are recognizing that improving quality in all aspects of their businesses improves customer satisfaction and increases customer loyalty.

Expansion of OM Concepts into Other Functions

MARKETING
FINANCE
ACCOUNTING

As inferred in Mark Longa's story at the beginning of this chapter, successful companies are also recognizing that, in addition to quality, many of the tools and concepts that are now widely used within the operations function also have application in the other functional areas of an organization such as marketing, finance, and accounting. For example (as we shall see in Chapter 4), process analysis is a major tool which provides insight into understanding how inputs are converted into outputs, and can be applied to processes which exist everywhere in an organization. The hiring of personnel in human resources is a process, as is the design of a new product in engineering and the rolling out of a new product by marketing. In accounts receivable, the preparing and mailing of an invoice to a customer is also a process.

A New Paradigm for OM

For many years following World War II, the United States was the obvious world leader in manufacturing. U.S. dominance was the result of several factors, including: (a) available capacity built to support the war effort, (b) pent-up demand for consumer goods during the war, and (c) the virtually total destruction of most of the production capabilities of the other leading industrialized nations of the world. As Tom Peters said, "You couldn't screw up an American Fortune 500 company between 1946 and 1973 if you tried."[3] With demand significantly exceeding capacity at this time, emphasis was placed on output, and the operations function reacted to situations as they arose. Corporate managers during this period typically told operations managers to focus only on controlling costs.

As we shall see in Chapter 2, in the early 1970s, Wickam Skinner at Harvard Business School introduced the notion of operations strategy. He proposed that the operations function could take a proactive role in developing the overall strategy for an organization. In other words, Skinner suggested that the operations function could actually add value to the products a company manufactured (that is, adding value in terms of what a customer is willing to pay for the products). In developing this concept of operations strategy, he suggested that a firm could compete on dimensions other than cost to increase profit margins. These dimensions included *quality, speed of delivery, and process flexibility.* Each of these dimensions, in their own way, adds value to the end product. Skinner's notion of an operations strategy resulted in a new paradigm for the operations function. The new paradigm for the OM function in successful companies is to be proactive in the corporate decision-making process and to maximize the value added to the goods and services that are provided in whatever way best meets the specific needs of their customers.

THE EVER-CHANGING WORLD OF OPERATIONS MANAGEMENT

Operations management is continuously changing to meet the new and exciting challenges of today's business world. This ever-changing world is characterized by increasing global competition and advances in technology. Emphasis is also shifting within the operations function to link it more clearly with both customers and suppliers.

Increased Global Competition

global economy, global village, global landscape
Terms describing that companies are competing on an international level.

The world is rapidly transforming itself into a single **global economy,** which is also referred to as a **global village** or **global landscape.** Markets once dominated by local or national companies are now vulnerable to competition from firms in all corners of the world. For example, in the 1960s, only 7 percent of the firms in the United States were exposed to foreign competition; by the late 1980s, this figure exceeded 70 percent and that percentage has continued to grow.[4] Consequently, as

companies expand their businesses to include foreign markets, so too must the operations management function take a broader, more global perspective in order for companies to

[3]Tom Peters and KQED Golden Gate Productions, *The Power of Excellence: The Forgotten Customer,* Jack Hilton Productions, Video Publishing House, Inc., 1987.

[4]S. C. Gwynne, "The Long Haul," *Time,* September 25, 1992, pp. 34–38.

EXHIBIT 1.7

Ford's Global Network to Support the Manufacturing of the Escort

Assembling a World Car

France Alternator, cylinder head, master cylinder	
Sweden Hose clamps, cylinder bolt	
United Kingdom Carburetor, clutch, ignition, exhaust, oil pump	
Netherlands Paints, hardware	
Germany Pistons, front disc, speedometer, fuel tank, rear wheel spindle	

Canada Glass, radio

Belgium Seat pads

Assembly in Halewood, U.K., or Saarlouis, Germany

Spain Wiring harness, battery

Austria Radiator, heater hoses

Italy Cylinder head, defroster grills

Japan Starter

Denmark Fan belt

Norway Exhaust flanges, tires

Switzerland Speedometer, gears

United States EGR valves, wheel nuts, hydraulic tappet

Source: From Joseph E. Stiglitz, *Principles of Micro-economics,* 2nd ed. (New York: W. W. Norton and Company, 1997), p. 58.

remain competitive. To survive and prosper in such a global marketplace companies must excel in more than one competitive dimension, which previously was the norm. With the rise of the global economy, companies are no longer limited as to where they can make or buy their products and components. As seen in Exhibit 1.7, Ford's Escort in Europe is assembled in two locations, England and Germany, using components that are produced in no less than 15 countries from all over the world. This trend toward globalization has placed increased emphasis on the logistics of where to locate facilities and the issues associated with moving material long distances, both of which are addressed in Chapter 11.

Advances in Technology

Advances in technology in recent years have also had a significant impact on the operations management function. Information technology (IT) now allows us to collect data on individual customers so that we can "mass customize" products to meet the needs of individual customers. The increased use of automation and robotics has also permitted us to improve the quality of the goods that are being manufactured. Automated teller machines (ATMs), which can provide customers with 24-hour service, are a good example of technology being applied in service operations, particularly in those countries with high labor costs.

 However, advances in technology place new requirements on the workforce and even on customers, especially in service operations. (For example, customers must now have computer skills to access companies that are now advertising on the Internet or the World Wide Web.) Consequently, skilled workers are replacing unskilled workers in all types of operations. As we shall see in Chapter 9, an organization's workforce should be considered its most valuable asset, only increasing in value as it becomes more educated.

Operations Management in Practice

THE CUSTOMER FRIEND PROGRAM AT FOXBORO'S SYSTEMS MANUFACTURING OPERATION

The Foxboro Company's systems manufacturing operation, which produces control systems for process industries like refineries, chemical plants and breweries, has a Customer Friend Program that directly links customers to manufacturing. This program is offered free of charge and provides each customer with a contact person or "friend" in manufacturing who is responsible for helping the customer resolve any and all product- and service-related problems. Since its inception in 1992, more than 40 individuals from manufacturing have taken part in the Customer Friend Program involving more than 300 customer systems, both large and small.

The benefits of this program to manufacturing are to: (a) identify more closely with the customer's needs, (b) feel the customer's pain when a problem does occur, (c) gain a better understanding of how manufacturing can improve its support to its customers, and (d) obtain direct feedback from "where the rubber meets the road" in terms of how manufacturing can improve its processes and products.

The program benefits the customer by (a) identifying more closely the customer's needs, (b) passing the pain directly to the source when a problem does occur, (c) having a dedicated individual within manufacturing who has a personal commitment to customer satisfaction, (d) having direct contact with manufacturing to analyze product failures, and (e) acting as a conduit for new and improved ideas.

Foxboro's Customer Friend Program is proactive rather than reactive. Depending on the needs and desires of the customer, the Foxboro friend will call his assigned customer every one to four weeks just to make sure everything is running smoothly. Many of these customer-friend relationships are long standing. Ray Webb, the employee involvement manager at Foxboro's Systems Manufacturing Operation, for example, has had a five-year association with Ergon Refining of Mississippi.

Source: Special thanks to Ray Webb, Systems Manufacturing Operation, The Foxboro Company.

MARKETING
FINANCE
PURCHASING
HUMAN RESOURCES

Linking Operations Management to Customers and Suppliers

In the past, most manufacturing organizations viewed operations as an internal function that had to be buffered from the external environment by other organizational functions. Orders were generated by the marketing function; supplies and raw materials were obtained through the purchasing function; capital for equipment purchases came from the finance function; the labor force was obtained through the human resources function; and the product was delivered by the distribution function.

Buffering the transformation process from direct environmental influence has been traditionally desirable for several reasons:

- Interaction with environmental elements (e.g., customers and salespeople on the production floor) could be a disturbing influence on the transformation process.
- The transformation process was often more efficient than the processes required for obtaining inputs and distributing finished goods.
- With certain processes (e.g., auto assembly lines and continuous flow processes such as petroleum refining), maximum productivity was achieved only by operating at a continuous rate which assumed that the market could absorb all of the product being manufactured. This meant that the production process had to shift at least some of the input and output activities to other parts of the firm.
- The managerial skills required for the successful operation of the transformation process were often different from those required for the successful operation of boundary functions like marketing and human resources, for example.

However, there were some inherent disadvantages when the transformation process was totally isolated as an internal function. One was that information lagged between the process and the boundary functions; this inevitably led to inflexibility. Another was that for high-tech products in particular, communications between the shop floor and the customer could

At Ford Motor Company's Valencia, Spain, plant more than 20 suppliers are located in an adjacent industrial park that feed parts, like these bumpers, directly to the assembly line as needed.

be extremely valuable in solving technical problems during production. As shown in the OM in Practice box, Foxboro Company's Customer Friend Program provides a good example of how manufacturing is now directly interacting with customers.

More and more firms are recognizing the competitive advantage achieved when the transformation process is not isolated, as when customers are invited to view their operating facilities firsthand. For example, Green Giant believes that the tours of their production facilities that they provided to Japanese distributors was a major factor in their ability to penetrate that market with their Green Giant food products.[5] Similarly, National R_x Services, which offers a mail-order prescription service, encourages insurance companies and HMOs to visit their facilities to assure themselves of the high quality of its prescription-filling process.

In a like manner, companies are working more closely with suppliers. Firms like Toyota, for example, have suppliers deliver product directly to the factory floor, eliminating any need for a stockroom. General Scanning of Watertown, Massachusetts, encourages its vendors to automatically replenish items on the factory floor without purchase orders or incoming reports.

value chain
Steps an organization requires to produce a good or a service regardless of where they are performed.

This trend toward having the transformation process work more closely with both suppliers and customers alike is often referred to as a product's **value chain.** We can define a value chain as consisting of all those steps that actually add value to the product without distinguishing where they are added. This concept attempts to eliminate all nonvalue-added steps (such as inspections and inventory), and consequently results in a higher degree of dependence among the value-added functions that are linked in the chain. The relationship between the transformation process, its support functions, and the other value-added functions is shown in Exhibit 1.8.

[5]J. Ammeson, "When in Rome," *Northwest Airlines World Traveler,* March 1993.

EXHIBIT 1.8

The Value Chain and Its
Support Functions

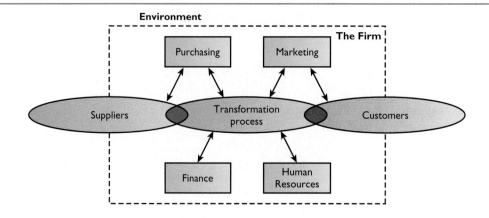

EXHIBIT 1.9

Line and Staff Jobs in
Operations Management

Organizational Level	Manufacturing Industries	Service Industries
Upper	Vice president of manufacturing	Vice president of operations (airline)
	Regional manager of manufacturing	Chief administrator (hospital)
Middle	Plant manager	Store manager (department store)
	Program manager	Facilities manager (wholesale distributor)
Lower	Department supervisor	Branch manager (bank)
	Foreman	Department supervisor (insurance company)
	Crew chief	Assistant manager (hotel)
Staff	Production controller	Systems and procedures analyst
	Materials manager	Purchasing agent
	Quality manager	Inspector
	Purchasing agent	Dietician (hospital)
	Work methods analyst	Customer service manager
	Process engineer	

virtual enterprise
Company whose
boundaries are not
clearly defined due to the
integration of customers
and suppliers.

This integration of both suppliers and customers into the transformation process begins to blur the boundaries between what were previously totally independent organizations. What appears to be emerging now is a concept known as the **virtual enterprise,** which is a full integrated and interlocked network in *inter*dependent organizations. With this new approach, it is often difficult to determine where one organization leaves off and the next one begins. As one example, FedEx has several employees who work full time at the L.L. Bean Mail Order Distribution Center in Freeport, Maine.

Job Opportunities in Operations Management: Relating OM to Other Business Functions

Exhibit 1.9 lists some of the line and staff jobs that are frequently viewed as relating to the operations function. There are more staff specializations in manufacturing than in services because of the focus on materials management and control.

Operations Management is a required course in many business schools, not only because it deals with the basic question of how goods and services are created, but also because many of the concepts developed in OM have applications in every other functional area within an organization. As seen in Exhibit 1.10, processes exist within every function.

Functional Area	Processes within Function	Interaction with OM
Accounting	Customer billing Tax returns Financial statement preparation	Inventory management Capacity utilization Labor and material costs
Finance	Capital investment analysis Cash flow management Budget preparation	Capacity utilization Make or buy decisions Plant expansion/location
Marketing	New product introduction Customer orders Customer service	Degree of customization Delivery dates New product introduction
Human resources	Hiring Training	Skills requirements Job descriptions
MIS	Software evaluation Hardware requirements analysis Web site design	Terminal locations Data requirements

These processes can be continuously improved by applying OM tools and techniques. In addition, as also seen in Exhibit 1.10, each of these functional areas interacts with the OM function. Therefore, in order to do their jobs correctly, it is important for individuals working in these areas to understand the fundamental concepts of operations management.

HISTORICAL DEVELOPMENT OF OM

Prior to 1900

Up through the end of the eighteenth century, agriculture was the predominant industry in every country. Manufacturing, as we know it today, did not exist. Items were usually custom made by skilled artisans who spent many years in apprenticeship learning every facet of how to make a good or provide a service. No two products were ever the same. For many products, trades or guilds were established to provide a common basis of knowledge for these apprenticeship programs.

This cottage industry approach to manufacturing began to change in the nineteenth century, however. Watt invented the steam engine in England in 1765, which provided a source of power for manufacturing. In 1801, Eli Whitney introduced the concept of standardized parts to President Jefferson with a demonstration in which he selected parts at random to assemble and then fire a musket. (Prior to this every musket was hand crafted with customized parts.) The middle of the nineteenth century saw the onrush of the Industrial Revolution with its large manufacturing facilities that were powered either by steam or water. However, even with the advent of these large facilities, manufacturing, to a large degree, still remained an art rather than a science.

Scientific Management

scientific management
Systematic approach to increasing worker productivity introduced by Frederick W. Taylor.

This all changed with the introduction of **scientific management** at the beginning of the twentieth century. Although we could claim that operations management has existed since the dawn of civilization, scientific management was probably the first historical landmark in the field in that it represented for the first time a systematic approach to manufacturing. This concept was developed by Frederick W. Taylor, an imaginative engineer and insightful observer of organizational activities.

The essence of Taylor's philosophy was that scientific laws govern how much a worker can produce per day and that it is the function of management to discover and use these laws in the operation of productive systems (and the function of the worker to carry out management's wishes without question). Taylor's philosophy was not greeted with approval by all his contemporaries. On the contrary, some unions resented or feared scientific management—and with some justification. In too many instances, managers of the day were quick to embrace the mechanisms of Taylor's philosophy—time study, incentive plans, and so forth—but ignored their responsibility to organize and standardize the work to be done. For many firms, workers were often viewed as just another interchangeable asset, like plant and equipment.

Taylor's ideas were widely accepted in contemporary Japan, and a Japanese translation of Taylor's book, *Principles of Scientific Management* (titled *The Secret of Saving Lost Motion*), sold more than two million copies. To this day, there is a strong legacy of Taylorism in Japanese approaches to manufacturing management.[6]

Notable co-workers of Taylor were Frank and Lillian Gilbreth (motion study, industrial psychology) and Henry L. Gantt (scheduling, wage payment plans). Their work is well known to management scholars. However, it is probably not well known that Taylor, a devout Quaker, requested "cussing lessons" from an earthy foreman to help him communicate with workers; that Frank Gilbreth defeated younger champion bricklayers in bricklaying contests by using his own principles of motion economy; or that Gantt won a presidential citation for his application of the Gantt chart to shipbuilding during World War I.

Moving Assembly Line

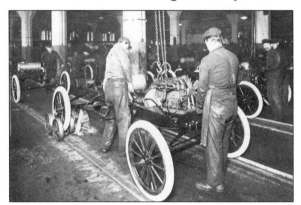

The year 1913 saw the introduction of one of the machine age's greatest technological innovations—the moving assembly line for the manufacture of Ford automobiles. (Ford is said to have gotten the idea for an assembly line from observing a Swiss watch manufacturer's use of the technology. Incidentally, all Model-T Fords were painted black. Why? Because black paint dried the fastest.) Before the assembly line was introduced, in August of that year, each auto chassis was assembled by one worker in about 12½ hours. Eight months later, when the line was in its final form, with each worker performing a small unit of work and the chassis being moved mechanically, the average labor time per chassis was reduced to 93 minutes. This technological breakthrough, coupled with the concepts of scientific management, represents the classic application of labor specialization and still exists today in both manufacturing and service operations.

Hawthorne Studies

Mathematical and statistical developments dominated the evolution of operations management from Taylor's time up to around the 1940s. One exception was the Hawthorne studies, conducted during the late 1920s and early 1930s by a research team from Harvard Business School and supervised by the sociologist Elton Mayo. These experiments were designed to study the effects of certain environmental changes on the output of assembly workers at Western Electric's Hawthorne plant in Chicago, Illinois. The unexpected findings, reported in *Management and the Worker* by F. J. Roethlisberger and W. J. Dickson,[7] intrigued sociologists and students of "traditional" scientific management alike. To the surprise of the researchers, changing the level of illumination, for example, had much less

---

[6]C. J. McMillan, "Production Planning in Japan," *Journal of General Management* 8, no. 4, 1984, pp. 44–71.

[7]F. J. Rothlisberger and W. J. Dickson, *Management and the Worker.* (Cambridge, MA: Harvard University Press, 1939).

effect on the output than the way in which the changes were introduced to the workers. That is, reductions in illumination in some instances led to increased output because workers felt an obligation to their group to keep output high. Discoveries such as these had tremendous implications for work design and worker motivation and ultimately led to the establishment of personnel management and the human resources departments in most organizations.

Operations Research

World War II, with its complex problems of logistics control and weapons-systems design, provided the impetus for the development of the interdisciplinary, mathematically oriented field of operations research. Operations research (OR) brings together practitioners in such diverse fields as mathematics, psychology, and economics. Specialists in these disciplines customarily form a team to structure and analyze a problem in quantitative terms so that a mathematically optimal solution can be obtained. Operations research, or its approximate synonym *management science,* now provides many of the quantitative tools that are used today in operations management as well as in other business disciplines.

OM Emerges as a Field

In the late 1950s and early 1960s, scholars began to write texts dealing specifically with operations management as opposed to industrial engineering or operations research. Writers such as Edward Bowman and Robert Fetter (*Analysis for Production and Operations Management* [1957]) and Elwood S. Buffa (*Modern Production Management* [1961]) clearly noted the commonality of problems faced by all manufacturing organizations and emphasized the importance of viewing a production operation as a system.

Today, operations management is acknowledged as a legitimate functional area within many organizations, be they for profit or not-for-profit, public or private, manufacturing or service. Those companies that recognize the important contributions that the operations management function can make toward achieving their respective corporate goals will lead the way into the next century.

The Marriage of OM and Information Technology

Today, information technology (IT) plays a critical role in the design and management of production processes. Business process reengineering, supply chain management, and sophisticated tools for systems integration such as SAP (all defined later in the book) require "integrated solutions" which marry OM and IT. To illustrate, a recent survey of consulting practice areas showed that 31 percent of the services offered by the 40 largest consulting firms were in the process/operations management area which implies the blending of OM and IT.[8] Thus, while information technology has always been a key factor in the management of factory operations, its application throughout the firm to other functional areas such as marketing and finance suggests a major evolutionary step in the development of the field.

OM in Services

As stated earlier, Theodore Levitt was probably one of the first to demonstrate how many of the concepts and tools that had been developed for manufacturing operations could also be applied to service operations. By using these tools, services could also realize many of the efficiencies of operation that had previously been limited to manufacturing. McDonald's provided several good examples of these applications, from the efficient cooking and

---

[8]"Consultant News," cited in the *Economist,* March 22, 1997, p. 40.

assembly of hamburgers in a batch operation to the use of specially designed scoops that quickly package french fries in consistent portion sizes.

Integration of Manufacturing and Services

More recently, managers have recognized the importance of both manufacturing and services, and the need to integrate the two. A primary objective of this text is to emphasize this integration. Companies that want to succeed as world class operations must therefore devote resources to both areas. In addition, production and service must be compatible with each other and strategically aligned with the firm's overall goals.

CONCLUSION

Operations management is recognized today as a critical functional area within every organization. No longer is operations management considered to be subservient to the finance and marketing areas; instead, it is now treated as equal. Firms that fail to recognize the significant contribution of the operations management function will lose profits and market share to those firms that do. The once-reactive role of operations management, which concentrated solely on minimizing costs, has been replaced by a more proactive position of maximizing the value added to the goods and services that the organization provides.

Some of the major issues facing operations management executives today in this constantly changing business environment include:

1. Reducing the development and manufacturing time for new goods and services.
2. Achieving and sustaining high quality while controlling cost.
3. Integrating new technologies and control systems into existing processes.
4. Obtaining, training, and keeping qualified workers and managers.
5. Working effectively with other functions of the business (marketing, engineering, finance, and human resources) to accomplish the goals of the firm.
6. Integrating production and service activities at multiple sites in decentralized organizations.
7. Working effectively with suppliers and being user-friendly for customers.
8. Working effectively with new partners formed by strategic alliances (for example, IBM and Apple Computers).

All of these issues are interrelated. The key to success is for operations management to do all of these at a level that is competitive in both global and domestic markets.

KEY TERMS

global economy   p. 10
global landscape   p. 10
global village   p. 10
operations management   p. 5

scientific management   p. 15
transformation process   p. 7
value chain   p. 13
virtual enterprise   p. 14

REVIEW AND DISCUSSION QUESTIONS

1. What is operations management and how is it different from operations research?
2. What were the underlying reasons for the lack of emphasis on operations management in the post–World War II years?
3. What are the advantages of bringing customers into the transformation process or technical core?

4. Take a look at the want ads in *The Wall Street Journal* and evaluate the opportunities for an OM major with several years of experience.

5. What are the major factors leading to the resurgence of interest in OM today?

6. Explain the difference, from an operations management perspective, between cost minimization and value maximization.

7. Using Exhibit 1.4 as a model, describe the input-transformation-output relationships found in the following systems.

   a. An airline.

   b. A state penitentiary.

   c. A branch bank.

   d. A bakery.

   e. A clothing manufacturer.

   f. A dry cleaner.

   g. An automobile assembly line.

   h. An accounting firm.

8. What do we mean by the expression *value chain,* as it applies to the transformation process of a good or service?

9. Identify a product that is 100 percent goods without any service component. Identify a product that is 100 percent service without any goods component.

10. Speculate on the future role of the OM function within an organization and the future role of the operations manager.

 ## INTERNET UPDATE

Conduct a search on the Internet to find some of the various job openings or positions that are currently available in the field of operations management. As an alternative search, identify some individuals in operations and give a brief description of their backgrounds. Suggested key words to help you in your search are OPERATIONS, MANAGEMENT, and POSITIONS.

SELECTED BIBLIOGRAPHY

Ammeson, Jane. "When in Rome." *Northwest Airlines World Traveler,* March 1993.

Chase, Richard B., and Eric L. Prentis. "Operations Management: A Field Rediscovered." *Journal of Management* 13, no. 2 (October 1987), pp. 351–66.

Chase, Richard B., and David A. Garvin. "The Service Factory." *Harvard Business Review* 67, no. 4 (July–August 1989), pp. 61–69.

"Consultant News," cited in the *Economist,* March 22, 1997, p. 40.

Duclos, Leslie K.; Samia M. Siha; and Rhonda R Lummus. "JIT in Services: A Review of Current Practices and Future Directions for Research." *International Journal of Service Industry Management* 6, no. 5, 1995.

Flaherty, M. Therese. *Global Operations Management.* New York: The McGraw-Hill Companies, Inc., 1996.

Greene, Constance. *Eli Whitney and the Birth of American Technology.* Boston: Little, Brown and Company, 1956.

Gwynne, S. C. "The Long Haul." *Time,* September 25, 1992, pp. 34–38.

Hammonds, K. H., and M. Roman. "Itching to Get onto the Factory Floor." *Business Week,* October 14, 1991.

Levitt, Theodore. "Production-Line Approach to Service." *Harvard Business Review* 50, no. 5, (September–October 1972), pp. 41–52.

Levitt, Theodore. "The Industrialization of Service." *Harvard Business Review* 54, no. 5, (September–October 1976), pp. 63–74.

McMillan, Charles J. "Production Planning in Japan." *Journal of General Management* 8, no. 4, 1984, pp. 44–71.

Peters, Tom, and KQED Golden Gate Productions. *The Power of Excellence: The Forgotten Customer.* Jack Hilton Productions, Video Publishing House, Inc., 1987.

Rothlisberger, F. J. and W. J. Dickson. *Management and the Worker.* Cambridge, MA: Harvard University Press, 1939.

Skinner, Wickham. "Manufacturing—Missing Link in Corporate Strategy." *Harvard Business Review,* May–June 1969, pp. 136–45.

_____."The Focused Factory." *Harvard Business Review,* May–June 1974, pp. 113–21.

COMPETITIVENESS AND OPERATIONS STRATEGY

Chapter Objectives

- Define operations strategy and the need for alignment with other functional strategies as well as with the overall business strategy of the firm.

- Identify the different ways in which the operations strategy can provide an organization with a competitive advantage.

- Introduce the concept of trade-offs between various strategies and the need for a firm to prioritize its operations strategies.

- Differentiate between order-qualifiers and order-winners as they pertain to operations strategy.

- Describe the need for the firm to integrate goods and services as "bundles" of benefits.

I n 1995, 70 percent of product sales at Hewlett-Packard (HP) were from new products that were less than two years old. The operations strategy in the Medical Products Group (MPG) has focused on developing manufacturing processes that are both fast and flexible: fast, in terms of time-to-market in new product development and in delivery time after receipt of customer orders; flexible, in terms of quickly introducing new products into production while at the same time accommodating a wide variety of product types and configurations.

The average time-to-market for developing new products has been significantly reduced over the years. This reduction can be attributed to the use of defined product generation processes, product platforms (standardized building blocks), and product evolution strategies. Because manufacturing is an integrated part of the new product development process, MPG can quickly introduce new products into production.

Moreover, production processes have been designed to minimize final assembly and test time. The final assembly and test for a typical patient monitoring system (which has an average list price of $20,000) is 30 minutes. Thus products are built to order because the process is sufficiently flexible to accommodate different product configurations.

The rapid build times of products and subassemblies eliminates the need to keep track of work-in-process (WIP) inventories at every stage in the manufacturing process. Instead, using bar code technology, all of the components and raw material that go into completed components and end products are "backflushed" from inventory, much in the same way that all of the ingredients in a Whopper at Burger King are subtracted from inventory when that item is rung up on the cash register. This alignment between business and manufacturing strategies has been a key ingredient in the success of the Medical Products Group. Sales and profit margins have continued to increase in recent years in a market that is considered to be highly competitive. ■

Source: Special thanks to Rick La Fratta and Steve Smyth, Hewlett-Packard Medical Products Group, Andover, Massachusetts.

BEING COMPETITIVE IS ALL ABOUT WINNING

Competition in most industries has intensified significantly in recent years, especially among international firms, and this trend is expected to continue. This increase in competition is largely because the world is quickly becoming a global village.

This movement towards a single world economy has occurred for several reasons, including: (a) continued advances in information technology which facilitate the rapid transfer of data across vast distances, (b) the growing trend to lower trade barriers as evidenced by NAFTA and the formation of the European Union, (c) the lowering of transportation costs, and (d) the emergence of high-growth markets with associated high-profit margins, in **newly industrialized countries (NIC)**.[1] These new markets can be compared to the saturated markets and shrinking profit margins that are being experienced in the more highly developed countries. For example, McDonald's growth in the United States between 1984 and 1994 was 6.4 percent annually while its international sales grew 19.0 percent annually during this same time period.[2]

As a consequence, in order to not only survive but also prosper in such a fiercely competitive marketplace, a company needs to differentiate itself from its competition. In such an environment, customers will buy solely on the basis of price, thereby driving prices down and shrinking profit margins. In this highly competitive situation, only the low cost producer in an industry can be successful and Michael Porter, a professor at the Harvard Business School and perhaps today's leading authority on competitive strategy, has suggested that even this isn't guaranteed.[3]

He recommends, therefore, that beyond a **low cost strategy**, there are two other business strategies that a firm can adopt: **market segmentation** and **product differentiation**. Companies that are considered to have world-class operations have been able to develop an operations strategy that is properly aligned with corporate strategy which, in turn, is compatible with the overall goals and mission of the firm.

newly industrialized countries (NIC)
Emerging countries that compete in global markets with their goods and have populations with a high standard of living.

types of business strategies:
low cost
Producing the lowest cost products.
market segmentation
Satisfying the needs of a particular market niche.
product differentiation
Offering products that differ significantly from the competition.

Definitions

There often develops within an industry or company a unique set of terms that are familiar only to those associated with that industry or company. This is also true for the functional areas within an organization. Since operations strategy is a relatively new and evolving concept, several of the terms more commonly used are defined here.

Today, many corporations, especially the larger conglomerates, consist of several stand-alone businesses which are often referred to as **strategic business units** or **SBUs**. Within this context, **corporate strategy** pertains to the overall *financial strategy* that has been adopted by the umbrella organization, in terms of how capital is generated (that is, debt versus equity), which SBUs receive infusions of investment, and which are treated as cash generators or "cash cows."

Business strategy refers to the individual strategy adopted by each SBU, in terms of how it addresses the specific markets that it serves and the products that it provides.

strategic business unit (SBU)
Stand-alone business within a conglomerate which operates like an independent company.

corporate strategy
Overall financial strategy adopted by the parent corporation.

business strategy
How a strategic business unit (SBU) addresses the specific markets it serves and products it provides.

---

[1]J. Naisbitt and P. Aburdene, *Megatrends 2000* (New York: William Morrow and Co., 1990).

[2]G. Loveman, "The Globalization of Services: Four Strategies That Drive Growth across Borders," *Proceedings of the 4th International Research Seminar in Service Management,* Agelonde-LaLonde les Maures, France, June 4–7, 1996.

[3]M. Porter, *Competitive Strategy: Techniques for Analyzing Industries and Competitors* (New York: The Free Press, 1980).

functional strategy
Strategy developed by a function within an organization to support the business strategy.

competitiveness
Company's position in the marketplace relative to its competition.

operations strategy
How the operations function contributes to competitive advantage.

competitive priorities
How the operations function provides a firm with a competitive advantage.

Functional strategies (for example, operations, marketing, human resources) are developed to support or align with the established business strategy.

A company or SBU's **competitiveness** refers to its relative position in the marketplace in terms of how it competes with the other firms in its industry. **Operations strategy** refers to how the operations management function contributes to a firm's ability to achieve its competitive advantage in that marketplace.

Operations strategy can be divided into two major categories: *structural elements* consisting of facility location, capacity, vertical integration, and choice of process (all of which are considered to be long term or "strategic" in nature) and *infrastructural elements* consisting of the workforce (in terms of size and skills), quality issues, planning and control, and organizational structure (all of which are often viewed as "tactical" because they can be changed in a relatively short time).

Operations strategies are developed from the **competitive priorities** of an organization which include (a) **low cost,** (b) **high quality,** (c) **fast delivery**, (d) **flexibility,** and (e) **service.**

Core capabilities are the means by which competitive priorities are achieved. Consequently, core capabilities must align directly with competitive priorities.

OPERATIONS STRATEGY—AN OVERVIEW

MARKETING
FINANCE

In the period following World War II, corporate strategy in the United States was usually developed by the marketing and finance functions within a company. With the high demand for consumer products that had built up during the war years, U.S. companies could sell virtually everything they made at comparatively high prices. In addition, there was very little international competition. The main industrial competitors of the United States today, Germany and Japan, lay in ruins from massive bombings. They could not even satisfy their own markets, let alone export globally.

Within the business environment that existed at that time, the manufacturing or operations function was assigned the responsibility to produce large quantities of standard products at minimum costs, regardless of the overall goals of the firm. To accomplish this, the operations function focused on obtaining low-cost, unskilled labor and installing highly automated assembly line type facilities.

The Emergence of Operations Strategy

With no global competition and continued high demand, the role of operations management (that is, to minimize costs) remained virtually unchanged throughout the 1950s and early 1960s. By the late 1960s, however, Wickham Skinner of the Harvard Business School, who is often referred to as the grandfather of operations strategy, recognized this weakness among U.S. manufacturers. He suggested that companies develop an operations strategy that would complement the existing marketing and finance strategies. In one of his early articles on the subject, Skinner referred to manufacturing as the missing link in corporate strategy.[4]

[4]C. W. Skinner, "Manufacturing—The Missing Link in Corporate Strategy," *Harvard Business Review* 47, no. 3 (May–June 1969), pp. 136–45.

Subsequent work in this area by researchers at the Harvard Business School, including Abernathy, Clark, Hayes, and Wheelwright, continued to emphasize the importance of using the strengths of a firm's manufacturing facilities and people as a competitive weapon in the marketplace, and also take a longer-term view of how to deploy them.

What Is Operations Strategy?

Operations strategy is thus concerned with the development of a long-term plan for determining how to best utilize the major resources of the firm so that there is a high degree of compatibility between these resources and the firm's long-term corporate strategy. Operations strategy addresses very broad questions about how these major resources should be configured in order to achieve the desired corporate objectives. Some of the major long-term issues addressed in operations strategy include:

How big do we make the facilities?
Where do we locate them?
When do we build them?
What type of process(es) do we install to make the products?

Each of these issues is addressed in greater detail in subsequent chapters. In this chapter we want to take a more macroscopic perspective to better understand how these issues are interrelated.

In developing an operations strategy, management needs to take many factors into consideration. These include: (a) the level of technology that is or will be available, (b) the required skill levels of the workers, and (c) the degree of vertical integration, in terms of the extent to which outside suppliers are used.

As shown in Exhibit 2.1, operations strategy supports the long-range strategy developed at the SBU level. One might say that decisions at the SBU level focus on being effective, that is, "on doing the right things." These decisions are sometimes referred to as **strategic planning.** Strategic decisions impact intermediate-range decisions, often referred to as **tactical planning,** which focus on being efficient, that is, "doing things right." Here the emphasis is on when material should be delivered, when products should be made to best meet demand, and what size the workforce should be. Finally, we have **operational planning and control** which deals with the day-to-day procedures for doing work, including scheduling, inventory management, and process management.

strategic planning
Long range planning such as plant size, location, and type of process to be used.

tactical planning
Focuses on producing goods and services as efficiently as possible within the strategic plan.

operational planning and control
Scheduling of daily tasks to determine which operator is assigned to work on which job and machine.

EXHIBIT 2.1
Hierarchy of Operational Planning

Type of Planning	Time Frame	Typical Issues
Strategic	Long range	Plant size, location, type of process
Tactical	Intermediate range	Workforce size, material requirements
Operational planning and control (OPC)	Short range	Daily scheduling of workers, jobs, and equipment; process management; inventory management

COMPETITIVE PRIORITIES

competitive priorities
cost
Providing low cost products.
quality
Providing high quality products.
delivery
Providing products quickly.
flexibility
Providing a wide variety of products.
service
How products are delivered and supported.

The key to developing an effective operations strategy lies in understanding how to create or add value for customers. Specifically, value is added through the competitive priority or priorities that are selected to support a given strategy.

Skinner and others initially identified *four basic competitive priorities.* These were **cost, quality, delivery,** and **flexibility.** These four priorities translate directly into characteristics that are used to describe various processes by which a company can add value to the products it provides. There now exists a fifth competitive priority—**service**, and it currently is the primary way in which companies are differentiating themselves in the 1990s.

Cost

Within every industry, there is usually a segment of the market that buys strictly on the basis of low cost. To successfully compete in this niche, a firm must necessarily, therefore, be the low-cost producer. But, as noted earlier, even doing this doesn't always guarantee profitability and success.

Products sold strictly on the basis of cost are typically commodity-like. (Examples of commodities include flour, petroleum, and sugar.) In other words, customers cannot distinguish the products made by one firm from those of another. As a result, customers use cost as the primary determinant in making a purchase.

However, this segment of the market is frequently very large and many companies are lured by the potential for significant profits, which are associated with large unit volumes of product. As a consequence, the competition in this segment is exceedingly fierce—and so is the failure rate. After all, there can only be one low-cost producer, and that firm usually establishes the selling price in the market.

Quality

Quality can be divided into two categories: product quality and process quality. The level of quality in a product's design will vary as to the particular market that it is aimed to serve. Obviously, a child's first two-wheel bicycle is of significantly different quality than the bicycle of a world-class cyclist. The use of thicker sheetmetal and the application of extra coats of paint are some of the product quality characteristics that differentiate a Mercedes-Benz from a Hyundai. One advantage of offering higher-quality products is that they command higher prices in the marketplace.

The goal in establishing the "proper level" of product quality is to focus on the requirements of the customer. Overdesigned products with too much quality will be viewed as being prohibitively expensive. Underdesigned products, on the other hand, will lose customers to products that cost a little more but are perceived by the customers as offering much greater benefits.

Process quality is critical in every market segment. Regardless of whether the product is a child's first two-wheeler or a bicycle for an international cyclist, or whether it is a Mercedes-Benz or a Hyundai, customers want products without defects. Thus, the goal of process quality is to produce error-free products.

Delivery

Another market niche considers speed of delivery to be an important determinant in its purchasing decision. Here, the ability of a firm to provide consistent and fast delivery allows

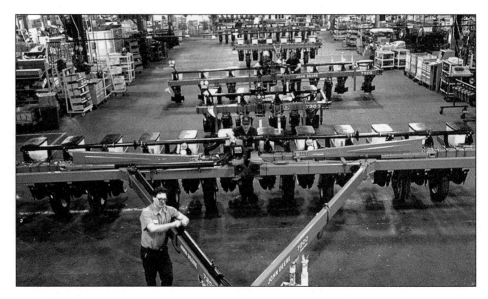

The flexibility of the manufacturing process at John Deere's Harvester Works in Moline, Illinois, allows the firm to respond to the unpredictability of the agricultural industry's equipment needs. By manufacturing such small volume products as seed planters in "modules" or factories within a factory, Deere can offer farmers a choice of 84 different planter models with such a wide variety of options that farmers, with a choice of 1.6 million different types of planters, can have planters virtually customized to meet their individual needs. Its manufacturing process thus allows Deere to compete on both speed and flexibility.

it to charge a premium price for its products. George Stalk, Jr., of the Boston Consulting Group, has demonstrated that both profits and market share are directly linked to the speed with which a company can deliver its products relative to its competition.[5] In addition to fast delivery, the reliability of the delivery is also important. In other words, products should be delivered to customers with minimum variance in delivery times.

Flexibility

Flexibility, from a strategic perspective, refers to the ability of a company to offer a wide variety of products to its customers. Flexibility is also a measure of how fast a company can convert its process(es) from making an old line of products to producing a new product line. Product variety is often perceived by the customer to be a dimension of quality.

 ### Service

With product life cycles becoming shorter and shorter, the actual products themselves tend to quickly resemble those of other companies. As a consequence, these products are often viewed as commodities in which price is the primary determinant in deciding which one to buy. A good example of this is the personal computer (PC) industry. Today, the differences in the products offered among the different PC manufacturers are relatively insignificant, so price is the prime selection criterion.

[5]George Stalk, Jr., "Time—The Next Source of Competitive Advantage," *Harvard Business Review* 66, no. 4 (July–August 1988), pp. 41–51.

To obtain an advantage in such a competitive environment, firms are now providing "value-added" service. This is true for firms that provide goods and services. The reason is simple. As Sandra Vandermerwe puts it, "The market power is in the services, because the value is in the results." For example, Hendrix Veeders, a Dutch producer of livestock feed for pig farmers, now provides a range of value-added services for these farmers, including consulting on pig breeding, nutrition management, delivery of pigs to the slaughter house, and distribution of pork products to retail outlets. Another example is SKF, a Swedish manufacturer of ball bearings that advises its customers on spare parts management, training and installation, and good preventive maintenance practices to extend the life of ball bearings.[6]

Within the service sector Putnam Investments in Boston offers a wide range of mutual funds through independent brokers. To obtain a competitive advantage over other mutual fund companies, Putnam now provides brochures and prospectuses of their mutual funds to brokers within 24 hours of request.

The Next Competitive Advantage?

Companies are always looking toward the future to find the next competitive advantage that will distinguish their products in the marketplace. Currently, there appears to be a trend toward offering environmentally friendly products that are made through environmentally friendly processes. As consumers become more aware of the fragility of the environment, they are increasingly turning towards products that are safe for the environment. Ford now advertises an environmentally friendly automobile. The Body Shop, an international retail chain headquartered in England, sells various cosmetics and skin lotions that are made without harming the environment. Veryfine Products of Westford, Massachusetts, which produces a line of fruit drinks, promotes its concern for the environment by noting that it uses a very high percentage of recycled products in its containers and packaging.

BUILDING AN OPERATIONS STRATEGY FROM COMPETITIVE PRIORITIES

Factory Focus and Trade-Offs

The notion of factory focus and trade-offs was central to the concept of operations strategy during the late 1960s and early 1970s. The underlying logic was that a factory could not excel simultaneously on all four competitive priorities. Consequently, management had to decide which priorities were critical to the firm's success, and then concentrate or focus the resources of the firm on those particular characteristics. For firms with very large manufacturing facilities, Skinner suggested the creation of a Plant-within-a-Plant (PWP) concept, in which different locations within the facility would be allocated to different product lines, each with their own competitive priority. Even the workers, under the PWP concept, would be separated in order to minimize the confusion associated with shifting from one type of priority to another.[7]

For example, if a company wanted to focus on speed of delivery, then it could not be very flexible in terms of its ability to offer a wide range of products. As an example,

[6]S. Vandermerwe, *From Tin Soldiers to Russian Dolls: Creating Added Value through Services* (Oxford, England: Butterworth-Heinemann, 1993).

[7]C. W. Skinner, "The Focused Factory," *Harvard Business Review* 52, no. 3 (May–June 1974), pp. 113–22.

McDonald's provides very fast service but offers a very limited menu of highly standardized products; in contrast, Wendy's makes your request to order but takes longer to deliver. Similarly, a low-cost priority was not seen to be compatible with either speed of delivery or flexibility. High quality was also viewed as a trade-off to low cost.

The need for focus has been recognized in other service operations as well. Hotel chains like Marriott and Holiday Inn have segmented the hotel industry and now offer a variety of products, each focused on a different market segment. For example, within the Marriott group there is Fairfield Inns for economy-minded customers; Marriott Hotels and Resorts for conferences and for customers wanting full-service hotels; Residence Inns for customers wanting more than just a hotel room; and Marriott Courtyards for those wanting certain hotel conveniences like meals, but who are still concerned about price. Skinner's PWP concept is now also being applied to the healthcare industry where "hospitals-within-hospitals" allow specialized firms to focus only on specific ailments. For example, Intensiva accepts only long-term acute patients and operates independently within the facilities of St. Francis Hospital in Beech Grove, Indiana. Because it specializes in only one area (intensive care), Intensiva's operating costs are 50 percent lower than those of a typical intensive care ward.[8]

Other examples of focused operations in the service sector include BankBoston's Private Bank Division, which focuses on providing a full line of banking services to wealthy customers ("A bank within a bank," which is again not unlike Skinner's Plant-within-a-Plant concept) and Shouldice Hospital in Toronto, Canada, which performs only one type of hernia operation. The benefits of a focused operation can be readily demonstrated at Shouldice Hospital, whose very unusual product is a "hernia vacation." Patients are admitted to a mansionlike hospital in a beautiful setting outside Toronto. Every detail of the hospital's operations is focused on providing high-quality hernia care and a congenial, restful atmosphere. Patients mingle, mix, and generally relax, enjoying the experience so much that the annual reunion dinner is oversubscribed. This highly focused care permits Shouldice to keep operating costs low while maintaining high quality, both in terms of medical care and customer service. However, by becoming a specialist facility, Shouldice does not have the capabilities to perform other types of medical treatments.

Questioning the Trade-Offs

With the world becoming a single global village, there has emerged a group of companies that have adopted an international perspective toward both manufacturing and marketing. Within this global arena, competition is significantly more intense, due to both the greater number of "players" and the tremendous profit opportunities that exist.

Those companies that have excelled on this global level have often been referred to as *world-class operations*. Events in the world marketplace during the 1970s and 1980s, in terms of the growing intensity in competition, forced these companies to reexamine the concept of operations strategy, especially in terms of the so-called "necessary" trade-offs. Managers began to realize that they didn't have to make trade-offs to the same extent that they had previously thought. What emerged instead was a realization of the need to establish a hierarchy among the different priorities, as dictated by the marketplace. Exhibit 2.2 presents the sequence or priorities in which these priorities were introduced over time.

---

[8]Keith Hammonds and Nicole Harris, "Medical Lessons from the Big Mac," *Business Week*, February 10, 1997, pp. 94–98.

EXHIBIT 2.2

Time Line for Operations Strategies

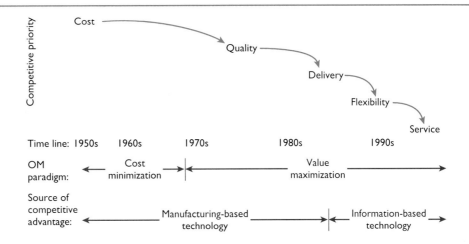

Specifically, in the late 1960s and early 1970s, cost was the primary concern, a holdover from the philosophy of the 1950s that manufacturing's only objective was to minimize production costs. However, as more and more companies began to produce low-cost products, the need became apparent to develop other ways to differentiate themselves from their competitors. The priority thus shifted to quality. Companies at this time obtained a competitive advantage by producing high-quality products, which allowed them to charge more—although price still was a factor in the consumer's buying decision. However, competition again soon caught up, and everyone was offering high-quality products that were reasonably priced.

Companies, in looking to obtain another competitive advantage in the marketplace, turned to speed and reliability of delivery as a means of differentiating themselves from the rest of the pack. Now the ante into the "game" was high-quality products that were reasonably priced and which could be delivered quickly and reliably to the customer.

In the 1980s, George Stalk, Jr., a leading management "guru," as previously noted, identified speed of delivery as a major factor in determining the success of a company.[9] Companies therefore concentrated their resources on reducing product lead times with very dramatic results. Products that once took weeks or months to deliver were now being shipped within hours or days of the receipt of an order.

Eventually, the competition again caught up and the more aggressive firms looked for still another means to obtain a competitive advantage. This time flexibility was selected, as manifested by the ability of the firm to produce customized products. Now the marketplace dictated that for firms to be successful, they had to produce reasonably priced, customized products of high quality that could be quickly delivered to the customer.

 A good example of a firm that has accomplished this is the National Bicycle Company in Japan.[10] (See the OM in Practice box on Japan's Personalized Bike Production.) An example of a retail operation that competes on more than one dimension is Custom Foot of Westport, Connecticut, that offers custom-fitted shoes on a mass-market basis (see the OM in Practice box).

---

[9]George Stalk, Jr., "Time—The Next Source of Competitive Advantage," *Harvard Business Review,* July–August 1988, pp. 41–51.

[10]Susan Moffat, "Japan's New Personalized Production," *Fortune,* October 22, 1990, pp. 132–35.

Operations Management in Practice

JAPAN'S PERSONALIZED BIKE PRODUCTION

Does your bike fit you to a "t"? Would you like one that does? If you are willing to pay 20 to 30 percent more than you would pay for a mass-produced bike, you can get a Panasonic bike manufactured to exactly match your size, weight, and color preference. You can even get your bike within three weeks of your order (only two weeks if you visit Japan). This is accomplished via a process called the Panasonic Individual Customer System (PICS), which skillfully employs computers, robots, and a small factory workforce to make one-of-a-kind models at the National Bicycle Industrial Company factory in Kokubu, Japan.

The National Bicycle Industrial Company (NBIC), a subsidiary of electronics giant Matsushita, began making the bikes under the Panasonic brand in 1987. With the introduction of its personalized order system (POS) for the Japanese market (PICS was developed for overseas sales), the firm gained international attention as a classic example of mass customization—producing products to order in lot sizes of one.

The factory itself has 21 employees and a computer-aided design (CAD) system, and is capable of producing any of 8 million variations on 18 models of racing, road, and mountain bikes in 199 color patterns for virtually any size person.

The PIC system works in the following way. A customer visits a local Panasonic bicycle store and is measured on a special frame. The storeowner then faxes the specifications to the master control room at the factory. There an operator punches the specs into a minicomputer, which automatically creates a unique blueprint and produces a bar code. (The CAD blueprint takes about three minutes as opposed to three hours required by company draftspeople prior to computerization.) The bar code is then attached to metal tubes and gears that ultimately become the customer's personal bike. At various stages in the process, line workers access the customer's requirement using the bar code label and a scanner. This information, displayed on a CRT terminal at each station, is fed directly to the computer-controlled machines that are part of a local area computer network. At each step of production, a computer reading the code knows that each part belongs to a specific bike, and tells a robot where to weld or tells a painter which pattern to follow.

Despite the use of computers and robots, the process is not highly automated. Gears are hand-wired, assembly is manual, and the customer's name is silk-screened by hand with the touch of an artisan. The entire manufacturing and assembly time required to complete a single bike is 150 minutes, and

---

As the "rules" for operations strategy shifted from that of primarily reducing costs to that of including quality, speed of delivery, flexibility and service, the strategy for the operations management function has also shifted. The strategy of minimizing production costs has been replaced with that of maximizing the value added.

This emphasis on being competitive on more than one dimension might lead to the conclusion that there are no longer any trade-offs. This is not the case. As Wickham Skinner said at a breakfast meeting of the Boston P/OM Pancake Society in April 1995, "There will always be trade-offs." Today, however, those trade-offs occur on what can be described as a higher performance curve, as shown in Exhibit 2.3. A firm can either improve delivery at the same cost (A_1 to B_1) or reduce cost while maintaining the same speed of delivery (A_2 to B_2) or any combination of the two (A_3 to B_3).

Order Qualifiers and Order Winners

order-qualifiers
Minimum characteristics of a firm or its products to be considered as a source of purchase.

order-winners
Characteristics of a firm that distinguish it from its competition so that it is selected as the source of purchase.

Terry Hill of the London Business School has developed the strategic concept of **order-qualifiers** and **order-winners**.[11] Order qualifiers can be defined as the minimum elements or characteristics that a firm or its products must have in order to even be considered as a potential supplier or source. In Europe, for example, the vast majority of companies today require that their vendors be ISO-9000 certified. (This certification ensures that a firm has documented all of its processes.) Thus, ISO-9000 certification is an order-qualifier in

---

[11]T. Hill, *Manufacturing Strategy: Text and Cases*, 2nd ed. (Burr Ridge, IL: Irwin, 1994).

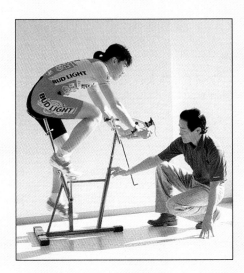

Customers are custom-fitted in the retail store with options for 11,231,862 possible variations.

a customer must wait two to three weeks given that it takes less than three hours to make a custom model. According to the general manager of sales, "We could have made the time shorter, but we want people to feel excited about waiting for something special."

To provide a more personal touch to mass customization, the factory is given the responsibility to communicate directly with the customer. Immediately after the factory receives the customer's order, a personalized computer-generated drawing of the bicycle is mailed with a note thanking the customer for choosing the bike. This is followed up with a second personal note, three months later, inquiring about the customer's satisfaction with the bicycle. Finally, a "bicycle birthday card" is sent to commemorate the first anniversary of the bicycle.

NBIC is now contemplating extending the Panasonic system to all of its bicycle production, while Matsushita is considering applying the concept to industrial machinery.

the factory can make about 60 a day. NBIC's mass-production factory (which makes 90 percent of its annual production) can make a standard model in 90 minutes. One might ask why

Source: Surech Kotha, "The National Bicycle Industrial Company: Implementing a Strategy of Mass-Customization," case study from the International University of Japan, 1993; and Susan Moffat. "Japan's New Personalized Production," *Fortune*, October 22, 1990, pp. 132–35.

Europe. In contrast, most companies in the United States at this time are not ISO-9000 certified (those firms that are certified in the United States have done so primarily to do business in Europe). As a consequence, ISO-9000 certified companies in the United States use their certification as an order-winner (that is, ISO-9000 certification distinguishes them as being better than their competition).

Basically, when very few firms offer a specific characteristic, like high quality, customization, or outstanding service, that characteristic can be defined as an order-winner. However, over time, as more and more firms begin to offer that same enhancement, the order-winner becomes an order-qualifier. In other words, it becomes the minimum acceptable level for all competitors. As a result, the customer uses some other new enhancement or characteristic to make the final purchase. The shift of a product characteristic from being an order-winner to an order-qualifier is shown in Exhibit 2.4. We have arbitrarily selected 50 percent to represent the point at which an order-winner becomes an order qualifier, as that is when the majority of firms provide a particular enhancement.

The Information Age

As we enter the twenty-first century, world-class companies are again looking for a breakthrough that will provide them with another competitive advantage in the marketplace. The 1996 annual meeting of the Operations Management Association (OMA) focused on the topic of service as the next source of competitive advantage, with several presentations suggesting that service (as shown in Exhibit 2.2), in particular post-purchase service,

EXHIBIT 2.3

Example of Trade-Offs on
Higher Performance Curves

EXHIBIT 2.4

Distinguishing between Order Qualifiers and Order Winners

is the current method by which companies now differentiate themselves. Cadillac and Lexus, for example, are already offering extensive warranty packages which include such things as road service, travel planning, and the use of loaner vehicles during the warranty period.

Warranty packages such as these now permit companies to capture all the data pertaining to product defects and malfunctions (at least those that occur during the warranty period). Such information can then be fed back into the product design process to further refine the product. These types of product warranties are very similar to the service guarantees advocated by Hart.[12]

With the incorporation of this type of consumer information into the operations process, companies will officially make the transition from the manufacturing age into the infor-

[12]C. W. L. Hart, "The Power of Unconditional Service Guarantees," *Harvard Business Review* 66, no. 4 (July–August 1988), pp. 56–62.

Operations Management in Practice

SHOES THAT FIT LIKE A GLOVE

Custom Foot, Inc. of Westport, Connecticut, offers its customers fashionable, custom-made Italian shoes for men and women at prices that start as low as $128.00. Customers can choose from 75 different styles (25 men's and 75 women's) which are offered in 670 different sizes that range from a woman's size 3-AAAAAA to a man's size 16-EEEEEEEEE.

As no two feet are exactly alike, a state-of-the-art digitized scanner takes a three-dimensional image of each foot. The scanner provides the exact measurements and precision required for hand-crafted shoes. The shoe specifications are then transferred via computer to Custom Foot's factories in Italy where production begins immediately. With this close link between the retail operations and the factory, the shoes are typically available for the customer to pick up within three weeks. Because customer foot sizes are kept on file in a database, subsequent orders can be placed on the telephone without a visit to the retail store.

As each pair of shoes is custom made, Custom Foot stocks no inventories in any of its retail locations. It therefore does not have to worry at the end of a season about getting rid of shoes which might go out of style. In addition, expensive retail space is not required to stock large inventories of

shoes, but can instead be devoted to increasing customer sales and providing better service.

Custom Foot provides a good example of a firm that is competing on several dimensions—namely, price, speed, customization, and quality.

Source: Special thanks to Jim Metscher and Mary Jo Vincent of Custom Foot.

---

mation age. Previously, competitive advantages were achieved through the operations processing capability of the company. Now, the competitive advantage is achieved primarily by using information from the marketplace.

In summary, the evolution of operations strategy, from being virtually nonexistent in the 1950s and 1960s to playing a critical role in the success of an organization, is shown in Exhibit 2.2. Also included in this figure is the change in paradigms for the operations management function and the transition from the manufacturing age to the information age.

A FRAMEWORK FOR IMPLEMENTING OPERATIONS STRATEGY

Core Capabilities

core capabilities
Specific strengths that allow a company to achieve its competitive priorities.

In order to successfully implement an operations strategy, be it within a manufacturing firm or within a service, certain **core capabilities** must be identified. These core capabilities allow the firm to establish its competitive priorities in the marketplace. Core capabilities can thus be defined as that skill or set of skills that the operations management function has developed that allows the firm to differentiate itself from its competitors. Similar core capabilities need to be identified in the other functional areas too, and each of these functional capabilities should be aligned to meet the overall goals of the firm. For example, in the opening vignette to this chapter, Hewlett-Packard's engineering function has developed a core capability for being the new product technology leader in its industry. Manufacturing

ENGINEERING

produces these new products both quickly and in a wide variety to meet the specific needs of individual customers.

In order to focus on these core capabilities, firms, both in manufacturing and services, have begun to divest themselves of those activities that are not considered to be critical to their success. In manufacturing, more and more components and subassemblies which were previously built in-house are now being subcontracted or outsourced to suppliers. As a result, the material cost in most manufacturing companies, as a percentage of total manufacturing costs, has substantially increased in recent years. On the other hand, the labor cost, as a percentage, has been drastically reduced, often to less than 5 percent of total costs.

This focus on core capabilities has also impacted services. More and more service operations are now subcontracting out ancillary support services which were previously provided in-house. Again, this strategy has allowed these services to concentrate on improving their core capabilities. For example, many colleges and universities now subcontract their food service operations to firms like Marriott and their bookstore operations to retailers like Barnes and Noble. As another example, ServiceMaster has built a very successful business providing housekeeping services to hospitals and office buildings at substantial savings to these businesses. In many instances, the companies that have subcontracted these support services have discovered that the subcontractors can perform them better and at a lower cost than when they were done internally. This focus on core capabilities further supports the concept of a value chain. Here each company focuses on its core capabilities thereby allowing it to maximize its value contribution to the end product that is provided to the customer. (A word of caution, however. Casually subcontracting a function that is not viewed as a core competency may result in losing knowledgeable people who know how the broader system operates and who can deal with unexpected emergencies that might shut down a core activity.)

MANUFACTURING'S ROLE IN CORPORATE STRATEGY

Wheelwright and Hayes have identified four stages in the integration of operations strategy into the overall support of corporate goals of a manufacturing firm. Top management and production managers view the decisions and choices that must be made in these stages very differently. A summary of these stages is found in Exhibit 2.5.

Stage 1: Internally Neutral Manufacturing operations capability is viewed as the result of a few simple decisions about capacity, location, technology, and vertical integration. Typically, top management makes these decisions with the aid of consultants. The company's own production staff handles only day-to-day, "get-the-product-out-the-door" decisions. The workers and managers in the operations departments tend to be low-skilled. There is constant performance measurement because top management wants to know immediately of any variance in order to take corrective action. Operations' potential negative impact needs to be minimized. Innovation in process technology is very slow. Management takes few investment risks in the manufacturing area.

Stage 2: Externally Neutral This stage is frequently seen in manufacturing-intensive organizations such as steel. Here operations management is viewed as relatively standardized and unsophisticated. Investment in process technology is reactive, being made only when competitors make changes. Top management is primarily concerned with decisions about

EXHIBIT 2.5

Stages in Operations
Manufacturing Strategic Role

Stage I	Minimize manufacturing's negative potential: "internally neutral"	Outside experts are called in to make decisions about strategic manufacturing issues. Internal, detailed management control systems are the primary means for monitoring manufacturing performance. Manufacturing is kept flexible and reactive.
Stage 2	Achieve parity with competititors: "externally neutral"	"Industry practice" is followed. The planning horizon for manufacturing investment decisions is extended to incorporate a single business cycle. Capital investment is the primary means for catching up with competition or achieving a competitive edge.
Stage 3	Provide credible support to the business strategy: "internally supportive"	Manufacturing investments are screened for consistency with the business strategy. A manufacturing strategy is formulated and pursued. Longer-term manufacturing developments and trends are addressed systematically.
Stage 4	Pursue a manufacturing-based competitive advantage: "externally supportive"	Efforts are made to anticipate the potential of new manufacturing practices and technologies. Manufacturing is involved "up front" in major marketing and engineering decisions (and vice versa). Long-range programs are pursued in order to acquire capabilities in advance of needs.

Source: Reprinted by permission of the *Harvard Business Review*. An exhibit from "Competing through Manufacturing" by Steven C. Wheelwright and Robert H. Hayes (January/February 1985). Copyright © 1985 by the President and Fellows of Harvard College; all rights reserved.

resource allocation (capital investments), with emphasis on economy-of-scale criteria. In acquiring new technologies, parity with competitors is sought and new technologies are purchased rather than developed. America's failing smokestack industries (such as steel) and the loss of their markets to foreign competition are evidence of the lack of effectiveness of this stage.

Stage 3: Internally Supportive   In this stage—a considerable change from the neutrality of the preceding two stages—all the manufacturing decisions are used to support corporate strategy. The operations staff is given the authority to make decisions, and those decisions are expected to be consistent with the overall goals of the firm. The corporate strategy is translated into terminology that is meaningful to manufacturing. A longer-term, creative view of the operations function is taken, but only as long as the creative direction is consistent and in alignment with the already existing strategy.

Stage 4: Externally Supportive   In this stage, operations is expected not only to support corporate strategy but also to contribute to its initial development. The operations management function gives the company its competitive advantage, such as low cost or high quality. The scope of decisions is long-term. Investment is made not only in the capital resources but also in workforce and systems.

In a true Stage 4 company, the operations management function, like all other business functions, takes a proactive role. The formal and informal communication between finance,

EXHIBIT 2.6

Stages of Service Firm Competitiveness

Stage	Service Dimensions					
	Service Quality	Back Office	Customer	Introduction of New Technology	Work Force	First-Line Management
I. Available for service	Second to cost: • High variability	Counting room	Satisfy unspecified customer at minimum cost	Only when necessary for survival: • Under duress	Negative constraint	Controls workers
II. Journeyman	Attempts to meet customer expectations: • Consistent on a few key dimensions	Plays important role in total service: • Given attention, but still a separate role	Market segment whose basic needs are understood	When justified by cost savings	Efficient resource; disciplined (follows procedures)	Controls process
III. Distinctive competence achieved	Exceeds customer expectations: • Consistent on multiple dimensions	Equally valued with front office; plays integral role	Collection of individuals whose various needs are understood	When promises to enhance service	Adaptive— permitted to select among alternative procedures	Listens to customers; coaches/facilitates workers
IV. World-class service delivery	Raises customer expectations; seeks challenges: • Continuous improvement	Proactive— develops own capabilities, generates opportunities	Source of stimulation, ideas, and opportunity	Source of firstmover advantages, creates ability to do things competitors can't do	Innovative— creates procedures	Listened to by top management as source of new ideas; mentors workers to enhance career growth

Source: Reprinted from "Beefing-Up Operations in Service Firms," by R. B. Chase and R. H. Hayes, *Sloan Management Review*, Fall 1991, pp. 17–28, by permission of publisher. Copyright 1991 by Sloan Management Review Association. All rights reserved.

marketing, accounting, personnel, and other functions is considerable. There is a horizontal structure, with no one function being more important than another.

OPERATIONS' ROLE IN A SERVICE FIRM'S COMPETITIVENESS

 The competitiveness of a service firm is generally *more* dependent on the strength of its operations capabilities than it is for a manufacturing company. For example, a manufacturing company may be outstanding in its design capabilities but only so-so in its operations, yet still be a market leader. Such a situation cannot exist in a service operation, where the operations activities constitute all or part of the product. The inseparability of product from process means that a service firm's competitiveness and its operations competitiveness are always closely linked. This linkage between operations strategy and corporate goals is shown in the four-stage model presented in Exhibit 2.6.

The first column of the exhibit lists four proposed stages of service firm competitiveness which are defined in Exhibit 2.7. Across the top are the major service dimensions that operations executives must address in strategy development. The entries in the table reflect our interpretation of the views held by senior management of companies that fit into each stage.

Some additional comments about the framework: First, the stage attained by any given firm is a composite. Every service delivery system embodies a unique set of choices about service quality, workforce policies, and so forth. A company may be at a different stage for a given dimension, or have service units that are further or less advanced than others. What determines a firm's overall stage is where the balance falls along these different dimensions—where, in a sense, the firm's center of gravity lies. Second, a firm can be very competitive (Stage III or even Stage IV) even if it is not outstanding on all dimensions. This could happen when it is doing an exceptional job on its critical success factors. Third, it is difficult or impossible to skip a stage in moving up the ladder. A company obviously must achieve journeyman performance before distinctive competence, and distinctive competence before becoming world class. (It is, however, possible to move through the stages

	Stage	Characteristics
	I. Available for service	• Firm survives for reasons other than performance (e.g., a government agency)
		• Operations reactive, at best
	II. Journeyman	• Firm neither sought out nor avoided
		• Operations reliable but uninspired
	III. Distinctive competence achieved	• Firm sought out based on reputation for meeting customer expectations
		• Operations continually excels, reinforced by management and systems supporting intense customer focus
	IV. World-class service delivery	• Firm name synonymous with service excellence; exceeds customer's expectations, delighting rather than satisfying; leaves competitors in the dust
		• Operations is quick learner, fast innovator; masters every step of service delivery process; provides capabilities superior to competitors

EXHIBIT 2.7

Defining the Four Stages of Service Firm Competitiveness

relatively rapidly. For example, Scandinavian Airlines System [SAS] instituted some 120 service improvements that moved it from Stage I to Stage III within the space of a year and a half.) Finally, it is all too easy to slip back a stage.

The Integration of Goods and Services

Many firms are now looking to integrated and user-friendly service as a means of obtaining a competitive advantage in the marketplace. In so doing they are recognizing the need to align and integrate the products that are being offered. This is true for both manufacturing and service operations.

For example, Ritz-Carlton, a hotel chain which focuses on the top 5 percent of the hotel market, has operators answering its 800 reservation number instead of having a more efficient menu-driven system. Although the menu-driven system is more cost efficient, management at the Ritz knows that its high income customers will not waste their time with such a system. Similarly, CTI-Cryogenics in Mansfield, Massachusetts, a leading producer of vacuum pumps that are critical items in the manufacture of computer chips, now has a "GUTS" program (Guaranteed Up-Time Service). When a pump fails, it impacts the production of a computer chip fabrication facility which typically costs more than a billion dollars. A call to the 800 number, therefore, puts the customer in contact with an engineer who diagnoses the problem and ships out the required parts within 24 hours. This high level of service allows the computer fabrication plant to resume operations as quickly as possible, thereby minimizing downtime.

By integrating goods and services into a total package, companies are better able to address the overall needs of their customers. In so doing, they are actually helping their customers solve problems rather than just selling them products. To provide a foundation for properly aligning the goods and services being offered, Vandermerwe suggests that a firm understand its customer's activity cycle, as shown in Exhibit 2.8. This cycle, in general terms, is divided into three major categories: (a) prepurchase activities, (b) purchase activities, and (c) postpurchase activities. The better a firm can identify and understand each of the elements that take place within these categories, the greater an advantage it will have in the marketplace. In other words, the more of the customer's activity cycle that a company addresses, the stronger is its position. Providing service through an

EXHIBIT 2.8

Customer's Activity Cycle

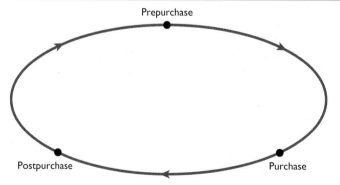

Source: S. Vandermerwe, *From Tin Soldiers to Russian Dolls* (Oxford, England: Butterworth-Heinemann, 1993).

understanding of the customer's activity cycle can also be viewed as an order-winner in the marketplace.

CONCLUSION

Competitiveness and the various operations strategies through which it is achieved are the underlying themes throughout the study of operations management. Decisions made at the operations strategy level impact most of the management decisions within the other functions of the organization. With global competition becoming only more intense in the foreseeable future, companies, in order to succeed, must adopt the operations strategy that best meets the needs of its customers. To satisfy these needs, firms must clearly understand their core capabilities and focus their resources on maintaining and improving these capabilities.

KEY TERMS

business strategies   p. 22
  low cost   p. 22
  market segmentation   p. 22
  product differentiation   p. 22
competitive priorities   p. 23
  cost   p. 25
  quality   p. 25
  delivery   p. 25
  flexibility   p. 25
  service   p. 25
competitiveness   p. 23

core capabilities   p. 33
corporate strategy   p. 22
functional strategy   p. 23
newly industrialized countries (NIC)   p. 22
operational planning and control   p. 24
operations strategy   p. 23
order-qualifiers   p. 30
order-winners   p. 30
strategic business unit (SBU)   p. 22
strategic planning   p. 24
tactical planning   p. 24

REVIEW AND DISCUSSION QUESTIONS

1. What is meant by competitiveness?
2. Identify the different types of competitive priorities. How has their relationship to each other changed over the years?
3. For each of the different competitive priorities, describe the unique characteristics of the market niche with which it is most compatible.
4. Describe the difference between order-qualifiers and order-winners. What is the relationship between the two over time?
5. Explain the concept of the core capabilities within an organization.
6. How does understanding a customer's activity cycle allow a firm to achieve a competitive advantage in the marketplace?
7. In your opinion, do business schools have competitive priorities?
8. Why does the "proper" operations strategy keep changing for companies that are world-class competitors?
9. What is meant by the expression "manufacturing is entering the information age"?
10. What is a "value-added" service? How does it differ from providing good service?
11. Describe the customer activity cycle involved in taking a transcontinental flight. What could be done to facilitate the process for the customer?

INTERNET UPDATE

Conduct a search on the Internet and identify the different types of operations strategies that companies have adopted in order to compete. Suggested key words to help you in your search are OPERATIONS and STRATEGY. As an alternate, go to the McGraw-Hill homepage at www.mhhe.com/pom and take several company tours for the purpose of describing some of their competitive priorities. For each tour identify the company, the product it makes, and its competitive priorities.

CASE: MOTOROLA'S PLANTATION, FLORIDA, FACTORY

Motorola strives to measure every task performed by every one of its 120,000 employees, and calculates that it saved $1.5 billion by reducing defects and simplifying processes last year. While that figure is hard to verify, here's one that isn't: Since 1986, productivity (sales per employee) has increased 126 percent, even though Motorola has expanded its work force.

What does the company do with all the money it saves? Some goes into R&D, some goes to workers as bonuses keyed to return on net assets, and some goes straight to the bottom line. But mostly, says corporate quality director Richard Buetow, "we've been giving it away at the marketplace." Motorola cut the price of cellular telephones 25 percent last year yet still raised its net profit margins.

At some Motorola factories quality is so high that they've stopped counting defects per million and started working on defects per *billion*. Overall, the company aims to reduce its error rate tenfold every two years and to increase the speed of its processes—cut its cycle time—tenfold every five years. At those levels, says Buetow, "you are hitting the limits of the capabilities of many of your machines." And those of your people as well.

Jerry Mysliwiec, manufacturing director at the Land Mobile Products factory in Plantation, Florida, begins each morning meeting of his factory supervisors with a singular request: "Okay, guys, tell me what records you broke, because if you didn't break records, you didn't improve."

Four years ago the Plantation factory wasn't breaking much of anything except the patience of its managers. It took Motorola as long as 10 days to turn out a finished radio. To decide which models to make, analysts crunched out elaborate forecasts of consumer demand, which were rarely on target. The company began building the radios at a "feeder plant" in Malaysia, where labor costs were low, then shipped them to Plantation for final assembly.

These days Plantation's Jedi line (named after the good guys in *Star Wars*) can make a specific radio—any one of more than 500 variations—for a specific customer in just two hours. They no longer rely on a forecast or a feeder plant. As the radios zip around the U-shaped assembly line, pallets marked with binary codes tell the robots, and the casually clad workers who monitor them, what to do. Plantation's most useful innovation: inventing a computer-controlled soldering process that eliminates the need for costly and time-consuming tool changes. Motorola is now converting the two-way radio plant in Malaysia, along with its other major operation in Ireland, into clones of Plantation's "focused flexible factory."

As part of its quality drive, Motorola has given new meaning to the phrase "team spirit." At the cellular equipment plant in Arlington Heights. Illinois, self-directed teams hire and fire their coworkers, help select their supervisors and schedule their own work (in consultation with other teams). Last year, the factory's 1,003 workers also mustered into no fewer than 168 special teams dedicated to improving quality, cutting costs, and reducing cycle time.

QUESTION

1. What operations capabilities is Motorola using to compete?

SELECTED BIBLIOGRAPHY

Davidow, W. H., and B. Uttal. "Service Companies: Focus or Falter." *Harvard Business Review* 67, no. 4 (July–August 1989), pp. 77–85.

Garvin, D. A. *Operations Strategy: Text and Cases*. Englewood Cliffs, NJ: Prentice Hall, 1992.

Hammonds, Keith, and Nicole Harris. "Medical Lessons from the Big Mac." *Business Week,* February 10, 1997, pp. 94–98.

Hart, C. W. L. "The Power of the Unconditional Service Guarantees." *Harvard Business Review* 66, no. 4 (July–August 1988), pp. 56–62.

Hayes, Robert, and Gary Pisano. "Beyond World Class: The New Manufacturing Strategy." *Harvard Business Review* 72, no. 1 (January–February 1994), pp. 77–86.

Henkoff, Ronald. "Keeping Motorola on a Roll." *Fortune*, April 18, 1994, pp. 67–78.

Hill, T. *Manufacturing Strategy: Text and Cases*. 2nd ed. Burr Ridge, IL: Irwin, 1994, pp. 67–78.

Loveman, G. "The Globalization of Services: Four Strategies That Drive Growth Across Borders." *Proceedings of the 4th International Research Seminar in Service Management*. Agelonde-LaLonde les Maures, France, June 4–7, 1996.

Martin, Justin. "Give 'Em Exactly What They Want." *Fortune,* November 10, 1997, pp. 238–85.

Naisbitt, J., and P. Aburdene. *Megatrends 2000.* New York: William Morrow Co., 1990.

Normann, Richard, and Rafael Ramirez. "From Value Chain to Value Constellation: Designing Interactive Strategy." *Harvard Business Review* 71, no. 3 (July–August 1993), pp. 65–77.

Porter, M. *Competitive Strategy: Techniques for Analyzing Industries and Competitors*. New York: The Free Press, 1980.

Porter, Michael E., and Claas van der Linde. "Green and Competitive: Ending the Stalemate." *Harvard Business Review* 73, no. 5 (September–October 1995), pp. 120–34.

Skinner, C. Wickham. "Manufacturing—The Missing Link in Corporate Strategy." *Harvard Business Review* 47, no. 3 (May–June 1969), pp. 136–45.

Skinner, C. Wickham. "The Focused Factory." *Harvard Business Review* 52, no. 3 (May–June 1974), pp. 113–22.

Stalk, George, Jr. "Time—The Next Source of Competitive Advantage." *Harvard Business Review* 66, no. 4 (July–August 1988), pp. 41–51.

Vandermerwe, S. *From Tin Soldiers to Russian Dolls: Creating Added Value Through Services*. Oxford, England: Butterworth-Heinemann, 1993.

Chapter 3

PROCESSES IN MANUFACTURING AND SERVICES

Chapter Outline

Chapter Objectives

- Demonstrate that processes within an organization need to address not only the technical aspects of manufacturing the goods but also the customer-related aspects of delivery and service.

- Introduce the product design process and the concept of a product's life cycle.

- Identify the various processes by which goods and services can be produced and how these processes relate to a product's life cycle.

- Present a framework for classifying services to identify common threads which can facilitate their analysis.

- Demonstrate the impact of technology on the processes that provide us with these goods and services.

P

rocess management at FedEx is viewed as a systematic examination of how the actual work of operating a business gets done. This approach, which cuts across divisional, functional, and departmental lines, entails collaborative investigation, analysis, and then refinement of the basic processes, activities, and tasks by which a business operates.

The five core business processes defined at FedEx are: (*a*) providing direction, (*b*) acquiring and retaining customers, (*c*) servicing customers, (*d*) moving, tracking, and delivering the product, and (*e*) invoicing and collecting payment. Process management at FedEx is customer-driven. It focuses first on customer requirements to assure that the process is designed to meet the expectations of the customer. It utilizes analytical techniques to identify high-leverage opportunities for standardizing work processes, as well as for creating opportunities for continuous improvement.

Measurement is also important at FedEx. The old business maxim, "You cannot manage what you cannot measure," has been an inspiration for measuring both customer satisfaction and service quality. Measurement is accomplished through the use of process quality indicators (PQIs), which measure the outputs of processes, as well as other process indicators, which measure such factors as the quality of the process results, the cycle time of each operation within a process, and the cost of the process. An example of a PQI within the moving, tracking, and delivering the product core process is "the total number of conveyances (trucks and aircraft) arriving late at Hubs, destination ramps, and destination stations, which is measured on a daily basis at the corporate level."

FedEx recognizes that its future success depends on many factors, including its ability to improve its business processes. It believes that only if it can adopt and fully utilize analytical business tools, such as process management, to improve operations will it be able to compete against other companies in the marketplace. However, the full utilization of the techniques of process management depends on the motivation and competencies of its front-line management. Its managers must have analytical, communication, and decision-making skills, and that the training is available to ensure that these managers obtain these required skills. ■

Source: Adapted from a letter from Fred Smith, CEO, FedEx, to FedEx management, October 7, 1996.

As confirmed by Fred Smith at FedEx, managers today recognize that processes exist everywhere within their organizations. We define a *process* as any step or series of steps that are involved in the conversion or transformation of inputs into outputs. We use the terms *process, conversion process,* and *transformation process* interchangeably throughout this text. Exhibit 3.1 presents some examples of the various types of processes that can exist within an organization. Within the operations function, some processes focus on the development of new products; some focus on the day-to-day production of existing products; still others focus on customer service.

This chapter provides a framework for addressing some of the basic issues that are associated with the design and on-going production of goods and services. We also identify the factors that need to be considered in selecting the proper processes for producing these products. We include here a discussion of the product/process relationship and how technology can impact these processes.

THE ORIGINS OF NEW PRODUCTS

Davis and Tumolo have identified five different types of new products that are a function of the process by which they are developed. These include: (*a*) revolutionary products, (*b*) evolutionary products, (*c*) product extensions, (*d*) core research products, and (*e*) partnership products. How a firm decides to develop new products can have a significant impact on resources (such as plant and equipment), cash flow, and scheduling.[1]

Revolutionary Products

Revolutionary products are the result of major breakthroughs in science and technology, in terms of new product materials and/or new processes by which the product is made. Ford's Model T car, nylon fabric, the Polaroid camera, Xerox copiers, and compact disks (CDs) provide good examples of revolutionary products.

Typically, a firm with a revolutionary product has a tremendous advantage in the marketplace over its competition. Such new products are often protected by patents, which prevent competition from producing identical or similar products for a significant amount of time. Consequently, these companies often enjoy a captive audience for the first few years

EXHIBIT 3.1

Examples of Processes within an Organization

Process Description	Inputs	Outputs
Market research	Surveys, interviews, focus groups	Customer preferences, suggestions
Payroll	Time sheets, time cards	Paychecks
Customer service	Complaints, inquiries	Resolution of issues
Hiring new employees	Advertisements, interviews, tests	New employees

[1]Mark M. Davis and Paul L. Tumolo, *Operations Management in Manufacturing* (Watertown, MA: American Management Association, 1994), pp. 29–31.

after these new products are introduced, which translates into high-profit margins. However, revolutionary products also have some negative aspects. They usually require large investments in new manufacturing facilities, or at the minimum, major changes to existing processes. Another critical element of revolutionary products is the integration of the new product with existing product(s), both in terms of manufacturing and marketing. IBM's introduction of the personal computer provides a good example of a revolutionary product in that it affected their market for minicomputers and at the same time opened up new markets that were previously nonexistent.

Evolutionary Products

Evolutionary products represent significant enhancements to existing products in terms of lower costs, increased reliability, and/or major improvements to the manufacturing processes by which they are made. One example of an evolutionary product is the Sony Sport Walkman CD player which is a waterproofed version of a previously existing product. (Waterproofing increases its reliability outdoors.)

Evolutionary products usually have a relatively small impact on a company's resources because the changes are considered to be incremental. These changes to existing products are often provided by customers in several ways, including (*a*) data on warranty work, (*b*) direct feedback through written surveys, telephone interviews and/or focus groups, and (*c*) the use of service guarantees (which are discussed in Chapter 5). These incremental improvements to existing products typically will have a minor impact on material requirements and processes that are already in place.

Product Extensions

Product extensions are products that have been derived from a common product base or "platform." As we saw in the opening vignette in Chapter 2, the use of such platforms allows Hewlett-Packard's Medical Products Group to quickly introduce a wide variety of new products. Another good example was Chrysler's K-car, which consisted of a frame and drive train that formed the basis for approximately a dozen different automobile models. Likewise, Apple's MacIntosh computer is the underlying platform for a whole family of personal computers.

Through the use of product extensions or platforms, a company can introduce a wide variety of products in a relatively short time period. The common basis for these products translates into relatively small changes that focus primarily on improving performance, features, and appearance. The common product platform also permits a firm to use previously designed components, which further reduces design time, procurement costs, and manufacturing cycles.

Unlike revolutionary products, no major changes are made to any specific product within a particular platform group. Nevertheless, it is important to properly plan for the integration of these new products into existing manufacturing processes. With investments in plant and equipment already in place, another advantage of this type of product is that it can extend the life cycle of current manufacturing processes—provided that those processes are sufficiently flexible to accommodate these new products.

Core Research Products

New products that are the result of core or basic research are very often high risk ventures because the ratio of successful new products (as defined by consumer acceptance) to failures is very low. Unlike revolutionary products which are the result of "applied" research to achieve a specific end product, new products that result from core or basic research are often a byproduct or "stumble-on product" that were not the primary goal of the research. A good example of a new product that was developed from core research is the Post-It paper that resulted from 3M company's research study of adhesives. It has become one of the most successful office supply products ever made.

Partnership Products

New product development costs continue to escalate. The ability for one firm to absorb all of these costs without exposing itself to significant financial risk has, therefore, become increasingly difficult. Consequently, companies often look for one or more partners to share both the expenses and benefits that are associated with the development of a new product. There are, however, added difficulties when such partnerships are formed. For example, communication between partners is often slower and less effective than it is within an existing organization.

NEW PRODUCT DESIGN AND DEVELOPMENT PROCESSES IN MANUFACTURING

In today's fiercely competitive environment, no company can rest on the successful introduction of any one new product. Product life cycles are growing increasingly shorter, and the more successful firms are reducing new product development times to a fraction of what they once were. As noted in Chapter 2, 70 percent of the sales in 1995 at Hewlett-Packard's Medical Products Group were derived from products that were less than two years old. The 3M Corporation in Minneapolis introduced 500 new products in 1996 alone and now requires that 30 percent of revenues come from new products every year.[2] Consequently, competition has the ability to react more quickly to changes in the marketplace, thereby substantially reducing the advantages of any one new product introduction, regardless of how innovative it is. The speed with which a company can introduce a new product can, therefore, significantly affect both its profit margins and market share.

With the trend towards shorter product life cycles, successful companies must be able to: (*a*) continuously generate new product ideas, (*b*) convert these ideas into reliable functional designs that are user-friendly, (*c*) ensure that these designs are readily producible, and (*d*) select the proper processes that are most compatible with the needs of the customer from a technical aspect as well as from a customer service perspective. In addition, all of this must be accomplished within an increasingly shorter time frame (see Exhibit 3.2).

MARKETING
PRODUCT DEVELOPMENT
MANUFACTURING

Designing new products and delivering them to the market quickly is the challenge facing manufacturers in all industries, from computer chips to potato chips. (See OM in Practice box on Successful Product Design.) As shown in Exhibit 3.3, three major functions are involved in these activities: marketing, product development, and manufacturing. Marketing has the responsibility for collecting customer data on new products; product development has the responsibility for translating the customer requirements into technical specifications; and manufacturing has the responsibility for designing the processes for producing the items.

Typically, most American firms generate the majority of their product ideas from R&D departments augmented by listening to their customers. In addition, many companies encourage their own employees to generate new product ideas and to contribute to the development of those currently being investigated. At Hewlett-Packard, for example, product design engineers leave whatever they are working on out on their desks so that others may come by and tinker with their projects.

---

[2]K. M. Eisenhardt and S. L. Brown, "Time-Pacing: Competing in Markets That Won't Stand Still," *Harvard Business Review,* March–April 1998, pp. 59–69.

EXHIBIT 3.2

The Trend toward Shorter
Product Development Times

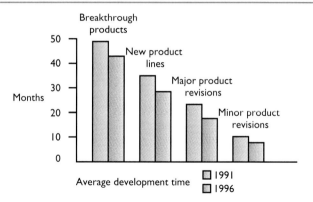

Note: From a survey of 200 U.S. companies.

Source: Data: Product Development & Management Association, *Business Week*, January 27, 1997, p. 6.

EXHIBIT 3.3

Flow of Activities in Product Design and Process Selection

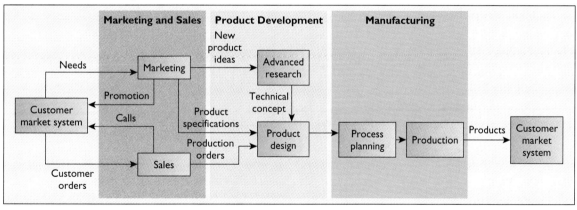

Source: Reprinted with the permission of the Free Press, an imprint of Simon & Schuster from *Fast Cycle Time: How to Align Purpose, Strategy, and Structure for Speed* by Christopher Meyer. Copyright © 1993 by Christopher Meyer.

Design for Manufacturability

In translating the functional product design into a manufacturable product, designers must consider many aspects. They can use a variety of methods and alternative materials to make a product. Material choices can be ferrous (iron and steel), aluminum, copper, brass, magnesium, zinc, tin, nickel, titanium, or several other metals. The nonmetals include polymers (thermoplastics, thermosetting plastics, and elastomers), wood, leather, rubber, carbon, ceramics, glass, gypsum, concrete, as well as several others. Further, all of these materials can be formed, cut, and shaped in many ways. There are extrusions, stampings, rolling, powder-metal, forgings, castings, injection molding, along with a very large selection of machining processes.

In designing for manufacturability, it is also desirable to keep the number of individual parts to a minimum. In electronics, manufacturers accomplish this by combining circuits that have been in different components into larger and larger integrated circuits. Not only does this increase the speed within the circuits, because electrons don't have to travel as far,

Operations Management in Practice

FACTORS THAT CONTRIBUTE TO SUCCESSFUL PRODUCT DESIGNS

A recent review of successful product designs, ranging from razors and laptop computers to power tools and outdoor grills, identified several factors that these products and their manufacturers shared, including:

- *Design from the outside in.* Make the customer's use of the product the focus of all product development.
- *Partner deeply.* Involve all of the relevant functional areas (e.g., marketing, engineering, purchasing, and manufacturing) early in the design process to assist in defining the new product. (This is often referred to as concurrent engineering.)
- *Partner widely.* With the emergence of the virtual enterprise, organizational boundaries are becoming unclear. Designers must, therefore, partner with all stakeholders—both internal and external.
- *Design the product upfront.* Match the right product to the right market niche. Upfront design analysis will eliminate faulty concepts early.
- *Get physical fast.* Use prototypes to visualize a concept and to obtain quick feedback from both users and managers.
- *Design for manufacturability.* Always design a product that will meet established quality, cost, and delivery parameters. Manufacturing issues are as important to success as ergonomics, aesthetics, and function.
- *Surprise the user.* Always build something extra into the product that will unexpectedly delight the customer. This creates customer loyalty and increases the chances of having a truly "hot" product.

One example of a successful product design is the "smart" bottle cap. Forgetful and/or reluctant patients who don't take their medicine accumulate an estimated $25 billion in avoidable hospital bills annually and billions more in unnecessary nursing home admissions. To reduce these costs, Aprex Corp, located in Fremont, California, now offers a smart bottle cap. Built with a computer chip, alarm clock and a small display panel, the smart cap maintains a record of how frequently the bottle is opened, and is also equipped with a beeper to remind those patients who forget to take their medications. The addition of a modem reads the cap's memory and automatically transmits it to Aprex. If the number of times the bottle has been open is incorrect, the patient receives a "reminder call."

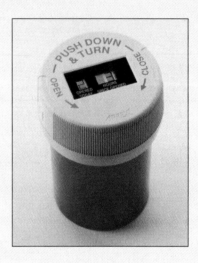

Source: B. Nussbaum, "Hot Products: Smart Design Is the Common Thread," *Business Week,* June 7, 1993 and Otis Port, "These Bottles Nag You to Take Your Medicine," *Business Week,* February 13, 1995.

---

but it also reduces the physical size and increases reliability. Reliability is increased by eliminating the many connections necessary when the circuits were in separate parts. Exhibit 3.4 shows how to reduce a simple bracket from five parts to one by focusing on the purpose of the part, the fabrication, and the assembly procedure used for its manufacture.

product's specifications: Output from the design activity that states all criteria for building a product.

The output of the product design activity is the **product's specifications.** These specifications provide the basis for production-related decisions such as the purchase of materials, selection of equipment, assignment of workers, and the size and layout of the production facility. Product specifications, while commonly thought of as blueprints or engineering drawings, often take other forms ranging from precise quantitative and qualitative statements to rather fluid guidelines. Physical products tend to have traditional blueprint specifications, while a service firm's design specifications tend to be more general.

While designing for manufacturability, we must still remember to design for the consumer. A basic rule in design is to:

Be obvious. Design a product so that a user can look at it, understand it, and figure out how to use it—quickly, and without an instruction manual.

EXHIBIT 3.4

Design Change to Reduce the Number of Parts in a Bracket

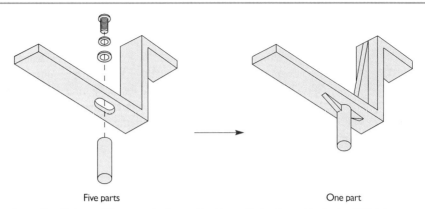

Five parts   One part

Source: Bart Huthwaite. "Managing at the Starting Line: How to Design Competitive Products," Workshop at the University of Southern California–Los Angeles, January 14, 1991, p. 7.

Customer Support Services

MARKETING

More and more firms are looking to service as a means for obtaining a competitive advantage in the marketplace. This includes customer support services after the purchase has been made. It is important that these services properly focus on the needs of the customer and do so in a customer-friendly manner that will continue to foster customer loyalty. Properly designed customer support services understand how a customer uses a product. This information can be obtained through focus groups, and more recently, with "storytelling." With storytelling, market researchers seek out real-life anecdotes that reflect how customers behave and what they actually feel. These stories provide some newfound insights into what customers really want in a product. Using this approach, Kimberly-Clark developed a new $500 million diaper market and Intuit similarly was able to develop software that totally changed the way in which people conduct their financial transactions.[3] Information gathered through these various approaches reduces the need for customer support services by anticipating customer issues before they occur. In addition, when these support services are requested, the firm can respond quickly and properly to satisfy the customer.

Frequency of Design Changes

Should products be changed every year, twice a year, every two years? How often a firm changes designs depends, in large part, on its marketing strategy. An example of very frequent design changes is Sony Corporation's Walkman cassette player. Sony introduced its Walkman to the market in 1979. It was an immediate success. Two years later, Sony brought out a new model to keep ahead of its competitors. Since 1979, the rate of new Walkman products introduced by Sony has accelerated; Sony has brought out more than 160 models of the Walkman.

Sony has relied on "design-based incrementalism." That is, product families are upgraded and enhanced throughout their life cycles. Such changes are small, frequent, and both technological and topological. *Technological innovation* is introducing new technology that enhances the function, adds higher quality, and/or lowers production costs (e.g., developing a new motor). *Topological design* is the rearrangement or remanufacture of well-understood components (e.g., making smaller parts, a more compact unit, easier functioning,

[3]Ronald B. Lieber, "Storytelling: A New Way to Get Close to Your Customer," *Fortune,* February 3, 1997, pp. 102–10.

a more appealing product, or creating product distinction, etc.). Due to its policy of incrementalization, Sony could bring out its "My First Sony" line for children in less than one year because it was built on existing products.

One of the main reasons for the success of Japanese companies is their ability to quickly introduce new products to the market. Their speed of introduction is also compatible with their philosophy of "Ready, Fire, Aim." In the same time that a typical U.S. company takes to conduct extensive and time-consuming market analyses, their Japanese counterparts will launch several new products, letting the market itself determine which ones are good and which ones are not. The key in successfully implementing this strategy is the flexibility of the manufacturing function to easily convert existing production capacity from one product to another.

Opportunity for Product Design Change   In the overall development of a new product, the concept and design phases typically commit about 70 percent of the product's manufacturing costs while expending only about 5 percent of the total costs. (Committed costs are defined here as the production costs directly resulting from the design, including materials, labor, processes and so forth.[4]) Often, manufacturers spend far too little time and resources in identifying all the flaws during the design stage of a new product. Therefore, a more prudent approach might suggest expending a bit more to ensure a good, reliable user-friendly design and expecting to profit through reduced committed cost.

Concurrent Engineering   A major trend in manufacturing companies is early and continuing involvement with new products by production, materials planning, and engineering support groups and even vendors to ensure that the products are effectively managed throughout their life cycles. At Hewlett-Packard, this responsibility is seen as carrying through product development, transition to manufacturing, volume production, and obsolescence.

concurrent engineering
Integration of functional areas in an organization which results in faster design and development of new products.

MARKETING
PURCHASING

Concurrent engineering can be used interchangeably with the terms *simultaneous engineering* or *concurrent design*. Obviously, as these terms imply, continual interaction and parallel actions are necessary throughout that entire process from initial product design through production. Other areas such as marketing and purchasing need to be involved and interact with the different phases of design and development. Their input is critical concerning production planning, productive capacity, and the availability of parts and materials. The sequence from product design to delivery to the marketplace is not a series of consecutive steps. Continual interaction throughout the process ensures that a well-designed product is released to the market at a good price and on time.

NEW PRODUCT DESIGN AND DEVELOPMENT PROCESSES IN SERVICES

Services differ from manufacturing operations in many respects. In services, customers typically interact directly with the service delivery process, and production and consumption take place simultaneously. Services are considered to be intangible, and they cannot be stored. An empty seat on an airline or a vacant hotel room cannot be saved for a busy period when all of the available seats or rooms are being used.

Because of these differences, specifically the direct interaction of the customer with the process, the analysis of service systems must be broader in approach and also include the marketing and human resource management functions within an organization.

---

[4]Bart Huthwaite, "Managing at the Starting Line: How to Design Competitive Products," Presented at a Workshop at the University of Southern California, Los Angeles, CA, January 14, 1991.

Karl Albrecht and Ron Zemke's *Service America!* gets to the heart of the issue of managing service operations in stating: "Every time a customer comes into contact with any aspect of the company it is a 'moment of truth,' and it can create either a positive or a negative impression about the company."[5] How well these moments of truth are managed depends on a carefully designed service delivery system.

In order to better understand the various processes with respect to services, we begin by presenting several approaches to classifying services. Next, we introduce different service strategies and how to design a service delivery system that is compatible with a specific strategy. Finally, we present three different approaches to designing service delivery systems.

A Framework for Designing Service Processes

Service systems are generally classified along industry lines (financial services, health services, transportation services, and so on). These groupings, though useful in presenting aggregate economic data, are not particularly appropriate for OM purposes because they tell us little about the process. In manufacturing, by contrast, there are fairly well-defined terms for classifying production activities that transcend industry lines (such as *intermittent* and *continuous production*); when applied to a manufacturing setting, they readily convey the essence of the process. While it is possible to describe services in these same terms, we need another item of information to reflect the level of customer involvement in the process. That item, which we believe operationally distinguishes one service system from another in its production function, is the extent of customer contact in the creation of service.

Customer contact refers to the presence of the customer in the system, and *creation of the service* refers to the work process that is involved in providing the service itself. *Extent of contact* here may be roughly defined as the percentage of time the customer must be involved in the system relative to the total time it takes to perform the customer service. Generally speaking, the greater the percentage of contact time between the service system and the customer, the greater the degree of interaction between the two during the production process.

high degree of customer contact
Service operations which require a high percentage of customer contact time.

From this concept of customer contact, it follows that service systems with a **high degree of customer contact** are usually more difficult to manage and consequently harder to justify than those with a **low degree of customer contact.** In high-contact systems, the customer can affect the time of demand, the exact nature of the service, and the quality of service since the customer is involved in the process.

low degree of customer contact
Service operations which require a low percentage of customer contact time.

Exhibit 3.5 illustrates the difference between high- and low-contact service systems in a bank. Here we see that each design decision is impacted by whether or not the customer is present during the service delivery. We also see that when work is done behind the scenes (in this case a bank's processing center), it is performed on substitutes for the customer, that is, customer reports, databases, and invoices. We can, therefore, design these behind-the-scenes operations according to the same principles we would use in designing a factory. That is, to maximize the amount of items processed during the production day.

Obviously, there can be tremendous diversity of customer influence and hence system variability within high-contact service systems. For example, a bank branch offers both simple services such as cash withdrawals that take just a minute or so, as well as complicated services such as loan application preparation that can take in excess of an hour. Moreover, these activities may range from being self-service through an ATM, to coproduction

---

[5]Jan Carlzon, president, Scandinavian Airlines System, quoted in Karl Albrecht and Ron Zemke, *Service America! Doing Business in the New Economy* (Homewood, IL: Dow Jones-Irwin, 1985), p. 19.

Design Decision	High-Contact System (a branch office)	Low-Contact System (a check processing center)
Facility location	Operations must be near the customer.	Operations may be placed near supply, transport, or labor.
Facility layout	Facility should accommodate the customer's physical and psychological needs and expectations.	Facility should focus on production efficiency.
Product design	Environment as well as the physical product define the nature of the service.	Customer is not in the service environment so the product can be defined by fewer attributes.
Process design	Stages of production process have a direct, immediate effect on the customer.	Customer is not involved in majority of processing steps.
Scheduling	Customer is in the production schedule and must be accommodated.	Customer is concerned mainly with completion dates.
Production planning	Orders cannot be stored, so smoothing production flow will result in loss of business.	Both backlogging and production smoothing are possible.
Worker skills	Direct workforce constitutes a major part of the service product and so must be able to interact well with the public.	Direct workforce need only have technical skills.
Quality control	Quality standards are often in the eye of the beholder and hence variable.	Quality standards are generally measurable and hence fixed.
Time standards	Service time depends on customer needs, and therefore time standards are inherently loose.	Work is performed on customer surrogates (e.g., forms), thus time standards can be tight.
Wage payment	Variable output requires time-based wage systems.	"Fixable" output permits output-based wage systems.
Capacity planning	To avoid lost sales, capacity must be set to match peak demand.	Storable output permits capacity at some average demand level.

where bank personnel and the customer work together as a team to develop the loan application.

In another attempt to better understand services in general, Roger Schmenner proposes a method for classifying services along two dimensions.[6] The first dimension, degree of customer interaction and customization, closely parallels the degree of customer contact we discuss above. In addition, Schmenner also includes the degree of labor intensity required to deliver the service. From these two factors he develops a service process matrix, as shown in Exhibit 3.6.

Within this matrix, Schmenner defines four broad categories of services:

1. *Service factory* is characterized by a low degree of labor intensity and a low degree of customer interaction and customization.

2. *Service shop* has the same low degree of labor intensity, but has a higher degree of customer interaction and customization.

---

[6]Roger W. Schmenner, "How Can Service Businesses Survive and Prosper?" *Sloan Management Review* 27, no. 3 (Spring 1986).

EXHIBIT 3.6

The Service Process Matrix

		Degree of Interaction and Customization	
		Low	**High**
Degree of Labor Intensity	Low	Service factory: Airlines Trucking Hotels Resorts and recreation	Service shop: Hospitals Auto repair Other repair services
	High	Mass service: Retailing Wholesaling Schools Retail aspects of commercial banking	Professional service: Doctors Lawyers Accountants Architects

Source: Roger W. Schmenner, "How Can Service Businesses Survive and Prosper?", *Sloan Management Review* 27, no. 3 (Spring 1986), pp. 21–32, by permission of publisher. Copyright 1986 by Sloan Management Review Association. All rights reserved.

3. *Mass service* is defined by a high degree of labor intensity, but has a relatively low degree of customer interaction.

4. *Professional service* requires both a high degree of labor intensity as well as a high degree of customer interaction and customization.

This type of classification scheme provides service managers with some insights in developing strategies for their respective organizations. For example, those services that exhibit a low degree of labor intensity are usually capital intense with high fixed costs. These firms cannot easily adjust capacity to meet changes in demand and must, therefore, attempt to smooth out the demand during peak periods by shifting it to off-peak times.

The issues confronting service managers with high labor intensity operations require a different focus. Here, workforce management is paramount, with emphasis being placed on hiring, training, and scheduling.

More important, this approach to classifying services cuts across industry lines, providing service managers with a better understanding of the strengths and weaknesses within their own operations. Through this perspective, managers can look to similar operations in other service industries to seek ways for improving their respective operations.

Designing a New Service Organization

Designing a service organization entails the execution of four elements of what James Heskett refers to as the "Service Vision."[7] The first element is identification of the target market (Who is our customer?); the second is the service concept (How do we differentiate our service in the market?); the third is the service strategy (What is our service package and the operating focus of our service?); and the fourth is the service delivery system (What are the actual processes, staff requirements, and facilities by which the service is created?).

Choosing a target market and developing the service package are top management decisions setting the stage for the direct operating decisions of service strategy and delivery system design.

Several major factors distinguish service design and development from typical manufactured product development. First, the process and the product must be developed simultaneously; indeed, in services the process is the product. (We make this statement with the

[7]James L. Heskett, "Lessons from the Service Sector," *Harvard Business Review,* March–April 1987, pp.118–26.

general recognition that many manufacturers are using such concepts as concurrent engineering and DFM [design for manufacture] as approaches to more closely link product design and process design.)

Second, although equipment and software that support a service can be protected by patents and copyrights, a service operation itself lacks the legal protection commonly available to goods production. Third, the service package, rather than a definable good, constitutes the major output of the development process. Fourth, many parts of the service package are often defined by the training individuals receive before they become part of the service organization. In particular, in professional service organizations (PSOs) such as law firms and hospitals, prior certification is necessary for hiring. Fifth, many service organizations can change their service offerings virtually overnight. Routine service organizations (RSOs) such as barbershops, retail stores, and restaurants have this flexibility.

Designing the Customer Service Encounter

service-system design matrix
Framework for relating sales opportunities with ways a service can interact with a customer.

Service encounters can be structured in a number of different ways. The **service-system design matrix** in Exhibit 3.7 identifies six common alternatives.

The top of the matrix shows the degree of customer/server contact: the *buffered core,* which is physically separated from the customer; the *permeable system,* which the customer can penetrate via phone or face-to-face contact; and the *reactive system,* which is both penetrable and reactive to the customer's requirements. The left side of the matrix shows what we believe to be a logical marketing proposition, namely, that the greater the amount of contact, the greater the opportunity to generate additional sales; the right side shows the impact on production efficiency as the customer exerts more influence on the operation.

EXHIBIT 3.7

Service-System Design Matrix

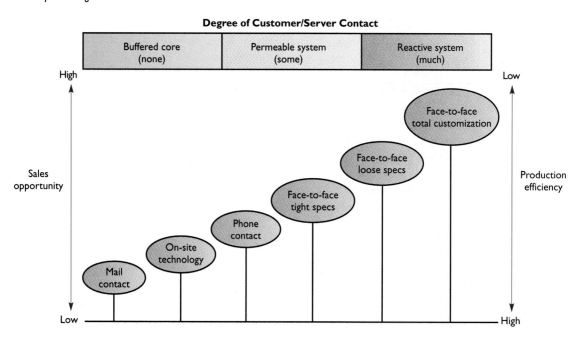

As one would anticipate, production efficiency decreases as the customer contact time increases, thereby giving the customer more influence on the system. To offset this, however, the face-to-face contact provides greater opportunity to sell additional products. Conversely, low contact, such as mail, allows the system to work more efficiently because the customer is unable to significantly affect (or disrupt) the system. However, there is relatively little, if any, sales opportunity for additional product sales at this end of the spectrum.

There can be some shifting in the positioning of each entry. Consider the "face-to-face tight specs" entry in Exhibit 3.7. This refers to those situations where there is little variation in the service process—neither customer nor server has much discretion in creating the service. Fast-food restaurants and Disneyland come to mind. "Face-to-face loose specs" refers to situations where the service process is generally understood, but there are options in the way it will be performed or the physical goods that are a part of it. A full-service restaurant or a car sales agency are examples. "Face-to-face total customization" refers to service encounters whose specifications must be developed through some interaction between the customer and server. Legal and medical services are of this type, and the degree to which the resources of the system are mustered for the service determines whether the system is reactive or merely permeable. Examples would be the mobilization of an advertising firm's resources in preparation for an office visit by a major client, or an operating team scrambling to prepare for emergency surgery.

Strategic Uses of the Matrix   The service-system design matrix has both operational and strategic uses. Its operational uses are reflected in its identification of worker requirements, focus of operations, and innovations previously discussed. Some of its strategic uses are

1. *Enabling systematic integration of operations and marketing strategy.* Trade-offs become more clear-cut, and, more important, at least some of the major design variables are crystalized for analysis purposes. For example, the matrix indicates that it would make little sense relative to sales for a service firm to invest in high-skilled workers if it plans to operate using tight specs.
2. *Clarifying exactly which combination of service delivery the firm is actually providing.* As the company incorporates the delivery options listed on the diagonal, it is becoming diversified in its production process.
3. *Permitting comparison with other firms in the way specific services are delivered.* This helps to pinpoint a firm's competitive advantage.
4. *Indicating evolutionary or life cycle changes that might be in order as the firm grows.* Unlike the product-process matrix for manufacturing, where natural growth moves in one direction (from intermittent to line-flow as a volume increases), the evolution of service delivery can move in either direction along the diagonal as a function of the trade-off between efficiency and the potential to generate additional sales.
5. *Providing flexibility.* The user of the matrix can go into depth, placing particular service products of a small firm or individual department on it, or cover a large service organization at a more aggregated level.

PROCESS SELECTION IN MANUFACTURING

Types of Processes

Manufacturing operations, as shown in Exhibit 3.8, are categorized into three broad types of process structures, each category depending to a large extent on the volume of item(s) to be produced. These three categories are often referred to as **project processes, intermittent**

EXHIBIT 3.8

Types of Processes

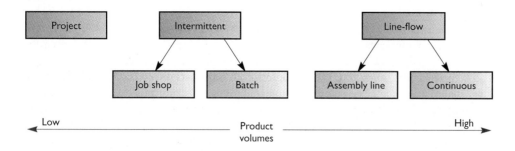

processes, and **line-flow processes.** While we identify three discrete categories, we should emphasize that the different types of manufacturing processes that exist should be viewed as a continuum, and that any one company may incorporate a combination of these processes in the manufacture of its products.

project process
Process that focuses on making one-of-a-kind products.

Project Process   A project-oriented process usually involves the manufacture of a single, one-of-a-kind product. Examples here include the production of a movie and the erection of a skyscraper. Building a customized car to compete in the Indianapolis 500 race is another good example. The major strength of a project-type process is that it is totally flexible to meet the individual needs of the customer. Projects are usually analyzed using network-solving techniques like those presented in Chapter 10.

Variable costs in this category are comparatively very high. On the other hand, fixed costs are negligible or even nonexistent. (In the extreme case, when there is truly only one product to build, all costs are expensed and consequently there are no fixed costs.)

Highly skilled personnel are usually required for this type of process, as they must often work independently, with minimal guidance and supervision. In addition, workers here need to be well trained in a variety of tasks.

intermittent process
Process that produces products in small lot sizes.

Intermittent Process   As shown in Exhibit 3.8, intermittent type processes can be further subdivided into job shop and batch processes. We define a *job shop* as a process where a specific quantity of a product is produced only once. Numbered prints from a painting, programs for concerts, and T-shirts commemorating specific events are good examples of products made in a job shop process.

A batch process produces the same item again and again, usually in specified lot sizes. McDonald's is a good example of a batch process where hamburgers are cooked throughout the day in lot sizes of 12. The manufacture of shoes provides another example of a batch process. Here a batch consists of one size and style of shoe.

Variable costs are still relatively high with intermittent processes, although they are usually lower than those of a project-type process. However, higher fixed costs are incurred with these processes. Similarly, worker skills remain high, though somewhat less than those required for projects.

line-flow process
Continuous process that produces high volume, highly standardized products.

Line-Flow Process   As with intermittent processes, line-flow processes are also frequently subdivided into two processes: assembly line and continuous. Assembly-line processes manufacture individual, discrete products. Examples here include electronic products such as VCRs and CD players, as well as automobiles and kitchen appliances. Continuous processes are exactly what their name implies—continuous, producing products that are not discrete. Petroleum refineries and chemical plants provide good examples of continuous processes.

Line-flow processes can produce a wide variety of products ranging from filling and capping of bottled beer in a continuous flow process at the Miller Brewing Company to motorcycles that are made on an assembly line at Kawasaki Motors Manufacturing Company.

Line-flows are characterized by high fixed costs and low variable costs, and are often viewed as the most efficient of the three types of processes. Labor skill, especially in assembly-line operations, is typically very low, as workers are required to learn only a very few simple operations. Line-flows are used for only the highest volumes of products, are very focused, and consequently are the most inflexible of the three processes.

The Product-Process Matrix

The relationship between the different types of processes and their respective volume requirements is often depicted on a product-process matrix, shown in Exhibit 3.9, which is adapted from the widely cited Hayes and Wheelwright product-process matrix. In this matrix, as volume increases and the product line narrows (the horizontal dimension), specialized equipment and standardized material flows (the vertical dimension) become economically feasible. This evolution in process structure is frequently related to the different stages of a product's life cycle (introduction, growth, and maturity).

The industries listed within the matrix are presented as ideal types that have found their process niche. It certainly is possible for an industry member to choose another position on the matrix, however. For example, Volvo makes cars on movable pallets rather than on an assembly line. Thus, on the matrix it would be at the intersection of process stage II and product stage III. Volvo's production rate is lower than its competitors because it is giving up the speed and efficiency of the line. On the other hand, the Volvo system has more flexibility and better quality control than the classic automobile production line. Similar kinds of analysis can be carried out for other types of process-product options through the matrix.

In looking at Exhibit 3.9, it is interesting to note that companies that try to operate in either of the corners opposite the diagonal are doomed to failure. Companies in the upper right-hand corner reflect those firms that are too slow to react to changes in the marketplace. As a result, they try to compete in a market that requires high volume, low-cost products with a project-type process that not only has very high variable costs, but also has very limited capacity. As a consequence, these firms incur very high opportunity costs from lost sales because high prices encourage customers to take their business elsewhere.

EXHIBIT 3.9

Matching Major Stages of Product and Process Life Cycles

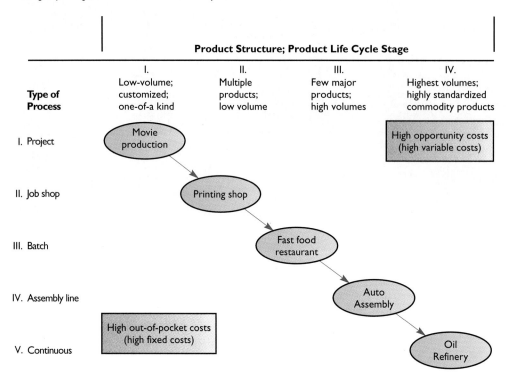

Source: Adapted from Robert Hayls and Steven Wheelwright, *Restoring Competitive Edge: Competing through Manufacturing* (New York: John Wiley & Sons, 1984).

In the lower left-hand corner are companies that anticipated selling greater volumes of product than actually materialized. As a result, these firms have incurred very high out-of-pocket costs in the form of very high fixed costs, which are associated with the capital intensive processes that were installed.

It may be a little easier to understand the logic of a product-process matrix if we divide it into its component parts. Part A of Exhibit 3.10 shows a traditional product life cycle from product conception through product termination. Part B relates the frequency of changes made in the product design to the stages of the product life cycle. Logically, most of the product changes occur during the initial stages of the life cycle, before major production starts. This suggests that a project-type process is appropriate for this stage. The product then tends to go through many changes—simplification, adding features, newer materials, and so forth. The motivation here is for more performance and perhaps greater appeal to a broader market. The flexibility of an intermittent-type process allows for these changes. During the maturity stage of the product very few additional changes are made and the focus is on low costs, which can be provided by a line-flow process.

Changes in the production process, as shown in Part C of Exhibit 3.10, occur most rapidly during the early stages of production design and startup. This is where choices are made in the production layout, equipment, tooling, and so on. The goal here is to reduce production costs. Also, both product and process engineers work together to reduce costs and increase product performance. When full production occurs, few additional changes

EXHIBIT 3.10

Product and Process Life Cycles

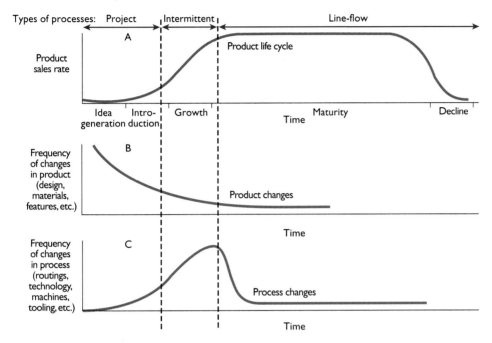

are made. During the decline phase of the product, however, some additional process changes occur; these are due in part to switching the smaller production volumes to different equipment and facilities.

During the early stages in a product's life cycle when production quantities are small (certainly during the product research and development stages), manufacturing likely takes place in a functional type layout, which we usually call a *process-oriented layout*. Here, all similar machines and processes are grouped together in one location and are used for many different products. As production volumes increase, machines and processes may be grouped to simplify the product's flow through the factory. This ultimately results in assembly lines, which are considered to be *product-oriented layouts*.

Choosing among Alternative Processes

break-even analysis
Determination of product volume where the costs associated with two alternative processes are the same.

A standard approach for deciding which among several alternatives is best suited for a particular business is to use **break-even analysis.** (The specific steps involved in conducting a break-even analysis are presented in Chapter 3S which follows this chapter.)

The results of such an analysis can be presented in graph form, as shown in Exhibit 3.11. The horizontal axis represents the volume of product to be produced, while the vertical axis represents the total costs. As discussed previously, projects have little or no fixed costs but very high variable costs. On the other hand, line-flow processes have very high fixed costs but very low variable costs. Intermittent processes fall in between. Using a lowest cost criterion, the choice of which process to adopt is therefore dependent on the volume to be produced. For example, if the anticipated volume is less than V_1, then the project process should be selected; if the volume is expected to be between V_1 and V_2, then the intermittent process is the proper choice; and if the volume will be greater than V_2, then the line-flow

EXHIBIT 3.11

Determining the Least Cost Process as a Function of Volume

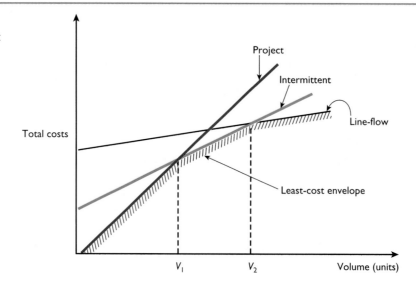

least-cost envelope
Lowest total costs to produce various volumes of a product.

process gives us the lowest total cost and unit cost. The lowest cost line for each type of process is often referred to as the **least-cost envelope,** as noted by the shaded area on the graph.

PROCESS SELECTION IN SERVICES

Types of Service Organizations

Service management issues exist in three broad organizational contexts:

1. *Service businesses* are organizations whose primary business requires interaction with the customer to produce the service. Familiar examples of service businesses include banks, airlines, hospitals, law firms, retail stores, restaurants, and so on. Within this category, we can make a further major distinction: **facilities-based services,** where the customer must go to the service facility, and **field-based services,** where production and consumption of the service take place in the customer's environment (e.g., cleaning and home repair services).

facilities-based services
Services which require the customer to go to the service facility.

Technology has allowed for the transfer of many facility-based services to field-based services. Dental vans bring the dentist to your home. Some auto repair services have repairmobiles. Telemarketing brings the shopping center to your TV screen.

field-based services
Services which can be performed at the customer's location.

2. *Customer support services* provide support to external customers who have already purchased the goods and/or services of the company. Included here are 800-numbers for registering complaints and obtaining additional information on the firm's products. Product maintenance and repair services also fall into this category.

3. *Internal services* are the services required to support the activities of the larger organization. These services include such functions as data processing, accounting, engineering, and maintenance. Their customers are the various departments within the organization that require such services. (It is not uncommon for an internal service to start marketing its services outside the parent organization and become a service business itself.)

MIS
ACCOUNTING
ENGINEERING
MARKETING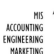

The three general approaches to delivering on-site services are the production line approach made famous by McDonald's Corporation, the customer involvement approach made famous by ATMs and gas stations, and the personal attention approach made famous by Nordstrom department stores.

The Production Line Approach

The production line approach pioneered by McDonald's refers to more than just the steps required to assemble a Big Mac. Rather, as Theodore Levitt notes, it is treating the delivery of fast food as a manufacturing process rather than a service process.[8] The value of this philosophy is that it overcomes many of the problems inherent in the concept of service itself. That is, service implies subordination or subjugation of the server to the served; manufacturing, on the other hand, avoids this connotation because it focuses on things rather than people. Thus, in manufacturing and at McDonald's, "the orientation is toward the efficient production of results not on the attendance on others." Levitt notes that besides McDonald's marketing and financial skills, the company carefully controls "the execution of each outlet's central function—the rapid delivery of a consistently uniform, high-quality mix of prepared foods in an environment of obvious cleanliness, order, and cheerful courtesy. The systematic substitution of equipment for people, combined with the carefully planned use and positioning of technology, enables McDonald's to attract and hold patronage in proportions no predecessor or imitator has managed to duplicate."

Levitt cites several aspects of McDonald's operations to illustrate the concepts:

- The McDonald's french fryer allows cooking of the optimum number of french fries at one time.
- A wide-mouthed scoop is used to pick up the precise amount of french fries for each order size. (The employee never touches the product.)
- Storage space is expressly designed for a predetermined mix of prepackaged and premeasured products.
- Cleanliness is pursued by providing ample trash cans in and outside each facility (and the larger outlets have motorized sweepers for the parking area).
- Hamburgers are wrapped in color-coded paper.
- Through painstaking attention to total design and facilities planning, everything is built integrally into the (McDonald's) machine itself—into the technology of the system. The only choice available to the attendant is to operate it exactly as the designers intended.

The Customer Involvement Approach

In contrast to the production line approach, C. H. Lovelock and R. F. Young propose that the service process can be enhanced by having the customer take a greater participatory role in the production of the service.[9] Automatic teller machines (ATMs), self-service gas stations, salad bars, and in-room coffee-making equipment in motels are good examples of where the burden of providing service is shifted to the consumer. Obviously, this philosophy requires some selling on the part of the service organization to convince customers that this is beneficial to them. To this end, Lovelock and Young propose a number of steps, including developing customer trust, promoting the benefits of cost, speed, and convenience, and following up to make sure that the procedures are being effectively used. In essence, this turns customers into "partial employees" who must be trained in what to do and be compensated primarily through low prices charged for the service.

[8]Theodore Levitt, "Production-Line Approach to Service," *Harvard Business Review* 50, no. 5 (September–October 1972), pp. 41–52.

[9]C. H. Lovelock and R. F. Young, "Look to Customers to Increase Productivity," *Harvard Business Review* 57, no. 2, (May–June 1979), pp. 168–78.

The Personal Attention Approach

 The following example by Tom Peters describes how Nordstrom department store operationalizes its personal attention philosophy.[10]

> After several visits to a store's men's clothing department, a customer's suit still did not fit. He wrote the company president, who sent a tailor to the customer's office with a new suit for fitting. When the alterations were completed, the suit was delivered to the customer—free of charge.
>
> This incident involved the $1.3 billion, Seattle-based Nordstrom, a specialty clothing retailer. Its sales per square foot are about five times that of a typical department store. Who received the customer's letter and urged the extreme (by others' standards) response? Co-chairman John Nordstrom.
>
> The frontline providers of this good service are well paid. Nordstrom's salespersons earn a couple of bucks an hour more than competitors, plus a 6.75 percent commission. Its top salesperson moves over $1 million a year in merchandise. Nordstrom lives for its customers and salespeople. Its only official organization chart puts the customer at the top, followed by sales and sales support people. Next come department managers, then store managers, and the board of directors at the very bottom.
>
> Salespersons religiously carry a "personal book," where they record voluminous information about each of their customers; senior, successful salespeople often have three or four bulging books, which they carry everywhere, according to Betsy Sanders, the vice president who orchestrated the firm's wildly successful penetration of the tough southern California market. "My objective is to get one new personal customer a day," says a budding Nordstrom star. The system helps him do just that. He has a virtually unlimited budget to send cards, flowers, and thank-you notes to customers. He also is encouraged to shepherd his customer to any department in the store to assist in a successful shopping trip.
>
> He also is abetted by what may be the most liberal returns policy in this or any other business: Return *anything,* no questions asked. Sanders says that "trusting customers," or "our bosses" as she repeatedly calls them, is vital to the Nordstrom philosophy. President Jim Nordstrom told the *Los Angeles Times,* "I don't care if they roll a Goodyear tire into the store. If they say they paid $200, give them $200 (in cash) for it." Sanders acknowledges that a few customers rip the store off—"rent hose from us," to use a common insider's line. But this is more than offset by goodwill from the 99 percent-plus who benefit from the "No Problem at Nordstrom" logo that the company lives up to with unmatched zeal.
>
> No bureaucracy gets in the way of serving the customer. Policy? Sanders explains to a dumbfounded group of Silicon Valley executives, "I know this drives the lawyers nuts, but our whole 'policy manual' is just one sentence, 'Use your own best judgment at all times.'" One store manager offers a translation, "Don't chew gum. Don't steal from us."

No matter what approach is taken, seven common characteristics of well-designed service systems have been identified:

1. *Each element of the service system is consistent with the operating focus of the firm.* For example, when the focus is on speed of delivery, each step in the process should help to foster speed.
2. *It is user-friendly.* This means that the customer can interact with it easily—that is, it has good signage, understandable forms, logical steps in the process, courteous service workers that are available to answer questions, and is easily accessible.
3. *It is robust.* That is, it can cope effectively with variations in demand and resource availability. For example, if the computer goes down, effective backup systems are in place to permit service to continue.
4. *It is structured so that consistent performance by its people and systems is easily maintained.* This means that the tasks required of the workers can be performed

[10]Tom Peters, *Quality!* Palo Alto, CA: TPG Communications, 1986, pp. 10–12.

repeatedly with a high level of consistency, and the supporting technologies are truly supportive and reliable.

5. *It provides effective links between the back office and the front office so that nothing falls between the cracks.* In other words, the barriers between the different functional areas are reduced or eliminated.

6. *It manages the evidence of service quality in such a way that customers see the value of the service provided.* Many services do a great job behind the scenes but fail to make this visible to the customer. This is particularly true where a service improvement is made. Unless customers are made aware of the improvement through explicit communication about it, the improved performance is unlikely to gain maximum impact.

7. *It is cost-effective.* There is minimum waste of time and resources in delivering the service.

THE ROLE OF TECHNOLOGY

Technology in Manufacturing

The term *automation* is familiar to all, but a commonly agreed upon definition still eludes us. Some authorities view automation as a totally new set of concepts that relate to the automatic operation of a production process; others view it simply as an evolutionary development in technology in which machinery performs some or all of the process-control function. Automation is a set of concepts, but it is also evolutionary in the sense that it is a logical and predictable step in the development of equipment and processes.

Some major developments in manufacturing automation include machining centers, numerically controlled machines, industrial robots, computer-aided design and manufacturing systems, flexible manufacturing systems, computer-integrated manufacturing, and islands of automation.

machining centers
Operations where machine tools are changed automatically as part of the process.

Machining centers not only provide automatic control of a machine but carry out automatic tooling changes as well. For example, a single machine may be equipped with a shuttle system of two worktables that can be rolled into and out of the machine. While work is being done at one table, the next part is mounted on the second table. When machining on the first table is complete, it is moved out of the way and the second part is moved into position.

numerically controlled (NC) machines
Manufacturing equipment that is directly controlled by a computer.

Numerically controlled (NC) machines are under the control of a digital computer. Feedback control loops determine the position of the machine tooling during the work, constantly compare the actual location with the programmed location, and correct as needed. This eliminates time lost during setups, and applies to both high-volume, standardized types of products as well as low-volume, customized products.

industrial robots
Programmable machines that can perform multiple functions.

Industrial robots are substitutes for human manipulation and other highly repetitive functions. A robot is a reprogrammable machine with multiple functions that can move devices through specialized motions to perform any number of tasks. It is essentially a mechanized arm that can be fitted with a variety of handlike fingers or grippers, vacuum cups, or a tool such as a wrench. Robots are capable of performing many factory operations ranging from machining processes to simple assembly.

One of the major contemporary approaches to the product design process is **computer-aided (or -assisted) design (CAD)**. *CAD* may be defined as carrying out all structural or mechanical design processes of a product or component at a specially equipped computer terminal. Engineers design through a combination of console controls and a light pen that draws on the computer screen or electronic pad. Different perspectives of the product can be visualized by rotating the product on the screen, and individual components can be enlarged to examine particular characteristics. Depending on the sophistication in software, on-screen testing may replace the early phases of prototype testing and modification.

> **computer-aided (or -assisted) design (CAD)**
> Designing a product using a specially equipped computer.

CAD has been used to design everything from computer chips to potato chips. Frito-Lay, for example, used CAD to design its O'Grady's double-density, ruffled potato chip. CAD is also now being used to custom design swimsuits. Measurements of the wearer are fed into the CAD program, along with the style of suit desired. Working with the customer, the designer modifies the suit design as it appears on a humanform drawing on the computer screen. Once the design is decided upon, the computer prints out a pattern, and the suit is cut and sewn on the spot.

> **computer-aided design and manufacturing system (CAD/CAM)**
> Integration of design and production of a product through use of a computer.

Computer-aided design and manufacturing (CAD/CAM) uses a computer to integrate component design and processing instructions. In current CAD/CAM systems, when the design is finalized, the link to CAM is made by producing the manufacturing instructions. Because of the efficiency of CAD/CAM systems, design and manufacture of small lots can be both fast and low in cost.

Even though CAD/CAM systems are usually limited to larger companies because of the high initial cost, they do increase productivity and quality dramatically. More alternative designs can be produced, and the specifications can be more exact. Updates can be more readily made, and cost estimates more easily drawn. In addition, computer-aided process planning (CAPP) can shorten and, in some cases, even eliminate traditional process planning.

> **flexible manufacturing system (FMS)**
> Manufacturing facility that is automated to some extent and produces a wide variety of products.

A **flexible manufacturing system (FMS)** actually refers to a number of systems that differ in the degree of mechanization, automated transfer, and computer control and are sufficiently flexible to produce a wide variety of products.

A flexible manufacturing module is a numerically controlled (NC) machine supported with a parts inventory, a tool changer, and a pallet changer. A flexible manufacturing cell consists of several flexible manufacturing modules organized according to the particular product's requirements. A flexible manufacturing group is a combination of flexible manufacturing modules and cells located in the same manufacturing area and joined by a material handling system, such as an automated guided vehicle (AGV).

A flexible production system consists of flexible manufacturing groups that connect different manufacturing areas, such as fabrication, machining, and assembly. A flexible manufacturing line is a series of dedicated machines connected by automated guided vehicles (AGVs), robots, conveyors, or some other type of automated transfer devices.

> **computer-integrated manufacturing (CIM)**
> Integration of all aspects of manufacturing through computers.

Computer-integrated manufacturing (CIM) integrates all aspects of production into one automated system. Design, testing, fabrication, assembly, inspection, and materials handling may all have automated functions within the area. However, in most companies, communication between departments still flows by means of paperwork. In CIM, these islands of automation are integrated, thus eliminating the need for the paperwork. A computer links all sectors together, resulting in more efficiency, less paperwork, and less personnel expense.

The speed with which a company can design and develop new products is a critical element in its ability to quickly introduce new products into the marketplace. Rapid prototyping machines are a new generation of CAD equipment that can quickly produce three dimensional prototypes early in the product design cycle. These rough draft models of new designs result in higher quality products and lower development costs.

This flexible manufacturing system from Cincinnati Milacron automates the machining of structural aerospace components at Boeing's plant in Auburn, Washington. The demand for this technology is driven by industry's need to shorten lead times and improve flexibility.

islands of automation
Automated factories or portions which include NC equipment, automated storage/ retrieval systems, robots and machining centers.

Islands of automation refers to the transition from conventional manufacturing to the automated factory. Typical islands of automation include numerically controlled machine tools, robots, automated storage/retrieval systems, and machining centers.

Technology in Services

The advances in technology, especially information technology, have had a significant impact on how services are provided. Technology, in one form or another, has penetrated almost every type of service. In-room check-out at hotels, automatic teller machines (ATMs) at banks, airline reservation systems, and the emergence of the Internet provide good examples of how technology affects the delivery of services. As an illustration, using e-mail to provide technical support instead of a telephone allows a company to "inventory" demand, and thus level out the workload over a 24-hour period. In addition, by making documents available at a Web site, the cost and time to obtain these documents are placed on the customer. At the same time, these documents are always available when the customer wants them.

However, management must clearly understand how the technology is to be used and then define its role in the overall organization to avoid many of the pitfalls that have been previously experienced. For example, many service firms have looked to technology to increase worker productivity and ultimately to increase profits. However, as Roach has pointed out, the large investments in technology that these service companies have made have not yielded the expected increases in productivity.[11] In order to better understand the various ways in which technology can contribute to services, Quinn and Bailey have identified the following reasons, other than increasing productivity, that a company would want to invest in technology:

- Maintaining market share.
- Avoiding catastrophic losses.
- Creating greater flexibility and adaptability.
- Improving responsiveness for new products.
- Improving service quality.
- Enhancing quality of life.
- Increasing predictability of operations.[12]

When investing in technology, service managers must therefore realize that technology investments may not result in increased productivity. In fact, managers must realize that such investments are often required just to maintain the status quo (and the lack of such investments would have resulted in significant decreases in sales and associated profits) with respect to competition. Managers must also realize that some of the benefits of technology investments are difficult to measure and quantify in dollars, such as improved worker morale and shortened customer service times, both of which may be of considerable importance to the organization. As an example, Norwalk Furniture Corporation of Norwalk, Ohio, uses technology to simplify a customer's furniture selection process. (See OM in Practice box.)

Technology can significantly alter the way in which a company does business. Adopting the proper strategy and associated technology can result in substantial increases in market share and profits. Failure to do so can result in customers defecting to competitors. We suggest there are four major strategies that service firms can adopt in terms of why they should invest in technology. These are: (*a*) strengthen customer relations, (*b*) provide rapid and controlled growth, (*c*) improve performance, and (*d*) increase efficiency.

Strengthen Customer Relationships   One reason why services are adopting new technologies is to strengthen their relationships with their customers. For example, during the 1950s, Holiday Inn was probably one of the first companies to recognize the importance of information technology as a way in which it could achieve a competitive advantage. With its *Holidex* reservation system network, customers were able to make reservations at any Holiday Inn in the country from any other Holiday Inn with only a single, toll-free telephone call. Similarly, American Airlines SABRE system has linked that airline's reservation systems directly to travel agents, thereby giving them online, real-time capability to provide information to customers. Instead of dealing with a reservation agent, which can be time consuming and inefficient, the travel agent, with the SABRE system, can quickly explore all of the flight and pricing options for a customer.

[11]S. S. Roach, "Services Under Seige—The Restructuring Imperative," *Harvard Business Review,* September–October 1991, pp. 82–91.

[12]J. B. Quinn and M. N. Bailey, "Information Technology: Increasing Productivity in Services," *Academy of Management Executive* 8, no. 3, 1994, pp. 28–51.

Operations Management in Practice

COMPUTERS ASSIST CUSTOMERS IN CHOOSING FABRICS AT NORWALK— THE FURNITURE IDEA STORES

When customers visit a retail outlet of Norwalk Furniture, they can actually see what a chair or sofa will look like with different types of fabrics. To simplify the customer selection process, Norwalk has installed in each of its retail locations a computer with a software package that will allow customers to view a particular style of sofa or chair with a variety of fabric designs. The computer and software are part of a larger overall process that Norwalk has recently developed which allows it to deliver customized furniture to its customers in about five weeks—half the normal delivery time in the furniture industry.

Even though it is the leader in the industry, in terms of fast delivery, Norwalk isn't resting on its laurels. Instead, Norwalk is continuously looking at new ways and processes which will allow them to deliver furniture even faster than they currently do.

Source: Special thanks to Barb Myers at Norwalk Furniture.

Provide Rapid and Controlled Growth   A second reason that service companies are investing in new technologies is to achieve rapid and controlled growth. Services that interact directly with their customers must be located where these customers are. Examples include retail operations, restaurants, hotels and car rental agencies. For example, one of the key factors to the sustained and managed growth of Mrs. Fields' Cookies was the management information system that was custom designed and installed for its operations. As a result, the headquarters for Mrs. Fields' Cookies, located in Utah, receives on a daily basis a detailed performance report on every outlet throughout the world. In addition to providing operational measures of performance, the system also has the capability to conduct initial interviews with prospective workers.

Wal-Mart provides another good example of how technology can provide a firm with the ability to have rapid growth while maintaining consistency across all locations. Through advances in technology, Wal-Mart has installed in its headquarters in Arkansas a satellite hookup with all of its retail operations. With this new system, the president of Wal-Mart can now have weekly meetings with all of his store managers. With this satellite system, all company news is quickly disseminated to all its employees, thereby eliminating rumors. Since all employees are receiving the same message at the same time, possible sources of miscommunication and unnecessary delays are also eliminated.

Improve Performance   Service managers must recognize that the decision to adopt technology is often driven by the need to increase the existing performance of their current operations rather than only to increase productivity. Often, however, with the proper technology, both performance and productivity can be improved to create a win-win situation for the firm. Performance here can be defined as (*a*) faster service, (*b*) improved knowledge about their customers and (*c*) increased customization.

For example, to provide faster service, many hotels now provide their guests with an in-room checkout option. Guests who want to take advantage of this option simply follow the menu-driven instructions on the television in their rooms, leave their room keys in the rooms, and never have to wait in line at the front desk to check out.

Databases are now available that can provide managers with detailed information on their customers' purchasing characteristics. As part of their focus on attention to personal detail, for example, the Ritz-Carlton hotel chain, with its management information system, can track individual guest preferences including the type of bed they like to sleep in (such as a queen or king-size bed) and the type of wine they prefer. Any previous incidents involving the customer, particularly complaints, are also recorded in the database to assure that similar incidents do not occur again. Another method of using technology for obtaining data on individual customers is through membership cards. Many retail operations now require membership cards or provide discount incentives to encourage the use of these cards. For example, BJ's Wholesale Club, Costco, and Sam's Club all require their customers to have membership cards.

micro-niching
Dividing the market into very small segments that often comprise only one customer.

mass customization
Ability to provide customized products to a large group of customers.

Technology also allows service managers to provide their customers with a wider variety of options than they could offer previously. The terms **micro-niching** and **mass customization** have evolved, in part, as a direct result of advances in technology that permit firms to identify and provide customized goods and services to individual customers. As an example, Levi Strauss now provides customers in its retail stores with the option of buying jeans that are made to the customer's exact size. The customer's measurements are entered into the computer and a few weeks later the jeans are delivered to the customer's home. Additional pairs can be ordered with only a telephone call, thereby eliminating the need to visit the store.

Increased Efficiency   Another goal in using technology in services is to reduce operating costs. Just as capital equipment is often used to reduce costs in a manufacturing company, technology can be similarly applied in a service environment. The two primary ways in which the efficiency or productivity of the operation can be increased are through (*a*) economies of scale and (*b*) reduced direct labor costs, recognizing that there is some overlap between the two.

In making the decision to adopt new technologies for their operations, service managers must recognize the fact that these technologies require a significant amount of training and support in order for both workers and customers to reap the full benefits. The lack of proper training and support, in many instances, will not only fail to yield the expected improvements in performance and/or productivity, but could also prove disastrous financially as frustrated workers quit and customers defect.

It is also critical that managers, when investing in technology, review the long-term goals of the firm to ensure that compatibility in the form of strategic alignment exists between the technology being adopted and these goals. For example, the customers of a five-star hotel chain want personalized, individual attention (and are willing to pay for it) will probably be turned off by an automated, menu-driven room reservation system that is very time consuming (from the customer's perspective).

Conclusion

It is becoming more and more apparent that successful firms are not simply a collection of vaguely related activities acting independently. Rather, the successful companies of today and tomorrow are well-integrated and well-disciplined organizations. Just like a physical machine, each part of the firm—labor, equipment and management—has an important role to play in achieving that success. The choice of process is also a contributing factor. Goods and services can be produced by several different types of processes, each of which has its own distinctive characteristics. It is important for management to identify these process characteristics in selecting a process to ensure that the goods and services being delivered meet the needs of the firm's customers. In other words, to succeed in the marketplace, a company's processes should be compatible with the customer requirements of the specific market niche that it is trying to serve.

The understanding of how to better manage services clearly lags behind manufacturing. In fact, many of the concepts that have been successfully developed in manufacturing have been adopted by service operations. Nevertheless, services are different from manufacturing, and managers must recognize these differences (the prime difference being the interaction of the customer with the service delivery process). Although service design was once considered an art form, specific logical approaches to better design and management of service systems are slowly emerging.

It is also apparent that advances in technology will continue to alter the ways in which goods and services are designed, produced and delivered. How much of an impact such innovations will have is one of the most intriguing questions to be answered in the coming years. We do know, however, that product life cycles and delivery times will continue to decrease and that customer demand for more customized products will continue to grow. Both of these factors will only increase the pressure on organizations to maintain state-of-the-art technologies in their processes.

 At the same time, there also appears to be a blurring between what we typically think of as manufacturing firms and what we think of as service firms. For example, companies such as Bally Manufacturing, Turner Construction, and Exxon Pipeline, which started out as manufacturing firms, are now listed among the Fortune 500 service companies. IBM, which is considered to be a manufacturer, derives a major portion of its revenues and profits from various services that it provides. We anticipate that this "blurring" between manufacturing and services will continue. The key to success in the future will be dependent on the ability of firms to properly integrate their manufacturing and services elements so that the customer perceives it as a seamless, total entity rather than as independent and separate components.

KEY TERMS

break-even analysis   p. 59
computer-aided (or -assisted) design
   (CAD)   p. 64
computer-aided design and manufacturing
   system (CAD/CAM)   p. 64
computer-integrated manufacturing
   (CIM)   p. 64
concurrent engineering   p. 50
facilities-based services   p. 60
field-based services   p. 60
flexible manufacturing system (FMS)   p. 64
industrial robots   p. 63
islands of automation   p. 65
least-cost envelope   p. 60

levels of customer interaction in
   services   p. 51
   high degree of customer contact   p. 51
   low degree of customer contact   p. 51
machining centers   p.63
mass customization   p. 68
micro-niching   p. 68
numerically controlled machines (NC)   p. 63
product's specifications   p. 48
service-system design matrix   p. 54
types of processes   p. 55
   project   p. 56
   intermittent   p. 56
   line-flow   p. 56

REVIEW AND DISCUSSION QUESTIONS

1. What factors have contributed to the increased emphasis on faster product development and introduction?

2. Discuss the product design phases of design for manufacturability and customer service support. Which do you think is the more important?

3. Discuss the "ready, fire, aim" philosophy of many Japanese companies with respect to new product introduction. How does it compare with that of the typical U.S. company?

4. Why is daily contact between engineering and production groups so important in making early involvement effective?

5. What are the three major categories of processes, and how do they differ in terms of operational characteristics?

6. What is the product-process matrix telling us? How does automation change its basic premise?

7. Assume that a firm would like to manufacture a new product. What are the areas of responsibility for each of the functional business areas (marketing, finance, accounting, human resources, operations)?

8. Why is it important that managers understand the relationship between the various stages of a product's life cycle and the different types of processes that are available for manufacturing that product?

9. Is it possible for a service firm to use either a production line approach or a self-serve design approach and still keep a high customer focus (personal attention)? Explain and support your answer with examples.

10. Identify the high-contact and low-contact operations that exist in the following services:

    a. A dental office.

    b. An airline.

    c. An accounting office.

    d. An automobile agency.

11. Some suggest that customer expectation is the key to service success. Give an example from your own experience to support or refute this assertion.

12. Where would you place a drive-in church, a campus food vending machine, and a bar's automatic mixed drink machine on the service-system design matrix?

13. Using Schmenner's classification scheme that is shown in Exhibit 3.6, identify different segments within a broad service industry (e.g., food service, health care, transportation, etc.) that meet the characteristics found in at least two of the four quadrants, and discuss the key managerial issues in each segment.

14. What are the different ways in which technology can impact an operation? Use examples in both manufacturing and service operations.

 INTERNET UPDATE

Conduct a search on the Internet to locate companies where specific products are identified and the various types of processes that are required to make them are described. Suggested key words to assist you in this search include: OPERATIONS, MANUFACTURING, SERVICES, and PRO-CESSES.

PROBLEMS

1. *a.* List specific products that you especially like. What do you like most about them?

    b. Create a list of products that you dislike or are unhappy with. What don't you like about them?

    c. Are there some common reasons for your lists? For example, is it more important for products that you don't see or see very little to be functional rather than attractive (e.g., the furnace or air conditioning in the house, the transmission or engine in the car)? Is it more important for things to be well designed that other people see and relate to you such as your car, your clothes, or your apartment or home furnishings?

    Can you formulate some general design guidelines based on your answers?

2. Pick a product and make a list of issues that need to be considered in its design and manufacture. The product can be something like a stereo, a telephone, a desk, a kitchen appliance, etc. Consider the functional and aesthetic aspects of design as well as the important concerns for manufacturing.

3. Place the following functions of a department store on the service-system design matrix: Mail order (i.e., catalog), phone order, hardware, stationery, apparel, cosmetics, customer service (i.e., complaints).

4. Place the following functions of a hospital on the service-design system matrix: Physician/patient, nurse/patient, billing, medical records, lab tests, admissions, diagnostic tests (e.g., X-rays).

5. The first step in studying a production process is to develop a description of that process. Once the process is described, we are better able to determine why it works well or poorly and to recommend production-related improvements. Since we are all familiar with fast-food restaurants, try your hand at describing the production process employed at, say, a McDonald's. In doing so, answer the following questions:

   a. What are the important aspects of the service package?
   b. Which skills and attitudes are needed by the service personnel?
   c. How can customer demand be altered?
   d. Can the customer/provider interface be changed to include more technology? More self-serve?
   e. How does it measure up on the seven characteristics of a well-designed service?

CASE: THE BEST ENGINEERED PART IS NO PART

Putting together NCR Corp.'s new 2760 electronic cash register is a snap. In fact, William R. Sprague can do it in less than two minutes—blindfolded. To get that kind of easy assembly, Sprague, a senior manufacturing engineer at NCR, insisted that the point-of-sale terminal be designed so that its parts fit together with no screws or bolts.

The entire terminal consists of just 15 vendor-produced components. That's 85 percent fewer parts, from 65 percent fewer suppliers, than in the company's previous low-end model, the 2160. And the terminal takes only 25 percent as much time to assemble. Installation and maintenance are also a breeze, says Sprague. "The simplicity flows through to all of the downstream activities, including field service."

The new NCR product is one of the best examples to date of the payoffs possible from a new engineering approach called "design for manufacturability," mercifully shortened to DFM. Other DFM enthusiasts include Ford, General Motors, IBM, Motorola, Perkin-Elmer, and Whirlpool. Since 1981, General Electric Co. has used DFM in more than 100 development programs, from major appliances to gearboxes for jet engines. GE figures that the concept has netted $200 million in benefits, either from cost savings or from increased market shares.

NUTS TO SCREWS

One U.S. champion of DFM is Geoffrey Boothroyd, a professor of industrial and manufacturing engineering at the University of Rhode Island and the co-founder of Boothroyd Dewhurst Inc. This tiny Wakefield (R.I.) company has developed several computer programs that analyze designs for ease of manufacturing.

The biggest gains, notes Boothroyd, come from eliminating screws and other fasteners. On a supplier's invoice, screws and bolts may run mere pennies apiece, and collectively they account for only about 5 percent of a typical product's bill of materials. But tack on all of the associated costs, such as the time needed to align components while screws are inserted and tightened, and the price of using those mundane parts can pile up to 75 percent of total assembly costs. "Fasteners should be the first thing to design out of a product," he says.

Had screws been included in the design of NCR's 2760, calculates Sprague, the total cost over the lifetime of the model would have been $12,500—per screw. "The huge impact of little things like screws, primarily on overhead costs, just gets lost," he says. That's understandable, he admits, because for new-product development projects "the overriding factor is hitting the market window. It's better to be on time and over budget than on budget but late."

But NCR got its simplified terminal to market in record time without overlooking the little details. The product was formally introduced last January, just 24 months after development began. Design was a paperless, interdepartmental effort from the very start. The product remained a computer model until all members of the team—from design engineering, manufacturing, purchasing, customer service, and key suppliers—were satisfied.

That way, the printed-circuit boards, the molds for its plastic housing, and other elements could all be developed

simultaneously. This eliminated the usual lag after designers throw a new product "over the wall" to manufacturing,
which then must figure out how to make it. "Breaking
down the walls between design and manufacturing to facilitate simultaneous engineering," Sprague declares, "was the
real breakthrough."

The design process began with a mechanical computer-
aided engineering program that allowed the team to fashion three-dimensional models of each part on a computer
screen. The software also analyzed the overall product and
its various elements for performance and durability. Then
the simulated components were assembled on a computer
workstation's screen to assure that they would fit together
properly. As the design evolved, it was checked periodically with Boothroyd Dewhurst's DFM software. This
prompted several changes that trimmed the parts count
from an initial 28 to the final 15.

NO MOCK-UP

After everyone on the team gave their thumbs-up, the data
for the parts were electronically transferred directly into

computer-aided manufacturing systems at the various suppliers. The NCR designers were so confident everything
would work as intended that they didn't bother making a
mock-up.

DFM can be a powerful weapon against foreign competition. Several years ago, IBM used Boothroyd Dewhurst's software to analyze dot-matrix printers it was
sourcing from Japan—and found it could do substantially
better. Its Proprinter had 65 percent fewer parts and slashed
assembly time by 90 percent. "Almost anything made in
Japan," insists Professor Boothroyd, "can be improved
upon with DFM—often impressively."

QUESTION

What development problems has the NCR approach overcome?

Source: Otis Port, "The Best-Engineered Part Is No Part at All," *Business Week,* May 8, 1989, p. 150.

CASE: KINKO'S COPIER STORES

"We're not your average printer," says Annie Odell,
Kinko's regional manager for Louisiana. She's right. She
may have the only printshops in town where customers
come as much for the company as for the copies. It's a free-
wheeling, high-tech operation that marches to the beat of a
different drum machine. It looks chaotic; it is chaotic. Yet
it produces profit as well as fun.

Odell's copy shop empire has grown from one to seven
in six years, including five in the greater New Orleans area.

Kinko's keeps its sales figures a secret, but Odell estimates her New Orleans stores make about 40 million
copies a year. At the firm's advertised 4 1/2 cents-per-copy
price, that would mean around $1.8 million a year in sales,
or an average of over $300,000 per shop. The New Orleans
operations rank among Kinko's top 25 percent nationally,
reports Becky Barieau of Kinko's of Georgia.

Sales in New Orleans have climbed even while the
marketplace has been sinking. At the Carrollton store, revenues increased 10 percent over last year, an excellent
showing considering the 4½ cents-per-copy rate has not
budged since 1980.

"Depression seems to generate more need for copies,"
says Wallis Windsor, manager of the Carrollton store,
"There are bankruptcies, legal documents and resumes—
hundreds of people who want 50 copies of their resumes on
specialty paper."

PRINTERS SNEER

Kinko's is unique. For one thing, it doesn't do a lick of offset printing. It makes copies, copies, and almost nothing
but copies. On the side it binds, folds, staples, collates,
makes pads, and takes passport photos.

Kinko's is also unique among quick printing chains in
that it doesn't franchise. All 300 or so Kinko's stores are
divided among a few closely held corporations, and
founder Paul Orfalea holds a piece of virtually all of them.
Odell explains that the company avoids franchising to ensure tight control over quality at its outlets.

Others attribute the structure to a desire to avoid the
legal restrictions and paperwork demanded by setting up
franchises in different states. How it's been kept together is
a management feat in itself.

Even the name sticks out. The Yellow Pages list dozens
of quick printers with some reference to speed in their
names, often intentionally misspelled. "Kinko's" denotes a
place that's . . . well, a little kinky. For the record, Orfalea,
who plugged in his first photocopier when he was in college, was nicknamed by classmates as "Kinko" for his
curly head of hair.

BROADWAY AND BENIHANA

Kinko's management style draws on both the restaurant
business and the stage. Fast copies are like fast food, say

the managers. It's not just that every Big Mac is a copy of every other one. Images of eating come up again and again as they try to explain what keeps their customers coming back.

"Making copies is addictive," says Windsor, and points to her clientele of "regulars," who "have made this their office. They will spend four or five hours here although they don't spend more than \$5 or \$6. People have suggested we open a bar in here."

"Instant gratification is what Kinko's is offering," says another manager.

The last time managers from around the country huddled in Santa Barbara for the company "picnic," they studied looseleaf binders crammed full of floor plans for McDonald's and Benihana of Tokyo—a variation on the acclaimed art of Japanese management.

"You'd find it hard to believe," says Odell, "but Benihana is a lot like Kinko's. They're masters of efficiency. We'll try to set up the floor to get one person operating two copiers, just like Benihana puts one cook between two tables. Our paper is centrally located, just as they have all the chopping prepared ahead of time. Then there's the floater, who floats around and pops in wherever he's needed."

Both Kinko's and Benihana's use theater to attract clients, charging their employees with putting on a good show as well as putting out good service. At the Japanese restaurant, the show is the cook, who sizzles a sukiyaki right in front of your table. At Kinko's, it's the clatter of copy machines and the Charlie Chaplinlike spectacle of operators running back and forth between them.

"They do it right in front of you and you get instant quality control," says Odell, "There's no way you're going to drop that document with the customer watching you."

She deliberately displays all her machines and personnel in one big room. "We work out with the public. That's why it's fun," says Odell, "The other guys are behind closed doors."

Windsor enjoys working in a fishbowl. "My personality changes," she says. "I'll be a little more dramatic and louder than I would be in a closed group. I walk quickly. I'll wad up and throw papers a lot."

She believes customers unconsciously get into the act. "Some of the mildest-mannered people get aggressive in here. I've seen a little old lady elbow her way in ahead of people, where if she were in a bank she'd stand in line neatly."

Kinko's does no broadcast and little print advertising, counting on price and word-of-mouth to draw customers, and ambience doesn't hurt. Each Kinko's has its "regulars," who get friendly with particular operators and who favor particular machines. The area in front of the counter is strewn with typewriters, lettering machines and light tables, all the better to hook people into making themselves comfortable and coming back.

A recent addition to that melange is the customer comment form. The customer mails the postage-paid form straight to headquarters in Santa Barbara, where senior management review it and send a thank-you note to the author before routing it back to the shop manager for action. Odell has several inches of forms on file, along with notes on the follow-up calls she made to the customers.

"We don't choose our market so much as our market chooses us," she says. Each shop keeps a different mix of machines, depending on the needs of its patrons. An operator learns quickly that the Xerox 1000 series picks up blue but not yellow, while the 9000 series picks up yellow and black but not blue. Thus, the store adjoining the Tulane campus does not have a 9000 because students tend to bring in notes and books highlighted with yellow markers.

Another adaptation to the market is "Professor Publishing," a service which lets professors excerpt chapters from several books and print them up together as a single textbook. During the first two weeks of every semester, the Broadway office works virtually around-the-clock on this specialty.

Odell maintains that her managers clear all material with publishers before printing a professor's anthology. Indeed, Kinko's says it is one of the most scrupulous of the copy chains about observing copyright laws.

PRINTING IN A FISHBOWL

If working at the Kinko's shops in New Orleans is like working in a fishbowl, it's a two-way fishbowl where the fish are always peering back at their audience. The crazy-quilt mix of customers provides endless entertainment and a fund of oddball stories to exchange over beers. A sampling:

- One woman insisted that the manager throw away the ribbon on the self-service typewriter she'd just used, fearing that someone might try to use it to recreate her document. Another customer wanted several confidential pages typed, and asked, "Can you get me a typist who won't read them?"
- Some artists enjoy using the photocopiers for the oddest things. One woman brings in stuffed dead birds for reproduction. Another brought in a box of pecans purported to be from the backyard of a house where Tennessee Williams once lived.
- A tipsy woman, about 25 years of age, meandered in from a Mardi Gras parade, curled up next to a window, and fell asleep. There she remained for four hours, while the copiers and binding machines pounded and rattled. Manager Raynell Murphy called the home office. "What should I do?" she asked.

"Get a picture," came the word from California, "We can use it as a promotion, you know, to show what a relaxed atmosphere we have at Kinko's."

Finally, a hulking woman who had just bought some copies walked over to the sleeper, kicked her a couple of times, and asked, "Are you ready yet?" The sleeper arose and groggily headed out the door.

QUESTIONS

1. Can general operational standards be developed and implemented in all or a majority of Kinko's shops?

2. Discuss the idea of grouping copiers in machine centers so that certain copiers are available for specific tasks.

3. How do the different services offered (private copying versus copying services provided) present separate types of problems for management?

4. Kinko's Professor Publishing apparently did not pan out. What might have been the cause?

Source: Mark Ballard, "Working in a Fishbowl," *Quick Printing*, May 1987, pp. 30–32. Reprinted by permission.

SELECTED BIBLIOGRAPHY

Adler, Paul S.; Henry E. Riggs; and Steven C. Wheelwright. "Product Development Know-How: Trading Tactics for Strategy." *Sloan Management Review,* Fall 1989, pp. 7–17.

Albrecht, Karl, and Ron Zemke. *Service America! Doing Business in the New Economy* (Homewood, IL: Dow Jones-Irwin, 1985).

Bitran, Gabriel R., and Johannes Hoech. "The Humanization of Service: Respect at the Moment of Truth." *Sloan Management Review,* Winter 1990, pp. 89–96.

Bolwijn, P. T., and T. Kumpe. "Manufacturing in the 1990s—Productivity, Flexibility, and Innovation." *Long Range Planning* 23, no. 4 (1990), pp. 44–57.

Chase, R. B. "The Customer Contact Approach to Services: Theoretical Bases and Practical Extensions." *Operations Research* 21, no. 4 (1981), pp. 698–705.

Cohen, Morris A., and Hau L. Lee. "Out of Touch with Customer Needs?" *Sloan Management Review,* Winter 1990, pp. 55–66.

Collier, D. A. *Service Management: The Automation of Services.* Reston, VA: Reston Publishing, 1986.

Davis, Mark M., and Paul L. Tumolo. *Operations Management in Manufacturing.* Watertown, MA: American Management Association, 1994, pp. 29–31.

Davidow, William H., and Bro Uttal. "Service Companies: Focus or Falter," *Harvard Business Review* 67, no. 4 (July–August 1989), pp. 77–85.

Dixon, John R., and Michael R. Duffy. "The Neglect of Engineering Design." *California Management Review,* Winter 1990, pp. 9–23.

Drucker, Peter F. "The Emerging Theory of Manufacturing." *Harvard Business Review,* May–June 1990, pp. 94–102.

Edmondson, Harold E., and Steven C. Wheelwright. "Outstanding Manufacturing in the Coming Decade." *California Management Review,* Summer 1989, pp. 70–90.

Eisenhardt, K. M., and S. L. Brown, "Time Pacing: Competing in Markets That Won't Stand Still," *Harvard Business Reivew,* March–April 1998, pp. 59–69.

Fitzsimmons, James A., and Mona J. Fitzsimmons. *Service Management: Operations, Strategy, and Information Technology.* 2nd ed. New York: McGraw-Hill, 1998.

Galsworth, G. D. *Smart, Simple Design.* Essex Junction, VT: Oliver Wight Productions, 1994.

Hackett, Gregory P. "Investment in Technology: The Service Sector Sinkhole?" *Sloan Management Review,* Winter 1990, pp. 97–103.

Heskett, James L. *Managing in the Service Economy.* Cambridge, MA: Harvard University Press, 1986.

_____. "Lessons from the Service Sector." *Harvard Business Review,* March–April 1987, pp. 118–26.

Huthwaite, Bart. "Managing at the Starting Line: How to Design Competitive Products." Presented at a Workshop at the University of Southern California, Los Angeles, CA, January 14, 1991.

Levitt, Theodore. "Production-Line Approach to Service." *Harvard Business Review* 50, no. 5 (September–October 1972), pp. 41–52.

Lieber, Ronald B. "Storytelling: A New Way to Get Close to Your Customer." *Fortune,* February 4, 1997, pp. 102–10.

Lovelock, C. H., and R. F. Young. "Look to Customers to Increase Productivity." *Harvard Business Review* 57, no. 3 (May–June 1979), pp. 168–78.

Machlis, Sharon. "Three Shortcuts to Better Design," *Design News,* November 19, 1990, pp. 89–91.

Main, Jeremy. "Manufacturing the Right Way." *Fortune,* May 21, 1990, pp. 54–64.

Meyers, Christopher. *Fast Cycle Time: How to Align Purpose, Strategy and Structure for Speed.* New York: Free Press, 1993.

Nussbaum, Bruce. "Hot Products: Smart Design Is the Common Thread." *Business Week,* June 7, 1993.

Nussbaum, Bruce, and Robert Neff. "I Can't Work This Thing!" *Business Week,* April 29, 1991, pp. 58–66.

Pare, Terence P. "Why Some Do It the Wrong Way." *Fortune,* May 21, 1990, pp. 75–76.

Peavey, Dennis E. "It's Time for a Change." *Management Accounting,* February 1990, pp. 31–35.

Peters, Tom. *Quality!* Palo Alto, CA: TPG Communications, 1986.

Port, Otis. "The Best Engineered Part Is No Part at All." *Business Week,* May 8, 1989, p. 150.

Quinn, J. B., and M. N. Bailey. "Information Technology: Increasing Productivity in Services." *Academy of Management Executive* 8, no. 3, 1994.

Rao, Ashok, et al. *Total Quality Management: A Cross Functional Perspective*. New York: John Wiley and Sons, 1996.

Roach, S. S. "Services Under Siege—The Restructuring Imperative." *Harvard Business Review,* September–October 1991, pp. 82–91.

Roehm, Harper A.; Donald Klein; and Joseph F. Castellano. "Springing to World-Class Manufacturing." *Management Accounting,* March 1991, pp. 40–44.

Sakai, Kuniyasu. "The Feudal World of Japanese Manufacturing." *Harvard Business Review,* November–December 1990, pp. 38–49.

Sanderson, Susan Walsh, and Vic Uzumeri. "Strategies for New Product Development and Renewal: Design-Based Incrementalism." Center for Science and Technology Policy, School of Management, Rensselaer Polytechnic Institute, May 1990.

Schmenner, Roger W. "How Can Service Businesses Survive and Prosper?" *Sloan Management Review* 27, no. 3 (Spring 1986), pp. 21–32.

Schmenner, Roger. *Service Operations Management.* Englewood Cliffs, NJ: Prentice Hall, 1995.

Shina, Sammy G. *Concurrent Engineering and Design for Manufacture of Electronic Products.* New York: Van Nostrand Reinhold, 1991.

Shunk, Dan L. *Integrated Process Design and Development.* Homewood, IL: Business One Irwin, 1992.

Spenser, William J. "Research to Product: A Major U.S. Change." *California Management Review,* Winter 1990, pp. 45–53.

Stalk, George, Jr. "Time—The Next Source of Competitive Advantage." *Harvard Business Review,* July–August 1988, pp. 41–51.

Wheelwright, Steven C., and W. Earl Sasser, Jr. "The New Product Development Map," *Harvard Business Review,* May–June 1989, pp. 112–27.

Ziemke, M. Carl, and Mary S. Spann. "Warning: Don't Be Half-Hearted in Your Efforts to Employ Concurrent Engineering." *Industrial Engineering,* February 1991, pp. 45–49.

FINANCIAL ANALYSIS IN OPERATIONS MANAGEMENT

3

Supplement Outline

Supplement Objectives

- Introduce various cost definitions and demonstrate how they are applied in operations management.

- Demonstrate how break-even analysis is used within an operations management context.

- Demonstrate how the concepts of obsolescence, depreciation, and taxes impact the decision-making process within an operations management context.

- Introduce and demonstrate how the time value of money can be used as a financial tool in the decision-making process with respect to various types of operations management issues.

ACCOUNTING
FINANCE

OM focuses primarily on the transformation of inputs (resources) into outputs (goods and services). Nevertheless, it is important for operations managers to have a thorough understanding of various financial techniques and concepts. Why? Because they must be able to assess the financial performance of their operations. In addition, this knowledge will allow them to evaluate the financial consequences of alternative courses of action, especially with respect to capital investment decisions. The goal of this supplement, therefore, is to provide a basic understanding of these various financial tools and concepts as they relate to OM.

COST DEFINITIONS

We begin this supplement with some basic definitions of standard financial terms.

Fixed Costs

fixed costs
Expenses such as rent that remain constant over a wide range of output volumes.

A **fixed cost** is any expense that remains constant regardless of the level of output. Although no cost is truly fixed, there are many types of expenses that remain virtually fixed over a wide range of outputs. Typical examples of fixed costs include rent, property taxes, most types of depreciation, insurance payments and salaries of top management, all of which remain the same whether the firm is producing one unit or 10,000 units.

Variable Costs

variable costs
Expenses such as material and direct labor that vary proportionately with changes in output volume

Variable costs are expenses that fluctuate directly with changes in the level of output. For example, to clean a hotel room requires a specific amount of material (soap, shampoo, clean towels, etc.) and labor. The incremental cost of this material and labor can be isolated and assigned to each hotel room that is cleaned. Typically, these costs are directly proportional to the output, that is, to clean two hotel rooms costs exactly twice as much as to clean one room.

Exhibit 3S.1 illustrates the fixed and variable cost components of total cost. Note that total costs increase at the same rate as variable costs because fixed costs remain constant.

Sunk Costs

sunk costs
Expenses already incurred that have no salvage value.

Sunk costs are expenses that have previously been incurred or investments that have no salvage value; therefore they should not be taken into account when considering investment alternatives. Sunk costs could also be current costs that are essentially fixed, such as

EXHIBIT 3S.1

Fixed and Variable Cost Components of Total Costs

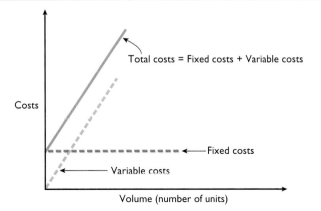

rent on a building with a long term lease. For example, suppose an ice cream manufacturing firm occupies a rented building and is considering making sherbet in the same building. If the company decides to enter sherbet production, its cost accountant will assign some of the rental expense to the sherbet operation. However, the building rent remains unchanged and therefore is not a relevant expense to be considered in making the decision. The rent is *sunk;* that is, it continues to exist and does not change in amount regardless of the decision.

Opportunity Costs

opportunity costs
Profits lost when one alternative is chosen over another that would have provided greater financial benefits.

Opportunity costs represent the benefits *foregone,* or the advantage *lost,* as a result of choosing one alternative over another that could have provided a greater financial return. For example, suppose a firm has $100,000 to invest, and two alternatives of comparable risk present themselves, each requiring a $100,000 investment. Investment A will net $25,000; Investment B will net $23,000. Investment A is clearly the better choice, with a $25,000 net return. If the decision is made to invest in B instead of A, the opportunity costs associated with B are $2,000.

Avoidable Costs

avoidable costs
Expenses such as higher labor costs resulting from poor productivity incurred if an investment is not made.

Avoidable costs include any expense that is *not* incurred if an investment is made but that *must* be incurred if the investment is *not* made. Suppose a company owns a metal lathe that is not in working condition, but the firm needs a working lathe. Since the lathe must be repaired or replaced, the repair costs are avoidable if a new lathe is purchased. Avoidable costs reduce the cost of a new investment because they are not incurred if the investment is made. Avoidable costs are an example of how it is possible to "save" money by spending money.

Out-of-Pocket Costs

out-of-pocket costs
Actual cash outflows associated with a particular alternative.

Out-of-pocket costs are actual expenses that are incurred by the firm and are typically related to the selection of a particular alternative. For example, if a company is considering the conversion of an empty warehouse into office space, then the out-of-pocket costs with respect to the cost of this space (that is, the rent if the building was leased or the amortization if the building was purchased) would be zero. There would be, however, out-of-pocket expenses with respect to renovations, equipment purchases, and other items that would have to be bought in order to convert this space into working offices. Thus, out-of-pocket costs represent actual cash that leaves the firm.

Cost of Capital

cost of capital
Usually expressed as an annual percentage rate, it reflects the cost of the money that is invested in a project.

The **cost of capital** is usually expressed as a percentage cost on an annual basis. The determination of the actual percentage to use is dependent on the financial condition of the company. We present here three different scenarios for determining the cost of capital.

If a company has to go out and borrow the money required to pay for the project under consideration, then the cost of capital is the cost of borrowing that money. On the other hand, if a company is cash rich, then the cost of capital is the interest lost on short term notes like certificates of deposit where the money could otherwise be invested. Finally, if the firm has a limited amount of cash and has a choice on investing it in one of several projects, then the cost of capital is the opportunity cost of forgoing the other projects. Larger corporations usually calculate a weighted average of the three approaches while at the same time taking into consideration the expected return on investment of the owners of the firm.

ACTIVITY-BASED COSTING

In order to determine the total costs involved with making a certain product or delivering a service, some method of allocating overhead costs must be applied. The traditional approach has been to allocate overhead costs to products on the basis of direct labor dollars or hours. The overhead rate can be established by dividing the total estimated overhead costs by total budgeted direct labor hours. The problem with this approach is that direct labor as a percentage of total costs has fallen dramatically over the past decade, especially in manufacturing companies. For example, the introduction of advanced manufacturing technology and other productivity improvements has driven direct labor to less than 10 percent of total manufacturing costs in many industries. As a result, overhead rates of 600 percent or even 1,000 percent are found in some highly automated plants.[1]

This traditional accounting practice of allocating overhead to direct labor can lead to questionable investment decisions; for example, automated processes may be chosen over labor-intensive processes based on a comparison of projected costs. Unfortunately, overhead does not disappear when the equipment is installed and overall costs may actually be lower with the labor-intensive process. It can also lead to wasted effort since an inordinate amount of time is spent tracking direct labor hours. For example, one plant spent 65 percent of its computer costs tracking information about direct labor transactions even though direct labor accounted for only 4 percent of total production costs.[2]

activity-based costing
Accounting technique that allocates overhead costs in actual proportion to the overhead consumed by the production activity.

Activity-based costing techniques have been developed to alleviate these problems by refining the overhead allocation process to more directly reflect actual proportions of overhead consumed by the production activity. Causal factors, known as cost drivers, are identified and used as the means for allocating overhead. These factors might include machine hours, beds occupied, computer time, flight hours, or miles driven. The accuracy of overhead allocation, of course, depends on the selection of the appropriate cost drivers.

Activity-based costing involves a two-stage allocation process with the first stage assigning overhead costs to cost activity pools. These pools represent activities such as performing machine setups, issuing purchase orders, and inspecting parts. In the second stage, costs are assigned from these pools to activities based on the number or amount of pool-related activity required in their completion. Exhibit 3S.2 shows a comparison of traditional cost accounting and activity-based costing.

Consider the example of activity-based costing in Exhibit 3S.3. Two products, A and B, are produced using the same number of labor hours. Applying traditional cost accounting methods, identical overhead costs (usually expressed as a percentage of direct labor costs) would be charged to each product. For example, in Exhibit 3S.3, the $875,000 would be divided by the total labor costs required to make products A and B in order to obtain an overhead rate. By applying activity-based costing, traceable costs are assigned to specific activities. Because each product requires a different amount of transactions, different overhead amounts, expressed here as $s per transaction, are allocated to these products from the pools.

---

[1]Matthew J. Libertore. *Selection and Evaluation of Advanced Manufacturing Technologies* (New York: Springer-Verlag, 1990), pp. 231–56.

[2]Thomas Johnson and Robert Kaplan, *Relevance Lost: The Rise and Fall of Management Accounting* (Boston: Harvard Business School Press, 1987), p. 188.

EXHIBIT 3S.2

Traditional and Activity-Based Costing

EXHIBIT 3S.3

Overhead Allocations by an Activity Approach

Basic Data

		Events or Transactions		
Activity	Traceable Costs	Total	Product A	Product B
Machine setups	$230,000	5,000	3,000	2,000
Quality inspections	160,000	8,000	5,000	3,000
Production orders	81,000	600	200	400
Machine-hours worked	314,000	40,000	12,000	28,000
Material receipts	90,000	750	150	600
	$875,000			

Overhead Rates by Activity

	(a) Traceable Costs	(b) Total Events or Transactions	(a) ÷ (b) Rate per Event or Transaction
Machine setups	$230,000	5,000	$46/setup
Quality inspections	160,000	8,000	$20/inspection
Productuon orders	81,000	600	$135/order
Machine-hours worked	314,000	40,000	$7.85/hour
Material receipts	90,000	750	$120/receipt

Overhead Cost per Unit of Product

	Product A		Product B	
	Events or Transactions	Amount	Events or Transactions	Amount
Machine setups, at $46/setup	3,000	$138,000	2,000	$ 92,000
Quality inspections, at $20/inspection	5,000	100,000	3,000	60,000
Production orders at $135/order	200	27,000	400	54,000
Machine-hours worked, at $7.85/hour	12,000	94,200	28,000	219,800
Material receipts, at $120/receipt	150	18,000	600	72,000
Total overhead cost assigned (a)		$377,200		$497,800
Number of units produced (b)		5,000		20,000
Overhead cost per unit, (a) ÷ (b)		$75.44		$24.89

Source: Ray Garrison, *Managerial Accounting*, 6th ed. (Homewood, IL: Richard D. Irwin, 1991), p. 94.

As stated earlier, activity-based costing overcomes the problem of cost distortion by creating a cost pool for each activity or transaction that can be identified as a cost driver, and by assigning overhead costs to products or jobs on the basis of the number of separate activities required for their completion. Thus, in the previous situation, the low-volume product would be assigned the bulk of the costs for machine setup, purchase orders, and quality inspections, thereby showing it to have high unit costs compared to the other product.

Finally, activity-based costing is sometimes referred to as *transactions costing*. This transactions focus gives rise to another major advantage over other costing methods; that is, it improves the traceability of overhead costs and thus results in more accurate *unit* cost data for management.

BREAK-EVEN ANALYSIS

break-even analysis
Determination of product volume where revenues equal total costs or costs associated with two alternative processes are the same.

Break-even analysis, as we define it here, can be viewed from two perspectives. From the overall view of the company, break-even analysis usually refers to determining how much volume of business the company must do in order to break-even, that is, to have neither profits nor losses. The *break-even point,* in this case is where total revenues equal total costs. Break-even analysis from a purely operational perspective usually focuses on the choice of processes. Here, break-even implies that the two processes have equal costs for a specific level of volume, which is again referred to as the break-even point. We will address both of these types of break-even analysis. In each case we apply a simple linear model that uses only fixed costs and variable costs.

Revenues versus Costs

As stated above, the objective here is to determine how much volume of business a company has to do to break-even. The volume can be stated in either monetary units or product units, although the latter is usually easier to conceptualize from an operational perspective.

The underlying assumptions in this linear model are:

- *The selling price per unit is constant.* In other words, there is one selling price for a unit, with no allowances for quantity discounts or special terms for major customers.

- *Variable costs per unit remain constant.* Here, the cost to produce each unit remains the same over the range of volume that we are concerned with. (Consequently, there are no allowances for economies of scale.) Since variable costs refer to the material and direct labor that go into making each unit, additional unit costs such as overtime, second shift premiums or subcontracting are, therefore, excluded from consideration.

- *Fixed costs remain constant.* Over the range of volume that we are concerned with, the fixed costs of the operation do not change regardless of the volume produced. As defined earlier, these fixed costs usually include rent, insurance and taxes on the facility, senior management salaries, and other overhead expenses.

Example | The West Pacific Toy Company, a small manufacturing firm located in Manila, Philippines, produces cloth dolls for export to the United States. The company sells these dolls to major retail chains for US$3.00 each, which does not include shipping costs of US$0.50 per doll. (These dolls are then marked up to a retail selling price in the United

States of US$14.95 per doll.) The workers in the factory are paid, on the average, the equivalent of US$8.00 per day, and it is estimated that the average daily output per worker is 50 dolls. The cost of the material is estimated at US$1.25 per doll. Fixed costs for this operation are estimated to be US$160,000 per year.

a. What is the break-even point for this company, in terms of the number of dolls per year?

b. If the company sold 135,000 dolls last year, how much profit (loss) did it have for the year?

Solution

a. As seen in Exhibit 3S.4, the break-even point is that point on the graph where the total sales line intersects with the total cost line. This point can be calculated as follows:

Selling price = SP = US$3.00 per doll

Variable cost = VC = Material cost + Labor cost

$$= 1.25 + 8.00/50$$
$$= US\$1.41 \text{ per doll}$$

Fixed costs = FC = US$160,000 per year

X = Number of dolls sold per year

As seen in Exhibit 3S.4, total annual sales

$$= TS = (SP)(X)$$

Total annual costs equals fixed costs plus variable costs

$$= TC = FC + (VC)(X)$$

The point at which the total sales line and the total costs line intersect is the break-even point, which is where they are equal to each other.
Thus

$$TS = TC$$
$$(SP)(X) = FC + (VC)(X)$$

Solving for X we have

$$X = \frac{FC}{(SP - VC)}$$

Substituting the values for SP, VC, and FC we have

$$X = \frac{160,000}{(3.00 - 1.41)}$$

$$X = 100,629 \text{ dolls per year}$$

b. Profits = P = Total sales − Total costs

$$P = TS - TC$$
$$P = (SP)(X) - [FC + (VC)(X)]$$

$$P = (3.00)(135,000) - [160,000 + (1.41)(135,000)]$$
$$P = 405,000 - [160,000 + 190,350]$$
$$P = 405,000 - 350,350$$
$$\text{Profits for the year} = \text{US\$54,650}$$

EXHIBIT 3S.4

Break-Even Analysis for Revenues versus Costs

Choice of Processes

Break-even analysis can also be used to choose from among alternative processes a company can use. Again, we assume that both the variable costs per unit and the fixed costs over the range of volumes being evaluated remain constant. Sales are not considered in this analysis, in terms of identifying the break-even points. (Although the forecasted level of sales is definitely a factor in selecting the process to be used.) Here, we define the break-even point as that volume where we are indifferent with respect to the costs of the two alternative processes.

Example

Allison and Jon, to earn extra money while they are in high school, have a small catering business. They provide a variety of freshly made sandwiches in the evenings to college students. Currently, they prepare the sandwiches at their home which is about 15 miles away. The average cost per sandwich, including the transportation, material and direct labor is approximately $2.55. The school has recently offered to lease them a small kitchen on campus. The rent for this kitchen is $360.00 per month for each of the nine months that the school is open full time. (The building in which the kitchen is located is closed for the other three months, so the kitchen is also closed.) Allison and Jon estimate that they will be able to produce the sandwiches at this new location at an average cost of $1.80 per sandwich. (The savings are attributed to working more efficiently in a professional kitchen.)

a. How many sandwiches a month do Allison and Jon have to sell in order to be indifferent to the costs of working at home versus working in the kitchen on campus?

b. The parents of Allison and Jon have decided that they are going to charge them $120.00 per month because of the additional out-of-pocket costs involved with preparing the sandwiches at home (electricity, cleaning supplies, etc.). What is the new break-even point under these circumstances between working at home and working on campus?

Solution

a. *Alternative 1: Working at Home*

Total costs = $TC_1 = VC_1X$

where

   VC_1 = Variable costs per sandwich of $2.55

   X = Number of sandwiches sold

or

   $TC_1 = 2.55X$

Alternative 2: Working on Campus

Total costs = $TC_2 = FC_2 + VC_2X$

where

   FC_2 = Fixed costs of $360.00 per month

   VC_2 = Variable cost per sandwich of $1.80

As seen in Exhibit 3S.5, the break-even point between these two alternatives is where the two total costs lines intersect.

The break-even point is calculated as follows:

$$TC_1 = TC_2$$

Substituting for TC_1 and TC_2 from above, we have

$$VC_1X = FC_2 + VC_2X$$

$$2.55X = 360 + 1.80X$$

$$0.75X = 360$$

$$X = 480 \text{ Sandwiches a month.}$$

Note that when we analyze process alternatives, we do not need to know the selling price per unit. The decision here is based upon the forecasted volume to be sold, with the goal being to select that process which has the lowest total costs at the forecasted volume. In this example, if the forecast per month is greater than 480 sandwiches, then they should rent the kitchen on campus, otherwise they should continue working at home.

b. *Alternative 1: Working at Home*

Total costs = $TC_1 = FC_1 + VC_1X$

where

   FC_1 = Fixed costs of $120.00 per month

   VC_1 = Variable cost per sandwich of $2.55

   X = Number of sandwiches sold

or

   $TC_1 = 120 + 2.55X$

Alternative 2: Working on Campus

Total costs $= TC_2 = FC_2 + VC_2X$
where

$FC_2 =$ Fixed costs of \$360.00 per month
$VC_2 =$ Variable cost per sandwich of \$1.80

As seen in Exhibit 3S.6, the new break-even point between these two alternatives is again where the two total costs lines intersect. Under these conditions, the break-even point is calculated as follows:

$$TC_1 = TC_2$$
$$FC_1 + VC_1X = FC_2 + VC_2X$$
$$120 + 2.55X = 360 + 1.80X$$
$$.75X = 240$$
$$X = 320 \text{ Sandwiches a month.}$$

Here, if the forecast is more than 320 sandwiches a month, they should use the kitchen at school, if it is less, they should continue working at home.

EXHIBIT 3S.5

Break-Even Analysis for Alternative Types of Processes

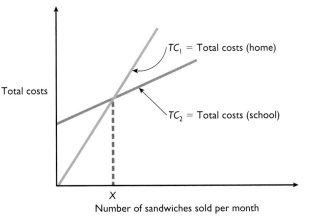

EXHIBIT 3S.6

Break-Even Analysis for Alternative Types of Processes

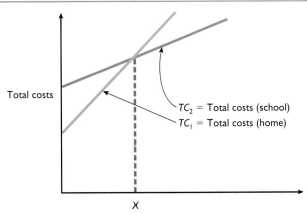

OBSOLESCENCE, DEPRECIATION, AND TAXES

Economic Life and Obsolescence

obsolete
Status of an asset when it has worn out or been surpassed by a superior performing asset.

When a firm invests in an income-producing asset, the economic life of the asset is estimated. For accounting purposes, the asset is depreciated over this period. It is assumed that the asset will perform its function during this time and then be considered **obsolete** or worn out, and replacement will be required. However, this view of asset life rarely coincides with reality.

To illustrate this, assume that a machine with an expected productive life of 10 years is purchased. If at any time during the ensuing 10 years a new machine is developed that can perform the same task more efficiently or economically, the old machine is considered to be obsolete. Whether it is "worn out" or not is irrelevant.

economic life
Useful life of an asset in which it provides the best method of operation to an organization.

The **economic life** of a piece of equipment is the period over which it provides the best method for performing its task. When a new, superior method is developed, the actual value of the existing equipment is usually significantly less than the stated *book value* of a machine (that is, the "official" remaining value).

Types of Depreciation

depreciation
Method for allocating capital equipment costs over more than one time period.

Depreciation is a method for allocating the costs of capital equipment over more than one time period (for discussion here, we will use years). The value of any capital asset—buildings, machinery, and so forth—decreases as its useful life is expended. *Amortization* and *depreciation* are often used interchangeably. Through convention, however, *depreciation* refers to the allocation of costs due to the physical or functional deterioration of *tangible* (physical) assets, such as buildings or equipment, while *amortization* refers to the allocation of costs over the useful life of *intangible* assets, such as patents, leases, franchises, or goodwill.

Depreciation procedures may not reflect an asset's true value at any point in its life because obsolescence at any time may result in a large difference between the true value and book value of the asset. Also, since depreciation rates significantly affect taxes, a firm may choose a particular depreciation method from the several alternatives that are available, giving more consideration to its effect on taxes than its ability to make the book value of an asset reflect the true resale value.

We describe five commonly used methods of depreciation:

1. *Straight-line method.*   With this method, an asset's value is reduced in uniform annual amounts over its estimated useful life. The general straight-line depreciation formula is:

$$\text{Annual amount to be depreciated} = \frac{\text{Cost} - \text{Salvage value}}{\text{Estimated useful life}}$$

For example, a machine costing $10,000, with an estimated salvage value of $0 and an estimated life of 10 years, would be depreciated at the rate of $1,000 per year for each of the 10 years. If its estimated salvage value at the end of the 10 years is $1,000, the annual depreciation then becomes:

$$\frac{\$10,000 - \$1,000}{10} = \$900 \text{ per year}$$

2. *Sum-of-the-years'-digits (SYD) method.*   The purpose of the SYD method is to reduce the book value of an asset rapidly in the early years of its life and at a lower rate in its later years. This is done both for tax purposes and to more accurately reflect the true value of an asset.

To illustrate this, suppose that the estimated useful life of a piece of equipment is five years. Here, the sum of the years' digits is $1 + 2 + 3 + 4 + 5 = 15$. Therefore, the asset is depreciated by $5 \div 15$ (or 33 percent) after the first year, $4 \div 15$ (or 26.7 percent) after the second year, and so on, down to $1 \div 15$ (or 6.7 percent) in the last year. (We are assuming here that the salvage value at the end of the fifth year is zero.)

3. *Declining-balance method.* This method also provides for an accelerated depreciation. The asset's value is decreased each year by reducing its book value by a constant percentage each year. The percentage rate selected is often the one that just reduces book value to salvage value at the end of the asset's estimated life. In any case, the asset should never be reduced below estimated salvage value. Use of the declining-balance method and allowable rates is controlled by Internal Revenue Service regulations. As a simplified illustration, the example in the next table uses an arbitrarily selected rate of 40 percent. (Salvage value after five years is estimated at $2,000.) Depreciation with this method is based on full cost, *not* cost minus salvage value.

Year	Depreciation Rate	Beginning Book Value	Depreciation Charge	Accumulated Depreciation	Ending Book Value
1	0.40	$17,000	$6,800	$ 6,800	$10,200
2	0.40	10,200	4,080	10,880	6,120
3	0.40	6,120	2,448	13,328	3,672
4	0.40	3,672	1,469	14,797	2,203
5		2,203	203	15,000	2,000

Note that in the fifth year, reducing book value by 40 percent would have caused it to drop below salvage value. Consequently, the asset was depreciated by only $203, which decreased book value to salvage value.

4. *Double-declining-balance method.* Again, for tax advantages, the double-declining-balance method offers higher depreciation early in the economic life of the asset. The double-declining-balance method uses a percentage that is equal to twice the straight line rate over the life of the item but applies this rate to the undepreciated original cost. The method is the same as the declining-balance method, but the term *double-declining balance* means double the straight-line rate. Thus, equipment with a 10-year lifespan would have a straight line depreciation rate of 10 percent per year and a double-declining-balance rate (applied to the undepreciated amount) of 20 percent per year. (At some point, usually near the end of the equipment's life span, one switches to straight-line depreciation.)

5. *Depreciation-by-use method.* The purpose of this method is to depreciate a capital investment in proportion to its use. It is applicable, for example, to a machine that performs the same operation many times. The life of the machine is not estimated in years but rather it is estimated in the total number of operations it may reasonably be expected to perform before wearing out. Suppose that a metal-stamping press has an estimated life of 1 million stampings and costs $100,000. The charge for depreciation per stamping is then $100,000 \div 1,000,000$, or $0.10. Assuming a $0 salvage value, the depreciation charges are as shown:

Year	Total Yearly Stampings	Cost per Stamping	Yearly Depreciation Charge	Accumulated Depreciation	Ending Book Value
1	150,000	0.10	$15,000	$15,000	$85,000
2	300,000	0.10	30,000	45,000	55,000
3	200,000	0.10	20,000	65,000	35,000
4	200,000	0.10	20,000	85,000	15,000
5	100,000	0.10	10,000	95,000	5,000
6	50,000	0.10	5,000	100,000	0

The depreciation-by-use method is an attempt to allocate depreciation charges in proportion to actual use and thereby coordinate expense charges with productive output more accurately. Also, since a machine's resale value is related to its remaining productive life, it is expected that with this method the book value will more closely approximate the resale value.

The Effects of Taxes

Tax rates and the methods of applying them occasionally change. When analysts evaluate investment proposals, tax considerations often prove to be the deciding factor since depreciation expenses directly affect taxable income and, therefore, profit. The ability to write off depreciation in early years provides an added source of funds for investment.

TYPES OF ECONOMIC DECISIONS

The capital investment decision has become highly rationalized, as evidenced by the variety of techniques that are now available. In contrast to pricing or marketing decisions, the capital investment decision can usually be made with a higher degree of confidence because the variables affecting the decision are relatively well known and can be quantified with a relatively high degree of accuracy.

Investment decisions may be grouped into six general categories:

1. Purchase of new equipment or facilities.
2. Replacement of existing equipment or facilities.
3. Make-or-buy decisions.
4. Lease-or-buy decisions.
5. Temporary shutdown or plant-abandonment decisions.
6. Addition or elimination of a product or product line.

Investment decisions are usually made with regard to the *lowest acceptable rate of return* on investment. This is often referred to as the "threshold" rate of return. As a starting point, the threshold rate of return may be considered to be the cost of investment capital needed to underwrite the expenditure. Certainly an investment will not be made if it does not return at least the cost of capital.

Investments are generally ranked according to the return they yield in excess of their cost of capital. In this way a business with only limited investment funds can select investment alternatives that yield the highest *net returns*. (*Net return* is the earnings an investment yields after gross earnings have been reduced by the cost of the funds used to finance the investment.) In general, investments should not be made unless the return in funds exceeds the *marginal* cost of investment capital (*marginal cost* is the incremental cost of each new acquisition of funds from outside sources).

FINANCIAL DEFINITIONS

There are two basic methods to account for the effects of interest accumulation. One is to compute the total amount accumulated over the time period into the future as the *compound value*. The other is to remove the interest rate effect over time by reducing all future sums to present-day dollars, or the *present value*.

Compound Value of a Single Amount

Albert Einstein was once quoted as saying that compound interest is the eighth wonder of the world. After reviewing this section, with its dramatic growth effects during a longer term of years, you might wish to propose a new government regulation: on the birth of a child, the parents must put, say, $1,000 into a retirement fund for that child at age 65. This might be one way to reduce the pressure on Social Security and other state and federal pension plans. While inflation will decrease the value significantly, there is still a lot left over. At 14 percent interest, our $1,000 increased to $500,000 after subtracting the $4.5 million for inflation (assuming that inflation erodes 90 percent of the gain!). That's still 500 times larger than the original $1,000.

Most calculators make such computation easy. However, many people still refer to tables for compound values. Using Appendix A, Table 1 (compound sum of $1), for example, we see that the value of $1 at 10 percent interest after three years is $1.331. (Note: Tables 1 through 4 are in Appendix A.)

Compound Value of an Annuity

An *annuity* is the receipt of a constant sum each year for a specified number of years. Usually an annuity is received at the end of a period and does not earn interest during that period. Therefore, an annuity of $10 for three years would bring in $10 at the end of the first year (allowing the $10 to earn interest if invested for the remaining two years), $10 at the end of the second year (allowing the $10 to earn interest for the remaining one year), and $10 at the end of the third year (with no time to earn interest). If the annuity receipts were placed in a bank savings account at 5 percent interest, the total or compound value of the $10 at 5 percent for the three years would be:

Year	Receipt at End of Year	Compound Interest Factor $(1 + i)^n$	Value at End of Third Year
1	$10.00 ×	$(1 + 0.05)^2 =$	$11.02
2	10.00 ×	$(1 + 0.05)^1 =$	10.50
3	10.00 ×	$(1 + 0.05)^0 =$	10.00
			$31.52

The general formula for finding the compound value of any annuity is

$$S_n = R[(1 + i)^{n-1} + (1 + i)^{n-2} + \cdots + (1 + i)^1 + 1]$$

where

S_n = Compound value of an annuity

R = Periodic receipts in dollars

n = Length of the annuity in years

Applying this formula to the above example, we get

$$S_n = R[(1 + i)^2 + (1 + i) + 1]$$
$$= \$10[(1 + 0.05)^2 + (1 + 0.05) + 1]$$
$$= \$31.52$$

Appendix A, Table 2 lists the compound value factor of $1 for 5 percent after three years as 3.152. Multiplying this factor by $10 yields $31.52.

Consider the beneficial effects of investing $2,000 each year, starting at the age of 21. Assume investments in AAA-rated bonds are available today yielding 9 percent. From Table 2 in Appendix A, after 30 years (age 51) the investment is worth 136.3 times $2,000, or $272,600. Fourteen years later (age 65) this would be worth $962,993 (using a hand calculator, since the table only goes up to 30 years, and assuming the $2,000 is deposited at the end of each year)! But what 21-year-old thinks about retirement?

Present Value of a Future Single Payment

Compound values are used to determine the future value of a stream of cash flows after a specified period has elapsed; present-value (PV) procedures accomplish just the reverse. They are used to determine the current value of a sum or stream of receipts expected to be received in the future. Most investment decision techniques use present-value concepts rather than compound values. Since decisions affecting the future are made in the present, it makes more sense to convert future returns into their present value at the time the decision is being made. In this way, investment alternatives are viewed from a better perspective in terms of current dollars.

Example

If a rich uncle offers to make you a gift of $100 today or $250 after 10 years, which should you choose? You must determine whether $250 in 10 years will be worth more than the $100 now. Suppose that you base your decision on the rate of inflation in the economy and believe that inflation will be 10 percent per year. But deflating the $250, you can compare its relative purchasing power with $100 received today. Procedurally, this is accomplished by solving the compound formula for the present sum, P, where V is the future amount of $250 in 10 years at 10 percent.

Solution

The general formula for compound value is

$$V_n = P(1 + i)^n$$

where

V_n = Value of principal at the end of year n
n = Length of the compounding period in years
P = Present value of principal
i = Interest rate

Dividing both sides by $(1 + i)^n$ gives:

$$P = \frac{V_n}{(1 + i)^n}$$

$$= \frac{250}{(1 + 0.10)^{10}}$$

$$= \$96.39$$

This shows that, at a 10 percent inflation rate, $250 in 10 years will be worth $93.39 today. The rational choice is to take the $100 now based on a belief that inflation will remain constant at 10 percent per year for the next 10 years.

The use of tables is also standard practice in solving present-value problems. With reference to Appendix A, Table 3, the present-value factor for $1 received 10 years hence is 0.386. Multiplying this factor by $250 yields $96.50.

Present Value of an Annuity

The present value of an annuity is the value of an annual amount to be received over a future period expressed in terms of the present. To find the value of an annuity of $100 for three years at 10 percent, find the factor in the present-value table that applies to 10 percent in *each* of the three years in which the amount is received and multiply each receipt by this factor. Then sum the resulting figures. Remember that annuities are usually received at the end of each period.

Year	Amount Received at End of Year		Present-Value Factor at 10%		Present Value
1	$100	×	0.909	=	$ 90.90
2	100	×	0.826	=	82.60
3	100	×	0.751	=	75.10
Total receipt	$300		Total present value	=	$248.60

The general formula used to derive the present value of an annuity is

$$A_n = R \left[\frac{1}{(1+i)} + \frac{1}{(1+i)^2} + \cdots + \frac{1}{(1+i)^n} \right]$$

where

A_n = Present value of annuity of n years

R = Periodic receipts

n = Length of the annuity in years

Applying the formula to the above example gives

$$A_n = \$100 \left[\frac{1}{(1+0.10)} + \frac{1}{(1+0.10)^2} + \frac{1}{(1+0.10)^3} \right]$$

$$= \$100 \ (2.488)$$

$$= \$248.80$$

Appendix A, Table 4 contains present values of an annuity for varying maturities. The present-value factor for an annuity of $1 for three years at 10 percent (from Appendix A, Table 4) is 2.487. Since our sum is $100 rather than $1, we multiply this factor by $100 to arrive at $248.70. The slight variance from the previous answers results from rounded figures in the table.

When the stream of future receipts is uneven, the present value of each annual receipt must be calculated. The present values of the receipts for all years are then summed to determine the total present value. This process can sometimes be tedious, if done manually. Fortunately, today's software programs can accomplish this easily.

Discounted Cash Flow

The term *discounted cash flow,* or DCF, refers to the total stream of payments that an asset will generate in the future discounted to the present time. This is simply present value analysis that includes all flows: single payments, annuities, and all others.

METHODS FOR EVALUATING INVESTMENT ALTERNATIVES

Net Present Value

net present value
Present cash value of a stream of future cash flows.

The **net present value** method is commonly used in business. With this method, decisions are based on the amount by which the present value of a projected income stream exceeds the cost of an investment.

Example

A firm is considering two alternative investments: the first, Alternative A, costs $30,000 and the second, Alternative B, costs $50,000. The expected yearly cash income streams for each of the two alternatives are shown in the next table.

	Cash Inflow	
Year	Alternative A	Alternative B
I	$10,000	$15,000
2	10,000	15,000
3	10,000	15,000
4	10,000	15,000
5	10,000	15,000

To decide which of the two alternatives is better, we need to determine which has the highest net present value. (For this calculation we need the cost of capital; let's assume it is 8 percent.)

Solution

Alernative A

$$3.993 \text{ (PV factor)} \times \$10,000 = \$39,930$$
$$\text{Less cost of investment} = \underline{30,000}$$
$$\text{Net present value} = \$9,930$$

Alternative B

$$3.993 \text{ (PV factor)} \times \$15,000 = \$59,895$$
$$\text{Less cost of investment} = \underline{50,000}$$
$$\text{Net present value} = \$9,895$$

Based purely on economic criteria, management would prefer Alternative A because its net present value exceeds that of Alternative B by $35 ($9,930 − $9,895 = $35).

Payback Period

payback period
Time necessary for the firm to recover its initial investment.

The **payback period** method ranks investments according to the time required for each investment to return earnings equal to the cost of the investment. The rationale is that the sooner the investment capital can be recovered, the sooner it can be reinvested in new revenue-producing projects. Thus, supposedly, a firm will be able to get the most benefit from its available investment funds.

Consider two alternatives, each requiring a $1,000 investment. The first will earn $200 per year for six years; the second will earn $300 per year for the first three years and $100 per year for the next three years.

If the first alternative is selected, the initial investment of $1,000 will be recovered at the end of the fifth year. The income produced by the second alternative will total $1,000 after only four years. The second alternative will permit reinvestment of the full $1,000 in new revenue-producing projects one year sooner than the first.

Although the payback period method is declining in popularity as the sole measure for evaluating investments, it is still frequently used in conjunction with other methods to give an indication of the time commitment of funds. The major problems with the payback period method are that it does not consider income beyond the payback period and it ignores the time value of money. Any method that ignores the time value of money must be considered questionable.

Internal Rate of Return

internal rate of return
Interest rate which
equates present value of
future cash flows with
cost of an investment.

The **internal rate of return** (IRR) can be defined as the interest rate that equates the present value of an income stream with the cost of an investment. There is no procedure or formula that may be used directly to compute the internal rate of return—it must be found by interpolation or iterative calculation (in other words, trial and error which can be performed quite easily with a computer).

Example	Suppose we wish to find the internal rate of return for an investment costing $12,000 that will yield a cash inflow of $4,000 per year for four years.
Solution	We see that the present value factor sought is

$$\text{PV factor} = \frac{\$12,000}{\$4,000} = 3.000$$

and we seek the interest rate that will provide this factor over a four-year period. The interest rate must lie between 12 percent and 14 percent because 3.000 lies between 3.037 and 2.914 (in the fourth row of Appendix A, Table 4). Linear interpolation between these two values, according to the following equation

$$i = 12 + (14 - 12)\frac{(3.037 - 3.000)}{(3.037 - 2.914)}$$

$$= 12 + 0.602 = 12.602\%$$

provides us with a good approximation to the actual internal rate of return.

When the income stream is discounted at 12.6 percent, the resulting present value closely approximates the cost of the investment. Thus, the internal rate of return for this investment is 12.6 percent. The cost of capital can be compared with the internal rate of return to determine the net rate of return on the investment. If, in this example, the cost of capital were 8 percent, the net rate of return on the investment would be 4.6 percent.

The net present value and internal rate of return methods involve procedures that are essentially the same. They differ in that the net present value method enables investment alternatives to be compared in terms of the dollar value in excess of cost, whereas the internal rate of return method permits a comparison of rates of return on alternative investments. Moreover, the internal rate of return method occasionally encounters problems in calculation, as multiple rates frequently appear in the computation.

Ranking Investments with Uneven Lives

When proposed investments have the same life expectancy, comparison among them using the preceding methods will give a reasonable picture of their relative value. When lives are unequal, however, there is the question of how to relate the two different time periods. Should replacements be considered the same as the original? Should productivity for the shorter-term unit that will be replaced earlier be considered to have higher productivity? How should the cost of future units be estimated?

No estimate dealing with investments unforeseen at the time of decision can be expected to reflect a high degree of accuracy. Still, the problem must be dealt with, and some assumptions must be made in order to determine a ranking. The following section presents several different examples of how different methods can be applied to OM-related investment decisions.

SAMPLE PROBLEMS ON INVESTMENT DECISIONS

An Expansion Decision

Example

William J. Wilson Ceramic Products, Inc., leases plant facilities in which firebrick is manufactured. Because of rising demand, Wilson could increase sales by investing in new equipment to expand output. The selling price of $2.50 per brick will remain unchanged if output and sales increase. Based on engineering and cost estimates, the accounting department provides management with the following cost estimates based on an annual increased output of 400,000 bricks:

Cost of new equipment having an expected life of five years	$500,000
Equipment installation cost	20,000
Expected salvage value	0
New operation's share of annual lease expense	40,000
Annual increase in utility expenses	40,000
Annual increase in labor costs	160,000
Annual additional cost for raw materials	400,000

The sum-of-the-years'-digits method of depreciation will be used, and taxes are paid at a rate of 40 percent. Wilson's policy is not to invest capital in projects earning less than a 20 percent rate of return. Should the proposed expansion be undertaken?

Solution

Compute cost of investment:

Acquisition cost of equipment	$500,000
Equipment installation costs	20,000
Total cost of investment	$520,000

Determine yearly cash flows throughout the life of the investment.

The lease expense is a sunk cost. It will be incurred whether or not the investment is made and is therefore irrelevant to the decision and should be disregarded. Annual production expenses to be considered are utility, labor, and raw materials. These total $600,000 per year.

Annual sales revenues are $2.50 × 400,000 units of output, or $1,000,000. Yearly income before depreciation and taxes is thus $1,000,000 gross revenues, less $600,000 expenses, or $400,000.

Next, determine the depreciation charges to be deducted from the $400,000 income each year using the SYD method (sum-of-years'-digits $= 1 + 2 + 3 + 4 + 5 = 15$):

Year	Proportion of $500,000 to Be Depreciated		Depreciation Charge
1	5/15 × $500,000	=	$166,667
2	4/15 × 500,000	=	133,333
3	3/15 × 500,000	=	100,000
4	2/15 × 500,000	=	66,667
5	1/15 × 500,000	=	33,333
Accumulated depreciation			$500,000

Find each year's cash flow when taxes are 40 percent. Cash flow for only the first year is illustrated:

Earnings before depreciation and taxes	$400,000
Less depreciation	−$167,667
Earnings before taxes	$233,333
Less federal taxes (40%)	−93,333
Net earnings	$140,000
Net cash flow = Net earnings + Depreciation	$306,667
(first year)	

Determine present value of the cash flow. Since Wilson demands at least a 20 percent rate of return on investments, multiply the cash flows by the 20 percent present-value factor for each year. The factor for each respective year must be used because the cash flows are not an annuity.

Year	Present Value Factor (20%)		Cash Flow		Present Value
1	0.833	×	$306,667	=	$255,454
2	0.694	×	293,333	=	203,573
3	0.579	×	280,000	=	162,120
4	0.482	×	266,667	=	128,533
5	0.402	×	253,334	=	101,840
Total present value of cash flows (discounted at 20%)				=	$851,520

Now find whether net present value is positive or negative:

Total present value of cash flows	$851,520
Total cost of investment	520,000
Net present value	$331,520

The net present value is positive when returns are discounted at 20 percent. Wilson will earn an amount in excess of 20 percent on the investment and the proposed expansion should be undertaken.

A Replacement Decision

Example

For five years Bennie's Brewery has been using a machine that attaches labels to bottles. The machine was purchased for $4,000 and is being depreciated over 10 years to a $0 salvage value using straight-line depreciation. The machine can be sold now for $2,000. Bennie can buy a new labeling machine for $6,000 that will have a useful life of five years and cut labor costs by $1,200 annually. The old machine will require a major overhaul in the next few months at an estimated cost of $300. If purchased, the new machine will be depreciated over five years to a $500 salvage value using the straight-line method. The company will invest in any project earning more than the 12 percent cost of capital. The tax rate is 40 percent. Should Bennie's Brewery invest in the new machine?

Solution Determine the cost of investment:

Price of new machine		$6,000
Less: Sale of old machine	$2,000	
Avoidable overhaul costs	300	2,300
Effective net cost of investment		$3,700

Determine the increase in cash flow resulting from investment in the new machine:

Yearly cost savings = $1,200

Differential depreciation:

Annual depreciation on old machines: $\dfrac{\text{Cost} - \text{Salvage}}{\text{Expected life}} = \dfrac{\$4,000 - \$0}{10} = \$400$

Annual depreciation on new machines: $\dfrac{\text{Cost} - \text{Salvage}}{\text{Expected life}} = \dfrac{\$6,000 - \$500}{5} = \$1,100$

Differential depreciation = $1,100 - $400 = $700

Yearly net increase in cash flow into the firm:

Cost savings		$1,200
Deduct: Taxes at 40%	$480	
Add: Advantage of increase in depreciation (0.4 × 700)	280	200
Yearly increase in cash flow		$1,000

Determine the total present value of the investment:

The five-year cash flow of $1,000 per year is an annuity.

Discounted at 12 percent, the cost of capital, the present value is 3.605 × $1,000 = $3,605

The present value of the new machine, if sold at its salvage value of $500 at the end of the fifth year, is 0.567 × $500 = $284

Total present value of the expected cash flows: $3,605 + $284 = $3,889

Determine whether the net present value is positive:

Total present value	$3,889
Cost of investment	3,700
Net present value	$ 189

Bennie's Brewery should make the purchase because the investment will return slightly more than the cost of capital.

Note: The importance of depreciation has been shown in this example. The present value of the yearly cash flow resulting from operation is only

$$\dfrac{(\text{Cost savings} - \text{Taxes}) \times (\text{Present value factor})}{(\$1,200 - \$480) \qquad \times \qquad (3.605)} = \$2,596$$

This figure is $1,104 less than the $3,700 cost of the investment. Only a very large depreciation advantage makes this investment worthwhile. The total present value of the advantage is $1,009:

$$(\text{Tax rate} \times \text{Differential depreciation}) \times (\text{P.V. factor}) = \$1,009$$
$$(0.4 \times \$700) \qquad\qquad \times \quad 3.605$$

A Make-or-Buy Decision

Example

The Triple X Company manufactures and sells refrigerators. It makes some of the parts for the refrigerators and purchases others. The engineering department believes it might be possible to cut costs by manufacturing one of the parts currently being purchased for $8.25 each. (It is assumed that there is an unlimited supply of these parts at this price.) The firm uses 100,000 of these parts each year, and the accounting department compiles the following list of costs based on engineering estimates.

Fixed costs will increase by $50,000.
Labor costs will increase by $125,000.
Factory overhead, currently running $500,000 per year, may be expected to increase 12 percent.
Raw materials used to make the part will cost $600,000.

Given these estimates, should Triple X make the part or continue to buy it?

Solution

Find total cost incurred if the part were manufactured:

Additional fixed costs	$ 50,000
Additional labor costs	125,000
Raw materials cost	600,000
Additional overhead costs = 0.12 × $500,000	60,000
Total cost to manufacture	$835,000

Find cost per unit to manufacture:

$$\frac{\$835,000}{100,000} = \$8.35 \text{ per unit}$$

Triple X should continue to buy the part. Manufacturing costs exceed the present cost to purchase by $0.10 per unit.

An Example Using Excel

Example

It is July 1, 1990, and you are currently operating a re-export business in Hong Kong. Your warehouse where you store the products you receive from Ghuangzhou in the People's Republic of China is old and very poorly laid out. Consequently, your operating expenses are very high.

You have just been approached by a developer who has an empty warehouse that he built for a client that went bankrupt. He offers to sell you the warehouse for HK$8,250,000. However, the warehouse is located on land that is leased from the government, and the lease expires on June 30, 1997, when Hong Kong becomes part of the People's Republic of China. As a result, you do not anticipate that you will be able to renew this lease.

Your current annual operating expenses is HK$3,200,000. You hire a consultant to conduct an analysis of the new warehouse. The consultant estimates that because of its efficiencies your annual operating expenses in the new warehouse will be HK$1,750,000. In addition, the developer has told you that he can sell your current warehouse for HK$2,600,000.

a. If your current cost of capital is 15 percent, what is the net present value of purchasing this new warehouse?

b. What is the internal rate on return of this investment?

c. Should you buy this new warehouse?

Solution

a. Using Excel, set up a worksheet showing the net cost of the warehouse and the projected savings for the next seven years, as shown in Exhibit 3S.7. Using the Net Present Value (NPV) function, as shown in Exhibit 3S.7, determine the net present value of the project, which is HK$1,060,000. Since the NPV is positive, this means that the overall return on this investment exceeds your cost of capital of 15 percent.

b. Again using the same Excel worksheet, use the Internal Rate of Return (IRR) function, as shown in Exhibit 3S.7, to determine the internal rate of return for this investment which is 22 percent. (Note: the .15 in the IRR function is an estimate that is needed to start the IRR calculation.)

c. Inasmuch as the project has a 22 percent return on investment that exceeds your minimum requirement of 15 percent, you should buy the new warehouse, even though the lease expires in seven years.

EXHIBIT 3S.7

Application of Excel to Determining Net Present Value and Internal Rate of Return

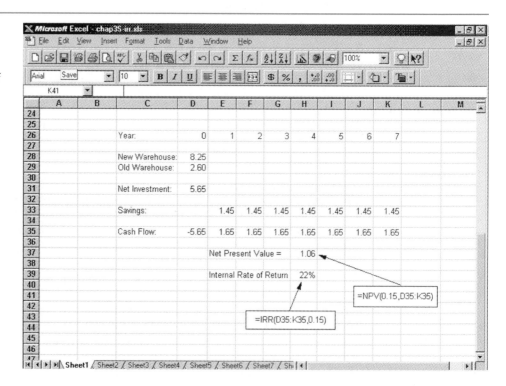

KEY FORMULAS

Compound value of an annuity

$$S_n = R[(1+i)^{n-1} + (1+i)^{n-2} + \cdots + (1+i)^1 + 1]$$

where

S_n = Compound value of an annuity

R = Periodic receipts in dollars

n = Length of the annuity in years

Present value of a future single payment

$$V_n = P(1+i)^n$$

where

V_n = Value of principal at the end of year n

n = Length of the compounding period in years

P = Present value of principal

i = Interest rate

Present value of an annuity

$$A_n = R\left[\frac{1}{(1+i)} + \frac{1}{(1+i)^2} + \cdots + \frac{1}{(1+i)^n}\right]$$

where

A_n = Present value of annuity of n years

R = Periodic receipts

n = Length of the annuity in years

KEY TERMS

activity-based costing   p. 79
avoidable costs   p. 78
break-even analysis   p. 81
cost of capital   p. 78
depreciation   p. 86
economic life   p. 86
fixed costs   p. 77
internal rate of return   p. 93

net present value   p. 92
obsolete   p. 86
opportunity costs   p. 78
out-of-pocket costs   p. 78
payback period   p. 92
sunk costs   p. 77
variable costs   p. 77

REVIEW AND DISCUSSION QUESTIONS

1. List three examples of capital investments in operations management.
2. Define the following terms: *fixed, variable, opportunity, and avoidable costs; obsolescence* and *depreciation.*
3. What are the goals of the two types of break-even analysis?

4. What are the main advantages of activity-based costing techniques?

5. How do taxes affect profits? Why?

6. How does depreciation affect capital investment? Why?

7. If a firm is short of capital, what action might it take to conserve the capital it has and to obtain more?

8. What are the reasons for using present-value analysis rather than "future-value" analysis?

9. Why might a decision maker like to use the payback period method as well as the rate of return and the net present value?

10. Discuss why the comparison of alternative investment decisions is especially difficult when the investment choices have different life lengths.

11. Compare the advantages and disadvantages of the following depreciation methods: straight-line, sum-of-the years' digits, double-declining balance.

PROBLEMS

1. Jana and Marla, two recent business school graduates, have decided to open their own copy-service business on a part-time basis. They estimate that their annual fixed costs are $32,000 and their average variable cost for each copy sold at $.03. They expect their selling price to average $.07 per copy.

    a. Draw the break-even chart for their business, and indicate all of the relevant costs.

    b. What is their break-even point in dollars? In number of copies?

    c. After their first year of operations, in which they generated $84,000 in revenues, Jana and Marla decide to pay themselves each $5,000 per year in salaries. What do their annual sales have to be in the second year if they want to make the same amount of profit as they did in their first year?

2. Peter McWalters is president of Transformonics, a firm that produces power transformers for personal computer manufacturers. Peter's analysis of the various methods by which a new model of transformer can be built has been narrowed down to one of three alternatives. Because of the rapidly changing technology in the industry, Peter estimates the product life of the transformer to be one year. Marketing has estimated that it can sell 5,000 of these new transformers within that time period. The three alternative processes are:

    • Use existing equipment and fixtures, and hire high-skilled machinists and technicians at $16.00 per hour (including benefits). With this method, each transformer will require two (2) labor-hours to assemble.

    • Use existing equipment, but invest $30,000 in new fixtures and instruction manuals to simplify some of the more complicated operations. Semiskilled workers could be employed at $12.00 per hour (including benefits), with each transformer requiring one (1) labor-hour to complete.

    • Invest $75,000 in new equipment, fixtures, and instruction manuals. This approach would eliminate all of the complicated procedures, thereby requiring only unskilled labor, which could be hired at $6.00 per hour (including benefits). With this method, each transformer would require only 20 labor-minutes to complete.

    a. Draw a break-even chart using total cost versus volume for the above processes.

    b. Calculate the two break-even volumes (i.e., those volumes at which you shift from one process to another).

c. Which alternative would you recommend, and why?

3. Marisa Strauss, a financial analyst for Green Garden Salads, Inc., is currently evaluating three different sites for locating its plant in the greater San Francisco area. This plant will produce prepackaged tossed salads in five and ten pound bags. The three locations are: (*a*) Oakland, (*b*) Petaluma and (*c*) San Jose. Marisa estimates that the fixed costs and variable unit costs associated with each site are as follows:

Location	Fixed Costs per Year	Variable Costs per Unit
Oakland	$250,000	$10.00/100 lb.
Petaluma	$100,000	$30.00/100 lb.
San Jose	$150,000	$20.00/100 lb.

a. Plot the total costs curves for each of these locations on a single graph and identify the range of outputs for which each alternative site is the most economical.

b. If the vice-president of marketing has estimated that the demand for prepackaged salads to be 500,000 lb per year, which location would you pick and why?

4. What is the depreciation expense for the third year, using the sum-of-the-years'-digits method, for the following cost of a new machine?

Cost of machine	$35,000
Estimated life	6 years
Estimated salvage value	$5,000

5. Disregarding tax considerations, is it cheaper to buy or to lease a piece of equipment with the following costs for a five-year term? (Assume the cost of capital is 10 percent.)

	To Buy	To Lease
Purchase (or lease) cost	$50,000	$10,000/yr.
Annual operating cost	4,000/yr.	4,000/yr.
Maintenance cost	2,000/yr.	0
Salvage value at end of 5 years	$20,000	0

6. A new piece of office equipment must be purchased, and the choice has been narrowed down to two styles, each capable of meeting the intended needs. With a 10-year horizon and an interest rate of 8 percent, which piece of equipment should be purchased?

	Equipment A	Equipment B
Initial cost	$10,000	$7,000
Salvage value (10 years hence)	4,000	2,000
Estimated annual operation and maintenance cost	1,000	1,500

7. The local university is accepting bids for the hot dog and cold drink concession at the new stadium. The contract is for a five-year period, and it is your feeling that a bid of $40,000 will win the contract. A preliminary analysis indicates that annual operating costs will be $35,000 and average annual sales will be $50,000. The contract can be written off during the five

years. Taxes are at the 40 percent rate, and your goal is to make a 20 percent return on your investment.

a. Will you meet your goal if you use straight-line depreciation?

b. Would you meet your goal using sum-of-the-years'-digits depreciation?

8. In adding a new product line, a firm needs a new piece of machinery. An investigation of suitable equipment for the production process has narrowed the choice to the two machines listed.

	Machine A	Machine B
Type of equipment	General purpose	Special purpose
Installed cost	$8,000	$13,000
Salvage value	800	3,000
Annual labor cost	6,000	3,600
Estimated life (years)	10	5

Assume that at the end of five years, a comparable replacement for Machine B will be available. Using present-value analysis with a 10 percent interest rate, which machine would you choose?

9. ABC's business has been going so well that the firm decides to diversify with a sideline business. Ballard, a partner and an experienced cabinetmaker, has a great deal of know-how in making cabinets for kitchens and vanities for bathrooms. (Countertops would be subcontracted because of the specialized equipment needed for molding and pressing.) The company is anticipating putting out a standard line of cabinets available in birch, walnut, mahogany, or oak veneer at no extra charge.

   Three manufacturing methods are feasible for producing the cabinets. The first is largely manual, the second uses some semiautomated equipment, and the third is largely automatic. The semiautomatic equipment requires an investment of $45,000. ABC expects this equipment to generate incremental after-tax cash flows of $15,000 for each of the next four years. What is the net present value for this equipment? What is the payback period? What should ABC do?

10. Matt Koslow, having just graduated from business school, has decided to open his own brewery, which he named JoJo Brewery in honor of his grandparents, Joe and Joan. He purchases the necessary brewing and fermenting equipment to get started for $60,000, and locates his brewery in an old brick building that was previously a textile mill. His annual fixed costs are estimated to be $45,000. In addition, the variable costs are estimated to be $14.00 per barrel of beer. Initially, to save money, he will produce only kegs of beer, which he will sell to local bars and restaurants. Based on a market survey that he had conducted, Matt forecasts his sales for the first five years to be as follows:

Year:	1	2	3	4	5
Barrels:	3,000	4,400	6,200	7,000	7,800

Currently, the cost of money is 15 percent and the tax rate is 35 percent. The average selling price per barrel is estimated to be $35.00.

Using a spreadsheet software program, answer the following questions:

a. If Matt uses straight-line depreciation and a five-year life on the equipment with no salvage value, what is the net present value (NPV) of his investment? If he uses sum-of-the-years' digits method of depreciation, what is his NPV?

b. What is the internal rate of return (IRR) on this investment with the current tax rate of 35 percent? If the tax rate was increased to 42 percent?

c. What is the NPV at the current cost of money (15 percent) and tax rate (35 percent) if sales each year are 20 percent lower than his original forecast?

SELECTED BIBLIOGRAPHY

Brigham, Eugene F. *Fundamentals of Financial Management,* 7th ed. Fort Worth, TX: The Dryden Press, 1995.

Gitman, Lawrence. *Principles of Managerial Finance,* 7th ed. New York: HarperCollins, 1994.

Hodder, James E., and Henry E. Riggs. "Pitfalls in Evaluating Risky Projects." *Harvard Business Review,* January–February 1985, pp. 128–35.

Johnson, Thomas, and Robert Kaplan. *Relevance Lost: The Rise and Fall of Management Accounting.* Boston: Harvard Business School Press, 1987, p. 188.

Libertore, Matthew J. *Selection and Evaluation of Advanced Manufacturing Technologies.* New York: Springer-Verlag, 1990, pp. 231–56.

Pringle, John J., and Robert S. Harris. *Essentials of Managerial Finance,* Glenview, IL: Scott Foresman, 1984.

Ross, Stephen A.; Randolph W. Westerfield; and Jeffrey Jaffe. *Corporate Finance.* Burr Ridge, IL: Irwin/McGraw-Hill, 1996.

Van Horne, James C. *Financial Management and Policy,* 9th ed. Englewood Cliffs, NJ: Prentice Hall, 1992.

Welsch, Glenn A., and Robert N. Anthony. *Fundamentals of Financial Accounting.* Burr Ridge, IL: Richard D. Irwin, 1984.

PROCESS MEASUREMENT AND ANALYSIS

Chapter Outline

Chapter Objectives

- Identify the different measures of performance that can be used to evaluate a process.

- Introduce the concept of benchmarking and demonstrate why it is an important tool for those companies that want to have world class operations.

- Demonstrate how process analysis can provide management with an in-depth understanding of a process and explain the difference between demand and the capacity of a process.

- Introduce the concept of service blueprinting and illustrate how it is used to evaluate service operations.

- Introduce the concept of business process reengineering and show how it is changing the way in which managers view their operations.

Prior to the fast food era, hamburgers, like any other sandwich in a restaurant, were made to order. To begin the process the cook, upon receipt of the order, reached into the refrigerator for a raw hamburger patty and placed it on the grill. The customer could specify the degree of doneness (e.g., rare, medium, or well done) and request certain condiments. The roll could be toasted or not. However, the quality of the hamburger produced in this fashion was highly dependent on the skill of the cook, and consequently the quality could vary significantly between cooks, even within the same restaurant. In addition, hamburgers prepared using this method took a relatively long time to deliver, as they were cooked only after the order was received (see Exhibit 4.1A).

The arrival of Burger King and McDonald's in the 1950s, and later Wendy's totally changed the way in which hamburgers were cooked and delivered to the customer. Unlike most restaurants at that time, which offered a wide variety of food items, Burger King and McDonald's were highly focused operations with very limited menus. In addition, both firms offered low-cost products that were delivered quickly. However, each has taken a different approach in the type of process they have adopted to cook and deliver hamburgers and the particular markets that they serve. This chapter focuses on processes and how they contribute to the overall success of the firm. ▪

PROCESS ANALYSIS

An analysis of the methods used by various food service operations to prepare and deliver hamburgers provides us with some insight into the trade-offs that managers face when selecting one particular process over another. This type of analysis also allows us to identify the strengths and weaknesses of each process, which can then be related to the specific market segments that each firm is focusing on.

To continue the chapter opener, McDonald's cooks its hamburgers on grills in batches, with 12 hamburgers per batch. The rolls are similarly toasted or caramelized in batches of 12. After cooking, the hamburgers are assembled (that is, placed on rolls with condiments, etc.) and wrapped, also in batch sizes of 12. The finished products are then stored in holding bins for immediate delivery to the customer. This low-cost, highly efficient, make-to-stock process produces highly standardized products that can be delivered quickly to the customer (see Exhibit 4.1B). As a result, a major market for McDonald's is families with small children for whom speed of delivery is important. Thus, fast service is emphasized in many of McDonald's advertisements.

Burger King, on the other hand, cooks its hamburgers with a conveyor-broiler, which is a highly specialized piece of equipment. Using this method, a worker places raw hamburgers on one end of a moving conveyor which proceeds under a broiler where they are cooked from both the top and bottom. Ninety seconds later the hamburgers emerge from the other end of the conveyor, cooked to the desired degree. The rolls also are toasted in the conveyor-broiler. The use of this highly focused process ensures consistency of product quality with minimum dependence on worker skill; however, the process is very limited in terms of flexibility. Because all hamburgers are cooked in 90 seconds, the thickness of the patty cannot vary. Consequently, when Burger King came out with the Whopper, the only way it could make the bigger burger was to make it wider because the thickness had to remain the same as that of the regular-sized patties.

Once cooked, the hamburgers at Burger King are placed on rolls and stored in a steam cabinet. This work-in-process (WIP) inventory is then used to replenish standard items in the holding bins (or finished goods inventory). It is also used as the starting point for assembling hamburgers to meet individual customer requests. The WIP inventory of cooked hamburgers allows Burger King to custom assemble hamburgers in a relatively short time (as compared to cooking them from the raw state) while simultaneously reducing the level of finished goods inventory in holding bins (as compared to McDonald's) because replenishment time is shorter (see Exhibit 4.1C). The strength of Burger King's process lies in its ability to quickly deliver assembled-to-order products; therefore, it tries to attract individuals who "want it their way."

Wendy's has adopted still a different approach. Here hamburgers are cooked on a grill, awaiting individual customer orders. Upon receipt of the order, the hamburger is taken off the grill and placed on a bun with the specific condiments requested, all within view of the customer. Customers perceive this assemble-to-order process as higher quality in comparison to that at McDonald's or Burger King, due, in part, to the fact that everything is done in front of the customer. The trade-off here is that an average hamburger takes longer to prepare than a special request at Burger King because the order begins farther upstream in the process (see Exhibit 4.1D).

As we have noted, each of these operations has its strengths and weaknesses. All three fast food chains are successful because they recognize their strengths and focus advertising and promotional efforts on attracting those segments of the market that value their particular process characteristics.

EXHIBIT 4.1

Process Flowcharts for Making Hamburgers

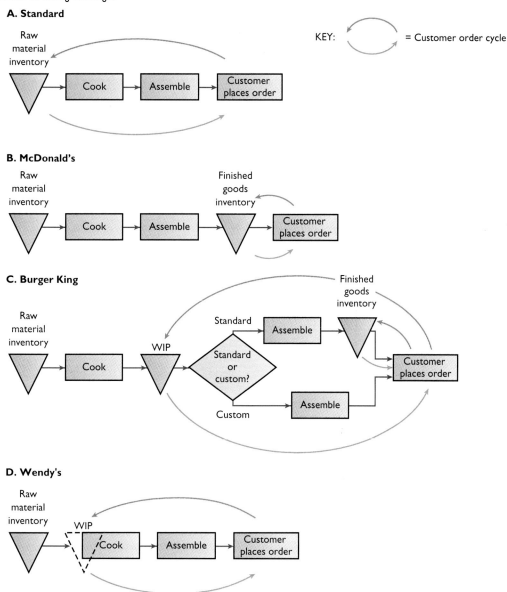

A. Standard

KEY: = Customer order cycle

B. McDonald's

C. Burger King

D. Wendy's

PROCESS MEASUREMENT

A key factor in the success of every organization is its ability to measure performance. Such feedback on a continuous basis provides management with data to determine if established goals or standards are being met. As Peter Drucker, a well-known management guru has said, "If you can't measure it, you can't manage it." Without proper measures of performance, managers could not assess how well their organizations do or compare their performance with that of their competitors. Managers would be like ships' captains, adrift on the ocean with no land in sight and no compass or other navigational instruments to guide them.

However, with a growing number of performance measures available, managers must be selective in choosing only those measures that are critical to their firm's success. Depending on the specific industry and market niche within that industry, some measures of performance are more important to management than others. For example, in a fast food outlet, a key performance indicator is the speed with which food is delivered to the customer. In an upscale restaurant, on the other hand, key performance measures may be the variety of items offered on the menu and the quality of food served.

Today, in the information age, management, like everyone else, is swamped with reams of reports containing data on all aspects of a company's performance. It is, therefore, essential for management to identify those key indicators that measure those parameters that are critical to the success of their firms.

Types of Performance Measures

productivity
Efficiency of a process.

Productivity   The efficiency with which inputs are transformed into outputs is a measure of the process's **productivity.** In other words, productivity measures how well we convert inputs into outputs. In its broadest sense, productivity is defined as:

$$\text{Productivity} = \frac{\text{Outputs}}{\text{Inputs}}$$

Ideally, we would like to measure the total productivity of a process, which would be the total outputs divided by the total inputs. Unfortunately, the inputs come in various forms. For example, labor is measured in hours, a building is measured in square feet, raw material is measured in pounds, units, and so forth. It would therefore be impossible to obtain a measure for the total inputs into a process unless we converted all of the inputs to a common denominator like money. However, in doing so, the operations manager loses an understanding of how the process is performing. Consequently, management will adopt one or more partial measures of productivity, which is the output of the process (in either revenues or units) divided by a single input. Some commonly used partial measures of productivity are presented in Exhibit 4.2. Such measures give managers the necessary information in familiar units, thereby allowing the manager to more easily relate to the actual performance of the operation.

Productivity is what we call a *relative measure.* In other words, to be meaningful it needs to be compared with something else. For example, what can we learn from the fact that we operate a restaurant, and that its productivity last week was 8.4 customers/labor hour? (Nothing!)

Productivity comparisons can be made in two ways. First, a company can compare itself with similar operations within its industry, or can use industry data when it is available (e.g., comparing productivity among the different stores in a franchise).

EXHIBIT 4.2

Partial Measures of Productivity

Type of Business	Productivity Measure (Output/Input)
Restaurant	Customers (meals)/labor hour
Retail store	Sales/square foot
Chicken farm	Pounds of meat/pound of feed
Utility plant	Kilowatts/ton of coal
Paper mill	Tons of paper/cord of wood

Another approach is to measure productivity over time within the same operation. Here we would compare our productivity in one time period with that of the next.

capacity
Output of a process in a given time period.

Capacity   The output capability of a process is referred to as the **capacity** of the process. This performance measure is typically presented in units of output per unit of time, although, as we shall see later in the section, this is not always practical. Examples of measures of capacity are shown in Exhibit 4.3.

As noted by these examples, measures of capacity exist for both manufacturing and services. The major difference between manufacturing and services, in terms of measuring capacity, is that with service operations the measures of capacity usually include the customer, since the customer is typically an integral part of the process. (Because customers very often participate in the service delivery process, they can be viewed as both an input and an output.)

Design capacity is defined as the ideal output rate at which a firm would like to produce under normal circumstances and for which the system was designed. Depending on the product or process and goals of the company, design capacity could even be established using a five-day-a-week, single-shift operation. *Maximum capacity* is used to define the maximum potential output rate that could be achieved when productive resources are used to their maximum. Typically, most firms can operate effectively at maximum capacity for only short periods of time. Operating at maximum capacity, for example, results in higher energy costs, the need for overtime wage premiums, and increased machine breakdowns due to the lack of time to conduct scheduled preventive maintenance. Worker fatigue resulting from extended hours on the job can also cause an increase in defective products as well as a decrease in labor productivity.

capacity utilization
Percentage of available capacity that is actually used.

The degree to which a firm utilizes its productive capacity is referred to as **capacity utilization,** which is defined as follows:

$$\text{Capacity utilization} = \frac{\text{Actual output}}{\text{Design capacity}}$$

For example, if an automobile assembly plant had a design capacity of 3,600 cars per week, and actually produced only 2,700 cars in one week, then its capacity utilization for that week would be:

$$\text{Capacity utilization} = \frac{2,700}{3,600} = 75\%$$

With this definition of capacity utilization, it is possible to have utilization rates that are in excess of 100 percent, which should be a warning to management that excessive production costs are being incurred.

So far, we have measured capacity in terms of units of output per unit of time, which is appropriate as long as the output is relatively homogeneous (e.g., cars, stereos, etc.). However,

EXHIBIT 4.3

Measures of Capacity

Type of Operation	Measure of Capacity
Fast-food restaurant	Customers per hour
Brewery	Barrels of beer per year
Hotel reservation call center	Telephone calls per hour
Automobile assembly plant	Cars per hour
Paper mill	Tons of paper per year

when the output units are highly variable, especially in terms of process requirements, a more meaningful measure of capacity is often expressed in terms of one of the inputs. Consider, for example, a flexible machining center that can make parts that take anywhere from five minutes to two hours to produce. The capacity of the center, in terms of units produced per week, could vary significantly depending on which particular units were being produced. In this case, a better measure of capacity utilization would be:

$$\text{Capacity utilization} = \frac{\text{Actual machine hours used}}{\text{Total machine hours available}}$$

Such measures of capacity utilization will become more popular as the flexibility of processes increases to permit wider varieties of products to be made. This approach to measuring capacity utilization is also more applicable to many service operations that have a very high labor content and also require that labor to perform a wide variety of tasks. Examples here include medical doctors, whose tasks can vary from performing surgical operations to having office visits and attending required meetings. College professors provide another good example. In addition to teaching students, they are also required to conduct research and be of service to the college and the community. In both these instances, capacity as measured in terms of available hours per week is clearly the appropriate measure.

Quality   The quality of a process is usually measured by the defect rate of the products produced. Defects include those products that are identified as nonconforming, both internally (prior to shipping the product to the customer) as well as externally (i.e., products whose defects are found by the customer). The topic of process quality measurement and control is presented in greater detail in Chapter 5 and its supplement.

There are additional measures of a process's overall quality. With increasing awareness and concern for the environment, for example, the amount of toxic waste generated is also a measure of a process's quality. Similarly, the amount of scrap and waste material produced is another process quality indicator.

Speed of Delivery   Many companies are experiencing increased pressure with respect to speed of delivery. Firms that once took weeks and months to deliver a product are now delivering those products in hours and days. (See the OM in Practice on MBNA.)

Speed of delivery has two dimensions to measure. The first is the amount of time from when the product is ordered to when it is shipped to the customer, which is known as a product's *lead time*. Companies that produce standard products significantly reduce lead times by producing products for finished goods inventory. For such situations, orders are immediately filled from existing inventories, thereby eliminating any lead times. Companies that produce customized products, however, do not have the luxury of a finished goods inventory. Firms producing such products typically require a significant lead time before the finished product can be shipped.

The other dimension in measuring speed of delivery is the variability in delivery time. In many cases, this dimension is more critical than the estimated lead time itself. In other words, customers, whether they be other companies or end users, do not like uncertainty. Uncertainty affects work scheduling, capacity utilization, and so forth, which negatively affects the overall efficiency of the process. Thus, the less variability in delivery times, the better.

Flexibility   Currently, the competitive advantage for many companies lies in their ability to produce customized products to meet individual customer needs. The capability of a

Operations Management in Practice

MBNA IS TRULY A SPEED FREAK

Credit card issuer MBNA sets up scoreboards in its various offices to keep employees up to speed on how quickly they're serving customers.

"MBNA, the Wilmington, Delaware, credit card company, has developed a very loyal customer base due, in large part, to its ability to provide outstanding service. To accomplish this, MBNA has developed 15 different measures of performance, many of which pertain directly to speed. For example, customer address changes must be processed within one day; telephones must be answered within two rings; switchboard calls must be transferred to the appropriate individual within 21 seconds. State-of-the-art technology allows MBNA to monitor performance on a continuous basis.

At any given moment it is possible to obtain a performance measurement that shows, for example, that employees are achieving "two-ring pick-up" 99.7 percent of the time, as shown in the picture. The current standard for the minimum level of service that is acceptable for each of the 15 performance measures is 98.5 percent, which was increased recently from 98.0 percent and is significantly up from 10 years ago when it was 90 percent.

Source: Martin, J. and J. E. Davis, "Are You As Good As You Think?" *Fortune*, September 30, 1996.

---

agile manufacturing
Ability of a manufacturing process to respond quickly to the demands of the customer.

company to provide such customized products in a timely manner is often referred to as **agile manufacturing.** Flexibility is the measure of how readily the company's transformation process can adjust to meet the ever-changing demands of its customers.

There are three dimensions of flexibility. The first type of flexibility indicates how quickly a process can convert from producing one product or family of product(s) to another. For example, many U.S. automobile assembly plants still require a minimum of several weeks shutdown annually in order to convert from one model year to the next, indicating a degree of inflexibility in this area.

Another measure of a process's flexibility is its ability to react to changes in volume. Those processes that can accommodate large fluctuations in volume are said to be more flexible than those that cannot. Most service operations need to be very flexible in this dimension because of their inability to inventory demand. (For example, customers wanting to eat at a restaurant on Saturday night will not wait until Monday morning.) Thus, service operations such as retail stores, restaurants, and health clinics can adjust to meet the demand from a few customers per hour to several hundred customers per hour. The typical assembly line operation in a manufacturing facility cannot similarly adjust. The volume of output from an assembly line is fixed, and consequently companies with this type of process must resort to other means of balancing supply and demand. For example, appliance makers and automobile companies offer discounts and low-cost financing to encourage consumer buying during slow periods of demand, due in part to their inability to adjust the outputs of their manufacturing facilities without shutting them down entirely.

The third dimension of flexibility is the ability of the process to produce more than one product simultaneously. Thus, the more products that a process can produce at a time, the more flexible it is said to be.

process velocity
Ratio of total throughput time for a product to the value-added time.

Process Velocity   A relatively new measure of performance is **process velocity.** Also referred to as *manufacturing velocity,* process velocity is the ratio of the actual throughput time that it takes for a product to go through the process divided by the value-added time required to complete the product or service.

For example, if the throughput time for a product is six weeks, and the actual value-added time to complete the product is four hours, then the process velocity of this product is:

$$\text{Process velocity} = \frac{\text{Total throughput time}}{\text{Value-added time}}$$

$$\text{Process velocity} = \frac{6 \text{ weeks} \times 5 \text{ days per week} \times 8 \text{ hours per day}}{4 \text{ hours}} = 60$$

A process velocity of 60, in this case, means that it takes 60 times as long to complete the product as it does to do the actual work on the product itself. In other words, process velocity is like a golf score, the lower it is, the better.

 Process velocities in excess of 100 are not uncommon. For example, University Microfilms, Inc. (UMI), the largest publisher of dissertations in the United States, took 150 days to process a manuscript, although only two hours were actually spent adding value to the manuscript. For UMI, the process velocity for a manuscript was therefore:

$$\text{Process velocity} = \frac{150 \text{ days per manuscript} \times 8 \text{ hours per day}}{2 \text{ hours}} = 600$$

UMI was able to reduce the throughput time to 60 days, thereby lowering its process velocity to 240.[1]

As noted by the above example, the concept of process velocity is equally applicable to manufacturing and services. Process velocity can also be applied to any particular segment of the process, or to the overall process. For example, a firm may want to focus only on its manufacturing velocity, in which case it would look at the throughput time from when the product is first begun to when it is completed and ready to ship. A broader perspective may measure process velocity from the time when the customer first places the order for the product to when payment is finally received and the check has cleared.

In the past, especially in the United States, companies have focused solely on increasing the efficiency of the value-added time, which often constitutes only a very small portion of a product's overall time in the process.

---

[1]A. Bernstein, "Quality Is Becoming Job One in the Office, Too," *Business Week,* April 29, 1991.

BENCHMARKING[2]

benchmarking
Comparison of a company's measures of performance with those of firms that are considered to be world class.

Benchmarking is simply a comparison of a company's performance in certain areas with the performance of other firms in its industry and/or with those firms that are identified as world-class competitors in specific functions and operations. Benchmarking can cut across traditional industry lines, providing opportunities for new and innovative ways to increase performance. For example, Xerox, in its desire to deliver products quickly, studied how L.L. Bean of Freeport, Maine, a mail order company well-known for fast accurate service, accomplished this.

Firms that want to compete as world-class organizations in the highly competitive global arena must attain "best of breed" status in those performance parameters that are critical for success in their respective industries and market segments. This can be accomplished only through measuring and comparing their performance with that of others, and then instituting the necessary actions for improvement. Companies like AT&T, Du Pont, Ford Motor, IBM, Eastman Kodak, Milliken, Motorola, Xerox, and other industry leaders, in an attempt to increase both quality and productivity now use benchmarking as a standard management tool.

David T. Kearns, CEO of Xerox Corporation, defines benchmarking as follows:

> Benchmarking is the continuous process of measuring products, services, and practices against the toughest competitors or those companies recognized as industry leaders.[3]

Several key elements in this definition should be emphasized. Continuous measuring implies that benchmarking is an iterative process with no end. With competition constantly "raising the bar," accepted levels of performance yesterday will not be tolerated by the customer tomorrow. Only through constant monitoring of our performance and that of our competitors will we be able to know where we stand at any point in time.

Benchmarking means measurement. This can be accomplished internally within the organization as well as externally with competitors and world-class firms. It is important for management to be cognizant that benchmarking is not limited only to manufacturing, but can also be applied to all of the other functional areas in an organization. This means that it can be used for products, services, and processes/practices.

Benchmarking should not be limited only to direct competitors. Rather it should focus on those firms or business functions or operations within firms that have achieved recognition as world-class operations. In other words, as Robert Camp states in the title of his book, "benchmarking is the search for best practices that leads to superior performance."[4]

What Should We Benchmark?

Benchmarking can be applied to many areas within an organization. Robert Camp identifies three of these: (*a*) goods and services, (*b*) business processes, and (*c*) performance measures.

Goods and Services   Benchmarking identifies the features and functions of the goods and services that are desired by the firm's customers. This information is incorporated into

---

[2]This section has drawn heavily on the following two books: Robert C. Camp, *Benchmarking: The Search for Industry Best Practices That Lead to Superior Performance* (Milwaukee, WI: ASQC Quality Press, 1989) and Robert C. Camp, *Business Process Benchmarking: Finding and Implementing Best Practices* (Milwaukee, WI: ASQC Quality Press, 1995).

[3]Robert C. Camp, *Benchmarking: The Search for Industry Best Practices That Lead to Superior Performance*, p. 10.

[4]Ibid.

product planning, design, and development in the form of product goals and technology design practices.

Business Processes   Benchmarking in this area provides the basis for business process improvement and reengineering. These changes should be an integral part of the continuous quality improvement initiative.

Performance Measures   The end result of benchmarking goods, services, and processes is to establish and validate objectives for the vital few performance measures that have been identified as critical to the success of the organization.

Key Steps in Benchmarking

Robert Camp, based on his experience with Xerox Corporation, has identified five phases that are necessary for successfully implementing benchmarking within an organization. These phases are planning, analysis, integration, action, and maturity. (These five phases and the various steps within each phase are summarized in Exhibit 4.4.)

Planning   This phase of benchmarking identifies the areas that we should benchmark, the specific organizations against which we should be benchmarking, the types of data we should collect, and the ways we should collect that data.

Analysis   The analysis phase focuses on obtaining an in-depth understanding of our firm's existing practices and processes as well as those of the organizations against which we will be benchmarking.

Integration   Here we use the findings from the first two phases to define those target areas that we want to change. As part of this phase, we need to ensure that benchmarking concepts are implemented in the corporate planning process, and that benchmarking is accepted by all levels of management.

Action   The benchmarking findings and associated goals must be translated into action. Those individuals who actually perform the tasks should determine how the findings can best be incorporated into the existing process.

Maturity   An organization reaches maturity when the best business practices that have been identified have been incorporated into all of the relevant business processes, thereby ensuring superior performance for the organization as a whole.

Types of Benchmarking

There are four general categories of benchmarking: (*a*) internal, (*b*) competitive, (*c*) functional, and (*d*) generic.

MARKETING
MANAGEMENT
ACCOUNTING
FINANCE

Internal Benchmarking   This type of benchmarking provides for a comparison among similar operations or processes within a firm's own organization. It is often the starting point for identifying best practices that currently exist with the company. Internal benchmarking also provides the first step to documenting processes, which is necessary for identifying future areas for improvement. Internal benchmarking is especially appropriate for organizations (both manufacturing and services) with multiple locations.

Competitive Benchmarking   This provides a comparison between an organization's performance and that of its best direct competitors. The relative information obtained here will show how the company compares to other firms in its industry. Benchmarking within an

EXHIBIT 4.4

Benchmarking Process Steps

Planning
- 1. Identify what is to be benchmarked.
- 2. Identify comparative companies.
- 3. Determine data collection method and collect data.

Analysis
- 4. Determine current performance "GAP".
- 5. Project future performance levels.

Integration
- 6. Communicate benchmark findings and gain acceptance.
- 7. Establish functional goals.

Action
- 8. Develop action plans.
- 9. Implement specific actions and monitor progress.
- 10. Recalibrate benchmarks.

Maturity
- Leadership position attained.
- Practices fully integrated into processes.

Source: Robert C. Camp, *Benchmarking: The Search for Industry Best Practices That Lead to Superior Performance,* (Milwaukee, WI: ASQC Quality Press, 1989).

industry is often difficult because of the natural unwillingness of competitors to share critical information.

 Functional Benchmarking   This type of benchmarking addresses performance comparisons with the best functional areas, regardless of the industry in which they are located. The benefits to this are several. First, a firm may have less difficulty in obtaining benchmarking partners in other industries which are not direct competitors. In addition, it is often

Technology has allowed John Deere, the farm equipment manufacturer, to be more responsive to the needs of its customers. Dealers, through satellites and CD-ROM technology, can now directly communicate electronically with John Deere warehouses. Farmers, through their own computers, also have ready access to Deere parts and other equipment.

easy to identify those firms that are considered to be the "best of breed" in performing a specific function. The L.L. Bean example presented at the beginning of this section provides a good example of functional benchmarking. Other examples of leaders in specific functional areas include General Electric (information systems), John Deere (service parts logistics, see photo) and Ford (assembly automation).

 Generic Benchmarking   Here performance measures are concerned with specific work processes that are virtually the same for all industries that use these processes. Generic benchmarking can easily identify those firms that have adopted innovative processes, thereby providing targets that can be more readily acceptable by members of the organization. Examples of leaders in generic benchmarking include the Federal Reserve Bank (bill scanning) and Citicorp (document processing).

PROCESS ANALYSIS IN MANUFACTURING

Definitions

As a first step in understanding the important characteristics of processes, we have defined some of the more commonly used terms.

multistage process
Process that consists of more than one step.

hybrid process
Multistage process that consists of more than one type of process.

Hybrid Process   Most of the processes that we encounter consist of more than one stage or step to produce the required goods or services. These are often referred to as **multistage processes.** Within a multistage process a different type of process can exist at each stage. When this occurs, these multistage processes are frequently referred to as **hybrid processes.** For example, in making potato chips at Cape Cod Potato Chips in Hyannis, Massachusetts, the potatoes are first washed in a continuous process, cooked in a batch process, and then packaged in an assembly line type of operation. Within a given industry, different firms may adopt different types of processes to produce the same or similar products. As an example, some potato chip manufacturers cook their potatoes with a continuous process instead of a batch process. To further illustrate, at McDonald's, the hamburgers are both cooked and assembled in batches. This approach produces a highly standardized product. Burger King, on the other hand, cooks its hamburgers on a continuous flow broiler, but assembles them individually to meet specific customer requests.

Make-to-Stock versus Make-to-Order Which type of process is chosen for each stage is dependent on the firm's operations strategy and the type of product being manufactured. A **make-to-stock system** is compatible with producing a highly standardized product that can be stored in a finished goods inventory for quick delivery to the customer. As a result, these products are usually forecasted in anticipation of future customer orders. In contrast, a **make-to-order system** focuses on producing customized items which have already been ordered by the customer. It is important to note here that a make-to-order system requires more flexibility than a make-to-stock system, and as a result tends to be slower and more inefficient and, therefore, more expensive.

However, the choice of a make-to-stock system tends to limit the number of product variations to a few highly standardized items. In order to achieve maximum process efficiency while at the same time increase product variety, firms will delay the customization step until the last possible moment. A good example of this application is the mixing of custom colored paints at home improvement centers while the customers wait.

Modularization Another approach that attempts to combine process efficiency with some degree of customization is called **modularization.** With this approach, the end product is designed so it can be assembled from several individual components that are considered to be standard items. The concept of modularization is used extensively throughout the computer industry. As an illustration, suppose a computer firm produces four different types of central processors, three different kinds of input/output devices, and two varieties of printers. From a customer's perspective, this firm offers a choice of 24 different computer configurations ($4 \times 3 \times 2$), although manufacturing has to produce only nine standard products ($4 + 3 + 2$). The final assembly of automobiles provides another good example. Here standard components are delivered to the automobile assembly plant and the selection of a particular combination of these components produces a "custom-made" car. Modularization also has application in services. For example, an Italian restaurant can offer its customers a choice of 60 different dishes by combining four types of pasta, three types of sauces and five varieties of meat ($4 \times 3 \times 5$).

Exhibit 4.5 shows a comparison of the process flow charts for make-to-stock, make-to-order, and modularized production processes.

Tightness and Dependence The relationship between the various stages in a process is frequently referred to as the degree of *tightness* in the process. Processes that are considered very tight, like assembly lines, have a great deal of *dependence* between stages. In other words, if production stops due to a machine breakdown at an early stage in the process, work ceases almost immediately at all of the subsequent operations. This high degree of dependence among the stages is caused by a lack of buffer inventories between adjacent stages. The greater the buffer inventories, the greater the independence between stages and the "looser" the process. Batch processes typically exhibit a high degree of independence between stages as shown by the large amounts of buffer inventories in the form of work-in-process (WIP). With these types of processes, a failure at one stage in the process does not impact any other stages until the WIP between them is depleted.

Bottlenecks The capacity of each stage in a multistage process often varies for several reasons, including dissimilar output rates of the different pieces of equipment that comprise

make-to-stock system
Process for making highly standardized products for finished goods inventory.

make-to-order system
Process for making customized products to meet individual customer requirements.

modularization
Use of standard components and subassemblies to produce customized products.

EXHIBIT 4.5

A Comparison of Make-to-Stock, Make-to-Order, and Modularized Processes

Make-to-Stock
Process for
Standardized Products

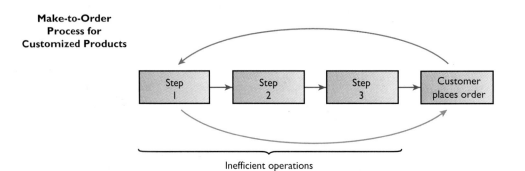

Make-to-Order
Process for
Customized Products

Modularized
Process for
Semicustomized Products

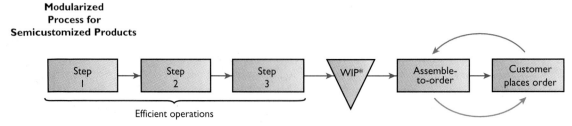

* WIP consists of standardized components and subassemblies.

the overall process. In these situations, the stage of the process with the lowest capacity is referred to as the **bottleneck** in the process. Adding additional capacity to alleviate the bottleneck at one stage in the process will shift the bottleneck to another stage. When this occurs, the full capacity potential of the additional equipment may not be realized.

bottleneck
Stage or stages that limits the total output of a process.

Example   A commercial bread bakery wants to evaluate its capacity, in terms of how many pounds of bread it can produce per hour. A simplified version of the process is shown below:

In the mixing stage, all of the ingredients are combined to form the dough. The dough must then rise in a controlled environment called a proofing box or proofing oven, which monitors humidity and temperature. Following the proofing, the bread is then formed into loaves and baked. In the final stage, the bread is packaged prior to distribution to retail outlets. The bakery currently has the following equipment:

Stage	Capacity (Lb/Hr/Machine)	Number of Machines
Mixing	60	3
Proofing	25	6
Baking	40	4
Packaging	75	3

a. What is the current capacity of the bakery in pounds of bread per hour?
b. Where is the bottleneck in the process?
c. If an additional piece of equipment is purchased to increase the capacity of the bottleneck, what is the new capacity of the bakery?

Solution

a. The total capacity of the bakery is determined by calculating the total capacity at each stage of the process as follows:

Stage	Equipment Capacity (Lb/Hr/Machine)	Number of Machines	Total Capacity (Lb/Hr/Machine)
Mixing	60	3	180
Proofing	25	6	150
Baking	40	4	160
Packaging	75	3	225

The overall capacity of the bakery is 150 pounds per hour, as determined by the proofing operation, which is that stage with the smallest capacity.

b. Currently, the bottleneck is at the proofing stage because that has the smallest hourly capacity.

c. If another proofing oven is purchased, the capacity of the proofing stage is now 175 pounds per hour. However, with the addition of the new proofing oven, the bottleneck in the process now shifts to the baking stage because that has the lowest capacity of 160 pounds per hour. Thus the new overall capacity of the bakery with the addition of another proofing oven is only 160 pounds per hour.

Capacity versus Demand

In the above example, we have focused entirely on the available capacity of the process without considering the demand for the bread. It is important when analyzing the capacity requirements for a process that we do not confuse the capacity of the process with the demand for the firm's products. For example, if the demand for a product is less than the capacity of the smallest stage, then no bottleneck really exists (In the bakery example, if demand was less than 150 pounds per hour, there would not be any bottleneck). As a result no additional equipment is needed. Only when demand exceeds the capacity at one or more stages do we have to address the problem of a bottleneck and consider installing additional equipment.

Process Flowcharts

process flowchart
Schematic diagram for describing a process.

A **process flowchart** provides management with an opportunity to view the entire process step by step. The traditional symbols used in drawing a process flowchart are presented in Exhibit 4.6.

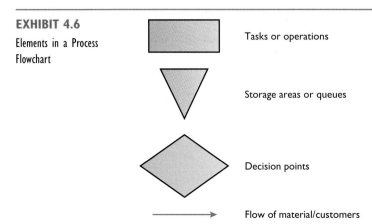

EXHIBIT 4.6
Elements in a Process
Flowchart

Tasks or operations

Storage areas or queues

Decision points

Flow of material/customers

Example

A potato chip manufacturer in Hawaii produces "Maui-style, kettle-cooked" potato chips for distribution throughout the Hawaiian Islands to retail outlets as well as to hotels and resort areas. The process of making potato chips is relatively simple. Raw potatoes, which are delivered once a week to the factory, are first washed and peeled. After a visual inspection to ensure all of the peel and eyes are removed, the potatoes are then sliced and immediately fried in a large kettle. (The peeling and frying operations are done in batches while the slicing is a continuous operation.) After frying, the cooked chips are inspected and any burnt ones are removed. The chips are then salted and stored in large cartons. This first phase of the process is done on two shifts of eight hours each. In contrast, the packaging operation is run only eight hours a day because of the large capacity of the equipment. The cooked chips are packaged in either one-ounce or eight-ounce packages. The last step in the process places the packages in cartons for delivery. (There are 24 one-ounce packages to a carton and 12 eight-ounce packages to a carton.

Draw the process flowchart for this operation.

Solution

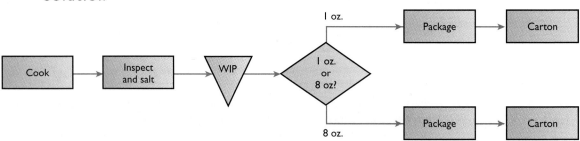

Example

To continue with a more in-depth analysis of the potato chip company, the following information is given about the capacities of the different stages in the operation.

Stage	Capacity per Machine	Number of Machines
Peeling	600 lb./hr.	2
Slicing	1,500 lb./hr.	1
Cooking	250 lb./hr.	2
Packaging (1 oz.)	160 pkgs./min.	2

Stage	Capacity per Machine	Number of Machines
Packaging (8 oz.)	30 pkgs./min.	1
Cartoning (1 oz.)	5 cartons/min.	2
Cartoning (8 oz.)	4 cartons/min.	1

The weekly demand is 30,000 cartons of 1 ounce chips and 5,000 cartons of 8 ounce chips.

a. Using Excel, set up a worksheet that shows all of the stages involved in producing potato chips and determine the capacity of each stage in pounds per week.

b. Identify the bottleneck(s) in the process.

c. Make recommendations for eliminating the bottleneck(s).

Solution   a. See spreadsheet.

b. The bottlenecks are the cooking stage, 1 ounce packaging and the cartoning of the 1 ounce packages, because the demand in each case exceeds the available capacity.

c. Add two additional fryers for cooking the potatoes, one additional 1 ounce packaging machine and one additional operation for putting the 1 ounce packages into cartons.

The use of process flowcharts in conjunction with a capacity analysis of each stage in the process provides management with a thorough understanding of the major process issues that need to be addressed. In addition, as part of the process analysis, it is often necessary to draw three different flowcharts. These three flowcharts define (*a*) what the official or documented method is, (*b*) how the work is actually being performed and (*c*) what the proper procedures should be.

EXHIBIT 4.7

Service Blueprint for a Cash Account at a Discount Brokerage

Source: Adapted from G. Lynn Shostack, "Designing Services That Deliver," *Harvard Business Review* 62, no. 1 (January–February 1984), p. 138.

PROCESS ANALYSIS IN SERVICES

Service Blueprinting

service blueprint
Process flowchart for services that includes the customer.

As with manufacturing process analysis, the standard tool for service process analysis is the flowchart. In 1978, Lynn Shostack added to the standard process flowchart the concept of the *line of visibility* and emphasized the identification of potential fail points in her version of the flowchart, calling it a **service blueprint.**[5] She has also made a compelling argument for having blueprints on every aspect of a service, and for having the "keeper of the blueprint" as a specific job function in any large service organization. Current practice in some companies is to have blueprints available on computers so when problems arise, senior managers can zero in on any portion of a service process, thereby making more informed decisions about how to resolve them. One example is the service blueprint for a cash account at a discount brokerage, as shown in Exhibit 4.7.

A key element in developing the service blueprint is the *line of visibility.* All activities above the line take place in direct contact with the customer. Those activities below the line are considered to be "backroom" operations, taking place without the customer's presence. Activities above the line of visibility, therefore, need to focus on providing good service; backroom operations, on the other hand, should focus on increasing process efficiency.

As an example, the steps involved in developing a blueprint for a simple shoeshine process, including a profitability analysis, are as follows:

1. *Identify processes* The first step in creating such a blueprint is mapping the processes that constitute the service. Exhibit 4.8 maps out the various steps in providing a

[5]G. Lynn Shostack, "Designing Services That Deliver," *Harvard Business Review* 62, no. 1 (January–February 1984), p. 135.

EXHIBIT 4.8

Blueprint for a Corner Shoeshine

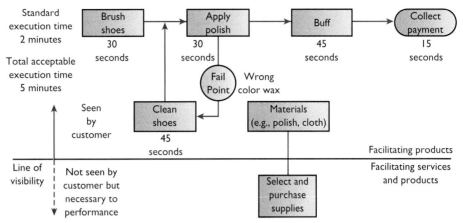

EXHIBIT 4.9

Shoeshine Profitability Analysis

	Execution Time		
	2 Minutes	**3 Minutes**	**4 Minutes**
Price	$.50	$.50	$.50
Costs			
Time @ $.10 per minute	.20	.30	.40
Wax	.03	.03	.03
Other operating expenses	.09	.09	.09
Total costs	$.32	$.42	$.52
Pretax profit	$.18	$.08	($.02)

shoeshine. As the service is simple and clear-cut, the map is straightforward. It might be useful to specify how the proprietor will perform the step called *buff.*

2. *Isolate fail points* Having diagrammed the processes involved, the designer can now see where the system might go awry. For example, the shoeshiner may pick up and apply the wrong color wax, so the process designer must build in a subprocess to correct this possible error. The identification of fail points and the design of fail-safe processes are critical. The consequences of service failures can be greatly reduced by analyzing fail points at the design stage.

3. *Establish a time frame* Since all services depend on time, which is usually the major cost determinant, the process designer should establish a standard execution time.

4. *Analyze profitability* The customer can spend the three minutes between standard and acceptable execution time at the shoeshine parlor waiting in line or during service, if an error occurs or if the shoeshiner does certain things too slowly. Whatever its source, a delay can affect profits dramatically. Exhibit 4.9 quantifies the cost of delay; after four minutes the proprietor loses money. A service designer must establish a time-of-service-execution standard to ensure a profitable business.

BUSINESS PROCESS REENGINEERING[6]

For many years, dating well back into the 19th century, companies were organized and structured both to maximize efficiency and also to control growth. However, with the emergence of a single world economy and increased competition from all corners of the globe, today's competitive priorities for success have shifted from efficiency to innovation, speed, service, and quality.

To increase efficiency in the factory, job design was dominated by the division of labor concept in which the work to be done was subdivided into a series of tasks that could be performed by less-skilled individuals. However, this approach, while increasing productivity among lower-skilled workers, had its disadvantages. With each individual focusing primarily on his or her assigned task, no one assumed overall responsibility for the process itself. The result was that these conventional process structures were fragmented and piecemeal, and consequently lacked the integration necessary to support the current competitive priorities, for example, quality and service. This shift in priorities has forced managers to rethink how their firms operate, and to focus on redesigning their core business processes. This is the goal of reengineering. To accomplish this, we need to "get back to the basics," by applying some of the concepts presented in this chapter that allow us to better understand these processes.

Reengineering Defined

reengineering
Process of rethinking and restructuring an organization.

This process of rethinking and restructuring an organization is referred to as **reengineering.** Reengineering means literally starting from the beginning with a clean sheet of paper in terms of how we design our organizations to better serve our customers. It focuses on processes, not individuals performing individual tasks. A key element of reengineering is the notion of "discontinuous thinking"—identifying and discarding antiquated rules and assumptions that are often the foundation for current business operations, and that continue to exist when only small, incremental changes are made.

 MIS

A cornerstone of reengineering is the use of computer technology. With advances in database management, speed of processing, and networking capabilities, today's computers should be used to formulate new approaches that are based on the computer's strengths. Instead, many companies simply transfer existing manual systems onto the computers and wonder why their problems still exist even though they have "automated" their systems.

 ACCOUNTING

An example of reengineering is shown with Ford's desire to reduce its accounts payable department in the early 1980s. Initially, through traditional methods, management determined that the 500-person department should be reduced by 100 people (a 20 percent reduction in that workforce). However, investigation revealed that Mazda's accounts payable department consisted of only five people. Even though Mazda was smaller than Ford, this didn't explain the tremendous difference in department sizes. Subsequently, Ford decided to completely rethink its accounts payable department.

Under the old system, the 500 workers in accounts payable were constantly shuffling paper—matching vendor invoices to purchase orders and receiving documents, for example. Most of their time was spent trying to reconcile the paperwork when it didn't match up. This was the biggest cause of delayed payments. Under the new system, all of the paperwork has been virtually eliminated, thanks to the computer. When goods are received, a clerk on the dock uses the computer to instantly reconcile each delivery with its purchase order. The clerk now has the authority to accept the goods and to issue an order to the computer to pay the vendor. As a result, the bill is paid when the goods are received, not when the invoice is received. With the significant reduction in paperwork, the accounts payable

[6]Adapted from Michael Hammer and James Champy, *Reengineering the Corporation: A Manifesto for Business Revolution* (New York: HarperCollins, 1993).

Using business process reengineering concepts, this team of workers at Union Carbide's factory in Taft, Louisiana, tore up their old process map and created a new one, and in the process saved Union Carbide more than $20 million, a 50 percent increase over what management had expected.

department has been reduced to 125 people, who can now accomplish the same work previously done by 500 people, and do it faster.

Citicorp provides another good example of how effective reengineering can be. Over a two-year period, Citicorp slashed its workforce by 15 percent (14,000 employees), and trimmed its operating expenses by 12 percent. The number of data processing centers has been reduced from 240 to 60, with the goal of eventually consolidating them down to 20. Although much of these savings were attributed to traditional expense reduction, a substantial portion was the result of reengineering. In fact, John Reed, Citicorp's chief executive, believes another $1 billion in costs can be saved by reengineering the method by which Citicorp processes products and data. Consultants contend that banks in general could cut their operating expenses 25 percent to 35 percent through reengineering.[7]

Characteristics of a Reengineered Process

Based on their many years of experience with companies that have successfully reengineered their processes to better meet the needs of the marketplace, Michael Hammer and James Champy have identified several characteristics of reengineered processes, which are described below, that they have observed on a recurring basis.

Several Jobs Are Combined into One   Assembly lines are no longer used because of their inherent fragmentation of work. Specialists are replaced with "case workers," who have the responsibility for overseeing the entire process. This is referred to as horizontal work compression. By combining tasks and jobs under one person, errors that occur in transferring information from one individual to another are eliminated. In addition, the cycle time is significantly reduced because only one person has responsibility.

Workers Make Decisions   Decision making becomes a part of every person's job, eliminating the need for the traditional and costly hierarchical organizational structure with its many layers of management. This is referred to as vertical work compression. The benefits include faster customer response, lower overhead costs, and increased worker empowerment.

The Steps in the Process Are Performed in a Natural Order   With reengineering, processes no longer have to be forced into a sequential order. Instead, a natural sequence of

[7]Steven Lipin, "A New Vision," *The Wall Street Journal* (June 25, 1993).

	Tactical	Strategic
Scope	Function	Strategic business unit (SBU)
Focus	Single Process	All critical core processes
Targets	Process workflow	Holistic: workflow, systems, structure, incentives, culture
Role	Isolated improvement initiative	Focused vision for all improvement initiatives
Results	Decrease in expense, headcount, space	Increase in profit, return, market share

Source: Gateway Management Consulting.

events is permitted, based on what needs to be done next. This allows many jobs to be performed simultaneously, thereby reducing the throughput time.

Processes Have Multiple Versions   Unlike assembly lines, which are totally inflexible and therefore can produce only standardized products, reengineered processes have several versions to meet the unique requirements of different market niches as well as individual customers. An advantage of the multiple version approach is that these processes tend to be relatively clean and simple in comparison to the traditional assembly processes, which are usually quite complex.

 Work Is Performed Where It Makes the Most Sense   This involves shifting work across traditional functional boundaries. No longer, for example, are all purchases made by the purchasing department. For small purchases, such as office supplies, it may be more efficient to have each department do its own purchasing.

Issues with Reengineering

In recent years, many companies, both manufacturing and service, have adopted business process reengineering in an attempt to be more responsive to the marketplace as well as to increase the overall efficiency of their operations. However, very few of these reengineering efforts have been successful. One reason for this is the inability of management to link the reengineering effort to the overall corporate strategy. The result is often a piecemeal approach where the reengineering program has to compete for scarce resources along with other management initiatives such as total quality management, self-directed work teams, and outsourcing.

A successful reengineering program must be linked to the corporate strategy of the firm. In other words, reengineering is a strategic issue that must be addressed by the entire organization, at least at the strategic business unit (SBU) level, rather than being viewed as a tactical program. The differences in these two approaches to implementing reengineering are shown in Exhibit 4.10.[8]

As with all major projects that require significant organizational changes, the successful implementation of a reengineering effort is highly dependent upon the commitment and participation of top management.

CONCLUSION

No matter where we work or what we do, be it in manufacturing or services, we need to measure the performance of our organization in order to know where we are and where we should be in comparison to our competition. Performance measures come in various shapes

---

[8]Raymond L. Manganelli and Steven P. Raspa, "Why Reengineering Has Failed," *Management Review,* July 1995.

and sizes. It is therefore essential for managers to identify those performance measures that best provide them with the proper information that will allow intelligent and effective decision making.

To be most meaningful, performance measures should be compared with something. Traditionally these comparisons have been made within an organization, looking at trends over a period of time. Other comparisons were made with industry data that was readily available.

More recently, however, companies have begun looking outside their industries in order to find those firms that have the best practices in a particular functional area or in a specific type of process. This policy of seeking out the best of the best is referred to as benchmarking.

Proper performance measurement and benchmarking are critical elements for those firms that want to compete successfully in the global marketplace. In such a fiercely competitive environment, where rules are constantly changing and standards are constantly being raised, only those firms that are cognizant of both their capabilities and those of their competitors will survive.

Managers are now recognizing that processes exist everywhere within an organization. Process flowcharts and analysis, which were once used solely within the manufacturing function, can also be applied to other business processes such as those that exist in marketing and accounting, for example.

The lessons learned in manufacturing can also be applied in a service environment. Here, however, the customer's direct interaction with the service process must be taken into consideration. This type of analysis of service operations is often referred to as service blueprinting.

In an effort to improve processes, both in terms of effectiveness and efficiency, business process reengineering often starts from ground zero in redesigning a process. This approach provides an opportunity for new and innovative ideas to be introduced while at the same time taking advantage of the latest state-of-the-art technology that is available.

KEY TERMS

agile manufacturing   p. 111
benchmarking   p. 113
bottleneck   p. 118
capacity   p. 109
capacity utilization   p. 109
hybrid process   p. 116
make-to-order system   p. 117
make-to-stock system   p. 117

modularization   p. 117
multistage process   p. 116
process flowchart   p. 119
process velocity   p. 112
productivity   p. 108
reengineering   p. 124
service blueprint   p. 122

REVIEW AND DISCUSSION QUESTIONS

1. Why are performance measures important?

2. What do we mean when we say productivity is a "relative" measure?

3. What are the typical performance measures for quality, speed of delivery, and flexibility?

4. What should the criteria be for management to adopt a particular performance measure?

5. What is benchmarking? Why is it important for firms that want to compete globally to adopt benchmarking?

6. What are the different types of benchmarking?

7. What is the difference between a make-to-stock and a make-to-order process?

8. How does modularization allow a company to increase efficiency while at the same time provide its customers with a wide variety of products?

9. What is the definition of *bottleneck?* How does a bottleneck impact the output of a process?

10. Identify the major elements in a process flowchart.

11. How does service blueprinting differ from process flow analysis?

12. What is meant by *business process reengineering?* Why have so many of these types of projects failed in recent years?

INTERNET UPDATE

Go to the Irwin/McGraw-Hill Operations Management homepage at http://www.mhhe.com/pom and take a plant tour. Describe the firm's process in detail and draw a process flow chart for the operation.

PROBLEMS

1. Your parents are visiting you, and you decide to take them out to dinner at a fancy restaurant. As you drive up to the restaurant, a parking attendant greets you and takes your car to the parking lot. Upon entering the restaurant, you give your name to hostess, who tells you there will be a short wait. You go into the lounge where you order drinks. Your name is called shortly thereafter, and you are seated in the main dining room where all of you enjoy your meal.

   a. Draw a service blueprint for your visit to this restaurant. Be sure to include the line of visibility and identify all of the processes associated with your visit.

   b. Identify what you think are the strengths and weaknesses of this process.

2. You have just dropped your car off at the local gas station for an oil change and tune-up. When you pick up your car, you drive up to a gas pump and fill up. You then pay for the gas and the work that you had done.

   a. Draw a service blueprint for your visit to this gas station, including the line-of-visibility.

3. As the regional manager of a small chain of pizza stores, you have just received the following data from two of your locations:

	Store A	Store B
Sales (week)	$8,500	$12,500
Number of customers (week)	2,150	4,175
Total labor hours worked (week)	440	535
Total square feet of operation	1,275	1,650

   a. Define at least three measures of productivity for these two operations and calculate the productivity for each of these measures for the two stores.

   b. Based on these productivity measures, briefly analyze and compare these two operations.

   c. What might be some of the reasons for the differences in productivity?

4. The Top Hat Popcorn Company produces high quality gourmet popcorn that is delivered to independently owned specialty food shops. Currently, the weekly demand is 6,000 cartons of 2-ounce bags and 5,000 cartons of 8-ounce packages. (There are 24 2-ounce packages and 12 8-ounce packages per carton.) The facility where the popcorn is made is operating on a five day a week, eight hour a day schedule. Currently, this facility has the following equipment and respective capacities:

Equipment	Capacity	Batch Time	Number
Corn popper	50 lb/batch	6 min.	3
Packaging (2 oz.)	40 pkgs/min.		2
Packaging (8 oz.)	20 pkgs/min.		1
Carton operation (2 oz.)	1 min./carton		2
Carton operation (8 oz.)	1 min./carton		1

     a. Draw a process flowchart for producing and packaging the popcorn.

     b. Determine the capacity utilization of each stage in the process when the daily demand is produced, and identify any bottlenecks that exist.

     c. If bottleneck(s) do exist, what are your recommendations for meeting the daily demand?

5.   Speedy Tax Service offers low-cost tax preparation services in many locations throughout New England. In order to efficiently expedite a client's tax return, Speedy's operations manager has established the following process: Upon entering a tax preparation location, each client is greeted by a receptionist who, through a series of short questions, can determine which type of tax service the client needs. This takes about five minutes. Clients are then referred to either a professional tax specialist, if their tax return is complicated, or to a tax preparation associate, if the return is relatively simple. The average time for a tax specialist to complete a return is one hour, while the average time for an associate to complete a return is 30 minutes. Typically during the peak of tax season an office is staffed with six specialists and three associates, and it is open for 10 hours a day. After the tax returns have been completed, the clients are then directed to see a cashier (there are two at a location) to pay for having their tax return prepared. This takes about six minutes per client to complete. During the peak of tax season, an average of 100 clients per day come into a location of which 70 percent require the services of a tax specialist.

     a. Draw a flowchart for the above process.

     b. Identify any bottleneck(s) that exist during tax season.

     c. Calculate the average client throughput times (assuming there is no waiting) for a client seeing a specialist and for a client seeing an associate.

6.   The Dainty Donuts Store has both a take-out section and an eat-in area. The take-out section consists of four stations, and there are 10 seats in the eating area. The average take-out order takes about three minutes to fill. The average eat-in customer consumes his or her coffee and donut(s) in an average time of 12 minutes, although the server is only required to spend two minutes to complete these orders. The peak hour of the day is from 7:00 A.M.–8:00 A.M. during which approximately 100 customers will typically arrive. Of these, 60 percent are take-out orders.

     a. In order to prevent worker burn-out, management believes that worker utilization should not exceed 80 percent. Using this criterion, how many workers should be scheduled during the peak hour of 7:00 A.M.–8:00 A.M.?

     b. Determine the capacity utilization for both the take-out counters and the seats during this peak period.

7.   The walk-in clinic at a local hospital has received a grant from the federal government to analyze how well it is treating its patients. In order to conduct this analysis, a business student has been hired to identify and define the various steps required to process a patient through the clinic. Her report contains the following information:

> Upon entering the clinic, each patient is given a form to complete, which takes about five minutes, and then has to wait an additional three minutes before being seen by a triage nurse, who assesses the severity of the patient's illness. This step in the process takes about two minutes per patient. Based on the nurse's evaluation, the patient is assigned to see either a doctor, a nurse practitioner, or is sent immediately to the hospital's emergency room.
>
> Patients assigned to see a doctor wait an average of about 12 minutes before actually seeing the doctor. The average treatment time with a doctor is 15 minutes. Patients directed to nurse practitioners wait an average of 18 minutes. With nurse practitioners, the average treatment time is 17 minutes.
>
> Following treatment by either the doctor or nurse practitioner, each patient must then check-out with a cashier to settle how they are going to pay for their visit. The wait to see a cashier is five minutes, and the time spent with the cashier is approximately six minutes.

     a. What is the average throughput time in the walk-in clinic for a patient seeing a doctor? For a patient seeing a nurse practitioner? For a patient who is transferred to the emergency room?

     b. Determine the process velocity for a patient seeing a doctor and for a patient seeing a nurse practitioner.

CASE: KRISTEN'S COOKIE COMPANY (A)

You and your roommate are preparing to start Kristen's Cookie Company in your on-campus apartment. The company will provide fresh cookies to starving students late at night. You need to evaluate the preliminary design for the company's production process to figure out many variables, including what prices to charge, whether you will be able to make a profit, and how many orders to accept.

Business Concept   Your idea is to bake fresh cookies to order, using any combination of ingredients that the buyer wants. The cookies will be ready for pickup at your apartment within an hour.

Several factors will set you apart from competing products such as store-bought cookies. First, your cookies will be completely fresh. You will not bake any cookies before receiving the order; therefore, the buyer will be getting cookies that are literally hot out of the oven.

Second, like Steve's Ice Cream,[1] you will have a variety of ingredients available to add to the basic dough, including chocolate chips, M&M's, chopped Heath bars, coconut, walnuts, and raisins. Buyers will telephone in their orders and specify which of these ingredients they want in their cookies. You guarantee completely fresh cookies. In short, you will have the freshest, most exotic cookies anywhere, available right on campus.

The Production Process   Baking cookies is simple: mix all the ingredients in a food processor; spoon out the cookie dough onto a tray; put the cookies into the oven; bake them; take the tray of cookies out of the oven; let the cookies cool; and, finally, take the cookies off the tray and carefully pack them in a box. You and your roommate already own all the necessary capital equipment: one food processor, cookie trays, and spoons. Your apartment has a small oven that will hold one tray at a time. Your landlord pays for all the electricity. The variable costs, therefore, are merely the cost of the ingredients (estimated to be $.60/dozen), the cost of the box in which the cookies are packed ($.10 per box; each box holds a dozen cookies), and your time (what value do you place on your time?).

A detailed examination of the production process, which specifies how long each of the steps will take, follows. The first step is to take an order, which your roommate has figured out how to do quickly and with 100 percent accuracy. (Actually, you and your roommate devised a method using the campus electronic mail system to accept orders and to inform customers when their orders will be ready for pickup. Because this runs automatically on your personal computer, it does not take any of your time.) Therefore, this step will be ignored in further analysis.

You and your roommate have timed the necessary physical operations. The first physical production step is to wash out the mixing bowl from the previous batch, add all of the ingredients, and mix them in your food processor. The mixing bowls hold ingredients for up to three dozen cookies. You then dish up the cookies, one dozen at a time, onto a cookie tray. These activities take six minutes for the washing and mixing steps, regardless of how many cookies are being made in the batch. That is, to mix enough dough and ingredients for two dozen cookies takes the same six minutes as one dozen cookies. However, dishing up the cookies onto the tray takes two minutes per tray.

The next step, performed by your roommate, is to put the cookies in the oven and set the thermostat and timer, which takes about one minute. The cookies bake for the next nine minutes. So total baking time is 10 minutes, during the first minute of which your roommate is busy setting the oven. Because the oven only holds one tray, a second dozen takes an additional 10 minutes to bake.

Your roommate also performs the last steps of the process by first removing the cookies from the oven and putting them aside to cool for five minutes, then carefully packing them in a box and accepting payment. Removing the cookies from the oven takes only a negligible amount of time, but it must be done promptly. It takes two minutes to pack each dozen and about one minute to accept payment for the order.

That is the process for producing cookies by the dozen in Kristen's Cookie Company. As experienced bakers know, a few simplifications were made in the actual cookie production process. For example, the first batch of cookies for the night requires preheating the oven. However, such complexities will be put aside for now. Begin your analysis by developing a process flow diagram of the cookie-making process.

Key Questions to Answer before You Launch the Business   To launch the business, you need to set prices and rules for accepting orders. Some issues will only be resolved after you get started and try out different ways of producing the cookies. Before you start, however, you at least want a preliminary plan, with as much as possible specified, so that you can do a careful calculation of how much time you will have to devote to this business each night, and how much money you can expect to make. For example, when you conduct a market survey to determine the likely demand, you will want to specify exactly what your order policies will be. Therefore, answering the following operational questions should help you:

1. How long will it take you to fill a rush order?
2. How many orders can you fill in a night, assuming you are open four hours each night?

---

[1] Steve's Ice Cream was started in the Boston area by a young entrepreneur to provide make-to-order ice cream, using mix-ins.

3. How much of your own and your roommate's valuable time will it take to fill each order?

4. Because your baking trays can hold exactly one dozen cookies, you will produce and sell cookies by the dozen. Should you give any discount for people who order two dozen cookies, three dozen cookies, or more? If so, how much? Will it take you any longer to fill a two-dozen cookie order than a one-dozen cookie order?

5. How many food processors and baking trays will you need?

6. Are there any changes you can make in your production plans that will allow you to make better cookies or more cookies in less time or at lower cost? For example, is there a bottleneck operation in your production process that you can expand cheaply? What is the effect of adding another oven? How much would you be willing to pay to rent an additional oven?

Problems for Further Thought

1. What happens if you are trying to do this by yourself without a roommate?

2. Should you offer special rates for rush orders? Suppose you have just put a tray of cookies into the oven and someone calls up with a "crash priority" order for a dozen cookies of a different flavor. Can you fill the priority order while still fulfilling the order for the cookies that are already in the oven? If not, how much of a premium should you charge for filling the rush order?

3. When should you promise delivery? How can you look quickly at your order board (list of pending orders) and tell a caller when his or her order will be ready? How much of a safety margin for timing should you allow?

4. What other factors should you consider at this stage of planning your business?

5. Your product must be made to order because each order is potentially unique. If you decide to sell standard cookies instead, how should you change the production system? The order-taking process?

SELECTED BIBLIOGRAPHY

Albrecht, Karl, and Ron Zemke. *Service America! Doing Business in the New Economy.* Homewood, IL: Dow Jones-Irwin, 1985.

Bernstein, A. "Quality Is Becoming Job One in the Office, Too." *Business Week,* April 29, 1991.

Bitran, Gabriel R., and Johannes Hoech. "The Humanization of Service: Respect at the Moment of Truth." *Sloan Management Review,* Winter 1990, pp. 89–96.

Camp, Robert C. *Benchmarking: The Search for Industry Best Practices That Lead to Superior Performance.* Milwaukee, WI: American Society for Quality Control, Quality Press, 1989.

Camp, Robert C. *Business Process Benchmarking: Findings and Implementing Best Practices.* Milwaukee, WI: ASQC Quality Press, 1995.

Chase, R. B. "The Customer Contact Approach to Services: Theoretical Bases and Practical Extensions." *Operations Research* 21, no. 4 (1981), pp. 698–705.

Fitzsimmons, James A., and Mona J. Fitzsimmons. *Service Management: Operations, Strategy, and Information Technology.* 2nd edition. Burr Ridge, IL: Irwin/McGraw-Hill, 1998.

Hall, Gene; Jim Rosenthal; and Judy Wade. "How to Make Reengineering Really Work." *Harvard Business Review,* November–December 1993.

Hammer, Michael. "Reengineering Work: Don't Automate, Obliterate." *Harvard Business Review,* July–August 1990, pp. 104–12.

Hammer, Michael, and James Champy. *Reengineering the Corporation.* New York: HarperCollins Books, 1993.

Levitt, Theodore. "Production-Line Approach to Service." *Harvard Business Review* 50, no. 5 (September–October 1972), pp. 41–52.

Lipin, Steven. "A New Vision." *The Wall Street Journal,* June 25, 1993.

Main, Jeremy. "How to Steal the Best Ideas Around." *Fortune,* October 19, 1992.

Manganelli, Raymond L., and Steven P. Raspa. "Why Reengineering Has Failed." *Management Review,* July 1995, pp. 39–43.

Port, Otis, and Geoffrey Smith. "Beg, Borrow and Benchmark." *Business Week,* November 30, 1992.

Roehm, Harper A.; Donald Klein; and Joseph F. Castellano. "Springing to World-Class Manufacturing." *Management Accounting,* March 1991, pp. 40–44.

Shostack, G. Lynn. "Designing Services That Deliver." *Harvard Business Review* 62, no. 1 (January–February 1984), pp. 133–39.

Stoddard, Donna; B. Sirkka; L. Jarvenpaa; and Michael Littlejohn. "The Reality of Business Reengineering: Pacific Bell's Centrex Provisioning Process." *California Management Review* 38, no. 3 (Spring 1996), pp. 57–76.

Rikert, David C. *Burger King.* Harvard Business School Case No. 681–045. Boston: Harvard Business School, 1980.

Rikert, David C. *McDonald's Corporation.* Harvard Business School Case No. 681–044. Boston: Harvard Business School, 1980.

Chapter

QUALITY MANAGEMENT

Chapter Objectives

- Identify the different dimensions of quality in both goods and services and show how they relate to a firm's overall strategy.

- Present a framework for the development of Total Quality Management (TQM) within an organization.

- Define the various elements that comprise the cost of quality.

- Identify the various tools that can be used to assess and improve the quality of a process.

- Introduce the Malcolm Baldrige National Quality Award and its criteria for evaluating companies.

- Introduce the ISO 9000 standards and describe the steps a company must take to obtain certification.

IBM Rochester, 1990 winner of the Malcolm Baldrige National Quality Award, manufactures intermediate computer systems and has more than 400,000 systems installed worldwide. The concept of quality at IBM Rochester is linked directly to its customers, who are involved in every step of the process from product design to delivery. As a result of this focus on quality, productivity increased 30 percent between 1986 and 1989. Product development time for new mid-range computer systems has been reduced by more than 50 percent, while the manufacturing cycle has been trimmed by more than 60 percent. Customers have benefited from a threefold increase in product reliability; an increase from 3 to 12 months in the product warranty period; and a cost of ownership that is among the lowest in the industry.

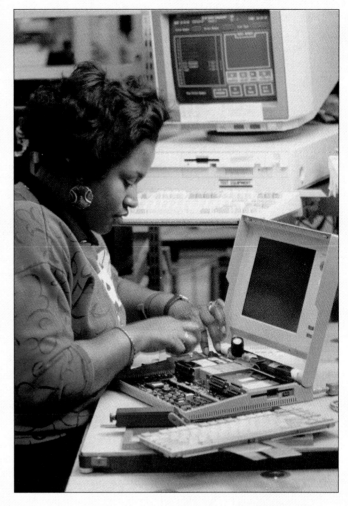

IBM Rochester strengthened its strategic quality initiatives by formulating improvement plans that are based upon six critical success factors: (a) improved product and service requirements definition, (b) an enhanced product strategy, (c) a six-sigma defect elimination strategy, (d) further cycle time reductions, (e) improved employee education and (f) increased employee involvement and ownership. Each senior manager "owns" one of these six factors and assumes responsibility for its plans and implementation.

Quality at IBM Rochester is viewed as continuous journey where the objective is always excellence in customer satisfaction. ∎

In today's highly competitive markets, managers are recognizing the value of customer loyalty. To maintain customer loyalty it is not sufficient for a firm to satisfy its customers. Now goods and services must "delight" customers in order to retain them, and this is achieved by providing only the highest quality goods and services.

The quality movement can trace its roots back to Walter Shewhart's development of the first process control chart in the 1920s, while he was employed as a statistician at Bell Labs. During World War II, the use of statistics to monitor the quality of wartime production increased out of necessity, due in part to both the vast quantities of material being produced and the shortage of labor on the home front. After the war, demand for consumer goods in the United States was high. As a result, the quality emphasis that was so important during the war gave way to a focus on production volume. Meanwhile, W. Edwards Deming and Joseph Juran were teaching managers in Japan how to lower costs and improve quality by "doing it right the first time." As a result of their efforts, Japanese goods, by the 1970s, were considered to be among the best in the world.

In the United States, the importance of quality as a key element in the success of an organization didn't begin to be recognized until the late 1970s. In 1980, NBC presented a documentary entitled "If Japan Can, Why Can't We?" which highlighted Deming's significant contribution to improving the quality of Japanese products. Only after this documentary was aired was Deming asked to assist U.S. companies in improving the quality of their products. The shift in focus of U.S. companies to quality has not gone unnoticed. Consumers have recognized significant improvements in the quality of U.S. products. The Ford Taurus, for example, is now the best-selling car in the United States, a distinction previously held for many years by the Honda Accord.

total quality management (TQM)
Approach for integrating quality at all levels of an organization.

In this chapter we introduce some of the basic concepts of **total quality management (TQM),** which are critical elements in the successful implementation of quality programs not only in Japan, but around the world. As part of this discussion, we present traditional as well as emerging topics relating to quality with which all managers should be familiar. While we emphasize the technical aspects that are required for a successful quality effort, we also recognize the importance of providing proper leadership and the need for worker involvement as integral parts of the quality improvement process. To quote Tom Peters, "Most quality programs fail for one of two reasons: They have system without passion, or passion without system."[1]

THE STRATEGIC ROLE OF QUALITY

For many years following World War II, quality was viewed primarily as a defensive function rather than as a competitive weapon for use in developing new markets and increasing market share. In this role, the quality emphasis was on quality control (QC): reducing the number of customer complaints that were received. As a result, there was a heavy reliance on inspection (sorting the good from the bad) rather than on prevention. Identifying defective output and either fixing it (rework) or disposing of it (scrap) incurred costs. It was therefore believed that higher quality must be more costly. Quality control managers often reported to manufacturing managers, who were measured primarily on output; consequently they had little or no power to either halt production or delay the shipment of faulty products.

Today, however, more and more companies recognize the value of using quality as an offensive, strategic weapon. In adopting this approach, these firms are able to both identify new market niches as well as increase their market share in existing ones. However, in

---

[1]Tom Peters, *Thriving on Chaos* (New York: Knopf, 1987), p. 74.

quality dimensions
Recognition that quality can be defined in many ways and that companies can use quality as a competitive advantage.

taking the offensive with quality, managers must realize that there is more than one facet or dimension on which it can focus, and, in fact, some of these may even be in conflict. David Garvin[2] has identified eight different **quality dimensions** on which a company can compete. These are: (1) performance, (2) features, (3) reliability, (4) conformance, (5) durability, (6) serviceability, (7) aesthetics, and (8) perceived quality.

Quality in Goods

Performance   Performance is a measure of a product's primary operating characteristics. Since performance can usually be measured in specific quantitative terms, a product's performance characteristics are often compared and ranked with those of the competition. With an automobile, for example, performance characteristics would include how fast it can accelerate from 0 to 60 mph and its fuel efficiency in terms of miles per gallon. For a personal computer, performance characteristics would include operating speed and random access memory capacity.

Features   Features are the "bells and whistles" that are offered with a product. While features are not the primary operating characteristics of a product, they may, nonetheless, be very important to the customer. For example, a moon roof and stereo system may be the deciding factors for a new car buyer while a specific type of refrigerator may appeal to a customer because it offers an icemaker and water dispenser.

Reliability   The reliability of a product relates to the probability that the product will fail within a specified time. Reliability is often measured as the mean time between failures (MTBF) or the failure rate per unit of time or other measure of usage. High product reliability is important in such products as airplanes, computers, and copying machines. Stratus Computers, for example, has successfully carved out a niche for itself in the highly competitive computer industry by offering "fault-free" computer systems. The bored Maytag repairman with no service calls offers another good example of product reliability.

Durability   The durability dimension of quality relates to the expected operational life of a product. In some instances, like with a light bulb, the filament eventually burns out and the entire product must be replaced. In other cases, such as with an automobile, the consumer must evaluate the trade-off between replacing the product entirely versus spending money on repairs for the existing one.

Conformance   A product's conformance to design specifications is primarily process oriented, in that it reflects how well the product and its individual components meet the established standards.

Serviceability   Serviceability is concerned with how readily a product can be repaired and the speed, competence, and courtesy associated with that repair. This dimension of quality is sometimes overlooked in the design stage. For example, Chevrolet in the 1970s designed a car in which one of the spark plugs could not be removed without pulling out the entire engine. The speed of the repair is also important, in that it affects the overall number of products needed in those circumstances where constant coverage is required. Using a city's paramedic service as an example, the frequency and the amount of time a paramedic vehicle requires repair and maintenance impacts directly on the total number of vehicles needed to provide the proper level of coverage.

---

[2]David Garvin, "Competing on the Eight Dimensions of Quality," *Harvard Business Review* (November–December 1987), pp. 101–9.

Aesthetics   Aesthetics is obviously a dimension of quality for which there is a high de-gree of individual judgment. In fact, in terms of aesthetics, good quality to one group of customers might even be perceived as poor quality to another group. Companies, therefore, have an opportunity with this quality dimension to seek out a very specific market niche.

Perceived Quality   According to David Garvin, perceived quality is directly related to the reputation of the firm that manufactures the product. Often, total information about the var-ious quality aspects of a product is not available, especially when it is a new product that is being introduced for the first time. Consequently, customers rely heavily on the past per-formance and reputation of the firm making the product, attaching a perceived value based on the previous performance of the company's other products.

Quality in Services

Parasuraman, Zeithaml, and Berry (1986, 1990)[3,4] identified the following ten "generic" factors or dimensions that contribute to the level of service quality a firm provides to its customers.

Tangibles   Tangibles are the physical evidence of the service. The boxy brown UPS truck or the clean white FedEx truck is an easily recognized tangible. The type of uniform a restaurant's waitstaff wears and the cleanliness of the uniforms are some of the tangibles that you observe when you go out to eat. The food served at the music festival and the t-shirts that celebrate that festival are also examples of tangibles.

Reliability   As previously described, reliability relates to the consistency of performance and dependability of the service.

Responsiveness   This refers the willingness and/or readiness of employees to provide ser-vice. How easily you can get the attention of the clerk at Bloomingdale's Department Store is a measure of responsiveness. The length of time it takes to receive a return call on a com-plaint or a solution to a problem is also a measure of a firm's responsiveness.

Competence   Competence relates to workers having the required skills and knowledge to properly perform the service. How qualified are the tellers at your bank? Are they able to correctly handle your transaction, or do they often seem uncertain or seek assistance from others? When you call your computer's technical support hotline, does the person on the other end appear to be knowledgeable in terms of understanding your problem?

Courtesy   This refers to the politeness, respect, consideration, and friendliness of contact personnel. Once you've gotten the attention of the clerk at Macy's, is she pleasant, or does she continue her discussion of her parents with her co-worker while you wait awkwardly for her to ring up your purchases and accept your payment?

Credibility   Credibility refers to the characteristics of trustworthiness, believability, and honesty of the service worker. Do you feel more or less comfortable with paying for a major repair after you discuss it with your auto mechanic? How much trust do you place in the sales clerk that is trying to sell you a computer?

Security   Security refers to freedom from any danger, risk, or doubt. This is a particularly important dimension of professional service quality. Most consumers of health care or

---

[3]A. Parasuraman, V. A. Zeithaml, and L. L. Berry, "SERVQUAL: A Multiple-Item Scale for Measuring Consumer Perceptions of Service Quality," *Marketing Science Institute,* Cambridge, MA, 1986.

[4]L. L. Berry, V. A. Zeithaml, and A. Parasuraman, "Five Imperatives for Improving Service Quality," *Sloan Man-agement Review* 29, Summer 1990.

legal services, for example, are unable to assess the appropriateness of the recommendations of their physicians or attorneys, but their services are often sought when there are significant risks involved.

Access   Access relates to approachability and ease of contact. How difficult is it to find a repair service for your computer? How many times are you transferred when you call your credit card company to resolve a billing problem?

Communication   This is a very important dimension of quality in some services. When you are in an emergency room with a sick child, how well are you kept informed of the process of your child's care? How well do the nurses, doctors, and clerks listen to you?

Understanding the Customer   This dimension refers to how well the service worker makes the effort to understand the specific needs of each customer.

Parasuraman, Berry, and Zeithaml used these definitions and key elements as a basis for identifying five principal service quality gaps. These gaps address the *customer's perception* of service performance rather than the managerial decisions around changing *actual* service performance.

HOUSE OF QUALITY

Businesses today recognize the need to involve their customers in all aspects of the design, production, and delivery of the goods and services that they offer. In the past, this was often not the case. However, with the trend towards increased competition, companies who do not listen to their customers on a continuous basis will find them taking their business to firms who will listen. While there are many approaches for obtaining information from customers, such as surveys, focus groups, and so forth, we present one that links directly to the processes that produce these goods and services.

MARKETING
ENGINEERING
MANUFACTURING

quality function deployment (QFD)
Process for translating customer requirements into a product's design.

voice of the customer
Customer feedback used in quality functional deployment process to determine product specifications.

house of quality
Part of the quality function deployment process that uses customer feedback for product design criteria.

Quality Function Deployment

A fairly rigorous method for translating the needs of the customer into the design specifications of a product is **quality function deployment (QFD)**. This approach, which uses interfunctional teams from marketing, design engineering, and manufacturing, has been credited by Toyota Motor Corporation for reducing the costs on its cars by more than 60 percent by significantly shortening design times.

The QFD process begins with studying and listening to customers to determine the characteristics of a superior product. This customer feedback is often referred to as the **voice of the customer.** Through market research, the consumers' product needs and preferences are defined and broken down into categories called *customer attributes*. For example, an automobile manufacturer would like to improve the design of a car door. Through customer surveys and interviews, it determines that two important customer attributes desired in a car door are that it "stays open on a hill" and is "easy to close from the outside." After the customer attributes are defined, they are weighted based on their relative importance to the customer. Next, the consumer is asked to compare and rate the company's products with those of its competitors. This process helps the company to determine those product characteristics that are important to the consumer and to evalute its product in relation to others. The end result is a better understanding and focus on the product characteristics that require improvement.

Customer attribute information forms the basis for a matrix called the **house of quality** (see Exhibit 5.1). By building a house of quality matrix, the cross-functional QFD team can use customer feedback to make engineering, marketing, and design decisions. The matrix

EXHIBIT 5.1

Completed House of Quality
Matrix for a Car Door

helps the team to translate customer attribute information into concrete operating or engineering goals. The important product characteristics and goals for improvement are jointly agreed on and detailed in the house. This process encourages the different departments to work closely together and results in a better understanding of one another's goals and issues. However, the most important benefit of the house of quality is that it helps the team to focus on building a product that satisfies customers.

THE ELEMENTS OF TQM

Total quality management (TQM) can be viewed as an organizationwide approach that focuses on producing high quality goods and services. TQM, when properly used, is an integral part of an organization, not a separate, stand alone program, and it encompasses all of the functional areas and levels within the organization, including suppliers.

There are four primary elements that are integral to every successful TQM program. These elements are (*a*) leadership, (*b*) employee involvement, (*c*) product/process excellence, and (*d*) customer focus.

Leadership

The leadership provided by an organization's management is a major cornerstone in the development and implementation of a successful TQM program. When properly executed, a TQM program is companywide, transcends traditional functional areas, and involves all of the firm's employees. It therefore requires vision, planning, and communication, all of which are the responsibility of top management. Studies have indicated that total commitment from management is considered to be a critical element in successfully implementing such programs.

Top management can demonstrate its commitment to a TQM program in several ways. These include incorporating TQM into the firm's overall strategy, and demonstrating by actions as well as by words that quality is the number one operating priority of the organization.

Employee Involvement

Employee involvement is another critical element in successfully implementing a TQM program. By involving all employees in the decision-making process, management is able to receive inputs from those nearest the problems and in the best position to recommend viable solutions. Employee involvement also takes advantage of the skills and knowledge of all employees, which appears to be prevalent in world-class operations.

A key element in employee involvement is that each worker assumes the responsibility for inspecting the quality of his or her own work. This is referred to as quality at the source and extends beyond the worker to include the work group, all departments, and the suppliers of parts and services to the organization. This view changes the often adversarial practice of having a QC inspector, typically from the QC department, making decisions about good or bad quality.

Product/Process Excellence

Product/process excellence involves the quality of the product's design and analysis of field failures. It also includes statistical process control (SPC) and other analytical tools (which are discussed later in this chapter and in Supplement 5).

Process control is concerned with monitoring quality *while the product is being produced or the service is being performed.* Typical objectives of process control plans are to provide timely information on whether currently produced items are meeting design specifications and to detect shifts in the process that signal that future products may not meet the customer's requirements. The actual control phase of process control occurs when corrective action is taken, such as when a worn part is replaced, a machine is overhauled, or a new supplier is found. Process control concepts, especially statistically based control charts, are used in services as well as in manufacturing.

continuous improvement
Concept that recognizes that quality improvement is a journey with no end and that there is a need for continually looking for new approaches for improving quality.

An underlying philosophy in achieving product/process excellence is the concept of **continuous improvement.** This has a general meaning as well as a specific TQM meaning. Its general meaning is an ongoing effort to improve in every part of the organization and all of its outputs. Its more specific meaning focuses on continual improvement in the processes by which work is accomplished.

In Japanese companies, the concept of continuous improvement is referred to as *kaizen.* It can be interpreted to mean a systematic approach to eliminating errors and improving the

poka-yoke
Simple devices, such as automatic shutoff valves or fixtures to orient parts, which prevent defects from being produced.

quality of the product that is delivered to the customer. One of the ways kaizen is achieved is through the use of **poka-yoke** or foolproofing in the methods that are used to make the products. United Electric Controls in Watertown, Massachusetts, a winner of the Shingo Prize in Manufacturing, attributes much of its quality improvements to introducing poka-yoke into its manufacturing processes. In manufacturing, poka-yoke often requires that a part be redesigned so that it can fit only one way. A good example of poka-yoke in services is the bathroom onboard an airplane. Here the light will not go on until the door is locked, ensuring privacy. Also, height bars at amusement parks, as shown in the photo, ensure proper height for the rides.

Customer Focus

MARKETING

The customer's perception of quality must be taken into account in setting acceptable quality levels. In other words, a product isn't reliable unless the customer says it's reliable and a service isn't fast unless the customer says it's fast. Translating customer quality demands into specifications requires marketing (or product development) to accurately determine what the customer wants and product designers to develop a product (or service) that can be produced to consistently achieve that desired level of quality. This, in turn, requires that we have an operational definition of quality, an understanding of its various dimensions, and a process for including the voice of the customer in those specifications. The quality of a product or service may be defined by the quality of its design (product quality) and the quality of its conformance to that design (process quality). **Design quality** refers to the inherent value of the product in the marketplace and is thus a strategic decision for the firm, as discussed earlier.

design quality
Specific characteristics of the product that determines its value in the marketplace.

conformance quality
Defines how well the product is made with respect to its design specifications.

Conformance quality refers to the degree to which the product or service meets design specifications. It, too, has strategic implications, but the execution of the activities involved in achieving conformance are of a tactical day-to-day nature. It should be evident that a product or service can have high design quality but low conformance quality, and vice versa.

The operations function and the quality organization within the firm are primarily concerned with quality of conformance. Achieving all the quality specifications is typically the responsibility of manufacturing management (for products) and branch operations management (for services).

Both design quality and conformance quality should provide products that meet the customer's objectives for those products. This is often termed the product's *fitness for use,* and it entails identifying those dimensions of the product (or service) that the customer wants and developing a quality control program to ensure that these dimensions are met.

THE GURUS OF QUALITY MANAGEMENT

quality gurus
Individuals who have been identified as making a significant contribution to improving the quality of goods and services.

Over the years there have been many individuals involved in the quality revolution. Several have been recognized as **quality gurus** for their valuable contributions and forward thinking. They are Walter A. Shewhart, W. Edwards Deming, Joseph M. Juran, Armand Feigenbaum, Philip Crosby, and Genichi Taguchi. While they share much in common in terms of how they view quality, each has left his own unique stamp on the quality movement. Consequently, their philosophical approaches to quality are significantly different. A comparison of the philosophies of three of the more prominent quality gurus is presented in Exhibit 5.2.

Walter A. Shewhart

Walter A. Shewhart as mentioned earlier was a statistician at Bell Laboratories who studied randomness in industrial processes. He developed a system that permitted workers to determine whether the variability of a process was truly random or due to assignable causes. If a process exhibited only random variation, it was considered to be "in control." If a process exhibited nonrandom variation, the cause for the variation had to be identified and addressed in order for the process to be brought back into control. In addition to

EXHIBIT 5.2

Three of the Quality Gurus Compared

	Crosby	Deming	Juran
Definition of quality	Conformance to requirements	A predictable degree of uniformity and dependability at low cost and suited to the market	Fitness for use
Degree of senior management responsibility	Responsible for quality	Responsible for 85% of quality problems	Less than 20% of quality problems are due to workers
Performance standard/motivation	Zero defects	Quality has many "scales": use statistics to measure performance in all areas; critical of zero defects	Avoid campaigns to do perfect work
General approach	Prevention, not inspection	Reduce variability by continuous improvement; cease mass inspection	General management approach to quality, especially human elements
Structure	14 steps to quality improvement	14 points for management	10 steps to quality improvement
Statistical process control (SPC)	Rejects statistically acceptable levels of quality	Statistical methods of quality control must be used	Recommends SPC but warns that it can lead to tool-driven approach
Improvement basis	A process, not a program; improvement goals	Continuous to reduce variation; eliminate goals without methods	Project-by-project team approach; set goals
Teamwork	Quality improvement teams; quality councils	Employee participation in decision making; break down barriers between departments	Team and quality circle approach
Costs of quality	Cost of nonconformance; quality is free	No optimum, continuous improvement	Quality is not free, there is an optimum
Purchasing and goods received	State requirements; supplier is extension of business; most faults due to purchasers themselves	Inspection too late; allows defects to enter system through AQLs; statistical evidence and control charts required	Problems are complex; carry out formal surveys
Vendor rating	Yes and buyers; quality audits useless	No, critical of most systems	Yes, but help supplier improve
Single sourcing of supply		Yes	No, can neglect to sharpen competitive edge

Source: Modified from John S. Oakland, *Total Quality Management* (London: Heinemann Professional Publishing Ltd., 1989), pp. 291–92.

EXHIBIT 5.3

Shewhart's Plan-Do-Check-Act (PDCA) Cycle

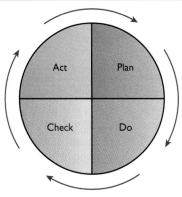

Source: Mary Walton, *Deming Management at Work* (New York: Perigree Books, 1991), p. 22.

developing the foundations for modern statistical process control, Shewhart also developed the "plan-do-check-act" (PDCA) cycle shown in Exhibit 5.3. Prior to the PDCA cycle, organizations typically managed activities as though they had identifiable beginning and end points. The PDCA cycle uses a circular model to emphasize the need for continuous improvement. Shewhart's pioneering work in statistical process control had a strong influence on both Deming and Juran.

W. Edwards Deming

statistical process control (SPC)
Methods, such as control charts, which signal shifts in a process that will likely lead to products and/or services not meeting customer requirements.

A thorough understanding of **statistical process control (SPC)** is the basic cornerstone of Deming's approach to quality. In fact, the Japanese were so impressed with his knowledge of SPC that they invited him back to teach the subject to Japanese managers and workers. Deming emphasized the importance of having an overall organizational approach for quality management. He therefore insisted that top managers attend his lectures, knowing that the QC staff by itself could not support and sustain an ongoing organizationwide quality effort. The Japanese have recognized Deming's tremendous contribution to the success of their companies by naming their highest award for industrial excellence after him—the Deming Prize. (Another indicator that U.S. companies are making significant progress toward improving quality is that Florida Power & Light, a non-Japanese company, was awarded the Deming Prize.)

One of Deming's major contributions focused on disproving the fallacy that it costs more to make better-quality products. He demonstrated that just the opposite is true: a high-quality process is, in fact, less costly than a low-quality one. When products are made properly the first time, substantial savings accrue from the elimination of unnecessary labor for rework and repairs and the cost to scrap nonconforming material.

Deming also introduced the plan-do-check-act (PDCA) cycle to the Japanese.

According to Deming, 85 percent of the quality problems generated by a company can be attributed to management, because they have the power to make the decisions that impact on the current systems and practices. His extensive consulting experiences with such companies as Ford, Nashua Corp., and Florida Power & Light have supported this claim. Over the years, Deming identified 14 points that he believed to be critical for improving quality. These 14 points are presented in Exhibit 5.4.

Joseph M. Juran

Like Deming, Juran also visited Japan shortly after the end of World War II to assist in rebuilding its industrial base. Also like Deming, Juran emphasized the importance of

EXHIBIT 5.4

Deming's 14-Point Program
for Improving Quality

1. Create constancy of purpose for improvement of product and service.
2. Adopt the new philosophy.
3. Cease dependence on mass inspection.
4. End the practice of awarding business on the price tag alone.
5. Improve constantly and forever the system of production and training.
6. Institute training.
7. Institute leadership.
8. Drive out fear.
9. Break down barriers between staff areas.
10. Eliminate slogans, exhortations, and targets for the workforce.
11. Eliminate numerical quotas.
12. Remove barriers to pride in workmanship.
13. Institute a vigorous program of education and retraining.
14. Take action to accomplish the program.

Source: Mary Walton, *Deming Management at Work* (New York: Perigree Books, 1991),
pp. 17–18.

producing quality products, and thus directed his efforts while in Japan toward teaching quality concepts and their application to the factory floor. Based on his experiences with Japanese companies, Juran developed an approach to quality that focuses primarily on three areas: (*a*) quality planning, (*b*) quality control, and (*c*) quality improvement.

According to Juran, the quality of a product is defined as fitness for use, as viewed by the customer. Juran further defines fitness for use as consisting of five components: (*a*) quality of design, (*b*) quality of conformance, (*c*) availability, (*d*) safety, and (*e*) field use. In evaluating a product's fitness for use, Juran takes into account the total life cycle of the product.

Juran uses the cost of quality as his framework for introducing his approach to quality. In doing so, he divides the cost of quality into three major categories: (*a*) cost of prevention, (*b*) cost of detection/appraisal, and (*c*) cost of failure, all of which are presented in greater detail later in this chapter.

Armand Feigenbaum

In 1956, Armand Feigenbaum proposed the concept of "total quality control," which begins with the recognition that quality is the responsibility of everyone in the organization. He stressed interdepartmental communication, particularly with respect to product design control, incoming material control, and production control. Like Juran, he believed in the power of the cost-of-quality framework, and emphasized careful measurement and reporting of these costs. Also like Juran, he believed that a new type of quality professional was needed, the quality control engineer, who would oversee cross-functional elements. The application of statistics by itself was no longer enough. The Japanese embraced this concept and expanded it to "companywide quality control." In recognition of his contribution to improving quality, The Massachusetts Quality Award is named in honor of Armand Feigenbaum.

Philip Crosby

Unlike Deming and Juran, both of whom were trained initially as statisticians, Crosby was educated as an engineer and began his career in manufacturing. After working for several large companies, primarily in quality-related positions, he founded his own "Quality College" in Florida in 1979.

Crosby's philosophy, which is similar in some respects to Deming's, states that any organization can reduce its total overall costs by improving the quality of its processes. In one of his first books, Crosby preached that "quality is free." According to Crosby, the cost of providing poor-quality goods and services is significant. He estimated that the cost of producing poor quality can run as high as 25 percent of revenues for manufacturing companies and 40 percent of operating expenses in service operations. Crosby also claims that companies that have successfully implemented quality programs can expect to reduce their costs of quality to less than 2.5 percent of sales.[5]

Genichi Taguchi

Genichi Taguchi has contributed importantly to both the refinement of quality management philosophy and the development of quality tools. Taguchi takes an engineering approach to design quality, focusing on the design of experiments to improve both the yield and performance quality of products. He emphasizes the minimization of variation, which is also the cornerstone of his philosophical approach. While Juran emphasized the cost of quality to the firm, Taguchi is also concerned with the cost of quality to society as a whole. He takes Juran's concept of external failure much further, including not only the cost to the firm that ships the defective product, but also the cost to the firm that accepts it, the customer that buys and uses it, and so on. His dual engineering-philosophical perspective shows how much is lost when products fail to meet specifications, which "ups the stakes" for managers concerned with the quality of their products and services.

THE COST OF QUALITY

cost of quality
Framework for identifying quality components that are related to producing both high quality products and low quality products, with the goal of minimizing the total cost of quality.

Following Juran's model, we divide the **cost of quality** into three major categories: (*a*) cost of prevention, (*b*) cost of detection/appraisal, and (*c*) cost of failure. The third category, the cost of failure, is further subdivided into internal failure costs and external failure costs.

The total cost of quality is the sum of the costs in all three categories. The typical percentages of total quality costs that are estimated for each of the three categories are shown in Exhibit 5.5.

Cost of Prevention

cost of prevention
Costs associated with the development of programs to prevent defectives from occurring in the first place.

Costs of prevention, by definition, are those costs incurred by an organization in its effort to prevent defective goods and services from being produced. Included in this category are investments in machinery, technology, and education programs that are designed to reduce the number of defects that the process produces. Also included in this category are the costs to administer the firm's quality program, data collection and analysis, and vendor certification. All of the quality gurus strongly support investments in this category because the returns are so high, including the benefits gained from increasing customer satisfaction and reducing scrap losses and rework expenses.

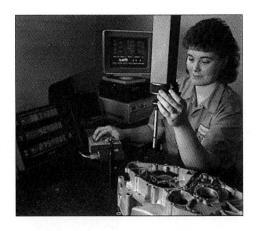

[5]Philip B. Crosby, *Quality Is Free* (New York: New America Library, 1979), p. 15.

Source: A.V. Feigenbaum, *Total Quality Control*, 3rd ed. (New York: McGraw-Hill, 1983), p. 112; and Joseph M. Juran, and F. M. Gryna, *Quality Planning and Analysis* (New York: McGraw-Hill, 1970), p. 60.

EXHIBIT 5.5
Typical Quality Cost Ratios

Category	Feigenbaum	Juran and Gryna
Prevention costs	5%–10%	0.5%–5%
Detection/appraisal costs	20%–25%	10%–50%
Failure costs	65%–70%	Internal : 25%–40%
		External: 20%–40%
Total cost of quality	100%	100%

Cost of Detection/Appraisal

cost of detection/appraisal
Costs associated with the test and inspection of subassemblies and products after they have been made.

Costs of detection or appraisal are those costs associated with evaluating the quality of the product. Costs included in this category are: incoming material inspection, tests and inspection throughout the transformation process, test equipment maintenance, and products destroyed during destructive testing.

Cost of Failure

cost of failure
Costs associated with the failure of a defective product.

Costs of failure pertain to nonconforming and nonperforming products. Also included in this category are the costs associated with the evaluation and disposition of customer complaints. As stated earlier, we further subdivide failure costs into internal and external failure costs.

internal failure costs
Costs associated with producing defective products that are identified prior to shipment.

Internal failure costs are identified as those costs that are eliminated when no defects are produced within the system. They include only those costs attributed to defects that are found before the products are delivered to the customer. Examples of internal failure costs include: scrap, rework/repair, retesting of reworked/repaired products, downtime, yield losses due to process variability, and the disposition of the defective items.

external failure costs
Costs associated with producing defective products that are delivered to the customer.

External failure costs are those costs that are incurred after the product has been delivered to the customer. Included in this category are: the cost of returned material, warranty charges, field survey costs, legal expenses from lawsuits, customer dissatisfaction, loss of revenues due to downgrading products as seconds, and costs of allowances/concessions made to customers.

It is generally now recognized that increased spending on prevention provides significant returns in the form of reductions in detection/appraisal and failure costs—and in the overall cost of quality. Thus the old adage, "An ounce of prevention is worth a pound of cure" is also most appropriate for quality.

At the same time, Deming suggested that total quality costs can be decreased by improving the process itself. An improved process reduces both the number of defects produced and the costs of prevention and appraisal. A comparison of Deming's model with the previously traditional view toward quality is presented in Exhibit 5.6.

When defective products or services are eliminated, there are two direct effects. First, there are more good units produced (and capacity is therefore increased) and second, each unit produced costs less because the cost of the failures is both reduced and also spread over a larger number of nondefective goods or services. For example, if a plastic injection molding process scraps 15 defective pen barrels out of every 100 that are produced, the cost to produce the 15 scrapped units must be spread over the remaining 85 units—and there are only 85 units available to sell. If the quality of the process is improved and only five units are scrapped per 100 produced, then there are 95 units that are available for sale, and the cost of only the five scrapped units is now spread over the 95 good units rather than 85 as was previously the case.

EXHIBIT 5.6

Two Views of the Cost of Improved Quality

A bank, for example, that set out to improve quality and reduce its costs found that it had also boosted productivity. The bank developed this productivity measure for the loan processing area: the number of tickets processed divided by the resources required (labor cost, computer time, ticket forms). Before the quality improvement program, the productivity index was 0.2660 [2,080/($11.23 × 640 hours + $0.05 × 2,600 forms + $500 for systems costs)]. After the quality improvement project was completed, labor time fell to 546 hours and the number of forms processed increased to 2,100 for a change in the index to 0.3088, or an increase in productivity of 16 percent.

THE SEVEN BASIC QUALITY CONTROL TOOLS

seven basic quality control tools
Quantitative techniques that can assist a manager in collecting, grouping, presenting and analyzing data that is process-generated.

Within the quality literature, seven basic tools have been identified that can assist managers in organizing, displaying, and analyzing process-generated data. These **seven basic quality control (QC) tools** are (*a*) process flowcharts (or diagrams), (*b*) run (or trend) charts, (*c*) checksheets, (*d*) scatter plots (or diagrams), (*e*) cause and effect diagrams (or fishbone charts), (*f*) Pareto charts, and (*g*) histograms. These different quality control tools are shown in Exhibit 5.7.

Process Flowcharts

Process flowcharts or diagrams show each of the steps that are required to produce either a good or a service. As stated previously in Chapter 4, actions are usually depicted as rectangles, waits or inventories are shown as inverted triangles, and decision points as diamonds. Arrows connecting these activities show the direction of flow in the process. In service operations, this procedure is often referred to as "blue-printing" the process, as discussed in detail in the previous chapter.

Checksheets

Checksheets are used to record the frequency of occurrence of problems and/or errors.

Run Charts

Run charts show data that is plotted over time, for example, hamburgers sold per hour throughout a day or patients seen per day over a month. The visual representation of the data in a run chart makes it easy to identify unusual points or patterns that might have managerial significance. (As an illustration, Exhibit 5.8 shows a run chart of on-time departures for an airline.)

EXHIBIT 5.7

The Seven Basic Quality Control Tools

Process Flow Diagram

Run Chart

Checksheet

Scatter Plot

Histogram

Pareto Chart

Cause-and-Effect Diagram

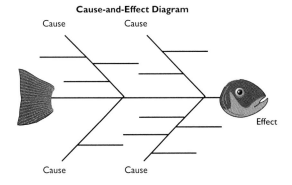

EXHIBIT 5.8

Run Chart of Midway
Airlines On-Time Departures

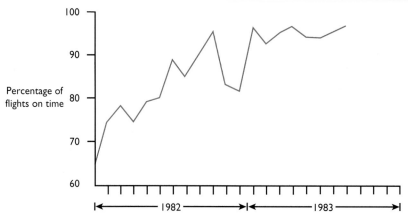

Source: Adapted from D. D. Wychoff, "New Tools for Achieving Service Quality," *Cornell Hotel and Restaurant Administration Quarterly* (November 1984), p. 246.

For example, if a hotel manager plotted complaints on a run chart by the day of the week, she might notice that complaints are unusually high on Wednesdays in comparison to other days of the week. The manager could then investigate the cause for this difference—perhaps low staffing or inexperienced personnel—and take the appropriate action to correct the situation.

Statistical process control (SPC) charts are a specialized version of run charts which incorporate statistics which show the mean and measures of variation in a process. Supplement 5S which follows this chapter addresses SPC in detail.

Scatter Diagrams

Scatter diagrams or scatter plots are used to determine whether or not a relationship exists between two variables or product characteristics. For example, a restaurant manager might look at the relationship between customer satisfaction values on a survey and the length of wait prior to being seated at a table.

Cause-and-Effect Diagrams

Cause-and-effect diagrams, first introduced by Kaoru Ishikawa, are also referred to as fishbone diagrams because of their shape. They attempt to identify all of the potential causes for a recurring defect or failure.

First the major causes are identified. Then, for each cause, "Why?" is asked until the root cause for that category can be identified. Consider the example in Exhibit 5.9, a cause-and-effect diagram for customer complaints in a restaurant. If customers complain about the rudeness of the waitstaff, the cause of the rudeness must first be identified before the manager can take the appropriate action. In this example, the servers are rude because they are rushed, and they are rushed because they have been assigned too many tables. Thus the table assignment process should be the focus of the manager's action rather than admonishing the servers to be more polite.

Histograms and Bar Charts

Histograms and bar charts visually display data variation. A bar chart is used to graph nominal data (also referred to as "categorical" or "attribute" data), which are data that can be counted rather than measured. For example, one can count the number of people in a room with brown, blue, or hazel eyes. Similarly, a manufacturing company can count the number

EXHIBIT 5.9

Cause-and-Effect Diagram for Restaurant Customer Complaints

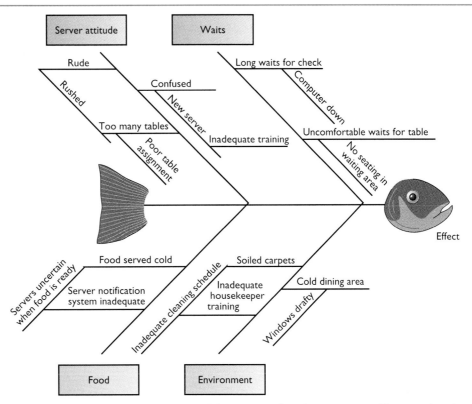

This cause-and-effect diagram demonstrates the search for root causes of complaints in a restaurant. The reason why each cause exists is assessed until the root cause is identified.

 of customers it has in various countries. An example of a bar chart is shown in Exhibit 5.10 which shows the train service regularity for different lines of the London Underground subway system.

Histograms are used to display continuous data: data that can be measured. For example, one can weigh the ounces in different boxes of cereal. The scale for ounces is continuous. Therefore, if we want to show the variation in weight of a number of cereal boxes, we would first have to determine how to divide the ounces scale into appropriate intervals. We could use intervals of one-half ounce, one ounce, or five ounces, depending on how much detail we wanted to show and how much variation in weight there was in our sample. It is important to note here that the histogram interval, once chosen, must remain constant and must not overlap.

Pareto Charts

Pareto charts are specialized bar charts. The frequency of occurrence of items is sorted in descending order and a cumulative percent line is usually added to make it easy to determine how the categories add up. Pareto charts can help to establish priorities for managerial action, focusing attention on those categories of variables that occur most frequently. Exhibit 5.11 shows a Pareto chart in a hotel in the People's Republic of China.

 There are times when frequency of occurrence, however, does not determine the importance of a factor. For example, when making a bar chart of student complaints about the food served at a university, it might be known that complaints about waiting in line are twice as common as complaints about food availability, but that students consider food availability to be five times more important than waiting. The Pareto diagram can weight

EXHIBIT 5.10

Bar Chart Showing
Performance of Different
Subway Lines in London

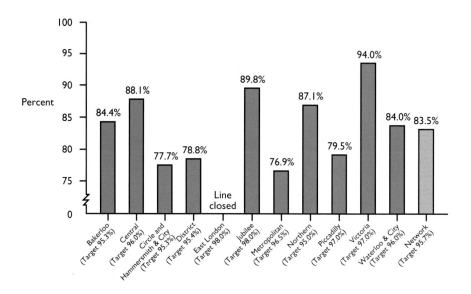

Train Service Regularity
4 weeks ending Friday 19 July 1996

This graph shows how each Underground line and the Underground as a whole performed against its target for service regularity. We measure this by timing the intervals between a sample of the trains we run each weekday. If the time between trains is twice the scheduled interval, this counts as a failure to meet the target.

Information is expressed in percentage terms for comparison, and the Hammersmith & City and Circle line figures are unified because the intervals between trains are measured at the same location.

the factors being considered, which will enable managers to take action on those items that most need attention.

Service Guarantees

Warrantees are common for products such as automobiles, washing machines, and televisions. Such warrantees guarantee that these products will work throughout a stated period of time or else they will either be repaired or replaced free of charge. Less common are guarantees for services. Nevertheless, Christopher Hart has suggested that the service guarantee can be a powerful tool for obtaining feedback from customers on how your operations are performing.

In order for a service guarantee to be effective it must contain the following elements: It must be (*a*) unconditional, (*b*) easy to understand and communicate, (*c*) meaningful, (*d*) easy and painless to invoke, and (*e*) easy and quick to collect on. For example, at FedEx, the service guarantee is simple, if your package is not delivered on time, then there is no charge. At L. L. Bean, a leading mail order firm located in Freeport, Maine, the guarantee is "100 percent satisfaction in every way." If you buy an L. L. Bean product and are not satisfied with it, you can return it for an exchange or a refund, regardless of how long you have owned it.

From a quality standpoint, the unconditional service guarantee provides management with continuous customer feedback. If it is easy to invoke and collect on, then customers will use the service guarantee to voice their complaints rather than just taking their business elsewhere. (See OM in Practice on a Guarantee of Service Excellence.)

EXHIBIT 5.11

Examples of a Cause-and-Effect Diagram and a Histogram in a Hotel in Guangzhou, People's Republic of China

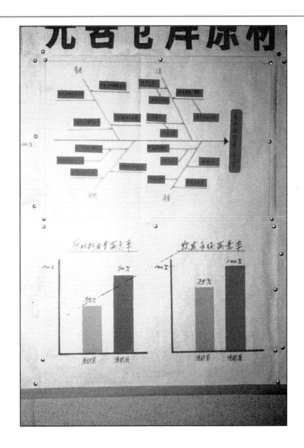

THE MALCOLM BALDRIGE NATIONAL QUALITY AWARD

Background

On August 20, 1987, President Ronald Reagan affixed his signature to Public Law 100–107. This groundbreaking legislation, known commonly as the Malcolm Baldrige National Quality Improvement Act, established the nation's annual award to recognize total quality management in American industry. The Malcolm Baldrige National Quality Award (MBNQA) named after Malcolm Baldrige, who served as secretary of commerce from 1981 until his death in 1987, represents the United States government's endorsement of quality as an essential part of successful business strategy.

Operations Management in Practice

A GUARANTEE OF SERVICE EXCELLENCE (GOSE) PLAYS A MAJOR ROLE IN THE SUCCESS OF NORTHEAST DELTA DENTAL

Northeast Delta Dental, a nonprofit dental insurance company located in Concord, New Hampshire, attributes much of its growth and success in recent years to its Guarantee of Service Excellence (GOSE).

According to Tom Raffio, President of Northeast Delta Dental, having a service guarantee is ". . . like putting water through a hose. You turn on the pressure and you find out where all the holes are. An unconditional service guarantee like GOSE, when properly designed and implemented, quickly identifies all of the flaws that exist in the current system."

The Guarantee of Service Excellence Program at Northeast Delta Dental consists of the following seven elements:

1. Smooth implementation to Northeast Delta Dental.
2. Exceptional customer service.
3. Quick processing of claims.
4. No inappropriate billing by participating dentists.
5. Accurate and quick turnaround of identification cards.
6. Timely employee booklets.
7. Marketing service contacts.

With each element, the guarantee is clearly explained and the customer is refunded a stated amount when the service in that element is not provided—no hassles, no questions asked!

Source: Special thanks to Tom Raffio, President of Northeast Delta Dental.

By establishing a national quality improvement act, Congress sought to encourage greater U.S. competitiveness in global markets through the recognition and commendation of exceptional quality in American business. As an instrument of the U.S. government, the Baldrige Award seeks to improve quality and productivity by:

1. Helping to stimulate American companies to improve quality and productivity for the pride of recognition while obtaining a competitive advantage through decreased costs and increased profits.
2. Establishing guidelines and criteria that can be used by business, industrial, governmental, and other organizations in evaluating their quality improvement efforts.
3. Recognizing the achievements of those companies that improve the quality of their goods and services and thereby provide an example to others.
4. Providing specific guidance for other American organizations that wish to learn how to manage for high quality by making available detailed information on how winning organizations were able to change their cultures and achieve quality eminence.

Without question, the MBNQA and its comprehensive criteria for evaluating total quality in an organization have had considerable impact. Some observers have begun referring to the award as the Nobel Prize for business. As seen in Exhibit 5.12, the MBNQA is awarded in three categories: manufacturing, services, and small business. Beginning in 1995, two additional categories, health care and education, have been undergoing evaluation through a pilot program.

The Baldrige Criteria

To evaluate and recognize effective quality systems, Baldrige administrators created a comprehensive process and set of quality criteria based on the comments and observations

EXHIBIT 5.12

Baldrige Award Winners, by Category

Manufacturing	Service	Small Business
Motorola Inc. (1988)	Federal Express (1990)	Globe Metallurgical Inc.(1988)
Westinghouse Commercial Nuclear Fuel Division (1989)	AT&T Universal Card Services (1992)	Wallace Co. (1990)
Milliken & Co. (1989)	The Ritz-Carlton Hotel (1992)	Marlow Industries (1991)
Xerox Business Products (1989)	AT&T Consumer Communications Services (1994)	Granite Rock Co. (1992)
Cadillac (1990)		Ames Rubber Co. (1993)
IBM Rochester (1990)	GTE Directories Corp. (1994)	Wainwright Industries (1994)
Solectron (1991)	Dana Commercial Credit Corp. (1996)	Custom Research, Inc. (1996)
Zytec Corp. (1991)	Merrill Lynch Credit Corp. (1997)	Trident Precision Manufacturing, Inc. (1996)
AT&T Network Systems Group (1992)	Xerox Business Services (1997)	
Texas Instruments, Inc. (1992)		
Eastman Chemical Company (1993)		
Armstrong Building Products Operation (1995)		
Corning Telecommunication Products Division (1995)		
ADAC Laboratories (1996)		
3M Dental Products Division (1997)		
Solectron (1997)		

Baldrige criteria
Process for assessing the overall quality of an organization and for determining the winner(s) of the Malcolm Baldrige National Quality Award.

of experts from throughout the country. The **Baldrige criteria** consequently reflects the combined experience and wisdom of many people. As a set of principles, it is nondenominational in the sense that it does not favor any one system. Instead, the Baldrige criteria are designed to be flexible, evaluating quality on three broad dimensions: (*a*) the soundness of the approach or systems; (*b*) the deployment or integration of those systems throughout the entire organization; and (*c*) the results generated by those systems (see Exhibit 5.13).

The Baldrige quality criteria focuses on seven broad topical areas that are dynamically related, as seen in Exhibit 5.14 which provides an integrated framework for the Baldrige criteria.

In short, the Baldrige criteria create an integrated set of indicators of excellence and continuity that describes total quality. In the Baldrige view, total quality is a value system. It is a way of life, an approach to doing business that affects every corporate decision and permeates the entire organization.

When a company applies for the Baldrige Award or uses the Baldrige criteria internally to evaluate its quality program, its organization must address 20 subcategories that fall under the seven broad topical areas. Each topical area and subcategory are weighted according to general importance (see Exhibit 5.15).

For evaluation purposes, a maximum of 1,000 points are allocated for the seven Baldrige quality categories. Just as the Japanese stress the importance of both the means and ends when considering quality, the Baldrige criteria tie approximately half their points to the quality process (methods and means) and half to the results (ends and trends). The means or process is a leading indicator of the ends that will be attained. In turn, the results verify that the appropriate process is in place and being used effectively.

EXHIBIT 5.13

Scoring Guidelines for the Malcolm Baldrige National Quality Award

Score	Approach/Deployment
0%	■ No systematic approach evident; anecdotal information
10% to 30%	■ Beginning of a systematic approach to the primary purposes of the item ■ Early stages of a transition from reacting to problems to a general improvement orientation ■ Major gaps exist in deployment that would inhibit progress in achieving the primary purposes of the item
40% to 60%	■ A sound, systematic approach, responsive to the primary purposes of the item ■ A fact-based improvement process in place in key areas; more emphasis is placed on improvement than on reaction to problems ■ No major gaps in deployment, though some areas or work units may be in very early stages of deployment
70% to 90%	■ A sound, systematic approach, responsive to the overall purposes of the item ■ A fact-based improvement process is a key management tool; clear evidence of refinement and improved integration as a result of improvement cycles and analysis ■ Approach is well-deployed, with no major gaps; deployment may vary in some areas or work units
100%	■ A sound, systematic approach, fully responsive to all the requirements of the item ■ A very strong, fact-based improvement process is a key management tool; strong refinement and integration—backed by excellent analysis ■ Approach is fully deployed without any significant weaknesses or gaps in any areas or work units

Score	Results
0%	■ No results or poor results in areas reported
10% to 30%	■ Early stages of developing trends; some improvements and/or early good performance levels in a few areas ■ Results not reported for many to most areas of importance to the applicant's key business requirements
40% to 60%	■ Improvement trends and/or good performance levels reported for many to most areas of importance to the applicant's key business requirements ■ No pattern of adverse trends and/or poor performance levels in areas of importance to the applicant's key business requirements ■ Some trends and/or current performance levels—evaluated against relevant comparisons and/or benchmarks—show areas of strength and/or good to very good relative performance levels
70% to 90%	■ Current performance is good to excellent in most areas of importance to the applicant's key business requirements ■ Most improvement trends and/or performance levels are sustained ■ Many to most trends and/or current performance levels—evaluated against relevant comparisons and/or benchmarks—show areas of leadership and very good relative performance levels
100%	■ Current performance is excellent in most areas of importance to the applicant's key business requirements ■ Excellent improvement trends and/or sustained excellent performance levels in most areas ■ Strong evidence of industry and benchmark leadership demonstrated in many areas

Source: *1997 Criteria for Performance Excellence*, U.S. Dept. of Commerce, National Institute of Standards and Technology.

EXHIBIT 5.14

The Integrated Framework of the Baldrige Award Criteria

BALDRIGE AWARD CRITERIA FRAMEWORK
A Systems Perspective

Source: *1997 Criteria for Performance Excellence,* U.S. Dept. of Commerce, National Institute of Standards and Technology.

EXHIBIT 5.15

1997 Award Criteria—Item Listing

Categories/Items	Points Values
1.0 Leadership	**110**
1.1 Leadership system	80
1.2 Company responsibility and citizenship	30
2.0 Strategic planning	**80**
2.1 Strategy development process	40
2.2 Company strategy	40
3.0 Customer and market focus	**80**
3.1 Customer and market knowledge	40
3.2 Customer satisfaction and relationship enhancement	40
4.0 Information and analysis	**80**
4.1 Selection and use of information and data	25
4.2 Selection and use of comparative information and data	15
4.3 Analysis and review of company performance	40
5.0 Human resource development and management	**100**
5.1 Work systems	40
5.2 Employee education, training, and development	30
5.3 Employee well-being and satisfaction	30
6.0 Process management	**100**
6.1 Management of product and service processes	60
6.2 Management of support processes	20
6.3 Management of supplier and partnering processes	20
7.0 Business results	**450**
7.1 Customer satisfaction results	130
7.2 Financial and market results	130
7.3 Human resource results	35
7.4 Supplier and partner results	25
7.5 Company-specific results	130
Total Points	**1,000**

Source: *1997 Criteria for Performance Excellence,* U.S. Dept. of Commerce, National Institute of Standards and Technology.

Application of the Baldrige Quality Criteria

For companies using them, the Baldrige criteria serve many purposes. Indeed, part of the Baldrige criteria's power lies in the fact that they can be applied in many different ways to organizations whose quality improvement programs are of different maturities.

As a practical tool for assessing operations, the Baldrige guidelines can be used:

1. To help define and design a total quality system.
2. To evaluate ongoing internal relationships among departments, divisions, and functional units within an organization.
3. To assess and assist outside suppliers of goods and services to a company.
4. To assess customer satisfaction.

Early-stage companies can literally use the Baldrige guidelines as a checklist or blueprint to help them design their overall quality programs. Middle-stage companies can use them as a road map to guide them down the road to continued quality improvement. Finally, advanced-stage companies can use them as an evaluative tool to help fine-tune their quality programs and benchmark them against other industry and world leaders.

The Baldrige guidelines also provide a common language for discussing quality across companies, functional areas, industries, and disciplines. By providing a broad, flexible approach to assessing total quality, the Baldrige system fosters improved information sharing and overall communications. These activities, in turn, lead employees and management to develop a shared meaning of total quality that can be built into the organization's goals and policies. From such shared meaning develops an organizational value system that is customer-focused, quality-driven, and central to the culture of the company. So deeply does Motorola believe in the value of total quality control that the company has ordered all 3,500 of its suppliers to apply for the Baldrige Award, as tangible evidence of their commitment to total quality management, or lose Motorola's business.

The role of the Baldrige Award as an instructor of quality is also rapidly growing. The application process compels management and employees:

1. To recognize the far-reaching importance of quality.
2. To examine the organization's total quality progress and current standing.
3. To exchange information between departments, divisions, and organizational levels.

Assimilating the Baldrige view of total quality can also lead to actions with profound long-term consequences. At Baldrige winners such as Globe, Motorola, and Westinghouse's CNFD, quality planning has been elevated to the same level as strategic planning and integrated with it. Indeed, all these organizations have wrought significant cultural and organizational changes to support companywide total quality. (See OM in Practice on Quality Pays.)

Award Process

The Baldrige applications are scored by quality experts from business, consulting, and academia. Of the 1,000 points that can possibly be awarded on the overall application, none of the applicants received more than 751 points in 1994. A good company usually falls in the 500 range on the Baldrige scoring.

Only about 10 percent of the applicants become Baldrige finalists and receive site visits from a team of examiners. From this group of finalists, the Baldrige winners are chosen. All companies applying for the award receive from the examiners written feedback reports summarizing the examiners' findings of the company's organizational strengths and weaknesses.

Operations Management in Practice

QUALITY PAYS

Between 1988, when the Malcolm Baldrige National Quality Awards were first initiated, and 1995, the 16 winners outperformed the Standard and Poor's (S&P) 500 Stock Index by a margin of three to one when using return on investment as the measurement. In addition, the 48 companies who made it to the final round but did not win the award have outperformed the S&P 500 Stock Index by a margin of two to one (see chart).

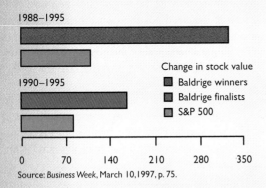

QUALITY PAYS

1988–1995

Change in stock value
- Baldrige winners
- Baldrige finalists
- S&P 500

1990–1995

0   70   140   210   280   350

Source: *Business Week*, March 10, 1997, p. 75.

These gains can be directly attributed to the application of the Baldrige criteria within these companies. For example:

- GTE Directories Corporation (1994 winner) reduced publishing errors by 9 percent between 1991 and 1993 and lowered billing and collection errors by 71 percent.
- Ames Rubber Corporation (1993) reports that by sharing their quality techniques, their suppliers have achieved a 99.9 percent quality and on-time delivery status.
- AT&T Network Transmission Group, Transmission Systems Business Unit (1992) improved customer satisfaction in part by a 15 percent improvement in product reliability.
- The Ritz-Carlton Hotel Company has eliminated $75 million in costs through the initiation of improvement projects.

Source: National Institute of Standards and Technology.

The response to the Baldrige criteria for evaluating total quality has been very positive. The Baldrige guidelines are proving to be useful and inspirational to scores of companies at all different stages of developing and deploying total quality systems. Moreover, the award itself has brought international attention and prestige to a handful of American companies that have clearly demonstrated their preeminent leadership in total quality management.

 The experience of the award's winners suggests that companies throughout the country—indeed, around the world—are deeply interested and concerned about quality. In fact,

EXHIBIT 5.16

Combined Award Applications State and National

Total number of applications

Key
- Baldrige applications
- State applications

Note: 36 state programs in 34 states, 2 of these keep this information confidential.

many of the leading companies in the United States that plan to do business in the European Union (EU) are adopting the Baldrige Award criteria as their vision to be followed beyond the basic requirements of the ISO 9000 standards.

Although the total number of Baldrige applications has decreased in recent years, there has been significant growth in the number of applications at the state level. Between 1991 and 1995, the combined number of applications increased from 216 to 621, as shown in Exhibit 5.16.

ISO 9000

During the 1980s and into the 1990s, organizations around the world became more concerned about efficiently and effectively meeting the needs of their customers. Managers often found the quality literature to be too philosophical and vague about exactly *what* to do to achieve quality and *how* to do it. Though national quality awards like the Deming Prize in Japan and the Malcolm Baldrige National Quality Award in the United States had been bestowed on companies that had achieved high quality in their goods and services, increasing international trade made universal standards for quality more important. However, until 1987, there was no standardized way for supplier organizations around the world to demonstrate their quality practices or to improve the quality of their manufacturing or service processes. In that year, the International Organization for Standardization (ISO) published its first standards for quality management.

The International Organization for Standardization

ISO, headquartered in Geneva, Switzerland, is made up of representatives from each of the national standards bodies from over 90 countries. ISO and the International Electrotechnical Commission (IEC), both nongovernmental organizations, work together to develop and publish voluntary standards, introducing as many as 800 new and revised standards each year. In 1986, after several years of development, ISO Technical Committee 176 completed the **ISO 9000 series quality standards.** It immediately became apparent that the ISO 9000 standards were different from the usual engineering standards, which often related to units of measure, standardization of terminology, and methods of testing. Instead, these new standards incorporated the belief that management practice can be standardized to the benefit of both the producers of goods and services and their customers.

ISO 9000 series quality standards International set of standards for documenting the processes that an organization uses to produce its goods and services.

The ISO 9000/Q90 Series of Standards

The purpose of the ISO 9000/Q90 standards is to satisfy the customer organizations' quality assurance requirements and to increase the level of confidence of the customer organizations in their suppliers. The five ISO standards consist of two guideline standards (ISO 9000 and ISO 9004) and three contractual standards (ISO 9001, ISO 9002, and ISO 9003). The guideline standards provide a framework for managers on how to develop and/or improve their quality processes. ISO 9000 (Q90) provides a broad view of quality management and quality assurance standards, sets guidelines for their selection and use, and explains the philosophy behind the other standards. Basically, it provides a framework for the application of the more specific standards. ISO 9004 (Q94) serves as a primer on quality management, focusing on the specific elements of quality systems.

More and more U.S. companies, especially small to medium sized firms, are obtaining ISO 9000 certification in order to gain a competitive advantage by entry into export markets and can lead to significant cost savings. The certification effort at Canon Virginia was led by calibration supervisor Donna Voshell (left) and quality assurance manager Doug Grossenbaugh. Canon, which is located in Newport News, Virginia, assembles copiers, laser printers, and printer cartridges.

On the other hand, the contractual standards are prescriptive in nature, and are very specific, using terms like "you shall . . .". The most comprehensive of the three contractual standards, ISO 9001 (Q91), is a model for quality assurance in design/development, production, installation, and servicing. ISO 9002 (Q92) focuses on quality assurance in production and installation, and ISO 9003 (Q93) provides a model for quality assurance in final test and inspection.

ISO 9000 standards played a particularly important role in the formation of the European Union because they promoted a single worldwide quality standard which would foster international trade and cooperation. Before long, organizations recognized that service management could also be improved through the application of the fundamentals of management practice that were set forth in the ISO 9000 standards.

ISO 9000 Certification

In the United States, there are three ways an organization can become ISO 9000 certified. A company can audit itself against the appropriate standards and issue a conformance statement to achieve *first-party* certification. Customers can audit their suppliers for *second-party* certification which can mean considerable duplication of effort because most customers will have similar requirements for their suppliers. Companies can also be assessed by *third-party* registrars for ISO 9000 certification.

The Role of the Registrars   The quality processes that are used by firms seeking third-party ISO 9000/Q90 are assessed by an external organization called a registrar; the individuals from the registrar who conduct the assessment are called auditors. To govern the process in the United States, ASQC has established a separate corporation called the Registration Accreditation Board (RAB). In 1991, the ANSI and the RAB signed an agreement establishing the American National Accreditation Program for Registrars of Quality Systems. Its 11 member Board of Directors consists of volunteers, the RAB president, and the ASQC executive director.

Registrars apply to the RAB, which reviews their application information in order to determine if there is a conflict of interest (for example, a consultant organization who has been advising a company on ISO certification cannot be a registrar for that company). Registrars must develop their own Quality Manual (described below) and documentation of the procedures they use to apply their quality policies. The RAB then evaluates the registrar against the criteria for accreditation.

Preparing for ISO 9000/Q90 Registration   Preparing for ISO 9000 registration generally requires developing documentation of the organization's quality practices and how they relate to ISO standards. The *Quality Manual* addresses the company's entire quality system. It is written at a very general level and tends to be fairly brief (20–40 pages). *Procedures* must also be documented, describing the process flows for addressing each of the ISO standards. *Work instructions* consist of the steps that must be followed to get the work done. These may already exist within the applicant's organization as "standard operating procedures." Finally, *forms and records* must be provided to demonstrate that the company is complying with its own stated quality procedures.

The ISO 9000/Q90 Registration Process   Supplier companies follow a fairly straightforward process to obtain ISO 9000/Q90 registration. First, the firm submits an application to a registrar. Generally this involves providing information about the size and locations of the company, its products, what products will be included in the scope of the registration, who the firm's ISO contact people will be, and how the 20 elements of the standard are documented and supported by procedures. The registrar reviews the Quality Manual prior to the on-site audit.

The next step in the audit is a preliminary assessment, which can either be an on-site document review or a mock audit lasting several days. The preliminary assessment determines the current state of operations at the supplier firm. The registrar provides feedback to the supplier firm and suggestions for corrective action. When the issues of concern have been addressed, a full audit is performed.

The full audit typically takes two or three auditors two to four days to complete. Auditors review the supplier's facility and determine how processes have been documented. The auditor's final report is submitted to the registrar's Review Board, which makes a final determination about registration. If a supplier is not approved for registration, it has the right to appeal, first to the registrar, then to the RAB. Once a supplier firm has been registered, it has the right to use its registrar's mark on stationary and advertising, along with the mark of the RAB. However, it may not use these marks on its products because ISO 9000 registration certifies processes rather than products.

Registration audits cost between $10,000 and $30,000. Companies will typically take 18–24 months to prepare for and undergo the registration process. Some companies undertake the registration process on their own; others engage outside consultants. The usual registration period is three years, although this can vary by registrar. During the registration period, surveillance audits are conducted every six months.

 ## Toward a Global Market

The ISO 9000 standards have been important in facilitating the formation of the European Union and of the development of worldwide markets. Today, over 40,000 companies are ISO certified, with the vast majority of them located within the 12 nations that currently comprise the European Union. When customer organizations have an objective way to evaluate the quality of a supplier's processes, the risk of doing business with that supplier is significantly reduced. When quality standards are truly standardized around the world, customer firms can be more confident that supplier firms will produce the goods and services that will satisfy their needs.

CONCLUSION

The production and delivery of high-quality goods and services are critical elements in determining the success of an organization. No longer is quality relegated to a passive, defensive role; rather, quality now contributes offensively as a strategic weapon in defining market niches. Total quality management (TQM) consists of four integral components, all of which are necessary for a TQM program to succeed. High quality is not more expensive; in fact, just the reverse is true. High quality is cost effective, especially when emphasis is placed on preventing defects from occurring in the first place.

EXHIBIT 5.17

Three Schools of Total Quality Management Programs

	Total Quality Harangue	Total Quality Tools	Total Quality Integration
Noticeable characteristics	Exhortation, lots of talk about quality; generally a marketing campaign intended to create buying signals without incurring the expense of fundamental changes	Introduction of specific tools; viz, statistical process control, employee involvement programs, and/or quality circles	Serious review of all elements of the organization; efforts to involve suppliers and customers
Rationale	Management may believe that quality is better than generally known or may be creating a smoke screen; viz, "everybody's doing it," "it's the thing to do these days"	Valued customers insist on implementation of a team program; or competitors have introduced successful programs creating a "bandwagon" effect	Systematic effort to improve earnings through differentiation based on quality
Responsibility for quality	Unchanged; specific function within organization assigned responsibility for quality	Lower-level members of organization regardless of function	Shared responsibility, senior management accepts responsibility to create an environment encouraging quality
Structural changes	None; the organization remains unchanged	Incremental changes within functional areas or processes	Dramatic changes integrating functions within the organization and involving customers and suppliers in the total production process
Representative employee attitudes and behaviors	Total quality is just a fad, "this too shall pass"; smart employees learn to keep their heads down, they talk about quality when expected to but know that business continues as usual	"It's a nice idea, too bad management isn't really serious about quality"; clever employees participate in seminars and use appropriate tools to fix obvious flaws in their areas of responsibility, but are careful not to rock the boat	"At last, we've got a chance to do it right"; committed employees study the total quality vision, actively search for opportunities to improve performance across the organization, challenge conventional assumptions, and seek to involve customers and suppliers
Role of the quality professional	Police officer, watchdog	Resident expert, advisor	Strategic leaders, change agent

Source: Eric W. Skopec, Strategic Visions Inc. (used by permission).

Thus, quality management as a strategic issue should not be approached with an off-the-shelf program devised by others. Quality must be integrated internally and externally (see Exhibit 5.17). Managers are paid to use new concepts, but more important, to lead customization and integration of these concepts into their organizations.

KEY TERMS

Baldrige criteria   p. 153
conformance quality   p. 140
continuous improvement   p. 139
cost of quality   p. 144
cost of prevention   p. 144
cost of detection/appraisal   p. 145
cost of failure   p. 145
  internal failure costs   p. 145
  external failure costs   p. 145
design quality   p. 140

house of quality   p. 137
ISO 9000 series quality standards   p. 158
poka-yoke   p. 140
quality dimensions   p. 135
quality function deployment (QFD)   p. 137
quality gurus   p. 140
seven basic quality control tools   p. 146
statistical process control (SPC)   p. 142
total quality management (TQM)   p. 134
voice of the customer   p. 137

REVIEW AND DISCUSSION QUESTIONS

1. Is quality free? Debate!
2. Identify the quality dimensions for each of the following:
   a. IBM personal computer
   b. School registration process
   c. Steakhouse
   d. University
   e. Travel agency
   f. Television
3. An agreement is made between a supplier and a customer such that the supplier must ensure that all parts are within tolerance before shipment to the customer. What is the effect on the cost of quality to the customer?
4. In the situation described in Question 3, what would be the effect on the cost of quality to the supplier?
5. If line employees are required to assume the quality control function, their productivity will decrease. Discuss this.
6. "You don't inspect quality into a product; you have to build it in." Discuss the implications of this statement.
7. How could you apply the Baldrige Award criteria to your college or university?
8. How is the Baldrige award process beneficial to companies who do not win?
9. What is the major contribution of the ISO 9000 standards?
10. Compare the ISO certification process with the Malcolm Baldrige National Quality Award criteria. What are the main differences?

INTERNET UPDATE

a. Conduct a search on the Web to identify the various ways in which companies are applying TQM to improve the quality of the products that they make. Suggested key words are MANUFACTURING and TQM.
b. Referring to Exhibit 5.12, which lists the annual winners of the Malcolm Baldrige National Quality Award (MBNQA), find the homepage of at least one winner and describe in detail its operations.

c. Using ISO 9000 and CERTIFICATION as key words, identify two firms that provide ISO 9000 certification and describe their certification process in detail.

PROBLEMS

1. A company currently using an inspection process in its material receiving department is trying to install an overall cost reduction program. One possible reduction is the elimination of one of the inspection positions. This position tests material that has a defect rate on the average of 4 percent. By inspecting all items, the inspector is able to remove all defects. The inspector can inspect 50 units per hour. The hourly rate, including fringe benefits, for this position is $9. If the inspection position is eliminated, defects will go into product assembly and will have to be replaced later at a cost of $10 each when they are detected in final product testing.

   a. Should this inspection position be eliminated?

   b. What is the cost to inspect each unit?

   c. Is there benefit (or loss) from the current inspection process? How much?

2. You have just returned from a trip to New York City where you stayed at a first-class hotel. After spending $250 per night for the room plus an additional $35 per night to park your car, you are very unhappy with the level of service you received during your stay at this hotel.

   a. Draw a fishbone diagram identifying the major causes for your dissatisfaction and possible secondary causes within each of these categories (do not include price).

   b. You call the hotel to voice your complaint and the manager asks you if you would be willing to collect some data for her so she can get at the root cause of the problem. You collect the following data on 100 complaints:

Cause (Select from part *a*)	Frequency
1. _____	16
2. _____	11
3. _____	27
4. _____	42
5. _____	4

   c. Draw a Pareto diagram for the above data, labeling the axes appropriately. How does this information assist the manager in improving the service quality of her operation?

3. You have just returned from an airline trip to California and are very unhappy with your onboard experience.

   a. Draw a fishbone diagram identifying the different possible primary causes (within each of these categories) for your dissatisfaction with your trip. Also identify several possible secondary causes.

   b. You call the airline to voice your complaint and the manager asks you if you will collect some data for him so that he can get at the root cause of the problem. You collect the following data on 100 complaints:

Cause (Select from part *a*)	Frequency
1. _____	6
2. _____	22
3. _____	14
4. _____	43
5. _____	10
6. _____	5

c. Draw a Pareto diagram for the above data, labeling the axes appropriately. How does this information assist the manager in improving the service quality of his operation?

4. The following is a partial house of quality for a golf facility. Provide an importance weighting from your perspective (or that of a golfing friend) in the unshaded areas. If you can, compare it to a club where you or your friend plays using the QFD approach.

WHATs versus HOWs — Strong relationship: ● / Medium relationship: ○ / Weak relationship: △	Physical aspects	Course location	Ground maintenance	Landscaping	Pin placement	Course tuning	Tee placement	Service facilities	Customer-trained attendants	Top quality food	Highly rated chefs	Attractive restaurant	Tournament activities	Calloway handicapping	Exciting door prizes	Perception issues	Invitation only	Types of guests	Income level	Celebrity
Physical aspects																				
Manicured grounds																				
Easy access																				
Challenging																				
Service facilities																				
Restaurant facilities																				
Good food																				
Good service																				
Good layout																				
Plush locker room																				
Helpful service attendant																				
Tournament facilities																				
Good tournament prize																				
Types of players																				
Fair handicapping system																				
Perception issues																				
Prestigious																				

CASE: SHORTENING CUSTOMERS' TELEPHONE WAITING TIME

This case illustrates how a bank applied some of the basic seven quality tools shown in Exhibit 5.7 and storyboard concepts to improve customer service. It is the story of a QC program implemented in the main office of a large bank. An average of 500 customers call this office every day. Surveys indicated that callers tended to become irritated if the phone rang more than five times before it was answered, and often would not call the company again. In contrast, a prompt answer after just two rings reassured the customers and made them feel more comfortable doing business by phone.

Selection of a Theme

Telephone reception was chosen as a QC theme for the following reasons: (a) Telephone reception is the first impression a customer receives from the company, (b) this theme coincided with the company's telephone reception slogan, "Don't make customers wait, and avoid needless switching from extension to extension," and (c) it also coincided with a companywide campaign being promoted at that time which advocated being friendly to everyone one met.

First, the staff discussed why the present method of answering calls made callers wait. Case Exhibit C5.1 illustrates a frequent situation, where a call from customer B comes in while the operator is talking with customer A. Let's see why the customer has to wait.

At (1), the operator receives a call from the customer but, due to lack of experience, does not know where to connect the call. At (2), the receiving party cannot answer the phone quickly, perhaps because he or she is unavailable, and no one else can take the call. The result is that the operator must transfer the call to another extension while apologizing for the delay.

Cause-and-Effect Diagram and Situation Analysis

To fully understand the situation, the quality circle members decided to conduct a survey regarding callers who waited for more than five rings. Circle members itemized factors at a brainstorming discussion and arranged them in a cause-and-effect diagram. (See Exhibit C5.2.) Operators then kept checksheets on several points to tally the results spanning 12 days from June 4 to 16. (See Exhibit C5.3A.)

Results of the Checksheet Situation Analysis

The data recorded on the checksheets unexpectedly revealed that "one operator (partner out of the office)" topped the list by a big margin, occurring a total of 172 times. In this case, the operator on duty had to deal with large numbers of calls when the phones were busy. Customers who had to wait a long time averaged 29.2 daily, which accounted for 6 percent of the calls received every day. (See Exhibits C5.3B and C5.3C.)

Setting the Target

After an intense but productive discussion, the staff decided to set a QC program goal of reducing the number of waiting callers to zero. That is to say that all incoming calls would be handled promptly, without inconveniencing the customer.

Measures and Execution

(a) Taking Lunches on Three Different Shifts, Leaving at Least Two Operators on the Job at All Times: Up until this resolution was made, a two-shift lunch system had been employed, leaving only one operator on the job while the other was taking a lunch break. However, since the survey revealed that this was a major cause of customers waiting on the line, the company brought in a helper operator from the clerical section.

(b) Asking All Employees to Leave Messages When Leaving Their Desks: The objective of this rule was to simplify the operator's chores when the receiving party was not at his desk. The new program was explained at the employees' regular morning meetings, and companywide support was requested. To help implement this practice, posters were placed around the office to publicize the new measures.

(c) Compiling a Directory Listing the Personnel and Their Respective Jobs: The notebook was specially designed to aid the operators, who could not be expected to know the details of every employee's job or where to connect her incoming calls.

Confirming the Results

Although the waiting calls could not be reduced to zero, all items presented showed a marked improvement as shown in Exhibits C5.4A and C5.4B. The major cause of delays, "one operator (partner out of the office)," plummeted from 172 incidents during the control period to 15 in the follow-up survey.

Source: From "The Quest for Higher Quality—the Deming Prize and Quality Control," Ricoh Company, Ltd., in Masaaki Imai, *Kaizen: The Key to Japan's Competitive Success* (New York: The McGraw-Hill Companies, 1986), pp. 54–58.

EXHIBIT C5.1

Why Customers Had to Wait

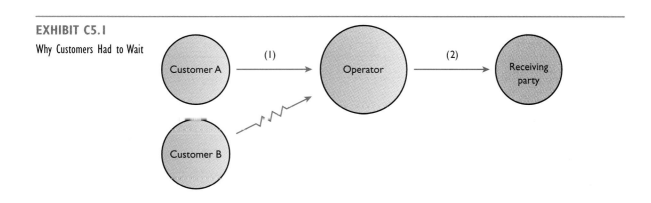

EXHIBIT C5.2

Cause-and-Effect Diagram

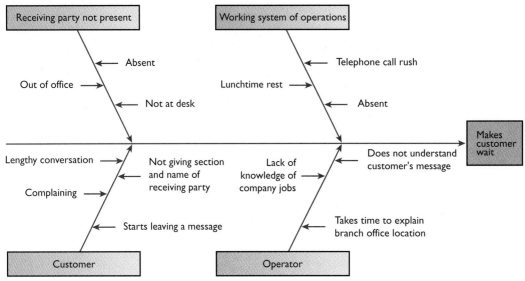

EXHIBIT C5.3

Causes of Callers' Waits

A. Checksheet—Designed to Identify the Problems

Reason / Date	No one present in the section receiving the call	Receiving party not present	Only one operator (partner out of the office)	Total
June 4	\\\\\	⊬⊬⊤ \	⊬⊬⊤ ⊬⊬⊤ \	24
June 5	⊬⊬⊤	⊬⊬⊤ \\\	⊬⊬⊤ ⊬⊬⊤ \\\\	32
June 6	⊬⊬⊤ \	\\\\	⊬⊬⊤ ⊬⊬⊤ \\	28
June 15	⊬⊬⊤	⊬⊬⊤	⊬⊬⊤ \\\	25

B. Reasons Why Callers Had to Wait

		Daily average	Total number
A	One operator (partner out of the office)	14.3	172
B	Receiving party not present	6.1	73
C	No one present in the section receiving the call	5.1	61
D	Section and name of receiving party not given	1.6	19
E	Inquiry about branch office locations	1.3	16
F	Other reasons	0.8	10
	Total	29.2	351

Period: 12 days from June 4 to 16, 1980

C. Reasons Why Callers Had to Wait (Pareto Diagram)

EXHIBIT C5.4

Effects of QC

A. Effects of QC (Comparison Before and After QC)

	Reasons why callers had to wait	Total number		Daily average	
		Before	After	Before	After
A	One operator (partner out of the office)	172	15	14.3	1.2
B	Receiving party not present	73	17	6.1	1.4
C	No one present in the section receiving the call	61	20	5.1	1.7
D	Section and name of receiving not given	19	4	1.6	0.3
E	Inquiry about branch office locations	16	3	1.3	0.2
F	Others	10	0	0.8	0
	Total	351	59	29.2	4.8

Period: 12 days from Aug. 17 to 30.

Problems are classified according to cause and presented in order of the amount of time consumed. They are illustrated in a bar graph. 100% indicates the total number of time-consuming calls.

B. Effects of QC (Pareto Diagram)

Selected Bibliography

Berry, L. L.; V. A. Zeithaml; and A. Parasuraman. "Five Imperatives for Improving Service Quality." *Sloan Management Review,* no. 29 (Summer 1990), pp. 29–38.

Bounds, Greg; Lyle Yorks; Mel Adams; and Gipsie Rannet. *Total Quality Management: Towards the Emerging Paradigm.* New York: McGraw-Hill, Inc., 1994.

Crosby, Philip B. *Quality Is Free.* New York: McGraw-Hill, Inc., 1979.

Crosby, Philip B. *Quality Without Tears.* New York: McGraw-Hill, Inc., 1984.

Deming, W. Edwards. *Quality, Productivity and Competitive Position.* Cambridge, MA: MIT Center for Advanced Engineering Study, 1982.

Feigenbaum, A. V. *Total Quality Control.* 3rd ed. New York: McGraw-Hill, 1983.

Garvin, David. "Competing on the Eight Dimensions of Quality." *Harvard Business Review,* November–December 1987, pp. 101–109.

Gitlow, Howard; Allan Oppenheim; and Rosa Oppenheim. *Quality Management: Tools and Methods for Improvement.* 2nd ed. Burr Ridge, IL: Irwin/McGraw-Hill, 1995.

Goetsch, David L., and Stanley B. Davis. *Introduction to Total Quality: Quality Management for Production, Processes and Services.* 2nd ed. Upper Saddle River, NJ: Prentice Hall, 1997.

Hart, Christopher W. L. "The Power of Unconditional Service Guarantees." *Harvard Business Review,* July–August 1988, pp. 54–62.

Huyink, David S., and Craig Westover. *ISO 9000: Motivating the People; Mastering the Process; Achieving Registration!* Burr Ridge, IL: Irwin Professional Publishing, 1994.

Ishikawa, Kaoru. Translated by David J. Lu. *What Is Total Quality Control?—The Japanese Way.* Englewood Cliffs, NJ: Prentice Hall, 1985.

Juran, Joseph M. *Juran on Quality by Design: The New Steps for Planning Quality in Goods and Services.* New York: The Free Press, 1992.

March, A. "A Note on Quality: The Views of Deming, Juran and Crosby." Note No. 9-687-011. ICCH, Harvard Business School, Cambridge, MA, 1986.

Oakland, John S. *Total Quality Control.* London: Heinemann, 1989.

Parasuraman, A.; L. L. Berry; and V. A. Zeithaml. "SERVQUAL: A Multiple-Item Scale for Measuring Consumer Perceptions of Service Quality." Marketing Science Institute, Cambridge, MA, 1986.

Parasuraman, A; L. L. Berry; and V. A. Zeithaml. "Understanding, Measuring, and Improving Service Quality: Findings From a Multiphase Research Program." *Service Breakthroughs: Changing the Rules of the Game.* New York: The Free Press, 1989.

Peters, Tom. *Thriving on Chaos.* New York: Knopf, 1987.

————. and Robert H. Waterman, Jr. *In Search of Excellence.* New York: Harper and Row, 1982.

Rabbitt, John T., and Peter A. Bergh. *The ISO 9000 Book: A Global Competitor's Guide to Compliance and Certification.* 2nd ed. White Plains, NY: Quality Resources, a Division of The Kraus Organization Limited, 1994.

Reichhold, F. F., and W. E. Sasser. "Zero Defections: Quality Comes to Services." *Harvard Business Review* 68, no. 5 (September–October 1990), pp. 105–11.

Rao, Ashok; L. P. Carr et al. *Total Quality Management: A Cross Functional Perspective.* New York: John Wiley & Sons, Inc., 1996.

Ross, Joel E. *Total Quality Management: Text, Cases and Readings.* Delray Beach, FL: St. Lucie Press, 1993.

Taguchi, G. *On-Line Quality Control During Production.* Tokyo: Japanese Standards Association, 1987.

Tenner, A. R., and I. J. DeToro. *Total Quality Management.* Reading, MA: Addison-Wesley, 1992.

Turner, Joseph. "Is an Out-of-Spec Product Really Out of Spec?" *Quality Progress.* December 1990, pp. 57–59.

Walton, Mary. *Deming Management at Work,* New York: Perigree Books, 1991.

Zeithaml, V. A.; L. L. Berry; and A. Parasuraman. "Communication and Control Processes in the Delivery of Service Quality." *Journal of Marketing* 52, (April 1988), pp. 35–48.

STATISTICAL QUALITY CONTROL METHODS

5

Supplement Objectives

- Provide a brief history of the introduction of statistical methods into companies for the purpose of monitoring and improving the quality of goods and services.

- Define the two different types of sampling errors that can occur when statistical sampling is used.

- Distinguish between attributes and variables with respect to statistical quality control.

- Introduce the concept of acceptance sampling and how it is applied in industry.

- Introduce the concept of statistical process control and how it is applied in industry.

- Discuss Taguchi methods and how they are different from traditional statistical quality control methods.

There are two major reasons why we use statistical quality methods. As discovered during World War II, testing and/or inspecting a sample rather than the entire population of items is both faster and more economical because it requires significantly less labor. In addition, for certain products and for certain types of tests, the product must be destroyed when it is tested. Examples of products that fall into this category include bullets and flashbulbs. An example of destructive testing is the crash testing of automobiles to assess the damage to the passenger compartment. In both of these situations it would never make sense to conduct 100 percent testing.

Statistical quality methods can be divided into two broad categories: (*a*) acceptance sampling which assesses the quality of products that have already been produced and (*b*) statistical process control which assesses whether or not a process is performing within established limits. The mathematical calculations are the same for each category. The interpretation of the results, however, varies as we shall see later in this chapter.

ATTRIBUTES AND VARIABLES

types of data:
attribute data
Data which count items, such as the number of defective items on a sample.

variable data
Data which measure a particular product characteristic such as length or weight.

The application of statistical quality control methods can be further divided into two additional categories: the first approach uses **attribute data** (that is, data which are counted, such as the number of defective parts produced or the number of dissatisfied customers); the second approach uses **variable data** (that is, data which are measured, such as the length of a wire or the weight of a package of cereal). Each approach can be used in either acceptance sampling or in statistical process control, as shown in Exhibit S5.1.

EXHIBIT S5.1

Statistical Quality Control Methods

EXHIBIT S5.2

Types of Sampling Errors

	The population or process is actually:	
	Good or in control	Bad or out of control
The sample says that the population or process is: Good or in control	In agreement	β or Type II error
Bad or out of control	α or Type I error	In agreement

SAMPLING ERRORS

types of sampling errors:

α error, Type I error, or producer's risk Occurs when a sample says parts are bad or the process is out of control when the opposite is true.

β error, Type II error, or consumer's risk Occurs when a sample says parts are good or the process is in control when just the reverse is true.

When we use a sample from a larger population or from the output generated by a process instead of monitoring the entire population or output, there is the possibility that the sample results are not representative of the actual population or process. When this occurs, we have a sampling error. There are two types of sampling errors that can occur, as shown in Exhibit S5.2. The first occurs when the population is considered bad or the process is considered out of control, when neither is the case. This type of error is referred to as an **α error, Type I error, or producer's risk.** The second type of sampling error occurs when the population is considered good or the process is considered in control, when they really are not. This type of error is referred to as a **β error, Type II error, or consumer's risk.** Balancing the risk of occurrence between the Type I and Type II errors is a major consideration in determining the sample size and the control limits.

ACCEPTANCE SAMPLING

Designing a Sampling Plan for Attributes

Acceptance sampling, as previously stated, is performed on goods that already exist to determine if they conform to specifications. These products may be items received from another company and evaluated by the receiving department or they may be components that have passed through a processing step and are evaluated by company personnel either in production or later in the warehousing function. Whether inspection should be done at all is addressed in the following example.

Acceptance sampling is executed through a sampling plan. In this section, we illustrate the planning procedures, with respect to attributes, for a single sampling plan—that is, a plan in which the quality is determined from the evaluation of one sample. (Other plans may be developed using two or more samples. See J. M. Juran and F. M. Gryna's *Quality Planning and Analysis* for a discussion of these plans.)

An employee inspects the manufacture of Reese's peanut butter cups. This is the last stage of full quality control where defective cups are removed.

Costs to Justify Inspection   Total or 100 percent inspection is justified when the cost of a loss incurred by not inspecting is greater than the cost of inspection. For example, suppose a faulty item results in a $10 loss. If the average percentage of defective items in a lot is 3 percent, the expected cost of faulty items is $0.03 \times \$10$, or $0.30 each. Therefore, if the cost of inspecting each item is less than $0.30, the economic decision is to perform 100 percent inspection. Not all defective items will be removed, however, since inspectors will pass some bad items and reject some good ones.

The purposes of a sampling plan are to test the lot to either (a) find its quality or (b) ensure that the quality is what it is supposed to be. Thus, if a quality control supervisor already knows the quality (such as the 0.03 given in the example), he or she does not sample for defects. Either all of the items must be inspected to remove the defects or none of them should be inspected, and the rejects pass into the process. The choice simply depends on the cost to inspect and the cost incurred by passing a reject.

A single sampling plan when we are looking at attributes is defined by n and c, where n is the number of units in the sample and c is the acceptance number. The size of n may vary from one to all the items in the lot (usually denoted as N) from which it is drawn. The acceptance number c denotes the maximum number of defective items that can be found in the sample before the lot is rejected. Values for n and c are determined by the interaction of four factors (AQL, α, LTPD, and β) that quantify the objectives of the product's producer and its consumer. The objective of the producer is to ensure that the sampling plan has a low probability of rejecting good lots. Lots are defined as good if they contain no more than a specified level of defectives, termed the **acceptable quality level (AQL).**[1] The objective of the consumer is to ensure that the sampling plan has a low probability of accepting bad lots. Lots are defined as bad if the percentage of defectives is greater than a specified amount, termed *lot tolerance percent defective* (LTPD). As presented earlier, the probability associated with rejecting a good lot is denoted by the Greek letter alpha (α) and is termed the *producer's risk*. The probability associated with accepting a bad lot is denoted by the Greek letter beta (β) and is termed the *consumer's risk*. The selection of particular values for AQL, α, LTPD, and β) is an economic decision based on a cost trade-off or, more typically, on company policy or contractual requirements.

There is a humorous story supposedly about Hewlett-Packard during its first dealings with Japanese vendors, who place great emphasis on high-quality production. HP had insisted on 2 percent AQL in a purchase of 100 cables. During the purchase agreement some heated discussion took place wherein the Japanese vendor did not want this AQL specification; HP insisted that they would not budge from the 2 percent AQL. The Japanese vendor finally agreed. Later, when the box arrived, there were two packages inside. One contained 100 good cables. The other package had 2 cables with a note stating: "We have sent you 100 good cables. Since you insisted on 2 percent AQL, we have enclosed 2 defective cables in this package, though we do not understand why you want them."

The following example, using an excerpt from a standard acceptance sampling table, illustrates how the four parameters—AQL, α, LTPD, and β—are used in developing a sampling plan.

acceptable quality level (AQL)
Maximum percentage of defects that a company is willing to accept.

---

[1]There is some controversy surrounding AQLs, based on the argument that specifying some acceptable percent of defectives is inconsistent with the philosophical goal of zero defects. In practice, even in the best companies, there is an acceptable quality level. The difference is that it may be stated in parts per million rather than in parts per hundred. This is the case in Motorola's six-sigma quality standard which holds that no more than 3.4 defects per million parts are acceptable.

EXHIBIT S5.3

Excerpt from a Sampling Plan Table for $\alpha = 0.05$, $\beta = 0.10$

c	LTPD ÷ AQL	n • AQL	c	LTPD ÷ AQL	n • AQL
0	44.890	0.052	5	3.549	2.613
1	10.946	0.355	6	3.206	3.286
2	6.509	0.818	7	2.957	3.981
3	4.890	1.366	8	2.768	4.695
4	4.057	1.970	9	2.618	5.426

Example

Values of n and c: Hi-Tech Industries manufactures Z-Band radar scanners used to detect speed traps. The printed circuit boards in the scanners are purchased from an outside vendor. The vendor produces the boards to an AQL of 2 percent defectives and is willing to run a 5 percent risk (α) of having lots of this level or fewer defectives rejected. Hi-Tech considers lots of 8 percent or more defectives (LTPD) unacceptable and wants to ensure that it will accept such poor-quality lots no more than 10 percent of the time (β). A large shipment has just been delivered. What values of n and c should be selected to determine the quality of this lot?

Solution

The parameters of the problem are AQL = 0.02, $\alpha = 0.05$, LTPD = 0.08, and $\beta = 0.10$. We can use Exhibit S5.3 to find c and n.

First divide LTPD by AQL ($0.08 \div 0.02 = 4$). Then find the ratio in column 2 that is equal to or just greater than that amount (i.e., 4). This value is 4.057, which is associated with $c = 4$.

Finally, find the value in column 3 that is in the same row as $c = 4$ and divide that quantity by AQL to obtain n ($1.970 \div 0.02 = 98.5$).

The appropriate sampling plan is $c = 4$, $n = 99$.

Operating Characteristic Curves

operating characteristic (OC) curves
Curves which show the probability of accepting lots that contain different percent defectives.

While a sampling plan such as the one just described meets our requirements for the extreme values of good and bad quality, we cannot readily determine how well the plan discriminates between good and bad lots at intermediate values. For this reason, sampling plans are generally displayed graphically through the use of **operating characteristic (OC) curves**. These curves, which are unique for each combination of n and c, simply illustrate the probability of accepting lots with varying percent defectives. The procedure we have followed in developing the plan, in fact, specifies two points on an OC curve—one point defined by AQL and $1 - \alpha$, and the other point defined by LTPD and β. Curves for common values of n and c can be computed or obtained from available tables.[2] (See Exhibit S5.4.)

A sampling plan discriminating perfectly between good and bad lots has an infinite slope (vertical) at the selected value of AQL. In Exhibit S5.4, percent defectives to the left of 2 percent would always be accepted and to the right, always rejected. However, such a curve is possible only with complete inspection of all units and thus is not a possibility with a true sampling plan.

---

[2]See, for example, H. F. Dodge and H. G. Romig, *Sampling Inspection Tables—Single and Double Sampling* (New York: John Wiley & Sons, 1959), and *Military Standard Sampling Procedures and Tables for Inspection by Attributes* (MIL-STD-105D) (Washington, DC: U.S. Government Printing Office, 1983).

EXHIBIT S5.4

Operating Characteristic Curve for AQL = 0.02, $\alpha = 0.05$, LTPD = 0.08, $\beta = 0.10$

An OC curve should be steep in the region of most interest (between the AQL and the LTPD), which is accomplished by varying n and c. If c remains constant, increasing the sample size n causes the OC curve to be more vertical. While holding n constant, decreasing c (the maximum number of defective units) also makes the slope more vertical, moving closer to the origin.

The size of the lot that the sample is taken from has relatively little effect on the quality of protection. Consider, for example, that samples—all of the same size of 20 units—are taken from different lots ranging from a lot size of 200 units to a lot size of infinity. If each lot is known to have 5 percent defectives, the probability of accepting the lot based on the sample of 20 units ranges from about 0.34 to about 0.36. This means that so long as the lot size is several times the sample size, it makes little difference how large the lot is. It seems a bit difficult to accept, but statistically (on the average in the long run) whether we have a carload or box full, we'll get about the same answer. It just seems that a carload should have a larger sample size.

Designing a Sampling Plan for Variables

When we use variables to determine if we should accept an entire lot, we again take a sample of the items. However, instead of counting the number of defectives in the sample, we measure the variable of interest for each item in the sample and compute the mean for the sample. We then compare the mean of the sample with **control limits** that have been previously established to determine whether or not we accept the entire lot.

control limits
Points on an acceptance sampling chart that distinguish the accept and reject region(s). Also, points on a process control chart that distinguish between a process being in and out of control.

There are three factors that must be taken into consideration in designing a sampling plan for an item where variables are used as the criterion for acceptance. These are: (*a*) the probability of rejecting a lot that is actually good (that is, committing an α error), (*b*) the probability of accepting a lot that is actually bad (that is, committing a β error), and (*c*) the sample size, n.

Example

ABC Electronics Company buys a 50-ohm resistor from an outside vendor. (A resistor is an electrical component used in electrical circuits to retard current. An ohm is the measure of how much a resistor retards the current.) From historical data, the standard deviation for this resistor is 3 ohms. Determine the appropriate control limits if we use a sample size of $n = 100$ and we want to be 95 percent confident that the sample results are truly representative of the total population. (In other words, the probability of committing an α error is $1 - 0.95$ or 5 percent.)

Solution

The equation for determining the control limits (CL) is:

$$CL = \mu \pm z_{\alpha/2} \frac{\sigma}{\sqrt{n}} \qquad (S5.1)$$

where

$\mu =$ The desired mean of the population.

$z_{\alpha/2} =$ The number of standard deviations from the mean that corresponds to the given level of α. ($\alpha/2$ indicates that this is a two-tail test and that the α error is equally divided between the two tails of the distribution.) The value of z is obtained from the normal distribution table in Appendix B or C at the end of this book. (As noted in the table, the z-value for a two-tailed test with 95 percent confidence is 1.96.)

$\sigma =$ The value of the population's standard deviation.

Substituting we have:

$$CL = 50 \pm 1.96 \frac{(3)}{\sqrt{100}}$$
$$= 50 \pm 0.588$$

The lower control limit (LCL) is therefore 49.412 and the upper control limit (UCL) is 50.588, as shown in Exhibit S5.5.

The inspection procedure for this resistor therefore is to (a) take a random sample of 100 resistors, (b) measure the number of ohms in each resistor in the sample, (c) compute the mean of the sample, and finally (d) compare the sample mean with the established control limits; in other words, if the sample mean falls within the range of 49.412–50.588, then the lot is accepted, otherwise the lot is rejected.

EXHIBIT S5.5

Establishing Control Limits for Acceptance Sampling Using Variables

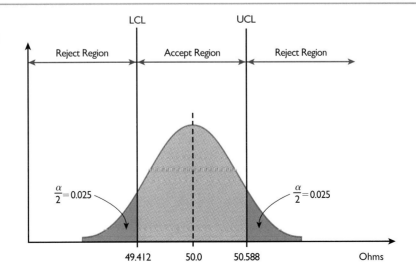

Example   Continuing with the resistor problem, we can tolerate some variation in the number of ohms in each resistor. However, if the number of ohms falls below 49, then we would have a serious problem in our electrical circuit. What is the probability of us accepting a lot when the average resistance is 49 ohms or less?

Solution   This situation is depicted in Exhibit S5.6. It is important to note that the control limits that were previously established do not change. The probability of accepting a bad lot or committing a β error is defined by that percentage of the area under the curve with a mean of 49 that falls within the acceptance range. (Note that this is a one-tailed test because the β error occurs only in the right tail under the curve.)

The probability of committing this error is determined as follows:

$$LCL = \mu + z_\beta \frac{\sigma}{\sqrt{n}}$$

where

$z_\beta =$ The number of standard deviations from the mean that corresponds to the given level of β.

Substituting, we have:

$$49.412 = 49 + z_\beta \frac{(3)}{\sqrt{100}}$$

$$0.412 = (z_\beta)0.3$$

$$z_\beta = 1.373$$

Again, using the normal distribution table at the end of this book, we look up the value of $z = 1.373$ and find the corresponding area under the curve of 0.0853. Thus the probability of committing a β error under these conditions is 8.53 percent.

EXHIBIT S5.6

Determining the Probability of Committing a β Error

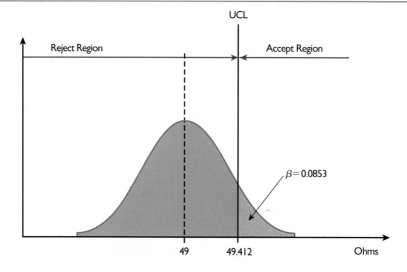

STATISTICAL PROCESS CONTROL

statistical process control (SPC)
Statistical method for determining whether a particular process is in or out of control.

Statistical process control (SPC) is a quantitative method for monitoring a repetitive process to determine whether that process is operating properly. SPC uses process data collected in real time and compares current measures to baseline process performance measures. It then applies simple statistical techniques similar to those used in acceptance sampling to determine whether or not the process has changed. SPC allows management and workers to distinguish between random fluctuations inherent in the process and variation that might indicate that the process has changed.

At its core, SPC is about understanding process variation. Every process varies in some unique way. Some processes vary a great deal; some vary only slightly. A careful analysis of the inherent variation in a given process makes it possible to compare its current performance with its expected performance, as determined by how the process has performed in the past.

As an illustration, a person uses an axe to chop logs into one-foot lengths for firewood. Over many days of chopping, he has discovered that he consistently chops the logs into lengths that can vary as much as three inches from his target length of 12 inches (in other words, the lengths he chops are 12 inches plus or minus three inches). It could be said that the expected variation—due to the random variation in his chopping process—is three inches from the target. He would expect that unless something in his chopping process changes, he would continue to chop pieces of length 12 ± 3 inches. If suddenly he was producing pieces that were shorter than nine inches and/or longer than 15 inches, he might question why his usual process has changed. He might look for nonrandom causes of variation: Is he tired or distracted? Has he changed his chopping style? Has his axe become dull? Is the wood he is currently chopping somehow different from the wood he has consistently cut within three inches of the target?

This simple example demonstrates the difference between the inherent, random variation that can be associated with a particular process, and the nonrandom, or assignable causes of variation. Assignable causes can usually be categorized as relating to the worker or to the equipment or materials being used.

SPC uses statistics—in particular, the power of sampling—to refine this basic understanding of variation in processes. The *central limit theorem* tells us that no matter what the actual shape of a distribution is, when samples of a given size are repeatedly drawn from that distribution and the means of the samples are calculated and plotted on a graph, these sample means will be normally distributed. If you are not convinced of this, think about a deck of cards. If each of the cards takes its face value (an ace = 1, numbered cards take their number value, a jack = 11, a queen = 12, and a king = 13), the deck represents a uniform distribution of cards: there are four of each value. The overall average value of a card in a deck would be seven. If you draw several samples of four cards each from the deck, how many will have an mean value of one? It will be a very rare sample that contains four aces. How many samples will have an mean value of 13? Again, only four kings will produce that sample mean, so that outcome will be very rare. On the other hand, think of how many ways a sample mean of seven could be produced: four sevens, three sixes and one nine, and so on in many different combinations. If you shuffle the deck, draw a sample, calculate its mean, plot the sample mean on a graph, reshuffle the deck and begin again, you will find that your sample mean distribution will quickly take on the shape of a bell curve, rather than the uniform flat shape of the underlying distribution of cards in the deck.

What about distributions other than the uniform? Does the central limit theorem hold true? You can do the same experiment with cards, assigning the value of four to all red cards and 10 to all black cards. The overall or grand mean of the deck is still seven, but the

EXHIBIT S5.7

Areas under the Normal Distribution Curve Corresponding to Different Numbers of Standard Deviations from the Mean

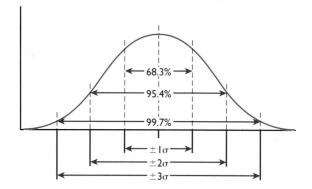

shape of the distribution of cards is now bimodal. Draw samples as before, calculate the mean value of each sample, plot the means on a graph, and the graph will shortly begin to look bell-shaped. Of course, the larger the sample size, the smoother the curve.

If the distribution of sample means is assumed to be normal, then we can use the well-understood properties of the normal distribution to understand variation in processes. For example, as shown in Exhibit S5.7, we know that if we have a normal distribution:

- The distribution is bilaterally symmetrical.
- 68.3 percent of the distribution lies between plus and minus one standard deviation from the mean;
- 95.4 percent of the distribution lies between plus and minus two standard deviations from the mean; and
- 99.7 percent of the distribution lies between plus and minus three standard deviations from the mean.

If we plot the means of successive samples drawn from a process whose long-run pattern of variation is known, we can look at the pattern of the sample means and decide whether the process is behaving the way we expect it to behave, or whether it has changed.

Statistical control means that a process is exhibiting only its inherent random variation and that it is not showing any signs of "assignable" variation. Statistical control does *not* mean that a process is producing goods or services that are good or bad.

SPC Charts

SPC charts are actually a specialized category of run charts that are based on the central limit theorem. The mean value for the process is calculated (usually from past performance) and, for the sample size being used, control limits are calculated. These control limits are usually established at three standard deviations above and below the mean because plus and minus three standard deviations from the mean value encompasses 99.7 percent of the area under a normal distribution. The x-axis of the SPC chart is time; the y-axis is the variation from the mean value for the process. The center line of an attribute chart is the long-run average for that attribute, such as percent defective, and the center line of a variables chart is the target value for the process.

For each sample, we calculate the sample mean (either the percentage of an attribute that occurs in the sample or the average measured value) and plot that point on the graph. As each sample mean is plotted, we look to see if the process is exhibiting variation that does

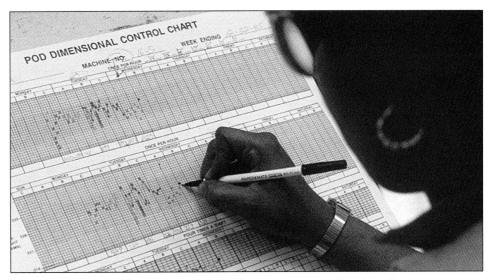

Statistical process control charts can be generated with computers, or manually, as shown. Samples are taken from the process at stated time intervals and their average parameter values are plotted on the charts. As long as these values remain within established control limits, the process is in control. However, a value falling outside the control limits might indicate the process is no longer in control and further investigation is required.

not look random. For example, we would expect to see the points distributed around the center line in the proportion described above because of what we know about normal distributions. If we see too little or too much variation, it may indicate that there is a nonrandom factor affecting the process. If we see evidence that the points are not distributed symmetrically around the center line, it may also indicate that there is a nonrandom factor affecting the process. If we see patterns such as several points in a row going up or several points in a row going down, it may again indicate that there is a nonrandom factor affecting the process. When we look at an SPC chart, we are looking for evidence of nonrandom behavior—the process behaving in a way we would not expect it to behave, given what we know about it.

Because points on an SPC chart are plotted as the sample is drawn, the ambiguity of "too little or too much variation" or "evidence of a nonrandom pattern" has prompted the development of rules of thumb for interpreting control charts, as shown in Exhibit S5.8. These rules of thumb, or heuristics, are simply methods of standardizing the way variation in a control chart is interpreted.

A process that exhibits nonrandom variation is said to be "out of control." (Remember that "out of control" does not mean that the process is producing bad output. A process can be out of control and producing fewer defects than usual. The key is that the process is not behaving in the way it is expected to behave given what is known about the process.) When we see evidence of nonrandom variation in a process, we try to identify the factors that may have caused that variation. In other words, we look for assignable cause: changes in workers, equipment, or materials.

SPC Using Attribute Measurements

Attribute data are data that are counted, such as good or bad units produced by a machine. If we draw samples during our production run on that machine, we can count, for each

EXHIBIT S5.8

Control Chart Evidence for Investigation

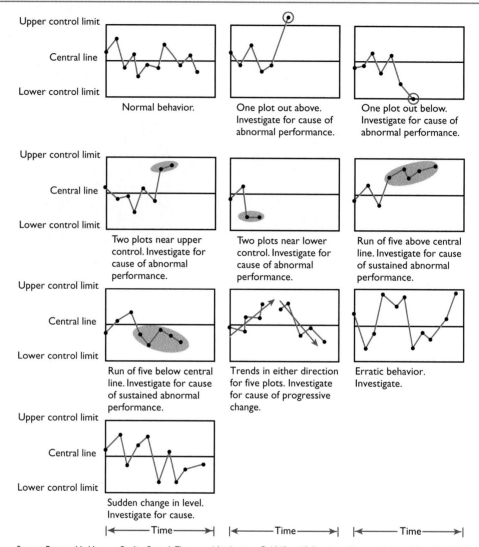

Source: Bertrand L. Hansen, *Quality Control: Theory and Applications*, © 1963, p. 65. Reprinted by permission of Prentice Hall, Inc., Englewood Cliffs, NJ.

sample, the number of units that are good and the number of units that are bad, based on our quality criteria. We can then compare the number of bad units in each sample to the long-run percentage of bad units for that particular machine and determine whether the process is behaving the way we expect it to behave. A process can be in control and producing bad output. For example, if the long-run percent defectives for a particular process is 20 percent, that means that 20 percent of the output is bad! The process may continue to produce the same level of defectives—in other words, be in control—but the defectives are still defectives. On the other hand, if a process usually produces 20 percent defectives and something changes so that the process now produces only 5 percent defectives, the process is out of control—but has improved! The goal is to find the cause of any nonrandom variation and either eliminate it (if it is producing more defects) or sustain it (if it has resulted in process improvement).

Calculating Control Limits The center line for an attribute chart is the long-run average for the attribute in question. For example, for a p-chart, or percent defective chart, the center line is $\overline{p}$ (said "p-bar"), the long-run average percent defective.

$$\text{Center line} = \overline{p} = \text{Long-run average}$$

$$\text{Standard deviation of sample} = s_p = \sqrt{\frac{\overline{p}(1 - \overline{p})}{n}}$$

Thus, we have:

$$\text{CL} = \overline{p} \pm z_{\alpha/2} \sqrt{\frac{\overline{p}(1 - \overline{p})}{n}} \tag{S5.2}$$

The upper control limit (UCL) and the lower control limit (LCL) are usually established at plus and minus three standard deviations from p ($z_{\alpha/2} = 3$). Thus:

$$\text{Upper control limit} = \text{UCL} = \overline{p} + 3s_p$$
$$\text{Lower control limit} = \text{LCL} = \overline{p} - 3s_p$$

If the calculated LCL is a negative number, the LCL is set equal to zero.

Sample Size in Attribute SPC The size of a sample is extremely important for successful SPC implementation. If attribute data are being collected, the sample must be large enough to be able to count the attribute. For example, if we know that a machine produces, in the long-run, 5 percent defects, we are very unlikely to be able to answer the question, Is the process producing defects at the rate it usually does, if we have a sample of size 5. The usual rule of thumb for attribute SPC is that the sample should be large enough to be able to include the attribute twice, on average. So if the defect rate is 5 percent, the sample size would need to be at least 40 to expect to count two defects. Of course, since we are not looking at every unit, some samples will, just by chance, have more than two defects, while some will have fewer than two. We are looking for a pattern of defects in the samples over time that will tell us whether the process is exhibiting nonrandom variation.

Determining the Long-Run Attribute Level Because the long-run attribute percentage is critical in determining the center line and for calculating the control limits for the SPC chart, it is important to have adequate historical information about the process.

Variable Measurements Using $\overline{X}$ and R Charts

Variable data are data that are measured, such as length or weight. There are four main issues in creating a control chart that uses variable data. These are: (*a*) the size of the sample, (*b*) the number of samples, (*c*) the frequency of the samples, and (*d*) the control limits.

Size of Samples For industrial applications in process control, it is preferable to keep the sample size small. There are two main reasons: first, the sample needs to be taken within a reasonable length of time, otherwise the process might change while the sample is being taken. Second, the larger the sample, the more it costs to take.

Sample sizes of four or five units seem to be the preferred numbers. The *means* of samples of this size have an approximately normal distribution, no matter what the distribution of the parent population looks like. Sample sizes greater than five give narrower control limits and, thus, are more sensitive. For detecting finer variations of a process it may be necessary, in fact, to use larger sample sizes. However, when sample sizes exceed 15 or so, it would be more appropriate to use the standard deviation (σ) and $\overline{X}$ charts rather than R

and $\overline{X}$ charts. One advantage of using the R charts is that the range is easier to calculate than the standard deviation.

Number of Samples   Once the chart has been set up, each sample taken can be compared to the chart and a decision can be made about whether the process is acceptable. To set up the charts, however, prudence (and statistics) suggest that 25 or so samples be taken.

Frequency of Samples   How often to take a sample is a trade-off between the cost of sampling (along with the cost of the unit if it is destroyed as part of the test) and the benefit of adjusting the system. Usually, it is best to start off with frequent sampling of a process and taper off as confidence in the process builds. For example, one might start with a sample of five units every half hour and end up feeling that one sample per day is adequate.

Control Limits   Standard practice in statistical process control for variables is to set control limits at three standard deviations above the mean and three standard deviations below. This means that 99.7 percent of the sample means are expected to fall within these control limits (i.e., within a 99.7 percent confidence interval). Thus, if one sample mean falls outside this obviously wide band, we have strong evidence that the process is out of control.

How to Construct $\overline{X}$ and R Charts

An $\overline{X}$ chart tracks the changes in the means of the samples by plotting the means that were taken from a process. $\overline{\overline{X}}$ is the average of the means.

An R chart tracks the changes in the variability by plotting the range within each sample. The range is the difference between the highest and the lowest value in that sample. As stated earlier, R values provide an easily calculated measure of variation used like a standard deviation. $\overline{R}$ is the average of the ranges of each sample. More specifically, these terms are defined:

$$\overline{X} = \frac{\sum_{i=1}^{n} X_i}{n} \tag{S5.3}$$

where

$\overline{X}$ = Mean of the sample

i = Item number

n = Total number of items in the sample

$$\overline{\overline{X}} = \frac{\sum_{j=1}^{m} \overline{X}_j}{m} \tag{S5.4}$$

where

$\overline{\overline{X}}$ = The average of the means of the samples

j = Sample number

m = Total number of samples

$$\overline{R} = \frac{\sum_{j=1}^{m} R_j}{m} \tag{S5.5}$$

EXHIBIT S5.9

Factors for Determining from $\bar{R}$ the 3-Sigma Control Limits for $\bar{X}$ and R Charts

Number of Observations in Subgroup n	Factor for X̄ Chart A₂	Factors for R Chart	
		Lower Control Limit D₃	Upper Control Limit D₄
2	1.88	0	3.27
3	1.02	0	2.57
4	0.73	0	2.28
5	0.58	0	2.11
6	0.48	0	2.00
7	0.42	0.08	1.92
8	0.37	0.14	1.86
9	0.34	0.18	1.82
10	0.31	0.22	1.78
11	0.29	0.26	1.74
12	0.27	0.28	1.72
13	0.25	0.31	1.69
14	0.24	0.33	1.67
15	0.22	0.35	1.65
16	0.21	0.36	1.64
17	0.20	0.38	1.62
18	0.19	0.39	1.61
19	0.19	0.40	1.60
20	0.18	0.41	1.59

Upper control limit for $\bar{X}$ = UCL$_{\bar{x}}$ = $\bar{\bar{X}}$ + A₂$\bar{R}$ Upper control limit for $\bar{R}$ = UCL$_R$ = D₄$\bar{R}$
Lower control limit for $\bar{X}$ = LCL$_{\bar{x}}$ = $\bar{\bar{X}}$ − A₂$\bar{R}$ Lower control limit for $\bar{R}$ = LCL$_R$ = D₃$\bar{R}$

Note: All factors are based on the normal distribution.

Source: E. L. Grant, *Statistical Quality Control*, 6th ed. (New York: McGraw-Hill, 1988). Reprinted by permission of McGraw-Hill, Inc.

where

$\overline{R}$ = Average of the measurement differences R for all samples

R_j = Difference between the highest and lowest values in sample j

E. L. Grant and R. Leavenworth computed a table that allows us to easily compute the upper and lower control limits for both the $\overline{X}$ chart and the R chart.[3] These are defined as:

$$\text{Upper control limit for } \overline{X} = \overline{\overline{X}} + A_2\overline{R}$$
$$\text{Lower control limit for } \overline{X} = \overline{\overline{X}} - A_2\overline{R}$$
$$\text{Upper control limit for } R = D_4\overline{R}$$
$$\text{Lower control limit for } R = D_3\overline{R}$$

Where the values for A_2, D_3 and D_4 are obtained from Exhibit S5.9.

[3]E. L. Grant and R. Leavenworth, *Statistical Quality Control* (New York: McGraw-Hill, 1964), p. 562. Reprinted by permission.

EXHIBIT S5.10

Measurements in Samples of
Five from a Process

Sample Number	Each Unit in Sample					Average X̄	Range R
1	10.60	10.40	10.30	9.90	10.20	10.28	.70
2	9.98	10.25	10.05	10.23	10.33	10.17	.35
3	9.85	9.90	10.20	10.25	10.15	10.07	40
4	10.20	10.10	10.30	9.90	9.95	10.09	.40
5	10.30	10.20	10.24	10.50	10.30	10.31	.30
6	10.10	10.30	10.20	10.30	9.90	10.16	.40
7	9.98	9.90	10.20	10.40	10.10	10.12	.50
8	10.10	10.30	10.40	10.24	10.30	10.27	.30
9	10.30	10.20	10.60	10.50	10.10	10.34	.50
10	10.30	10.40	10.50	10.10	10.20	10.30	.40
11	9.90	9.50	10.20	10.30	10.35	10.05	.85
12	10.10	10.36	10.50	9.80	9.95	10.14	.70
13	10.20	10.50	10.70	10.10	9.90	10.28	.80
14	10.20	10.60	10.50	10.30	10.40	10.40	.40
15	10.54	10.30	10.40	10.55	10.00	10.36	.55
16	10.20	10.60	10.15	10.00	10.50	10.29	.60
17	10.20	10.40	10.60	10.80	10.10	10.42	.70
18	9.90	9.50	9.90	10.50	10.00	9.96	1.00
19	10.60	10.30	10.50	9.90	9.80	10.22	.80
20	10.60	10.40	10.30	10.40	10.20	10.38	.40
21	9.90	9.60	10.50	10.10	10.60	10.14	1.00
22	9.95	10.20	10.50	10.30	10.20	10.23	.55
23	10.20	9.50	9.60	9.80	10.30	9.88	.80
24	10.30	10.60	10.30	9.90	9.80	10.18	.80
25	9.90	10.30	10.60	9.90	10.10	10.16	.70
					$\overline{\overline{X}} =$	10.21	
					$\overline{R} =$		.60

Example

We would like to create an $\overline{X}$ and an R chart for a process. Exhibit S5.10 shows the measurements that were taken of all 25 samples. The last two columns show the average of the sample $\overline{X}$ and the range R.

Solution

$$\text{Upper control limit for } \overline{X} = \overline{\overline{X}} + A_2\overline{R}$$
$$= 10.21 + 0.58(0.60) = 10.56$$
$$\text{Lower control limit for } \overline{X} = \overline{\overline{X}} - A_2\overline{R}$$
$$= 10.21 - 0.58(0.60) = 9.86$$
$$\text{Upper control limit for } R = D_4\overline{R}$$
$$= 2.11(0.60) = 1.26$$
$$\text{Lower control limit for } R = D_3\overline{R}$$
$$= 0(0.60) = 0$$

Exhibit S5.11 shows the $\overline{X}$ chart and R chart with a plot of all the sample means and ranges of the samples. All the points are well within the control limits, although sample 23 is close to the $\overline{X}$ lower control limit. The $\overline{X}$ chart shows how well the process is centered about the target mean. The R chart demonstrates the degree of variability in the process.

EXHIBIT S5.11

$\overline{X}$ Chart and R Chart

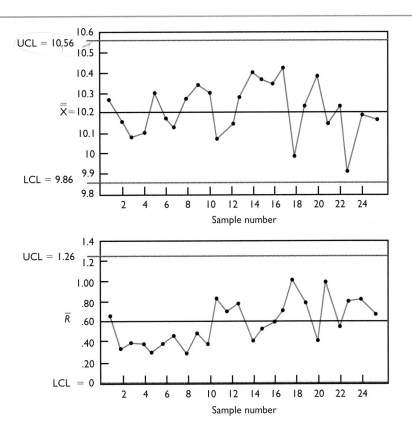

Process Capability

Process control chart limits can be compared to design specification limits to determine if the process itself is not capable of making products within design specification (or tolerance) limits. In Exhibit S5.12A, we see a process that on average is producing items within the control limits, but its variation is such that it can't meet specifications for all items. Exhibit S5.12B shows reduction in this variability, but the process is still deficient. Finally, in Exhibit S5.12C, we see that the process variability has been brought under control. How is this accomplished? By working to improve the performance of each source of variance: workers, machine, tooling, setup, material, and the environment.

Process Capability Ratio In order for a process to be both in control and within tolerance, the part tolerance limits must be equal to or wider than the upper and lower limits of the process control chart. Since these control limits are at plus or minus three standard deviations (3 sigma), the tolerance limits must exceed 6 sigma. A quick way of making this determination is through the use of a process capability ratio. This ratio is calculated by dividing the tolerance width by 6 sigma (the process capability), as shown in the following formula in which s, the sample standard deviation, is substituted for σ, the population standard deviation.

$$\text{Process capability ratio} = C_p = \frac{\text{Upper tolerance limit} - \text{Lower tolerance limit}}{6s} \quad \text{(S5.6)}$$

The larger the ratio, the greater the potential for producing parts within tolerance from the specified process. A ratio that is greater than 1 indicates that the tolerance limit range is wider than the actual range of measurements. If the ratio is less than 1, then some parts will be out of tolerance. The minimum capability index is frequently established at 1.33. Below

EXHIBIT S5.12

Reducing Process Variance So That All Parts Are within Specification (Tolerance)*

A. Process Not Capable, but in Statistical Control

Normal variance pattern, but variance is too great for all individual unit measurements to be within tolerance limits. (Seven of 35 are outside.)

B. Process Variance Reduced, but Still Not Capable of Defect-Free Production

One individual measure out

Variance is reduced so that control limits for sample means are inside the tolerance limits, but individual units will still be produced outside the tolerance limits just through normal variation.

C. Process Capable of Defect-Free Production

Upper specification limit (USL)

Upper control limit (UCL)

Lower control limit (LCL)

Lower specifications limit (LSL)

Variance now is so greatly reduced that no individual measurements should fall outside tolerance even if the central tendency of the process is not centered in the tolerance range.

* Tolerance: The range within which all individual measurements of units produced is desired to fall.

Source: Robert W. Hall, *Attaining Manufacturing Excellence: Just-in-Time Manufacturing, Total Quality, Total People Involvement* (Homewood, IL: Dow Jones–Irwin, 1987), p. 66. By permission of The McGraw-Hill Companies.

this value, design engineers have to seek approval from manufacturing before the product can be released for production.

Capability Index (C_{pk})   The process capability ratio does not specifically indicate how well the process is performing relative to the target dimension. Thus, a second performance index, called C_{pk}, must be employed to determine whether the process mean is closer to the upper specification limit, USL, or the lower specification limit, LSL.

$$C_{pk} = \min\left[\frac{\overline{X} - \text{LSL}}{3s}, \frac{\text{USL} - \overline{X}}{3s} \right] \qquad (S5.7)$$

When C_{pk} equals the capability ratio, then the process mean is centered between the two specification limits. Otherwise, the process mean is closest to the specification limit corresponding to the minimum of the two C_{pk} ratios. Consider the following example.

Example

A manufacturing process produces a certain part with a mean diameter of 2 inches and a standard deviation of 0.03 inches. The upper specification limit equals 2.05 inches, and the lower specification limit equals 1.9 inches.

Solution

From this information, a process capability ratio (C_p) and a capability index (C_{pk}) were calculated.

$$\text{Process capability ratio} = C_p = \frac{2.05 - 1.90}{6(0.03)} = 0.833$$

$$C_{pk} \text{ for LSL} = \frac{2 - 1.90}{3(0.03)} = 1.11$$

$$C_{pk} \text{ for USL} = \frac{2.05 - 2}{3(0.03)} = 0.56$$

From the process capability ratio, we can conclude that the process is not capable of producing parts within the design's specification. The C_{pk} analysis points out that the process mean is closer to the upper tolerance limit. Given this information, work can be done on the manufacturing process to increase the process capability ratio and also to center the mean between the two specification limits. This may involve, for example, a simple adjustment of a machine tool setting.

EXHIBIT S5.13

The Goal of Six Sigma

A. Process Variation Equals Design Tolerance

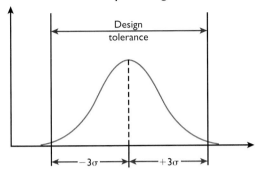

B. Process Variation Is 50 Percent of Design

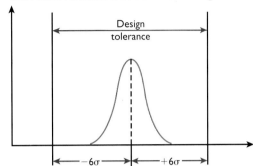

Six Sigma

six sigma
Quality improvement program developed by Motorola to reduce process variation to 50 percent of design tolerance.

Motorola, in large part to respond to the very high quality products that were being manufactured in Japan, introduced a quality improvement program during the 1980s known as **six sigma.** The goal of this program is to reduce the process variation to 50 percent of the design tolerance, thereby achieving a process capability ratio or $C_p = 2.0$.

As seen in Exhibit S5.13A, where the design tolerance is equal to the process variation, we have a $C_p = 1.0$. In this case, there is $+/- 3$ standard deviations of process variation within the design tolerance. This results in 99.7 percent good parts or 2,700 defects per million parts produced.

With the six sigma program, the process variation is reduced to 50 percent of the design tolerance as shown in Exhibit S5.13B. This results in a $C_p = 2.0$ and only 3.4 defects per million parts produced.

Other companies, like General Electric and the Foxboro Company, have introduced the six sigma program into their organizations. These companies, like Motorola, are able to achieve six sigma quality due in large part to their ability to automate operations which were previously done manually. The automation of these processes significantly reduces process variation.

TAGUCHI METHODS

Taguchi methods
Statistical technique for identifying the cause(s) of process variation that reduces the number of tests that are necessary.

Throughout this chapter we have discussed statistical quality control methods from the point of view of acceptance sampling and process adjustments. In what many have termed a revolution in quality thinking, Genichi Taguchi of Japan has suggested the following: Instead of constantly fiddling with production equipment to ensure consistent quality, design the product to be robust enough to achieve high quality despite fluctuations on the production line. This simple idea has been employed by such companies as Ford Motor Company, ITT, and IBM; as a result, they have saved millions of dollars in manufacturing costs.

Taguchi methods are basically statistical techniques for conducting experiments to determine the best combinations of product and process variables to make a product. *Best* means lowest cost with highest uniformity. This can be a complicated, time-consuming procedure. For example, in designing the process for a new product, one might find that a single processing step with only eight process variables (machine speed, cutting angle, and so on) could be combined in up to 5,000 different ways (a full factorial design). Thus, finding the combination that makes the product with the highest uniformity at the lowest cost can't be done efficiently by trial and error. Taguchi has found a way around this problem by focusing on only a fraction of the combinations that represent the overall spectrum of product/process outcomes. He developed a visual way to choose the best subset of the full number of experiments. This approach makes use of fractional factorial design significantly easier for people who do not have extensive training in statistics.

Taguchi is also known for the development of the concept of a *quality loss function* (QLF) that relates the cost of quality directly to the variation in a process. Essentially, with this function Taguchi is saying that any deviation from the target quality level results in a loss to society. For example, if a defective tire goes flat, society loses the productive time of the owner who needs to either change it and/or have it repaired. If the owner doesn't change the tire, society loses the time the repair person spends on fixing the tire because he or she could have been doing work that was not repair, but instead contributed value to society (either by producing value or enjoying leisure). The following discussion from an article by Joseph Turner develops this concept in detail.

Is an Out-of-Spec Product Really Out of Spec?

VARIATION AROUND US

It is generally accepted that, as variation is reduced, quality is improved. Sometimes that knowledge is intuitive. If a train is always on time, schedules can be planned more precisely. If clothing sizes are consistent, time can be saved by ordering from a catalog. But rarely are such things thought about in terms of the value of low variability. With engineers, the knowledge is better defined. Pistons must fit cylinders, doors must fit openings, electrical components must be compatible, and boxes of cereal must have the right amount of raisins—otherwise quality will be unacceptable and customers will be dissatisfied.

However, engineers also know that it is impossible to have zero variability. For this reason, designers establish specifications that define not only the target value of something, but also acceptable limits about the target. For example, if the target value of a dimension is 10 inch, the design specifications might then be 10.00 inch ± 0.02. This would tell the manufacturing department that, while it should aim for exactly 10 inch, anything between 9.98 inch and 10.02 inch is OK.

The traditional way of interpreting such a specification is that any part that falls within the allowed range is equally good, while any part falling outside the range is totally bad. This is illustrated in Exhibit S5.14. (Note that the cost in this model is zero over the entire specification range, and then there is a quantum leap in cost once the limit is violated.)

Taguchi has pointed out that such a view is nonsense for two reasons:

1. From the customer's view, there is often practically no difference between a product just inside specifications and a product just outside. Conversely, there is a far greater difference in the quality of a product that is at the target and the quality of one that is near a limit.
2. As customers become more demanding, there is pressure to reduce variability. The underlying philosophy in Exhibit S5.14 does not recognize this pressure.

Taguchi suggests that a more correct picture of the loss is shown in Exhibit S5.15. Notice that in this graph the cost is represented by a smooth curve. There are dozens of illustrations of this notion: the meshing of gears in a transmission, the speed of photographic film, the temperature in a workplace or department store. In nearly anything that can be

EXHIBIT S5.14

A Traditional View of the Cost of Variability

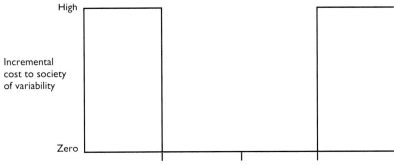

Source: Adapted from Joseph Turner, "Is an Out-of-Spec Product Really Out of Spec?" *Quality Progress*, December 1990, pp. 57–59.

EXHIBIT S5.15

Taguchi's View of the Cost of Variability

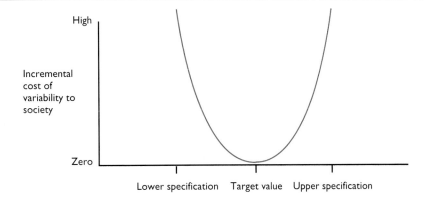

measured, the customer sees not a sharp line, but a gradation of acceptability. Customers see the loss function as Exhibit S5.15 rather than Exhibit S5.14.

What are the elements of loss to society? Internally, the more variable the manufacturing process, the more scrap generated and the more a company will have to spend on testing and inspecting for conformance. Externally, customers will find that the product does not last as long or work as well if it is not close to target. Perhaps, when used in adverse situations, the product will not perform at all, even though it meets specifications that were developed based on normal usage.

CONCLUSION

Statistical quality methods provide the necessary foundation for producing high-quality goods and services. Acceptance sampling provides us with a method for evaluating products after they have been made. The purpose of statistical process control is to focus on the process while the product is made.

If the inherent variation of a process is understood, managers and workers can watch the process to make sure that it is performing as expected. When the process exhibits nonrandom variation, the cause of the variation (assignable cause) needs to be sought, and eliminated (if the process has deteriorated) or continued (if the process has improved). Because variation can easily be seen on an SPC chart, managers and workers can readily identify nonrandom variation and look for its assignable causes.

KEY FORMULAS

Control limits for a variable

$$CL = \mu \pm z_{\alpha/2} \frac{\sigma}{\sqrt{n}} \tag{S5.1}$$

Control limits for an attribute

$$CL = \overline{p} \pm z_{\alpha/2} \sqrt{\frac{\overline{p}(1 - \overline{p})}{n}} \tag{S5.2}$$

Mean of a sample

$$\overline{X} = \frac{\sum_{i=1}^{n} X_i}{n} \tag{S5.3}$$

Average of means of all samples

$$\overline{\overline{X}} = \frac{\sum_{j=1}^{m} \overline{X}_j}{m} \tag{S5.4}$$

Average range of all samples

$$\overline{R} = \frac{\sum_{j=1}^{m} R_j}{m} \tag{S5.5}$$

Process capability ratio

$$C_p = \frac{\text{Upper tolerance limit} - \text{Lower tolerance limit}}{6s} \tag{S5.6}$$

Capability index

$$C_{pk} = \min \left[\frac{\overline{X} - \text{LSL}}{3s}, \frac{\text{USL} - \overline{X}}{3s} \right] \tag{S5.7}$$

KEY TERMS

acceptable quality level (AQL)　p. 172
control limits　p. 174
operating characteristic (OC) curves　p. 173
six sigma　p. 187
statistical process control (SPC)　p. 177
Taguchi methods　p. 187

types of data:
　attribute data　p. 170
　variable data　p. 170
types of sampling errors:
　α error, Type I error, or producer's risk　p. 171
　β error, Type II error, or consumer's risk　p. 171

REVIEW AND DISCUSSION QUESTIONS

1. Discuss the trade-off between achieving a zero AQL (acceptable quantity level) and a positive AQL (e.g., an AQL of 2 percent).

2. The capability index allows for some drifting of the process mean. Discuss what this means in terms of product quality output.

3. Discuss the purposes and differences between p-charts and $\overline{X}$ and R charts.

4. In an agreement between a supplier and a customer, the supplier must ensure that all parts are within tolerance before shipment to the customer. What is the effect on the cost of quality to the customer?

5. In the situation described in Question 4, what would be the effect on the cost of quality to the supplier?

6. Discuss the logic of Taguchi methods.

7. Can you think of a way to use a deck of cards to simulate other distributions and test the central limit theorem?

SOLVED PROBLEM

Problem 1

Completed forms from a particular department of an insurance company were sampled on a daily basis as a check against the quality of performance of that department. In order to establish a tentative norm for the department, one sample of 100 units was collected each day for 15 days, with these results:

Sample	Sample Size	Number of Forms with Errors	Sample	Sample Size	Number of Forms with Errors
1	100	4	8	100	3
2	100	3	9	100	4
3	100	5	10	100	2
4	100	0	11	100	7
5	100	2	12	100	2
6	100	8	13	100	1
7	100	1	14	100	3
			15	100	1

a. Develop a p-chart using a 95 percent confidence interval.

b. Plot the 15 samples collected.

c. What comments can you make about the process?

Solution
Insurance company forms.

a. $$\overline{p} = \frac{46}{15(100)} = 0.031$$

$$s_p = \sqrt{\frac{\overline{p}(1 - \overline{p})}{n}} = \sqrt{\frac{0.031(1 - 0.031)}{100}} - \sqrt{0.0003} - .017$$

$$\text{UCL} = \overline{p} + 1.96s_p = 0.031 + 1.96(0.017) = 0.064$$

$$\text{LCL} - \overline{p} - 1.96s_p = 0.031 - 1.96(0.017) = -0.002 \text{ or zero}$$

b. The defectives are plotted here.

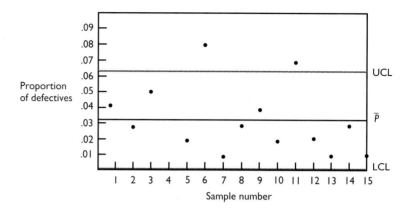

c. Of the 15 samples, 2 were out of the control limits. Since the control limits were established as 95 percent, or 1 out of 20, we would say that the process is out of control. It needs to be examined to find the cause of such widespread variation.

PROBLEMS

1. A metal fabricator produces connecting rods with an outer diameter that has a $1 \pm .01$ inch specification. A machine operator takes several sample measurements over time and determines the sample mean outer diameter to be 1.002 inches with a standard deviation of 0.003 inches.

   a. Calculate the process capability ratio and the capability index for this example.

   b. What do these figures tell you about the process?

2. Ten samples of 15 parts each were taken from an ongoing process to establish a p-chart for control. The samples and the number of defectives in each are shown here.

Sample	n	Number of Defects in Sample		Sample	n	Number of Defects in Sample
1	15	3		6	15	2
2	15	1		7	15	0
3	15	0		8	15	3
4	15	0		9	15	1
5	15	0		10	15	0

   a. Develop a p-chart for 95 percent confidence.

   b. Based on the plotted data points, what comments can you make?

3. Resistors for electronic circuits are being manufactured on a high-speed automated machine. The machine is being set up to produce a large run of resistors of 1,000 ohms each.

   To set up the machine and to create a control chart to be used throughout the run, 15 samples were taken with 4 resistors in each sample. The complete list of samples and their measured values are as follows:

Sample Number	Readings (in ohms)				Sample Number	Readings (in ohms)			
1	1010	991	985	986	9	1006	989	1005	1007
2	995	996	1009	994	10	992	1007	1006	979
3	990	1003	1015	1008	11	996	1006	997	989
4	1015	1020	1009	998	12	1019	996	991	1011
5	1013	1019	1005	993	13	981	991	989	1003
6	994	1001	994	1005	14	999	993	988	984
7	989	992	982	1020	15	1013	1002	1005	992
8	1001	986	996	996					

Develop an $\overline{X}$ chart and an R chart and plot the values. From the charts, what comments can you make about the process? (Use the table in Exhibit S9.5.)

4. You are the newly appointed assistant administrator at a local hospital, and your first project is to investigate the quality of the patient meals put out by the food-service department. You conducted a 10-day survey by submitting a simple questionnaire to the 400 patients with each meal, asking that they simply check off either that the meal was satisfactory or unsatisfactory. For simplicity in this problem, assume that the response was 1,000 returned questionnaires from the 1,200 meals each day. The results ran as follows:

	Number of Unsatisfactory Meals	Sample Size
December 1	74	1,000
December 2	42	1,000
December 3	64	1,000
December 4	80	1,000
December 5	40	1,000
December 6	50	1,000
December 7	65	1,000
December 8	70	1,000
December 9	40	1,000
December 10	75	1,000
	600	10,000

a. Construct a *p*-chart based on the questionnaire results, using a confidence interval of 95.4 percent, which is two standard deviations.

b. What comments can you make about the results of the survey?

5. The state and local police departments are trying to analyze crime rate areas so that they can shift their patrols from decreasing crime rate areas to areas when rates are increasing. The city and county have been geographically segmented into areas containing 5,000 residences. The police recognize that all crimes and offenses are not reported; people either do not want to become involved, consider the offenses too small to report, are too embarrassed to make a police report, or do not take the time, among other reasons. Every month, because of this, the police are contacting by phone a random sample of 1,000 of the 5,000 residences in one area for data on crime (the respondents are guaranteed anonymity). The data collected for the past 12 months for one area are as follows:

Month	Crime Incidence	Sample Size	Crime Rate
January	7	1,000	0.007
February	9	1,000	0.009
March	7	1,000	0.007
April	7	1,000	0.007
May	7	1,000	0.007
June	9	1,000	0.009
July	7	1,000	0.007
August	10	1,000	0.010
September	8	1,000	0.008
October	11	1,000	0.011
November	10	1,000	0.010
December	8	1,000	0.008

Construct a $\overline{p}$-chart for 95 percent confidence and plot each of the months. If the next three months show the number of crime incidences (out of 1,000 residences sampled) in this area as:

$$\text{January} = 10 \quad \text{February} = 12 \quad \text{March} = 11$$

What comments can you make regarding the crime rate?

6. Some of the citizens complained to city council members that there should be equal protection under the law against the occurrence of crimes. The citizens argued that this equal protection should be interpreted as indicating that high-crime areas should have more police protection than low-crime areas. Therefore, police patrols and other methods for preventing crime (such as street lighting or cleaning up abandoned areas and buildings) should be used proportionately to crime occurrence.

In a fashion similar to Problem 5, the city has been broken down into 20 geographical areas, each containing 5,000 residences. The 1,000 sampled from each area showed the following incidence of crime during the past month.

Area	Number of Crimes	Sample Size	Crime Rate	Area	Number of Crimes	Sample Size	Crime Rate
1	14	1,000	0.014	11	20	1,000	0.020
2	3	1,000	0.003	12	15	1,000	0.015
3	19	1,000	0.019	13	12	1,000	0.012
4	18	1,000	0.018	14	14	1,000	0.014
5	14	1,000	0.014	15	10	1,000	0.010
6	28	1,000	0.028	16	30	1,000	0.030
7	10	1,000	0.010	17	4	1,000	0.004
8	18	1,000	0.018	18	20	1,000	0.020
9	12	1,000	0.012	19	6	1,000	0.006
10	3	1,000	0.003	20	30	1,000	0.030
					$\overline{300}$		

Suggest a reallocation of crime protection effort, if indicated, based on a *p*-chart analysis. In order to be reasonably certain in your recommendation, select a 95 percent confidence level.

7. The Eau de Fawcett Beverage Company has developed a line of sophisticated beverages targeted for couples who both work and have no children. This segment of the consumer market is often referred to as "DINKS" (i.e., Double Income, No Kids). This new line of beverages is thus being produced under the label "Drinks for Dinks." The bottles for this product are filled on automatic equipment which has been adjusted so that the average fill per bottle is 11 ounces. Historically, it has been determined that the standard deviation of the filling equipment is 0.16 ounces. Every hour, a sample of 36 bottles is taken at random from the process, and the average volume is calculated and plotted on an $\overline{X}$ chart.

   a. Draw an $\overline{X}$ process control chart with limits of ± 3 standard deviations, correctly labeling the UCL and LCL.

   b. The average sample volumes for Monday morning were as follows:

Hour	7:00 AM	8:00 AM	9:00 AM	10:00 AM	11:00 AM
Average volume	11.09	10.95	10.82	11.06	11.23

   Plot the average volume for each hour on the process control chart. Do you think that the process is in control?

8. Allison Jon, the manager of the 800 number reservation service for a nationwide chain of luxury hotels, is concerned about the productivity of her operation. Analysis of past data shows that it should take an average of five minutes to properly process a reservation and that

the standard deviation is 30 seconds. Every day, Allison randomly samples how long it takes to make each of 25 reservations.

    a. Set up a process control chart with 95 percent confidence limits.

    b. If the sample results show that the average reservation time is significantly above the upper control limit, what might be some of the causes for the longer reservation times? How would you correct these problems?

    c. Should Allison have any concern if the average reservation time was significantly below the lower control limit? Why?

SELECTED BIBLIOGRAPHY

Aslup, Fred, and Ricky M. Watson. *Practical Statistical Process Control: A Tool for Quality Manufacturing.* New York: Van Nostrand Reinhold, 1993.

Hradesky, John L. *Productivity and Quality Improvement: A Practical Guide to Implementing Statistical Process Control.* New York: McGraw-Hill, 1988.

Juran, J. M., and F. M. Gryna. *Quality Planning and Analysis.* 2nd ed. New York: McGraw-Hill, 1980.

Taguchi, G. *On-Line Quality Control during Production.* Tokyo: Japanese Standards Association, 1987.

Thompson, James R., and Jacek Koronacki. *Statistical Process Control for Quality Improvement.* New York: Chapman & Hall, 1993.

Turner, Joseph. "Is an Out-of-Spec Product Really Out-of-Spec?" *Quality Progress,* December 1990, pp. 57–59.

Wetherill, G. Barrie, and Don W. Brown. *Statistical Process Control: Theory and Practice.* New York: Chapman & Hall, 1991.

Wheeler, Donald J. *Understanding Variation: The Key to Managing Chaos.* Knoxville, TN: SPC Press, Inc., 1993.

6

FORECASTING

Chapter Objectives

- Introduce the basic concepts of forecasting and its importance within an organization.

- Identify several of the more common forecasting methods and how they can improve the performance of both manufacturing and service operations.

- Provide a framework for understanding how forecasts are developed.

- Demonstrate that errors exist in all forecasts and show how to measure and assess these errors.

- Introduce the concept of neural networks and show how they are used to make forecasts.

- Discuss some of the software programs that are available for developing forecasting models.

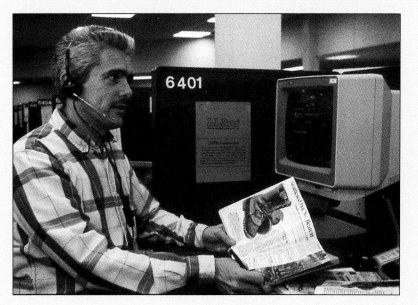

L. Bean, the outdoor mail order company located in Freeport, Maine, depends on customer telephone orders for 72 percent of its business. Scheduling telephone operators at its call centers is therefore a critical element in its success. Having too few operators results in long customer waiting times and the real possibility of losing customers to competitors. On the other hand, having too many telephone operators results in unnecessary labor costs which impacts negatively on profits. The key to scheduling the proper number of operators to be on duty at any given time depends on the ability to accurately forecast the number and type of customer calls that will occur in a given time period. Using a time series forecasting model developed by professors at the University of Southern Maine, L.L. Bean has been able to save approximately $300,000 annually in labor costs by scheduling their operators more efficiently. This has been done without incurring any decrease in service quality! ∎

Source: Bruce H. Andrews and Shawn M. Cunningham, "L.L. Bean Improves Call Center Forecasting," *Interfaces* 25, no. 6 (November–December 1995), pp. 1–13.

FINANCE
ACCOUNTING
MARKETING

As with L.L. Bean, many companies now recognize the importance of forecasting at all levels of the organization. At the highest levels, it is the basis for corporate, long-range, strategic planning. In the functional areas of finance and accounting, forecasts provide the basis for budgetary planning and cost control. Marketing relies on sales forecasting to plan new products, compensate sales personnel, and make other key decisions. The operations management function uses forecasts to make periodic decisions involving process selection, capacity planning, facility layout, and for continual decisions about production planning, scheduling, and inventory. More recently, a growing number of service operations, like L.L. Bean, are using forecasting techniques to predict customer demand so they can better serve their customers while at the same time control their labor costs.

However, while forecasting can provide managers with future information that will allow them to run their operations more effectively and efficiently, managers must also recognize that these forecasts are not perfect. There are simply too many factors in the business environment that cannot be predicted or controlled with certainty. Rather than search for the perfect forecast, it is far more important for managers to establish the practice of continually reviewing these forecasts and to learn to live with their inaccuracies. This is not to say that we should not try to improve the forecasting model or methodology, but that we should try to find and use the best forecasting method available, *within reason.* In this respect, it is important to note that the cost of obtaining small improvements in forecasting accuracy is very high after *reasonable* forecasts have been developed.

The goal of this chapter is to present an introduction to several different forecasting techniques and models (both qualitative and quantitative) that are commonly used in business, recognizing that additional and more sophisticated forecasting techniques and models are available for people seeking more in-depth knowledge in this area. We address primarily time series techniques and causal relationships, including a discussion of the sources of errors and their measurement.

TYPES OF FORECASTING

The various types of forecasting techniques can be classified into three broad categories—*qualitative, time series analysis,* and *causal relationships.*

qualitative techniques
Nonquantitative forecasting techniques based upon expert opinions and intuition. Typically used when there are no data available.

Qualitative techniques are subjective or judgmental in nature, and are based on estimates and opinions. Such techniques are used primarily when there are no data available. **Time series analysis,** the primary focus of this chapter, is based on the idea that data relating to past demand can be used to predict future demand. In other words, the trends that generated demand in the past will continue to generate demand in the future. **Causal forecasting** assumes that demand is related to some underlying factor or factors in the environment, and that cause-and-effect relationships are at work.

time series analysis
Analyzing data by time periods (for example, hours, days, weeks) to determine if trends or patterns occur.

Time series analysis is typically used in short-range situations, like forecasting worker schedules. Causal forecasting is usually used for longer-term issues, such as selecting a site for a retail operation. Exhibit 6.1 briefly describes some of the different varieties of the three basic types of forecasting models. In this chapter we present the three time series analysis methods in the exhibit and the first of the causal techniques.

causal forecasting
Relating demand to an underlying factor other than time.

Exhibit 6.2 shows a comparison of the strengths and weaknesses of these different forecasting methods. The moving average and exponential smoothing tend to be the best and easiest techniques to use for short-term forecasting with little data required, and provide average results. The long-term models are more complex, requiring much more data input, but provide a higher degree of accuracy. In general, the short-term models compensate for random variation and adjust for short-term changes (such as consumers' responses to a new product). Medium-term forecasts are useful for seasonal effects, and long-term

EXHIBIT 6.1

Forecasting Techniques and Common Models

I. Qualitative	*Subjective, judgmental. Based on intuition, estimates and opinions.*
Delphi method	An interactive learning process involving a group of experts who respond to a questionnaire. A moderator compiles results and formulates a new questionnaire which is again submitted to the same group of experts.
Market research	Sets out to collect data in a variety of ways (surveys, interviews, etc.) to test hypotheses about the market. These are typically used to forecast long-range and new-product sales.
Historical analogy	Ties what is being forecast to a similar item. Important in planning new products where a forecast may be derived by using the history of a similar existing product.
II. Time Series Analysis	*Based on the idea that the history of occurrences over time can be used to predict the future.*
Simple moving average	A time period containing a number of data points is averaged by dividing the sum of the point values by the number of points. Each, therefore, has equal influence. These points may be weighted equally or unequally, as seen fit by experience.
Exponential smoothing	Recent data points are weighted more, with weighting declining exponentially as data become older.
Regression analysis	Fits a straight line to past data generally relating the data value to time. Most common fitting technique is least squares.
Trend projections	Fits a mathematical trend line to the data points and projects it into the future.
III. Causal	*Tries to understand the system underlying and surrounding the item being forecast. For example, sales may be affected by advertising, quality, and competitors.*
Regression analysis	Similar to least squares method in time series but may contain multiple variables. Basis is that forecast is caused by the occurrence of other events.
Input/output models	Focuses on sales of each industry to other firms and governments. Indicates the changes in sales that a producer industry might expect because of purchasing changes by another industry.
Leading indicators	Statistics that move in the same direction as the series being forecast but move before the series, such as an increase in the price of gasoline indicating a future drop in the sale of large cars.

EXHIBIT 6.2

Comparison of Forecasting Techniques

Technique	Time Horizon	Model Complexity	Model Accuracy	Data Requirements
I. Qualitative				
Delphi method	Long	High	Varies	High
II. Time Series				
Moving average	Short	Very low	Medium	Low
Exponential smoothing	Short	Low	Fair	Very low
Linear regression	Long	Medium high	Medium high	High
III. Causal				
Regression analysis	Long	Fairly high	High	High

models detect general trends and are especially useful in identifying major turning points. Which forecasting model or models a firm should adopt depends on several factors, including: (*a*) forecasting time horizon, (*b*) data availability, (*c*) accuracy required, (*d*) size of the forecasting budget, and (*e*) availability of qualified personnel.

COMPONENTS OF DEMAND

In most cases, the demand for products or services can be broken down into five components: (*a*) average demand for the period, (*b*) trends, (*c*) seasonal influence, (*d*) cyclical elements, and (*e*) random variation. Exhibit 6.3 illustrates a plot of demand over a four-year period, showing the trend, cyclical, and seasonal components, and randomness around the smoothed demand curve.

Cyclical factors are more difficult to determine since either the time span or the cause of the cycle may not be known. For example, cyclical influence on demand may come from such occurrences as political elections, war, economic conditions, or sociological pressures.

Random variations are caused by chance events. Statistically, when all the known causes for demand (average, trend, seasonal, and cyclical) are subtracted from the total demand, what remains is the unexplained portion of demand. If one is unable to identify the cause of this remainder, it is assumed to be purely random chance.

In addition to these five components there is often autocorrelation, which denotes the persistence of occurrence. More specifically, the demand expected at any point is highly correlated with its own past values. For example, if demand has been high during December for the past 10 years, then one would expect high demand during December for the coming year. When demand is random, the demand from one time period to another may vary widely. Where high autocorrelation exists, the demand is not expected to change very much from one time period to the next.

Trend lines are the usual starting point in developing a forecast. These trend lines are then adjusted for seasonal effects, cyclical, and any other expected events that may influence the final forecast. Exhibit 6.4 shows four of the most common types of trends. A linear trend obviously reflects a straight continuous relationship. An S-curve is typical of a product's growth and maturity cycle. The critical points on the S-curve are where the trend makes a transition from slow growth to fast growth and from fast to slow. An asymptotic trend starts with the highest demand growth at the beginning, which then tapers off. Such a curve could happen when a firm enters an existing market with the objective of saturating and capturing a large share of the market. An exponential curve is common in products with explosive growth. The exponential trend suggests that sales will continue to increase rapidly for some period of time—an assumption that may be questionable for longer time periods.

EXHIBIT 6.3

Historical Monthly Product Demand Consisting of a Growth Trend, Cyclical Factor, and Seasonal Demand

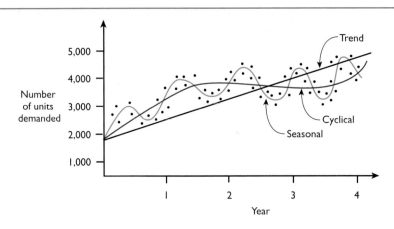

EXHIBIT 6.4

Common Types of Trends

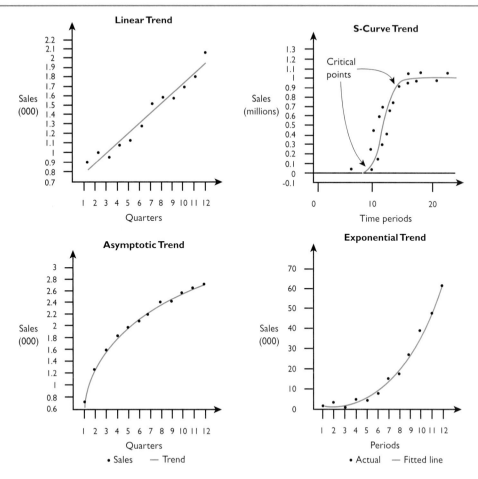

TIME SERIES ANALYSIS

Time series forecasting models try to predict the future based on past data. For example, sales figures collected for each of the past six weeks can be used to forecast sales for the seventh week. Quarterly sales figures collected for the past several years can be used to forecast the sales in future quarters.

Simple Moving Average

simple moving average
Average over a given number of time periods that is updated by replacing the data in the oldest period with that in the most recent period.

If the demand for a product is neither growing nor declining rapidly, and also does not have any seasonal characteristics, a **simple moving average** can be useful in identifying a trend within the data fluctuations. For example, if we want to forecast sales in June with a five-month moving average, we can take the average of the sales in January, February, March, April, and May. When June passes, the forecast for July would be the average of February, March, April, May, and June. The formula for a simple moving average forecast is:

$$F_t = \frac{A_{t-1} + A_{t-2} \cdots + A_{t-n}}{n} \qquad (6.1)$$

where

F_t = Forecasted sales in period t

A_{t-1} = Actual sales in period $t-1$

n = Number of periods in the average

Example

Suppose we want to forecast weekly demand using both a three-week and a nine-week moving average, as shown in Exhibits 6.5 and 6.6. These forecasts are computed as follows:

Solution

To illustrate, the three-week forecasting for week 4 is:

$$\frac{800 + 1,400 + 1,000}{3} = 1,067$$

and the nine-week forecast for week 10 is:

$$\frac{800 + 1,400 + 1,000 + \cdots + 1,300}{9} = 1,367$$

EXHIBIT 6.5

Forecast Demand Based on a Three- and a Nine-Week Simple Moving Average

Week	Demand	Forecast (3-Week)	Forecast (9-Week)	Week	Demand	Forecast (3-Week)	Forecast (9-Week)
1	800			16	1,700	2,200	1,811
2	1,400			17	1,800	2,000	1,800
3	1,000			18	2,200	1,833	1,811
4	1,500	1,067		19	1,900	1,900	1,911
5	1,500	1,300		20	2,400	1,967	1,933
6	1,300	1,333		21	2,400	2,167	2,011
7	1,800	1,433		22	2,600	2,233	2,111
8	1,700	1,533		23	2,000	2,467	2,144
9	1,300	1,600		24	2,500	2,333	2,111
10	1,700	1,600	1,367	25	2,600	2,367	2,167
11	1,700	1,567	1,467	26	2,200	2,367	2,267
12	1,500	1,567	1,500	27	2,200	2,433	2,311
13	2,300	1,633	1,556	28	2,500	2,333	2,311
14	2,300	1,833	1,644	29	2,400	2,300	2,378
15	2,000	2,033	1,733	30	2,100	2,367	2,378

EXHIBIT 6.6

Moving Average Forecast of Three- and Nine-Week Periods versus Actual Demand

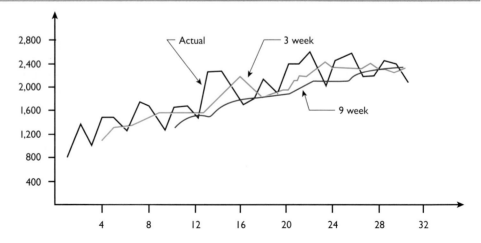

FORECASTING SALES AT TACO BELL REDUCES LABOR COSTS

Labor is a major cost component at Taco Bell, a large fast food chain specializing in Mexican food, averaging 30 percent of sales. Scheduling the proper number of workers for a given time period is critical in the highly competitive fast food industry. Too many workers results in excessive costs and reduced profits. Too few workers, on the other hand, results in lost sales and/or poor service. With the demand being highly variable throughout the day (52 percent of daily sales occur between 11:00 AM and 2:00 PM), Taco Bell needs to accurately forecast sales to schedule the proper number of workers.

After evaluating several forecasting techniques, Taco Bell adopted a six-week moving average. The number of cus-

tomer transactions are recorded in 15-minute time intervals for each day of the week. For example, the forecasted number of customers to be served next Friday between 10:30 AM and 10:45 AM is the six-week average of the number of customers served in that same time period for the previous six Fridays.

This forecasting model is a major element in Taco Bell's labor-management system, which is estimated to have saved Taco Bell $16.4 million in labor costs in 1996 (in comparison to the previously existing management system).

Source: Jackie Hueter and William Swart, "An Integrated Labor-Management System for Taco Bell, Interfaces 28, no. 1, January–February, 1998, pp. 75–91.

As noted in the OM in Practice, Forecasting Sales at Taco Bell Reduces Labor Costs, it is important to select the proper number of periods to include in the moving average. However, there are several conflicting effects that need to be taken into consideration in determining the "right" number of periods. As noted in Exhibit 6.6, the larger the number of periods included in the average, the greater the random elements are "smoothed," which may be desirable in some cases. However, if a trend exists in the data—either increasing or decreasing—the resulting moving average has the adverse affect of constantly lagging this trend. Therefore, while a smaller number of periods in the moving average produces more oscillation, the resulting forecast will more closely follow the existing trend. Conversely, the inclusion of more periods in the moving average will give a smoother forecast but at the same time it will lag the trend by a greater amount.

Exhibit 6.6 graphs the data shown in Exhibit 6.5, illustrating the effects of the number of periods that are included in the moving average. We see that the growth trend levels off at about the 23rd week. The three-week moving average responds better in following this change than the nine-week, although overall, the nine-week average is smoother.

The main disadvantage in calculating a moving average is that all individual elements must be carried as data since a new forecast period involves adding the newest data and dropping the oldest data. For a three- or six-period moving average, this is not too severe; but plotting a 60-day moving average of the daily demand for each of 20,000 items in inventory would involve a significant amount of data. However, today even small PCs are fast and efficient at doing multiproduct moving averages for a long time period. For example, using a 60-day average for 20,000 products would require 61 calculations per product × 20,000 products or 1,220,000 calculations. With the speed of today's PCs these calculations would probably take one or two seconds, at most, to complete.

weighted moving average
Simple moving average where weights are assigned to each time period in the average. The sum of all of the weights must equal one.

Weighted Moving Average

Whereas the simple moving average gives equal weight to each component of the moving-average database, a **weighted moving average** allows each element to be weighted by a factor, where the sum of all the weighting factors equals one. The formula for a weighted moving average forecast is:

$$F_t = \frac{w_{t-1}A_{t-1} + w_{t-2}A_{t-2} \cdots + w_{t-n}A_{t-n}}{n} \tag{6.2}$$

where

F_t = Forecasted sales in period t

A_{t-1} = Actual sales in period $t-1$

w_{t-1} = Weight assigned to period $t-1$

n = Number of periods in the average

An additional constraint when using the weighted moving average forecast is:

$$\sum_{i=1}^{n} w_{t-i} = 1$$

Example

A department store may find that in a four-month period the best forecast is derived by using 40 percent of the actual sales (in units) for the most recent month, 30 percent of two months ago, 20 percent of three months ago, and 10 percent of four months ago. The actual unit sales were as follows,

Month 1	Month 2	Month 3	Month 4	Month 5
100	90	105	95	?

Solution

The forecast for month 5 would therefore be:

$$F_5 = 0.40(95) + 0.30(105) + 0.20(90) + 0.10(100)$$
$$= 38 + 31.5 + 18 + 10$$
$$= 97.5 \text{ units.}$$

Suppose sales for month 5 actually turned out to be 110; then the forecast for month 6 would be:

$$F_6 = 0.40(110) + 0.30(95) + 0.20(105) + 0.10(90)$$
$$= 44 + 28.5 + 21 + 9$$
$$= 102.5 \text{ units.}$$

The weighted moving average has a definite advantage over the simple moving average in being able to vary the effects between older data and more recent data. With the forecasting software that is now available, there is little computational difference between using a weighted moving average and a simple moving average. Both can be obtained in "real time." If there is a disadvantage to the weighted moving average, it is that someone must determine the weights to be used.

Exponential Smoothing

In the previous methods of forecasting that have been presented (that is, simple and weighted moving averages), a major issue is the need to continually carry a large amount of historical data. As new data are added in these methods, the oldest data are dropped and the new forecast is calculated. In many applications (perhaps even in most), the most recent data points tend to be more indicative of the future than those in the distant past. If this premise is valid—that the importance of data diminishes as the past becomes more distant—then **exponential smoothing** may be the most logical and easiest method to use.

exponential smoothing
Time series forecasting technique that does not require large amounts of historical data.

The reason this is called "exponential smoothing" is because each increment in the past is decreased by $(1 - \alpha)$, or

	Weighting at $\alpha = 0.05$
Most recent weighting $= \alpha(1 - \alpha)^0$	0.0500
Data 1 time period older $= \alpha(1 - \alpha)^1$	0.0475
Data 2 time periods older $= \alpha(1 - \alpha)^2$	0.0451
Data 3 time periods older $= \alpha(1 - \alpha)^3$	0.0429

Therefore, the exponents 0, 1, 2, 3 … , etc. give this method its name.

Exponential smoothing is the most used of all forecasting techniques. It is an integral part of virtually all computerized forecasting programs, and is widely used for ordering inventory in retail firms, wholesale companies, and other service operations.

exponential smoothing constant alpha (α)
Value between 0 and 1 that is used in exponential smoothing to minimize the error between historical demand and respective forecasts.

Exponential smoothing accomplishes virtually everything that can be done with moving average forecasts, but requires significantly less data. The **exponential smoothing constant alpha (α)** is a value between 0 and 1. If the actual demand tends to be relatively stable over time, we would choose a relatively small value for α to decrease the effects of short-term or random fluctuations, which is similar to having a moving average that involves a large number of periods. If the actual demand tends to fluctuate rapidly, we would choose a relatively large value for α to keep up with these changes. This is similar to using a moving average with a small number of periods.

The major reasons that exponential smoothing techniques have become so well accepted are:

1. Exponential models are surprisingly accurate.
2. Formulating an exponential model is relatively easy.
3. The user can readily understand how the model works.
4. There is very little computation required to use the model.
5. Computer storage requirements are small because of the limited use of historical data.
6. Tests for accuracy as to how well the model is performing are easy to compute.

In the exponential smoothing method, only three pieces of data are needed to forecast the future: the most recent forecast, the actual demand that occurred for that forecast period, and a smoothing constant alpha (α). This smoothing constant determines the level of smoothing and the speed of reaction to differences between forecasts and actual occurrences. The value for the constant is arbitrary and is determined both by the nature of the product and the manager's sense of what constitutes a good response rate. However, error measuring techniques, such as MAD (which is discussed later in this chapter) can be used to evaluate different values for α until that value is found which minimizes the historical error. For example, if a firm produced a standard item with relatively stable demand, the reaction rate to differences between actual and forecast demand would tend to be small, perhaps just a few percentage points. However, if the firm were experiencing growth, it would be desirable to have a higher reaction rate, to give greater importance to recent growth experience. The more rapid the growth, the higher the reaction rate should be. Sometimes users of the simple moving average switch to exponential smoothing but like to keep the forecasts about the same as the simple moving average. In this case, α is approximated by $2 \div (n + 1)$ where n was the number of time periods that were used in the moving average.

The equation for an exponential smoothing forecast is:

$$F_t = (1 - \alpha)F_{t-1} + \alpha A_{t-1}$$

or rewritten as

$$F_t = F_{t-1} + \alpha(A_{t-1} - F_{t-1}) \tag{6.3}$$

where

$\quad F_t =$ Exponentially smoothed forecast for period t

$\quad F_{t-1} =$ Exponentially smoothed forecast made for the prior period

$\quad A_{t-1} =$ Actual demand in the prior period

$\quad \alpha =$ Desired response rate, or smoothing constant

This equation states that the new forecast is equal to the old forecast plus a portion of the error (the difference between the previous forecast and what actually occurred).[1]

When exponential smoothing is first introduced, the initial forecast or starting point may be obtained by using a simple estimate or an average of preceding periods. If no historical forecast data are available, then the forecast for the previous period (that is, last month) is set equal to the demand for that period.

Example

To demonstrate the exponential smoothing method, assume that the long-run demand for the product under study is relatively stable and a smoothing constant (α) of 0.05 is considered appropriate. If the exponential smoothing method were used as a continuing policy, a forecast would have been made for last month. Assume that last month's forecast (F_{t-1}) was 1,050 units, and 1,000 were actually demanded, rather than 1,050.

Solution

The forecast for this month would then be calculated as follows:

$$\begin{aligned} F_t &= F_{t-1} + \alpha(A_{t-1} - F_{t-1}) \\ &= 1,050 + 0.05(1,000 - 1,050) \\ &= 1,050 + 0.05(-50) \\ &= 1,047.5 \text{ units} \end{aligned}$$

Because the smoothing coefficient is relatively small, the reaction of the new forecast to an error of 50 units is to decrease the next month's forecast by only 2.5 units.

Example

Kevin Alexander owns a small restaurant that is open seven days a week. Until just recently he forecasted the number of customers using his "gut feel." However, he wants to open another restaurant and recognizes the need to adopt a more formal method of forecasting that can be used in both locations. He decided to compare a three-week moving average, and exponential smoothing with $\alpha = .7$ and $\alpha = .3$. The actual sales for the past three weeks are shown below, along with his forecast for last week.

---

[1]Some writers prefer to call F_t a smoothed average.

	Customers per Day						
Week	Sun	Mon	Tue	Wed	Thu	Fri	Sat
Actual:							
3 weeks ago	138	183	182	188	207	277	388
2 weeks ago	143	194	191	200	213	292	401
Last week	157	196	204	193	226	313	408
Forecast:							
Last week	155	191	192	198	204	286	396

a. Forecast sales for each day of the next week using:

- A three-week moving average
- Exponential smoothing with $\alpha = .7$
- Exponential smoothing with $\alpha = .3$

b. The actual sales for the next week were as follows:

	Customers per Day						
Week	Sun	Mon	Tue	Wed	Thu	Fri	Sat
Actual:	160	204	197	210	215	300	421

Evaluate each of the three forecasting techniques based on the one week's data. Which technique would you recommend to Kevin?

Solution   a. The forecasts for each of the three methods is presented below.

b.

Using the average MAD as a criterion, Kevin should use the exponential smoothing method with $\alpha = .7$, as that method has the lowest average MAD of 8.27.

As discussed above, exponential smoothing has the shortcoming of lagging changes in demand. Exhibit 6.7 shows actual data plotted as a smooth curve to show the lagging effects of the exponential forecasts. The forecast lags the actual demand during an increase or decrease, but overshoots actual demand when a change in the direction occurs. Note that the higher the value of alpha, the more closely the forecast follows the actual. In order to more closely track actual demand, a trend factor may be added. What also helps is the ability to adjust the value of alpha. This is termed *adaptive forecasting.* Both trend effects and adaptive forecasting are briefly explained in the following sections.

Trend Effects in Exponential Smoothing   As stated earlier, an upward or downward trend in data collected over a sequence of time periods causes the exponential forecast to always lag behind (that is, to be above or below) the actual occurrence. Exponentially smoothed forecasts can be corrected somewhat by including a trend adjustment. To correct for the trend, we now need two smoothing constants. In addition to the smoothing constant α, the trend equation also requires a **trend smoothing constant delta (δ).** Like alpha, delta is limited to values between 0 and 1. The delta reduces the impact of the error which occurs between the actual and the forecast. If both alpha and delta are not included, the trend would overreact to errors.

To initiate the trend equation, the trend value must be entered manually. This first trend value can be an educated guess or a computation based on observed past data.

trend smoothing constant delta (δ)
Value between 0 and 1 that is used in exponential smoothing when there is a trend.

EXHIBIT 6.7

Exponential Forecasts versus
Actual Demands for Units of
a Product over Time
Showing the Forecast Lag

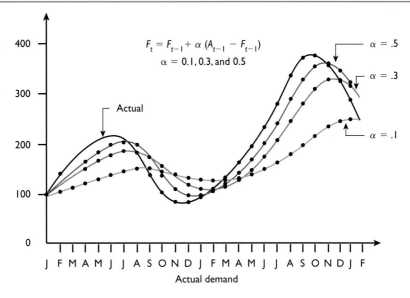

The equation to compute the forecast including trend (FIT) is:

$$\text{FIT}_t = F_t + T_t \tag{6.4}$$

where

$$F_t = \text{FIT}_{t-1} + \alpha(A_{t-1} - \text{FIT}_{t-1}) \tag{6.5}$$
$$T_t = T_{t-1} + \alpha\delta(A_{t-1} - \text{FIT}_{t-1}) \tag{6.6}$$

Example

Assume an initial starting point for F_t of 100 units, a trend of 10 units, an alpha of .20, and a delta of .30. If the actual demand turned out to be 115 rather than the forecast 100, calculate the forecast for the next period.

Solution

Adding the starting forecast and the trend, we have:

$$\text{FIT}_{t-1} = F_{t-1} + T_{t-1} = 100 + 10 = 110$$

The actual A_{t-1} is given as 115. Therefore,

$$
\begin{aligned}
F_t &= \text{FIT}_{t-1} + \alpha(A_{t-1} - \text{FIT}_{t-1}) \\
&= 110 + .2(115 - 110) = 111.0 \\
T_t &= T_{t-1} + \alpha\delta(A_{t-1} - \text{FIT}_{t-1}) \\
&= 10 + (.2)(.3)(115 - 110) = 10.3 \\
\text{FIT}_t &= F_t + T_t = 111.0 + 10.3 = 121.3
\end{aligned}
$$

If, instead of 121.3, the actual turned out to be 120, the sequence would be repeated and the forecast for the next period would be:

$$
\begin{aligned}
F_{t+1} &= 121.3 + .2(120 - 121.3) = 121.04 \\
T_{t+1} &= 10.3 + (.2)(.3)(120 - 121.3) = 10.22 \\
\text{FIT}_{t+1} &= 121.04 + 10.22 = 131.26
\end{aligned}
$$

Adaptive Forecasting   There are two approaches for adjusting the value of alpha. One uses various values of alpha and the other uses a tracking signal.

1. *Two or more predetermined values of alpha.* The amount of error between the forecast and the actual demand is measured. Depending on the degree of error, different values of alpha are used. For example, if the error is large, alpha is 0.8; if the error is small, alpha is 0.2.

2. *Computed values of alpha.* A tracking signal computes whether the forecast is keeping pace with genuine upward or downward changes in demand (as opposed to random changes). The tracking signal is defined here as the exponentially smoothed actual error divided by the exponentially smoothed absolute error. Alpha is set equal to this tracking signal and therefore changes from period to period within the possible range of 0 to 1.

In logic, computing alpha seems simple. In practice, however, it is quite prone to error. There are three exponential equations—one for the single exponentially smoothed forecast as done in the previous section of this chapter, one to compute an exponentially smoothed actual error, and the third to compute the exponentially smoothed absolute error. Thus, the user must keep three equations running in sequence for each period. Further, assumptions must be made during the initial time periods until the technique has had a chance to start computing values. For example, alpha must be given a value for the first two periods until actual data are available. Also, the user must select a second smoothing constant, in addition to alpha, which is used in the actual and absolute error equations. Clearly, those who use adaptive forecasting on a regular basis rely on technology for the calculations.

FORECASTING ERRORS

When we use the word *error,* we are referring to the difference between the forecast value and what actually occurred. So long as the forecast value is within the confidence limits, as we discuss below in "Measurement of Error," this is not really an error. However, common usage refers to the difference as an error.

Demand for a product is generated through the interaction of a number of factors which are too complex to describe accurately in a model. Therefore, all forecasts contain some degree of error. In discussing forecast errors, it is convenient to distinguish between *sources of error* and the *measurement of error.*

Sources of Error

Errors can come from a variety of sources. One common source that many forecasters are unaware of is caused by the projection of past trends into the future. For example, when we talk about statistical errors in regression analysis, we are referring to the deviations of observations from our regression line. It is common to attach a confidence band to the regression line to reduce the unexplained error. However, when we then use this regression line as a forecasting device by projecting it into the future, the error may not be correctly defined by the projected confidence band. This is because the confidence interval is based on past data; consequently it may or may not be totally valid for projected data points and therefore cannot be used with the same confidence. In fact, experience has shown that the actual errors tend to be greater than those predicted from forecasting models.

Errors can be classified as either bias or random. *Bias errors* occur when a consistent mistake is made, that is, the forecast is always too high. Sources of bias include: (*a*) failing to include the right variables, (*b*) using the wrong relationships among variables, (*c*) employing the wrong trend line, (*d*) mistakenly shifting the seasonal demand from where it normally occurs, and (*e*) the existence of some undetected secular trend. *Random errors* can be defined simply as those that cannot be explained by the forecast model being used. These random errors are often referred to as "noise" in the model.

Measurement of Error

Several of the common terms used to describe the degree of error associated with forecasting are *standard error, mean squared error* (or *variance*), and *mean absolute deviation*. In addition, *tracking signals* may be used to indicate the existence of any positive or negative bias in the forecast.

Standard error is discussed in the section on linear regression later in the chapter. Since the standard error is the square root of a function, it is often more convenient to use the function itself. This is called the *mean square error,* or variance.

The **mean absolute deviation (MAD)** was at one time very much in vogue but subsequently was ignored in favor of the standard deviation and standard error measures. In recent years, however, MAD has made a comeback because of its simplicity and usefulness in obtaining tracking signals. MAD is the average error in the forecasts, using absolute values. It is valuable because MAD, like the standard deviation, measures the dispersion (or variation) of observed values around some expected value.

MAD is computed using the differences between the actual demand and the forecast demand without regard to whether it is negative or positive. It is therefore equal to the sum of the absolute deviations divided by the number of data points, or, stated in equation form:

$$\text{MAD} = \frac{\sum\limits_{t=1}^{n} |A_t - F_t|}{n} \qquad (6.7)$$

where

t = Period number

A_t = Actual demand for period t

F_t = Forecast demand for period t

n = Total number of periods

$|\ |$ = A symbol used to indicate the absolute value of a number and thus disregarding positive and negative signs

When the errors that occur in the forecast are normally distributed (which is assumed to be the usual case), the mean absolute deviation relates to the standard deviation as

$$1 \text{ standard deviation} = \sqrt{\frac{\pi}{2}} \times \text{MAD}, \text{ or approximately 1.25 MAD.}$$

Conversely,

$$1 \text{ MAD} \approx 0.8 \text{ standard deviation}$$

The standard deviation is the larger measure. If the MAD for a set of points was found to be 60 units, then the standard deviation would be 75 units. And, in the usual statistical manner, if control limits were set at ±3 standard deviations (or ± 3.75 MADs), then 99.7 percent of the points would fall within these limits. (See Exhibit 6.8.)

A **tracking signal** is a measurement that indicates whether the forecast average is keeping pace with any genuine upward or downward changes in demand. As used in forecasting, the tracking signal is the *number* of mean absolute deviations that the forecast value is above or below the actual occurrence. Exhibit 6.8 shows a normal distribution with a mean of zero and a MAD equal to one. Thus, if we compute a tracking signal and find it equal to -2, we

mean absolute deviation (MAD) Average forecasting error based upon the absolute value between the forecast and actual demand.

tracking signal Measure of error to determine if the forecast is staying within specified limits of the actual demand.

EXHIBIT 6.8

A Normal Distribution with a Mean = 0 and a MAD = 1

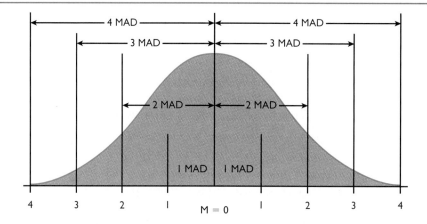

EXHIBIT 6.9

Computing the Mean Absolute Deviation (MAD), the Running Sum of Forecast Errors (RSFE), and the Tracking Signal from Forecast and Actual Data

Month	Demand Forecast	Actual	Deviation	(RSFE)	Abs Dev	Sum of Abs Dev	MAD*	TS = RSFE/MAD
1	1,000	950	−50	−50	50	50	50	−1.00
2	1,000	1,070	+70	+20	70	120	60	.33
3	1,000	1,100	+100	+120	100	220	73.3	1.64
4	1,000	960	−40	+80	40	260	65	1.23
5	1,000	1,090	+90	+170	90	350	70	2.43
6	1,000	1,050	+50	+220	50	400	66.7	3.31

* Mean absolute deviation (MAD). For Month 6, MAD = 400 ÷ 6 = 66.7.

† Tracking signal = $\dfrac{\text{RSFE}}{\text{MAD}}$. For Month 6. TS = $\dfrac{\text{RSFE}}{\text{MAD}}$ = $\dfrac{220}{66.7}$ = 3.3 MADs.

can conclude that the forecast model is providing forecasts that are quite a bit above the mean of the actual occurrences.

A tracking signal can be calculated using the arithmetic sum of forecast deviations divided by the mean absolute deviation, or

$$TS = \frac{RSFE}{MAD} \tag{6.8}$$

where

RSFE = Running sum of forecast errors

MAD = Mean absolute deviation

Exhibit 6.9 illustrates the procedure for computing MAD and the tracking signal for a six-month period where the forecast had been set at a constant 1,000 and the actual demands that occurred are as shown. In this example, the forecast, on the average, was off by 66.7 units and the tracking signal was equal to 3.3 mean absolute deviations.

We can obtain a better interpretation of the MAD and tracking signal by plotting the points on a graph. While not completely legitimate from a sample size standpoint, we plotted each month in Exhibit 6.10 to show the drifting of the tracking signal. Note that it

EXHIBIT 6.10

A Plot of the Tracking
Signals Calculated in
Exhibit 6.9

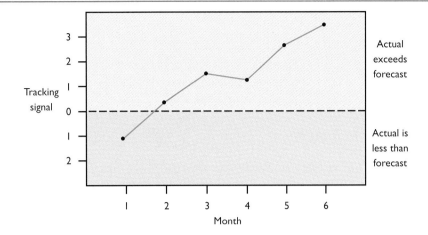

EXHIBIT 6.11

The Percentages of Points
Included within the Control
Limits for a Range of 0 to
4 MADs

Control Limits		
Number of MADs	**Related Number of Standard Deviations**	**Percentage of Points Lying within Control Limits**
=1	0.798	57.048
=2	1.596	88.946
=3	2.394	98.334
=4	3.192	99.856

drifted from minus 1 MAD to +3.3 MADs. This occurred because the actual demand was greater than the forecast in four of the six periods. If the actual demand doesn't fall below the forecast to offset the continual positive RSFE, the tracking signal would continue to rise and we would conclude that assuming a demand of 1,000 is a bad forecast. When the tracking signal exceeds a pre-established limit (for example, ±2.0 or ±3.0), the manager should consider changing the forecast model or the value of α.

Acceptable limits for the tracking signal depend on the size of the demand being forecast (high-volume or high-revenue items should be monitored frequently) and the amount of personnel time available (narrower acceptable limits cause more forecasts to be out of limits and therefore require more time to investigate). Exhibit 6.11 shows the area within the control limits for a range of zero to four MADs.

In a perfect forecasting model, the sum of the actual forecast errors would be zero; that is, the errors that result in overestimates should offset errors that are underestimates. The tracking signal would then also be zero, indicating an unbiased model, neither leading nor lagging the actual demands.

Often, MAD is used to forecast errors. It might then be desirable to make the MAD more sensitive to recent data. A useful technique to do this is to compute an exponentially smoothed MAD (often identified as MAD_t) to forecast the next period's error range. The procedure is similar to single exponential smoothing, which was presented earlier in this chapter. The value of the MAD_t forecast is to provide a range of errors; in the case of inventory control, this is useful in establishing safety stock levels.

$$MAD_t = \alpha |A_{t-1} - F_{t-1}| + (1 - \alpha)MAD_{t-1} \qquad (6.9)$$

where

MAD_t = Forecast MAD for the tth period

α = Smoothing constant (normally in the range of 0.05 to 0.20)

A_{t-1} = Actual demand in the period $t - 1$

F_{t-1} = Forecast demand for period $t - 1$

LINEAR REGRESSION ANALYSIS

linear regression analysis
Type of forecasting technique which assumes that the relationship between the dependent and independent variables is a straight line.

Linear regression analysis is used to define a functional relationship between two or more correlated variables. The relationship is usually developed from observed data where one parameter (the independent variable) is used to predict another (the dependent variable). Linear regression refers to a special class of regression where the relationship between the variables is assumed to be represented by a straight line. The equation for simple linear regression includes only one independent variable and takes the form:

$$Y = a + bX \qquad (6.10)$$

where

Y = Dependent variable we are solving for

a = Y intercept

b = Slope

X = Independent variable (in time series analysis, X represents units of time)

This forecasting method is useful for long-term forecasting of major occurrences and aggregate planning. For example, linear regression would be very useful to forecast demands for product families. Even though demand for individual products within a family may vary widely during a time period, demand for the total product family is surprisingly smooth.

The major restriction in using linear regression forecasting is, as the name implies, that past data and future projections are assumed to fall around a straight line. While this does limit its application, sometimes, if we use a shorter period of time, linear regression analysis can still be used.

Linear regression is used for both time series forecasting and for causal relationship forecasting. When the dependent variable (which is usually represented on the vertical axis of a graph) changes as a result of time (which is plotted on the horizontal axis), it is referred to as time series analysis. If the dependent variable changes due to the change in the independent variable, then it is a causal relationship (such as the number of deaths from lung cancer increasing with the number of people who smoke).

The following example illustrates time series analysis using the least squares method for obtaining the linear regression equation that forecasts sales for future quarters.

Example

A firm's sales for a product line during the 12 quarters of the previous three years were as follows:

Quarter	Sales	Quarter	Sales
1	600	7	2,600
2	1,550	8	2,900
3	1,500	9	3,800
4	1,500	10	4,500
5	2,400	11	4,000
6	3,100	12	4,900

Solution

The firm wants to forecast each quarter of the fourth year, that is, quarters 13, 14, 15, and 16. The least squares equation for linear regression is:

$$\hat{y} = a + bX$$

where
$\hat{y}$ = Dependent variable computed by the equation (sales in this example)
y = Dependent variable data point (see below)
a = Y intercept
b = Slope of the line
X = Independent variable (time period in this example)

The least squares method identifies that line which *minimizes the sum of the squares of the vertical distances* between each data point (y) and its corresponding point on the line (y). If a straight line is drawn through the general area of the points, the difference between the point and the line is ($y - \hat{y}$). Exhibit 6.12 shows these differences. The sum of the squares of the differences between the plotted data points and the line points is:

$$(y_1 - \hat{y}_1)^2 + (y_2 - \hat{y}_2)^2 + \cdots + (y_{12} - \hat{y}_{12})^2$$

The best line to use is the one that minimizes this total.

In the least squares method, the equations for solving for a and b are obtained using calculus and are:

$$a = \bar{Y} - b\bar{X}$$

$$b = \frac{\sum XY - n\bar{X}\bar{Y}}{\sum X^2 - n\bar{X}^2}$$

where
a = Y intercept
b = Slope of the line
$\bar{Y}$ = Arithmetic mean of all Ys
$\bar{X}$ = Arithmetic mean of all Xs
X = X value at each data point
Y = Y value at each data point
n = Number of data points
$\hat{y}_i$ = Value of the dependent variable computed with the regression equation

Exhibit 6.13 shows these computations carried out for the 12 data points. Note that the final equation for Y shows an intercept of 441.6 and a slope of 359.6. The slope shows that for every unit change in X, Y changes by 359.6.

Using this linear regression equation, the forecasts for periods 13 through 16 would be

$$Y_{13} = 441.6 + 359.6(13) = 5,116.4$$
$$Y_{14} = 441.6 + 359.6(14) = 5,476.0$$
$$Y_{15} = 441.6 + 359.6(15) = 5,835.6$$
$$Y_{16} = 441.6 + 359.6(16) = 6,195.2$$

EXHIBIT 6.12

Least Squares Regression Line

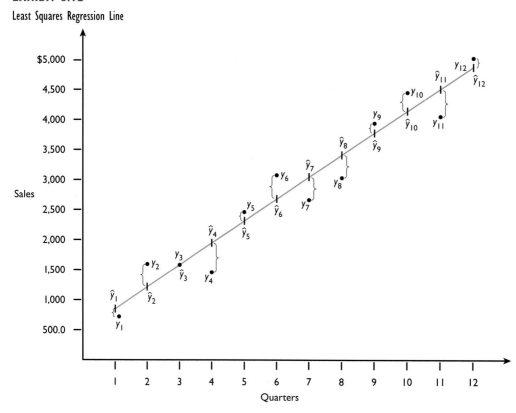

EXHIBIT 6.13

Least Squares Regression
Analysis

(1) X	(2) Y	(3) XY	(4) X^2	(5) Y^2	(6) $\hat{y}$
1	600	600	1	360,000	801.3
2	1,550	3,100	4	2,402,500	1,160.9
3	1,500	4,500	9	2,250,000	1,520.5
4	1,500	6,000	16	2,250,000	1,880.1
5	2,400	12,000	25	5,760,000	2,239.7
6	3,100	18,600	36	9,610,000	2,599.4
7	2,600	18,200	49	6,760,000	2,959.0
8	2,900	23,200	64	8,410,000	3,318.6
9	3,800	34,200	81	14,440,000	3,678.2
10	4,500	45,000	100	20,250,000	4,037.8
11	4,000	44,000	121	16,000,000	4,397.4
12	4,900	58,800	144	24,010,000	4,757.1
78	33,350	268,200	650	112,502,500	

$\overline{X} = 6.5$

$\overline{Y} = 2,779.17$

$b = 359.6153$

$a = 441.6666$

Therefore: $Y = 441.66 + 359.6 X$

$S_{YX} = 363.9$ which is the standard error of the estimate

A measure of how well the data fits the regression line can be determined by calculating the **standard error of the estimate** (S_{YX}). The standard error of the estimate is similar in many ways to the standard deviation (σ). Just as the standard deviation is a measure of how widely the data points are dispersed around the arithmetic mean, so does the standard error of the estimate reflect how widely the errors are dispersed around the regression line. If the error points are assumed to be normally distributed around the regression line, then, as with the standard deviation, we can conclude, for example, that 68.26 percent of the data points around the regression line fall within one standard error of the estimate.

standard error of
the estimate
Measure of dispersion of
the data about a
regression line.

The formula for the standard error of the estimate, or how well the line fits the data, is[2]

$$S_{YX} = \sqrt{\frac{\sum_{i=1}^{n} (y_i - \hat{y}_i)^2}{n - 2}} \tag{6.11}$$

The standard error of the estimate is computed from the first and last columns of Exhibit 6.13:

$$S_{YX} = \sqrt{\frac{(600 - 801.3)^2 + (1{,}550 - 1{,}160.9)^2 + (1{,}500 - 1{,}520.5)^2 + \cdots + (4{,}900 - 4{,}757.1)^2}{10}}$$

$$S_{YX} = 363.9$$

CAUSAL RELATIONSHIP FORECASTING

Any independent variable, to be of value from a forecasting perspective, must be a leading indicator. For example, if the weather service or the *Farmer's Almanac* predicted that next winter was to have an abnormally large number of snow storms, people would probably go out and buy snow shovels and snow blowers in the fall. Thus, the weather prediction or the *Farmer's Almanac* are said to be leading indicators of the sale of snow shovels and snow blowers. These relationships between variables can be viewed as causal relationships—the occurrence of one event causes or influences the occurrence of the other. Running out of gas while driving down a highway, however, does not provide useful data to forecast that the car will stop. The car will stop, of course, but we would like to know enough in advance in order to do something about it. A "low gas level" warning light, for example, is a good leading indicator which forecasts that the car will stop shortly.

The first step in causal relationship forecasting is to identify those occurrences that are really the causes. Often leading indicators are not causal relationships but in some indirect way may suggest that some other things might happen. Other noncausal relationships just seem to exist as a coincidence. One study some years ago showed that the amount of alcohol sold in Sweden was directly proportional to teachers' salaries. Presumably this was a spurious, or noncausal, relationship.

The following problem illustrates one example of how a forecast is developed using a causal relationship.

---

[2]An equation for the standard error that is often easier to compute is

$$S_{XY} = \sqrt{\frac{\sum Y_i^2 - a \sum Y_i - b \sum Y_i X_i}{n - 2}}$$

Example

The Carpet City Store in Carpenteria has kept records of its sales (in square yards) each year, along with the number of permits for new houses in its area. Carpet City's operations manager believes forecasting sales is possible if housing permits are known for that year.

Year	Number of Housing Permits	Sales (in sq. yds.)
1990	18	14,000
1991	15	12,000
1992	12	11,000
1993	10	8,000
1994	20	12,000
1995	28	16,000
1996	35	18,000
1997	30	19,000
1998	20	13,000

First, the data are plotted on Exhibit 6.14, with

X = Number of housing permits

Y = Sales of carpeting in square yards

Solution

Since the points appear to be in a straight line, the manager decides to use the linear relationship $Y = a + bX$. We solve this problem by using the least squares method. Solving for a and b, using the equations presented earlier in this chapter, we obtain the following forecasting equation:

$$Y = 5{,}576.0 + 387.2X$$

Now, suppose that there are 25 housing permits granted in 1999. The 1999 sales forecast would therefore be:

$$Y = 5{,}576.0 + 387.2(25) = 15{,}256.0 \text{ square yards}$$

In this problem, the lag between filing the permit with the appropriate agency and the new homeowner coming to Carpet City to buy carpet makes a causal relationship feasible for forecasting.

EXHIBIT 6.14

Causal Relationship: Sales to Housing Starts

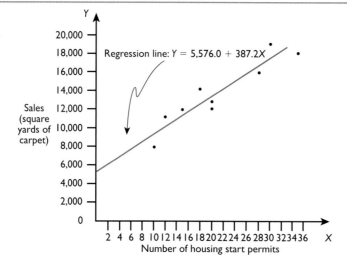

EXHIBIT 6.15

The Relationship between $\bar{Y}$, y_i, and $\hat{y}_i$ in Determining r^2

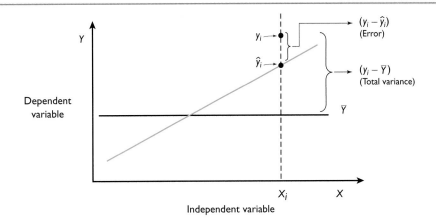

Reliability of the Data

coefficient of determination (r^2) Proportion of variability in demand that can be attributed to an independent variable.

With causal relationship forecasting, we are concerned with how much of the changes in the dependent variable are being "explained" by changes in the independent variable. This is measured by the variance. The greater the proportion of the variance that can be explained by the independent variable, the stronger the relationship. The **coefficient of determination (r^2)** measures the proportion of the variability in the dependent variable that can be explained by changes in the independent variable, and is calculated as follows:

$$r^2 = \frac{\sum (y_i - \bar{Y})^2 - \sum (y_i - \hat{y}_i)^2}{\sum (y_i - \bar{Y})^2} \tag{6.12}$$

where

y_i = Actual value of Y that has been observed for a given value of X

$\bar{Y}$ = Arithmetic mean for all values of y

$\hat{y}_i$ = Value of Y corresponding to a given value of X that has been calculated from the regression equation

The relationship between these variables is shown in Exhibit 6.15. In the equation above, the first term in the numerator and the term in the denominator are the same $(\sum (y_i - \bar{Y})^2)$. This term represents the total variation of the Y variable around the arithmetic mean $\bar{Y}$. The second term in the numerator represents the error or that variation in the Y variable that cannot be explained by the regression equation. Thus the numerator represents that amount of variation that can be explained by the regression equation, and the denominator represents the total variation. As stated above, the coefficient of determination therefore measures the proportion of variation in Y that can be explained by changes in X.

mean squared error (MSE) Measure of variability in the data about a regression line.

Another measure for evaluating the reliability of a regression forecast is the **mean squared error (MSE)**. Using the same notation as above, the MSE is calculated as follows:

$$MSE = \frac{\sum (y_i - \hat{y}_i)^2}{n - 2} \tag{6.13}$$

where n = the number of observations.

The following example will demonstrate the use of both of these terms.

Example

Using the data from the Carpet City Store example presented above, we can compute the coefficient of determination (r^2) and the MSE as follows:

Year	Actual Sales (Sq. Yds)	Predicted Sales (Sq. Yds)	Total Variance	Error Variance
1990	14,000	12,546	111,111	2,114,116
1991	12,000	11,384	2,777,778	379,456
1992	11,000	10,222	7,111,111	605,284
1993	8,000	9,448	32,111,111	2,096,704
1994	12,000	13,320	2,777,778	1,742,400
1995	16,000	16,418	5,444,444	174,724
1996	18,000	19,128	18,777,778	1,272,384
1997	19,000	17,192	28,444,444	3,268,864
1998	13,000	13,320	444,444	102,400
		Totals:	98,000,000	11,756,332

Solution

$$r^2 = \frac{98,000,000 - 11,756,332}{98,000,000} = .88$$

or 88 percent of the change in carpet sales from year to year can be attributed to a change in the number of housing permits issued.

Similarly, we compute the mean squared error:

$$\text{MSE} = \frac{11,756,332}{9 - 2} = 1,679,476$$

The operations manager can use these values for r^2 and MSE to evaluate other forecasting techniques with the technique that is currently being used.

Multiple Regression Analysis

Another forecasting technique is multiple regression analysis, in which more than one independent variable is considered, together with the effects of each of the items of interest. For example, in the home furnishings field, the effects of the number of marriages, housing starts, disposable income, and trend can be expressed in a multiple regression equation as

$$S = B + B_m(M) + B_h(H) + B_i(I) + B_t(T)$$

where

S = Gross sales for year
B = Base sales, a starting point from which other factors have influence
M = Marriages during the year
H = Housing starts during the year
I = Annual disposable personal income
T = Time trend (first year = 1, second = 2, third = 3, and so forth)

and B_m, B_h, B_i, and B_t represent the influence on expected sales of the number of marriages, housing starts, income, and trend, respectively.

Forecasting by multiple regression is very appropriate when a number of factors might influence a variable of interest—in this case, sales. The primary difficulty in applying multiple regression analysis is in the data gathering, and the mathematical computations. Fortunately, standard programs for multiple regression analysis are now available for most computers, relieving the need for tedious manual calculation.

NEURAL NETWORKS

neural networks
A forecasting technique simulating human learning that develops complex relationships between model inputs and outputs.

Neural networks represent a relatively new and growing area of forecasting. Unlike the more common statistical forecasting techniques like time series analysis and regression analysis, neural networks simulate human learning. Thus, over time and with repeated use, neural networks can develop an understanding of the complex relationships that exist between inputs into a forecasting model and the outputs. For example, in a service operation these inputs might include such factors as historic sales, weather, time of day, day of week, and month. The output would be the number of customers that are expected to arrive on a given day and in a given time period. In addition, neural networks perform computations much faster than traditional forecasting techniques. For example, the Southern Company, which is a utility company that provides electricity throughout the south, currently uses neural networks to forecast short-term power requirements a week to ten days ahead. Previously, only mid-term forecasting, that is three months ahead, was feasible with traditional forecasting techniques.[3]

Neural networks can be divided into two broad categories: supervised and unsupervised. In the supervised models, historical data are used to "train" the software. In the unsupervised models, no training takes place. Instead, the software seeks out and identifies patterns that exist in a given data set.[4]

THE APPLICATION OF FORECASTING IN SERVICE OPERATIONS

Service managers are recognizing the important contribution that forecasting can make in improving both the efficiency and the level of service in a service operation. Point-of-sale (POS) equipment can now provide the service manager with historical sales data in time increments that are as small as 15 minutes. The availability of this data permits accurate forecasting of future sales in similar time increments thereby permitting the service manager to schedule workers more efficiently. Davis and Berger[5] point out that, in addition to forecasting sales, such models can also forecast product usage which reduces the spoilage of perishable items.

Forecasting is also an integral part of *yield management* (also known as revenue management), which is discussed in more detail in a later chapter. In brief, yield management attempts to maximize the revenues of service operations that have high fixed costs and small variable costs. Examples of such service businesses include airlines, car rental agencies and hotels. The goal of yield management is to maximize capacity utilization, even if it means offering large price discounts, when necessary, to fill available capacity. At the same time, the manager does not want to turn away a full paying customer because the capacity was already sold to a discount customer. In order to accomplish this successfully, the manager must be able to forecast demand patterns for different market segments.

---

[3]Karl Moore, Robert Burbach, and Roger Heeler, "Using Neural Networks to Analyze Qualitative Data," *Marketing Research* 7 (January 1, 1995), p. 34.

[4]Scott Hample, "R U Ready for AI?" *Marketing Tools,* May 1, 1996, p. 60.

[5]Mark M. Davis and Paul D. Berger. "Sales Forecasting in a Retail Service Environment," *The Journal of Business Forecasting,* Winter 1989, pp. 8–17.

At GTE Laboratories, engineer Phil Rossoni examines a print generated by GRANET, a graphics-based software tool developed by GTE to help engineers worldwide plan cellular networks and forecast their performance.

COMPUTER PROGRAMS FOR FORECASTING

There are many commercial programs now available. Some of these programs exist as library routines within a mainframe computer system while some may be incorporated or "bundled" as part of a larger program package. Still other programs can be purchased separately from software companies specializing in this area. Many of these programs are available for PCs.

No longer does one have to be an expert in statistical forecasting techniques to use these programs, as most of them are easy to understand and user friendly. Anyone with working knowledge of an electronic spreadsheet such as Lotus 1-2-3®, Quattro Pro®, SuperCalc®, or Excel® can create a forecast on a PC.

Also, a wealth of information concerning forecasting is available on the Internet. This includes reviews of different forecasting programs. George Stewart, a former editor of *Byte Magazine,* has reviewed several of these forecasting programs. Some of the forecasting programs that he has reviewed include Forecast Pro for Windows, SmartForecast, Solo Statistical Software, and Autocast II. Inasmuch as this is a fast changing area, you should conduct your own search on the Internet to obtain the latest information on forecasting programs.

CONCLUSION

Forecasting is fundamental to any planning effort. In the short run, a forecast is needed to predict the requirements for materials, products, services, or other resources to respond to changes in demand. Forecasts permit adjusting worker schedules and varying labor and materials. In the long run, forecasting is required as a basis for strategic changes, such as developing new markets, developing new products or services, and expanding or creating new facilities.

For long-term forecasts that lead to heavy financial commitments, great care should be taken to derive the forecast. Several approaches should be used. Causal methods such as regression analysis or multiple regression analysis are beneficial. These provide a basis for discussion. Economic factors, product trends, growth factors, and competition, as well as a myriad of other possible variables, need to be considered and the forecast adjusted to reflect the influence of each.

Short- and intermediate-term forecasting, such as those required for inventory control, and labor and material scheduling, may be satisfied with simpler models, such as exponential smoothing with perhaps an adaptive feature or a seasonal index. In these applications, thousands of items are usually being forecast. The forecasting routine should therefore be simple and run quickly on a computer. The routines should also detect and respond rapidly to definite short-term changes in demand while at the same time ignoring the occasional spurious demands. Exponential smoothing, when monitored by management to adjust the value of alpha, is an effective technique.

A Chinese fortune cookie once stated that "Forecasting is difficult, especially about the future." A perfect forecast is like a hole-in-one in golf: great to get but we should be satisfied just to get close to the cup—or, to push the metaphor, just to land on the green. The ideal philosophy is to create the best forecast that you reasonably can and then have sufficient flexibility in the system to adjust for the inevitable forecast error. Managers must recognize the trade-offs that exist in developing forecasting models: the greater the accuracy required, the more expensive the model. At some point, the cost of improved accuracy cannot be economically justified.

KEY FORMULAS

Simple moving average forecast

$$F_t = \frac{A_{t-1} + A_{t-2} \cdots + A_{t-n}}{n} \tag{6.1}$$

Weighted moving average forecast

$$F_t = \frac{w_{t-1} A_{t-1} + w_{t-2} A_{t-2} \cdots + w_{t-n} A_{t-n}}{n} \tag{6.2}$$

and

$$\sum_{i=1}^{n} w_{t-i} = 1$$

Exponential smoothing

$$F_t = F_{t-1} + \alpha(A_{t-1} - F_{t-1}) \tag{6.3}$$

Exponential smoothing with trend effects

$$\text{FIT}_t = F_t + T_t \tag{6.4}$$

$$F_t = \text{FIT}_{t-1} + \alpha(A_{t-1} - \text{FIT}_{t-1}) \tag{6.5}$$

$$T_t = T_{t-1} + \alpha\delta(A_{t-1} - \text{FIT}_{t-1}) \tag{6.6}$$

Mean absolute deviation (MAD)

$$\text{MAD} = \frac{\sum\limits_{t=1}^{n} |A_t - F_t|}{n} \tag{6.7}$$

Tracking signal

$$\text{TS} = \frac{\text{RSFE}}{\text{MAD}} \tag{6.8}$$

Exponentially smoothed MAD

$$\text{MAD}_t = \alpha|A_{t-1} - F_{t-1}| + (1 - \alpha)\text{MAD}_{t-1} \tag{6.9}$$

Linear regression

$$Y = a + bX \tag{6.10}$$

Standard error of the estimate

$$S_{YX} = \sqrt{\frac{\sum\limits_{i-1}^{n}(y_i - \hat{y}_i)^2}{n - 2}} \tag{6.11}$$

Coefficient of determination

$$r^2 = \frac{\sum(y_i - \bar{Y})^2 - \sum(y_i - \hat{y}_i)^2}{\sum(y_i - \bar{Y})^2} \tag{6.12}$$

Mean squared error

$$\text{MSE} = \frac{\sum(y_i - \hat{y}_i)^2}{n - 2} \tag{6.13}$$

KEY TERMS

causal forecasting   p. 198
coefficient of determination (r^2)   p. 219
exponential smoothing   p. 205
exponential smoothing constant alpha (α)
   p. 205
linear regression analysis   p. 214
mean absolute deviation (MAD) p. 211
mean squared error (MSE)   p. 219

neural networks   p. 221
qualitative techniques   p. 198
simple moving average   p. 201
standard error of estimate   p. 217
time series analysis   p. 198
tracking signal   p. 211
trend smoothing constant delta (δ)   p. 208
weighted moving average   p. 203

REVIEW AND DISCUSSION QUESTIONS

1. Examine Exhibit 6.2 and suggest which forecasting technique you might use for: (*a*) bathing suits; (*b*) demand for new houses; (*c*) electrical power usage; (*d*) new plant expansion plans.

2. In terms of the errors, why would the operations manager wish to use the least squares method when doing simple linear regression?

3. All forecasting methods using exponential smoothing, adaptive smoothing, and exponential smoothing including trend require starting values to initialize the equations. How would you select the starting value for, say, F_{t-1}?

4. From the choice of simple moving average, weighted moving average, exponential smoothing, and single regression analysis, which forecasting technique would you consider the most accurate? Why?

5. What is the main disadvantage of daily forecasting using regression analysis?

6. What are the main problems with using adaptive exponential smoothing in forecasting?

7. What is the purpose of a tracking signal?

8. What are the main differences between traditional forecasting techniques and neural networks?

9. Discuss the basic differences between the mean absolute deviation (MAD) and the standard error of the estimate.

10. What implications do the existence of forecast errors have for the search for ultrasophisticated statistical forecasting models such as neural networks?

 INTERNET UPDATE

Conduct a search on the Web to identify:

a. What types of forecasting programs are available and describe these programs. Suggested key words are FORECASTING and SOFTWARE.

b. Various applications of neural networks. Suggested key words are FORECASTING, NEURAL, and NETWORKS.

c. Various applications of forecasting models in scheduling. Suggested key words are FORECASTING and SCHEDULING.

SOLVED PROBLEMS

Problem 1

Sunrise Baking Company markets doughnuts through a chain of food stores and has been experiencing over- and underproduction because of forecasting errors. The following data are their daily demands in dozens of doughnuts for the past four weeks. The bakery is closed Saturday, so Friday's production must satisfy demand for both Saturday and Sunday.

	4 Weeks Ago	3 Weeks Ago	2 Weeks Ago	Last Week
Monday	2,200	2,400	2,300	2,400
Tuesday	2,000	2,100	2,200	2,200
Wednesday	2,300	2,400	2,300	2,500
Thursday	1,800	1,900	1,800	2,000
Friday	1,900	1,800	2,100	2,000
Saturday } Sunday }	2,800	2,700	3,000	2,900

Make a forecast for this week on the following basis:

a. Daily, using a simple four-week moving average.

b. Daily, using a weighted average of 0.40 for last week, 0.30 for two weeks ago, 0.20 for three weeks ago, and 0.10 for four weeks ago.

c. Sunrise is also planning its purchases of ingredients for bread production. If bread demand had been forecast for last week at 22,000 loaves and only 21,000 loaves were actually demanded, what would Sunrise's forecast be for this week using exponential smoothing with $\alpha = 0.10$?

d. Supposing, with the forecast made in (*c*), this week's demand actually turns out to be 22,500. What would the new forecast be for the next week?

Solution

a. Simple moving average, 4 weeks.

Monday $\qquad \dfrac{2{,}400 + 2{,}300 + 2{,}400 + 2{,}200}{4} = \dfrac{9{,}300}{4} = 2{,}325$ doz.

Tuesday $\qquad\qquad\qquad\qquad\qquad\qquad = \dfrac{8{,}500}{4} = 2{,}125$ doz.

Wednesday $\qquad\qquad\qquad\qquad\qquad\; = \dfrac{9{,}500}{4} = 2{,}375$ doz.

Thursday $\qquad\qquad\qquad\qquad\qquad\;\; = \dfrac{7{,}500}{4} = 1{,}875$ doz.

Friday $\qquad\qquad\qquad\qquad\qquad\qquad = \dfrac{7{,}800}{4} = 1{,}950$ doz.

Saturday and Sunday $\qquad\qquad\quad = \dfrac{11{,}400}{4} = 2{,}850$ doz.

b. Weighted average with weights of .40, .30, .20, and .10.

	(.10)		(.20)		(.30)		(.40)		
Monday	220	+	480	+	690	+	960	=	2,350
Tuesday	200	+	420	+	660	+	880	=	2,160
Wednesday	230	+	480	+	690	+	1,000	=	2,400
Thursday	180	+	380	+	540	+	800	=	1,900
Friday	190	+	360	+	630	+	800	=	1,980
Saturday and Sunday	280	+	540	+	900	+	1,160	=	2,880
	1,300	+	2,660	+	4,110	+	5,600	=	13,670

c. $F_t = F_{t-1} + \alpha(A_{t-1} - F_{t-1})$
  $= 22{,}000 + 0.10(21{,}000 - 22{,}000)$
  $= 22{,}000 - 100$
  $= 21{,}900$ loaves

d. $F_{t+1} = 21{,}900 + \alpha(22{,}500 - 21{,}900)$
  $= 21{,}900 + .10(600)$
  $= 21{,}960$ loaves

Problem 2

A specific forecasting model was used to forecast demands for a product. The forecasts and the corresponding demands that subsequently occurred are shown below.

Month	Actual	Forecast
October	700	660
November	760	840
December	780	750
January	790	835
February	850	910
March	950	890

Use the MAD and tracking signal technique to evaluate the forecasting model.

Solution

Evaluate the forecasting model using MAD and tracking signal.

Month	Actual Demand	Forecast Demand	Actual Deviation	Cumulative Deviation (RSFE)	Absolute Deviation
October	700	660	40	40	40
November	760	840	−80	−40	80
December	780	750	30	−10	30
January	790	835	−45	−55	45
February	850	910	−60	−115	60
March	950	890	60	−55	60
				Total dev. =	$\overline{315}$

$$\text{MAD} = \frac{315}{6} = 52.5$$

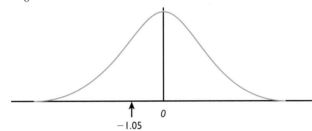

$$\text{Tracking signal} = \frac{-55}{52.5} = -1.05$$

Forecast model is well within the distribution.

PROBLEMS

1. Demand for stereo headphones and CD players for joggers has caused Nina Industries to experience a growth of almost 50 percent over the past year. The number of joggers is continuing to expand, so Nina expects demand for headsets to also expand, since there have, as yet, been no safety laws passed to prevent joggers from wearing them.

   Demands for the stereo units for last year were as follows:

Month	Demand (units)
January	4,200
February	4,300
March	4,000
April	4,400
May	5,000
June	4,700
July	5,300
August	4,900
September	5,400
October	5,700
November	6,300
December	6,000

   a. Using least squares regression analysis, what would you estimate demand to be for each month next year? Follow the general format in Exhibit 6.13.

b. To be reasonably confident of meeting demand, Nina decides to use three standard errors of estimate for safety. How many additional units should be held to meet this level of confidence?

2. The historical demand for a product is:

Month	Demand
January	12
February	11
March	15
April	12
May	16
June	15

a. Using a weighted moving average with weights of 0.60 for June, 0.30 for May, and 0.10 for April, find the July forecast.
b. Using a simple three-month moving average, find the July forecast.
c. Using single exponential smoothing with $\alpha = 0.2$ and a June forecast $= 13$, find the July forecast. Make whatever assumptions you wish. List these assumptions.
d. Using simple linear regression analysis, calculate the regression equation for the preceding demand data.
e. Using the regression equation in (d), calculate the forecast for July.

3. The following tabulations are actual sales of units for six months and a starting forecast in January.
a. Calculate the forecast for the remaining five months using simple exponential smoothing with alpha $= 0.2$.
b. Calculate the MAD for the forecasts.

	Actual	Forecast
January	100	80
February	94	
March	106	
April	80	
May	68	
June	94	

4. Sales data for two years is given below. The data is aggregated with two months of sales in each "period."

Period	Sales	Period	Sales
January–February	109	January–February	115
March–April	104	March–April	112
May–June	150	May–June	159
July–August	170	July–August	182
September–October	120	September–October	126
November–December	100	November–December	106

a. Plot the data on a graph.
b. Fit a simple linear regression model to the sales data.
c. Using the results from part (b), prepare bimonthly forecasts for the next year.

5. The tracking signals that were computed using the past demand history for three different products are shown below. Each product used the same forecasting technique.

	TS 1	TS 2	TS 3
1	−2.70	1.54	0.10
2	−2.32	−0.64	0.43
3	−1.70	2.05	1.08
4	−1.1	2.58	1.74
5	−0.87	−0.95	1.94
6	−0.05	−1.23	2.24
7	0.10	0.75	2.96
8	0.40	−1.59	3.02
9	1.50	0.47	3.54
10	2.20	2.74	3.75

Discuss the tracking signals for each product and what the implications are.

6. Prepare a forecast, using simple linear regression, for each quarter of the next year from the following past two years' quarterly sales information.

Quarter	Sales
1	160
2	195
3	150
4	140
5	215
6	240
7	205
8	190

7. Tucson Machinery, Inc., manufactures numerically controlled machines, which sell for an average price of $500,000 each. Sales for these NCMs for the past two years were as follows:

Quarter	Quantity (units)	Quarter	Quantity (units)
1996		1997	
I	12	I	16
II	18	II	24
III	26	III	28
IV	16	IV	18

a. Do a simple linear regression analysis.

b. Forecast sales for each quarter in 1998.

8. Following are the actual tabulated demands for an item for a nine-month period, from January through September. Your supervisor wants to test two forecasting methods to see which method was better over this period.

Month	Actual
January	110
February	130
March	150
April	170
May	160
June	180
July	140
August	130
September	140

a. Forecast April through September using a three-month simple moving average.

b. Use simple exponential smoothing to estimate April through September. (Use $\alpha = .3$ and assume that the forecast for March was 130.)

c. Use MAD to decide which method produced the better forecast over the six-month period.

9. A particular forecasting model was used to forecast monthly sales in a six-month period. The forecasts and the actual demands that resulted are as follows:

Month	Sales (Forecasted)	Sales (Actual)
April	250	200
May	325	250
June	400	325
July	350	300
August	375	325
September	450	400

Calculate the tracking signal and state whether you think the model being used is giving acceptable answers. Justify your conclusion.

10. Harlen Industries has a very simple forecasting model: take the actual demand for the same month last year and divide that by the number of fractional weeks in that month, producing the average weekly demand for that month. This weekly average is used as the weekly forecast this year.

The following eight weeks shows the forecast (based on last year) and the demand that actually occurred:

Week	Forecast Demand	Actual Demand
1	140	137
2	140	133
3	140	150
4	140	160
5	140	180
6	150	170
7	150	185
8	150	205

a. Compute the MAD of forecast errors.

b. Using the RSFE, compute the tracking signal.

c. Based on your answers to (*a*) and (*b*) what comments can you make about Harlen's method of forecasting?

11. The historical demand for a product is: January, 80; February, 100; March, 60; April, 80; and May, 90.

a. Using a simple four-month moving average, what is the forecast for June? If June experienced a demand of 100, what would your forecast be for July?

b. Using exponential smoothing with $\alpha = 0.20$, if the forecast for January had been 70, compute what the exponentially smoothed forecast would have been for the remaining months through June.

c. Using the least squares method, compute a forecast for June, July, and August.

d. Using a weighted moving average with weights of 0.30 (May), 0.25 (April), 0.20 (March), 0.15 (February), and 0.10 (January), what is June's forecast?

12. In this problem, you are to test the validity of your forecasting model. The following are the forecasts for a model you have been using along with the actual demands that occurred:

Week	Forecast	Actual
1	800	900
2	850	1,000
3	950	1,050
4	950	900
5	1,000	900
6	975	1,100

Use the method stated in the text to compute the MAD and the tracking signal and draw a conclusion as to whether the forecasting model you have been using is giving reasonable results. Justify your conclusion.

13. Assume that your stock of sales merchandise is maintained based on the forecast demand. If the distributor's sales personnel call on the first day of each month, compute your forecast sales for each of the three methods requested here.

Month	Actual
June	140
July	180
August	170

a. Using a simple three-month moving average, what is the forecast for September?

b. Using a weighted moving average, what is the forecast for September with weights of .20, .30, and .50 for June, July, and August, respectively?

c. Using simple exponential smoothing and assume that the forecast for June had been 130, calculate the forecasts for September with a smoothing constant alpha of .30.

14. The historical demand for a product is:

Month	Demand
April	60
May	55
June	75
July	60
August	80
September	75

a. Using a simple four-month moving average, calculate a forecast for October.

b. Using simple exponential smoothing with $\alpha = 0.2$ and a September forecast $= 65$, calculate a forecast for October.

c. Using simple linear regression, calculate the trend line for the historical data. To help in your calculations, the following data are given: The X axis is April $= 1$, May $= 2$, and so on. The Y axis is demand.

$$n = 6$$
$$\sum X = 21$$
$$\sum Y = 405$$
$$\sum X^2 = 91$$
$$\sum Y^2 = 27{,}875$$
$$\sum XY = 1{,}485$$

d. Using simple linear regression, calculate a forecast for October.

15. A forecasting method you have been using to predict product demand is shown in the following table along with the actual demand that occurred.

Forecast	Actual
1,500	1,550
1,400	1,500
1,700	1,600
1,750	1,650
1,800	1,700

    a. Compute the tracking signal using the mean absolute deviation (MAD) and running sum of forecast errors (RSFE).

    b. Comment on whether you feel the forecasting method is giving good predictions.

16. Sales during the past six months have been as follows:

January	115
February	123
March	132
April	134
May	140
June	147

    a. Using a simple three-month moving average, make forecasts for April through July. What is the main weakness of using a simple moving average with data that is patterned like this?

    b. Using simple exponential smoothing with $\alpha = 0.70$, if the forecast for January had been 110, compute the exponentially smoothed forecasts for each month through July. Is this method more accurate for this data? Why or why not?

    c. Using the least squares method, compute the forecasts for the rest of the year. Does your regression line seem to fit the January through June data well? If so, briefly describe a pattern of data with which linear regression would not work well.

    d. Calculate the mean absolute deviation (MAD) for January through June using the trend equation from (*c*).

17. Actual demand for a product for the past three months was:

Three months ago	400 units
Two months ago	350 units
Last month	325 units

    a. Using a simple three-month moving average, what would the forecast be for this month?

    b. If 300 units actually occurred this month, what would your forecast be for the next month?

    c. Using simple exponential smoothing, what would your forecast be for this month if the exponentially smoothed forecast for three months ago was 450 units and the smoothing constant was 0.20?

18. After using your forecasting model for a period of six months, you decide to test it using MAD and a tracking signal. Following are the forecasted and actual demands for the

six-month period:

Period	Forecast	Actual
May	450	500
June	500	550
July	550	400
August	600	500
September	650	675
October	700	600

a. Calculate the tracking signal.

b. Decide whether your forecasting routine is acceptable.

19. Consolidated Edison Company of New York, Inc., sells electricity, gas, and steam to New York City and Westchester County. Sales revenue for the years 1984 to 1994 are shown below. Forecast the revenues for 1995 through 1998. Use your own judgment, intuition, or common sense concerning which model or method to use, as well as the period of data to include. Obtain the actual revenues for three years and evaluate your forecasting model.

Year	Revenue ($ millions)	Year	Revenue ($ millions)
1984	5,728.8	1990	5,738.9
1985	5,497.9	1991	5,873.1
1986	5,197.7	1992	5,932.9
1987	5,094.4	1993	6,020.0
1988	5,108.8	1994	6,260.0
1989	5,550.6		

20. Dana and Kerry own a chain of aerobic and fitness centers for women. They recently hired a consultant to help identify which factors significantly affect the volume of sales at a location. Based on the consultant's analysis, the three most significant factors were: (1) average age of adult females within a three-mile radius, (2) number of adult females living or working within a three-mile radius, and (3) average household income within a three-mile radius. Using multiple regression analysis, the consultant developed the following equation to forecast sales for a new location:

Sales $= 410, 411 - 4, 417$(average age) $+ 4.62$(number of females) $+ 1.55$(average income)

Dana and Kerry are currently evaluating four potential sites. The data for each of these sites follows.

Site	Average Age	Number of Females	Average Income
A	47 yrs	14,000	$77,000
B	22	21,000	49,000
C	32	9,000	54,000
D	37	16,000	83,000

Calculate the forecasted sales for each site. Which one should Dana and Kerry select for their next location if their goal is to maximize their sales?

21. Josh Francis has been recently named Director of Marketing for a consumer products company. The company has divided up the United States into different territories, with a sales

manager assigned to each territory. The sales and populations for the current territories that her firm now does business in are as follows:

Territory	Population (millions)	Sales (thousands)
A	2.53	410
B	1,76	240
C	6.81	595
D	4.22	325
E	12.77	990
F	5.09	665
G	10.82	840
H	16.84	1,450
I	7.65	825
J	11.34	935
K	6.18	830

a. Using an electronic spreadsheet, calculate the least squares regression line that fits the above data.

b. What is the regression equation? What is the coefficient of determination?

c. Marisa's company is planning to expand into two additional territories in the coming year. The populations of these two territories are 7.43 million and 3.87 million. What are the estimated sales that Marisa can expect from these two territories?

22. Alex has recently graduated from a business school and has taken a position as the assistant manager at a small hotel with 35 rooms. One of his first assignments is to develop a model to forecast the number of room-nights that are expected to be sold in each month in 1999. (A room-night is the sale of one room for one night.) He has collected the following historical data on how many room-nights have been sold for each month in each of the past three years.

Month	Room-Nights Sold 1996	1997	1998
January	307	275	316
February	257	209	251
March	290	304	338
April	323	312	370
May	425	469	472
June	589	548	593
July	791	734	777
August	643	658	702
September	454	420	513
October	725	690	766
November	547	493	639
December	605	584	668

a. Using exponential smoothing with an electronic spreadsheet, develop a forecast for the number of room-nights to be sold in each month of 1999. Since this is the first time you are doing this forecast, use $\alpha = 0.3$ and $\alpha = 0.7$ and develop two forecasts. (Assume that the forecast for each month in 1996 is equal to the actual demand.)

b. Which α would you recommend using and why?

SELECTED BIBLIOGRAPHY

Andrews, Bruce H., and Shawn M. Cunningham. "L.L. Bean Improves Call Center Forecasting." *Interfaces* 25, no. 6 (November–December 1995), pp. 1–13.

Bowerman, B. L., and R. T. O'Connell. *Time Series Forecasting.* Boston: Duxbury, 1986.

Carlberg, Ralph. "BioComp Systems on Demand Forecasting." Biocomp Systems, Inc., Redmond, WA, 1996.

Cryer, J. *Time Series Analysis,* Boston: Duxbury, 1986.

Davis, Mark M., and Paul D. Berger. "Sales Forecasting in a Retail Service Environment." *The Journal of Business Forecasting,* Winter 1989, pp. 8–17.

DeLurgio, Stephen, and Carl Bhame. *Forecasting Systems for Operations Management.* Burr Ridge, IL: Richard D. Irwin, 1990.

Hample, Scott. "R U Ready for AI?" *Marketing Tools,* May 1, 1996, p. 60.

Hanke, John E., and Arthur G. Reitsch. *Business Forecasting.* 4th ed. Boston: Allyn and Bacon, 1992.

Hueter, Jackie, and William Swart. "An Integrated Labor-Management System for Taco Bell." *Interfaces* 28, no.1, January–February 1998, pp. 75–91.

Makridakis, Spyros; Steven C. Wheelwright; and Victor E. McGee. *Forecasting: Methods and Applications.* 2nd ed. New York: John Wiley & Sons, 1983.

————. "The Accuracy of Extrapolation (Time Series) Methods: Results of a Forecasting Competition." *Journal of Forecasting* 1 (1982), pp. 111–15.

Moore, Karl; Robert Burbach; and Roger Heeler. "Using Neural Networks to Analyze Qualitative Data." *Marketing Research* 7 (January 1, 1995), p. 34.

Newbold, Paul, and Theodore Bos. *Introductory Business Forecasting.* Cincinnati, OH: South-Western Publishing Co., 1990.

Chapter 7

FACILITY LOCATION, CAPACITY AND LAYOUT

Chapter Objectives

- Identify the various factors, both quantitative and qualitative, that should be taken into consideration when selecting a location for a manufacturing or service operation.

- Introduce a framework for evaluating alternative site locations.

- Introduce the concept of Geographical Information Systems (GIS) as a tool for evaluating locations.

- Present alternative strategies for increasing the capacity within an organization.

- Identify the different types of facility layouts that can be used in manufacturing and service operations.

- Define the various steps and elements that are involved in balancing an assembly line.

The success of most retail operations, especially restaurants and other food service outlets, has often been attributed to three factors: location, location, and location. Major chains now view site location as a two-stage process: the first involves locating the actual retail operations, the second focuses on locating a central commissary where the initial food preparation takes place.

Bruegger's Bagels, for example, mixes the dough and forms the bagels in its regional commissaries and then ships them to retail outlets where they are boiled and baked in front of customers. On the other hand, Au Bon Pain, a cafe and bakery chain that offers a variety of French breads, croissants, muffins, and other pastries, has decided to use a single central facility to support its approximately 250 Au Bon Pain and Saint Louis

Bread locations throughout the United States. Its goods are mixed and formed at the central location and then frozen, to be baked at the retail operations.

The site selection criteria are significantly different for each of the two stages of the site location process. For the retail site the criteria are determined by customer demographics such as average household income, average family size, population density, and automobile and/or pedestrian traffic counts; at the central production facility, the criteria are determined by labor costs, building costs, and distribution costs. ■

LOCATING MANUFACTURING FACILITIES

With the continued development of the global marketplace, businesses must take a more international perspective in determining where to locate their manufacturing operations. However, the complexity of the decision-making process increases several fold when a firm decides to shift from a national to an international site location strategy. Typically, with manufacturing, the facility location decision needs to include the location of both the manufacturing operations and the warehouse or distribution facilities. As a general rule, products that decrease in weight and volume during the transformation process tend to be located near sources of raw material. An example of this would be a lumber mill located near a forest. On the other hand, products that increase in weight and volume during the transformation process are usually located near points of consumption. An example of this would be a soft drink bottler located near a city.

In weighing the advantages and disadvantages of alternative sites, the analysis should include an evaluation of both qualitative and quantitative factors.[1]

Qualitative Factors

The qualitative factors include: (*a*) local infrastructure, (*b*) worker education and skills, (*c*) product content requirements, and (*d*) political/economic stability.

Local Infrastructure The local infrastructure that is necessary to support a manufacturing operation can be divided into two broad categories: institutional and transportational. With manufacturing operations becoming more flexible and responsive to customer requirements, there is a growing dependence on local institutions or suppliers to be more flexible and responsive. In addition the local transportation network that links the suppliers to the manufacturer must be efficient and reliable. For example, a lack of adequate transportation infrastructure in the Former Soviet Union (FSU) or the People's Republic of China would preclude a firm that uses just-in-time (JIT) concepts from locating in these areas.

Worker Education and Skills The increased sophistication of today's manufacturing processes requires that the workforce be highly educated and equipped with a wide variety of skills. Increased emphasis on automation requires specific worker skills to operate and maintain equipment. Modern manufacturing processes like just-in-time (JIT) also require a well-educated workforce. As an illustration, the significant growth of business in Singapore in recent years can be attributed, in large part, to the investment of its government in educating and training its population.

content requirements
Requirement that a percentage of a product must be made within a country for it to be sold there.

Product Content Requirements **Content requirements** state that a minimum percentage of a product must be produced within the borders of a country in order for that product to be sold in that country. This assures jobs in the local economy while reducing the difference between imports and exports. For example, for a car to be sold in the Philippines, it must be assembled there. Consequently, each of the major car manufacturers that wants to sell cars in the Philippines has an assembly plant there even though demand for cars in that country is sufficiently small to suggest that importing them would be more economical.

Political/Economic Stability The stability of a region refers to the number and intensity of economic and political fluctuations that might occur there. The dissolution of the Former

[1]Alan D. MacCormack, Lawrence J. Newmann, III, and Donald B. Rosenfeld, "The New Dynamics of Global Manufacturing Site Location, *Sloan Management Review*, Summer 1994.

Soviet Union provide ample evidence of the problems associated with locating a business in unstable economies.

Quantitative Factors

The quantitative factors include: (*a*) labor costs, (*b*) distribution costs, (*c*) facility costs, and (*d*) exchange rates.

 Labor Costs   Labor costs can vary dramatically, depending on location. In Western Europe, the United States, and Japan, the cost of labor can exceed US$20.00 per hour in comparison to countries in Asia where the cost can be as low as three or four U.S. dollars per day (see Exhibit 7.1). An important factor that must be considered is the skill requirements of the worker. Although the cost of labor in many areas is very cheap, the workers in these very same regions often lack adequate education and skills.

Distribution Costs   As we become more global, distribution and transportation costs take on added importance. In addition to the cost of transportation, the time required to deliver the products must also be taken into consideration. Consequently, in many cases the low costs associated with manufacturing products in Asia are offset by the long lead times and the high cost of delivery to markets in North America and Europe.

special economic zones
Duty-free areas in a country established to attract foreign investment in the form of manufacturing facilities.

Facility Costs   Undeveloped or third-world countries often offer incentives in the form of low-cost manufacturing facilities to attract companies. For example, within the People's Republic of China (PRC) many **special economic zones (SEZ)** have been established that are exempt from tariffs and duties—provided that the products made there are sold outside the PRC. In some countries, the local government will enter into a partnership with a firm, with the government providing the land, the building, and perhaps the training of the workforce.

Exchange Rates   The volatility of the exchange rates between countries can have a significant impact on sales and profits. For example, the change in rates between the Japanese

EXHIBIT 7.1

Comparison of 1995 Hourly Wages for Manufacturing Workers

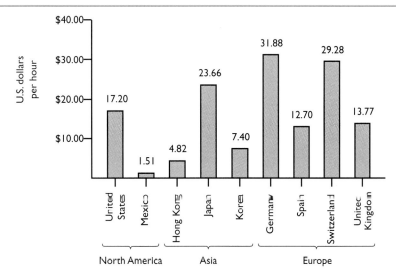

Source: Bureau of Labor Statistics, August 23, 1996.

yen and the U.S. dollar from below 90 yen per dollar to more than 120 yen per dollar between 1996 and 1997 increased the price competitiveness of Japanese products in the United States while decreasing the ability of U.S. products to compete in Japan.

Plant Location Methods

"If the boss likes Bakersfield, I like Bakersfield." The decisions that a company must make in choosing a location for a manufacturing facility are summarized in Exhibit 7.2. While the exhibit implies a step-by-step process, virtually all activities listed take place simultaneously. As suggested by the preceding vote for Bakersfield, political decisions may occasionally override systematic analysis.

center of gravity method
Quantitative approach for determining the location of facilities by minimizing transportation costs.

factor-rating systems
Qualitative approach for evaluating site locations.

The evaluation of alternative regions, subregions, and communities is commonly termed *macro analysis,* while the evaluation of specific sites in the selected community is often termed *micro analysis.* One technique used in macro analyses is the **center of gravity method.** This method provides a quantitative approach for determining where to locate a facility based upon minimizing the total transportation costs between where the goods are produced and where they are consumed. A more qualitative technique is **factor-rating systems,** which is described in detail below. A detailed cost analysis would accompany each of these methods.

EXHIBIT 7.2

Plant Search: Company XYZ

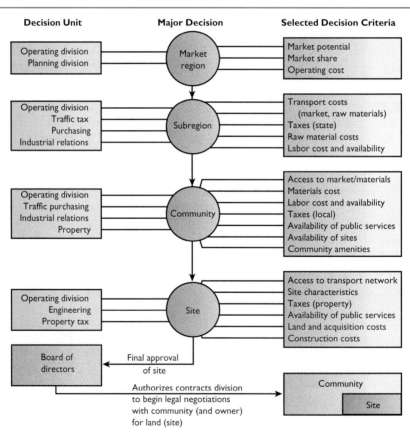

Source: Thomas M. Carroll and Robert D. Dean, "A Bayesian Approach to Plant-Location Decisions," *Decision Sciences* 11, no. 1 (January 1980), p. 87.

Factor-Rating Systems Factor-rating systems are perhaps the most widely used of the general location techniques because they provide a mechanism to combine diverse factors in an easy-to-understand format.

By way of example, a refinery assigned the following range of point values to major factors affecting a set of possible sites.

	Range
Fuels in region	0 to 330
Power availability and reliability	0 to 200
Labor climate	0 to 100
Living conditions	0 to 100
Transportation	0 to 50
Water supply	0 to 10
Climate	0 to 50
Supplies	0 to 60
Tax policies and laws	0 to 20

Each site was then rated against each factor, and a point value was selected from its assigned range. The sums of assigned points for each site were then compared, and the site with the maximum number of points was selected.

One of the major problems with simple point-rating schemes is that they do not account for the wide range of costs that may occur within each factor. For example, there may be only a few hundred dollars' difference between the best and worst locations on one factor and several thousands of dollars' difference between the best and the worst on another. The first factor may have the most points available to it, but it provides little help in making the location decision; the latter factor may have few points available but potentially shows a real difference in the value of locations.

Another problem with this approach is that often the values for some of the factors included in the decision analysis are highly subjective, such as the quality of the public education system and the quality of life in a certain location being good examples.

LOCATING SERVICE OPERATIONS

Within service organizations, the selection of the proper site is also a critical factor. However, unlike manufacturing operations where low production costs are an important consideration in selecting a location, services must focus primarily on customer-driven factors. As stated previously, these factors can include: (*a*) average family income, (*b*) average family size, (*c*) population density, and (*d*) pedestrian and automobile traffic. A manufacturing firm can expand its capacity by just building a larger facility at its current location. In contrast, because services must be located near the customer, the growth of a service business usually requires multiple locations, each focusing on serving a particular geographic market.

Many of the issues manufacturing companies have to address when expanding their operations internationally also must be addressed by service operations. (See the OM in Practice on Toys "R" Us in Japan.) For example, when McDonald's opened its first restaurant in Moscow, the lack of an existing institutional infrastructure to support its operation required that it build a central commissary. This commissary prepared everything for the retail outlet from hamburger patties to rolls and french fries. In addition, the Russian farmers had to be shown how to grow vegetables, such as potatoes and lettuce, that would meet

Operations Management in Practice

Toys "R" Us in Japan

Toys "R" Us has successfully entered the Japanese toy market through private-sector help—in this case, with the help of Nintendo.

On December 20, 1991, Toys "R" Us—the world's largest toy retailer—opened its first retail store in Japan. What may now sound like an American success story in Japan traveled a difficult road for two years. The retailer had established locations in Canada, the United Kingdom, Germany, France, Singapore, Hong Kong, Malaysia, and Taiwan well before it attempted to enter the Japanese market.

In January 1990, Toys "R" Us formally applied to open its first (large) toy store in Niigata, Japan. This caused local toy retailers to proclaim their opposition by invoking provisions contained in the Large-Scale Retail Store Act. Then they organized a lobbying group to mobilize support against the American firm. Toys "R" Us appealed for help directly through the U.S. trade representative and other channels. Sustained American political pressure and widespread publicity finally forced MITI to confront the local lobby and limit to 18 months the application process under the restrictive retail law. It was April 1990, and Toys "R" Us had overcome its first major hurdle.

But there was another hurdle to cross. Toys "R" Us succeeds in large part by selling below suggested retail price. It accomplishes this mainly through exploiting economies it obtains through volume purchases. Anticipating the threat posed by that strategy to their own profit margins, Japanese toy manufacturers banded together and vowed not to sell their wares to Toys "R" Us. But Nintendo depends heavily on Toys "R" Us for the distribution of its products in the United States and other major markets. Nintendo's defection triggered an ultimate end to this boycott.

Private sector countermeasures consciously adopted by numerous major Japanese corporations are replacing the falling barriers to entry of public sector regulation.

Source: Mark Mason, "United States Direct Investment in Japan: Trends and Prospects," Copyright © 1992 by The Regents at the University of California. Reprinted from the California Management Review, vol. 35, no. 1 by permission of The Regents.

McDonald's high-quality product specifications. In contrast, the opening of a McDonald's in the United States or Western Europe would only require a call to established, local suppliers.

Location Strategies

In an effort to better serve customers, service operations have adopted a variety of location strategies, depending on the particular customer requirements they are trying to address. Exhibit 7.3 presents several approaches to satisfying these customer needs.

EXHIBIT 7.3

Customer Requirements and Location Strategies for Service Operations

Customer Requirements	Strategy
Customers are hungry because airlines no longer serve food on short flights.	Locate "real" restaurants in airports (Legal Seafoods, Logan Airport, Boston, MA; Sam Adams Atlanta Brewhouse, Hartsfield International Airport, Atlanta, GA).
Customers want more convenient locations to save time.	Combine previously separate service operations into one location (Dunkin' Donuts in 7-Eleven; convenience stores with gas stations).
Customers are reluctant to shop frequently in large megastores because they are time consuming.	Add other services to increase convenience such as fast food and banking (McDonald's in Wal-Mart; Bank of Boston, and Barnes and Noble Bookstores at Super Stop & Shop Supermarkets).

Source: Adapted from Hal Reid, "Retailers Seek the Unique," *Business Geographics* 5, no. 2, February 1997, pp. 32–35.

Geographic Information Systems (GIS), shown here from MapInfo, are used by retailers, financial services groups, insurance companies, and utilities in the site selection process. Mapping relevant information on potential sites such as demographics, customers buying patterns, trade areas, competitors, and drive times allows this information to be seen in a single, comprehensive view for more informed and precise decision making.

Computer Programs for Site Selection

Geographic Information Systems (GIS)
Computer tool that assesses alternative locations for service operations.

With the growth in **Geographic Information Systems (GIS),** service operations are able to conduct location analysis more quickly and with greater accuracy than was previously possible. GIS allows large databases to be displayed graphically, thereby providing the service manager with a "bird's eye view" of a particular region of interest. These regional maps can display a wide variety of demographic data, depending on the needs of the service manager. (See OM in Practice on Using GIS to Locate Retail Operations.) Exhibit 7.4A, for example, shows the location of housing loans for a bank, including a

EXHIBIT 7.4

A. Distribution of a Bank's
   Housing Loans in an Area

B. Distribution of Sales for
   a Regional Mall by Area

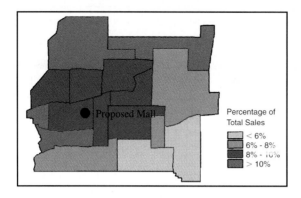

C. Demand for Healthcare
   in a Region and the
   Services That Are
   Available

Source: *Getting to Know Arc View GIS* (Redlands, CA: Environmental Systems
Research Institute, Inc., 1997).

breakdown by income of the different areas served by the bank. Exhibit 7.4B analyzes the percentage of total sales that would be generated from different areas if a regional mall were to be built. Exhibit 7.4C identifies the gap between the demand for noncritical emergency room visits and the availability of clinics and physicians to meet that demand.

In addition to GIS, there are many nongraphic computer programs available to assist the service manager in evaluating alternative site locations. Many of these models incorporate forecasting techniques like regression analysis which were introduced in the previous chapter.

Operations Management in Practice

USING GEOGRAPHICAL INFORMATION SYSTEMS (GIS) TO LOCATE RETAIL OPERATIONS

An analysis of Santa Clara County, California, using a computer-based geographical information system (GIS), indicated that retail operations specializing in child-related merchandise could take advantage of the area's growth in both the short and long term—provided they could obtain retail locations that would follow the path of new housing scheduled to be built to support expansion in Silicon Valley business. Using GIS, the analysis identified specific areas within the county where above average sales in children's toys and apparel are anticipated.

Source: Adapted from Len Strazewski,"Silicon Valley Holds Fertile Kids' Market," *Franchise Times*, February 1997.

EXHIBIT 7.5

Summary of the Variables That Correlated with Operating Margin in 1983 and 1986

Variable	1983	1986
ACCESS	.20	
AGE	.29	.49
COLLEGE		.25
DISTCBD		−.22
EMPLYPCT	−.22	−.22
INCOME		−.23
MILTOT		.22
NEAREST	−.51	
OFCCBD	.30	
POPULACE	.30	.35
PRICE	.38	.58
RATE		.27
STATE	−.32	−.33
SIGNVIS	.25	
TRAFFIC	.32	
URBAN	−.22	−.26

Source: Reprinted by permission of Sheryl E. Kimes and James A. Fitzsimmons,"Selecting Profitable Hotel Sites at La Quinta Motor Inns," *Interfaces* 20 (March–April 1990). Copyright 1990 The Institute of Management Sciences, 290 Westminster Street, Providence, Rhode Island 02903 USA.

Screening Location Sites at La Quinta Motor Inns

Selecting good sites plays a crucial role in the success of a service operation such as a hotel chain. Of the four major marketing considerations—price, product, promotion, and location—location and product have been shown to be the most important for multisite firms. As a result, hotel chain owners who can pick good sites quickly have a distinct competitive advantage.

Thirty-five variables were identified for inclusion in a study to assist La Quinta Motor Inns in screening potential locations for its new hotels.[2] Data were collected on 57 existing La Quinta Inns. A technique known as *exploratory data analysis* identified 16 variables that correlated with operating profit in 1983 and 1986 (see Exhibit 7.5).

---

[2]Sheryl E. Kimes and James A. Fitzsimmons, "Selecting Profitable Hotel Sites at La Quinta Motor Inns," *Interfaces* 20 (March–April 1990), pp. 12–20.

A multiple regression model was then constructed and in its final form appears as follows:

$$\text{Profitability} = 39.05 - 5.41 \times \text{State population per inn (1,000)}$$
$$+ 5.86 \times \text{Price of the inn}$$
$$- 3.91 \times \text{Square root of the median income of the area (1,000)}$$
$$+ 1.75 \times \text{College students within four miles.}$$

The model shows that profitability is negatively affected by market penetration, positively affected by price, negatively affected by higher incomes (the inns do better in lower median income areas), and positively affected by colleges nearby.

La Quinta implemented the model on a Lotus 1-2-3 spreadsheet and routinely uses the spreadsheet to screen potential real estate acquisitions. The founder and president of La Quinta has accepted the model's validity and no longer feels obligated to personally select the sites.

This example shows how a specific model can be developed from the requirements of a service organization and then be used to identify those features that are most important in making the right site selection. The OM in Practice discusses the expansion criteria and strategies of AM/PM International, a chain of convenience stores.

CAPACITY DECISIONS

The capacity of the production system defines the firm's competitive boundaries. Specifically, it sets the firm's response rate to the market, its cost structure, its workforce composition, its level of technology, its management and staff support requirements, and its general inventory strategy. If capacity is inadequate, a company may lose customers through slow service or by allowing competitors to enter the market. If capacity is excessive, a company may have to reduce its prices to stimulate demand, underutilize its workforce, carry excess inventory, or seek additional, less profitable products to stay in business.

HUMAN RESOURCES
MARKETING

Factors Affecting Capacity   Capacity is affected by both external and internal factors. The external factors include: (*a*) government regulations (working hours, safety, pollution), (*b*) union agreements, and (*c*) supplier capabilities. The internal factors include: (*a*) product and service design, (*b*) personnel and jobs (worker training, motivation, learning, job content, and methods), (*c*) plant layout and process flow, (*d*) equipment capabilities and maintenance, (*e*) materials management, (*f*) quality control systems, and (*g*) management capabilities.

Important Capacity Concepts

In service operations we often distinguish between *maximum capacity* and *optimum capacity* because of the customer's direct interaction with the service facility. Christopher Lovelock has identified four different situations that the service manager may encounter in trying to match customer demand with the existing capacity of the operation. These situations, illustrated in Exhibit 7.6, are: (*a*) demand exceeds maximum capacity causing customers to be turned away, (*b*) demand exceeds optimum capacity resulting in customers who receive poor service, (*c*) demand equals optimum capacity, and (*d*) demand is less than optimum capacity, resulting in idle capacity.

Best Operating Level   The *best operating level* is that capacity for which the average unit cost is at a minimum. This is depicted in Exhibit 7.7. Note that as we move down the unit

Operations Management in Practice

How AM/PM International Selects Its Sites

AM/PM convenience stores are a subsidiary of the ARCO Corporation. These stores are usually connected with service stations. The goals of AM/PM International are to leverage the existing AM/PM program through brand licensing agreements in foreign countries and joint-venture participation. Furthermore, ARCO wants to participate aggressively in emerging international markets and leverage its international presence. ARCO also wants to generate additional long-term profits.

To select a new potential country, AM/PM International looks at four main criteria:

1. The population should be over 1 million in a targeted city.
2. Annual per-capita income should be over $2,000.
3. The political system should be fairly stable.
4. The host country should have minimal restrictions on hard currency repatriation.

Once AM/PM has selected a potential country for its business, it evaluates further, the country's:

1. Stage of industrial development.
2. People/car ratio. (This is important because the AM/PM stores are located in service stations.)

3. Population density in rural and urban areas.
4. Availability and cost of labor.
5. Infrastructure (supply and distribution, equipment availability, real estate cost, and reliability of utilities).
6. Tax regulations.
7. Legal issues.

AM/PM International uses franchising as a rapid and convenient way to expand in the Pacific Rim, Europe, and North America. The company's prospective list of candidate countries for the next expansion includes Italy, France, Denmark, Mexico, Brazil, Malaysia, and Canada.

AM/PM's international expansion strategy is based on three points:

First, using the existing service station staff to run the convenience store.

Second, for the first year an American-trained manager works closely with the new licensee.

Third, to develop new stores in selected countries as quickly as possible.

Source: ARCO presentation to U.S.C. MBA students, June 5, 1991.

EXHIBIT 7.6

Comparing Capacity and Demand in a Service Operation

a. Customers turned away
b. Customers receive poor service
Maximum capacity
Demand capacity
Optimal capacity
c. Customer demand
d. Idle capacity
Time

Source: Adapted from Christopher Lovelock, "Strategies for Managing Capacity-Constrained Services," *Managing Services: Marketing, Operations Management and Human Resources,* 2nd ed. (Englewood Cliffs, NJ: Prentice Hall, 1992).

EXHIBIT 7.7

Economies of Scale

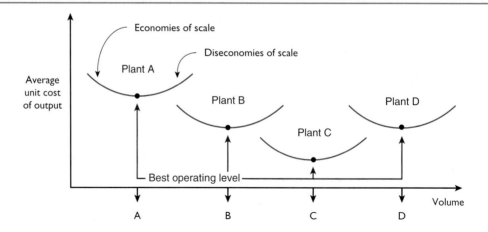

cost curve for each plant size, we achieve economies of scale until we reach the best operating level, and then we encounter diseconomies of scale as we exceed this point.

Economies and Diseconomies of Scale   The concept of economies of scale is well
known: As product volumes increase, the average cost per unit decreases. This concept can
be related to a best operating level for a given plant size. As shown in Exhibit 7.7,
economies of scale (as well as diseconomies of scale) are found not just between the cost
curves for each plant, but within each one as well.

Exhibit 7.7 also shows the best operating levels, V_A, V_B, V_C, and V_D, for plant sizes
A, B, C, and D, respectively. Economies of scale occur for several reasons. With larger volumes, fixed costs are spread out over a greater number of units, thereby reducing the
amount of overhead that is allocated to each product. With large volumes, a firm can also
take advantage of quantity discounts, thereby reducing material costs. Scale factors, which
are associated with larger facilities, are a third source of economies of scale. For example,
with processing operations like breweries and refineries, doubling the capacity of a facility
increases its costs by about 40 percent, which reflects the ratio of change in the volume in
a cylinder or pipe to its outside area (in other words, to double the volume through a pipe
requires about 141 percent more material for the larger pipe).

Diseconomies of scale can also occur for several reasons. When the best operating level
in a plant is exceeded, additional costs are incurred. These added costs can take the form of
overtime, inefficient scheduling, and machine breakdowns resulting from a lack of time to
perform preventive maintenance. Diseconomies of scale can also occur with larger plants,
as indicated by Plant D in Exhibit 7.7. This could be due to an inability to efficiently coordinate material flows and schedule workers. Organizational factors can also contribute to
diseconomies of scale. With larger facilities, the contribution of each individual is dimin-
ished. Management and workers become more segregated and communicate less with each
other. In operations that have a labor union, for example, grievances per 100 employees
tend to increase in relation to the size of the plant.

Although finding the best size and operating level is illusive, managers often set policies
regarding the maximum size for any one facility. As a result, the real challenge is predicting how costs will change for different output rates and facility sizes. This assessment requires careful attention to the different causes of economies of scale for each situation.

In the past several years, we have begun to see that diseconomies of scale come much
sooner than we previously anticipated. This recognition, along with technological capabil-

ity to do more in a plant, has resulted in a shift toward small facilities. The steel industry, with its declining number of large, integrated plants and its corresponding shift toward minimills, is a well-known case in point.

Capacity Flexibility   Having the capability to deliver what the customer wants within a relatively short lead time is how we define **capacity flexibility.** Such flexibility is achieved through flexible plants, processes, workers, and through strategies that use the capacity of other organizations. **Agile manufacturing** is another term that reflects the ability of a facility to react quickly to changes in the marketplace.

capacity flexibility
Ability to provide a wide range of products and volumes with short lead times.

agile manufacturing
Ability of a manufacturing process to respond quickly to changes in the marketplace.

Flexible Plants   Perhaps the ultimate in plant flexibility is the *zero-changeover-time* plant. Using movable equipment, knockdown walls, and easily accessible and reroutable utilities, such a plant can adapt to change in real time. An analogy to a familiar service business captures the flavor quite well—a plant with equipment "that is easy to install and easy to tear down and move—like the Ringling Bros., Barnum and Bailey Circus in the old tent-circus days."[3]

Flexible Processes   Flexible processes are epitomized by flexible manufacturing systems on the one hand, and simple, easy to set-up equipment on the other. Both of these technological approaches permit rapid low-cost switching from one product line to another, enabling what is sometimes referred to as *economies of scope.* (By definition, economies of scope exist when multiple products can be produced at a lower cost in combination than they can separately.)

Flexible Workers   Flexible workers have multiple skills and the ability to switch easily from one kind of task to another. They require broader training than specialized workers and need managers and staff support to facilitate quick changes in their work assignments.

Using External Capacity   Two common strategies for creating flexibility by using the capacity of other organizations are subcontracting and sharing capacity. An example of subcontracting is Japanese banks in California subcontracting check-clearing operations to the Wells Fargo Bank of California's check clearinghouse. An example of sharing capacity is two domestic airlines flying different routes with different seasonal demands exchanging aircraft (suitably repainted) when one's routes are heavily used and the other's are not.

Capacity Balance   In a perfectly balanced plant, the output of Stage 1 provides the exact input requirement for Stage 2, the output of Stage 2 provides the exact input requirement for Stage 3, and so on. In practice, however, achieving such a "perfect" design is usually both impossible and undesirable. One reason is that the best operating levels for each stage generally differ. For instance, Department 1 may operate most efficiently over a range of 90 to 110 units per month while Department 2, the next stage in the process, is most efficient at 75 to 85 units per month, and Department 3, the third stage, works best over a range of 150 to 200 units per month. Another reason is that variability in product demand and the processes themselves generally lead to imbalance except in automated production lines which, in essence, are just one big machine. There are various ways of dealing with imbalance. One is to add capacity to those stages that are bottlenecks. This can be done by temporary measures such as scheduling overtime, leasing equipment, or going outside the system and purchasing additional capacity through subcontracting. A second way is through the use of buffer inventories in front of the bottleneck stage to assure that it

[3]See R. J. Schonberger, "The Rationalization of Production," *Proceedings of the 50th Anniversary of the Academy of Management* (Chicago: Academy of Management, 1986), pp. 64–70.

always has something to work on. A third approach involves duplicating the facilities of that department which is the cause of the bottleneck (which, in essence, eliminates the bottleneck).

Capacity Strategies

For manufacturing firms, there are three major strategies for adding capacity: proactive, neutral, and reactive. Each has its strengths and weaknesses. Which strategy to adopt is dependent, to a large extent, on the operating characteristics of the facility and the overall strategy of the firm.

Proactive   With a proactive strategy, management anticipates future growth and builds the facility so that it is up and running when the demand is there, as seen in Exhibit 7.8A. With this strategy, opportunity costs resulting from lost sales due to an inability to meet demand are minimized, although the firm does have to allocate fixed costs over a relatively small volume of units during the plant's initial period of operation. This strategy is most compatible for a plant where the labor costs are a significant portion of total manufacturing costs, such as in low-volume assembly operations (e.g., footwear manufacturing).

Neutral   A neutral strategy for adding capacity simply takes a middle-of-the-road approach. As seen in Exhibit 7.8B, additional capacity becomes available when demand is about 50 percent of total capacity. The issue here, as with reactive strategy, is how best to satisfy demand before the plant is up and operating.

Reactive   When a reactive strategy is adopted, plant capacity is not added until all of the planned output from the facility can be sold. Thus, with this strategy, the plant is not brought on line until demand equals 100 percent of its capacity, as shown in Exhibit 7.8C. Operating costs are minimized with this approach, as the plant is producing at its desired optimal output, beginning with its first day of operation. This strategy is most conducive to process-oriented operations that have very high fixed costs, regardless of the volume produced, and low variable costs. Examples include paper mills, breweries, and refineries.

 The main problem with this strategy, as with the neutral strategy, is how best to meet the unfilled demand before the plant is in operation. One approach, if the firm has other plants that produce the same product(s), is to manufacture the products temporarily (albeit inefficiently) at these other locations, utilizing additional shifts and overtime as necessary.

Capacity Planning

capacity planning
Determination of which level of capacity to operate at to meet customer demand in a cost efficient manner.

The objective of **capacity planning** is to specify which level of capacity will meet market demands in a cost-efficient way. Capacity planning can be viewed in three time durations: long range (greater than one year), intermediate range (the next 6 to 18 months), and short range (less than six months).

 Our focus in this chapter is on long-range capacity planning, where the firm makes its major investment decisions. In addition to planning large chunks of capacity (such as a new factory) typical long-range capacity planning efforts must also address the demands for individual product lines, individual plant capabilities, and allocation of production throughout the plant network. Typically, these are carried out according to the following steps:

1. Forecast sales for each product line.
2. Forecast sales for individual products within each product line.
3. Calculate labor and equipment requirements to meet product line forecasts.
4. Project labor and equipment availabilities over the planning horizon.

EXHIBIT 7.8

Strategies for Adding Capacity

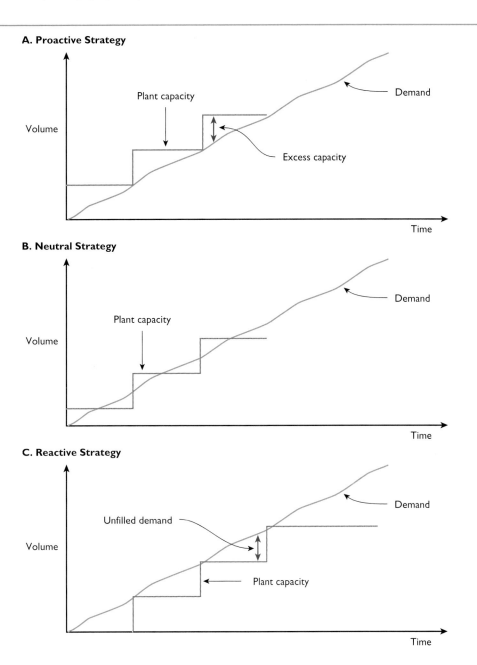

A. Proactive Strategy

Volume

Plant capacity

Demand

Excess capacity

Time

B. Neutral Strategy

Volume

Plant capacity

Demand

Time

C. Reactive Strategy

Volume

Unfilled demand

Demand

Plant capacity

Time

FACILITY LAYOUT

There are many factors that need to be taken into consideration when designing the layout for a facility, be it manufacturing or services. Decisions made at this point have long-range consequences, not only in terms of costs, but also in terms of the firm's ability to serve its market(s). It is therefore important that management devote ample time to properly identifying and evaluating alternative solutions for laying out the facility.

Many of the decisions made at the strategic level become constraints when designing the facility's layout. For example, the size of the facility, in terms of its capacity or output, will have been established, and the type of process used to make the product will have been selected.

Operations Management in Practice

IMPROVING A MANUFACTURING PROCESS USING PLANNING SOFTWARE

FactoryFLOW integrates material handling data and a layout drawing to compute material handling distances, costs, and equipment utilization.

A challenge many facilities planners face today is finding a way to quickly and effectively evaluate proposed layout changes and material handling systems so that the material handling costs and distances are minimized. This challenge was addressed during a three-day, on-site software training session conducted at an appliance manufacturer. The

The overall objective in designing a layout is to provide a smooth work flow of material through the factory, or an uncomplicated traffic pattern for both customers and workers in a service organization. Our emphasis is on quantitative techniques used in locating departments within a facility, and on workstation arrangements and balance in the important area of assembly lines. Before embarking on this discussion, however, it is useful to note the characteristics of a good layout, which are listed in Exhibit 7.9. The OM in Practice on Improving a Manufacturing Process Using Planning Software illustrates how layout planning is conducted using software packages.

Types of Layouts

How the different departments are arranged in a facility is defined by the general pattern of work flow. There are three basic types—product layout, process layout, and fixed-position layout—and one hybrid type, group technology or cellular layout. In this chapter we address all of these in detail except for the fixed-position layout.

process layout
Similar operations are performed in a common or functional area, regardless of the product in which the parts are used.

In a **process layout** (also called a *job-shop layout* or *layout by function*), similar equipment or functions are grouped together, such as in a machine shop where all the lathes are in one area and all the stamping machines are in another. A part being worked on travels from area to area, according to the specific sequence of operations required. This type of layout is often found in low-volume manufacturing plants that have an intermittent process. The support services in a hospital also provide a good example of process layout, with radiology, blood analysis, and pathology each being located in a specific area.

facilities planners were learning the basics on using the FactoryFLOW software package, a computer-based, facilities planning tool developed by Cimtechnologies Corp. The training group evaluated a current layout proposal of a console assembly area to see if any improvements could be made.

The FactoryFLOW software quantitatively evaluates facility layouts and material handling systems by showing the material flow paths and costs, both in output text reports and in a graphic overlay of an AutoCAD layout drawing. FactoryFLOW evaluates the material flow and material handling costs and distances using the following input information: an AutoCAD layout drawing, part routing data (i.e., part names, from/to locations, and move quantities), and material handling system characteristics (i.e., fixed and variable costs, load/unload times, and speeds).

The facilities planners had a drawing of the area, and the industrial engineers supplied the part routing and material equipment information; therefore data entry and analysis of the current layout took about one half of a day. Output diagrams and reports showed material handling distances of over 407 million feet per year and material handling costs of just over $900,000 per year.

The second half of the day was used to come up with alternative layouts by analyzing the output text reports and the material flow lines. One alternative was to rotate a line of 16 plastic presses 90-degrees, so they fed right into the subassembly area, and to rotate the main console assembly lines 90-degrees, so they were closer to the same area. Since the primary material handling system was an overhead conveyor, minimizing the length of conveyor was a major concern. FactoryFLOW was used to evaluate the alternative layout, and the output reports showed the material handling costs had been reduced by over $100,000 to $792,265 per year. Also, by decreasing the material travel distance, the length of overhead conveyor needed had been reduced from 3,600 feet to just over 700 feet.

The FactoryFLOW software made it possible to complete this project in a short amount of time, and the facilities planners at this company now have a tool for further evaluation of facility layouts and material handling systems.

Source: "Factory Planning Software Cimtechnologies Corp. (Ames, IA)," *Industrial Engineering*, December 1993, p. SS3.

EXHIBIT 7.9

Characteristics of a Good Layout

Manufacturing and Back-Office Service Operations	Face-to-Face Services
1. Straight-line flow pattern (or adaptation).	1. Easily understood service-flow pattern.
2. Backtracking kept to a minimum.	2. Proper waiting facilities.
3. Production time predictable.	3. Easy communication with customers.
4. Little interstage storage of materials.	4. Customer surveillance easily maintained.
5. Open plant floors so everyone can see what's going on.	5. Clear exit and entry points with sufficient check-out capabilities.
6. Bottleneck operations under control.	6. Departments and processes arranged so that customers see only what you want them to see.
7. Workstations close together.	7. Balance between waiting areas and service areas.
8. Minimum material movement.	8. Minimum walking.
9. No unnecessary rehandling of materials.	9. Lack of clutter.
10. Easily adjustable to changing conditions.	10. High sales volume per square foot of facility.

product layout
Equipment/operations are located according to the progressive steps required to make the product.

A **product layout** (also called a *flow-shop layout*) is one in which equipment or work processes are arranged according to the progressive steps by which the product is made. If equipment is dedicated to continual production of a narrow product line, this is usually called a *production line* or *assembly line*. Examples are the manufacture of small appliances (toasters, irons, beaters), large appliances (dishwashers, refrigerators, washing machines), electronics (computers, CD players), and automobiles.

group technology (G/T) layout
Groups of dissimilar machines brought together in a work cell to perform tasks on a family of products that share common attributes.

fixed-position layout
The product, because of its size and/or weight remains in one location and processes are brought to it.

A **group technology (GT) layout** brings together dissimilar machines into work centers (or cells) to work on products that have similar shapes and processing requirements. A GT layout is similar to process layout, in that cells are designed to perform a specific set of processes, and it is similar to product layout in that the cells are dedicated to a limited range of products. (*Group technology* also refers to the parts classification and coding system used to specify machine types that go into a GT cell.)

In a **fixed-position layout,** by virtue of its bulk or weight, the product remains stationary at one location. The manufacturing equipment is moved to the product rather than vice versa. Shipyards, construction sites, and professors' offices are examples of this format.

Many manufacturing facilities present a combination of two layout types. For example, a given floor may be laid out by process, while another floor may be laid out by product. It is also common to find an entire plant arranged according to general product flow (fabrication, subassembly, and final assembly), coupled with process layout within fabrication and product layout within the assembly department. Likewise, group technology is frequently found within a department that itself is located according to a plantwide process-oriented layout.

An operation's layout continually changes over time because the internal and external environments are dynamic. As demands change, so can layout. As technology changes, so can layout. In Chapter 3 we discussed a product/process matrix indicating that as products and volumes change, the most efficient layout is also likely to change. Therefore, the decision on a specific layout type may be a temporary one.

Process Layout

The most common approach for developing a process layout is to arrange departments consisting of similar or identical processes in a way that optimizes their relative placement. In many installations, optimal placement often translates into placing departments with large amounts of interdepartmental traffic adjacent to one another. The primary goal in laying out a manufacturing or distribution facility is to minimize material handling costs. In a service organization, the main objective is to minimize customer and worker travel time through the process.

Minimizing Interdependent Movement Costs   Consider the following simple example:

Example

Suppose that we want to arrange the six departments of a toy factory to minimize the interdepartmental material handling cost. Initially, let us make the assumption that all departments have the same amount of space, say 40 feet by 40 feet, and that the building is 80 feet wide and 120 feet long (and thus compatible with the department dimensions). The first thing we would want to know is the nature of the flow between departments and the way the material is transported. If the company has another factory that makes similar products, information about flow patterns might be obtained from these records. On the other hand, if this is a new product, such information would have to come from routing sheets or from estimates by knowledgeable personnel such as process or industrial engineers. Of course these data, regardless of their source, have to be adjusted to reflect the nature of future orders over the projected life of the proposed layout.

Let us assume that this information is available. We find that all material is transported in a standard-size crate by forklift truck, one crate to a truck (which constitutes one "load"). Now suppose that transportation costs are $1 to move a load between adjacent departments and $1 extra for each department in between. (We assume there is two-way traffic between departments.) The expected loads between departments for the first year of operation are tabulated in Exhibit 7.10; the available plant space is depicted in Exhibit 7.11.

Solution Given this information, our first step is to illustrate the interdepartmental flow by a model, such as Exhibit 7.12, which is Exhibit 7.10 displayed in the building layout in Exhibit 7.11. This provides the basic layout pattern, which we are trying to improve.

The second step is to determine the annual cost of this layout by multiplying the material handling cost per load by the number of loads moved between each department. Exhibit 7.13 presents this information, which is derived as follows: The annual material handling cost between Departments 1 and 2 is $175 ($1 × 175 moves), $460 between Departments 1 and 5 ($2 × 230 moves), and so forth. (The distances are taken from Exhibit 7.11 or 7.12, not Exhibit 7.10.)

The third step is a search for departmental changes that reduces costs. On the basis of the graph and the cost matrix, it appears desirable to place Departments 1 and 5 closer together to reduce their high move-distance costs. However, this requires shifting another department, thereby affecting other move-distance costs and the total cost of the second solution. Exhibit 7.14 shows the revised layout resulting from relocating Department 5 and an adjacent department (Department 3 is arbitrarily selected for this purpose). The revised cost matrix for the exchange, with the cost changes circled, is given in Exhibit 7.15. Note the total cost is now $345 less than in the initial solution. While this trial and error approach resulted in a lower total cost in this case, even in a small problem, it is often difficult to identify the correct "obvious move" on the basis of casual inspection.

EXHIBIT 7.10

Interdepartmental Flow

	1	2	3	4	5	6	
		175	50	0	230	20	1
			0	100	165	80	2
				17	213	99	3
					25	0	4
						554	5
							6

EXHIBIT 7.11

Building Dimensions and Departments

80′ / 120′

1 3 5
2 4 6

EXHIBIT 7.12

Interdepartmental Flow Graph with Number of Annual Movements

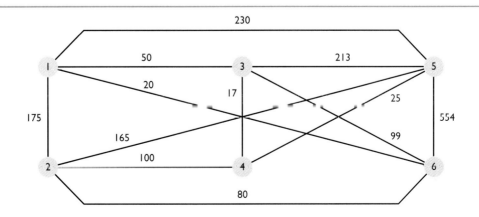

EXHIBIT 7.13

Cost Matrix—First Solution

	1	2	3	4	5	6	
		175	50	0	460	40	1
			0	100	330	160	2
				17	213	99	3
					25	0	4
						554	5
							6

Total cost: $2,223

EXHIBIT 7.14

Revised Interdepartmental Flowchart*

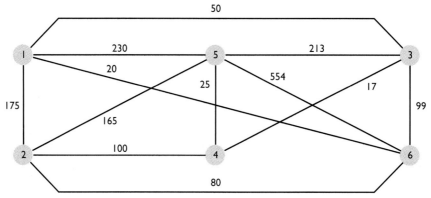

*Only interdepartmental flow with effect on cost is depicted.

EXHIBIT 7.15

Cost Matrix—Second Solution

	1	2	3	4	5	6		Net cost change
		175	100	0	230	40	1	+50 −230
			0	100	165	160	2	−165
				17	213	99	3	
					25	0	4	
						554	5	
							6	

Total cost: $1,878   Total difference: −345

Thus far, we have shown only one exchange among a large number of potential exchanges; in fact, for a six-department problem there are 6! (or 720) possible arrangements. Therefore, the procedure we have employed would have only a remote possibility of achieving an optimal combination in a "reasonable" number of tries. Nor does our problem stop here. Other factors must be taken into consideration.

Suppose that we are able to arrive at a good trial-and-error solution solely on the basis of material handling cost. Continuing with our toy factory example, locating the sewing department next to the painting department might not only be hazardous, but also may result in defective products with lint, thread, and cloth particles drifting onto the painted items. Thus, issues like these must also be incorporated into the final layout decision.

Product Layout

When product demand is high enough and sustainable over a long period of time, it is usually cost effective to rearrange resources from a process layout to a product layout as defined by the sequence required to make the product. We often call these *assembly* lines, although the ratio of direct manual labor to machine work can vary widely. Assembly lines can vary from virtually 100 percent parts assembly by workers, to the other extreme, a *transfer* line, where all direct work is done by machine. In between are all types: Automobile lines have tools ranging from simple hammers and wrenches to automatic welding and painting. Assembly lines in electronics can also range widely from manual parts assembly to equipment for automatic parts insertion, automatic soldering, and automatic testing.

Assembly Lines   Assembly lines are a special case of product layout. In a general sense, the term assembly line refers to a progressive assembly linked by some type of material handling device. The usual assumption is that some form of pacing is present, and the allowable processing time is equivalent for all workstations. Within this broad definition, there are important differences among line types. A few of these are: material handling devices (belt or roller conveyor, overhead crane); line configuration (U-shape, straight, branching); pacing (machine, human); product mix (one product or multiple products); workstation characteristics (workers may sit, stand, walk with the line, or ride the line); and length of the line (few or many workers).

The range of products partially or completely assembled on lines includes toys, appliances, autos, garden equipment, perfumes and cosmetics, and a wide variety of electronic components. In fact, it is probably safe to say that virtually any product with multiple parts and produced in large volume uses assembly lines to some degree. Clearly, assembly lines are an important technology; to really understand their managerial requirements one must have some familiarity with how a line is balanced.

An important consideration that should not be overlooked in designing assembly lines is the human factor. Early assembly lines were machine paced; that is, they moved at a predetermined pace, regardless of whether or not the work was completed at a station. Under this structure, workers who fell behind had to rush to complete their assigned tasks, with the result often being faulty workmanship.

In recent years, worker-paced assembly lines, advocated initially by Japanese manufacturers, have replaced machine-paced lines in many facilities. With the worker paced line, the operator continues to work on the product until the work assigned is satisfactorily completed. Only then is the product allowed to move on to the next station. The quality of the products made on a worker-paced line is significantly higher than that of products made on a comparable machine-paced line. When a Japanese manufacturer took over the production of televisions from a U.S. company, the number of defects dropped from 160 defects per

100 TVs to 4 defects per 100 TVs, even though the output per day and the workforce remained virtually unchanged. This dramatic increase in quality was attributed, in large part, to the installation of a worker-paced assembly line that replaced the previously existing machine-paced line.[4]

Assembly Line Balancing   An assembly line consists of a series of workstations, each with a uniform time interval called a **cycle time** (which is also the time between successive units coming off the end of the line). At each workstation, work is performed on a product by adding parts and/or by completing an assembly operation. The work performed at each station is made up of many *tasks* (also referred to as *elements,* or *work units*). Such tasks are described by motion-time analysis. Generally, they are groupings that cannot be subdivided on the assembly line without paying a high penalty in extra motions.

The total work to be performed at a workstation is equal to the sum of the tasks assigned to that workstation. The **assembly line balancing** problem is one of assigning all of the tasks required to a series of workstations so that the time required to do the work at each station does not exceed the cycle time, and at the same time, the unassigned (i.e., idle) time across all workstations is minimized. An additional consideration in designing the line is to assign the tasks as equitably as possible to the stations. The problem is further complicated by the relationships among tasks imposed by product design and process technologies. This is called the precedence relationship, which specifies the order in which the tasks must be performed in the assembly process.

Steps in Assembly Line Balancing   The sequence of steps required to balance an assembly line is straightforward:

1. Specify the sequential relationship among tasks using a precedence diagram. The diagram consists of circles and arrows. Circles represent individual tasks, arrows indicate the order of task performance.
2. Determine the required cycle time (C), using the following formula:

$$C = \frac{\text{Production time per day}}{\text{Output per day (in units)}}$$

3. Determine the theoretical minimum number of workstations (N_t) required to satisfy the cycle time constraint, using the following formula:

$$N_t = \frac{\text{Sum of task times }(T)}{\text{Cycle time }(C)}$$

4. Select a primary rule by which tasks are to be assigned to workstations, and a secondary rule to break ties.
5. Assign tasks, one at a time, to the first workstation until the sum of the task times is equal to the cycle time, or no other tasks are feasible because of time or sequence restrictions. Repeat the process for Workstation 2, Workstation 3, etc., until all tasks are assigned.
6. Evaluate the efficiency of the resulting assembly line using the following formula:

$$\text{Efficiency} = \frac{\text{Sum of task times }(T)}{\text{Actual number of workstations }(N_a) \times \text{Cycle time }(C)}$$

7. If efficiency is unsatisfactory, rebalance the line using a different decision rule.

cycle time
Maximum time allowed for a workstation in an assembly line to complete a set of assigned tasks.

assembly line balancing
Assignment of tasks to workstations within a given cycle time and with minimum idle worker time.

[4]Lloyd Dobyns and Frank Reuven, *If Japan Can, Why Can't We?* New York: NBC-TV News Presentation, June 24, 1980.

Example

A toy company produces a Model J Wagon that is to be assembled on a conveyor belt. Five hundred wagons are required per day. The company is currently operating on a one-shift, eight-hour-a-day schedule, with one hour off for lunch (i.e., net production time per day is seven hours). The assembly steps and times for the wagon are given in Exhibit 7.16. Assignment: Find the balance that minimizes the number of workstations, subject to cycle time and precedence constraints.

Solution

1. Draw a precedence diagram. Exhibit 7.17 illustrates the sequential relationships identified in Exhibit 7.16. (The length of the arrows has no meaning.)

2. Cycle time determination. Here we have to convert to seconds since our task times are in seconds.

$$C = \frac{\text{Production time per day}}{\text{Output per day}} = \frac{7 \text{ hrs./day} \times 60 \text{ min./hr.} \times 60 \text{ sec./min.}}{500 \text{ wagons}}$$

$$= \frac{25,200}{500} = 50.4 \text{ seconds}$$

3. Theoretical minimum number of workstations required (the actual number may be greater):

$$N_t = \frac{T}{C} = \frac{195 \text{ seconds}}{50.4 \text{ seconds}} = 3.86 \text{ stations} \rightarrow 4 \text{ stations}$$

(Since we cannot have a fraction of a station, we always round up to the next whole integer. For this example, the minimum number of stations is four.)

4. Select assignment rules. Research has shown that some rules are better than others for certain problem structures. In general, the strategy is to use a rule assigning tasks that either have many followers or are of long duration since they effectively limit the balance achievable. In this case, we use as our primary rule:

   a. Assign tasks in order of the largest number of following tasks. Our secondary rule, to be invoked where ties exist from our primary rule, is

   b. Assign tasks in order of longest operating time.

Task	Total Number of Following Tasks	Following Tasks
A	6	B, C, F, G, J, K
B or D	5	C, F, G, J, K (for B)
C or E	4	H, I, J, K (for E)
F, G, H, or I	2	J, K
J	1	K
K	0	—

5. Make task assignments to form Workstation 1, Workstation 2, and so forth, until all tasks are assigned. The actual assignment is given in Exhibit 7.18A and is shown graphically in Exhibit 7.18B.

6. Calculate the efficiency. This is shown in Exhibit 7.18C.

7. Evaluate solution. An efficiency of 77 percent indicates an imbalance or idle time of 23 percent (1.0 − 0.77) across the entire line. From Exhibit 7.18A we can see that there are 57 total seconds of idle time, and the "choice" job is at Workstation 5.

Is a better balance possible? In this case, yes. Try balancing the line with rule *b* and breaking ties with rule *a*. (This will give you a feasible four-station balance.)

EXHIBIT 7.16

Assembly Steps and Times for Model J Wagon

Task	Performance Time (in seconds)	Description	Tasks that Must Precede
A	45	Position rear axle support and hand fasten four screws to nuts	—
B	11	Insert rear axle	A
C	9	Tighten rear axle support screws to nuts	B
D	50	Position front axle assembly and hand fasten with four screws to nuts	—
E	15	Tighten front axle assembly screws	D
F	12	Position rear wheel #1 and fasten hub cap	C
G	12	Position front wheel #2 and fasten hub cap	C
H	12	Position front wheel #1 and fasten hub cap	E
I	12	Position rear wheel #2 and fasten hub cap	E
J	8	Position wagon handle shaft on front axle assembly and hand fasten bolt and nut	F, G, H, I
K	9	Tighten bolt and nut	J
	195		

EXHIBIT 7.17

Precedence Graph for Model J Wagon

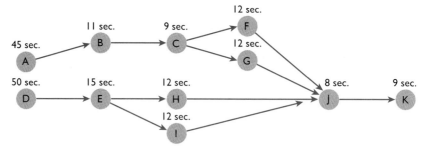

EXHIBIT 7.18

A. Balance Made According to Largest Number of Following Tasks Rule

	Task	Task Time (in seconds)	Remaining Unassigned Time (in seconds)	Feasible Remaining Tasks	Task with Most Followers	Task with Longest Operation Time
Station 1	A	45	5.4 idle	None		
Station 2	D	50	0.4 idle	None		
Station 3	B	11	39.4	C, E	C, E	E
	E	15	24.4	C, H, I	C	
	C	9	15.4	F, G, H, I	F, G, H, I	F, G, H, I
	F*	12	3.4 idle	None		
Station 4	G	12	38.4	H, I	H, I	H, I
	H*	12	26.4	I		
	I	12	14.4	J		
	J	8	6.4 idle	None		
Station 5	K	9	41.4 idle	None		

*Denotes task arbitrarily selected where there is a tie between longest operation times.

EXHIBIT 7.18 (Concluded)

B. Precedence Graph for Model J. Wagon

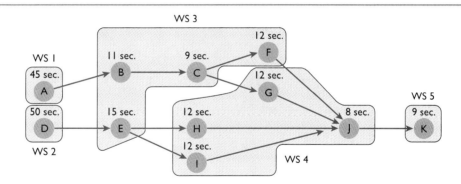

C. Efficiency Calculation

$$\text{Efficiency} = \frac{T}{NC} = \frac{195}{(5)\,(50.4)} = 0.77, \text{or } 77\%$$

Often the longest required task time dictates the shortest possible cycle time for the production line. This task time becomes the lower time bound, unless it is possible to split the task into two or more workstations.

Example

Consider the following illustration: Supposing that an assembly line contains the following task times in seconds: 40, 30, 15, 25, 20, 18, 15. The line runs for 7½ hours per day and demand for output is 750 wagons per day.

Solution

The cycle time required to produce 750 per day is 36 seconds ([7½ × 60 minutes × 60 seconds]/750). How do we deal with the task that is 40 seconds long?

There are several ways that we may be able to accommodate the 40-second task in a 36-second cycle. The possibilities include:

1. *Split the task.* Can we split the task so that complete units are processed in two workstations?

2. *Duplicate the station.* By duplicating the task at two stations, the effective task time is reduced by 50 percent. If necessary, additional stations can be assigned to the same task to further lower the effective task time. Often with this approach, several tasks may be combined into one station to increase efficiency. In the example given, the first two tasks with 40 and 30 seconds each would be combined into one station, which would then be duplicated. The effective cycle time for this station is then 35 seconds ([40 + 30]/2), which is below the required cycle time of 36 seconds.

3. *Share the task.* Can the task somehow be shared so an adjacent workstation does part of the work? This differs from the split task in the first option because the adjacent station acts to assist, not to do some units containing the entire task.

4. *Use a more skilled worker.* Since this task exceeds the cycle time by just 11 percent, a faster worker may be able to meet the 36-second time.

5. *Work overtime.* Producing at a rate of one every 40 seconds would produce 675 wagons per day, 75 short of the needed 750. The amount of overtime required to do the additional 75 wagons is 50 minutes (75 × 40 seconds/60 seconds).

6. *Redesign.* It may be possible to redesign the product to reduce the task time slightly.

Other possibilities to reduce the task time include equipment upgrading, a roaming helper to support the line, a change of materials, and multiskilled workers to operate the line as a team rather than as independent workers.

EXHIBIT 7.19

Flexible Line Layouts

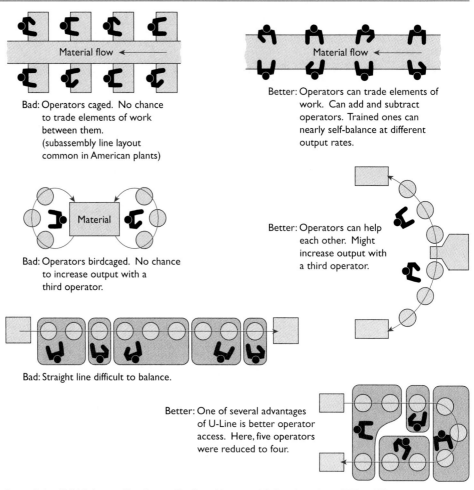

Bad: Operators caged. No chance
to trade elements of work
between them.
(subassembly line layout
common in American plants)

Better: Operators can trade elements of
work. Can add and subtract
operators. Trained ones can
nearly self-balance at different
output rates.

Bad: Operators birdcaged. No chance
to increase output with a
third operator.

Better: Operators can help
each other. Might
increase output with
a third operator.

Bad: Straight line difficult to balance.

Better: One of several advantages
of U-Line is better operator
access. Here, five operators
were reduced to four.

Source: Robert W. Hall, *Attaining Manufacturing Excellence* (Homewood, IL: Dow Jones-Irwin, 1987), p. 125.

Flexible Line Layouts As we saw in the preceding example, assembly line balancing frequently result in unequal workstation times. In fact, the shorter the cycle time, the greater the probability of a higher percentage of imbalance in the line. Flexible line layouts such as those shown in Exhibit 7.19 are a common way of dealing with this problem. In our toy company example, the U-shaped line with work sharing at the bottom of the figure could help resolve the imbalance.

Mixed-Model Line Balancing To meet the demand for a variety of products and to avoid building high inventories of one product model, many manufacturers often schedule several different models to be produced over a given day or week on the same line. To illustrate how this is done, suppose our toy company has a fabrication line to bore holes in its Model J Wagon frame and its Model K Wagon frame. The time required to bore the holes is different for each wagon type.

Example   Assume that the final assembly line downstream requires equal numbers of Model J and Model K wagon frames. Also assume that we want to develop a cycle time for the fabrication line, which is balanced for the production of equal numbers of J and K frames. Of course, we could produce Model J frames for several days and then produce Model

K frames until an equal number of frames has been produced. However, this would build up unnecessary work in-process inventory.

If we want to reduce the amount of work-in-process inventory, we could develop a cycle mix that greatly reduces inventory buildup while keeping within the restrictions of equal numbers of J and K wagon frames.

Solution

Process times: 6 minutes per J and 4 minutes per K.

The day consists of 480 minutes (8 hours $\times$ 60 minutes).

$6J + 4K = 480$

Since equal numbers of J and K are to be produced (or J = K), produce 48J and 48K per day, or 6J and 6K per hour.

The following shows one balance of J and K frames.

	Balanced Mixed-Model Sequence					
Model sequence	J J	K K K	J J	J J	K K K	Repeats
Operation time	6 6	4 4 4	6 6	6 6	4 4 4	8 times
Minicycle time	12	12	12	12	12	per day
Total cycle time			60			

This line is balanced at six wagon frames of each type per hour with a minicycle time of 12 minutes.

Another balance is J K K J K J, with times of 6, 4, 4, 6, 4, 6. This balance produces three J and three K every 30 minutes with a minicycle time of 10 minutes (JK, KJ, KJ).

The simplicity of mixed-model balancing (under conditions of a level production schedule) is seen in Yasuhiro Mondon's description of Toyota Motor Corporation's operations:

1. Final Assembly lines of Toyota are mixed product lines. The production per day is averaged by taking the number of vehicles in the monthly production schedule classified by specifications, and dividing by the number of working days.

2. In regard to the production sequence during each day, the cycle time of each different specification vehicle is calculated and in order to have all specification vehicles appear at their own cycle time, different specification vehicles are ordered to follow each other.[5]

The mixed-model line appears to be a relatively straightforward sequencing problem. This is because in our example the two models fit nicely into a common time period that also matched demand. From a mathematical standpoint, designing a mixed-model line is very difficult and no technique exists to provide the optimum assignment of tasks to workstations. This is because the mixed-model line involves multiple lot sizes, lot sequencing, setup times for each lot, differing workstation sizes along the line, and task variations. The problem is to design the assembly line and workstations and to specify exactly which tasks are to be done in each.

The objectives of a mixed-model line design are to minimize idle time and minimize the inefficiencies caused by changing from model to model. Researchers have used integer programming, branch and bound techniques, and simulation. They still are not able to find the optimal solution for a realistic sized, real-world problem.

---

[5]S. Manivannan and Dipak Chudhuri, "Computer-Aided Facility Layout Algorithm Generates Alternatives to Increase Firm's Productivity," *Industrial Engineering* (May 1984), pp. 81–84.

Current Thoughts on Assembly Lines

It is true that the widespread use of assembly-line methods in manufacturing has dramatically increased output rates. Historically, the focus has almost always been on full utilization of human labor; that is, to design assembly lines minimizing human idle times. Equipment and facility utilization stood in the background as much less important. Past research tried to find optimal solutions as if the problem stood in a never-changing world.

Newer views of assembly lines take a broader perspective. Intentions are to incorporate greater flexibility in the number of products manufactured on the line, more variability in workstations (such as size, number of workers), improved reliability (through routine preventive maintenance), and high-quality output (through improved tooling and training). Exhibit 7.20 compares some old and new ideas about production lines. (See also the OM in Practice on How Ford Achieves Flexibility on the Assembly Line.)

Group Technology (Cellular) Layout

A group technology (or cellular) layout allocates dissimilar machines into cells to work on products that have similar weights, shapes, and processing requirements. Group technology (GT) layouts are now widely used in metal fabricating, computer chip manufacture, and assembly work. The overall objective is to gain the benefits of product layout in job-shop kinds of production. These benefits include:

1. Better human relations. Cells consist of a few workers who form a small work team; a team turns out complete units of work.
2. Improved operator expertise. Workers see only a limited number of different parts in a finite production cycle, so repetition means quick learning.

EXHIBIT 7.20

Assembly Lines: Traditional versus New Focus

Traditional	New Focus
1. Top priority: line balance	Top priority: flexibility
2. Strategy: stability—long production runs so that the need to rebalance seldom occurs	Strategy: flexibility—expect to rebalance often to match output to changing demand
3. Assume fixed labor assignments	Flexible labor: move to the problems or to where the current workload is
4. Use inventory buffers to cushion effects of equipment failure	Employ maximal preventive maintenance to keep equipment from breaking down
5. Need sophisticated analysis (e.g., using computers) to evaluate and cull the many options	Need human ingenuity to provide flexibility and ways around bottlenecks
6. Planned by staff	Supervisor may lead design effort and will adjust plan as needed
7. Plan to run at fixed rate; send quality problems off line	Slow for quality problems: speed up when quality is right
8. Linear or L-shaped lines	U-shaped or parallel lines
9. Conveyorized material movement is desirable	Put stations close together and avoid conveyors
10. Buy "supermachines" and keep them busy	Make (or buy) small machines; add more copies as needed
11. Applied in labor-intensive final assembly	Applied even to capital-intensive subassembly and fabrication work
12. Run mixed models where labor content is similar from model to model	Strive for mixed-model production, even in subassembly and fabrication

Source: Reprinted with the permission of The Free Press, a division of Simon & Schuster from *Japenese Manufacturing Techniques: Nine Hidden Lessons in Simplicity* by Richard J. Schonberger. Copyright © 1982 by Richard J. Schonberger.

Operations Management in Practice

HOW FORD ACHIEVES FLEXIBILITY ON THE ASSEMBLY LINE

Ford Motor Company's assembly plant in Wixom, Michigan, provides another good example of how, with careful planning, several different products can be made on assembly lines. The Wixom plant produces the Mark VIII, the Lincoln Continental, and the Lincoln Town Car. To further complicate the situation, the Continental is a front-wheel drive vehicle on a unibody chasis, whereas the Town Car and the Mark VIII are rear-wheel drive models mounted on a stan-

dard frame chassis. The line producing the Continental and the Town Car can be balanced by having between 67 percent and 75 percent of the cars be rear-wheel drive models. Although the Mark VIII is assembled on its own line, all three models share the same paint shop. Currently, the output from the Mark VIII line is 10 cars per hour, and the Continental/Town Car line produces 42 cars per hour.

---

3. Less work-in-process inventory and material handling. A cell combines several production stages, so fewer parts travel through the shop.
4. Faster production setup. Fewer jobs mean reduced tooling and hence faster tooling changes.

Developing a GT Layout Shifting from process layout to a GT cellular layout entails three steps:

1. Grouping parts into families that follow a common sequence of steps. This step requires developing and maintaining a computerized parts classification and coding system. This is often a major expense with such systems, although many companies have developed short-cut procedures for identifying parts-families.
2. Identifying dominant flow patterns of parts-families as a basis for location or relocation of processes.
3. Physically grouping machines and processes into cells. Often some parts cannot be associated with a family and specialized machinery cannot be placed in any one cell because of its general use. These unattached parts and machinery are placed in a "remainder cell."

Layout Considerations in Services

In designing facility layouts for service operations, additional, service-unique issues need to be taken into consideration. First, the cost per square foot for retail locations is usually very expensive (in comparison to manufacturing space costs). Service retail operations must, therefore, design their facilities to maximize the sales generated per square foot (or square meter). To accomplish this, operations like restaurants have reduced the percentage of area devoted to the back-of-the-house operations, like the kitchen, to allow more area for the customer in the form of additional seating. One way this is done, as discussed earlier in this chapter, is through the use of a central commissary where food can be economically prepared in a relatively low-cost area. Another approach is taken by Benihana's of Tokyo, a chain of Japanese steak houses. There the strategy is to move the kitchen to the front of the house so customers can actually participate in the food preparation process.

Another service-unique factor that needs to be taken into consideration is the customer's presence in the transformation process. As a result, the decor package of the service operation plays an important role in determining the customer's overall satisfaction with the service encounter.

Mary Jo Bitner has introduced the expression **servicescape** to describe the physical surroundings in which the service takes place.[6] The servicescape of an operation comprises three major elements: (*a*) the ambient conditions, (*b*) the spatial layout and functionality, and (*c*) the signs, symbols, and artifacts.

Ambient Conditions   These refer to the background characteristics of the operation, including noise level, lighting, and temperature. (It is often said that the prices in restaurants are inversely related to the amount of lighting—the darker the restaurant, the more expensive the food.) Hanging lights over tables, as seen in some of the better restaurants, suggests privacy; recessed lighting in ceilings, on the other hand, as seen in many fast food operations, send different signals to the customer.

Spatial Layout and Functionality   Unlike manufacturing firms where the goal in designing a layout is to minimize the cost of moving material between areas, one of the goals of a service operation is to minimize the travel time of employees, and, in some instances, customers. At the same time, the service firm is trying to maximize revenues per customer by exposing them to as many opportunities as possible to spend their money. For example, the long lines to get into the shows at Las Vegas casinos wend their way through slot machine areas so customers will play the slots while waiting. Operations like IKEA, a chain of Swedish furniture stores, and Stu Leonard's Dairy Store in Norwalk, Connecticut, are designed so the customer, after entering the store, must go through the entire facility to exit, not unlike a maze with a single path through it.

Signs, Symbols, and Artifacts   These refer to aspects of the service operation that have social significance. For example, banks often include columns and stone to give the feeling of security. The offices of large law firms and consulting practices are often done in dark woods and thick carpets to connote success and traditional values. Waiters in tuxedos and waiters in white shirts, hats, and aprons each give certain signals, in terms of establishing the customers' expectations of the operation.

CONCLUSION

Like so many topics in operations management, location decisions, capacity planning, and facility layouts are becoming heavily affected by the information revolution and globalization of production. The emergence of the network firm that coordinates production of multiple suppliers rather than manufacturing the products in house has changed the way management views its available capacity, and the growth of international markets has altered its location strategies. It is already clear that the operations executives in many companies must catch a plane to see the multiple shop floors that constitute the capacity of their organizations.

A major issue to be addressed in facility layout decisions in manufacturing is: How flexible should the layout be in order to adjust to future changes in product demand and product mix? Some have argued that the best strategy is to have movable equipment that can be shifted easily from place to place to reduce material flow time for near-term contracts. However, while this is appealing in general, the limitations of existing buildings and firmly anchored equipment, and the general plant disruption that is created make this a very costly strategy.

[6]Mary Jo Bitner, "Servicescapes: The Impact of Physical Surroundings on Customers and Employees," *The Journal of Marketing,* April 1992, pp. 57–71.

In service systems, particularly franchises, the study of layout has become extremely important because the selected layout may become replicated at hundreds or even thousands of facilities. Indeed, a layout error in a fast-food chain has a more immediate, and generally a more far-reaching, effect on profits than a layout error in a factory.

KEY TERMS

agile manufacturing   p. 249
assembly line balancing   p. 258
capacity flexibility   p. 249
capacity planning   p. 250
center of gravity method   p. 240
content requirements   p. 238
cycle time   p. 258
factor-rating systems   p. 240

fixed-position layout   p. 254
Geographic Information Systems (GIS)   p. 243
group technology (G/T) layout   p. 254
process layout   p. 252
product layout   p. 253
servicescapes   p. 266
special economic zones   p. 239

REVIEW AND DISCUSSION QUESTIONS

1. List some practical limits to economies of scale; that is, when should a plant stop growing in size?

2. What are some capacity balance problems faced by the following organizations or facilities?

    a. An airline terminal.

    b. A university computing center.

    c. A clothing manufacturer.

3. What are the primary capacity planning considerations for foreign companies locating their facilities in the United States?

4. What are some major capacity considerations in a hospital? How do they differ from those of a factory?

5. What kind of layout is used in a health club?

6. What is the objective of assembly line balancing? How would you deal with the situation where one worker, although trying hard, is 20 percent slower than the other 10 people on a line?

7. How do you determine the idle-time percentage from a given assembly line balance?

8. What are some of the location factors that a manufacturer needs to take into consideration in locating a factory in a foreign country?

9. What is the essential requirement for mixed-model lines to be practical?

10. Why might it be difficult to develop a group technology layout?

11. In what respects is facility layout a marketing problem in services? Give an example of a service system layout designed to maximize the amount of time the customer is in the system.

INTERNET UPDATE

Using PLANT and LAYOUT as suggested key words, search the Web to identify and describe in detail the plant layout for an individual company. As an alternative, go to the McGraw-Hill Operations Management homepage at http://www.mhhe.com/pom and take a plant tour of a company and describe the physical layout of the operation.

SOLVED PROBLEMS

Problem 1

A university advising office has four rooms, each dedicated to specific problems: petitions (Room A), schedule advising (Room B), grade complaints (Room C), and student counseling (Room D). The office is 80 feet long and 20 feet wide. Each room is 20 feet by 20 feet. The present location of rooms is A, B, C, D; that is, a straight line. The load summary shows the number of contacts that each advisor in a room has with other advisors in the other rooms. Assume that all advisors are equal in this value.

$$\text{Load summary:} \quad AB = 10, AC = 20, AD = 30,$$
$$BC = 15, BD = 10, CD = 20.$$

a. Evaluate this layout according to one of the methods presented in this chapter.

b. Improve the layout by exchanging functions within rooms. Show your amount of improvement using the same method as in *a*.

Solution

a. Evaluate this layout according to one of the methods in the chapter.

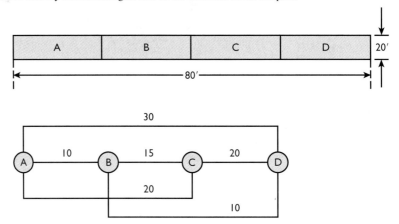

Using the material handling cost method shown in the toy company example we obtain the following costs, assuming that every nonadjacency doubles the initial cost/unit distance:

$$AB = 10 \times 1 = 10 \qquad BD = 10 \times 2 = 20$$
$$AC = 20 \times 2 = 40 \qquad CD = 20 \times 1 = 20$$
$$AD = 30 \times 3 = 90 \qquad \text{Current cost} = 195$$
$$BC = 15 \times 1 = 15$$

b. Improve the layout by exchanging functions within rooms. Show your amount of improvement using the same method as in *a*. A better layout would be either BCDA or ADCB.

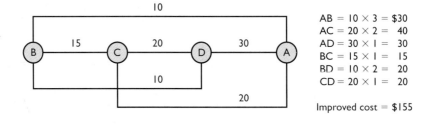

$$AB = 10 \times 3 = \$30$$
$$AC = 20 \times 2 = 40$$
$$AD = 30 \times 1 = 30$$
$$BC = 15 \times 1 = 15$$
$$BD = 10 \times 2 = 20$$
$$CD = 20 \times 1 = 20$$

Improved cost = \$155

Problem 2

The following tasks must be performed on an assembly line in the sequence and times specified.

Task	Task Time (seconds)	Tasks That Must Precede
A	50	—
B	40	—
C	20	A
D	45	C
E	20	C
F	25	D
G	10	E
H	35	B, F, G

a. Draw the schematic diagram.

b. What is the theoretical minimum number of stations required to meet a forecasted demand of 400 units per eight-hour day?

c. Use the longest operating time rule and balance the line in the minimum number of stations to produce 400 units per day.

d. Compute the efficiency of the line.

e. Does your solution generate any managerial concerns?

Solution

a. Draw the schematic diagram.

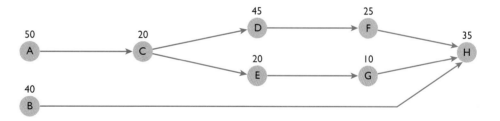

b. Theoretical minimum number of stations to meet D = 400 is:

$$N_t = \frac{T}{C} = \frac{245 \text{ seconds}}{\left(\dfrac{60 \text{ seconds} \times 480 \text{ minutes}}{400 \text{ units}}\right)} = \frac{245}{72} = 3.4 \to 4 \text{ stations}$$

c. Use the longest operating time rule and balance the line in the minimum number of stations to produce 400 units per day.

	Task	Task Time (seconds)	Remaining Unassigned Time	Feasible Remaining Tasks
Station 1	A	50	22	C
	C	20	2	None
Station 2	D	45	27	E, F
	F	25	2	None
Station 3	B	40	32	E
	E	20	12	G
	G	10	2	None
Station 4	H	35	37	None

d. Efficiency $= \dfrac{T}{N_a \times C} = \dfrac{245}{4(72)} = 85\%$

e. Yes. Station 4 is only half as busy as the other three stations.

PROBLEMS

1. An assembly line makes two models of trucks—a Buster and a Duster. Busters take 12 minutes each and Dusters take 8 minutes each. The daily output requirement is 24 of each per day. Develop a balanced mixed-model sequence to satisfy demand.

2. The tasks and the order in which they must be performed according to their assembly requirements are shown in the following table. These are to be combined into workstations to create an assembly line.

    The assembly line operates 7½ hours per day. The output requirement is 1,000 units per day.

Task	Preceding Tasks	Time (seconds)
A	—	15
B	A	24
C	A	6
D	B	12
E	B	18
F	C	7
G	C	11
H	D	9
I	E	14
J	F, G	7
K	H, I	15
L	J, K	10

a. What is the cycle time?

b. Balance the line based on the 1,000 unit forecast, stating which tasks would be done in each workstation.

c. For b above, what is the efficiency of your line balance?

d. After production was started, Marketing realized that they understated demand and will need to increase output to 1,100 units. What action would you take? Be specific in quantitative terms, if appropriate.

3. An assembly line operates seven hours per day and produces 420 units per day. The following tasks are required with their respective performance times and preceding tasks.

Task	Time (seconds)	Preceding Tasks
A	15	None
B	15	None
C	45	A, B
D	45	C

Compute the cycle time and the theoretical minimum number of workstations, and prepare an initial line configuration. Determine the efficiency of your assembly line.

4. An initial solution has been given to the following process layout problem. Given the flows described and a transportation cost of $2.00 per unit per foot, compute the total cost for the layout. Each location is 100 feet long and 50 feet wide as shown on the figure below. Use the centers of departments for distances and compute using rectilinear distances.

	Department			
	A	**B**	**C**	**D**
A	0	10	25	55
Department B		0	10	5
C			0	15
D				0

```
          100'   100'   100'
      50' ┌────┬────┬────┐
          │ A  │ B  │ C  │ 50'
          └────┴────┼────┤
                    │ D  │ 50'
                    └────┘
```

5. An assembly line will operate eight hours per day and produce 480 units per day. The task times and precedence relationships are summarized below. Prepare an initial assembly line configuration using the longest operating time rule, and determine the efficiency of your layout.

Task	Time (seconds)	Preceding Tasks
A	20	None
B	40	A
C	35	B
D	35	B
E	35	C, D

6. An assembly line is to be designed which will operate 7½ hours per day and supply a steady demand of 300 units per day. Following are the tasks and their task performance times.

Task	Preceding Tasks	Performance Time (seconds)
a	—	70
b	—	40
c	—	45
d	a	10
e	b	30
f	c	20
g	d	60
h	e	50
i	f	15
j	g	25
k	h, i	20
l	j, k	25

   a. Draw the precedence diagram.
   b. What is the cycle time?
   c. What is the theoretical minimum number of workstations?
   d. Assign tasks to workstations, stating what your logic rule is.
   e. What is the efficiency of your line balance?
   f. Suppose demand increases by 10 percent. How would you react to this?

7. Given the following data on the task precedence relationships for an assembled product and assuming that the tasks cannot be split, what is the theoretical minimum cycle time?

Task	Performance Time (minutes)	Tasks That Must Precede
A	3	
B	6	A
C	7	A
D	5	A
E	2	A
F	4	B, C
G	5	C
H	5	D, E, F, G

a. Determine the minimum number of stations needed to meet a cycle time of 10 minutes according to the "largest number of following tasks" rule.

b. Compute the efficiency of the balances achieved.

8. Simon's Mattress Factory is planning to introduce a new line of "pillow-top" mattresses. Current plans are to produce the mattresses on an assembly line. Mattresses will be built on individual platforms pulled by a chain in a track in the floor. This will allow workers to completely walk around the mattress. Tools will be suspended from the ceiling, so that there will not be a problem with tangling cords or wrapping them around the platform.

The assembly-line process starts with the basic spring foundation and builds the mattress as it progresses down the line. There are 12 operations required, and their times and process sequence are as follows:

Operation	Time (minutes)	Tasks That Must Precede
A	1	—
B	3	A
C	4	B
D	1	B
E	5	C
F	4	D
G	1	E, F
H	2	G
I	5	G
J	3	H
K	2	I
L	3	J, K

Tentative plans are to operate the line 7½ hours per day. Demand for the mattresses is expected to be 70 per day.

a. Draw the schematic diagram.

b. What is the cycle time?

c. What is the theoretical minimum number of workstations?

d. Create a reasonably balanced assembly line.

e. Supposing the plan was to produce these in a job shop layout. Discuss and compare the characteristics, pros, cons, etc. of a job shop versus assembly line for this mattress production.

9. XYZ Manufacturing Company received a contract for 20,000 units of a product to be delivered in equal weekly quantities over a six-month period. XYZ works 250 days per year on a single-shift 40-hour work week.

The table below states the tasks required and their precedence sequence and task times in seconds.

Task	Task That Must Precede	Time (seconds)
A	—	150
B	A	120
C	B	150
D	A	30
E	D	100
F	C, E	40
G	E	30
H	F, G	100

 a. Develop an assembly line that meets the requirements.

 b. State the cycle time.

 c. What is the "efficiency" of the line?

 d. Supposing the vendor asked you to increase output by 10 percent. State specifically how you would respond to this.

10. The following tasks are to be performed on an assembly line:

Task	Time (seconds)	Tasks That Must Precede
A	20	—
B	7	A
C	20	B
D	22	B
E	15	C
F	10	D
G	16	E, F
H	8	G

The workday is 7 hours long and the demand for completed product is 750 units per day.

 a. Find the cycle time.

 b. What is the theoretical number of workstations?

 c. Draw the precedence diagram.

 d. Balance the line using the longest operating time rule.

 e. What is the efficiency of the line balanced as in *d*?

 f. Suppose that demand rose from 750 per day to 800 units per day. What would you do?

 g. Suppose that demand rose from 750 per day to 1,000 units per day. What would you do?

CASE: COMMUNITY HOSPITAL

In 1983, Community Hospital, which had served the downtown area of a large West Coast city for more than 25 years, closed and then built a new hospital in a thinly populated area about 30 miles west of the city. The new hospital, also named Community Hospital, was located on a parcel of land owned by the original hospital for many years.

This new hospital, which opened October 1, 1983, is a four-story structure that includes all the latest innovations in health-care technology. The first floor houses the emergency departments; intensive care unit; operating room; radiology, laboratory, and therapy departments; pharmacy; housekeeping and maintenance facilities and supplies, as well as other supportive operations. All administrative offices, such as the business office, medical records department, special services, and so forth, are located on the second floor, as are the cafeteria and food service facilities. The two upper floors contain patient rooms divided into surgical, medical, pediatric, and obstetric units.

Community Hospital has a total capacity of 177 beds assigned as follows:

Unit	Number of Beds
Surgical	45
Medical	65
Pediatrics	35
Obstetrics	20
Intensive care	12

For the first six months of the hospital's operation, things were rather chaotic for the administrator, Sam Jones. All his time was occupied with the multitude of activities that go along with starting a new facility, such as seeing that malfunctioning equipment was repaired, arranging for new staff to be hired and trained, establishing procedures and schedules, making necessary purchasing decisions, and attending endless conferences and meetings.

All during this period, Mr. Jones had been getting some rather disturbing reports from his controller, Bob Cash, regarding Community Hospital's financial situation. But he decided that these financial matters would simply have to wait until things had settled down.

Finally, in April, Mr. Jones asked Mr. Cash to prepare a comprehensive report on the hospital's financial position and to make a presentation with his new assistant administrator, Tim Newman, who had recently received a degree in hospital administration.

In his report, Mr. Cash stated: "As you both know, we have been running at an operating cash deficit since we opened last October. We expected, of course, to be losing money at the start until we were able to establish ourselves in the community and draw in patients. We certainly were right. During our first month, we lost almost $221,000. Last month, in March, we lost $58,000.

"The reason, of course, is pretty straightforward. Our income is directly related to our patient census (i.e., patient load). On the other hand, our expenses are fixed and are running at about $235,000 a month for salaries and wages, $75,000 a month for supplies and equipment, and another $10,000 a month in interest charges. Our accumulated operating deficit for the six months we've been here totals $715,000, which we've covered with our bank line of credit. I suppose we can continue to borrow for another couple of months, but after that I don't know what we're going to do."

Mr. Jones replied, "As you said, Bob, we did expect to be losing money in the beginning, but I never expected the loss to go on for six months or to accumulate to almost three-quarters of a million dollars. Well, at least last month was a lot better than the first month. Do you have any figures showing the month-to-month trend?"

Bob Cash laid the following worksheet on the table:

COMMUNITY HOSPITAL
Six-Month Operating Statement October 1983–March 1984 (in thousands of dollars)

	1983 October	November	December	1984 January	February	March	Total
Income	$ 101	$ 163	$ 199	$ 235	$ 245	$ 262	$ 1,205
Expenses (excluding interest):							
Salaries, wages	232	233	239	235	235	235	1,410
Supplies, other	80	73	74	75	73	75	450
Total	312	306	313	310	309	310	1,860
Interest	10	10	10	10	10	10	60
Operating loss	$(221)	$(153)	$(124)	($ 85)	($ 74)	($ 58)	($ 715)
Average daily census	42	68	83	98	102	109	
Occupancy	24%	38%	47%	55%	58%	62%	

QUESTIONS

1. Evaluate the situation at Community Hospital with respect to trends in daily patient census, occupancy rate, and income.
2. Has there been any change in revenue per patient-day over the six-month period (assuming a 30-day month)?
3. At what capacity level will the hospital achieve breakeven?
4. What questions might we raise about the constant level of salaries and supplies relative to past and future operations?

Source: Reprinted with permission from *Hospital Cost Containment through Operations Management,* published by the American Hospital Association. Copyright 1984.

SELECTED BIBLIOGRAPHY

Blackburn, Joseph D. *Time-Based Competition: The Next Battle Ground in American Manufacturing.* Homewood, IL: Richard D. Irwin, 1991.

Choobineh, F. "A Framework for the Design of Cellular Manufacturing Systems." *International Journal of Production Research* 26, no. 7 (1988), pp. 1116–72.

Dobyns, Lloyd, and Reuven Frank. *If Japan Can, Why Can't We?* New York: NBC-TV News Presentation, June 24, 1980.

Francis, R. L.; L. F. McGinnis; and J. A. White. *Facility Layout and Location: An Analytical Approach.* 2nd ed. Englewood Cliffs, NJ: Prentice Hall, 1992.

Green, Timothy J., and Randall P. Sadowski. "A Review of Cellular Manufacturing Assumptions, Advantages and Design Techniques." *Journal of Operations Management* 4, no. 2 (February 1984), pp. 85–97.

Hayes, Robert H., and Steven C. Wheelwright. *Restoring Our Competitive Edge.* New York: John Wiley & Sons, 1984.

Heskett, J. L.; W. E. Sasser, Jr.; and C. W. L. Hart. *Service Breakthroughs: Changing the Rules of the Game.* New York: Free Press, 1990.

Hyer, Nancy Lea. "The Potential of Group Technology for U.S. Manufacturing." *Journal of Operations Management* 4, no. 3 (May 1984), pp. 183–202.

Kimes, Sheryl E., and James A. Fitzsimmons. "Selecting Profitable Hotel Sites at La Quinta Motor Inns." *Interfaces,* March–April 1990, pp. 12–20.

Lovelock, Christopher. "Strategies for Managing Capacity-Constrained Services." *Managing Services: Marketing, Operations Management and Human Resources.* 2nd ed. Englewood Cliffs, NJ: Prentice Hall, 1992.

MacCormack, Alan D.; Lawrence J. Newman, III; and Donald B. Rosenfeld. "The New Dynamics of Global Manufacturing Site Location." *Sloan Management Review,* Summer 1994, pp. 69–80.

Manivannan, S., and Dipak Chudhuri. "Computer-Aided Facility Layout Algorithm Generates Alternatives to Increase Firm's Productivity." *Industrial Engineering,* May 1984.

Mason, Mark. "United States Direct Investment in Japan: Trends and Prospects." *California Management Review,* Fall 1992, pp. 98–115.

Mondon, Yasuhiro, *Toyota Production System, Practical Approach to Production Management.* Atlanta, GA: Industrial Engineering and Management Press, 1983.

Moutinho, Luiz; Bruce Curry; and Fiona Davies. "Comparative Computer Approaches to Multi-Outlet Retail Site Location Decisions." *The Service Industries Journal* 13, no. 4 (October 1993), pp. 201–20.

Reid, Hal. "Retailers Seek the Unique." *Business Geographics* 5, no. 2 (February 1997), pp. 32–35.

Schonberger, Richard J. "The Rationalization of Production." *Proceedings of the 50th Anniversary of the Academy of Management.* Chicago: Academy of Management, 1986, pp. 64–70.

Strazewski, Len. "Silicon Valley Holds Fertile Kids' Market," *Franchise Times,* February 1997.

Tayman, Jeff, and Louis Pol. "Retail Site Selection and Geographic Information Systems." *Journal of Applied Business Research* 11, no. 2, pp. 46–54.

Vannelli, Anthony, and K. Ravi Kumar. "A Method for Finding Minimal Bottleneck Cells for Grouping Part-Machine Families." *International Journal of Production Research* 24, no. 2 (1986), pp. 387–400.

Wheelwright, Steven C., ed. *Capacity Planning and Facilities Choice: Course Module.* Boston: Harvard Business School, 1979.

WAITING LINE MANAGEMENT

Chapter Objectives

- Emphasize the importance of providing fast service as a competitive advantage to companies.

- Show the relationship between customer expectations, customer perceptions, and customer satisfaction as they pertain to waiting time.

- Identify the various factors that can affect customer satisfaction with waiting time and provide a framework for showing managers which of these factors are under their control.

- Demonstrate how service managers can design their operations and train their employees to provide faster service without incurring any additional costs.

- Illustrate how technology can assist companies in providing faster service to their customers.

You drive your car into the Hertz rental lot at the West Palm Beach, Florida, airport. As you begin to remove your luggage from the car, a service attendant greets you and asks for a copy of your rental car contract. The attendant quickly enters the contract number into a hand-held terminal, which prints a receipt before you have removed all of your luggage. Without further ado, you board the Hertz bus which takes you to your airline terminal.

At the Marriott Hotel in Newton, Massachusetts, guests who have preregistered can go directly to a self-service key rack to pick up their room keys and then can proceed directly to their rooms without the aggravation of waiting in line at the check-in desk. Guests who want to avoid the hassle of waiting in line to check out at Bally's Hotel in Las Vegas can take advantage of the express check-out feature available on the television in each room. A guest simply follows menu-driven options on the television screen. The final bill is then totaled and charged to the proper credit card. The guest simply deposits the room key in a box on the way out.

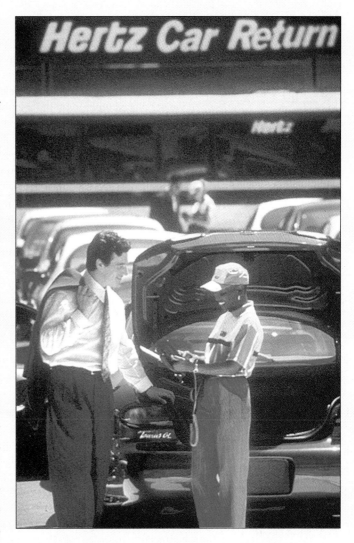

These examples illustrate a growing trend among companies in general, and service firms in particular, to provide continually faster service, and in some cases, as noted above, even totally eliminating customer waiting time. ∎

Every day we encounter waiting lines in one form or another. These include the checkout line at the supermarket where we shop or the line in the bank where we conduct our financial transactions. Other examples include the hotel or airline reservation line we wait in when we are placed on hold on the telephone.

Service managers need to properly manage these customer waiting times to ensure both efficiency and that customers are not so negatively affected by the wait that they take their future business elsewhere. To accomplish this, managers need to recognize that good waiting line management consists of two major components: the **actual waiting time** itself and the customer's **perceived waiting time.**

The determination of actual waiting times is presented in the supplement to this chapter; this supplement focuses on queuing theory and mathematical waiting line models for a variety of service delivery system configurations. The use of these models provides the manager with a framework for managing actual waiting times.

Providing improved levels of customer satisfaction through the management of the customer's perceived waiting time is the primary focus of this chapter. Understanding how customer satisfaction can be improved for a given waiting time provides service managers with an opportunity for managing their operations more effectively.

actual waiting time
Time, as measured by a stopwatch, of how long a customer has waited prior to receiving service.

perceived waiting time
Amount of time customers believe they have waited prior to receiving service.

THE IMPORTANCE OF GOOD SERVICE

 As stated previously in Chapter 2, those companies in both manufacturing and service operations that provide outstanding service to their customers can achieve a competitive advantage in the marketplace in the 1990s. And good service begins when the customer first comes in contact with an organization and waits in some type of line or queue prior to being served. There are many factors that contribute to good service, such as the friendliness and knowledge of workers, but customers' experiences with waiting lines, which are often their initial encounter with a firm, can significantly affect their overall level of satisfaction with the organization.

Providing ever-faster service, with the ultimate goal of having zero customer waiting time, has recently received managerial attention for several reasons. First, in the more highly developed countries, where standards of living are rising, time becomes more valuable as a commodity and, consequently, customers are less willing to wait for service. As a result, customers in many cases, are willing to pay a premium price to those firms that minimize their waiting time. (See OM in Practice Box on Time Is Money at Disney's Theme Parks.)

Another reason for this increased emphasis on providing fast and efficient service to customers is the realization by organizations that how they treat their customers today significantly impacts on whether or not they will remain loyal customers tomorrow. This differs from the past, when the treatment of customers in the present was viewed to be independent of any potential future sales. This attitude by management has persisted because the impact of future customer behavior does not appear anywhere on the firm's financial statements.

Finally, advances in technology, especially in information technology, have provided firms with the ability to provide faster service than was previously possible. Fax machines, e-mail, and satellite communications provide firms with this new capability to respond faster to the customer.

In providing fast service, however, the real goal of service managers should not be to ensure that customers are served within a specified time (e.g., a stated number of minutes), but rather to ensure that customers are sufficiently satisfied with the level of service provided so that they will want to return in the future.

Operations Management in Practice

TIME IS MONEY AT DISNEY'S THEME PARKS

Everyone goes to Disney theme parks. Everyone has to wait in lines. (Well, most people anyway.) And most people hate to wait in these lines.

Now some people have ways to avoid these lines. Disney's policy is that everyone is a VIP, but reality is that some are more VIP than others.

For an additional cost of $50–$60 per ticket, you can buy a theme park VIP tour. This will get you special privileges such as viewing shows from preferred seating to a personal escort on and off certain attractions. This service isn't very widely known, and you almost have to jump through hoops to obtain this type of service.

Another way to avoid the waiting line time is to be a celebrity or top business executive. Disney reasons that the top executive or celebrity is an attraction in and of itself, and tries to let that celebrity enjoy their stay at the park as well as retaining a modicum of anonymity.

Another way to get this so-called star treatment is to work for a company that sponsors the ride. It just takes a little savvy, like having a business card from your organization, knowing how to ask the right people with the right words, and you're there! Other rides (that your company may not be affiliated with) are available simply by networking.

Yet another way of avoiding these waiting lines is to spend big bucks at the hotel. Just put down an extra $300 a night for a stay on one of the special concierge floors and your concierge may even jump through hoops to accommodate your wishes and give you special passes.

And last, but not least, the old wheelchair game. For just $5 you can rent a wheelchair, which enables your group to get access to special lanes or side doors. This, too, has its drawbacks. Disney staff may deem certain rides unsafe for wheelchair victims and the group may have limited access to some attractions.

The best way to endure a theme park, unless you're exceptionally rich or a very special person? Grin and bear it, and wait in line. Who knows? You might even meet a new friend.

The Internet has become an increasingly important tool of companies in providing fast and convenient service to customers. The ability to shop, make reservations, and get information at any time and without a service representative, has changed how we do business.

CUSTOMER WAITING TIME VERSUS PROCESS EFFICIENCY: THE TRADE-OFF IN WAITING LINE MANAGEMENT

The classical operations management model relating service and cost, illustrated in Exhibit 8.1, shows the trade-off between the cost of providing fast service and the cost of having the customer wait. This trade-off between providing high levels of customer service (i.e., fast service) and obtaining high worker productivity results from the direct interaction of the customer with the service-producing process. Although easily understood in theory,

EXHIBIT 8.1

The Trade-Off in Waiting
Line Management

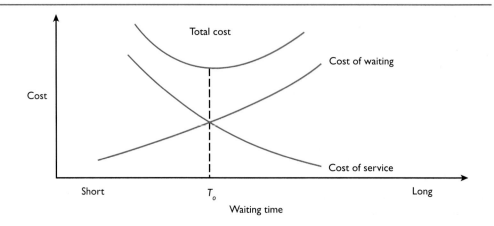

this model is not readily adaptable to real-world applications, due primarily to the difficulty associated with measuring the cost of having a customer wait.

In comparing a service operation with a manufacturing firm, customers waiting for service are often viewed as being analogous to inventory in the manufacturing process. Thus, a service firm that increases its process efficiency by having customers wait for service parallels a manufacturing firm that increases its process efficiency by maintaining a work-in-process inventory. In both instances, management faces a trade-off between improving process efficiency and increasing waiting time or inventory. The difference between the two, however, is that in the manufacturing facility, the parts that are waiting are inanimate objects, whereas in the service operation they are actual customers.

An inherent assumption in the model presented in Exhibit 8.1 is that the contact workers or available service capacity remain idle when there are no customers to serve. The basis for this assumption lies in queuing theory (which is discussed in detail in the supplement at the end of this chapter), which establishes the mathematical relationship between the number of servers or stations assigned and the average customer waiting time for a given level of demand. With this traditional approach to waiting line management, there exists an "optimal" waiting time, T_o, which minimizes the sum of the two cost components: the cost of having a customer wait and the cost of providing service. However, as presented later in this chapter, there are a variety of ways that service managers can reduce customer waiting times without increasing costs.

DEFINING CUSTOMER SATISFACTION

customer satisfaction
Measure of the
customer's reaction to a
specific service
encounter.

The customer's direct involvement in the service delivery system suggests a need to integrate both marketing and operations perspectives into the service system's design and evaluation. A marketing-related measure of customer reaction to waiting time would more clearly indicate the true customer waiting costs instead of just the actual waiting time itself. **Customer satisfaction** appears to be the marketing measure that fulfills this need.

customer's
expectations
Preconceived notions of
what will occur at a
service operation, often
influenced by prior
experience, advertising,
and word-of-mouth.

Definition of Customer Satisfaction

Drawing on work done in marketing, we define customer satisfaction as being related to the comparison between a **customer's expectations** of a service's performance and that customer's perception of that performance. If the perceived performance meets expectations,

EXHIBIT 8.2

The Role of Satisfaction in a Customer Behavior Model

Source: Oliver, R. L. "A Cognitive Model of the Antecedents and Consequences of Satisfaction Decisions," *Journal of Marketing Research* 17, November 1980.

disconfirmation
Marketing measure of the difference between a customer's expectations from an operation and a customer's perception of its performance.

then the customer is satisfied; if it exceeds expectations by a large amount, then the customer is highly satisfied or delighted; if the performance falls significantly short of expectations, then the customer is dissatisfied. In marketing terminology, satisfaction is said to be directly related to the **disconfirmation** (i.e., difference) between the customer's expected and perceived performance of the service.

Customer satisfaction is a good measure of how effective the delivery system is, because it appears to provide the necessary linkage between the level of service that the company is currently providing to a customer, the customer's perception of that service, and the customer's future behavior toward the firm. Oliver suggests that customer satisfaction is part of an overall model of customer behavior that develops over time, as shown in Exhibit 8.2.

Customer Expectations

Customer expectations are defined as the customers' preconceived notions of what level of service they should receive from a particular service business or organization. Expectations can be derived from several sources.

One source of expectations is advertising. Many restaurants, for example, promise in their advertising that your lunch will be served in 10 minutes or less. Thus, if you have to wait longer than 10 minutes, you will be dissatisfied; if your wait is much less than 10 minutes, you will be very satisfied. Expectations can also be predicated on the customer's prior experience with the company. Additional sources of expectations include word-of-mouth and previous experiences with similar types of operations.

The overall service delivery package also influences a customer's expectations with waiting time. People tend to associate little or no waiting with upscale or higher-priced services. These types of operations, therefore, often require appointments or reservations to ensure minimal, if any, waiting. The degree of customization provided to each customer is another factor that can influence expectations. The more a service is customized, the longer a customer might expect to wait.

Perceived Waiting Time

Perceived waiting time is the amount of time a customer believes he or she has waited before receiving service. While this is directly related to the actual time a customer waits, there are often significant differences between the two. In fact, studies have shown that perceived waiting time has a greater impact in determining customer satisfaction than does actual waiting time.[1] As we will discuss later in this chapter, management can have an influence on a customer's perceived waiting time if it has an understanding of the factors that affect it.

To illustrate the difference between perceived waiting time and actual waiting time, we look at the example of a newly designed hotel that was built with insufficient elevator capacity, especially in the morning hours when most guests were in a hurry to check out. Customer complaints about the long waits for elevators to take them to the ground floor prompted management to hire a consultant to reduce these waits. The consultant developed a scheduling algorithm for the elevators that significantly reduced the waiting times, but guest complaints still persisted. Another consultant was hired, who suggested placing full-length mirrors on both sides of the elevator doors on every floor. This was done and miraculously the complaints stopped, even though there was no further decrease in the actual waiting time. Why? Because the guests, after pushing the elevator button, now had something to occupy their time, and consequently weren't as cognizant of their wait for the elevator.[2]

FACTORS AFFECTING CUSTOMER SATISFACTION WITH WAITING[3]

As stated previously, service managers should focus on improving the customer's level of satisfaction with waiting rather than the actual waiting time itself. Maister[4] presented an initial framework for focusing on customer satisfaction with waiting, identifying many of the factors that can affect satisfaction. To further assist the service manager, these factors can be classified into three categories: (*a*) firm-related factors, (*b*) customer-related factors, and (*c*) both firm- and customer-related factors. Service managers, in order to effectively manage the customer's waiting time, must distinguish between those factors over which they have total or at least partial control from those over which they have no control at all.

Firm-Related Factors

Factors that fall primarily within the firm's control can be grouped into four types of waits: unfair versus fair waits, uncomfortable versus comfortable waits, unexplained versus explained waits, and initial versus subsequent waits.

Unfair versus Fair Waits   The successful management of the customer's perception of fairness with respect to waiting is dependent on queue design, service system design, and contact hours.

---

[1]Mark M. Davis, and Janelle Heineke, "How Disconfirmation, Perception and Actual Waiting Times Impact Customer Satisfaction," *International Journal of Service Industry Management* 9, no. 1, 1998, pp. 64–73.

[2]W. E. Sasser, R. P. Olsen, and D. D. Wyckoff, *Management of Service Operations: Text, Cases and Readings* (Boston: Allyn and Bacon, 1978).

[3]Adapted from Mark M. Davis and Janelle Heineke, "Understanding the Roles of the Customer and the Operation for Better Queue Management," *International Journal of Operations and Production Management* 14, no. 5 (1994), pp. 21–34.

[4]David Maister, "The Psychology of Waiting Lines," *The Service Encounter,* J. A. Czepiel, M. R. Solomon, and C. F. Surprenant (Eds.) (Lexington, MA: Lexington Books, D.C. Heath & Co., 1985).

A popular approach, to ensure fairness, is to group all customers into a single queue or line. When more than one server is available, the first person in line moves to the next server that is free. This method has been adopted by many bank and airline check-in counters. Not only is the combined queue perceived as fairer, but the average wait has also been shown to be considerably shorter, even though the line itself is longer. However, managers also need to take into consideration the physical elements of the operating system. For example, the physical space required by customers and their shopping carts has precluded most supermarkets from adopting the combined queue approach.

More subtle elements of service system design, beyond the physical waiting, can also affect customer perceptions of fairness. Interruptions by telephone calls during busy periods, for example, give the impression (which is correct!) that the answered call is receiving priority treatment.

So that customers do not perceive unfair treatment due to their watches being off by a few minutes, the actual hours of operation that a service is open for business should exceed the posted hours. For example, if a retail operation has posted hours of 10:00 AM to 10:00 PM, then the store should be ready to receive customers and the doors unlocked at 9:50 AM, and the doors should not be closed until 10:10 PM.

Uncomfortable versus Comfortable Waits   It is common sense to recognize the fact that when one is uncomfortable, time passes more slowly. There are many ways in which service organizations can affect comfort: temperature, lighting, seating, and sound levels should all be considered. Comfort and fairness can often be combined when a "take a number" system is employed. Full-service restaurants recognize the importance of comfort by providing a lounge in which customers can wait prior to being seated. This is a good example of a win-win situation. The restaurant can gain additional sales from drinks sold to waiting customers, and the customers enjoy a pleasant and comfortable environment in which to wait for their tables.

Unexplained versus Explained Waits   Customer dissatisfaction with waiting increases when the waits cannot be justified or explained. For example, when airline passengers are informed that they must wait for equipment arrival, for the weather to clear, or for the wings of their plane to be de-iced, they are less likely to be dissatisfied than if no explanation is given for the delay. A word of caution, however, is necessary here. The repeated use of the same reason, no matter how valid it is, will eventually negate any benefits gained from the explanation.

Unused capacity in terms of either idle workers or idle stations is another form of unexplained waits that increases the customer's level of dissatisfaction. Although there are many justifiable reasons for apparently idle capacity (e.g., worker rest breaks, the need to complete important off-line tasks, etc.), the customer should not be expected to recognize these. Consequently, workers on rest breaks should not be within the customer's view. Thus, idle service workers and service stations should be "camouflaged" when not in use.[5]

Waits of unknown duration always seem longer than waits of known duration. This relates, in part, to a customer's anxiety with waiting. Thus, it is important to provide customers with an estimate of the wait. When the actual waits cannot be determined, updates or status reports at predetermined intervals can be acceptable substitutes. For example, Federal Express will report back to a customer before the close of each business day with an update on the status of the search for a lost package.

---

[5]Richard B. Chase, "The Ten Commandments of Service System Management," *Interfaces* 15, no. 3 (May–June 1985).

Initial versus Subsequent Waits   As Maister points out, customers tend to become more dissatisfied with initial waits prior to entering a service delivery system than they are with subsequent waits after they are in the system. This can be due to the fact that prior to the initial wait, customers see themselves as being outside the system, whereas after the initial service has been received they consider themselves to be within the system and will, therefore, be served. Thus firms should emphasize minimizing a customer's initial wait when designing the service delivery system.

Customer-Related Factors

There are some factors that affect a customer's satisfaction with waiting time that a firm cannot control. For example, how customers arrive, and the various moods they are in when they do, cannot be controlled by the firm, but an awareness of these factors and how they can contribute to dissatisfaction with waiting can help the service manager to better control those aspects of the wait that are manageable.

Solo versus Group Waits   People waiting in line by themselves tend to grow more impatient with the wait in comparison to people who are waiting in groups. Although this is not something that can be changed by the service organization, recognition of this fact may suggest service-appropriate distractions or alternatives. Ski areas provide a good example in their lift lines, where there is usually a separate line for single skiers, and this line is typically much shorter than those for couples or larger groups.

Here is another case of designing the service delivery system in such a way as to create a win-win situation. The single skier has a much shorter waiting time, and the ski area can take maximum advantage of its lift capacity during periods of peak demand by using single skiers to fill otherwise empty seats as they appear.

Waits for More Valuable versus Less Valuable Services   When a product, be it a good or a service, is perceived to be of high value, customers are willing to wait longer than they would if they perceived the product to be of lower value. In other words, the perceived value of the product is large enough that customers are willing to absorb some of the cost in the form of waiting time. Firms should be forewarned, however, that in today's highly competitive environment, the ability to make customers wait extraordinarily long times will quickly result in a loss of market share to those competitors that provide the same or similar products in a shorter amount of time.

Customer Value Systems   Businesses need to recognize the importance of segmenting the market by customer value systems. Customers who place a premium on obtaining fast service do not mind paying for it, and these same customers do not want to waste their time, for example, on self-service, menu-driven service systems that many companies now provide, particularly with respect to telephone inquiries. To assure consistency from a customer's perspective, the market focus on the firm must therefore also be incorporated into its operational strategy for waiting line management. The importance of doing this is recognized by Ritz-Carlton Hotels which focuses on the top five percent of the hotel industry. Consequently, a real person answers the telephone when you call to make a reservation.

Customer's Current Attitude   The attitudes of customers just prior to entering the service operation can have a significant impact on their level of satisfaction with the service they receive. If customers enter upset, they are more likely to be dissatisfied with their wait, regardless of its length. This type of halo effect will also impact the customers' perception of all facets of the goods and/or services that they receive.

Both Firm- and Customer-Related Factors

There are some factors that relate to a customer's satisfaction with waiting that are under the influence of both the firm and the customer.

Unoccupied versus Occupied Waits   As illustrated with the example of the mirrors beside the elevator doors earlier in this chapter, customers who are unoccupied tend to perceive longer waiting times than do customers who are occupied during their waits. There are many options that are available to occupy a customer's time in line: reading material, interesting displays, mirrors, and music have all been demonstrated to be useful. Gambling casinos do an excellent job of keeping customers occupied while they are waiting to enter their nightclubs. The waiting lines to get into these clubs wend their way through the slot machine areas of the casino, creating another win-win situation: customers are kept occupied and slot machine revenues are increased.

Under certain circumstances, customers can also be kept busy while waiting in line doing meaningful activities that can improve the efficiency of the service. For example, customers waiting in line in a retail store can be informed, through the proper signage, of what they have to do to process a payment other than cash. Another approach to keeping customers occupied while waiting is to provide a waiting environment in which they can productively be working on their own tasks. Airport lounges with tables or private areas equipped with FAX machines, PCs, and so forth, are good examples of this.

Anxious versus Calm Waits   Customer anxiety regarding the nature of the service or the uncertainty of the wait can affect customer satisfaction. Any wait in a hospital emergency room or to hear the results from an important medical test may seem interminable, regardless of the actual length of the wait. Service organizations cannot totally eliminate the customer's anxiety associated with these types of waits, but they can, nevertheless, look critically at the nature of the service that they provide and take the necessary steps to try to reduce customer anxiety in such situations. Providing reading material that both occupies the wait and simultaneously explains the procedure to be followed can be very effective in reducing the customer's anxiety and the associated level of impatience with the wait.

At the Disney theme parks in Orlando, Florida, long lines are managed creatively. Posted signs estimate wait times while TV monitors provide entertainment. Guests are occupied by moving under runaway railroad cars, within a space mountain, or through theaters with movie memorabilia.

A FOCUS ON PROVIDING FAST SERVICE

 Ultimately, providing ever-better and ever-faster service to customers is the responsibility of the service operations manager. From an operations perspective, this can be accomplished in several ways, including the institution of good system design concepts and the proper cross-training of workers.

Service System Design Concepts

front-of-the-house
Portion of the service operation which is in full sight of the customer.

backroom
Behind-the-scenes portion of the service operation which the customer does not come into contact with.

Previous service system design theory advocated the splitting of the delivery system into two cores, with the goal of reducing customer contact time, thereby increasing the speed of delivery and the efficiency of the operation. With this approach, the first core, or **front-of-the-house,** interacts directly with the customer and consequently adopts a chase strategy. The second core, or **backroom,** includes all of those functions that can be accomplished without the presence of the customer, and therefore can be performed more efficiently with a level-type strategy. (Both chase and level strategies are presented in detail in a later chapter.) McDonald's provides an excellent example of this split core strategy, with packaged hamburgers in the bins acting as a buffer inventory between the two stages.

However, by adopting a properly designed concept that combines the backroom operations with those in the front-of-the-house, service workers can be kept productively occupied during idle periods when there are no customers to wait on. For example, with a proper design concept, service workers can answer telephones or perform nontime-dependent tasks during such periods.

In addition to the system design, benefits, in terms of faster customer service, can be accrued by reducing the set-up times required when a worker has to switch from one job function to another. This switching can occur frequently in a service operation whenever a customer requires service. Such reductions in set-up times permit the service manager to reassign workers from time-dependent tasks, such as waiting on customers, to nontime-dependent tasks, such as cleaning and paperwork, and vice versa, without incurring any additional costs.

The key factor in adopting these concepts is that there are sufficient nontime-dependent functions available to be accomplished during idle periods. This can be arranged, to a large extent, by carefully designing the service delivery system from the beginning.

Cross-Training of Employees

An integral part of providing a fast and efficient service operation is the flexibility of the service workers, in terms of their ability to perform a variety of tasks. With broader job skills, these workers can perform additional, noncustomer-related tasks during idle periods as they occur throughout the workday. Consequently, service managers should invest resources to cross-train workers so they can perform several tasks. What is essentially being accomplished through cross-training is that the firm is inventorying worker skills, instead of inventorying customers in the form of waiting lines; in the long run, this is more profitable to the firm.

As the standard of living improves, time becomes more important to individuals. As a consequence, the cost of having customers wait for service increases significantly. This is shown in Exhibit 8.3 as the Cost of Waiting line shifts from W_1 to W_2. At the same time, service managers who properly design their delivery systems and train their employees can dramatically reduce the cost of providing service without making customers wait longer. This is shown in Exhibit 8.3 in the shift of the Cost of Service line from S_1 to S_2. The result of these two trends is that there is now a new "optimal" waiting time, T_o', that minimizes

EXHIBIT 8.3

Why Faster Service Is Still "Optimal"

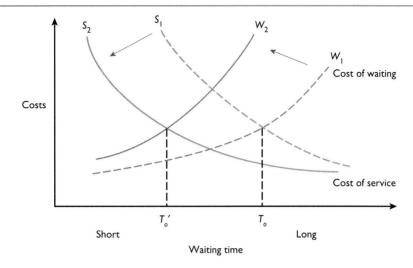

Total Cost and, at the same time, is lower than the initial T_o. As these trends continue in the future, the "optimal" waiting time will become shorter and shorter.

HOW TECHNOLOGY CAN PROVIDE FASTER SERVICE

 As shown in the beginning of this chapter, technology can used in many ways to reduce and, in many cases, totally eliminate customer waiting time. Automated teller machines (ATMs) now provide bank customers with 24-hour service, eliminating the need for customers to wait until the bank opens in the morning. Customers with personal computers can access their accounts any time, day or night, and request certain transactions to take place. (See OM in Practice box on ATMs Save Time by Sprouting Wings.)

Bar-code scanners at checkout counters in department stores and supermarkets reduce service processing times and also customer waiting times. Similar types of scanners are now being used on toll roads where commuters can obtain a "bar code" for their cars which is then electronically scanned each time the car passes a toll booth. (Currently under development for use in supermarkets are scanners that will be able to scan an entire shopping cart without having to unload it.)

Bar-code scanners are similarly used at many airports to scan tickets as passengers board airplanes. This permits passengers to board more quickly and with less waiting time.

Menu-driven computer databases provide telephone operators with quick access to customer information, thereby allowing them to be more responsive to customer inquiries.

Technology will continue to significantly impact the speed at which service operations can respond to customers. In designing new service delivery systems, managers should always keep in mind the idea that no wait is better than any wait!

CONCLUSION

As time becomes more critical in today's fast-paced environment, those firms that can provide fast service will have a competitive advantage over those that respond more slowly to customer requirements. Today, more than ever before, service managers need to constantly seek innovative ways to provide faster and better service to customers. Advances in

Operations Management in Practice

ATMs Save Time by Sprouting Wings

Cathay Pacific Airways now has ATMs onboard two of its 747 airplanes. These machines, supplied by Aero-Design Technology of Irvine, California, will dispense currency for bank cards as well as for all major credit cards. In addition, these ATMs will convert U.S. dollars into any one of 19 foreign currencies based on daily exchange rates that are provided by a satellite.

These airborne ATMs will eliminate the need for customers to wait in ATM lines at their own banks or at the airport. They also are attractive to security-minded passengers who are uncomfortable about using ATMs in strange airports.

Source: Dennis Blank, "ATMs at 12 o'Clock High," *Business Week*, October 13, 1997, p. 8.

technology, especially information technology, can assist the service manager in accomplishing this.

In providing faster service, however, managers should not lose sight of the fact that it is the customer's perception of the wait that is critical, rather than the actual wait itself. There are many factors that can affect customer perceptions of waits, and the service manager needs to know what these factors are and which of them can be effectively managed by the firm. Such an approach will provide a proper framework for the allocation of a firm's scarce resources to ensure faster service.

KEY TERMS

actual waiting time   p. 278
backroom   p. 286
customer's expectations   p. 280
customer satisfaction   p. 280

disconfirmation   p. 281
front-of-the-house   p. 286
perceived waiting time   p. 278

REVIEW AND DISCUSSION QUESTIONS

1. Explain the analogy between having inventory in a manufacturing company and having customers waiting in line in a service operation.

2. What are some of the factors that you think might affect your degree of satisfaction with waiting in line in a supermarket checkout line late at night? . . . in a bank during your lunch hour? . . . at a fast-food restaurant with young children (not necessarily your own!)?

3. Calculate the opportunity cost associated with a dissatisfied customer who stops frequenting a fast-food restaurant for a year. What are your assumptions?

4. Why is it important for a service manager to be able to distinguish between the different types of factors that can affect a customer's level of satisfaction with his or her wait?

5. From your own personal experiences, cite some actual examples of both good and bad waiting line management practices.

6. For each of the different types of service operations listed below, provide specific recommendations for improving both the efficiency of the operation and the customer's level of satisfaction with the waiting time.

   - Airline check-in counter
   - Hospital emergency room
   - Department of Motor Vehicles
   - Mail-order 800 number
   - Emergency hot line
   - Upscale restaurant

SELECTED BIBLIOGRAPHY

Anderson, R. E. "Consumer Dissatisfaction: The Effect of Disconfirmed Expectancy on Perceived Product Performance." *Journal of Marketing Research* 10 (February 1973).

Bearden, W. O., and J. E. Teele. "Selected Determinants of Consumer Satisfaction and Complaint Reports." *Journal of Marketing Research* 20 (February 1983).

Chase, Richard B. "The Customer Contact Approach to Services: Theoretical Bases and Practical Extensions." *Operations Research* 29, no. 4 (July–August 1981).

_____. "The Ten Commandments of Service System Management." *Interfaces* 15, no. 3 (May–June 1985).

Churchill, G. A., Jr., and C. Surprenant. "Investigation into the Determinants of Customer Satisfaction." *Journal of Marketing Research* 19 (November 1982).

Davis, Mark M., and Janelle Heineke. "How Disconfirmation, Perception and Actual Waiting Times Impact Customer Satisfaction." *International Journal of Service Industry Management* 9, no. 1, 1998, pp. 64–73.

_____. "Understanding the Roles of the Customer and the Operation for Better Queue Management." *International Journal of Operations and Production Management* 14, no. 5 (1994).

Davis, Mark M., and Michael J. Maggard. "Zero Waiting Time: A Model for Designing Fast and Efficient Service." In Teresa A. Swartz, David E. Bowen, and Stephen W. Brown (eds.), *Advances in Services Marketing and Management: Research and Practice* 3. Greenwich, CT: JAI Press (June 1994).

Day, R. L., and E. L. Landon. "Toward a Theory of Consumer Complaining Behavior." In A. G. Woodside, J. N. Sheth, and P. D. Bennett (eds.). *Consumer and Industrial Buying Behavior.* New York: North-Holland, 1977.

Katz, K. L.; B. M. Larson; and R. C. Larson. "Prescription for the Waiting Time Blues: Entertain, Enlighten, and Engage," *Sloan Management Review* 32, no. 2 (Winter 1991), pp. 44–53.

Maister, David. "The Psychology of Waiting Lines," In J. A. Czepiel, M. R. Solomon, and C. F. Surprenant (eds.), *The Service Encounter.* Lexington, MA: Lexington Books, D.C. Heath & Co., 1985.

Oliver, R. L. "A Cognitive Model of the Antecedents and Consequences of Satisfaction Decisions." *Journal of Marketing Research* 17 (November 1980).

Sasser, W. E.; R. P. Olsen; and D. D. Wyckoff. *Management of Service Operations: Text, Cases and Readings.* Boston: Allyn and Bacon, 1978.

WAITING LINE THEORY

Supplement Objectives

- Introduce the major characteristics that exist in waiting lines and describe how they can impact a customer's waiting time.

- Identify the various constraints and/or conditions which waiting line theory and its associated equations require for the results to be valid.

- Present waiting line theory in the form of a set of equations that represent various types of waiting line configurations that can be encountered.

What causes waiting lines in the first place? Whenever there is more than one user of a limited resource, a waiting line or queue forms. This delay phenomenon occurs in a wide range of activities affecting many types of users and resources.

In this supplement we discuss the basic elements of waiting line problems and provide standard steady-state formulas for solving them. These formulas, arrived at in the course of developing queuing theory, enable planners to analyze service requirements and establish service facilities appropriate to stated conditions. Queuing theory is broad enough to cover such dissimilar delays as those encountered by customers in a shopping mall or by aircraft awaiting landing slots.

Queuing theory is used extensively in both manufacturing and service environments, and is a standard tool of operations management in areas such as, service delivery system design, scheduling, and machine loading.

WAITING LINE CHARACTERISTICS

The waiting line (or queuing) phenomenon consists essentially of six major components: (*a*) the source population, (*b*) the way customers arrive at the service facility, (*c*) the physical line itself, (*d*) the way customers are selected from the line, (*e*) the characteristics of the service facility itself (such as how the customers flow through the system and how much time it takes to serve each customer), and (*f*) the condition of the customers exiting the system (back to the source population or not?). These six elements, shown in Exhibit S8.1, are discussed separately in the following sections.

Population Source

Arrivals at a service system may be drawn from either a *finite* or an *infinite* population. The distinction is important because the analyses are based on different premises and require different equations for their solution.

Finite Population   A *finite population* refers to the limited size of the customer pool which is the source that will use the service, and at times form a line. The reason this finite classification is important is because when a customer leaves his/her position as a member of the population of users, the size of the user group is reduced by one, which reduces the probability of a customer requiring service. Conversely, when a customer is serviced and returns to the user group, the population increases and the probability of a user requiring service also increases. This finite class of problems requires a separate set of formulas from that of the infinite population case.

EXHIBIT S8.1

Framework for Viewing Waiting Line Situations

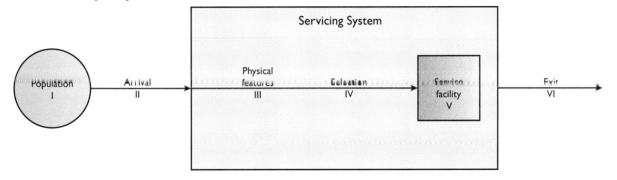

Infinite Population   An infinite population is one that is sufficiently large in relation to the service system, that any changes in the population size caused by subtractions or additions to the population (e.g., a customer needing service or a serviced customer returning to the population) does not significantly affect the system probabilities. If, for example, there were 100 machines that were maintained by one repairperson, and one or two machines broke down and required service, the probabilities for the next breakdowns would not be very different and the assumption could be made without a great deal of error that the population, for all practical purposes, was infinite. Nor would the formulas for "infinite" queuing problems cause much error if applied to a physician who has 1,000 patients, or a department store that has 10,000 customers.

 ## Arrival Characteristics

Another determinant in the analysis of waiting line problems is the *arrival characteristics* of the queue members. As shown in Exhibit S8.2, there are four main descriptors of arrivals: the *pattern of arrivals* (whether arrivals are controllable or uncontrollable); the *size of arrival units* (whether they arrive one at a time or in batches); the *distribution pattern* (whether the time between arrivals is constant or follows a statistical distribution such as a Poisson, exponential, or Erlang); and the *degree of patience* (whether the arrival stays in line or leaves). We describe each of these in more detail.

Arrival Patterns   The arrivals at a system are far more *controllable* than is generally recognized. Barbers may decrease their Saturday arrival rate (and hopefully shift it to other days of the week) by charging an extra $1 for adult haircuts or charging adult prices for children's haircuts. Department stores run sales during the off season or one-day-only sales in part for purposes of control. Airlines offer excursion and off-season rates for similar reasons. The simplest of all arrival-control devices is the posting of business hours.

Some service demands are clearly *uncontrollable,* such as emergency medical demands on a city's hospital facilities. However, even in these situations, the arrivals at emergency rooms in specific hospitals are controllable to some extent by, say, keeping ambulance drivers in the service region informed of the status of their respective host hospitals.

Size of Arrival Units   A *single arrival* may be thought of as one unit (a unit is the smallest number handled). A single arrival on the floor of the New York Stock Exchange (NYSE)

EXHIBIT S8.2

Arrival Characteristics in Queues

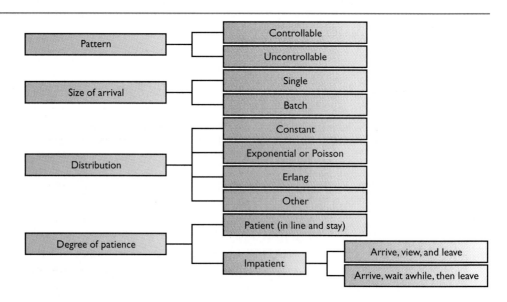

is 100 shares of stock; a single arrival at an egg-processing plant might be a dozen eggs or a flat of two and a half dozen.

A *batch arrival* is some multiple of the unit, as a block of 1,000 shares on the NYSE, a case of eggs at the processing plant, or a party of five at a restaurant.

arrival rate
Rate at which customers arrive into a service delivery system, usually expressed in terms of customers per hour.

Distribution of Arrivals   Waiting line formulas generally require an **arrival rate,** or the average number of customers or units per time period (e.g., 10 per hour). The time between arrivals is the interarrival time (such as an average of one every six minutes). A *constant* arrival distribution is periodic, with exactly the same time period between successive arrivals. In production processes, probably the only arrivals that truly approach a constant interarrival period are those that are subject to machine control. Much more common are *variable* random arrival distributions. The variable or random distribution patterns that occur most frequently in system models are described by the *negative exponential, Poisson,* or *Erlang* distributions.

Degree of Patience   A *patient* arrival is one who waits as long as necessary until the service facility is ready to serve him or her. (Even if arrivals grumble and behave impatiently, the fact that they wait is sufficient to label them as patient arrivals for purposes of waiting line theory.)

There are two classes of *impatient* arrivals. Members of the first class arrive, survey both the service facility and the length of the line, and then decide to leave. Those in the second class arrive, view the situation, and join the waiting line, and then, after some period of time, depart. The behavior of the first type is termed *balking,* and the second is termed *reneging*.

 ## Physical Features of Lines

Length   In a practical sense, an infinite line is very long in terms of the capacity of the service system. Examples of *infinite potential length* are a line of vehicles backed up for miles at a bridge crossing and customers who must form a line around the block as they wait to purchase tickets at a theater.

Gas stations, loading docks, and parking lots have *limited line capacity* caused by legal restrictions or physical space characteristics. This complicates the waiting line problem not only in service system utilization and waiting line computations but also in the shape of the actual arrival distribution as well. The arrival denied entry into the line because of lack of space may rejoin the population at a later time or may seek service elsewhere. Either action makes an obvious difference in the finite population case.

Number of Lines   A *single line* or single file is, of course, one line only. The term *multiple lines* refers either to the single lines that form in front of two or more servers or to single lines that converge at some central redistribution point.

Customer Selection

Queuing Discipline   A queuing discipline is a priority rule, or set of rules (some of which are listed in Exhibit S8.3), for determining the order of service to customers in a waiting line. The rules selected can have a dramatic effect on the system's overall performance. The number of customers in line, the average waiting time, the range of variability in waiting time, and the efficiency of the service facility are just a few of the factors affected by the choice of priority rules.

Probably the most common priority rule, particularly in service operations, is *first come, first served* (FCFS), also known as first in, first out (FIFO). This rule states that the customers in line are served on the basis of their chronological arrival; no other characteristics have any bearing on the selection process. This is popularly accepted as the fairest rule, even though in practice, it discriminates against the arrival requiring a short service time.

EXHIBIT S8.3

Factors in a Queuing
Discipline

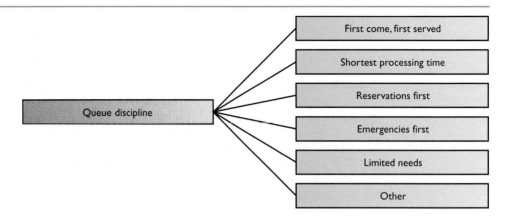

Reservations first, emergencies first, highest-profit customer first, largest orders first, best customers first, longest waiting time in line, and *soonest promised date* are other examples of priority rules. Each has its advantages as well as its shortcomings.

Directives such as "single transactions only" (as in a bank) or "cash only" express lanes (as in a supermarket) seem similar to priority rules, but in reality they are methodologies for structuring the line itself. Such lines are formed to serve a specific class of customers with similar characteristics. Within each line, however, priority rules still apply (as before) to the method of selecting the next customer to be served. A classic case of line structuring is the supermarket with the fast checkout line for customers with 12 items or less.

 ## Service Facility Structure

Several types of service facility structures are presented in Exhibit S8.4, four of which are discussed in detail in the following sections. The physical flow of items or customers to be serviced may go through a single line, multiple lines, or some combination of the two. The choice of format depends partly on the volume of customers served, partly on physical constraints, and partly on the restrictions imposed by sequential requirements governing the order in which the service must be performed.

Single Channel, Single Phase   This is the simplest type of waiting line structure, and straightforward formulas are available to solve the problem for standard distribution patterns of arrival and service. When the distributions are nonstandard, the problem is easily solved by computer simulation. A typical example of a single-channel, single-phase situation is the one-person barbershop.

Single Channel, Multiphase   A car wash is an illustration for a series of services—vacuuming, wetting, washing, rinsing, drying, window cleaning, and parking—performed in a fairly uniform sequence. A critical factor in the single-channel case with service in series is the amount of buildup of items allowed in front of each service, which in turn constitutes separate waiting lines.

Because of the inherent variability in service times, the optimal situation in maximizing the use of the service station is to allow an infinite waiting line to build in front of each station. The worst situation is that in which no line is permitted and only one customer at a time is allowed. When no sublines are allowed to build up in front of each station, as in a car wash, the use of the overall service facility is governed by the probability that a long service time will be required by any one of the servers in the system. This problem is common in most product-oriented systems, such as assembly lines.

Multichannel, Single Phase   Tellers' windows in a bank and checkout counters in supermarkets and high-volume department stores exemplify this type of structure. The difficulty

EXHIBIT S8.4

A Service Facility's Structure

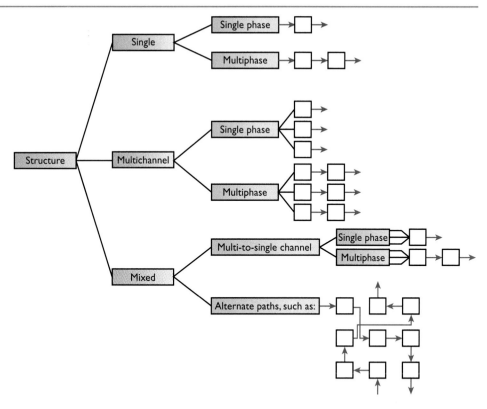

with this format is that the uneven service time given each customer results in unequal speed or flow among the lines. This results in some customers being served before others who arrived earlier as well as in some degree of line shifting. Varying this structure to assure the servicing of arrivals in chronological order would require forming a single line, from which, as a server becomes available, the next customer in the queue is assigned. This type of line structure is now commonly used at airport ticket counters and banks.

Multichannel, Multiphase   This case is similar to the preceding one except that two or more services are performed in sequence. The admission of patients in a hospital follows this pattern because a specific sequence of steps is usually followed: initial contact at the admissions desk, filling out forms, making identification tags, obtaining a room assignment, escorting the patient to the room, and so forth. Since several servers are usually available for this procedure, more than one patient at a time may be processed.

Service Rate   Waiting line formulas generally define **service rate** as the capacity of the server in number of units per time period (such as 12 completions per hour) and *not* as service time, which might average five minutes each. A *constant* service time rule states that each service takes exactly the same time. As in constant arrivals, this characteristic is generally limited to machine-controlled operations. As with arrival rates, Erlang and hyperexponential distributions represent variable service times.

A frequently used illustration of the *Erlang* distribution employs a single-channel, multiservice situation. However, the conditions that must be met for the Erlang approximation are so severe that practical application is rare.

The *exponential* distribution is frequently used to approximate the actual service distribution. This practice, however, may lead to incorrect results; few service situations are exactly represented by the exponential function since the service facility must be able to perform services much shorter than the average time of service.

service rate
Capacity of a service station, usually expressed in terms of customers per hour. The reciprocal of the service rate is the average time to serve a customer.

Most other services also have some practical minimum time. A clerk in a checkout line may have a three-minute average service time but a one-minute minimum time. This is particularly true where another checkout aisle provides a quick service. Likewise in a barbershop, while the average service time may be 20 minutes, a barber rarely cuts hair or gives a shave in fewer than 10 or more than 45 minutes. Hence, these and similar types of services that have strong time dependency are poorly characterized by the exponential curve.

Capacity Utilization   The percentage of time that a service station is busy attending to the needs of a customer is referred to as the **capacity utilization** of that station. This is the percentage of time that the station is busy. The remainder of the time there are no customers to be waited on and the station is, therefore, considered to be idle. In single channel service systems, the capacity utilization is simply the ratio of the arrival rate to the service rate. For example, if customers arrive into a system at the rate of eight per hour and the service rate is 12 customers per hour, then the capacity utilization of this service station is 8/12 or 66.7 percent. It is important to note that in determining the capacity utilization for a station both the arrival rate and the service rate must be expressed in the same units.

capacity utilization
Percentage of time a service station is busy serving a customer.

Exit

Once a customer is served, two exit scenarios are possible: (*a*) the customer may return to the source population and immediately become a competing candidate for service again or (*b*) there may be a low probability of reservice. The first case can be illustrated by a machine that has been routinely repaired and returned to duty but may break down again; the second can be illustrated by a machine that has been overhauled or modified and has a low probability of reservice over the near future. We might refer to the first as the "recurring-common-cold case" and to the second as the "appendectomy-only-once case."

It should be apparent that when the population source is finite, any change in the service performed on customers who return to the population modifies the arrival rate at the service facility. This, of course, alters the characteristics of the waiting line under study and necessitates reanalysis of the problem.

EXHIBIT S8.5

Properties of Some Specific Waiting Line Models

Model	Layout	Service Phase	Source Population	Arrival Pattern	Queue Discipline	Service Pattern	Permissible Queue Length	Typical Example
1	Single channel	Single	Infinite	Poisson	FCFS	Exponential	Unlimited	Drive-in teller at bank, one-lane toll bridge
2	Single channel	Single	Infinite	Poisson	FCFS	Constant	Unlimited	Roller coaster rides in amusement park
3	Single channel	Single	Infinite	Poisson	FCFS	Exponential	Limited	Ice cream stand, cashier in a restaurant
4	Single channel	Single	Infinite	Poisson	FCFS	Discrete distribution	Unlimited	Empirically derived distribution of flight time for a transcontinental flight
5	Single channel	Single	Infinite	Poisson	FCFS	Erlang	Unlimited	One-person barbershop
6	Multi-channel	Single	infinite	Poisson	FCFS	Exponential	Unlimited	Parts counter in auto agency, two-lane toll bridge

WAITING LINE EQUATIONS

To underscore the importance and wide range of applications of waiting line analysis, we describe in this section six different waiting line systems and their characteristics (Exhibit S8.5), and present their respective steady-state equations (Exhibit S8.6). The definitions of the terms used in these equations are presented in Exhibit S8.7. In addition, we present in

EXHIBIT S8.6

Equations for Solving Six Model Problems

Model 1

$$\bar{n}_l = \frac{\lambda^2}{\mu(\mu - \lambda)} \qquad \bar{t}_l = \frac{\lambda}{\mu(\mu - \lambda)} \qquad P_n = \left(1 - \frac{\lambda}{\mu}\right)\left(\frac{\lambda}{\mu}\right)^n$$

$$\bar{n}_s = \frac{\lambda}{\mu - \lambda} \qquad \bar{t}_s = \frac{1}{\mu - \lambda} \qquad \rho = \frac{\lambda}{\mu}$$

Model 2

$$\bar{n}_l = \frac{\lambda^2}{2\mu(\mu - \lambda)} \qquad \bar{t}_l = \frac{\lambda}{2\mu(\mu - \lambda)}$$

$$\bar{n}_s = \bar{n}_l + \frac{\lambda}{\mu} \qquad \bar{t}_s = \bar{t}_l + \frac{1}{\mu}$$

Model 3

$$\bar{n}_l = \left(\frac{\lambda}{\mu}\right)^2 \left[\frac{1 - Q\left(\frac{\lambda}{\mu}\right)^{-1} + (Q - 1)\left(\frac{\lambda}{\mu}\right)^Q}{\left(1 - \frac{\lambda}{\mu}\right)\left(1 - \left(\frac{\lambda}{\mu}\right)^{Q+1}\right)} \right]$$

$$\bar{n}_s = \left(\frac{\lambda}{\mu}\right)\left[\frac{1 - (Q + 1)\left(\frac{\lambda}{\mu}\right)^Q + Q\left(\frac{\lambda}{\mu}\right)^{Q+1}}{\left(1 - \frac{\lambda}{\mu}\right)\left(1 - \left(\frac{\lambda}{\mu}\right)^{Q+1}\right)} \right] \qquad P_n = \left[\frac{1 - \frac{\lambda}{\mu}}{1 - \left(\frac{\lambda}{\mu}\right)^{Q+1}} \right]\left(\frac{\lambda}{\mu}\right)^n$$

Model 4

$$\bar{n}_l = \frac{\left(\frac{\lambda}{\mu}\right)^2 + \lambda^2\sigma^2}{2\left(1 - \frac{\lambda}{\mu}\right)} \qquad \bar{t}_l = \frac{\frac{\lambda}{\mu^2} + \lambda\sigma^2}{2\left(1 - \frac{\lambda}{\mu}\right)}$$

$$\bar{n}_s = \bar{n}_l + \frac{\lambda}{\mu} \qquad \bar{t}_s = \bar{t}_l + \frac{1}{\mu}$$

Model 5

$$\bar{n}_l = \frac{K + 1}{2K} \cdot \frac{\lambda^2}{\mu(\mu - \lambda)} \qquad \bar{t}_l = \frac{K + 1}{2K} \cdot \frac{\lambda}{\mu(\mu - \lambda)}$$

$$\bar{n}_s = \bar{n}_l + \frac{\lambda}{\mu} \qquad \bar{t}_s = \bar{t}_l + \frac{1}{\mu}$$

Model 6

$$\bar{n}_l = \frac{\lambda\mu\left(\frac{\lambda}{\mu}\right)^M}{(M - 1)!(M\mu - \lambda)^2} P_0 \qquad \bar{t}_l = \frac{P_0}{\mu M M!\left(1 - \frac{\lambda}{\mu M}\right)^2}\left(\frac{\lambda}{\mu}\right)^M$$

$$\bar{n}_s = \bar{n}_l + \frac{\lambda}{\mu} \qquad \bar{t}_s = \bar{t}_l + \frac{1}{\mu}$$

$$P_0 = \frac{1}{\displaystyle\sum_{n=0}^{m-1} \frac{\left(\frac{\lambda}{\mu}\right)^n}{n!} + \frac{\left(\frac{\lambda}{\mu}\right)^M}{M!\left(1 - \frac{\lambda}{\mu M}\right)}} \qquad P_w = \left(\frac{\lambda}{\mu}\right)^M \frac{P_0}{M!\left(1 - \frac{\lambda}{\mu M}\right)}$$

EXHIBIT S8.7

Notations for Equations
(Exhibit S8.5)

Infinite Queuing Notation
σ = Standard deviation
λ = Arrival rate
μ = Service rate
$\dfrac{1}{\mu}$ = Average service time
$\dfrac{1}{\lambda}$ = Average time between arrivals
ρ = Potential capacity utilization of the service facility (defined as λ/μ)
$\bar{n}_l$ = Average number waiting in line
$\bar{n}_s$ = Average number in system (including any being served)
$\bar{t}_l$ = Average time waiting in line
$\bar{t}_s$ = Average total time in system (including time to be served)
Q = Maximum queue length
M = Number of channels

detail two sample problems and their solutions for the first two models. There are more types of models than these six, but the formulas and solutions become quite complicated and those problems are generally solved using computer simulation. Also, in using these formulas, keep in mind that they are steady-state formulas derived on the assumption that the process under study is ongoing. Thus, they may provide inaccurate results when applied to initial operations such as the manufacture of a new product or the start of a new business day by a service firm.

TWO TYPICAL WAITING LINE SITUATIONS

Here is a quick preview of the two problems we have used to illustrate the first two waiting line models in Exhibits S8.5 and S8.6.

Problem 1: Customers in line. A bank wants to know how many customers (or cars) are waiting for a drive-in teller, how long they have to wait, the utilization of the teller, and what the service rate would have to be so that 95 percent of the time there would not be more than three cars in the system at any one time.

Problem 2: Equipment selection. A franchisee for Robot Car Wash must decide which equipment to purchase out of a choice of three. Larger units cost more, but wash cars faster. To make the decision, costs are related to revenue.

The two problems are solved using the equations in Exhibit S8.6 with the notations defined in Exhibit S8.7.

 Problem 1: Customers in Line

Example

Western National Bank is considering opening a drive-in window for customer service. Management estimates that customers will arrive in their cars at the rate of 15 per hour. The teller who will staff the window can service customers at the rate of 20 per hour.

Assuming Poisson arrivals and exponential service, find the:

a. Capacity utilization of the teller.

b. Average number of cars in the waiting line.

c. Average number in the system.

d. Average waiting time in line.

e. Average waiting time in the system, including service.

Solution   a. The average capacity utilization of the teller is

$$\mu = 20 \text{ customers/hour}$$
$$\lambda = 15 \text{ customers/hour}$$
$$\rho = \frac{\lambda}{\mu} = \frac{15}{20} = 75 \text{ percent}$$

b. The average number of cars in the waiting line is

$$\bar{n}_l = \frac{\lambda^2}{\mu(\mu - \lambda)} = \frac{(15)^2}{20(20 - 15)} = 2.25 \text{ customers}$$

c. The average number in the system is

$$\bar{n}_s = \frac{\lambda}{\mu - \lambda} = \frac{15}{20 - 15} = 3 \text{ customers}$$

d. Average waiting time in line is

$$\bar{t}_l = \frac{\lambda}{\mu(\mu - \lambda)} = \frac{15}{20(20 - 15)} = 0.15 \text{ hour, or 9 minutes}$$

e. Average waiting time in the system is

$$\bar{t}_s = \frac{1}{\mu - \lambda} = \frac{1}{20 - 15} = 0.2 \text{ hour, or 12 minutes}$$

Example   Because of limited space availability and a desire to provide an acceptable level of service, the bank manager would like to ensure, with 95 percent confidence, that not more than three cars will be in the system at any one time. What is the present level of service for the three-car limit? What level of teller use must be attained and what must be the service rate of the teller to assure the 95 percent level of service?

Solution   The present level of service for three cars or less is the probability that there are 0, 1, 2, or 3 cars in the system.

From Model 1, Exhibit S8.6:

$$P_n = \left(1 - \frac{\lambda}{\mu}\right)\left(\frac{\lambda}{\mu}\right)^n$$

at $n = 0$ $P_0 = (1 - 15/20)$ $(15/20)^0 = 0.250$

at $n = 1$ $P_1 = (1/4)$ $(15/20)^1 = 0.188$

at $n = 2$ $P_2 = (1/4)$ $(15/20)^2 = 0.141$

at $n = 3$ $P_3 = (1/4)$ $(15/20)^3 = \underline{0.105}$

0.684 or 68.4 percent

The probability of having more than three cars in the system is 1.0 minus the probability of three cars or less ($1.0 - 0.684 = 0.316$ or 31.6 percent).

For a 95 percent service level to three cars or less, this states that $P_0 + P_1 + P_2 + P_3 = 95$ percent.

$$0.95 = \left(1 - \frac{\lambda}{\mu}\right)\left(\frac{\lambda}{\mu}\right)^0 + \left(1 - \frac{\lambda}{\mu}\right)\left(\frac{\lambda}{\mu}\right)^1 + \left(1 - \frac{\lambda}{\mu}\right)\left(\frac{\lambda}{\mu}\right)^2 + \left(1 - \frac{\lambda}{\mu}\right)\left(\frac{\lambda}{\mu}\right)^3$$

$$0.95 = \left(1 - \frac{\lambda}{\mu}\right)\left[1 + \frac{\lambda}{\mu} + \left(\frac{\lambda}{\mu}\right)^2 + \left(\frac{\lambda}{\mu}\right)^3\right]$$

We can solve this by trial and error for values of λ/μ. If $\lambda/\mu = 0.50$:

$$0.95 \overset{?}{=} 0.5(1 + 0.05 + 0.25 + 0.125)$$
$$0.95 \neq 0.9375$$

With $\lambda/\mu = 0.45$,

$$0.95 \overset{?}{=} (1 - 0.45)(1 + 0.45 + 0.203 + 0.091)$$
$$0.95 \neq 0.96$$

With $\lambda/\mu = 0.47$,

$$0.95 \overset{?}{=} (1 - 0.47)(1 + 0.47 + 0.221 + 0.104) = 0.95135$$
$$0.95 \approx 0.95135$$

Therefore, with the utilization $\rho = \lambda/\mu$ of 47 percent, the probability of three cars or less in the system is 95 percent.

To find the rate of service required to attain this 95 percent service level, we simply solve the equation $\lambda/\mu = 0.47$, where $\lambda =$ number of arrivals per hour. This gives $\mu = 31.92$ or about 32 per hour.

That is, the teller must serve approximately 32 people per hour—a 60 percent increase over the original 20-per-hour capability—for 95 percent confidence that not more than three cars will be in the system. Perhaps service can be speeded up by modifying the method of service, adding another teller, or limiting the types of transactions available at the drive-in window. (Many banks, in fact, now limit each customer to a maximum of three transactions at the drive-in window.) Note that with the condition of 95 percent confidence that three or fewer cars will be in the system, the teller will be idle 53 percent of the time.

Problem 2: Equipment Selection

Example

The Robot Company franchises combination gas and car wash stations throughout the United States. Robot gives a free car wash with a gasoline fill-up or, for a wash alone, charges $5.00. Past experience shows that the number of customers that have car washes following fill-ups is about the same as for a wash alone. The average gross profit on a gasoline fill-up is about $7.00, and the cost of the car wash to Robot is $1.00. Robot stays open 14 hours per day.

Robot has three power units with drive assemblies, and a franchise must select the unit preferred. Unit I can wash cars at the rate of one every five minutes and is leased for

$120 per day. Unit II, a larger unit, can wash cars at the rate of one every four minutes but costs $160 per day. Unit III, the largest, cost $220 per day and can wash a car in three minutes.

The franchisee estimates that customers will not wait in line more than five minutes for a car wash. A longer time will cause Robot to lose both gasoline sales and car wash sales.

If the estimate of customer arrivals resulting in washes is 10 per hour, which wash unit should be selected?

Solution

Using Unit I, calculate the average waiting time of customers in the wash line (μ for Unit I = 12 per hour). From the Model 2 equations (Exhibit S8.6),

$$\bar{t}_l = \frac{\lambda}{2\mu(\mu - \lambda)} = \frac{10}{2(12)(12 - 10)} = 0.208 \text{ hour, or } 12\frac{1}{2} \text{ minutes}$$

For Unit II at 15 per hour,

$$\bar{t}_l = \frac{10}{2(15)(15 - 10)} = 0.067 \text{ hour, or 4 minutes}$$

If waiting time is the only criterion, Unit II should be purchased. However, before we make the final decision, we must look at the profit differential between both units.

With Unit I, some customers would balk or renege because of the 12½-minute wait. And although this greatly complicates the mathematical analysis, we can gain some estimate of lost sales with Unit I by inserting $\bar{t}_l = 5$ minutes or $\frac{1}{12}$ hour (the average length of time customers will wait) and solving for λ. This would be the effective arrival rate of customers:

$$\bar{t}_l = \frac{\lambda}{2\mu(\mu - \lambda)}$$

$$\lambda = \frac{2\bar{t}_l\mu^2}{1 + 2\bar{t}_l\mu}$$

$$\lambda = \frac{2(1/12)(12)^2}{1 + 2(1/12)(12)} = 8 \text{ per hour}$$

Therefore, since the original estimate of λ was 10 per hour, an estimated two customers per hour will be lost. Lost profit of two customers per hour × 14 hours × ½ ($7.00 fill-up profit + $4.00 wash profit) = $154.00 per day.

Because the additional cost of Unit II over Unit I is only $40 per day, the loss of $154.00 profit obviously warrants the installation of Unit II.

The original constraint of a five-minute maximum wait is satisfied by Unit II. Therefore, Unit III is not considered unless the arrival rate is expected to increase in the future.

COMPUTER SIMULATION OF WAITING LINES

Some waiting line problems that seem very simple on first impression turn out to be extremely difficult or impossible to solve. Throughout this chapter we have been treating waiting line situations that are independent; that is, either the entire system consists of a single phase, or else each service that is performed in a series is independent. (This could happen if the output of one service location is allowed to build up in front of the next one so that this, in essence, becomes a calling population for the next service.) When a series of services is performed in sequence where the output rate of one becomes the input rate of the next, we can no longer use the simple formulas. This is also true for any problem where conditions do not meet the conditions of the equations, as specified in Exhibit S8.7. The analytical technique best suited for solving this type of problem is computer simulation.

CONCLUSION

Waiting line problems present both a challenge and a frustration to those who try to solve them. One of the main concerns in dealing with waiting line problems is what procedure or priority rule to use in selecting the next product or customer to be served.

Many queuing problems appear simple until an attempt is made to solve them. This supplement has dealt with the simpler problems. When the situation becomes more complex, such as when there are multiple phases and/or where services are performed only in a particular sequence, computer simulation is usually necessary to obtain the optimal solution.

KEY TERMS

arrival rate   p. 293   service rate   p. 295
capacity utilization   p. 296

REVIEW AND DISCUSSION QUESTIONS

1. How many waiting lines did you encounter during your last airline flight?
2. Distinguish between a *channel* and a *phase*.
3. Which assumptions are necessary to employ the formulas given for Model 1?
4. In what way might the first-come, first-served rule be unfair to the customers waiting for service in a bank or hospital?
5. Identify the various types of waiting lines you encounter in a "normal" day.

SOLVED PROBLEMS

Problem 1

Quick Lube, Inc. operates a fast lube and oil change garage. On a typical day, customers arrive at the rate of three per hour, and lube jobs are performed at an average rate of one every 15 minutes. The mechanics operate as a team on one car at a time.

Assuming Poisson arrivals and exponential service, determine the:

a. Utilization of the lube team.

b. Average number of cars in line.

c. Average time a car waits before it is lubed.

d. Total time it takes a car to go through the sytem (i.e., waiting in line plus lube time).

Solution

$\lambda = 3$, $\mu = 4$

a. Utilization $(\rho) = \dfrac{\lambda}{\mu} = \dfrac{3}{4} = 75\%$.

b. $\bar{n}_1 = \dfrac{\lambda^2}{\mu(\mu - \lambda)} = \dfrac{3^2}{4(4 - 3)} = \dfrac{9}{4} = 2.25$ cars in line.

c. $\bar{t}_l = \dfrac{\lambda}{\mu(\mu - \lambda)} = \dfrac{3}{4(4-3)} = \dfrac{3}{4} = .75$ hour $= 45$ minutes in line.

d. $\bar{t}_s = \dfrac{1}{\mu - \lambda} = \dfrac{1}{1} = 1$ hour (waiting + lube).

Problem 2

American Vending Inc. (AVI) supplies vended food to a large university. Because students kick the machines at every opportunity out of anger and frustration, management has a constant repair problem. The machines break down on an average of three per hour, and the breakdowns are distributed in a Poisson manner. Downtime costs the company $25/hour per machine, and each maintenance worker gets $4 per hour. One worker can service machines at an average rate of five per hour, distributed exponentially; two workers, working together, can service seven per hour, distributed exponentially; and a team of three workers can do eight per hour, distributed exponentially.

What is the optimum maintenance crew size for servicing the machines?

Solution

American Vending Inc.

Case I: One worker.

$$\lambda = 3/\text{hour Poisson}, \quad \mu = 5/\text{hour exponential}$$

The average number of machines (either broken down or being repaired) in the system is:

$$\bar{n}_s = \frac{\lambda}{\mu - \lambda} = \frac{3}{5 - 3} = \frac{3}{2} = 1\tfrac{1}{2} \text{ machines}$$

Downtime cost is $25 \times 1.5 = $37.50 per hour; repair cost is $4.00 per hour; and total cost per hour for 1 worker is $37.50 + $4.00 = $41.50.

$$\begin{aligned}
\text{Downtime } (1.5 \times \$25) &= \$37.50 \\
\text{Labor } (1 \text{ worker} \times \$4) &= \underline{4.00} \\
&\ \$41.50
\end{aligned}$$

Case II: Two workers.

$$\lambda = 3, \mu = 7$$

$$\bar{n}_s = \frac{\lambda}{\mu - \lambda} = \frac{3}{7 - 3} = 0.75 \text{ machines}$$

$$\begin{aligned}
\text{Downtime } (0.75 \times \$25) &= \$18.75 \\
\text{Labor } (2 \text{ workers} \times \$4.00) &= \underline{8.00} \\
&\ \$26.75
\end{aligned}$$

Case III: Three workers.

$$\lambda = 3, \mu = 8$$

$$\bar{n}_s = \frac{\lambda}{\mu - \lambda} = \frac{3}{8 - 3} = \frac{3}{5} = 0.60 \text{ machines}$$

$$\begin{aligned}
\text{Downtime } (0.60 \times \$25) &= \$15.00 \\
\text{Labor } (3 \text{ workers} \times \$4.00) &= \underline{12.00} \\
&\ \$27.00
\end{aligned}$$

Comparing the costs for one, two, or three workers, we see that Case II with two workers is the optimal decision.

PROBLEMS

1. Burrito King is a new fast-food franchise that is opening up nationwide. Burrito King has been successful in automating burrito production for its drive-up fast-food establishments. The Burro-Master 9000 requires a constant 45 seconds to produce a burrito (with any of the standard fillings). It has been estimated that customers will arrive at the drive-up window according to a Poisson distribution at an average of 1 every 50 seconds.

   a. What is the expected average time in the system?

   b. To help determine the amount of space (in terms of number of cars) needed for the line at the drive-up window, Burrito King would like to know the average line length (in cars) and the average number of cars in the system (both in line and at the window).

2. Big Jack's drive-through hamburger service is planning to build another stand at a new location and must decide how much land to lease to optimize returns. Leased space for cars will cost $1,000 per year per space. Big Jack is aware of the highly competitive nature of the quick-food service industry and knows that if his drive-through is full, customers will go elsewhere. The location under consideration has a potential customer arrival rate of 30 per hour (Poisson). Customers' orders are filled at the rate of 40 per hour (exponential) since Big Jack prepares food ahead of time. The average profit on each arrival is $0.60, and the stand is open from noon to midnight every day. How many spaces for cars should be leased?

3. To support National Heart Week, the Heart Association plans to install a free blood pressure testing booth in El Con Mall for the week. Previous experience indicates that, on the average, 10 persons per hour request a test. Assume arrivals are Poisson from an infinite population. Blood pressure measurements can be made at a constant time of five minutes each. Assume the queue length can be infinite with FCFS discipline.

   a. What is the average number of persons that can be expected to be in line?

   b. What is the average number of persons that can be expected to be in the system?

   c. What is the average amount of time that a person can expect to spend in line?

   d. On the average, how much time will it take to measure a person's blood pressure, including waiting time?

   e. On weekends, the arrival rate can be expected to increase to nearly 12 per hour. What effect will this have on the number in the waiting line?

4. A cafeteria serving line has a coffee urn from which customers serve themselves. Arrivals at the urn follow a Poisson distribution at the rate of three per minute. In serving themselves, customers take about 15 seconds, exponentially distributed.

   a. How many customers would you expect to see on the averge at the coffee urn?

   b. How long would you expect it to take to get a cup of coffee?

   c. What percentage of time is the urn being used?

   d. What is the probability that there would be three or more people in the cafeteria?

   If the cafeteria installs an automatic vendor that dispenses a cup of coffee at a constant time of 15 seconds, how does this change your answers to *a* and *b*?

5. L. Winston Martin is an allergist in Tuscon who has an excellent system for handling his regular patients who come in just for allergy injections. Patients arrive for an injection and fill out a name slip, which is then placed in an open slot that passes into another room staffed by one or two nurses. The specific injections for a patient are prepared and the patient is called through a speaker system into the room to receive the injection. At certain times during the day, the patient load drops and only one nurse is needed to administer the injections.

   Let's focus on the simpler case, when there is one nurse. Also assume that patients arrive in a Poisson fashion and the service rate of the nurse is exponentially distributed. During this slower period, patients arrive with an interarrival time of approximately three minutes. It takes the nurse an average of two minutes to prepare the patients' serum and administer the injection.

a. What is the average number you would expect to see in Dr. Martin's facilities?

b. How long would it take for a patient to arrive, get an injection, and leave?

c. What is the probability that there will be three or more patients on the premises?

d. What is the utilization of the nurse?

6. The NOL Income Tax Service is analyzing its customer service operations during the month prior to the April 15 filing deadline. On the basis of past data it has been estimated that customers arrive according to a Poisson process with an average interarrival time of 12 minutes. The time to complete a return for a customer is exponentially distributed with a mean of 10 minutes. Based on this information, answer the following questions.

a. If you went to NOL, how much time would you allow for getting your return done?

b. On average, how much room should be allowed for the waiting area?

c. If the NOL service were operating 12 hours per day, how many hours on average, per day, would the office be busy?

d. What is the probability that the system is idle?

e. If the arrival rate remained unchanged but the average time in the system must be 45 minutes or less, what would need to be changed?

f. A robotic replacement has been developed for preparing the new "simplified" tax forms. If the service time became a constant nine minutes, what would total time in the system become?

7. The law firm of Larry, Darryl and Darryl (L,D & D) specialize in the practice of waste disposal law. They are interested in analyzing their caseload. Data were collected on the number of cases they received in a year and the times to complete each case. They consider themselves a dedicated firm and will only take on one case at a time. Calls for their services apparently follow a Poisson process with a mean of one case every 30 days. Given the fact that L,D & D are outstanding in their field, clients will wait for their turn and are served on a first come, first served basis. The data on the number of days to complete each case for the last 10 cases are 27, 26, 26, 25, 27, 24, 27, 23, 22, and 23.

   Determine the average time for L,D & D to complete a case, the average number of clients waiting, and the average wait for each client.

SELECTED BIBLIOGRAPHY

Bartfai, P., and J. Tomko. *Point Processes Queuing Problems.* New York: Elsevier-North Holland Publishing, 1981.

Bruell, Steven C. *Computational Algorithms for Closed Queuing Networks.* New York: Elsevier-North Holland Publishing, 1980.

Cooper, Robert B. *Introduction to Queuing Theory.* 2nd ed. New York: Elsevier-North Holland Publishing, 1980.

Gorney, Leonard. *Queuing Theory: A Solving Approach.* Princeton, NJ: Petrocelli, 1981.

Griffin, Walter C. *Queuing: Basic Theory and Application.* Columbus, OH: Grid, 1978.

Hillier, Frederick S., et al. *Queuing Tables and Graphs.* New York: Elsevier-North Holland Publishing, 1981.

Newell, Gordon F. *Applications of Queuing Theory.* New York: Chapman and Hall, 1982.

_____. *Approximate Behavior of Tandem Queues.* New York: Springer-Verlag, 1980.

Solomon, Susan L. *Simulation of Waiting Lines.* Englewood Cliffs, NJ: Prentice Hall, 1983.

Srivastava, H. M., and B. R. Kashyap. *Special Functions in Queuing Theory: And Related Stochastic Processes.* New York: Academic Press, 1982.

Vinrod, B., and T. Altiok. "Approximating Unreliable Queuing Networks under the Assumption of Exponentiality." *Journal of the Operational Research Society* (March 1986), pp. 309–16.

HUMAN RESOURCES ISSUES IN OPERATIONS MANAGEMENT

Chapter Objectives

- Explain the role of an organization's human resources in providing high-quality goods and services and in maintaining a competitive advantage in the marketplace.

- Describe the changing role of the manager from command and control to team leader and coach, and the critical skills required for this emerging role.

- Define the concept of employee empowerment and demonstrate its impact on management and the organization.

- Distinguish between traditional work groups, self-managed teams, and cross-functional teams.

- Introduce behavioral and physical factors that should be taken into consideration when designing jobs.

"We Are Ladies and Gentlemen Serving Ladies and Gentlemen" is the motto of The Ritz-Carlton Hotel Company, L.L.C. which won the Malcolm Baldrige National Quality Award in 1992. In order to provide superior service to its hotel guests, Ritz-Carlton starts with a recruitment process that identifies those potential employees that have the personal characteristics necessary to succeed. Upon being selected, each employee goes through an in-depth orientation, followed by extensive on-the-job training and job certification. Every employee receives a card with the company's credo on it and is expected to learn the credo and practice it daily on the job. The values of Ritz-Carlton are continuously reinforced on a daily basis through "line-ups," frequent employee recognition for extraordinary achievement, and a performance appraisal based on specific expectations. To ensure that problems are resolved quickly, workers are required to act at the first notice of a customer complaint, regardless of the type of problem. *Every employee is empowered to take whatever action is necessary when a guest is dissatisfied.* Consequently, much of the responsibility for ensuring high-quality guest services and accommodations rests with employees. ▪

> "We Are Ladies and Gentlemen Serving Ladies and Gentlemen"

THE RITZ-CARLTON

CREDO

The Ritz-Carlton Hotel is a place where the genuine care and comfort of our guests is our highest mission.

We pledge to provide the finest personal service and facilities for our guests who will always enjoy a warm, relaxed yet refined ambience.

The Ritz-Carlton experience enlivens the senses, instills well-being, and fulfills even the unexpressed wishes and needs of our guests.

Source: Adapted from "Profiles of Winners of the Malcolm Baldrige National Quality Award." Photo: 1992 The Ritz-Carlton Hotel Company. All rights reserved. Reprinted with permission of The Ritz-Carlton Hotel Company, L. L. C.

As suggested by how the Ritz-Carlton treats its employees and the direct impact this treatment has on the high level of service provided to its guests, the role of workers has changed dramatically in recent years. This trend is expected to continue into the foreseeable future. In fact, both manufacturing and service operations today face more rapid and radical organizational changes than they have at any time since World War II. In order to remain competitive, today's organizations, as we previously discussed, must simultaneously focus on a wide range of issues to better meet the increasing demands of their customers. These issues include increasing quality, decreasing delivery time, and customizing products. Organizations must introduce new technologies, concentrate on process improvements and reengineering, increase efficiency, and create new organizational structures to succeed in an increasingly competitive and global marketplace. However, an organization's ability to first attain and then maintain world-class status in the manufacture of goods and the delivery of services depends on more than the introduction of new technologies and processes. It also depends on the activities of a trained and motivated workforce. In fact, the ability of managers to effectively manage the workforce has been shown to be three times more powerful than all other factors combined in accounting for the financial success of a firm when measured over a five-year period.[1]

The effective management of an organization's human resources is a very broad topic that cannot be covered adequately in one textbook, let alone one chapter. The purpose of this chapter, therefore, is to introduce you to several issues and emerging trends that organizations and managers must consider with respect to today's workforce and the ever changing, competitive environment that currently exists. These issues include the new managerial role, the growing emphasis on groups and teams to accomplish organizational tasks, and the new approaches to work design.

THE NEW MANAGERIAL ROLE

Managers in today's organizations face a rapidly changing and often unpredictable environment. Large-scale corporate restructuring, layoffs (or "downsizing"), and mergers and acquisitions mean that today's managers must identify new ways to produce more with fewer workers and fewer organizational layers. Attempts to create more profitable, "lean and mean" organizations have resulted in an unexpected byproduct: a sharp decline in perceptions of loyalty between the employee and the organization. In 1993, for example, 77 percent of workers surveyed said that companies were less loyal to employees than five years before. In addition, sixty percent of these workers judged that employees were less loyal to the organization.[2] As a consequence, today's managers are challenged to motivate employees who may feel less commitment to their organizations than was previously the norm.

The processes and technologies used to accomplish work are also changing, requiring managers to change with them. Total Quality Management, for example, emphasizes employee involvement. It also requires managers to assist workers in learning how to take responsibility for their work, and it requires managers to view workers from a new perspective, that of partners in the decision-making process rather than subordinates. No

[1]Gary Hanson, "Determinants of Firm Performance: An Integration of Economic and Organizational Factors" (Ph.D. diss., University of Michigan) cited in David A. Cameron and Kim S. Whetten, *Developing Manager Skills*, 3rd ed. (New York, Harper Collins, 1995).

[2]B. B. Moskal, "Company Loyalty Dies, a Victim of Neglect," *Industry Week*, March 1, 1993.

Operations Management in Practice

EMPLOYEE SUGGESTIONS PAY OFF AT DANA CORPORATION

The Dana Corporation is a multibillion-dollar conglomerate that produces truck and car parts and components for both automobile manufacturers and for the after purchase market. Its subsidiary, Dana Commercial Credit Corp., which provides leasing and financial services, won the 1996 Malcolm Baldrige National Quality Award. The employees of Dana Corp. submitted a total of 666,120 suggestions in 1996 or 1.22 suggestions per employee per month. The result of employee input is a steady stream of improvements to the existing operation in the form of lower costs, less labor, and increased productivity, all of which directly affects the bottom line. Taking advantage of employee knowledge has become somewhat of an obsession at Dana Corp. Says

CEO Woody Morcott, "It's a core part of our value system." It begins in the classroom where instructors at Dana University teach employees how to think about new ways of doing things. A major element for the success at Dana is emphasis on the fact that the workers are responsible for keeping the company competitive. Morcott admits he "stole" the idea when he visited a Japanese factory in the late 1980s. Each plant within Dana Corp. runs its own suggestion program, and it appears to be working. More than 70 percent of the suggestions submitted are adopted by the company.

Source: Adapted from Richard Teitelbaum, "How to Harness Gray Matter," *Fortune*, June 9, 1997, p. 168.

---

longer are employees expected "to leave their brains at the door" when they come to work each day. (See OM in Practice on Employee Suggestions Pay Off at Dana Corporation.) In addition, the introduction of fax machines, e-mail, and videoconferencing have influenced the speed with which information is available and the way in which employees work together. Wal-Mart, for example, as stated earlier in this text, holds weekly employee meetings via satellite communication, thereby ensuring that everyone in the company receives the same information at the same time. Moreover, the growing use of PC networks provides a new variety of ways to link organizations together that had never before been contemplated. These new technologies mean that managers, in many instances, must now oversee the work of employees with whom they rarely meet face to face.

The composition of the workforce is changing as well. In the United States, for example, the number of women and minority group members entering the workforce and advancing within organizations continues to increase. For example, by the year 2000, 85 percent of the new hires in organizations will be women, African-Americans, Hispanics, Asians, and Native Americans. Forty percent of the total workforce is expected to be women in the year 2000, and the total percentage of Hispanic and African-American employees is expected to increase to 25 percent by the year 2005.[3]

This growing diversity in the workforce, if properly managed, can improve creativity and decision making as well as make the organization more responsive to a wider variety of customers. On the other hand, failure to effectively manage a diverse workforce can lead to high turnover of valuable employees, unproductive conflicts, communication breakdowns, and expensive legal actions. For example, Southern California Edison agreed to pay $11.25 million to as many as 2,500 employees who were victims of job discrimination since 1989, and employees of Texaco filed a $520 million class-action discrimination lawsuit against the company in 1996.[4]

All of these changes, along with other issues like the increasing pressures generated by worldwide competition and/or the need to respond to new environmental regulations, mean that managers must now have a wide range of skills and be adept at playing a variety of organizational roles. In a study of 402 highly effective managers, Kim Whetten and David

---

[3]N. B. Songer, "Work Force Diversity," *Business and Economic Review*, April–June 1991.

[4]*USA Today*, November 15, 1996; *Boston Globe*, November 17, 1996.

Cameron identified ten skills that were most frequently cited as being critical to managerial effectiveness.[5] They are:

1. Verbal communication (including the ability to listen).
2. Managing time and stress.
3. Managing individual decisions.
4. Recognizing, defining, and solving problems.
5. Motivating and influencing others.
6. Delegating.
7. Setting goals and articulating a vision.
8. Self-awareness.
9. Team building.
10. Managing conflict.

At first, some of the skills may appear to be contradictory. Effective managers must have skills that foster employee participation and group work as well as skills in individual decision making and leadership. They must be visionary and, at the same time, manage day-to-day decision making. Robert Hoojberg and Robert Quinn use the term "behavioral complexity" to highlight the need for today's managers to use a variety of different, even conflicting, competencies and behaviors in an integrated way. A manager's ability to play multiple and competing roles has been related to a number of positive outcomes. These include better firm performance, higher overall managerial effectiveness as assessed by subordinates, better managerial performance, charisma, and the likelihood of making process improvements in the organization. Robert Quinn et. al. depict the behavioral complexity required of managers in a model that includes eight managerial leadership roles and the core competencies required for each role. These are shown in Exhibit 9.1.

A review of these eight roles and related core competencies highlights the need for managers to work through and with other people. Working through and with other people, however, has a different meaning for managers today than it did in the past. The traditional managerial role was based on the following set of assumptions: (a) a good manager always has more technical expertise than any subordinate; (b) a good manager can solve all the problems; (c) a good manager has the primary (or only) responsibility for how the department works; (d) a good manager knows at all times exactly what is going on in the department.

In contrast, today's effective manager is rarely someone who: (a) knows it all (and readily admits it!), (b) does it all alone, or (c) regularly instructs others in exactly what to do. Instead, a manager delegates, negotiates, communicates, develops, and is often a coach and teacher. In the emerging models of effective management, a key managerial skill is no longer "bossing" others around. "Bossing" may get the work done in the short term, but does little to develop a workforce that has either the creativity or the initiative to respond quickly to changing customer requirements, a new technology or competitor, or an unexpected obstacle. Increasingly, today's managers focus on developing employees who can manage and lead themselves to achieving the organization's goals both individually and by working in teams.

Charles Manz and Henry Sims describe managers who can lead others to lead themselves as "superleaders." A key to their managerial success is their ability to empower employees, helping them become "self-leaders." Empowered employees are highly motivated

---

[5]Kim Whetten and David Cameron, *Developing Management Skills* (New York: Harper Collins, 1995).

EXHIBIT 9.1

Eight Different Managerial Roles and Their Required Core Competencies

Type of Role	Core Competencies Required
Mentor	1. Understanding self and others. 2. Communicating effectively. 3. Developing subordinates.
Facilitator	1. Building teams. 2. Using participative decision making. 3. Managing conflict.
Monitor	1. Monitoring individual performance. 2. Managing collective performance. 3. Managing organizational performance.
Coordinator	1. Managing projects. 2. Designing work. 3. Managing across functions.
Director	1. Visioning, planning, and goal setting. 2. Designing and organizing. 3. Delegating effectively.
Producer	1. Working productively. 2. Fostering a productive work environment. 3. Managing time and stress.
Broker	1. Building and maintaining a power base. 2. Negotiating agreement and commitment. 3. Presenting ideas.
Innovator	1. Living with change. 2. Thinking creatively. 3. Creating change.

Source: R. E. Quinn, S. R. Faerman, M. P. Thompson, and M. R. McGrath, *Becoming a Master Manager: A Competency Framework* (New York: John Wiley and Sons, 1996), p. 23.

and committed to taking joint responsibility for the overall excellence of the organization. They find personal meaning in their work, know that they have the competence to perform their job well, believe that they have control over how to do their work, and understand that they have an impact on the outcomes that make a difference to the organization. (See OM in Practice on Employees Give Tours at Chrysler's Automobile Assembly Plant.)

In order to foster employee empowerment, managers, on a continuous basis, must share with frontline employees four organizational ingredients:

1. Information about the organization's performance.
2. Rewards based on the organization's performance.
3. Knowledge that enables employees to understand and contribute to organizational performance.
4. Power to make decisions that influence organizational direction and performance.[6]

These four ingredients of empowerment relate directly to what research and common sense tell us about what motivates individuals to achieve peak performance. Individuals

[6]David E. Bowen and Edward E. Lawler, "The Empowerment of Service Workers: What, Why, How and When," *Sloan Management Review,* Spring 1991, pp. 31–39.

Operations Management in Practice

EMPLOYEES GIVE TOURS AT CHRYSLER'S AUTOMOBILE ASSEMBLY PLANT

"In Detroit, the Viper-Prowler plant is the place to see." Employees are proud to show off their craftmanship.

"We run plant tours every single day. We are the hot ticket for tours in Detroit," said John Hinckley, manager of the Connor Avenue Plant. "If you bring a group in for a tour, I'm not going to lead it. I won't have one of my management people lead it. The people who build the cars are the people who know what's going on around here." The plant gets all kinds coming in for a tour, "... from Brownies to WWII veterans."

And the company goes even further. "Chrysler allows Viper customers to pick up their car as it comes out of final assembly, to meet the employees who built it ...," who in turn get a kick out of meeting the real people who drive their artwork.

Source: Gerald Scott, "A Look at the Goings-on inside Chrysler's Plant That Builds Viper and Prowler, Tour de Force," *Chicago Tribune*, March 8, 1998.

perform better when they understand the impact of their personal contribution on the success of the overall effort. They are more motivated when they can see the direct linkages between their contributions, the success of the overall effort, and the rewards they receive. They are also motivated to perform better if they know they have the requisite knowledge and skills to do the job well. And finally, individuals perform best when they have the autonomy and discretion to exercise their own best judgment about how to do the job.

The new managerial role of integrating seemingly contradictory competencies and creating empowered employees is not an easy one. It requires a manager to have not only technical and organizational skills, but also excellent people skills. An effective manager must be able to understand what it takes to effectively manage the organization's human resources.

INCREASING EMPHASIS ON TEAMWORK

Nowhere is the need for effective management and the focus on employee empowerment more obvious than in the increasing use of teamwork by organizations. Although some organizations, such as Volvo and Toyota, have successfully used team models for organizing work for more than twenty years, the surge in the number of American organizations now using teams has been relatively recent. The reasons for the growing popularity in teams are many, including that teams typically outperform individuals when doing tasks that require judgment, experience, and multiple skills. Companies using self-managed teams have found that they increase productivity, quality, customer satisfaction and flexibility, allow for the streamlining of functions, and produce higher worker commitment.[7]

In order to better understand the power of teams, it is important to highlight some of the differences between teams and traditional work groups. In traditional work groups, the emphasis is on sharing information and making decisions that help group members perform their functions more effectively. Work groups do not need to work collectively on tasks that require a group effort, and their members are individually accountable for their performance. Work teams, in contrast, emphasize collective performance. Work team members are both individually and mutually responsible for their contributions and performance. Work teams are characterized by a high degree of synergy. This synergy combines and improves the knowledge and skills of individual members to create products and/or decisions that are of higher quality than those made by individuals alone. Katzenbach and Smith define the difference between a team and a group of people with a common assignment as:

---

[7]J. D. Orsburn; L. Moran; E. Mussselwhite; and J. H. Zenger; *Self-Directed Work Teams: The New American Challenge* (Homewood, IL: Business One Irwin, 1990).

"a small number of people with complementary skills who are committed to a common purpose, performance goals, and approach for which they hold themselves mutually accountable." They go on to say that truly high-performance teams have the added ingredient of "members who are also deeply committed to another's personal growth and success."[8]

As more organizations embrace the use of work teams, the variety of team structures and projects on which teams work continues to increase. Two types of work teams that are prevalent in today's organizations are self-managed work teams and cross-functional teams.

Self-Managed Work Teams

self-managed work teams
Autonomous teams responsible for identifying problems, implementing solutions, and measuring outcomes.

Unlike traditional work groups, **self-managed work teams** tend to operate very autonomously. They have responsibility for not only solving problems, but also for implementing solutions and measuring outcomes. Typically composed of 10 to 15 employees, these teams take on many of the activities and responsibilities that were formerly the duties of their supervisors. Members of a self-managed team are likely to have collective control over (*a*) work assignments for team members, (*b*) the pace at which work gets done, (*c*) assessing the quality of team and individual output, and (*d*) who joins the team. For example, team members at Semco S/A were charged with making a decision about where to locate the company's new plant.[9] Self-managed teams at the General Motors plant in Fitzgerald, Georgia, which manufactures sealed, maintenance-free, automotive batteries, prepare annual material and labor budgets, evaluate group members for pay raises, and can shut down the production line to solve process and quality problems.[10]

There are, however, some unique problems with self-managed work teams, especially in service operations. For example, a guest at the front desk of a Ritz-Carlton Hotel became very upset when she was told that there was no manager for the front desk (it was a self-directed work team). To solve this type of problem, each team member becomes "manager for a day" on a rotating basis to address specific guest requests "requiring a manager."

Effective self-managed teams have produced some important benefits for organizations and their employees. The greater autonomy and responsibility given to employees in self-managed teams tend to increase worker motivation and job satisfaction. Employees are empowered and can see how their efforts contribute to organizational success. This motivation and satisfaction also results in positive effects on productivity and the organization's bottom line. For example, an employee on a self-managed team at ACES, an independent electric power producer, noticed that fans similar to those used in his plant were being sold at a local discount store for one-third the cost of those bought by ACES from the original manufacturer. He took the initiative to buy the discount store's entire inventory of fans. Because of his participation in a self-managed team, he knew the cost of the ACES fans, understood the purposes for which the fans were used and how often they would need to be replaced, and felt authorized by the company to implement a solution that would save money. The self-managed teams at the General Motors Fitzgerald plant also contributed to satisfaction and productivity. The plant was able to manufacture its products at costs significantly lower than similar plants run in a more traditional, top-down management style, and its levels of employee satisfaction were among the highest throughout the entire General Motors organization.[11]

[8]Jon R. Katzenbach and Douglas K. Smith, *The Wisdom of Teams: Creating the High Performance Organization* (Boston: Harvard Business School Press, 1993), pp. 45, 92.

[9]R. Wellins; W. Byham; and J. Wilson; *Empowered Teams* (San Francisco: Jossey-Bass, 1991).

[10]C. C. Manz and H. P. Sims, *Business without Bosses* (New York: John Wiley and Sons, 1995).

[11]Ibid.

The successful implementation of self-managed teams, however, is not easy. It takes considerable time, effort, and organizational commitment. Team members must not only have technical expertise but also develop skills in problem solving, decision making, interpersonal communication, and team management. The organization must be willing to create innovative reward and incentive systems that reflect both individual and team performance. Managers must learn to become facilitators and coaches of empowered, self-managed teams rather than directors and bosses of individual contributors.

Cross-Functional Work Teams

cross-functional work teams
Teams within an organization that have representatives from different areas of the firm.

Cross-functional work teams come together to tackle large, complex projects or solve organizational problems that cut across traditional functional lines and which, therefore, require the input and expertise from several areas within an organization. The members of a cross-functional team may come from the same organizational level but represent different departments and areas of expertise. Hallmark Cards' team reduced development of new cards and coordinated products from three years to less than a year. By using a cross-functional team to provide information from and coordinate the activities of various departments early in a project, organizations can save considerable time and money. For example, in developing the new 777 aircraft, Boeing created cross-functional teams that included designers, engineers, and maintenance and customer service personnel, as well as finance specialists and production employees. Instead of representatives from these functional areas working on the aircraft sequentially, they worked together on developing the new aircraft from the beginning of the process. Maintenance specialists were able to suggest ways to design an aircraft that would be faster to service and cheaper to operate. Production engineers helped designers develop solutions to potential production problems during the design phase. Designing these problems out rather than trying to fix them during the production phase was much less costly and time consuming.[12]

As in the case of self-managed work teams, the successful implementation of cross-functional teams requires organizational commitment. The members of a cross-functional team must learn to appreciate and understand the perspectives of representatives from other parts of the organization. They must also learn to communicate their expertise and opinions in ways that representatives from other functional areas can understand. Developing an effective cross-functional team can take considerable time and effort. The organizations that have done so, however, believe that the effort pays off. For example, the cross-functional team that designed the Chrysler Neon delivered the new subcompact in 42 weeks rather than taking the several years it usually takes to design a new car.[13]

---

[12]J. Main,"Betting on the 21st Century Jet," *Fortune,* April 20, 1992, pp. 102–17; D. J. Yang, "When the Going Gets Tough, Boeing Gets Touchy-Feely," *Business Week,* January 17, 1994, pp. 65–68.

[13]D. Woodruff, "Chrysler's Neon," *Business Week,* May 3, 1993, pp. 116–26.

JOB DESIGN

Central to an organization's ability to effectively manage its human resources is the appropriate design of jobs in the organization. Without the proper job design to support new styles of management, empowered employees, and teamwork, these innovative approaches to transform the workplace and increase organizational competitiveness are likely to fail. Many of the following trends in job design are directly linked to the issues and trends discussed earlier in this chapter.

Perhaps the most challenging (and also the most perplexing) design activity associated with the transformation process is the development of the jobs that each worker and work group are to perform. The reasons for this include:

1. There is often an inherent conflict between the needs and goals of the worker and work group, and the requirements of the process.
2. The unique personality of each individual results in a wide range of attitudinal, physiological, and productivity responses in performing any given task.
3. The character of the workforce and the work itself are changing, which challenges the traditional models of worker behavior and the efficacy of standard approaches to work development.

In this section, we explore these and other issues in job design and present some guidelines for carrying out the job-design function. We begin by noting some trends in job design, some of which were mentioned earlier:

1. *Quality as part of the worker's job.* Now often referred to as "quality at the source," improved quality is linked with the concept of **worker empowerment.** Empowerment, used in this context, refers to workers being given authority to stop a production line when there is a quality problem, or to give a customer an on-the-spot refund if service was not satisfactory.

worker empowerment Providing employees with authority to make decisions pertaining to the organization.

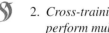 2. *Cross-training workers to perform multiskilled jobs.* This is more often seen in the factory than in the office despite pressures on the clerical workforce as described in the next OM in Practice on The New World of Work. Indeed, bank check processing centers and the majority of high-volume clerical jobs are far more factorylike than those in many factories.

3. *Employee involvement and team approaches to designing and organizing work.* This is a central feature in total quality management (TQM) and continuous improvement efforts. In fact, it is safe to say that virtually all TQM programs are team based.

 4. *"Informating" ordinary workers through telecommunications network and computers, thereby expanding the nature of their work and their ability to do it.* In this context,

Operations Management in Practice

THE NEW WORLD OF WORK

- London firms are now sending typing to Taipei. To survive, London typists must realize they are competing with Taipei typists. They must learn to "add value" (e.g., know more software programs or more languages than their Taiwanese counterparts) or else they'd better learn to love pounding the pavement.

- The FI Group, one of Britain's largest software systems houses, employs about 1,100 people, most of whom are part-time freelancers who need toil no more than 20 hours per week. More than two thirds of the firm's work is done at home: All told, employees live in 800 sites and serve 400 clients at any time. Life at FI is captured in the November 1988 issue of *Business:* "Chris Eyles, project manager, sat down in her office in Esher, Surrey, and called up the electronic 'chit chat' mailbox . . . The printer began to churn out messages. 'Help!' said [a message] from her secretary, based a few miles away in Weybridge. Somewhere in the Esher area, a computer analyst was in trouble . . . Eyles checked the team diary and her wall plan, located the

analyst and the problem, and set up a meeting at FI's work center in Horley, 25 miles away."

- So who's left to sweep the floor? A visit to a 3M facility in Austin, Texas, suggests that floor sweeping, food handling, and security guarding are fast becoming almost as sophisticated as engineering. Computer-based floor sweepers and new security systems call for a sophisticated worker in virtually every job. A new, highly automated facility belonging to the huge drug distributor, Bergen Brunswig, is illustrative: Most manual work is done by machine. Work teams that dot the facility are not so much in the business of "doing" (by old standards), but in the business of improving the system. They are brain-involved, improvement-project creators, not muscle-driven lump shifters. There is no room on the staff for anyone who sees himself or herself as a pair of hands, punching a time clock.

Source: Tom Peters, "Prometheus Barely Unbound," *The Executive* IV, no. 4 (November 1990), pp. 79–80, 83.

informating is more than just automating work, it is revising the fundamental structure of work. Northeast Utilities' computer system, for example, can pinpoint a problem in a service area before the customer service representative (CSR) answers the phone. The CSR uses the computer to troubleshoot serious problems, to weigh probabilities that other customers in the area have been affected, and to dispatch repair crews before other calls are even received.

5. *Any time, any place production.* The ability to do work away from the factory or office, again due primarily to advances in information technology, is a growing trend throughout the world. (See the OM in Practice.)

6. *Automation of heavy manual work.* Examples abound in both services (one-person trash pickup trucks) and manufacturing (robot spray painting on auto lines). These changes are driven by safety regulations as well as economics and personnel reasons. (See the OM in Practice.)

7. *Most important of all, organizational commitment to providing meaningful and rewarding jobs for all employees.* (See Exhibit 9.2.)

job design
Tasks and sequences that have to be accomplished and are within an individual's job assignment.

Job design may be defined as the specification of the work activities for an individual or group within an organizational setting. Its objective is to develop work assignments that meet the requirements of the organization and the technology, and that satisfy the personal and individual requirements of the jobholder. The term *job* (in the context of nonsupervisory work) and the activities involved in it are defined as follows:

1. *Micromotion:* the smallest work activity involving such elementary movements as reaching, grasping, positioning, or releasing an object.

2. *Element:* Two or more micromotions, usually thought of as a more or less complete entity, such as picking up, transporting, and positioning an item.

EXHIBIT 9.2

People-Related Objectives of Hewlett-Packard

1. Belief in our people.
   - Confidence in, and respect for, our people as opposed to depending upon extensive rules, procedures, and so forth.
   - Depend on people to do their job right (individual freedom) without constant directives.
   - Opportunity for meaningful participation (job dignity).

2. Emphasis on working together and sharing rewards (teamwork and partnership).
   - Share responsibilities; help each other; learn from each other; chance to make mistakes.
   - Recognition based on contribution to results—sense of achievement and self-esteem.
   - Profit sharing, stock purchase plan, retirement program, and so on are aimed at employees and company sharing in each other's successes.
   - Company financial management emphasis on protecting employee's job security.

3. A superior working environment that other companies seek but few achieve.
   - Informality—open, honest communications; no artificial distinctions between employees (first-name basis); management by walking around; and open-door communication policy.
   - Develop and promote from within—lifetime training, education, career counseling to help employees get maximum opportunity to grow and develop with the company.
   - Decentralization—emphasis on keeping work groups as small as possible for maximum employee identification with our businesses and customers.

EXHIBIT 9.3

Factors in Job Design

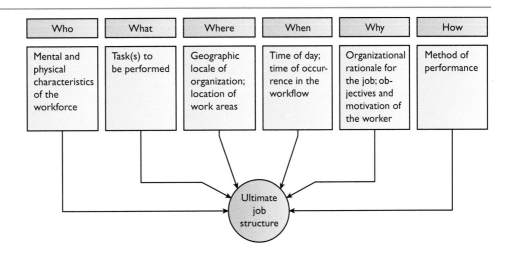

3. *Task:* Two or more elements that comprise a complete activity, such as wiring a circuit board, sweeping a floor, or cutting a tree.

4. *Job:* A set of all the tasks that must be performed by a given worker. A job may consist of several tasks, such as typing, filing, and taking dictation (as in secretarial work), or it may consist of a single task, such as attaching a wheel to a car (as in automobile assembly).

Job design is a complex function because of the variety of factors that enter into arriving at the ultimate job structure. Decisions must be made about who is to perform the job, where it is to be performed, and how. And, as we can see in Exhibit 9.3, each of these factors may have additional considerations.

Behavioral Considerations in Job Design

specialization of labor
Dividing tasks into small increments of work, resulting in efficient operations due to highly repetitive tasks.

Degree of Labor Specialization   **Specialization of labor** is a two-edged sword in job design. On one hand, specialization has made possible high-speed, low-cost production, and, from a materialistic standpoint, has greatly enhanced our standard of living. On the other hand, it is well known that extreme specialization, such as that encountered on traditional assembly lines in mass-production industries, often has serious adverse effects on workers, which in turn are often passed on to the production systems in the form of low-quality or defective work. In essence, the problem is to determine how much specialization is enough: At what point do the disadvantages outweigh the advantages? (See Exhibit 9.4.)

Recent research suggests that the disadvantages dominate the advantages much more than was thought in the past. However, simply stating that, for purely humanitarian reasons, specialization should be avoided is risky. The reason, of course, is that people differ in what they want from their work and what they are willing to put into it. Some workers prefer not to make decisions about their work, some like to daydream on the job, and others are simply not capable of performing highly complex work. Still, there is a good deal of worker frustration with the way many jobs are structured, leading organizations to try different approaches to job design. Two popular contemporary approaches are job enrichment and sociotechnical systems. The philosophical objective underlying these approaches is to improve the quality of work life of the employee, and so they are often applied as central features of what is termed a quality of work life (QWL) program.

EXHIBIT 9.4

Advantages and Disadvantages of Specialization of Labor

Advantages of Specialization	
To Management	**To Labor**
1. Rapid training of the workforce	1. Little or no education required to obtain work
2. Ease in recruiting new workers	2. Ease in learning job
3. High output due to simple and repetitive work	
4. Low wages due to ease of substitutability of labor	
5. Close control over workflow and workloads	

Disadvantages of Specialization	
To Management	**To Labor**
1. Difficulty in controlling quality since no one person has responsibility for entire product.	1. Boredom stemming from repetitive nature of work

2. "Hidden" costs of worker dissatisfaction, arising from
  a. Turnover
  b. Absenteeism
  c. Tardiness
  d. Grievances
  e. Intentional disruption of production process
	2. Little gratification from work itself because of small contribution to each item

	3. Little or no control over the work pace, leading to frustration and fatigue (in assembly-line situations)
3. Reduced likelihood of obtaining improvement in the process because of worker's limited perspective	4. Little opportunity to progress to a better job because significant learning is rarely possible on fractionated work
	5. Little opportunity to show initiative through developing better methods or tools
	6. Local muscular fatigue caused by use of the same muscles in performing the task
	7. Little opportunity for communication with co-workers because of layout of the work area

Job Enlargement and Job Enrichment   **Job enlargement** generally entails making adjustments to a specialized job to make it more interesting to the jobholder. A job is said to be *enlarged horizontally* if the worker performs a greater number or variety of tasks, and it is said to be *enlarged vertically* if the worker is involved in planning, organizing, and inspecting his or her own work. Horizontal job enlargement is intended to counteract oversimplification and to permit the worker to perform a "whole unit of work." Vertical enlargement (traditionally termed *job enrichment*) attempts to broaden the workers' influence in the transformation process by giving them certain managerial powers over their own activities. Today, common practice is to apply both horizontal and vertical enlargement to a given job and refer to the total approach as **job enrichment.**

Physical Considerations in Job Design

Beyond the behavioral components of job design, another aspect warrants consideration: the physical components. Indeed, while motivation and work-group structure strongly influence worker performance, they may be of secondary importance if the job is too demanding or is otherwise ill designed from a physical standpoint.

Work Task Continuum   One way of viewing the general nature of the physical requirements inherent in work is through the work task continuum shown in Exhibit 9.5. In this typology, *manual tasks* put stress on large muscle groups in the body and lead to overall fatigue. *Motor tasks* are controlled by the central nervous system, and their measure of effectiveness is the speed and precision of movements. While these tasks lead to fatigue, the effect is localized in the smaller muscle groups, such as the fingers, hands, and arms and, hence, cannot be adequately measured by indices of *general* fatigue. (In measuring the physiological stress of motor tasks, researchers are investigating the use of electromyography, which records the changes in electrical potential in the involved muscular extremity; i.e., the hands, arms, and fingers.) *Mental tasks* involve rapid decision making based on certain types of stimuli, such as blips on a radar screen or defects in a product. Here the measure of effectiveness is generally some combination of time to respond and the number and types of errors. Research in this area is usually predicated on concepts from the discipline of information theory, and as might be expected by the nature of the tasks, much of the source work has been provided by military agencies.

In the private sector, Westinghouse's Human Science Laboratory has been exploring the use of brain waves as a means of determining an individual's level of attention and

Oshkosh B'Gosh workers were plagued by tendonitis and numbness. The company redesigned the job and designed a pulley system allowing sewers to work with their arms at rest. In addition, jobs were enlarged through rotation so parts of the body could rest.

EXHIBIT 9.5

Work Task: Continuum
(Human Work)

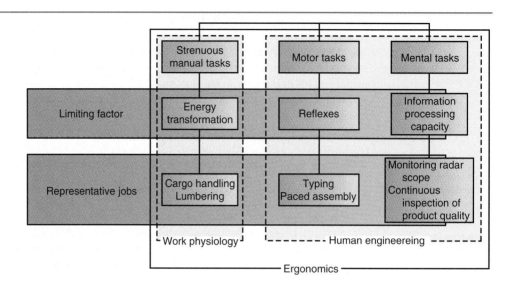

cognitive processing. The laboratory manager predicts that within the next decade West-inghouse could market a complete system that could monitor the mental processing efforts of employees as they work. A worker would wear something like a baseball cap fitted with an electronic monitoring device that would pick up and send relevant brain waves to a computer. The computer would then flash a warning if the brain-wave analysis indicated that the worker's attention had wandered too far, or that his or her mental stress level had climbed too high. Such a technology would be appropriate for such life-dependent jobs as air traffic controller, nuclear power plant controllers, and surgical staffs, and jobs where concentration is critical to work quality, such as inspection and accounting work.[14]

As noted in Exhibit 9.5, motor tasks and mental tasks fall under the heading *human engineering,* while the study of the physical aspects of work in general is called *ergonomics* (from the Greek noun for "work" and the Greek verb for "to manage").

CONCLUSION

Today's managers face increased pressure to improve performance within their organizations. This has come about for several reasons, including the growth in international competition and the need to excel simultaneously in a wide variety of areas. In order to produce more output with a smaller workforce, managers are now turning to their employees for ideas on how to improve worker productivity and performance. Much of the improvements in this area are the result of work teams which have been rapidly forming in many of the better companies. However, changes in management style are required for the successful implementation of these teams.

The human resource issues, in terms of how we manage our workforce, and the technical issues, in terms of how we specifically design jobs, are both critical elements in the success of a company. Many management gurus today, in fact, suggest that a firm's employees are the only sustainable competitive advantage that is possible.

[14]Michael Schrage, "Big Brother May Be Coming to the Workplace," *The Washington Post* (June 9, 1984).

KEY TERMS

cross-functional work teams p. 314
job design p. 316
job enlargement p. 319
job enrichment p. 319

self-managed work teams p. 313
specialization of labor p. 318
worker empowerment p. 315

REVIEW AND DISCUSSION QUESTIONS

1. Think of three examples of ways in which an organization has changed to become more competitive. What impact do you think these changes have on the employees of the organization?

2. Which of the eight managerial roles do you practice in your role as a student, . . . in activities in which you participate, . . . in your job? Which of Cameron and Whetten's ten skills do you use in these roles?

3. What problems might arise from empowering employees? What are some of the hurdles that managers must overcome in empowering employees? What could the organization do to address these issues?

4. Would you prefer to work in a traditional work group or in a self-managed work team? Why?

5. This chapter mentioned some of benefits of and the difficulties in implementing cross-functional and self-managed work teams. What other difficulties can you predict? What other benefits do you see?

6. Is there any inconsistency when a company requires precise time standards and, at the time, encourages job enlargement?

7. The study team from one American car manufacturer observed that the Japanese used techniques such as job rotation, making workers responsible for quality control, minimal work classifications, and indirect employee participation in management. What gains can be made with this approach, in contrast to the job specialization approach? If the Japanese approach were to be adopted in a specialized job environment, what changes would have to take place for it to be successfully implemented?

CASE: AT&T CREDIT CORP.

Millions of clerical employees toil in the back offices of financial companies, processing applications, claims, and customer accounts on what amounts to electronic assembly lines. The jobs are dull and repetitive and efficiency gains minuscule—when they come at all.

That was the case with AT&T Credit Corp. (ATTCC) when it opened shop in 1985 as a newly created subsidiary of American Telephone & Telegraph Corp. Based in Morristown, New Jersey, ATTCC provides financing for customers who lease equipment from AT&T and other companies. A bank initially retained by ATTCC to process lease applications couldn't keep up with the volume of new business.

ATTCC President Thomas C. Wajnert saw that the fault lay in the bank's method of dividing labor into narrow tasks and organizing work by function. One department

handled applications and checked the customer's credit standing, a second drew up contracts, and a third collected payments. So no one person or group had responsibility for providing full service to a customer. "The employees had no sense of how their jobs contributed to the final solution for the customer," Wajnert says.

UNEXPECTED BONUS

Wajnert decided to hire his own employees and give them "ownership and accountability." His first concern was to increase efficiency, not to provide more rewarding jobs. But in the end, he did both.

In 1986, ATTCC set up 11 teams of 10 to 15 newly hired workers in a high-volume division serving small businesses. The three major lease-processing functions were combined in each team. No longer were calls from customers shunted from department to department. The company also divided its national staff of field agents into seven regions and assigned two or three teams to handle business from each region. That way, the same teams always worked with the same sales staff, establishing a personal relationship with them and their customers. Above all, team members took responsibility for solving customers' problems. ATTCC's new slogan: "Whoever gets the call owns the problem."

The teams largely manage themselves. Members make most decisions on how to deal with customers, schedule their own time off, reassign work when people are absent, and interview prospective new employees. The only supervisors are seven regional managers who advise the team members, rather than give orders. The result: The teams process up to 800 lease applications a day versus 400 under the old system. Instead of taking several days to give a final yes or no, the teams do it in 24 to 48 hours. As a result, ATTCC is growing at a 40 percent to 50 percent compound annual rate, Wajnert says.

Extra Cash

The teams also have economic incentives for providing good service. A bonus plan tied to each team's costs and profits can produce extra cash. The employees, most of whom are young college graduates, can add $1,500 a year to average salaries of $28,000, and pay rises as employees learn new skills. "It's a phenomenal learning opportunity," says 24-year-old team member Michael LoCastro.

But LoCastro and others complain that promotions are rare because there are few managerial positions. And everyone comes under intense pressure from co-workers to produce more. The annual turnover rate is high: Some 20 percent of ATTCC employees either quit or transfer to other parts of AT&T. Still, the team experiment has been so successful that ATTCC is involving employees in planning to extend the concept throughout the company. "They will probably come up with as good an organizational design as management could," Wajnert says, "and it will work a lot better because the employees will take ownership for it."

Question

1. Besides few opportunities for promotion and intense peer pressure, what other factors might contribute to the high employee turnover rate?
2. What would you do to reduce the employee turnover rate at ATTCC?

Source: John Hoerr, "The Payoff from Teamwork" (July 10, 1989), p. 59, issue of *Business Week* by special permission © 1989 by The McGraw-Hill Companies.

SELECTED BIBLIOGRAPHY

Bowen, David E., and Edward E. Lawler. "The Empowerment of Service Workers: What, Why, How and When." *Sloan Management Review,* Spring 1991, pp. 31–39.

Carlisle, Brian. "Job Design Implications for Operations Managers." *International Journal of Production and Operations Management* 3, no. 3 (1983), pp. 40–48.

Cusumano, Michael. *Japan's Software Factories: A Challenge to U.S. Management.* New York: Oxford University Press, 1991.

Hanson, Gary. "Determinants of Firm Performance: An Integration of Economic and Organizational Factors." Ph.D. dissertation, University of Michigan. Cited in Cameron, David A., and Kim S. Whetten. *Developing Manager Skills.* 3rd ed. New York: Harper Collins, 1995.

Hoerr, John. "The Payoff from Teamwork." *Business Week,* July 10, 1989, p. 59.

Hoojberg, Robert, and Robert Quinn. "Behavioral Complexity and the Development of Effective Managers." In *Strategic Leadership: A Multiorganizational-Level Perspective,* eds. R. Phillips and J. Hunt. Westport, CT: Quorum Publishing, 1992.

Katzenbach, Jon R., and Douglas K. Smith. *The Wisdom of Teams: Creating the High Performance Organization.* Boston: Harvard Business School Press, 1993.

Konz, Stephan. *Work Design: Industrial Ergonomics.* 2nd ed. New York: John Wiley & Sons, 1983.

Lipin, Steven. "A New Vision." *The Wall Street Journal,* June 25, 1993.

Main, J. "Betting on the 21st Century Jet." *Fortune,* April 20, 1992, pp. 102–17.

Manz, Charles C., and Henry P. Sims, Jr. *Business Without Bosses.* New York: John Wiley and Sons, 1995.

Manz, Charles C., and Henry P. Sims, Jr. "Super-Leadership: Beyond the Myth of Heroic Leadership." *Organizational Dynamics* 19, no. 4 (1991), pp. 18–35.

Mondy, R. Wayne, and Robert N. Noe. *Human Resource Management.* Upper Saddle River, NJ: Prentice-Hall, 1996.

Moskal, B. B. "Company Loyalty Dies, A Victim of Neglect." *Industry Week,* March 1, 1993.

Orsburn J. D.; L. Moran; E. Mussselwhite; and J. H. Zenger. *Self-Directed Work Teams: The New American Challenge.* Homewood, IL: Business One Irwin, 1990.

Peters, Tom. "Prometheus Barely Unbound," *The Executive* IV, no. 4 (November 1990), pp. 79–83.

Quinn, R. E.; S. R. Faerman; M. P. Thompson; and M. R. McGrath. *Becoming a Master Manager: A Competency Framework.* New York: John Wiley and Sons, 1996, p. 23.

Sasser, W. Earl, and William E. Fullmer. "Creating Personalized Service Delivery Systems," in D. Bowen, R. Chase, and T. Cummings (eds.), *Service Management Effectiveness.* San Francisco: Jossey-Bass, 1990, pp. 213–33.

Schrage Michael. "Big Brother May Be Coming to the Workplace." *The Washington Post*, June 9, 1984.

Scott, Gerald. "A Look at the Goings-on inside Chrysler's Plant That Builds Viper and Prowler, Tour de Force." *Chicago Tribune*, March 8, 1998.

Songer, N. B. "Work Force Diversity." *Business and Economic Review,* April–June 1991.

Teitelbaum, Richard. "How to Harness Gray Matter." *Fortune,* June 9, 1997, p. 168.

Wellins, R.; W. Byham; and J. Wilson. *Empowered Teams.* San Francisco: Jossey-Bass, 1991.

Wetten, Kim, and David Cameron. *Developing Management Skills.* New York: Harper Collins, 1995.

Woodruff, D. "Chrysler's Neon." *Business Week,* May 3, 1993, pp. 116–26.

Yang, D. J. "When the Going Gets Tough, Boeing Gets Touchy-Feely." *Business Week,* January 17, 1994, pp. 65–68.

WORK PERFORMANCE MEASUREMENT

Supplement Objectives

- Introduce the basic elements involved in job design.

- Understand the fundamental issues involved in developing work measurements.

- Determine how to design a work sampling study and apply it to an actual operation.

- Recognize that there are many different methods to compensate employees including reward structures for good performance.

A fundamental building block in most organizations, whether manufacturing or service, is the proper design of work tasks and the measurement of how long it takes to accomplish these tasks. In the early part of this century, beginning with Frederick W. Taylor and continuing with Frank and Lillian Gilbreth, work measurements were done almost exclusively in manufacturing companies.The purpose of conducting these measurements was to determine the most efficient way to accomplish a specific task. In addition, management was able to compare worker performance to a set of established standards. These work standards, which stated how long it should take to complete a given set of tasks, also provided a basis for determining the labor costs associated with manufacturing.

While the specific methodology associated with work measurement has basically not changed since its inception with Taylor, the manner in which work measurements are conducted has changed significantly (See OM in Practice: Work Measurement Then and Now). In addition, with the development of sophisticated computerized worker scheduling systems for service operations, the length of time it takes service workers to complete various tasks is a critical element in determining how many workers to schedule to meet a forecasted level of customer demand in a given time period.

WORK METHODS

An integral part in the development of operational processes is the definition of the tasks that must be performed by the workers. But how should these tasks be done? Years ago, production workers were craftspeople who had their own (and sometimes secret) methods for doing things. However, over time products have become more complicated, as mechanization of a higher order was introduced, and output rates have increased. As a result, the responsibilities for work methods have been transferred to management. It was no longer logical or economically feasible to allow individual workers to produce the same product by different methods. Work specialization brought much of the concept of craftwork to an end, as less-skilled workers were employed to do the simpler tasks.

While in some large companies, the responsibility for developing work methods is typically assigned to either a staff department designated *methods analysis* or an industrial engineering department, in small firms this activity is often performed by consulting firms that specialize in work methods design. However, as illustrated in the NUMMI example (see OM in Practice), a growing number of firms are allowing their workers to design their own jobs and also to determine how long they should take.

The principal approach to the study of work methods is the construction of charts, such as operations charts, worker-machine charts, simo (simultaneous motion) charts, and activity charts, in conjunction with time study or standard time data. The choice of which charting method to use depends on the activity level of the task; that is, whether the focus is on (*a*) the overall operation, (*b*) the worker at a fixed workplace, (*c*) a worker interacting with equipment, or (*d*) a worker interacting with other workers (see Exhibit S9.1).

Overall Operation

The objective in studying the overall production system is to identify delays, transport distances, processes, and processing time requirements, in order to simplify the entire operation. The underlying philosophy is to eliminate any step in the process that does not add value to the product. The approach used here is to develop a process flowchart and then ask

Operations Management in Practice

WORK MEASUREMENT THEN AND NOW

JOB DESIGN THEN . . .

Frederick W. Taylor recounts his "motivation" of his trusty worker, Schmidt (in *Principles of Scientific Management*, 1910):

"Schmidt, are you a high-priced man?"

"Vell, I don't know vat you mean."

"Oh yes you do. What I want to know is whether you are a high-priced man or not. . . . What I want to find out is whether you want to earn $1.85 a day or whether you are satisfied with $1.15, just the same as all those cheap fellows are getting?"

"Vell, yes I vas a high-priced man."

"Now come over here. You see that pile of pig iron?"

"Yes."

"You see that car?"

"Yes."

"Well, if you are a high-priced man, you will load that pig iron on that car tomorrow for $1.85."

"You see that man over there? . . . Well, if you are a high-priced man, you will do exactly as this man tells you tomorrow, from morning till night. When he tells you to pick up a pig and walk, you pick it up and you walk, and when he tells

you to sit down and rest, you sit down. You do that straight through the day. And what's more, no back talk."

AND NOW . . .

Researcher Paul S. Adler describes job design at New United Motor Manufacturing Inc.'s (NUMMI) Fremont, California, plant. NUMMI is a joint venture between General Motors and Toyota.

Team members hold the stopwatch and design their own jobs. Team members begin by timing one another, seeking the most efficient way to do each task at a sustainable pace. They pick the best performance, break it down into its component parts, and then look for ways of improving each element. The team then takes the resulting methods, compares them with those used by teams working on the other shift at the same workstation, and writes detailed specifications that become the standard work definition for everyone on both teams.

Source: Discussions with Paul S. Adler; Paul S. Adler, "Time and Motion Regained," *Harvard Business Review* 71, no. 1 (January–February 1993), pp. 97–110; and "Return of the Stopwatch," *The Economist*, January 23, 1993, p. 69.

EXHIBIT S9.1

Work Methods and Design Aids

Activity	Objective of Study	Study Techniques
Overall production system	Eliminate or combine steps; shorten transport distance; identify delays	Flow diagram, service blueprint, process chart
Worker at fixed workplace	Simplify method; minimize motions	Operations charts, simo charts; apply principles of motion economy
Worker interacts with equipment	Minimize idle time; find number or combination of machines to balance cost of worker and machine idle time	Activity chart, worker-machine charts
Worker interacts with other workers	Maximize productivity, minimize interference	Activity charts, gang process charts

the following questions:

What is done? Must it be done? What would happen if it were not done?

Where is the task done? Must it be done at that location or could it be done somewhere else?

When is the task done? Is it critical that it be done then or is there flexibility in time and sequence? Could it be done in combination with some other step in the process?

How is the task done? Why is it done this way? Is there another way?

Who does the task? Can someone else do it? Should the worker be of a higher or lower skill level?

These types of questions usually help to eliminate much unnecessary work, as well as to simplify the remaining work, by combining a number of processing steps and changing the order of performance.

Use of the process chart is valuable in studying an overall operation, though care must be taken to follow the same item throughout the process. The subject may be a product being manufactured, a service being created, or a person performing a sequence of activities. An example of a process chart (and flow diagram) for a clerical operation is shown in Exhibit S9.2. Common notation in process charting is given in Exhibit S9.3.

Worker at a Fixed Workplace

There are many jobs that require workers to remain at a specified workstation in order to complete their assigned tasks. When the nature of the work is primarily manual (such as sorting, inspecting, making entries, or assembly operations), the focus of work design is on simplifying the work method and making the required operator motions as few and as simple as possible.

There are two basic ways to determine the best method when a method analyst studies a single worker performing an essentially manual task. The first is to search among the various workers performing a given task and find that one who performs the job best. That person's method is then accepted as the standard, and the other workers are trained to perform it in the same way. This was basically F. W. Taylor's approach. The second method is to observe the performance of a number of workers, analyze in detail each step of their work, and pick out the superior features of each worker's performance. This results in a composite method that combines the best elements of the group studied. This was the procedure used by Frank Gilbreth, the father of motion study, to determine the "one best way" to perform a work task.

therbligs
Basic units of measurement used in micromotion analysis.

Taylor observed actual performance to find the best method; Frank Gilbreth and his wife Lillian relied on movie film. Through micromotion analysis—observing the filmed work performance frame by frame—the Gilbreths studied work very closely and defined its basic elements, which was termed **therbligs** ("Gilbreth" spelled backward, with the *t* and *h* transposed). They also used the motion model—a wire representation of the path of a motion. Their study led to the rules or principles of motion economy listed in Exhibit S9.4.

Once the various motions for performing a task have been identified, an *operations chart* is then developed, listing the individual operations and their sequence of performance. For greater detail, a *simo* (simultaneous motion) *chart* may be constructed, listing not only the operations but also the times for both left and right hands. This chart may be assembled from the data collected with a stopwatch, from analysis of a film of the operation, or from predetermined motion-time data (discussed later in the chapter). Many aspects of poor design become immediately obvious with this technique—a hand being used as a holding device (rather than a jig or fixture), an idle hand, or an exceptionally long time for positioning.

EXHIBIT S9.2

Flow Diagram and Process Chart of an Office Procedure—Present Method*

Superintendent

Secretary

Purchasing agent

Research Laboratory

Offices

Supervisor's office

Present Method ☒ Proposed Method ☐			**PROCESS CHART**
SUBJECT CHARTED Requisition for small tools			DATE _____
Chart begins at supervisor's desk and ends at			CHART BY J.C.H.
typist's desk in purchasing department			CHART NO. R136
DEPARTMENT Research laboratory			SHEET NO. 1 OF 1

DIST. IN FEET	TIME IN MINS.	CHART SYMBOLS	PROCESS DESCRIPTION
		●⇨□D▽	Requisitions written by supervisor (one copy)
		O⇨□▶▽	On supervisor's desk (awaiting messenger)
65		O⇢□▶▽	By messenger to superintendent's secretary
		O⇨□▶▽	On secretary's desk (awaiting typing)
		●⇨□D▽	Requisition typed (original requisition copied)
15		O⇢□D▽	By secretary to superintendent
		O⇨□▶▽	On superintendent's desk (awaiting messenger)
		O⇨■D▽	Examined and approved
		O⇨□▶▽	On superintendent's desk (awaiting messenger)
20		O⇢□D▽	To purchasing department
		O⇨□▶▽	On purchasing agent's desk (awaiting approval)
		O⇨■D▽	Examined and approved
		O⇨□▶▽	On purchasing agent's desk (awaiting messenger)
5		O⇢□D▽	To typist's desk
		O⇨□▶▽	On typist's desk (awaiting typing of purchase order)
		●⇨□D▽	Purchase order typed
		O⇨□▶▽	On typist's desk (awaiting transfer to main office)
		O⇨□D▽	
105		3 4 2 8	Total

*Requisition is written by supervisor, typed by secretary, approved by superintendent, and approved by purchasing agent; then a purchase order is prepared by a stenographer.

Source: Ralph M. Barnes, *Motion and Time Study*, 8th ed. (New York: Wiley & Sons, 1980), pp. 76–79. Reprinted by permission of John Wiley & Sons, Inc.

EXHIBIT S9.3

Common Notation in Process Charting

● *Operation.* Something is actually being done. This may be work on a product, some support activity, or anything that is directly productive in nature.

➡ *Transportation.* The subject of the study (product, service, or person) moves from one location to another.

■ *Inspection.* The subject is observed for quality and correctness.

▶ *Delay.* The subject of the study must wait before starting the next step in the process.

▼ *Storage.* The subject is stored, such as finished products in inventory or completed papers in a file. Frequently, a distinction is made between temporary storage and permanent storage by inserting a T or P in the triangle.

EXHIBIT S9.4

Gilbreth's Principles of Motion Economy

Using the human body the way it works best:

1. The work should be arranged to provide a natural rhythm that can become automatic.

2. The symmetrical nature of the body should be considered:
   a. The motions of the arms should be simultaneous, beginning and completing their motions at the same time.
   b. Motions of the arms should be opposite and symmetrical.

3. The human body is an ultimate machine and its full capabilities should be employed:
   a. Neither hand should ever be idle.
   b. Work should be distributed to other parts of the body in line with their ability.
   c. The safe design limits of the body should be observed.
   d. The human should be employed at its highest use.

4. The arms and hands as weights are subject to the physical laws, and energy should be conserved:
   a. Momentum should work for the person and not against him or her.
   b. The smooth, continuous arc of the ballistic is more efficient.
   c. The distance of movements should be minimized.
   d. Tasks should be turned over to machines.

5. The tasks should be simplified:
   a. Eye contacts should be few and grouped together.
   b. Unnecessary actions, delays, and idle time should be eliminated.
   c. The degree of required precision and control should be reduced.
   d. The number of individual motions should be minimized along with the number of muscle groups involved.

Arranging the workplace to assist performance:

1. There should be a definite place for all tools and materials.

2. Tools, materials, and controls should be located close to the point of use.

3. Tools, materials, and controls should be located to permit the best sequence and path of motions.

Using mechanical devices to reduce human effort:

1. Vises and clamps can hold the work precisely where needed.

2. Guides can assist in positioning the work without close operator attention.

3. Controls and foot-operated devices can relieve the hands of work.

4. Mechanical devices can multiply human abilities.

5. Mechanical systems should be fitted to human use.

Source: Frank C. Barnes, "Principles of Motion Economy: Revisited, Reviewed, and Restored," *Proceedings of the Southern Management Association Annual Meeting,* Atlanta, 1983, p. 298.

Software from Deneb Robotics is designed to help companies strategically plan to meet production goals. Wearing a harness with 11 sensors, Brian Christensen of Deneb demonstrates software that helps engineers maximize efficiency on a production line by coordinating movements of humans and robots that work side by side (see the monitor).

Worker Interaction with Equipment

When a person and equipment operate together to perform a given set of tasks, interest focuses on the efficient use of both the person's time and the equipment's time. When the working time of the operator is less than the equipment run time, a worker-machine chart is a useful device in analysis. If the operator can operate several pieces of equipment, the problem is to find the most economical combination of operator and equipment, such that the combined cost of the idle time of the equipment and the idle time for the worker are at a minimum.

Worker-machine charts are always drawn to scale, the scale being time as measured by length. Exhibit S9.5 gives an example of a worker-machine chart in a service setting.

Workers Interacting with Other Workers

Increasingly, work in both manufacturing and services is being performed by teams. The degree of interaction may be as simple as one operator handing a part to another, or as complex as a cardiovascular surgical team consisting of doctors, nurses, an anesthesiologist, the operator of the artificial heart machine, an X-ray technician, standby blood donors, and the pathologist (and perhaps a minister to pray a little).

To facilitate analysis of team efforts, an activity or a gang process chart is used to plot the activities of each individual on a time scale similar to that of the worker-machine chart. A gang process chart is usually employed to trace the interaction of a number of workers with machines of a specified operating cycle, to find the best combination of workers and machines. An activity chart is less restrictive and may be used to follow the interaction of any group of operators, with or without equipment being involved. Such charts are often used to study and define each operator in an ongoing repetitive process, and they are extremely valuable in developing a standardized procedure for a specific task. Exhibit S9.6, for example, shows an activity chart for a hospital's emergency routine in performing a tracheotomy (an operation for opening a patient's throat surgically to allow him or her to breathe), where detailed activity analysis is of major importance because any unnecessary delay could be fatal.

EXHIBIT S9.5

Worker-Machine Chart for a Gourmet Coffee Store

	PERSON				MACHINE	
	Customer	Time in sec.	Clerk	Time in sec.	Coffee Grinder	Time in sec.
1.	Ask grocer for 1 pound of coffee (brand and grind)	5	Listen to order	5	Idle	5
2.	Wait	15	Get coffee and put in machine, set grind, and start grinder	15	Idle	15
3.	Wait	21	Idle while machine grinds	21	Grind coffee	21
4.	Wait	12	Stop grinder, place coffee in package, and close it	12	Idle	12
5.	Receive coffee from grocer, pay grocer, and receive change	17	Give coffee to customer, wait for customer to pay for coffee, receive money, and make change	17	Idle	17

Summary

	Customer	Clerk	Coffee grinder
Idle time	48 sec.	21 sec.	49 sec.
Working time	22	49	21
Total cycle time	70	70	70
Utilization in percent	Customer utilization = $\frac{22}{70} = 31\%$	Clerk utilization = $\frac{49}{70} = 70\%$	Machine utilization = $\frac{21}{70} = 30\%$

The customer, the clerk, and the coffee grinder (machine) are involved in this operation. It required 1 minute and 10 seconds for the customer to purchase a pound of coffee in this particular store. During this time the customer spent 22 seconds, or 31 percent of the time, giving the clerk his order, receiving the ground coffee, and paying the clerk for it. He was idle during the remaining 69 percent of the time. The clerk worked 49 seconds, or 70 percent of the time, and was idle 21 seconds, or 30 percent of the time. The coffee grinder was in operation 21 seconds, or 30 percent of the time, and was idle 70 percent of the time.

WORK MEASUREMENT

work measurement
Methodology used for establishing time standards.

The subject of **work measurement** for establishing time standards has been controversial since the days of Taylor. With the widespread adoption of Deming's ideas, it has become the subject of renewed criticism. (Deming argued that work standards and quotas inhibit process improvement, focusing all of the worker's efforts on speed rather than quality.) Nevertheless, all organizations need some form of standard time estimates to do planning

EXHIBIT S9.6

Activity Chart of Emergency Tracheotomy

Time in minutes	Nurse	First Doctor	Orderly	Second doctor	Nurse supervisor	Scrub nurse
0						
1	Detects problem; notifies doctor					
2	Gets mobile cart					
3		Makes diagnosis				
4						
5	Notifies nurse supervisor					
6	Notifies second doctor	Assists patient to breathe			Opens OR; calls scrub nurse	
7	Notifies orderly			Assures availability of laryngoscope and endotracheal tube		
8	Moves patient to OR	Moves to OR	Moves patient to OR			Moves to OR; sets up equipment
9		Scrubs				
10		Dons gown and gloves		Operates laryngoscope and inserts endotracheal tube		
11						
12				Calls for IPPB machine		
13		Performs tracheotomy				
14						
15						
16						

Source: Data taken from Harold E. Smalley and John Freeman, *Hospital Industrial Engineering* (New York: Reinhold, 1966), p. 409.

and budgeting, and many companies use them with success in work design demonstrated in the UPS case at the end of this chapter. In any event, it is important to understand the basic industrial engineering methods used to set standards. They are as follows:

1. Time study (stopwatch and micromotion analysis).
2. Elemental standard time data.
3. Predetermined motion-time data.
4. Work sampling.

Each method has its advantages over the others and has particular areas of application. Exhibit S9.7 lists these methods and relates them to a general class of jobs.

Time Study

time study
Determination, with use of a stopwatch, of how long it takes to complete a task or set of tasks.

A **time study** is generally conducted with a stopwatch, either on the job site or by analyzing a videotape of the job. Procedurally, the job or task to be studied is separated into measurable parts or elements, and each element is timed individually. After a number of repetitions,

EXHIBIT S9.7

Types of Work Measurement Applied to Different Tasks

Type of Work	Major Methods of Determining Task Time
Very short interval, highly repetitive	Videotape analysis
Short interval, repetitive	Stopwatch time study: predetermined motion-time data
Task in conjunction with machinery or other fixed-processing-time equipment	Elemental data
Infrequent work or work of a long cycle time	Work sampling

the collected times are averaged. (The standard deviation may be computed to give a measure of variance in the performance times.) The averaged times for each element are then added together, and the result is the performance time for the operator. However, to make this operator's time usable for all workers, a measure of speed, which is expressed as a *performance rating* and which reflects how hard the observed operator is working, must also be included to "normalize" the job. The application of a rating factor gives what is called *normal time.*

Example

An industrial engineer conducts a time study on an operator and determines that a specific task takes about two minutes to complete. The engineer estimates that the particular operator that she is observing is working about 20 percent faster than normal. The company has an allowance factor of 15 percent of job time for personal needs, delays, and fatigue. Calculate the standard time for this task.

Solution

$$\text{Normal time} = \text{observed performance time per unit} \times \text{Performance rating}$$

In this example, denoting normal time by NT,

$$NT = 2(1.2) = 2.4 \text{ minutes}$$

When an operator is observed over a long period of time, the number of units produced during this time, along with the performance rating, gives the normal time as

$$NT = \frac{\text{Total time observed}}{\text{Number of units produced}} \times \text{Performance rating}$$

Standard time is derived by adding allowances to normal time. These allowances include personal needs (washroom and coffee breaks, and so forth), unavoidable work delays (equipment breakdown, lack of materials, and so forth), and worker fatigue (physical or mental). There are two equations for calculating standard time:

$$\text{Standard time} = \text{Normal Time} + (\text{Allowances} \times \text{Normal time})$$

or

$$ST = NT(1 + \text{Allowances}) \tag{S9.1}$$

and

$$ST = \frac{NT}{1 - \text{Allowances}} \tag{S9.2}$$

Equation (S9.1) is most often used in practice. Here the allowances are stated as a percentage of the "job time." In other words, the allowance factor is added to the job time in order to obtain the standard time. However, if the allowances are stated as a percentage of the total "work time," then equation (S9.2) is the correct one to use.

In this example, the normal time to perform a task is 2.4 minutes and the allowances for personal needs, delays, and fatigue total 15 percent of the job time; then by equation (1),

$$ST = 2.4(1 + 0.15) = 2.76 \text{ minutes}$$

In an eight-hour day, a worker would produce $8 \times 60/2.76 = 174$ units. This implies 174×2.4 minutes per unit (normal time) $= 417.6$ minutes working and $480 - 417.6 = 62.4$ minutes for allowances.

However, if the allowance factor is stated as a percentage of the total work time, then we would use equation (S9.2):

$$ST = \frac{2.4}{1 - 0.15} = 2.82 \text{ minutes}$$

In the same eight-hour day, using equation (2), $8 \times 60/2.82$ (or 170) units are produced with 408 working minutes and 72 minutes for allowances. Depending on how the allowance factor is specified, there is a difference of 4 units produced and also approximately 10 minutes in the daily allowance time.

Before a time study is conducted, each task is broken down into elements or parts. Some general rules for this breakdown are:

1. Define each work element to be short in duration but sufficiently long enough so that each can be timed with a stopwatch and the time can be written down.
2. If the operator works with equipment that runs separately—the operator performs a task and the equipment runs independently—separate the actions of the operator and that of the equipment into different elements.
3. Define any delays by the operator or equipment into separate elements.

How many observations are enough? Time study is really a sampling process; that is, we take a relatively small number of observations as being representative of many subsequent cycles to be performed by the worker. A great deal of analysis and experience indicates that the number of observations is a function of cycle length and the number of repetitions of the job over a one-year planning period.

Elemental Standard-Time Data   Elemental standard-time data is obtained from previous time studies and codified in tables in a handbook or in a computer data bank. Such data are used to develop time standards for new jobs or to make time adjustments to reflect changes in existing jobs. They are more correctly viewed as *normal-time data,* because tabled values have been modified by an average performance rating, and allowances must be added to obtain a standard time.

time standard
Established time for completing a job, used in determining labor costs associated with making a product.

Calculating a **time standard** for a new job using elemental standard-time data tables entails the following steps:

1. Break down the new job into its basic elements.
2. Match these elements to the time for similar elements in the table.

3. Adjust element times for special characteristics of the new job. (In metal cutting, for example, this is often done by a formula that modifies the time required as a function of type of metal, size of the cutting tool, depth of the cut, and so forth.)

4. Add element times together and add delay and fatigue allowances as specified by company policy for the given class of work.

The obvious benefit of elemental standard data is cost savings in that it eliminates the need for a new time study every time there is a new job. This saves staff time and avoids disruption of the workforce. The main practical requirements of the approach is that the elemental data must be kept up to date and easily accessible.

Work Sampling

work sampling
Technique for estimating how workers allocate their time among various activities throughout a workday.

Whereas work measurement is concerned with how long it takes to perform a specific task or activity, **work sampling** is primarily concerned with how workers spend their time among several tasks or activities. For example, we may want to know how much time workers spend on indirect activities such as material handling to determine whether or not more cost-efficient material handling equipment should be purchased. Work sampling provides us with a method for determining the time spent on these activities, and involves observing a portion or sample of the work activity. Then, based on the findings in this sample, some statements can be made about how the employee or employees spend their time.

For example, if we were to observe a fire department rescue squad 100 random times during the day and found that it was involved in a rescue mission for 30 of the 100 times (en route, on site, or returning from a call), we would estimate that the rescue squad spends 30 percent of its time directly on rescue mission calls. (The time it takes to make an observation depends on what is being observed. Often only a glance is needed to determine the activity, and the majority of studies require only several seconds' observation.)

Observing an activity even 100 times may not, however, provide the accuracy desired in the estimate. To refine this estimate, three main issues must be decided (these points are discussed later in this section, along with an example):

1. What level of statistical confidence is desired in the results?
2. How many observations are necessary?
3. Precisely when should the observations be made?

The number of observations required in a work sampling study can be fairly large, ranging from several hundred to several thousand, depending on the activity and the desired degree of accuracy. The formula for computing the required number of observations is:

$$N = \frac{Z^2 p(1 - p)}{E^2} \tag{S9.3}$$

where

N = Number of observations to be made.

Z = Number of standard deviations associated with a given confidence level.

p = Estimated proportion of time that the activity being measured occurs.

E = Absolute error that is desired.

Example

For example, we want to determine what percentage of time clerks at a hotel registration desk are idle. We want our results to be 95 percent confident within an error of 3 percent. Our initial estimate of the clerks' idle time is 20 percent.

In this example:

$Z = 1.96$ (corresponding to 95% confidence).

$p = 0.20$ (estimated percentage idle time).

$E = 0.03$ (absolute error).

Solution Substituting these values into the above formula, we obtain the following:

$$N = \frac{(1.96)^2(0.2)(1-0.2)}{(0.03)^2}$$

$$N = \frac{(3.84)(0.16)}{(0.0009)}$$

$N = 682.95$ or 683 observations. (Note: We always round up here to ensure we meet the minimum requirements of the study.)

Thus, with the above work sampling study, we can state that we are 95 percent confident that the true percentage of time that the clerks are idle falls within 3 percent of the study results.

However, we don't always have an estimate of the proportion of time spent on a given activity (in fact, that is often why we are doing the work sampling study in the first place!). In these situations, we use $p = 0.5$ which will give us a worst case scenario. (If p is equal to anything other than 0.5 we have, in effect, overestimated the sample size.)

Suppose in the above example we don't have any estimate for the proportion of time the clerks are idle. In this case we would use $p = 0.5$, and the calculation of the sample size would be as follows:

$$N = \frac{(1.96)^2(0.5)(1-0.5)}{(0.03)^2}$$

$$N = \frac{(3.84)(0.25)}{(0.0009)}$$

$N = 1,067.11$ or 1,068 observations.

The specific steps involved in conducting a work sampling study are:

1. Identify the specific activity or activities that are the main purpose for the study. For example, determine the percentage of time equipment is working, idle, or under repair.
2. If it is possible, estimate the proportion of time of the activity of interest to the total time (e.g., that the equipment is working 80 percent of the time). These estimates can be made from the analyst's knowledge, past data, reliable guesses from others, or a pilot work-sampling study. If no estimate can be made, assume, as stated above, that the proportion is 0.50.
3. State the desired accuracy in the study results.
4. Determine the specific times when each observation is to be made.
5. If you are using an estimated time, recompute the required sample size at two or three intervals during the study period by using the data collected thus far. Adjust the number of observations if appropriate.

The number of observations to be taken in a work sampling study is usually divided equally over the study period. Thus, if 500 observations are to be made over a 10-day period, the observations are usually scheduled at 500/10, or 50 per day. Each day's observations are then assigned a specific time by using a random number generator. The need to divide the observations equally over the data collection period is even more important in service operations where workers can be extremely busy during certain periods and less busy at other times.

Example

There has been a long-standing argument that a large amount of nurses' hospital time is spent on non-nursing activities. This, the argument goes, creates an apparent shortage of well-trained nursing personnel, a significant waste of talent, a corresponding loss of efficiency, and increased hospital costs because nurses' wages are the highest single cost in the operation of a hospital. Further, pressure is growing for hospitals and hospital administrators to contain costs. With that in mind, let us use work sampling to test the hypothesis that a large portion of nurses' time is spent on non-nursing duties.

Assume at the outset that we have made a list of all the activities that are part of nursing and will make our observations in only two categories: nursing and non-nursing activities. (An expanded study could list all nursing activities to determine the portion of time spent in each.) Therefore, when we observe nurses during the study and find them performing one of the duties on the nursing list, we simply place a tally mark in the nursing column. If we observe a nurse doing anything besides nursing, we place a tally mark in the non-nursing column.

Solution

We can now proceed to design the work sampling study. Assume that we (or the nursing supervisor) estimate that nurses spend 60 percent of their time in nursing activities. Also assume that we would like to be 95 percent confident that the findings of our study are within the absolute error range of plus or minus 3 percent. In other words, if our study shows nurses spend 60 percent of their time on nursing duties, we are 95 percent confident that the true percentage lies between 57 and 63 percent. Using the above formula, we calculate that 1,025 observations are required for 60 percent activity time and ±3 percent error. If our study is to take place over 10 days, we start with 103 observations per day.

To determine when each day's observations are to be made, we assign specific numbers to each minute and a random number table to set up a schedule. If the study extends over an eight-hour shift, we can assign numbers to correspond to each consecutive minute. The list in Exhibit S9.8 shows the assignment of numbers to corresponding minutes. For simplicity, because each number corresponds to one minute, a three-number scheme is used, with the second and third number corresponding to the minute of the hour. A number of other schemes would also be appropriate. (If a number of studies are planned, a computer program may be used to generate a randomized schedule for the observation times.)

If we refer to a random number table and list three-digit numbers, we can assign each number to a time. The random numbers shown in Exhibit S9.9 demonstrate the procedure for seven observations.

This procedure is followed to generate 103 observation times, and the times are rearranged chronologically for ease in planning. Rearranging the times determined in Exhibit S9.9 gives the total observations per day shown in Exhibit S9.10 (for our sample of seven).

To be perfectly random in this study, we should also "randomize" the nurse we observe each time (the use of various nurses minimizes the effect of bias). In this study, our first observation is made at 7:13 AM for Nurse X. We walk into the nurse's area and check either a nursing or a non-nursing activity, depending on what we observe. Each observation need be only long enough to determine the class of activity—in most cases only a glance. At 8:04 AM we observe Nurse Y. We continue in this way to the end of the day and the 103 observations. At the end of the second day (and 206 observations), we decide to check for the adequacy of our sample size.

Let's say that we made 150 observations of nurses working and 64 of them not working, which gives 70.1 percent working. Again, using the formula given above, we calculate that the required number of observations is now 895. Inasmuch as we have already taken 206 observations, we only need to take another 689 over the next eight days or 86 per day. This recalculation of the sample size should be done several times during the data collection period.

If at the end of the study we find that 66 percent of nurses' time is involved with what has been defined as nursing activities, there should be an analysis to identify the remaining 34 percent. Approximately 12 to 15 percent is justifiable for coffee breaks and personal needs, which leaves 20 to 22 percent of the time that must be justified and compared to what the industry considers ideal levels of nursing activity. To identify the non-nursing activities, a more detailed breakdown could have been originally built into the sampling plan. Otherwise, a follow-up study may be in order.

EXHIBIT S9.8

Assignment of Numbers to Corresponding Minutes

Time	Assigned Numbers
7:00– 7:59 AM	100–159
8:00– 8:59 AM	200–259
9:00– 9:59 AM	300–359
10:00–10:59 AM	400–459
11:00–11:59 AM	500–559
12:00–12:59 PM	600–659
1:00– 1:59 PM	700–759
2:00– 2:59 PM	800–859

EXHIBIT S9.9

Determination of Observation Times

Random Number	Corresponding Time from the Preceding List
669	Nonexistent
831	2:31 PM
555	11:55 AM
470	Nonexistent
113	7:13 AM
080	Nonexistent
520	11:20 AM
204	8:04 AM
732	1:32 PM
420	10:20 AM

EXHIBIT S9.10

Observation Schedule

Observation	Scheduled Time	Nursing Activity (✓)	Non-Nursing Activity (✓)
1	7:13 AM		
2	8:04 AM		
3	10:20 AM		
4	11:20 AM		
5	11:55 AM		
6	1:32 PM		
7	2:31 PM		

FINANCIAL INCENTIVE PLANS

The third piece of the job design equation is the paycheck. In this section we briefly review common methods for setting financial incentives.

Basic Compensation Systems

The primary forms of basic compensation are hourly pay, straight salary, piece rate, and commissions. The first two are based on time spent on the job, with individual performance ultimately rewarded by an increase in the base rate. Piece-rate plans reward on the basis of direct daily output (a worker is paid $5 a unit and if he or she produces 10 units per day, he or she earns $50). Sometimes, a guaranteed base is included in a piece-rate plan; a worker would receive this base amount regardless of output, plus his or her piece-rate bonus. (For example, the worker's hourly base pay is $8, so this coupled with $50 piece-rate earnings would give him or her $114 for an eight-hour day.) Another approach with the guaranteed base is that the worker is paid either the piece rate or the guaranteed base, whichever is higher. Commissions may be thought of as sales-based piece rates and are calculated in the same general way.

The two broad categories of financial incentive plans are individual or small group incentive plans and organizationwide plans.

Individual or Small-Group Incentive Plans

Individual and work-group plans traditionally have rewarded performance by using output (often defined by piece rates) and quality measures. Quality is accounted for by a quality adjustment factor, say percent of rework (e.g., Incentive pay = Total output × [1 − Percent deduction for rework].[1] In recent years skill development has also been rewarded. Sometimes called *pay for knowledge,* this means that a worker is compensated for learning new tasks. This is particularly important in job shops using group technology, and in banking, where supervisors' jobs require knowledge of new types of financial instruments and selling approaches.

AT&T, for example, instituted incentive programs for its managers—an Individual Incentive Award (IIA) and a Management Team Incentive Award (MTIA). The IIA provides lump-sum bonuses to outstanding performers. These outstanding performers were determined by individual performance ratings accompanied by extensive documentation. The lump-sum bonus could range between 15 and 30 percent of base pay.

MTIAs are granted to members of specific divisions or units. Appropriate division or unit goals are established at the beginning of the year. The goals include department service objectives and interdepartmental goals. A typical MTIA could call for a standard amount equivalent to 1.5 percent of wages plus overtime for the next three years based on the performance in the current year.

Organizational Plans

Profit sharing and gain sharing are the major types of organizationwide plans. *Profit sharing* is simply distributing a percentage of corporate profits across the workforce. In the United States, at least one third of all organizations have profit sharing. In Japan, most major companies give profit-based bonuses twice a year to all employees. Such bonuses may go from as high as 50 percent of salaries in good years, to nothing in bad years.

---

[1]For a complete discussion of incentive plans including quality measures, see S. Globerson and R. Parsons, "Multi-factor Incentive Systems: Current Practices," *Operations Management Review* 3, no. 2 (Winter 1985).

Gain sharing also involves giving organizationwide bonuses, but differs from profit sharing in two important respects: First, it typically measures controllable costs or units of output, not profits, in calculating a bonus. Second, gain sharing is always combined with a participative approach to management. The original and best-known gainsharing plan is the Scanlon Plan (discussed next).

Scanlon Plan   In the late 1930s, the Lapointe Machine and Tool Company was on the verge of bankruptcy. Through the efforts of union president Joseph Scanlon and company management, a plan was devised to save the company by reducing labor costs. In essence, this plan started with the normal labor cost within the firm. Workers as a group were rewarded for any reductions in labor cost below this base cost. The plan's success depended on committees of workers throughout the firm whose purpose was to search out areas for cost saving and to devise ways of improvement. There were many improvements, and the plan did, in fact, save the company.

The basic elements of the **Scanlon Plan** are

a. The ratio. The ratio is the standard that serves as a measure for judging business performance. It can be expressed as:

$$\text{Ratio} = \frac{\text{Total labor cost}}{\text{Sales value of production}}$$

b. The bonus. The amount of bonus depends on the reduction in costs below the preset ratio.

c. The production committee. The production committee is formed to encourage employee suggestions to increase productivity, improve quality, reduce waste, and so forth. The purpose of a production committee is similar to that of a QC circle.

d. The screening committee. The screening committee consists of top management and worker representatives who review monthly bonuses, discuss production problems, and consider improvement suggestions.

Gain-sharing plans are now used by more than a thousand firms in the United States and Europe, and are growing in popularity. One recent survey in the United States indicated that about 13 percent of all firms have them, and that more than 70 percent were started after 1982.[2] Though originally established in small companies such as Lapointe, Lincoln Electric Company, and Herman Miller, gain sharing is now being installed by large firms such as TRW, General Electric Company, Motorola, and Firestone. These companies apply gain sharing to organizational units; Motorola, for example, has virtually all its plant employees covered by gain sharing. These plans are increasing because "they are more than just pay incentive plans; they are a participative approach to management and are often used as a way to install participative management."[3]

Scanlon Plan
One of the first incentive plans developed to reduce labor costs and reward employees.

CONCLUSION

Most readers of this book will encounter questions of work methods and measurement in the service sector. It appears that in services, as well as in manufacturing, the new performance metric will be speed, achieved through improved work methods and teamwork. ServiceMaster, for example, has been able to dominate the institutional custodial business

[2]C. O'Dell, *People, Performance, and Pay* (Houston: American Productivity Center, 1987).

[3]E. E. Lawler III, "Paying for Organizational Performance," Report G 87–1 (92), Center for Effective Organizations, University of Southern California, 1987.

Operations Management in Practice

ANATOMY OF A 15-MINUTE TURNAROUND

On a recent weekday a Southwest Airlines flight arrived at New Orleans from Houston. The scheduled arrival time was 8:00 AM, and departure for Birmingham, Alabama, was 8:15 AM. *Forbes* clocked the turnaround, half-minute by half-minute.

7:55	Ground crew chat around gate position.
8:03:30	Ground crew alerted, move to their vehicles.
8:04	Plane begins to pull into gate; crew move toward plane.
8:04:30	Plane stops; jetway telescopes out; baggage door opens.
8:06:30	Baggage unloaded; refueling and other servicing under way.
8:07	Passengers off plane.
8:08	Boarding call; baggage loading, refueling complete.
8:10	Boarding complete; most of ground crew leave.
8:15	Jetway retracts.
8:15:30	Pushback from gate.
8:18	Pushback tractor disengages; plane leaves for runway.

Source: Subrata N. Chakravarty, "Hit 'em Hardest with the Mostest" (September 16, 1991), p. 51. Reprinted by permission of FORBES Magazine © Forbes Inc., 1991.

(hospitals, schools, and offices) by applying fast cleaning methods to such basic tasks as mopping floors and washing windows. (Rather than using cumbersome ladders to wash windows, they employ specially designed, lightweight, long-handled squeegies using easy-to-remove velcro-backed washable cleaning cloths. Between uses, the clothes are soaked in fluids developed in ServiceMaster's laboratory.) Southwest Airlines uses teamwork (involving its ground crew, baggage handlers, and flight attendants) to achieve a 15-minute turnaround of its flights. (See the OM in Practice on Anatomy of a 15-Minute Turnaround.) Interestingly enough, these examples epitomize some of the fundamental ideas that Fredrick W. Taylor advocated almost a century ago.

KEY TERMS

Scanlon Plan   pp. 340
therbligs   pp. 327
time standard   pp. 334

time study   pp. 332
work sampling   pp. 335
work measurement   pp. 331

REVIEW AND DISCUSSION QUESTIONS

1. Why are work measurement and time study activities still necessary today?
2. How do the latest approaches for determining time standards, as shown in the NUMMI example, fit with the concepts of worker empowerment and team work?
3. What are the major differences between work measurement and work sampling? What are the objectives in each case?
4. Is there an inconsistency when a company requires precise time standards and, at the same time, encourages job enrichment?
5. Organizationwide financial incentive plans cover all the workers. Some groups or individuals may have contributed more to corporate profits than others. Does this detract from the

effectiveness of the incentive plan system? How would your incentive scheme for a small software development firm compare to an established automobile manufacturing firm?

6. The conclusion of this chapter describes Southwest Airlines's fast flight turnarounds. What do you think has to be done inside the terminal to attain this perfomance?

Solved Problems

Problem 1

Felix Unger is a very organized person and wants to plan his day perfectly. To do this, he has his friend Oscar time his daily activities. The following are the results of Oscar timing Felix on polishing two pairs of black shoes. What is the standard time for polishing one pair? (Assume a 5 percent allowance factor for Felix to get Oscar an ashtray for his cigar. Account for noncyclically recurring elements by dividing their observed times by the total number of cycles observed.) All times shown are in minutes.

			Observed Times				Performance	
Element	1	2	3	4	ST	$\bar{T}$	Rating	NT
Get shoeshine kit	0.50						125%	
Polish each shoe	0.94	0.85	0.80	0.81			110	
Put away kit				0.75			80	

Solution

	ST	$\bar{T}$	Performance Rating	NT
Get shoeshine kit	0.50	$0.50/2 = 0.25$	125%	0.31
Polish shoes (2 pair)	3.40	$3.40/2 = 1.70$	110	1.87
Put away kit	0.75	$0.75/2 = 0.375$	80	0.30
Normal time for one pair of shoes				2.48

Standard time for the pair $= 2.48 \times 1.05 = 2.61$ minutes.

Problem 2

A total of 15 observations have been taken on a head baker for a school district. The numerical breakdown of her activities is as follows:

Make Ready	Do	Clean Up	Idle
2	6	3	4

Based on this information, how many work sampling observations are required to determine how much of the baker's time is spent in "doing"? Assume a 5 percent desired absolute error and 95 percent confidence level.

Solution

Since the 95 percent confidence is required, use $Z = 1.96$. Also:

$$p = \text{``Doing''} = 6/15 = 40\%$$
$$E = .05 \text{ (given)}$$

To calculate the number of observations required we use the following formula:

$$N = \frac{Z^2 p(1-p)}{E^2} = \frac{(1.96)^2(0.4)(1-0.4)}{(0.05)^2} = 369 \text{ observations}$$

PROBLEMS

1. As a time-study analyst, you have observed that a worker has produced 40 parts in a one-hour period. From your experience, you rate the worker as performing slightly faster than 100 percent—so you estimate performance as 110 percent. The company allows 15 percent of job time for fatigue and delay.

   a. What is the normal time?

   b. What is the standard time?

   c. If a worker produces 300 units per day and has a base rate of $6 per hour, what would the day's wages be for this worker if payment was on a 100 percent wage incentive payment plan?

2. A time study was made of an existing job to develop new time standards. A worker was observed for a period of 45 minutes. During that period, 30 units were produced. The analyst rated the worker as performing at a 90 percent performance rate. Allowances in the firm for rest and personal time are 12 percent of job time.

   a. What is the normal time for the task?

   b. What is the standard time for the task?

   c. If the worker produced 300 units in an eight-hour day, what would the day's pay be if the basic rate was $6 per hour and the premium payment system paid on a 100 percent basis?

3. A time-study analysis has obtained the following performance times by observing a worker over 15 operating cycles:

Performance Number	Time (seconds)	Performance Number	Time (seconds)
1	15	9	14
2	12	10	18
3	16	11	13
4	11	12	15
5	13	13	16
6	14	14	15
7	16	15	11
8	12		

   The worker was rated as performing at 115 percent. Allowances for personal time and fatigue in the company are 10 percent of job time. The base rate for the worker is $5 per hour and the company operates on a 100 percent premium plan.

   a. What is the normal time?

   b. What is the standard time?

   c. If the worker produced 2,500 in a day, what would the gross pay for the day be if the premium rate was 100 percent?

4. A work sampling study is to be conducted over the next 30 consecutive days of an activity in the city fire department. Washing trucks, which is the subject of the study, is to be observed, and it is estimated that this occurs 10 percent of the time. A 3.5 percent accuracy with 95 percent confidence is acceptable. State specifically when observations should be made on one day. Use a 10-hour day from 8.00 AM to 6.00 PM.

5. In an attempt to increase productivity and reduce costs, Rho Sigma Corporation is planning to install an incentive pay plan in its manufacturing plant.

   In developing standards for one operation, time study analysts observed a worker for a 30-minute period. During that time the worker completed 42 parts. The analysts rated the worker as producing at 130 percent. The base wage rate of the worker is $5 per hour. The firm has established 15 percent as a fatigue and personal time allowance (as a percentage of job time).

    a. What is the normal time for the task?

    b. What is the standard time for the task?

    c. If the worker produced 500 units during an eight-hour day, what wages would the worker have earned?

6. Since new regulations will greatly change the products and services offered by savings and loan associations, time studies must be performed on tellers and other personnel to determine the number and types of personnel needed and incentive wage payment plans that might be installed.

    As an example of the studies that the various tasks will undergo, consider the following problem and come up with the appropriate answers:

    A hypothetical case was set up in which the teller (to be retitled later as an *account adviser*) was required to examine a customer's portfolio and determine whether it was more beneficial for the customer to consolidate various CDs into a single issue currently offered, or to leave the portfolio unaltered. A time study was made of the teller, with the following findings:

Time of study	90 minutes
Number of portfolios examined	10 portfolios
Performance rating	130 percent
Rest for personal time	15 percent
Teller's proposed new pay rate	$12 per hour

    a. What is the normal time for the teller to do a portfolio analysis for the CDs?

    b. What is the standard time for a portfolio analysis?

    c. If the S&L decides to pay the new tellers on a 100 percent premium payment plan, how much would a teller earn for a day in which he or she analyzed 50 customer portfolios?

7. It is estimated that a bank teller spends about 10 percent of this time in a particular type of transaction. The bank manager would like a work-sampling study that shows, within plus or minus 3 percent, whether the clerk's time is really 10 percent (i.e., from 7 to 13 percent). The manager is well satisfied with a 95 percent confidence level.

    You estimate that, for the first "cut" at the problem, a sample size of 400 is indicated for the 10 percent activity time and ± 3 percent absolute error.

    State how you would perform the work-sampling study. If the study were to be made over a five-week period with five days per week from the hours of 9:00 to 5:00, specify the exact time (in minute increments) that you would make Monday's observations.

CASE: UP TO SPEED: UNITED PARCEL SERVICE GETS DELIVERIES DONE BY DRIVING ITS WORKERS

Grabbing a package under his arm, Joseph Polise, a driver for United Parcel Service (UPS), bounds from his brown delivery truck and toward an office building here. A few paces behind him, Marjorie Cusack, a UPS industrial engineer, clutches a digital timer.

Her eyes fixed on Mr. Polise, she counts his steps and times his contact with customers. Scribbling on a clip-board, Mrs. Cusack records every second taken up by stoplights, traffic, detours, doorbells, walkways, stairways, and coffee breaks. "If he goes to the bathroom, we time him," she says.

Such attention to detail is nothing new at UPS, the nation's largest deliverer of packages. Through meticulous human-engineering and close scrutiny of its 152,000 employees, the privately held company, which is based in Greenwich, Connecticut, has grown highly profitable despite stiff competition. In fact, UPS is one of the most efficient companies anywhere, productivity experts say.

"You never see anybody sitting on his duff at UPS," says Bernard La Londe, a transportation professor at The Ohio State University. "The only other place you see the same commitment to productivity is at Japanese companies."

GETTING UP TO SPEED

At UPS, more than 1,000 industrial engineers use time studies to set standards for a myriad of closely supervised tasks. Drivers are instructed to walk to a customer's door at the brisk pace of three feet per second and to knock first lest seconds be lost searching for the doorbell. Supervisors then ride with the "least best drivers" until they learn to finish on time. "It's human nature to get away with as much as possible," says Michael Kamienski, a UPS district manager. "But we bring workers up to our level of acceptance. We don't go down to their level."

If UPS isn't quite a throwback to old-time work measurement, it nevertheless runs counter to the drift of many U.S. companies. To increase productivity, others are turning more often to employee-involvement techniques that stress consultation and reject the rigid monitoring of workers.

"Workers are better educated and want more to say about what happens to them," says Roger Weiss, a vice president of H. B. Maynard & Co., a consulting concern. "Time study is a dark-ages technique, and it's dehumanizing to track someone around with a stopwatch."

UPS dismisses the criticism. "We don't use the standards as hammers, but they do give accountability," says Larry P. Breakiron, the company's senior vice president for engineering. "Our ability to manage labor and hold it accountable is the key to our success."

NEW COMPETITION

Those techniques are about to be tested. Long engaged in a battle for parcels with the U.S. Postal Service, UPS recently has charged into overnight delivery against Federal Express Corporation, Purolator Courier, Airborne Freight, Emery Air Freight and others. What's more, it now is being challenged on its own turf by Roadway Services Inc., which in the early 1990s started a parcel delivery company called Roadway Package System that is implementing management ideas of its own.

The upstart competitor boasts that its owner-operator drivers, unlike UPS's closely scrutinized, but highly paid and unionized, drivers, are motivated by the challenge of running their own business. "Our people don't drive brown

trucks; they own their trucks," says Ivan Hoffman, a vice president of Roadway.

Roadway also is trying to gain the edge in productivity by eliminating people as much as possible through automation. Its package hubs use bar codes, laser scanners, computers, and special mechanical devices to sort packages, a task still handled at UPS by armies of workers. UPS calls its rival's methods unreliable, inflexible, and expensive. Those are the same epithets that Roadway hurls at UPS's human sorters.

The outcome of this budding competition interests package shippers. "UPS has taken the engineering of people as far as it can be taken," says Michael Birkholm, the director of transportation of American Greetings Corporation. "But the question is whether technologically sophisticated Roadway can dent the big brown UPS machine."

BURGEONING COMPETITION

If the competition intensifies, productivity improvements will be at the heart of UPS's counterattack. Indeed, UPS long has used efficiency to overcome rivals. Founded in Seattle in 1907 as a messenger service, UPS over the years won parcel deliveries from department stores and captured package business once handled by the U.S. Postal Service because of its lower rates and superior service.

UPS's founder, James E. Casey, put a premium on efficiency. In the 1920s, he turned to Frank B. Gilbreth and other pioneers of time study to develop techniques to measure the time consumed each day by each UPS driver. Later, UPS engineers cut away the sides of a UPS delivery truck, or "package car" as the company calls the vehicle, to study a driver at work. Resultant changes in package loading techniques increased efficiency 30 percent.

Mr. Casey also shaped the company culture, which stresses achievement and teamwork in addition to efficiency. Copies of his tract, "Determined Men," and of "Pursuit of Excellence," a pamphlet written by one-time UPS Chairman George Smith, are handed out to the company's managers. "We still use Jim's and George's quotes in everything we do," says George Lamb, Jr., a UPS director and past chairman.

Another guiding principle: a fair day's work for a fair day's pay. The company's drivers, all of them Teamsters, earn wages of $15 an hour, about $1 more than the best-paid drivers at other trucking companies earn. With overtime, many UPS drivers gross $35,000 to $40,000 a year.

In return, UPS seeks maximum output from its drivers as is shown by the time study Mrs. Cusack is conducting. On this day in suburban Whippany, she determines time allowances for each of Polise's 120 stops while watching for inefficiency in his methods. "What are you doing, Joe?"

she asks as Mr. Polise wastes precious seconds handling packages more than once. She says that a mere 30 seconds wasted at each stop can snowball into big delays by day's end.

Some UPS drivers with nicknames like Ace, Hammer, Slick, and Rocket Shoes take pride in meeting the standards day after day. "We used to joke that a good driver could get to his stop and back to the car before the seat belt stopped swaying," Mrs. Cusack says. (UPS has since redesigned its seat belts to eliminate sway.)

But not all UPS drivers enjoy the pace. For example, Michael Kipila, a driver in East Brunswick, New Jersey, says, "They squeeze every ounce out of you. You're always in a hurry, and you can't work relaxed." Some drivers say they cut their breaks in order to finish on time.

UPS officials maintain that the company's work standards are not just a matter of increasing output, but of making the job easier. "If you do it our way, you'll be less tired at the end of the day," says a UPS spokesman.

HAD ENOUGH

The pressure causes some UPS employees—supervisors and drivers alike—to quit. Jose Vega, a former UPS supervisor, says he would ride with one New York driver, noting each time "pace too slow, customer contact too long." Vega says he tried to embarrass the driver so as to speed him up: "Are you falling asleep? Do you want a sleeping bag?" After a while, "it's like you're abusing this person," says Vega, who now drives for Roadway.

"There's a fine line between motivation and harassment, and many times UPS crosses that line," says Mario Perrucci, the secretary-treasurer of Teamsters Local 177 in Hillside, New Jersey, Mr. Perrucci has battled UPS for years over a requirement that drivers tap their horns when they approach a stop in the hopes that the customer will hurry to the door seconds sooner.

UPS's efforts to increase productivity get mixed reactions from the Teamsters union. While some local Teamsters officials such as Perrucci say that UPS is driving its workers "beyond endurance," the union's national executives are grateful that the company is successful. "I'd rather see UPS pushing the men too hard," says a Team-

sters official in Washington, "than see UPS in bankruptcy court."

Many trucking companies employing Teamsters are shutting down or, like Roadway Package System, turning to nonunion workers. But, UPS continues to be the largest single employer of Teamsters members, with more than 100,000 unionized workers, a 33 percent rise since 1980.

A GAME OF INCHES

To sustain growth, UPS executives are looking for new efficiencies. For example, they are seeking to make work standards for truck mechanics more exact. And at UPS's Parsippany, New Jersey, package sorting hub, 1 of more than 100 that the company operates, officials are making the most of space by parking delivery trucks just five inches apart. But productivity has its price. New York City says that UPS drivers have received more than $1 million in unpaid parking tickets since March 1985 while making local deliveries. A company attorney says the amount is "much too high." UPS has contested the fines.

The new competition from Roadway Package System also looms large. Roadway is cutting labor expenses 20 percent to 30 percent by using independent drivers. Because Roadway drivers buy their own trucks, uniforms, and insurance, Roadway is saving money that it is using to automate package sorting. "We'll use technology to be the low-cost producer," says Bram Johnson, a Roadway vice president.

Roadway says it reduced personnel 25 percent at its five sorting hubs through automation. At its York, Pennsylvania, hub, for example, a moving belt of tilt trays following instructions from a computer drops packages down a series of chutes.

QUESTION

What are the advantages and disadvantages of the UPS approach to job design and work measurement?

Source: Daniel Machalaba, "Up to Speed: United Parcel Service Gets Deliveries Done by Driving Its Workers." Reprinted by permission of *The Wall Street Journal* (April 22, 1986), p. 1. © 1986 Dow Jones & Company, Inc. All rights reserved worldwide.

SELECTED BIBLIOGRAPHY

Adler, Paul S. "Time and Motion Regained." *Harvard Business Review* 71, no. 1 (January–February 1993), pp. 97–110.

Adler, Paul S. "The Return of the Stopwatch." *The Economist,* January 23, 1993, p. 69.

Barnes, Ralph M. *Motion and Time Study: Design and Measurement of Work.* 8th ed. New York: John Wiley & Sons, 1980.

Barnes, Frank C. "Principles of Motion Economy: Revisited, Reviewed and Restored." *Proceedings of the Southern Management Association Annual Meeting,* Atlanta, GA, 1983, p. 298.

Chakravarty, Subrata N. "Hit'em Hardest with the Mostest." *Forbes,* Steptember 16, 1991, p. 51.

Globerson, Shlomo, and Robert Parsons. "Multi-factor Incentive Systems: Current Practices." *Operations Management Review* 3, no. 2 (Winter 1985).

Lawler, E. E., III. "Paying for Organizational Performance." Report G 87–1 (92), Center for Effective Organizations, University of Southern California, 1987.

Machalaba, Daniel. "Up to Speed: United Parcel Service Gets Deliveries Done by Driving Its Workers." *The Wall Street Journal,* April 22, 1986, p. 1.

Niebel, Benjamin W. *Motion and Time Study.* 7th ed. Homewood, IL: Richard D. Irwin, 1982.

Niles, John L. "To Increase Productivity, Audit the Old Incentive Plan." *Industrial Engineering* (January 1980), pp. 20–23.

"The Promise of Reengineering." *Fortune* (May 3, 1993), p. 96.

Smalley, Harold E., and John Freeman. *Hospital Industrial Engineering.* New York: Reinhold, 1966, p. 409.

Chapter 10

PROJECT MANAGEMENT

Chapter Objectives

- Recognize that project management involves both people skills to coordinate and motivate individuals from a range of disciplines and technical skills to properly plan and schedule a project.

- Explain the role of the project manager in organizing and coordinating all activities performed in a project.

- Introduce critical path scheduling as a tool for identifying activities that require attention.

- Identify the time–cost trade-offs involved in expediting the completion of a project

- Discuss some of the criticisms often associated with project management techniques.

In the Los Angeles riots of 1992, a Taco Bell restaurant in Compton, California, was totally destroyed. Rather than abandon the site, Taco Bell decided to build a new restaurant there. Because the entire area where the restaurant was located had suffered significant damage from the riots, many jobs had been lost. Taco Bell therefore decided to make a major commitment to rebuilding and opening up the Compton restaurant in the shortest time possible.

To accomplish this, construction was coordinated with local subcontractors using project management tools and techniques. The goal was to have the entire restaurant rebuilt and open for business within 48 hours. (This was considerably shorter than the 60 days that was typically required to build and open a Taco Bell restaurant.) A large clock was erected on the site to mark the 48-hour countdown. Teams worked around the clock, and, as planned, 48 hours after the initial effort began, tacos were being served from the restaurant. ▪

The growing intensity of global competition is forcing companies to introduce new products at an accelerated pace. With product life cycles becoming shorter and shorter, the ability of a company to quickly introduce new products becomes one method of maintaining a competitive advantage in the marketplace. Intel, which introduces next generation computer chips while the demand for current generation chips is still high, provides a good example of a firm that has adopted such a strategy. Thus the time to market for such new products is a critical component for their success both in terms of market share and profit.

The speed with which a firm can introduce new products is dependent, in large degree, on understanding and applying the concepts of project management to the entire new product development cycle, beginning with product conception, design, and development, through to production.

Those firms that will succeed in such a dynamic environment where the time span from product design to full production is just a matter of months must understand and adopt the concepts of project management as a tool to plan, operate, and control operations.

Project management techniques are also very appropriate for exactly the opposite type of environment: one where a product's lead time may be long. The key factor in this case is that where frequency of production is low, each item produced tends to be viewed as a separate project. Examples include construction, shipbuilding, airplane manufacture, and the production of satellites. (See OM in Practice on Hughes Electronics.)

There are two main components in project management: one heavily emphasizes the organization and the behavior of *people;* the other focuses on the technology of the *method* (computing start and completion times, critical paths, etc.). In this chapter we address both elements, although we lean more toward describing the technical aspects of project management and leave the people issues to a course on management and organizational behavior.

DEFINITION OF PROJECT MANAGEMENT

project
Series of related jobs or tasks focused on the completion of an overall objective.

A project is simply an organized undertaking to accomplish a specific goal. In a technical sense, a **project** is defined as a series of related jobs or tasks that are usually directed toward some major output and require a significant period of time to perform. *Project management* can be defined as planning, directing, and controlling resources (i.e., people, equipment, material) to meet the technical, cost, and time constraints of the project.

While projects are often associated with single, one-of-a-kind type products, the fact is that many projects can be repeated or transferred to other settings or products. The result will be another project output. A contractor building houses or a firm producing low-volume products such as supercomputers, locomotives, or linear accelerators can effectively consider such products as individual projects.

A project starts out as a *statement of work (SOW).* The SOW may be a written description of the objectives to be achieved, with a brief statement of the work to be done and a proposed schedule specifying start and completion dates. It could also contain performance measures in terms of budget and completion steps (milestones) and the written reports to be supplied.

program
Synonym for a project, although it can also consist of several interrelated projects.

If the proposed work is a large endeavor, it is frequently referred to as a **program,** although the terms *project* and *program* are often used interchangeably. A program, which is the highest order of organizational complexity, may take several years to complete, and may consist of interrelated projects completed by many organizations. The development of a new missile system and the introduction of a new national medical health care system would be good examples of programs.

A *task* or *activity* is a subdivision of a project. It is usually not longer than several months in duration and is performed by one group or organization.

Operations Management in Practice

HUGHES ELECTRONICS LAUNCHES COMMUNICATION SATELLITES WITH PROJECT MANAGEMENT TECHNIQUES

Hughes Electronics markets direct broadcast satellite (DBS) services through PanAmSat Corporation, offering 150 channels of movies, cable TV programs, and sporting events directly to anyone in the United States, Canada, and parts of South America. It currently has three million subscribers with annual revenues of over $6 million. The factory where it produces the satellites for this venture is located in El Segundo, California, but it is unusual in that it is not a "traditional" manufacturing plant. There are no assembly lines, no conveyor belts, and no grinding tools. Instead, teams of workers gather around a half-dozen shiny objects doing the final assembly on satellites before they are launched. To successfully undertake the enormous challenges in this high-

technology growth industry, Hughes has adopted many project management concepts and applied them through a complex cross-functional team that reaches across company lines and international boundaries. During the implementation of this project, several technological breakthroughs occurred that ultimately resulted in the successful launching of Hughes into the DBS business. For example, in the world's first application of video compression technology, Hughes will at least quadruple the capacity of satellite transponders that are needed to receive radio signals from earth and then to rebroadcast them on designated frequencies.

Source: Special thanks to Hans Thamhain, Bentley College.

A *subtask* may be used if needed to further subdivide the project into more meaningful pieces.

A *work package* is a group of activities combined to be assignable to a single organizational unit. It still falls within the format of project management in that the package provides a description of what is to be done, when it is to be started and completed, the budget, measures of performance, and specific events to be reached at points in time which are called **milestones.** Typical milestones in the introduction of a new product might be the completion of the design, the production of a prototype, the completed testing of the prototype, and the approval of a pilot run.

milestones
Specific major events to be completed at certain times in the project.

Work Breakdown Structure

work breakdown structure (WBS)
Method by which a project is divided into tasks and subtasks.

The **work breakdown structure (WBS)** is the heart of project management. This subdivision of the objective into smaller and smaller pieces more clearly defines the system in detail and contributes to its understanding and success. Conventional use shows the work breakdown structure decreasing in size from top to bottom and shows this level by indentation to the right in the following format:

Level	
1	Program
2	Project
3	Task
4	Subtask
5	Work package

Exhibit 10.1 shows part of the work breakdown structure for a project to design a large optical scanner. Note the ease in identifying activities through the level numbers. For example, telescope design (the third item down) is identified as 1.1.1 (the first item in level 1, the first item in level 2, and the first item in level 3). Similarly, data recording (the 13th item down) is 1.2.4.

The key factors in having a good work breakdown structure are to:

- Allow the activities to be worked on independently.
- Make them manageable in size.

351

EXHIBIT 10.1

Part of a Work Breakdown Structure for a Large Optical Scanner Design

Level				
1	2	3	4	5
x				
	x			
		x		
		x		
		x		
		x		
	x			
		x		
			x	
			x	

Optical simulator design
Optical design
Telescope design/fab
Telescope/simulator optical interface
Simulator zoom system design
Ancillary simulator optical component specification
System performance analysis
Overall system firmware and software control
Logic flow diagram generation and analysis
Basic control algorithm design

- Give authority to carry out the program.
- Monitor and measure the program.
- Provide the required resources.

ORGANIZATIONAL CONSIDERATIONS IN PROJECT MANAGEMENT

As stated previously, the timely completion of successful projects requires an understanding of both the technical and human resource components of project management. The technical component is required to identify the critical activities that affect the overall length of time a project takes to complete. The human resource elements address the issues of leadership and worker motivation within a group or team environment. While Chapter 9 addressed many of these human resource issues as they pertain to working in teams, our focus here is to present a brief overview on those aspects that appear to exist in most projects.

ENGINEERING
OPERATIONS
MARKETING

Role of the Project Manager

Project managers typically have a unique role within the traditional organization structure. Most project management teams are multidisciplinary in nature, involving a wide variety of skills and organizational units. Often these teams include people from engineering, operations, and marketing, and from support services that include risk management, systems operations, auditing, and legal groups. Consequently, today's project managers must often cross traditional functional lines in order to obtain the support necessary for the completion of a project. In most instances, this support is requested without formal authority. Thus the project manager must create a collaborative culture that relies heavily on social skills as well as technical expertise.

Without the authority of a traditional functional manager and the associated system of rewards and punishments, project managers must earn their authority by building trust, respect, and credibility among project members, as well as by demonstrating sound decision making—all within a stimulating work environment.

High-Performance Project Teams

In today's complex and technologically sophisticated environment, the group has re-emerged in importance in the form of project teams. The characteristics of a project team and its ultimate performance depend on many factors that involve both people and structural issues. Although each organization has its own measures of performance, there is general agreement among project managers on which factors are necessary for the creation of a successful project team. These factors are divided into the following four categories:[1]

1. *Task-related variables* are direct measures of task performance, such as the ability to produce quality results on time and within budget, innovative performance, and the ability to change.

2. *People-related variables* affect the inner workings of the team and include good communications, high involvement, the capacity to resolve conflict, and mutual trust and commitment to project objectives.

3. *Leadership variables* are associated with the various leadership positions within the project team. These positions can be created formally, such as the appointment of project managers and task leaders, or emerge dynamically within the work process as a result of individually developed power bases such as expertise, trust, respect, credibility, friendship, and empathy. Typical leadership characteristics include the ability to organize and direct tasks, facilitate group decision making, motivate, assist in conflict and problem resolutions, and foster a work environment that satisfies the professional and personal needs of the individual team members.

4. *Organizational variables* include the overall organizational climate, command-control-authority structure, policies, procedures, regulations, and regional cultures, values, and economic conditions.

It is interesting to note that managers, in describing the characteristics of an effective, high-performing project team, not only focus on task-related skills for producing technical results on time and within budget, but also focus on team members and leadership qualities.

Barriers to High Team Performance   As a functioning group, the project team is subject to group dynamics. In addition, because it is usually a highly visible and focused work group, the project team often takes on special significance and is accorded high status with commensurate expectations of performance. Although a project team brings significant energy to a task, the possibility of the group malfunctioning is significant. This occurs because there are several barriers to high performance that can exist in a project team. These include: (*a*) different points of view, (*b*) role conflicts, and (*c*) power struggles. Each of these barriers must be overcome if the team is to successfully complete its assigned project. Hewlett-Packard's successful introduction of its Deskjet printer demonstrates that those firms that can overcome these barriers experience significant growth and profitability. (See OM in Practice on The Introduction of Hewlett-Packard's Deskjet Printer.)

PROJECT CONTROL

The Department of Defense was one of the earliest large users of project management and has published a variety of useful standard forms. Many are used directly or have been modified by firms engaged in project management. Since those early days, however, graphics software has been written for most computers, so management, the customer, and the project manager have a wide choice of how data are presented. Exhibit 10.2 shows a sample of available presentations.

---

[1]Hans J. Thamhain "Managing Technologically Innovative Team Efforts Towards New Product Success," *Journal of Production Innovation Management* 7, no. 1 (March, 1990), and Hans J. Thamhain, "Effective Leadership Style for Managing Project Teams." In *Handbook of Program and Project Management,* ed. P. C. Dinsmore (New York: AMACOM, 1992).

Operations Management in Practice

The Introduction of Hewlett-Packard's DeskJet Printer

The design and development of the DeskJet printer was one of Hewlett-Packard's (HP) first attempts to integrate its major functional areas such as manufacturing, marketing, and R&D. Its successful introduction was due, in large part, to HP's ability to apply many of the concepts in project management. The overall DeskJet printer project was subdivided into three project teams—firmware, electronics, and mechanical—with a project manager leading each team. The team members represented all of the functional areas of HP's Vancouver Division, including R&D, manufacturing, marketing, and quality assurance, with special assistance from personnel and finance. With all these functional groups in constant communication with each other, HP was able to identify specific project activities that could be performed concurrently, which significantly reduced both development time and manufacturing costs. As a result, the DeskJet printer provided HP with an unprecedented competitive advantage in the marketplace in both cost and speed of introduction.

Source: John D. Rhodes "Managing the Development of the Deskjet Printer," *Hewlett-Packard Journal*, October 1988.

Gantt chart
Graphical technique that shows the amount of time required for each activity and the sequence in which activities are to be performed.

Exhibit 10.2A is a sample **Gantt chart** showing both the amount of time involved and the sequence in which activities can be performed. For example, "long lead procurement" and "manufacturing schedules" are independent activities and can occur simultaneously. All of the other activities must be done in sequence from top to bottom. Exhibit 10.2B graphically shows the proportion of money spent on labor, material, and overhead. Its value is its clarity in identifying sources and amounts of cost.

Exhibit 10.2C shows the percentage of the project's labor hours that come from the various areas of manufacturing, finance, and so on. These labor hours are related to the proportion of the project's total labor cost. For example, manufacturing is responsible for 50 percent of the project's labor hours, but this 50 percent represents just 40 percent of the total labor dollars charged.

The top half of Exhibit 10.2D shows the degree of completion of these projects. The dotted vertical line signifies today. Project 1, therefore, is already late since it still has work to be done. Project 2, although on schedule, is not being worked on temporarily, which is why there is a space before the projected work. Project 3, also on schedule, continues to be worked on without interruption. The bottom of Exhibit 10.2D shows actual total costs compared to projected costs. The exhibit shows that two cost overruns occurred.

Exhibit 10.2E is a milestone chart. The three milestones mark specific points in the project where checks can be made to see if the project is on time and where it should be. The best place to locate milestones is at the completion of a major activity. In this exhibit, the major activities completed were "purchase order release," "invoices received," and "material received."

Other standard reports can be used for a more detailed presentation comparing cost to progress (such as a cost schedule status report—CSSR) or reports providing the basis for partial payment (such as an "earned value" report).

EXHIBIT 10.2

A Sample of Graphic Project Reports

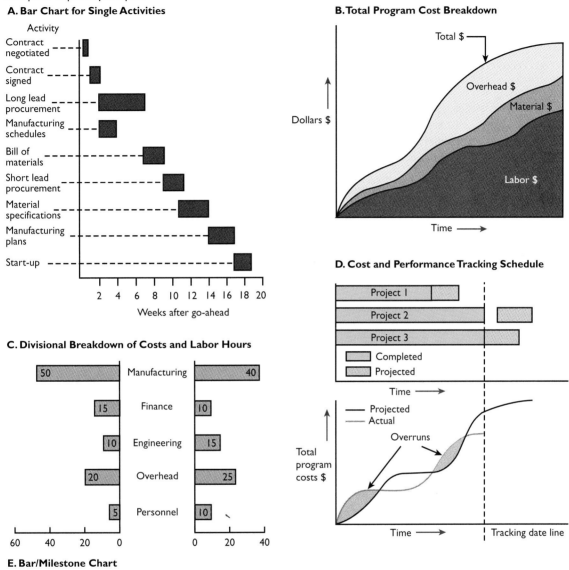

A. Bar Chart for Single Activities

Activity
- Contract negotiated
- Contract signed
- Long lead procurement
- Manufacturing schedules
- Bill of materials
- Short lead procurement
- Material specifications
- Manufacturing plans
- Start-up

Weeks after go-ahead: 2 4 6 8 10 12 14 16 18 20

B. Total Program Cost Breakdown

Total $
Overhead $
Material $
Labor $
Dollars $ / Time →

C. Divisional Breakdown of Costs and Labor Hours

	Manufacturing	
50		40
15	Finance	10
10	Engineering	15
20	Overhead	25
5	Personnel	10

60 40 20 0 — 0 20 40

D. Cost and Performance Tracking Schedule

Project 1
Project 2
Project 3
- Completed
- Projected
Time →

Projected
Actual
Overruns
Total program costs $
Time → | Tracking date line

E. Bar/Milestone Chart

Short lead procurement

⬇1 ⬇2 ⬇3

9 10 11
Weeks after go-ahead

Milestones
1 Purchasing order release
2 Invoices received
3 Material received

CRITICAL PATH SCHEDULING

PERT (program evaluation and review technique)
Technique developed by the U.S. Navy for planning the Polaris missile project.

CPM (critical path method)
Technique to schedule preventive maintenance shutdowns of chemical processing plants.

Critical path scheduling refers to a set of graphic techniques used in planning and controlling projects. In any given project, the three factors of concern are time, cost, and resource availability. Critical path techniques have been developed to deal with each of these, individually and in combination.

PERT (Program Evaluation and Review Technique) and **CPM (Critical Path Method)**, the two best-known techniques, were both developed in the late 1950s. PERT was developed under the sponsorship of the U.S. Navy Special Projects Office in 1958 as a management tool for scheduling and controlling the Polaris missile project. CPM was developed in 1957 by J. E. Kelly of Remington-Rand and M. R. Walker of Du Pont to aid in scheduling maintenance shutdowns of chemical processing plants.

Critical path scheduling techniques display a project in graphic form and relate its individual tasks in a way that focuses attention on those tasks that are critical to the project's completion. For critical path scheduling techniques to be most applicable, a project must have the following characteristics:

1. It must have well-defined jobs or tasks whose completion marks the end of the project.
2. The jobs or tasks are independent; they may be started, stopped, and conducted separately within a given sequence.
3. The jobs or tasks are ordered; certain ones must follow others in a given sequence.

The construction, aerospace, and shipbuilding industries commonly meet these criteria, and critical path techniques find wide application within them. We previously noted also that the applications of project management and critical path techniques are becoming much more common within firms in rapidly changing industries.

Project management techniques are also becoming more common in health care, with the objective of reducing a patient's overall stay in a hospital. Here, each patient is viewed as a project and the various procedures he or she undergoes are considered to be the tasks in that project. (It should be noted that there is a growing trend toward defining "care paths"

At Boeing, effective project management techniques were essential both in setting up the 777 assembly system and in scheduling and manufacturing the plane. Twenty percent of the 777 is built in Japan, along with manufacturing help from Australia (rudder), Northern Ireland and Singapore (nose gear), Korea (wingtip), Brazil (fin and wingtip assembly), and Italy (outboard wing flaps).

which provide standard steps that all patients follow. For example, Massachusetts General Hospital has established a paper checklist of what should happen with a patient on each day of a five-day stay for coronary artery bypass graft surgery.)

TIME-ORIENTED TECHNIQUES

The basic forms of PERT and CPM focus on identifying the longest time-consuming path through a network of tasks as a basis for planning and controlling a project. Both PERT and CPM use nodes and arrows for display. Originally, the basic differences between PERT and CPM were that PERT used the arrow to represent an activity and CPM used the node. The other original difference between these two techniques was that PERT used three estimates—optimistic, pessimistic, and best—of an activity's required time, whereas CPM used just a single, best time estimate. This distinction reflects PERT's origin in scheduling advanced scientific projects (like the lunar missions) that are characterized by uncertainty and CPM's origin in the scheduling of the fairly routine activity of plant maintenance. Thus PERT was often used when the primary variable of interest was time, whereas CPM was used when the primary variable of interest was cost. As years passed, these two features no longer distinguished PERT from CPM. This is because CPM users started to use three time estimates and PERT users often placed activities on the nodes.

We believe the activity on the node is much easier to follow logically than the activity on the arrow. However, the three time estimates are often very valuable in obtaining a measure of the probability of completion times. Therefore, in this chapter we use the activity on the node and either a single estimate for activity time or three time estimates, depending on our objective. We use the terms *CPM* and *PERT* interchangeably and mean the same thing, although we tend to use the term *CPM* more frequently.

In a sense, both techniques owe their development to their widely used predecessor, the Gantt chart. While the Gantt chart is able to relate activities to time in a visually usable fashion for very small projects, the interrelationship of activities, when displayed in this format, becomes extremely difficult to visualize and to work with for projects with more than 25 or 30 activities. Moreover, the Gantt chart provides no direct procedure for determining the critical path, which, despite its theoretical shortcomings, is of great practical value.

CPM with a Single Time Estimate

With the following as an example, we will develop the typical approach taken in project scheduling. The times for each activity have been given as a most likely estimate (rather than three estimates, which will be discussed in a later example).

Example | Many firms that have tried to enter the portable computer market have failed. Suppose your firm believes that there is a big demand in this market because existing products have not been designed correctly. They are either too heavy, too large, or too small to accommodate a standard-size keyboard. Your intended computer will be small enough to carry inside a jacket pocket if need be. The ideal size will be no larger than 4 inches $\times$ 9½ inches $\times$ 1 inch with a standard typewriter keyboard. It should weigh no more than 15 ounces, have a 4 to 8 line $\times$ 80 character back-lit display, have a micro disk drive, and a micro printer. It should be aimed primarily toward word processing use but have plug-in ROMs to accommodate an assortment of computer languages and programs.

These characteristics should appeal to traveling business people, but then could also have a much wider market. If it can be priced to sell retail in the $175–$200 range, the computer should appeal to a wide market.

The project, then, is to design, develop, and produce a prototype of this portable computer. In the rapidly changing computer industry, it is crucial to hit the market with a product of this type in less than a year. Therefore, the project team has been allowed approximately nine months, or 39 weeks, to produce the prototype.

The first assignment of the project team is to develop a project network chart to determine whether or not the prototype computer can be completed within the 39 weeks. Let's follow the steps in the development of this network.

Solution

Step 1: Activity identification
The project team decides that the following activities constitute the major components of the project: (A) designing the computer, (B) constructing the prototype, (C) evaluating automatic assembly equipment, (D) testing the prototype, (E) preparing an assembly equipment study report, (F) writing methods specifications (to be summarized in a report), and (G) preparing a final report summarizing all aspects of the design, equipment, and methods.

Step 2: Activity sequencing and network construction
On the basis of discussion with her staff, the project manager develops the precedence table and sequence network shown in Exhibit 10.3. Activities are indicated as nodes while arrows show the sequence in which the individual activities must be completed.

Using the precedence table, we can construct a network diagram, taking care to ensure that the activities are in the proper order and that the logic of their relationships is maintained. For example, it would be illogical to have a situation where Event A precedes Event B, B precedes C, and then C precedes A.

EXHIBIT 10.3
CPM Network for Computer Design Project

	CPM Activity/Designations and Time Estimates		
Activity	**Designation**	**Immediate Predecessors**	**Time in Weeks**
Design	A	—	21
Build prototype	B	A	4
Evaluate equipment	C	A	7
Test prototype	D	B	2
Write equipment report	E	C, D	5
Write methods report	F	C, D	8
Write final report	G	E, F	2

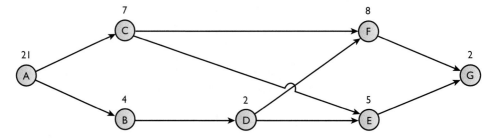

Step 3: Determine the critical path

The **critical path** is defined as the longest sequence of connected activities through the network. In other words, the shortest time in which the project can be completed is determined by the length of the critical path. To find the critical path, we simply identify all of the paths through the network and calculate their respective completion times. That path with the longest completion time is, by definition, the critical path. For our example, the different paths and their respective completion times are as follows:

Path	Completion Time (in weeks)
A–C–E–G	$21 + 7 + 5 + 2 = 35$
A–B–D–F–G	$21 + 4 + 2 + 8 + 2 = 37$
A–B–D–E–G 34	$21 + 4 + 2 + 5 + 2 =$
A–C–F–G	$21 + 7 + 8 + 2 = 38$

Path A–C–F–G takes the longest amount of time to complete, which is 38 weeks, and is therefore the critical path for this project. Consequently, this project as it now exists cannot be completed in fewer than 38 weeks. Inasmuch as the project has been allowed 39 weeks in which to be completed, there appears to be no problem. If the project were required to be completed in fewer than 38 weeks, then one or more of the activities on the critical path would have to be "crashed" or accelerated in order to meet the required project completion date.

Step 4: Determine slack times

The total **slack time** for an activity is defined as that amount of time that an activity can be delayed without affecting the overall completion time of the project. In order to calculate the slack time for each activity, the following terms are defined:

- *Early start time* (ES), the earliest possible time that the activity can begin.
- *Early finish time* (EF), the early start time plus the time needed to complete the activity.
- *Late finish time* (LF), the latest time an activity can end without delaying the project.
- *Late start time* (LS), the late finish time minus the time needed to complete the activity.

To determine the slack time for an activity requires the calculation of either the early start (ES) time and the late start (LS) time or the early finish (EF) time and the late finish (LF) time for that activity.

The difference between the early start time and the late start time (or between the early finish time and the late finish time) is the slack time. The difference between the ES and EF times, and the LS and LF times, is the same, being the amount of time required to complete that specific activity; hence $EF - ES = LF - LS = $ activity completion time.

These values and the resulting total slack time for each of the activities in our example will now be calculated with the following procedure.

Step 1: Find the ES for each activity

The early start time for each activity is determined with a "forward pass" through the network, beginning with the first activity A, for which we set the $ES = 0$, representing the start of the project. To find the ES for the activities that follow A, (i.e., B and C), we simply add the time it takes to complete activity A, which in this case is 21 weeks, to the ES for A, which is zero. Therefore, the earliest we could start either activity B or C is

21 weeks after we begin the project, which is when activity A is completed. (In other words, ES_B or $ES_C = 0 + 21 = 21$.) Likewise, the ES for activity D is the ES for activity B (21 weeks) plus the time to complete B (4 weeks) making ES = 25 weeks for activity D (i.e., $ES_D = 21 + 4 = 25$).

This procedure is repeated for each activity in the network. When more than one activity precedes the activity being evaluated, then the ES for each path leading to that activity is calculated, and the latest ES is selected, as that becomes the constraining factor as to when that activity can begin. For example:

$$ES_F = MAX (ES_C + C, ES_D + D)$$
$$ES_F = MAX (21 + 7, 25 + 2)$$
$$ES_F = MAX (28, 27) = 28 \text{ weeks}$$

where

C = Completion time for activity C

D = Completion time for activity D

Therefore, the earliest we could start activity F is 28 weeks after we begin the project. Likewise, through similar calculations, $ES_E = 28$ weeks and $ES_G = 36$ weeks.

Step 2: Find the LS for each activity

To obtain the LS for each activity, we simply reverse the procedure for calculating the ES, beginning at the end of the project. The LS for an activity is defined as the latest time that an activity can be started without delaying the completion of the overall project. Since we start at the end of the network and work our way back to the beginning, this is called a "backwards pass" through the network.

We begin with the last activity, G. As we determined earlier, the critical path for the project is 38 weeks. Therefore, the latest that we could start activity G and still complete the project in 38 weeks is 36 weeks, as it takes two weeks to do activity G. Similarly, $LS_F = LS_G - F = 36 - 8 = 28$ weeks, and $LS_E = LS_G - E = 36 - 5 = 31$ weeks. The other LS times for the remaining activities are likewise calculated.

When more than one activity follows the activity being evaluated, then the LS for all paths leading out of the activity must be calculated and that path with the earliest LS time is used, as that time becomes the constraining factor as to the latest time that activity can begin. For example:

$$LS_C = MIN (LS_F - C, LS_E - C)$$
$$LS_C = MIN (28 - 7, 31 - 7)$$
$$LS_C = MIN (21, 24) = 21 \text{ weeks}$$

Thus, the latest we can start activity C is 21 weeks after we begin the project. Similarly, $LS_D = 25$ weeks and $LS_A = 0$ weeks. The earliest start and the latest start times for all of the activities in the computer design project are shown in Exhibit 10.4. As stated earlier, the difference between the EF time and the ES time for an activity is simply the time it takes to complete that activity. This is also the difference between the LF and the LS times for the activity. The EF and LF times are, thus, also shown in Exhibit 10.4.

Step 3: Determine the total slack time for each activity

As stated previously, the total slack time for each activity is defined as either LS − ES or LF − EF. In the computer design project the slack time for activity E is three weeks, and for activities B and D, one week each. Notice that the activities on the critical path (i.e., A, C, F, and G) do not have any slack times, because, in fact, they are all on the critical path and any delay in these activities will therefore affect the overall project's completion time. Typically, the project completion time is calculated using network analysis and then compared with the desired deadline. Thus while there is no slack in any of the activities on the critical path with respect to the calculated project completion time, there can be slack in the critical path when the desired deadline is longer. In this example, with the desired deadline at 39 weeks and the calculated project completion time at 38 weeks, there is a one week slack time in the critical path.

Early start and late start schedules

early start schedule
Earliest time that each activity in the project can be started.

An **early start schedule** is one that lists all of the activities by their early start times. For activities not on the critical path, there is slack time between the activity completion and the start of the next activity that succeeds it. These slack times represent flexibility and should be used wisely by the project manager. The early start schedule completes the project and all of its activities as soon as possible.

late start schedule
Latest start time that each activity can be started without affecting the overall completion time.

A **late start schedule** lists the activities to start as late as possible without delaying the completion date of the project. One of the motivations for using a late start schedule is that savings are realized by postponing purchases of materials, the use of labor, and other costs until necessary.

EXHIBIT 10.4

CPM Network for Computer Design Project

Activity	LS − ES	Slack	On Critical Path
A	0 − 0	0	Yes
B	25 − 21	4	No
C	21 − 21	0	Yes
D	26 − 25	1	No
E	31 − 28	3	No
F	28 − 28	0	Yes
G	36 − 36	0	Yes

Slack Calculations and Critical Path Determinations

Activity	Normal Time	Crash Time	Normal Cost	Crash Cost
A	2	1	$6	$10
B	5	2	9	18
C	4	3	6	8
D	3	1	5	9

Summary of Activity Times and Costs

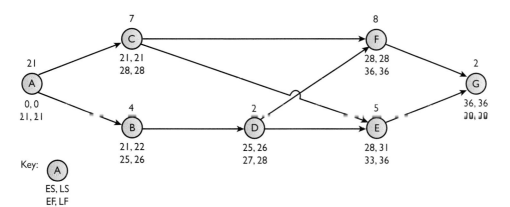

Key:

ES, LS
EF, LF

CPM with Three Activity Time Estimates

If a single estimate of the time required to complete an activity is not reliable, the alternative is to use three time estimates. By incorporating three estimates for each activity, we have the opportunity to obtain a probability for the completion time for the entire project. Briefly, the procedure using this approach is as follows: The estimated activity time is a weighted average, with more weight given to the best estimate and less to the maximum and minimum times. The estimated completion time of the network is then computed using basic statistics.

We continue with the computer design project, only now each of the activities has three time estimates associated with it, and the seven-step procedure for solving this problem is as follows:

Step 1: Identify each activity to be done in the project (which is identical to the CPM method with a single time estimate)

Step 2: Determine the sequence of activities and construct a network reflecting the precedence relationships (again, this is identical to the CPM method with a single time estimate)

Step 3: Define the three time estimates for each activity
The three time estimates for each activity are defined as:

$a = $ *Optimistic time:* the minimum reasonable period of time in which the activity can be completed. (There is only a small probability, typically assumed to be about 1 percent, that the activity can be completed in a shorter period of time.)

$m = $ *Most likely time:* the best guess of the time required. Since m would be the time thought most likely to appear, it is also the mode of the beta distribution (which is discussed in the next step).

$b = $ *Pessimistic time:* the maximum reasonable period of time the activity would take to be completed. (There is only a small probability, typically assumed to be about 1 percent, that it would take longer.)

Typically, the information about the three estimates is obtained from those people who are to perform the activity or others with expertise about the activity.

Step 4: Calculate the expected time (ET) for each activity
The formula to calculate the expected activity completion time is:

$$ET = \frac{a + 4m + b}{6}$$

This formula is developed from the beta probability distribution and weights the most likely time (m) four times more than either the optimistic time (a) or the pessimistic time (b). The beta distribution is an extremely flexible distribution. It can take on a variety of forms that typically arise in project management activities, and it has finite end points, which limit the possible activity times to the area between a and b and, in the simplified version, permits a straightforward computation of the activity mean and standard deviation. Four typical beta curves are illustrated in Exhibit 10.5.

Step 5: Calculate the variance (σ^2) for each activity
The variance, σ^2, associated with each ET is computed using the following formula:

$$\sigma^2 = \left(\frac{b - a}{6}\right)^2$$

EXHIBIT 10.5

Typical Beta Curves

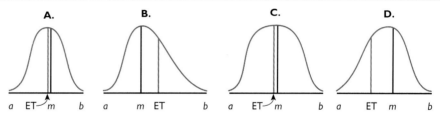

Curve A indicates very little uncertainty about the activity time, and since it is symmetrical, the expected time (ET) and the most likely or modal time (m) fall along the same point.

Curve B indicates a high probability of finishing the activity early, but if something goes wrong, the activity time could be greatly extended.

Curve C is almost a rectangular distribution, which suggests that the estimator sees the probability of finishing the activity early or late as equally likely, and $m \cong ET$.

Curve D indicates that there is a small chance of finishing the activity early, but it is more probable that it will take an extended period of time.

EXHIBIT 10.6

Activity Expected Times and Variances

Activity	Activity Designation	Time Estimates			Expected Times (ET) $\dfrac{a + 4m + b}{6}$	Activity Variances (σ^2) $\left(\dfrac{b - a}{6}\right)^2$
		a	m	b		
Design	A	10	22	28	21	9.00
Build prototype	B	1	4	7	4	1.00
Evaluate equipment	C	4	6	14	7	2.78
Test prototype	D	1	2	3	2	0.11
Write report	E	1	5	9	5	1.78
Write methods report	F	7	8	9	8	0.11
Write final report	G	2	2	2	2	0.00

As you can see, the variance is the square of one sixth the difference between the two extreme time estimates, and, of course, the greater this difference, the larger the variance. A summary of the expected time and variance for each activity involved in making the portable computer discussed previously is presented in Exhibit 10.6.

Step 6: Identify all of the paths in the network and their estimated completion times and variances

Using the data in Exhibit 10.6, the expected completion time for each path is simply the sum of the expected completion times for the activities that are on that path. Likewise, to calculate the variance for each path we simply add together the variances of the activities on the path. Again using the data in Exhibit 10.6, the path variances are calculated, and summarized in Exhibit 10.7, along with the path expected completion times.

Step 7: Determine the probability of completing the project by a given date

The probability of completing the project by a given date is dependent on the probability of each path in the network being completed by that date. In our example, the desired completion time for the project is 39 weeks. In other words, we want to calculate the probability of completing the project in 39 weeks or less. To do this we need to calculate the probability of each of the paths in the network being completed in 39 weeks or less. All of the paths need to be completed in 39 weeks or less for the project to be completed within that same time period. Thus, the probability of the project being completed within a given time is equal to the minimum of the probabilities of the different paths.

EXHIBIT 10.7

Path Estimated Completion Times and Variances

Path	Expected Completion Time (in weeks)	Variance (σ_p^2)
A–C–E–G	35	13.56
A–B–D–F–G	37	10.22
A–B–D–E–G	34	11.89
A–C–F–G	38	11.89

EXHIBIT 10.8

Probability of Each Path Being Completed in 39 Weeks or Less

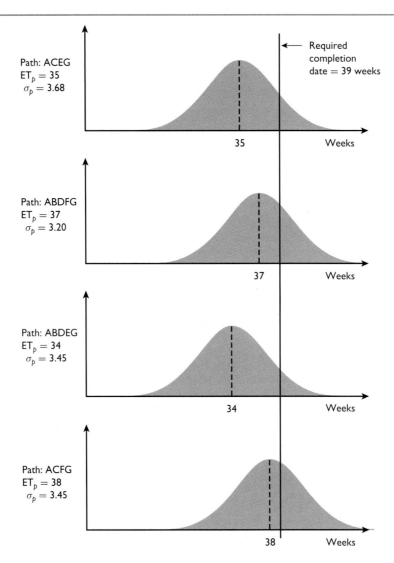

Using the data in Exhibit 10.7 we can now construct the probability distribution for each path and calculate the probability of each path being completed in 39 weeks or less. This is shown graphically in Exhibit 10.8. Note that in order to calculate the probability of completing each path in 39 days or less we use σ_p, which is the square root of the variance, σ_p^2.

In Exhibit 10.8, the shaded area to the left of the line representing 39 weeks is the probability of that path being completed within the 39 week period. To obtain the value of that

EXHIBIT 10.9

Path Z-Values and Probabilities of Completing Each Path in 39 Weeks or Less

Path	Z-Value	Completion Probability
A–C–E–G	1.09	0.8621
A–B–D–F–G	0.63	0.7357
A–B–D–E–G	1.45	0.9265
A–C–F–G	0.29	0.6141

probability, we use the normal table in Appendix B or C. In order to be able to use this table we need to calculate a Z-value associated with each path, indicating how many standard deviations the 39 weeks is from the expected completion time for that path. The formula for this is:

$$Z = \frac{D - ET_p}{\sigma_p}$$

where

$D =$ Desired completion date for the project

$ET_p =$ Expected completion time for the path

$\sigma_p =$ Standard deviation for the path

In this manner, the Z-value for each path is calculated and presented in Exhibit 10.9, along with the corresponding probability that we obtain from the normal table in Appendix B or C. As an approximation, one can determine the probability of completing the project within 39 weeks or less as the minimum of the individual path probabilities, or:

Prob (Proj < 39) = MIN [(0.8621), (0.7357), (0.9265), (0.6141)] = 0.6141

Thus, the probability of completing this project within 39 weeks is 61.41 percent, even though its expected completion time, as determined by the average activity times on the critical path, is 38 weeks.

Maintaining Ongoing Project Schedules

It is important to keep a project schedule accurate and current. The schedule tracks the progress of the project and identifies problems as they occur while time to correct the situation may still be available. It also monitors the progress of the costs and is often the basis for partial payments. In practice, however, schedules are often sloppily kept, or even totally abandoned.

Perhaps the most important reason for this happening is that managers are not committed enough to the technique to insist that the schedules be kept up to date. The resulting poor schedules consequently give project scheduling a bad name. Experience in project scheduling techniques is important and this job should not be carelessly relegated to the closest warm body. The project manager must support the schedule and see to it that it is maintained.

TIME–COST TRADE-OFF MODELS

time–cost trade-off models
Models that develop the relationship between direct project costs, indirect costs, and time to complete the project.

In practice, project managers are as much concerned with the cost to complete a project as they are with the time to complete the project. For this reason, **time–cost trade-off models** have been devised. These models, which are extensions of PERT and CPM, attempt to develop a minimum cost schedule for the entire project and to control budgetary expenditures during the project.

Minimum-Cost Scheduling (Time–Cost Trade-Off)

The basic assumption in minimum-cost scheduling is that there is a relationship between activity completion time and the cost of a project. On one hand, it costs money to expedite an activity; on the other, it costs money to sustain (or lengthen) the project. The costs associated with expediting activities in order to shorten their completion times are termed *activity direct costs* and add to the project's direct costs. These additional costs that are included when an activity is accelerated are also referred to as **crash costs.** Some of these may be worker related, such as overtime pay, hiring more workers, and transferring workers from other jobs, while others are resource related, such as buying or leasing additional or more efficient equipment and drawing on additional support facilities.

crash costs
Additional costs of an activity when time to complete it is shortened.

The costs associated with sustaining the project are termed *project indirect costs;* overhead, facilities, and resource opportunity costs, and, under certain contractual situations, penalty costs or lost incentive payments. Since *activity direct costs* and *project indirect costs* are opposing costs dependent on time, the scheduling problem is essentially one of finding that project duration which minimizes their sum or, in other words, finding the optimum point in a time–cost trade-off.

The procedure for finding this point consists of the following five steps and is illustrated using the simple four-activity network that is shown in Exhibit 10.10. Assume in this example that the indirect costs remain constant for eight days and then increase at the rate of $5 per day.

Step 1: Prepare a CPM-type network diagram
For each activity this diagram should list:

a. Normal cost (NC): The lowest expected activity cost (these are the lesser of the cost figures shown under each node in Exhibit 10.10).
b. Normal time (NT): The time associated with each normal cost.
c. Crash time (CT): The shortest possible activity time.
d. Crash cost (CC): The cost associated with each crash time.

EXHIBIT 10.10

Example of Time–Cost Trade-Off Procedure

Step 1. Prepare CPM Diagram with Activity Costs

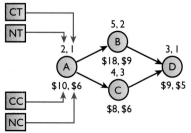

CT = Crash time
NT = Normal time
CC = Crash cost
NC = Normal cost

Step 2. Determine Cost per Unit of Time

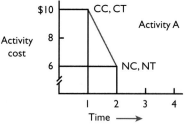

Step 3. Compute the Critical Path

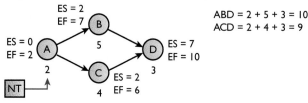

ABD = 2 + 5 + 3 = 10
ACD = 2 + 4 + 3 = 9

Step 2: Determine the cost per unit of time (assume days) to expedite (or crash) each activity

The relationship between activity time and cost may be shown graphically by plotting CC and CT coordinates and connecting them to the NC and NT coordinates by a concave, convex, or straight line—or some other form, depending on the actual cost structure of the activity's performance, as shown in Exhibit 10.10. For Activity A, we assume a linear relationship between time and cost. This assumption is common in practice and facilitates the derivation of the cost per day to expedite since this value may be found directly by taking the slope of the line using the formula: Slope = (CC − NC) ÷ (NT − CT). (When the assumption of linearity cannot be made, the cost of expediting must be determined graphically for each of the days the activity may be shortened.)

The calculations needed to obtain the cost of expediting the remaining activities are shown in Exhibit 10.11.

Step 3: Compute the critical path

For the simple network we have been using, this schedule would take 10 days. The critical path is A–B–D.

Step 4: Shorten the critical path at the least cost

The easiest way to proceed is to start with the normal schedule, find the critical path, and reduce the path time by one day using the lowest-cost activity. Then recompute and find the new critical path and reduce it by one day also. Repeat this procedure until the time of completion is satisfactory, or until there can be no further reduction in the project completion time. Exhibit 10.12 shows the reduction of the network one day at a time.

Step 5: Plot project direct, indirect, and total-cost curves and find minimum-cost schedule

Exhibit 10.13 shows the indirect cost plotted as a constant $10 per day for eight days and increasing $5 per day thereafter. The direct costs are plotted from Exhibit 10.12 and the total project cost is shown as the total of the two costs.

Summing the values for direct and indirect costs for each day yields the project total cost curve. As you can see, this curve is at its minimum for an eight-day schedule, which costs $40 ($30 direct + $10 indirect).

EXHIBIT 10.11

Calculation of Cost per Day to Expedite Each Activity

Activity	CC − NC	NT − CT	$\dfrac{\text{CC} - \text{NC}}{\text{NT} - \text{CT}}$	Cost per Day to Expedite	Number of Days Activity May Be Shortened
A	$10 − $6	2 − 1	$\dfrac{\$10 - 6}{2 - 1}$	$4	1
B	$18 − $9	5 − 2	$\dfrac{\$18 - \$9}{5 - 2}$	$3	3
C	$ 8 − $6	4 − 3	$\dfrac{\$8 - \$6}{4 - 3}$	$2	1
D	$ 9 − $5	3 − 1	$\dfrac{\$9 - \$5}{3 - 1}$	$2	2

EXHIBIT 10.12

Reducing the Project Completion Time One Day at a Time

Current Critical Path(s)	Remaining Number of Days Activity May Be Shortened	Cost per Day to Expedite Each Activity	Least Cost Activity to Expedite	Total Cost of All Activities in Network	Project Completion Time
A–B–D	All activity times and costs are normal			$26	10
A–B–D	A–1, B–3, D–2	A–4, B–3, D–2	D	28	9
A–B–D	A–1, B–3, D–1	A–4, B–3, D–2	D	30	8
A–B–D	A–1, B–3	A–4, B–3	B	33	7
A–B–D, A–C–D	A–1, B–2, C–1	A–4, B–3, C–2	A*	37	6
A–B–D, A–C–D	B–2, C–1	B–3, C–2	B&C†	42	5
A–B–D, A–C–D	B–1	B–3	B	45	5

*To reduce both critical paths by one day, reduce either A alone, or B and C together at the same time (since either B or C by itself modifies the critical path without shortening it).

†B &C must be crashed together to reduce both critical paths by one day.

EXHIBIT 10.13

Plot of Costs and Minimum Cost Schedule

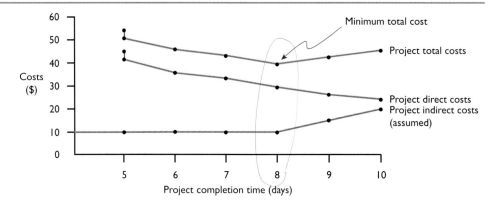

CRITICISMS OF PERT AND CPM

There are several assumptions that need to be made when applying CPM or PERT analysis to project networks. This section summarizes some of the more significant assumptions and their criticisms. One point of particular difficulty for the operating personnel is understanding the statistics when three time estimates are used. The beta distribution of activity times, the three time estimates, the activity variances, and the use of the normal distribution to arrive at project completion probabilities are all potential sources of misunderstandings, and with misunderstanding comes distrust and obstruction. Thus, management must be sure that the people charged with monitoring and controlling activity performance have a general understanding of the statistics.

1. *Assumption:* Project activities can be identified as entities (that is, there is a clear beginning and ending point for each activity).
   Criticism: Projects, especially complex ones, change in content over time, and therefore a network made at the beginning may be highly inaccurate later on. Also, the very fact that activities are specified and a network formalized tends to limit the flexibility that is required to handle changing situations as the project progresses.
2. *Assumption:* Project activity sequence relationships can be specified and networked.

Criticism: Sequence relationships cannot always be specified beforehand. In some projects, in fact, ordering certain activities is conditional on previous activities. (PERT and CPM, in their basic form, have no provision for treating this problem, although some other techniques have been proposed that present the project manager with several contingency paths, given different outcomes from each activity.)

3. *Assumption:* Project control should focus on the critical path.

   Criticism: It is not necessarily true that the longest time-consuming path (or the path in which each of the activities has zero slack) obtained from summing activity expected time values ultimately determines project completion time. What often happens as the project progresses is that some activity not on the critical path becomes delayed to such a degree (which exceeds the slack time for that activity) that it extends the entire project. For this reason it has been suggested that a "critical activity" concept replace the critical path concept as a focus of managerial control. Under this approach, attention would center on those activities that have a high potential variation and lie on a "near-critical path." A near-critical path is one that does not share any activities with the critical path and, though it has slack, could become critical if one or a few activities along it become delayed. Obviously, the more parallelism in a network, the more likely that one or more near-critical paths exist. Conversely, the more a network approximates a single series of activities, the less likely it is to have near-critical paths.

4. *Assumption:* The activity times in PERT follow the beta distribution, with the variance of the project assumed to be equal to the sum of the variances along the critical path.

   Criticism: Although originally the beta distribution was selected for a variety of good reasons, each component of the statistical treatment has been brought into question. First, the formulas are in reality a modification of the beta distribution mean and variance, which, when compared to the basic formulas, could lead to absolute errors on the order of 10 percent for expected time (ET) and 5 percent for the individual variances. Second, given that the activity-time distributions have the properties of unimodality, continuity, and finite positive end points, other distributions with the same properties would yield different means and variances. Third, obtaining three "valid" time estimates to put into the formulas presents operational problems—it is often difficult to arrive at one activity time estimate, let alone three, and the subjective definitions of *a* and *b* do not help the matter. (How optimistic and pessimistic should one be?)

Another problem that sometimes arises, especially when CPM or PERT is used by subcontractors working with the government, is the attempt to "beat" the network to get on or off the critical path. Many government contracts provide cost incentives for finishing a project early or on a "cost-plus-fixed-fee" basis. Contractors on the critical path generally have more leverage in obtaining additional funds since they have a major influence on the project duration. On the other hand—for political reasons that we will not go into here—some contractors deem it desirable to be less visible and therefore adjust their time estimates and activity descriptions to ensure they *won't* be on the critical path.

Finally, the cost of applying critical path methods to a project is sometimes used as a basis for criticism. However, the cost of applying PERT or CPM rarely exceeds 2 percent of the total project cost. When used with added features of a work breakdown structure and various reports it is more expensive but rarely exceeds 5 percent of total project costs. Thus, this added cost is generally justified by the additional savings resulting from improved scheduling and the resulting reduced project time.

The critical path techniques of PERT and CPM have proved themselves for more than three decades and promise to be of continued value in the future. With the rapidly changing business environment and the high costs associated with these changes, management needs to be able to both quickly and efficiently plan and control the activities of the firm. The inherent value of a tool that allows management to structure complex projects in an understandable way, to pick out possible sources of delay before they occur, to isolate areas of responsibility, and, of course, to save time in costly projects virtually ensures that the use of project management will expand. The availability of inexpensive yet powerful software programs for project scheduling, such as shown on this screen from Primavera Project Planner 2.0, further encourages the expanded use of project management.

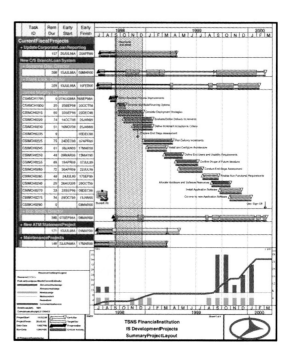

CONCLUSION

Product life cycles are becoming shorter as more new products are continuously being introduced into the marketplace. A key factor in the ability of a company to introduce these products quickly, add new facilities, or make major operational changes of any kind is an understanding of project management concepts and techniques.

Successful projects require both technical skills and people skills. Technical skills identify the critical activities on which the project team should focus its efforts. People skills provide the motivation and team efforts that are necessary for the project to be completed in a timely manner.

Although much of this chapter has dealt with network solving techniques used in project management, effective project management involves much more than simply setting up a CPM or PERT schedule. It requires, in addition, clearly identified project responsibilities, a simple and timely progress reporting system, and good people-management practices.

Projects fail for a number of reasons. The most significant reason is that those involved do not take project scheduling seriously. Often, personnel who have been newly exposed and those who have had unsatisfactory experiences do not comply with the procedure. They may neither spend the time to properly develop their parts of the network, nor even submit good time and cost estimates. This attitude usually continues throughout the project with a reluctance to revise schedules.

KEY TERMS

crash costs   p. 366
critical path   p. 359
CPM (critical path method)   p. 356
early start schedule   p. 361
Gantt chart   p. 354
late start schedule   p. 361

milestones   p. 351
PERT (program evaluation and review
  technique)   p. 356
program   p. 350
project   p. 350
slack time   p. 359
time–cost trade-off models   p. 365
work breakdown structure (WBS)   p. 351

REVIEW AND DISCUSSION QUESTIONS

1. Define project management.
2. Describe or define work breakdown structure, program, project, task, subtask, and work package.
3. How does the role of a project manager differ from that of a traditional functional manager?
4. What are some of the key characteristics of high performance work teams?
5. What are some of the reasons project scheduling is not done well?
6. Discuss the graphic presentations in Exhibit 10.2. Are there any other graphic outputs you would like to see if you were the project manager?
7. Which characteristics must a project have for critical path scheduling to be applicable? What types of projects have been subjected to critical path analysis?
8. What are the underlying assumptions of minimum-cost scheduling? Are they equally realistic?
9. "Project control should always focus on the critical path." Comment.
10. Why would subcontractors for a government project want their activities on the critical path? Under which conditions would they try to avoid being on the critical path?
11. Identify some of the advantages to Taco Bell if it can significantly shorten the construction time of new restaurants.

INTERNET UPDATE

The increasing application of project management techniques has resulted in the development of a large number of project management software packages. Your boss has asked you to conduct a search on the Internet to identify six different project management software packages that are currently available. She has requested that you prepare a one-page memo (plus any additional pages for exhibits, if necessary) that evaluates these different packages. You should include in your software evaluation the following information:

- Name of software.
- Name and location of company offering the software.
- Price.
- Computer requirements.
- Description.
- Unique features.
- Unique applications.

Suggested key words to help you in your search are PROJECT, MANAGEMENT, and SOFTWARE.

SOLVED PROBLEMS

Problem 1

A project has been defined to contain the following list of activities, along with their required times for completion:

Activity	Immediate Predecessors	Time (days)	Activity	Immediate Predecessors	Time (days)
A	—	1	F	C, D	2
B	A	4	G	E, F	7
C	A	3	H	D	9
D	A	7	I	G, H	4
E	B	6			

a. Draw the critical path diagram.

b. Show the early start and early finish times.

c. Show the critical path.

d. What would happen if Activity F were revised to take four days instead of two?

Solution

The answers to *a*, *b*, and *c* are shown in the following diagram.

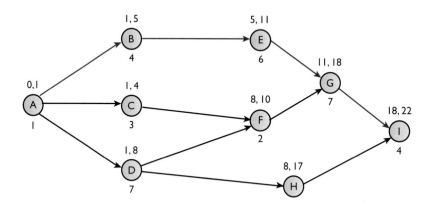

d. New critical path: A–D–F–G–I. Time of completion = 23 days.

Problem 2

Following are the precedence requirements, normal and crash activity times, and normal and crash costs for a construction project.

Activity	Preceding Activities	Required Time (weeks) Normal	Crash	Cost Normal	Crash
A	—	4	2	$10,000	$11,000
B	A	3	2	6,000	9,000
C	A	2	1	4,000	6,000
D	B	5	3	14,000	18,000
E	B, C	1	1	9,000	9,000
F	C	3	2	7,000	8,000
G	E, F	4	2	13,000	25,000
H	D, E	4	1	11,000	18,000
I	H, G	6	5	20,000	29,000

a. What is the critical path and the estimated completion time?

b. To shorten the project by three weeks, which tasks would be shortened and what would the final total project cost be?

Solution

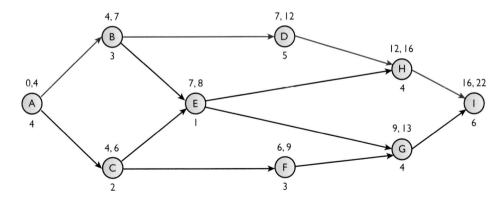

a. Critical path A–B–D–H–I.
    Normal completion time = 22 weeks.

b.

Activity	Crash Cost	Normal Cost	Normal Time	Crash Time	Cost per Week	Weeks
A	$11,000	$10,000	4	2	$ 500	2
B	9,000	6,000	3	2	3,000	1
C	6,000	4,000	2	1	2,000	1
D	18,000	14,000	5	3	2,000	2
E	9,000	9,000	1	1		0
F	8,000	7,000	3	2	1,000	1
G	25,000	13,000	4	2	6,000	2
H	18,000	11,000	4	1	2,333	3
I	29,000	20,000	6	5	9,000	1

1. 1st week: CP = A–B–D–H–I. Cheapest activity is A at $500. Critical path stays the same.

2. 2nd week: A is still the cheapest at $500. Critical path stays the same.

3. 3rd week: Since A is no longer available, the choices are B (at $3,000), D (at $2,000), H (at $2,333), or I (at $9,000).

Therefore, choose D at $2,000.
    Total cost for the project shortened three weeks is:

A	$11,000
B	6,000
C	4,000
D	16,000
E	9,000
F	7,000
G	13,000
H	11,000
I	20,000
	$97,000

PROBLEMS

1. The following activities are part of a project to be scheduled using CPM:

Activity	Immediate Predecessors	Time (weeks)
A	—	6
B	A	3
C	A	7
D	C	2
E	B, D	4
F	D	3
G	E, F	7

a. Draw the network.

b. What is the critical path?

c. How many weeks will it take to complete the project?

d. How much slack time does Activity B have?

2. American Steam Turbine and Generator Company manufactures electric power generating systems for the major electric power companies. Turbine/generator sets are made to specific order and generally require a three- to five-year lead time. Costs range from $8 to $15 million per set.

   Management has been planning their production using traditional planning techniques such as planning charts, Gantt charts, and other shop floor control methods. However, management would now like to introduce CPM project planning and control methods where each turbine/generator set is considered a separate project.

   Following is a segment of the total activities involved in the turbine/generator production:

Activity	Immediate Predecessors	Time (weeks)	Activity	Immediate Predecessors	Time (weeks)
a	—	8	i	h	9
b	a	16	j	i	13
c	a	12	k	i	7
d	a	7	l	j	36
e	b, c	22	m	k	40
f	c, d	40	n	l, m	9
g	e, f	15	o	g, n	10
h	—	14			

a. Draw the network.

b. Find the critical path.

c. If the project is to be cut by two weeks, show which activities would be on the list to be investigated for cutting performance time.

d. If the project is to be cut by 10 weeks, show which activities would be on the list to be investigated for cutting performance time.

3. The R&D department is planning to bid on a large project for the development of a new communication system for commercial planes. The table below shows the activities, times, and sequences required.

Activity	Immediate Predecessors	Time (weeks)	Activity	Immediate Predecessors	Time (weeks)
A	—	3	F	C, D	6
B	A	2	G	D, F	2
C	A	4	H	D	3
D	A	4	I	E, G, H	3
E	B	6			

    a. Draw the network diagram.

    b. What is the critical path?

    c. Supposing you wanted to shorten the completion time as much as possible, and had the option of shortening any or all of B, C, D, and G each two weeks (in effect, activity G takes zero time to complete). Which would you shorten?

    d. What is the new path and earliest completion time?

4. A construction project is broken down into the 10 activities listed below.

Activity	Preceding Activity	Time (weeks)
1	—	4
2	1	2
3	1	4
4	1	3
5	2, 3	5
6	3	6
7	4	2
8	5	3
9	6, 7	5
10	8, 9	7

    a. Draw the precedence diagram.

    b. Find the critical path.

    c. If activities 1 and 10 cannot be shortened, but activities 2 through 9 can be shortened to a minimum of 1 week each at a cost of $10,000 per week per activity, which activities would you shorten in order to shorten the project by four weeks?

5. A manufacturing concern has received a special order for a number of units of a special product that consists of two component parts, X and Y. The product is a nonstandard item that the firm has never produced before, and scheduling personnel have decided that the application of CPM is warranted. A team of manufacturing engineers has prepared the following table:

Activity	Description	Immediate Predecessors	Expected Time (days)
A	Plan production	—	5
B	Procure materials for Part X	A	14
C	Manufacture Part X	B	9
D	Procure materials for Part Y	A	15
E	Manufacture Part Y	D	10
F	Assemble Parts X and Y	C, E	4
G	Inspect assemblies	F	2
H	Completed	G	0

    a. Construct a graphic representation of the CPM network.

    b. Identify the critical path.

    c. What is the length of time to complete the project?

    d. Which activities have slack time and how much?

6. The following is a CPM network with activity times in weeks:

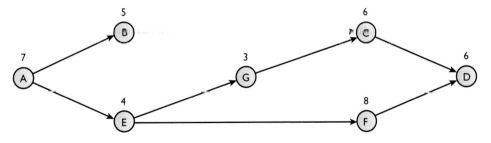

   a. Determine the critical path.

   b. How many weeks will the project take to complete?

   c. Supposing F could be shortened by one week and B by two weeks. What effect would this have on the completion date?

7. The following represents a plan for a project:

Job No.	Predecessor Job(s)	a	m	b
1	—	2	3	4
2	1	1	2	3
3	1	4	5	12
4	1	3	4	11
5	2	1	3	5
6	3	1	2	3
7	4	1	8	9
8	5, 6	2	4	6
9	8	2	4	12
10	7	3	4	5
11	9, 10	5	7	8

   a. Construct the appropriate network diagram.

   b. Identify the critical path.

   c. What is the expected completion time for the project?

   d. What is the probability that the project will be completed in 30 days or less?

8. Following is a network with the activity times shown under the nodes in days:

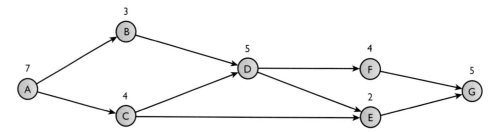

   a. Find the critical path.

   b. The following table shows the normal times and the crash times, along with the associated costs for each of the activities.

Activity	Normal Time	Crash Time	Normal Cost	Crash Cost
A	7	6	$7,000	$ 8,000
B	3	2	5,000	7,000
C	4	3	9,000	10,200
D	5	4	3,000	4,500
E	2	1	2,000	3,000
F	4	2	4,000	7,000
G	5	4	5,000	8,000

   If the project is to be shortened by four days, show which activities in order of reduction would be shortened and the resulting total project costs.

9. The home office billing department of a chain of department stores prepares monthly inventory reports for use by the stores' purchasing agents. Given the following information, use the critical path method to determine:

a. How long will the total process take?

b. Which jobs can be delayed without delaying the early start of any subsequent activity.

	Job and Description	Immediate Predecessors	Time (hours)
a	Start	—	0
b	Get computer printouts of customer purchases	a	10
c	Get stock records for the month	a	20
d	Reconcile purchase printouts and stock records	b, c	30
e	Total stock records by department	b, c	20
f	Determine reorder quantities for coming period	e	40
g	Prepare stock reports for purchasing agents	d, f	20
h	Finish	g	0

10. For the network and the data shown:

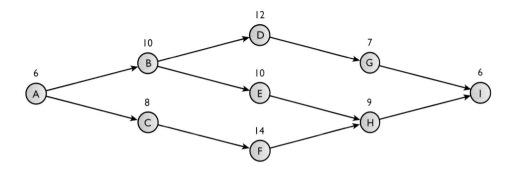

a. Determine the critical path and the early completion time for the project.

Activity*	Normal Time (weeks)	Normal Cost	Crash Time (weeks)	Crash Cost
A	6	$ 6,000	4	$12,000
B	10	10,000	9	11,000
C	8	8,000	7	10,000
D	12	12,000	10	14,000
E	10	10,000	7	12,000
F	14	14,000	12	19,000
G	7	7,000	5	10,000
H	9	9,000	6	15,000
I	6	6,000	5	8,000

*An activity cannot be shortened to less than its crash time.

b. Reduce the project completion time by four weeks. Assume a linear cost per day shortened and show, step by step, how you arrived at your schedule. Also indicate the critical path.

11. The following CPM network has estimates of the *normal time* listed for the activities:

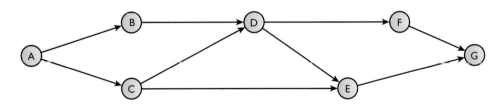

a. Identify the critical path.

b. What is the length of time to complete the project?

c. Which activities have slack, and how much?

Activity	Time (weeks)
A	7
B	2
C	4
D	5
E	2
F	4
G	5

d. The following is a table of normal and crash times and costs. Which activities would you shorten to cut two weeks from the schedule in a rational fashion? What would be the incremental cost? Is the critical path changed?

Activity	Normal Time	Crash Time	Normal Cost	Crash Cost	Possible Number of Weeks Decrease	Cost/Week to Expedite
A	7	6	$7,000	$ 8,000		
B	2	1	5,000	7,000		
C	4	3	9,000	10,200		
D	5	4	3,000	4,500		
E	2	1	2,000	3,000		
F	4	2	4,000	7,000		
G	5	4	5,000	8,000		

CASE: THE ADDITION TO HARVEY HALL AT BERKSHIRE SCHOOL OF BUSINESS

In an effort to improve the level of quality of its classroom instruction, the Berkshire School of Business recently decided to reduce the average size of its undergraduate classes. As a result of this decision, Lydia Keene, the undergraduate dean, calculated that she would have to hire an additional 35 faculty members, which meant that more offices were needed. An initial analysis determined that the most cost-effective way to add these new offices was to put an addition onto Harvey Hall, the existing faculty office building.

To complete the building addition in time for the faculty to be in their new offices before the start of the fall semester, John Yates, the school's VP for finance and who had overall responsibility for the Project's completion, decided to apply some project management techniques he learned in his undergraduate operations management course. This required that he identify all the various activities that were required as part of this project and understand how they were related.

John knew that the first step in this project was to obtain approval from the school's Board of Trustees. Once this was done, building permits could be obtained at the same time that bids for furniture were requested and the faculty recruitment process was initiated. With the necessary permits in hand, the actual construction of the addition could begin. Upon completion of the building exterior, the landscaping could be started and the interior work on the offices could be done simultaneously. Once the interiors were completed, a certificate of occupancy could be issued upon a final building inspection by the town fire marshal. A final cleanup of both the interior and the exterior of the building would then be done (landscaping had to be completed by this time). Following the cleanup, the office furniture would then be installed and the faculty allowed to move into their new offices.

John, in preparation for the upcoming board meeting, developed an initial budget for the project based on the normal costs associated with each of the project's individual activities. John's estimated cost for each activity is shown in the table below, along with the activity's estimated completion time. Also listed are crash costs and crash times, in the event it would be necessary to accelerate a specific activity so that the project would be completed on schedule before the start of the fall semester.

Activity	Normal Time*	Normal Costs†	Crash Time‡	Crash Costs¶
1. Board of Trustees approval	4	$ 10	2	$ 16
2. Obtain building permits	2	5	2	5
3. Construct building	21	1,500	17	1,700
4. Request bids for furniture	4	3	4	3
5. Recruit faculty	30	150	27	165
6. Order furniture	16	200	12	240
7. Complete interiors	6	110	3	131
8. Landscape site	4	68	2	80
9. Obtain certificate of occupancy	1	2	1	2
10. Final cleanup	2	20	1	26
11. Install furniture	1	12	1	12
12. Building occupied	—	—	—	—
Totals:		2,080		2,380

*Times listed are in weeks.
†Costs listed are in thousands of dollars.
‡Crash time is the minimum time in which an activity can be completed.
¶Crash costs are the total costs associated with the acceleration of an activity. The weekly increase in costs for a given activity is assumed to be constant.

QUESTIONS

1. What is the minimum time and overall cost in which the addition to Harvey Hall can be occupied by faculty under normal times and costs?

2. If you were operating under a very limited budget, how could you reduce the overall length of the project by one week at the least cost? By two weeks?

3. If John decides to complete this project in the shortest time possible, what is the minimum time and associated costs that the project can be completed (without incurring any unnecessary costs)?

4. After receiving approval from the school's board in the normal time of four weeks, John ran into a problem obtaining the necessary building permits. The original 125 acres on which the current campus is located was initially subdivided into one acre housing lots. As a result, permits are required for each of the building lots on which the addition was to be built, along with any immediately adjacent lots. These additional permits required an additional two weeks to obtain and increased the cost of obtaining the permits by $4,000. If John wants to complete the project in the original time that was determined in question 1, what specific actions must he now take to minimize costs while still completing the building as scheduled?

Source: © Mark M. Davis.

SELECTED BIBLIOGRAPHY

Cleland, David I., and William R. King. *Project Management Handbook.* New York: Van Nostrand Reinhold, 1983.

Hughes, Michael William. "Why Projects Fail: The Effects of Ignoring the Obvious." *Industrial Engineering* 18, no. 4 (April 1986), pp. 14–18.

Kerzner, Harold. *Project Management for Executives.* New York: Van Nostrand Reinhold, 1984.

Shtub, A.; J. F. Bard; and S. Globerson. *Project Management: Engineering, Technology and Implementation.* Englewood Cliffs, NJ: Prentice Hall, 1994.

Thamhain, Hans J. "Effective Leadership Style for Managing Project Teams." In *Handbook of Program and Project Management,* ed. P. C. Dinsmore. New York: AMACOM, 1992.

Thamhain, Hans J. "Managing Technologically Innovative Team Efforts Towards New Product Success." *Journal of Production Innovation Management* 7, no. 1 (March 1990).

Wheelwright, S., and J. Weber. "Massachusetts General Hospital: CABG Surgery (A)." Boston, MA: Harvard Business School Publishing, 1997.

SUPPLY CHAIN MANAGEMENT

Chapter Outline

Chapter Objectives

- Introduce the concept of supply chain management and describe how it has changed the supplier relationship.

- Present the different factors that have had an impact on the supply chain in recent years.

- Identify the requirements for the establishment of a successful supply chain.

- Define in-transit inventory costs and show their impact on the purchasing decision.

- Introduce the concept of disintermediation as a current trend that affects the structure of the supply chain.

General Scanning's Recorder Products Division in Bedford, Massachusetts, deals with its vendors using a concept that is often referred to as "the breadman method." With this approach, maximum inventory levels are established for each item. General Scanning's vendors are then empowered to determine how often these items should be replenished. Vendors have access to the manufacturing floor and restock the items directly at the points where they are used. There are no stockrooms at this facility.

The term "breadman" comes from commercial bakeries where the breadmen or salesmen determine the quantity of bread to deliver to each retail outlet on their route and are responsible for placing the bread on the shelves. The retail operations then receive credit for any unsold bread that is returned.

With this concept, paperwork is significantly reduced since no purchase orders are generated. The receiving function is also significantly reduced, as is the need for personnel to move the items onto the manufacturing floor. ▪

Source: Special thanks to Greg Baletsa, Vice President and General Manager, Recorder Products Division, General Scanning Corp., Bedford, Massachusetts.

Supply chain management has taken on increased importance in recent years. The reasons for its growing recognition include the fact that in many companies, purchased materials and components represent an increasing percentage of the manufacturing cost of an item. In many firms, for example, the cost of raw material and purchased components is often 60 to 70 percent of the cost of goods sold (and even higher in some cases). In addition, the logistical costs (that is, the transportation and distribution costs) associated with the delivery of products from suppliers have continued to escalate.

The trend toward using more purchased parts coupled with rising transportation and logistics costs has caused management to focus its attention on the firm's purchasing function. As a result, the purchasing function has undergone a significant transformation in the way it conducts business with the firm's suppliers.

In this chapter we present some of the underlying factors that have caused these changes to take place. In addition, we discuss the role of logistics in supply chain management and introduce the concept of in-transit inventories. Finally, we identify some of the current trends that appear to be taking place with respect to supply chain management.

DEFINITION OF SUPPLY CHAIN MANAGEMENT

supply chain
The steps and the firms that perform these steps in the transformation of raw material into finished products bought by customers.

A **supply chain** can be defined as a group of firms that provide all the various processes required to make a finished product. The chain begins with raw material and ends with a finished product that is delivered to the final customer. For example, if the finished product is a piece of wood furniture, then the supply chain, going backwards from the customer, would include: (*a*) the retail operation where the furniture was purchased, (*b*) the shipping company that delivered it, (*c*) the furniture manufacturer, (*d*) the hardware manufacturer, and (*e*) the lumber companies that harvested the wood from the forests. If the end product is fresh fish sold at a supermarket, then the supply chain would include: (*a*) the supermarket, (*b*) the fresh fish supplier who delivered the fish, (*c*) the fish processor who filleted it, and (*d*) the fishermen who caught it.

The structure of the supply chain can vary for different companies, even within the same industry. In addition, the role of an organization with respect to its span or degree of control over the supply chain can vary significantly. As an example, compare the supply chain for fish sold in a typical supermarket, described above, with that of Spenger's, a long established fish market and seafood restaurant located in Berkeley, California. Until recently, many of the various types of fish sold in its market and restaurant were caught on its own fishing boats and processed in its own operation. (Spenger's, founded in 1890, sold the last of its fishing boats in 1994 with the retirement of its owner and now buys fish either through brokers or from fishermen who work exclusively for Spenger's.)

As an another illustration, Henry Ford, in order to support his huge River Rouge automobile plant just outside of Detroit, Michigan, invested heavily in iron ore mines, forests, coal mines, and even cargo ships that transported raw material on the Great Lakes. His goal was to gain total control over his supply chain (which, in the end, he realized was not possible). The greater the degree or span of control that a firm has with respect to its supply chain, the more vertically integrated it is said to be. In other words, Ford's operation could be described as being very vertically integrated in comparison to other automotive manufacturers who focused solely on the manufacture and assembly of the cars themselves.

Supply chain management, therefore, can be defined as the ability of a firm to work with its suppliers to provide high quality material and components that are competitively priced. The closeness of the relationship between vendor and customer, in many respects, differentiates one type of supply chain from another. The adoption of the term *supply chain management* in lieu of materials management or purchasing reflects top management's recognition of the strategic role of suppliers in contributing to the long-term success of the

EXHIBIT 11.1

To Whom the Purchasing
Function Reports

Position to Whom the Purchasing Function Reports	Percent of Firms	
	1988	1995
President	16%	16%
Executive vice president	19	15
Sr. vice president/group vice president	*	19
Financial vice president	7	10
Mfg/prod/ops vice president	24	15
Materials/logistics vice president	8	7
Engineering vice president	1	1
Administrative vice president	13	9
Other (many of whom were VPs)	12	8
Total (less than 100% due to rounding)	99%	100%

*Category not identified in study.

Source: Michiel R. Leenders and Harold E. Fearon, *Purchasing and Supply Management,* (Burr Ridge, IL: Richard D. Irwin Co., 1997). By permission of The McGraw-Hill Companies.

firm. The growing importance of the purchasing function can also be seen by where the purchasing function now reports within an organization. As shown in Exhibit 11.1, between 1988 and 1995, there appears to be a significant shift in moving the purchasing function from reporting to the vice president of operations to reporting to a senior/group vice president or a financial vice president.

THE EVOLUTION OF SUPPLY CHAIN MANAGEMENT

Supply chain management is a relatively new concept in business. Previously, management theory suggested that the overall efficiency of the technical core or production function could be significantly improved if the core could be isolated or *buffered* to the greatest extent possible from an often erratic and uncertain external environment.

In order to isolate the technical core from suppliers (and also customers), companies established significant inventories of raw material and finished goods, as shown in Exhibit 11.2A. While this approach produced highly efficient operations, it simultaneously made the core less responsive to changes in the marketplace. This inability to react quickly to changes in customer demand, preferences, and so forth was caused primarily by the significant amounts of raw material and finished goods inventories that were maintained, and which first had to be depleted before the firm could begin supplying customers with new product.

Within this type of operating environment, companies very often had an antagonistic relationship with their suppliers. Every item that was purchased had several vendors. These vendors were played off against each other in order to obtain the lowest possible price, which was the primary criterion for being awarded a contract. Suppliers, recognizing that this relationship could very likely be terminated with the next contract, invested minimal time and money to address the specific needs of individual customers. Because of this short term perspective, very little information was shared between these firms. Under such conditions the purchasing function within a manufacturing company often reported to the operations manager, and its primary objective was to purchase raw material and components at the lowest possible cost.

Today, companies are working more closely with their suppliers to be more responsive to the changing needs of their customers. In so doing, they are significantly reducing, and in some cases eliminating, these previously established buffer inventories, as shown in

EXHIBIT 11.2

The Evolution of Supply Chain Management

A. Isolating the Technical Core

Suppliers (many) → Manufacturing Facility — Raw material inventory → Technical core → Finished goods inventory → Customer

B. Introduction of JIT Concepts

Suppliers (few) → Technical core → Customer

C. The Use of a Single Logistics Partner

Suppliers (few) → Logistics (inbound) → Technical core → Logistics (outbound) → Customer

(Partner)

D. Bringing Suppliers into the Plant

Suppliers (few) → Technical core → Logistics (outbound) → Customer

Exhibit 11.2B. Toyota is considered one of the early pioneers in this area with the development of the *just-in-time (JIT)* concept, which virtually eliminates all raw material and work-in-process inventories. In adopting JIT, however, companies become more dependent on their suppliers. (See related OM in Practice on Fire at Toyota's Supplier Stops Production.)

After JIT, the next stage in the supply chain management evolution was the use of a single logistics supplier to address all of the transportation and distribution functions for the firm, as shown in Exhibit 11.2C, which has led to the concept of *seamless logistics*. (Previously, firms dealt with many such transportation logistics vendors, again using cost as the primary criterion for selection.)

 As an example, Schneider Logistics of Green Bay, Wisconsin, was named, in January 1997, the logistics provider for General Motors' Canadian parts operation. In the fall of 1996, Schneider also established a long-term relationship with Case Corp., a manufacturer of construction and agricultural equipment. Under this agreement, Schneider handles all of

Operations Management in Practice

FIRE AT TOYOTA'S SUPPLIER STOPS PRODUCTION

Aisin Seiki provides 99 percent of the brake valves that Toyota uses in the assembly of its automobiles. Because Toyota uses a just-in-time (JIT) system with its vendors, it maintains only a four-hour supply of brake valves at each of its assembly plants. Consequently, when a fire destroyed Aisin Sekei's manufacturing facility on February 1, 1997, Toyota was forced to shut down its 20 automobile plants, which were producing 14,000 cars a day.

Although many experts predicted that it would take weeks before Aisin could begin producing valves, Toyota's plants were again turning out cars five days after the fire. This was accomplished through a concerted effort of all of Toyota's suppliers who worked together around the clock to provide an interim solution.

Source: Valerie Reitman, *The Wall Street Journal*, May 8, 1997, p. A1.

Ryder System manages Saturn's supply chain that links suppliers, factories, and dealers. Saturn turns its parts inventory quickly—over 300 times a year—so accurate information is essential. In the photo, drivers check the on-board computer that tells them where they should go, how to get there, and how long it should take.

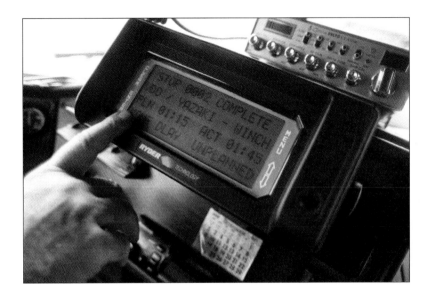

inbound
Relates to the logistics associated with receiving products from vendors.

outbound
Relates to the logistics associated with shipping products to customers.

Case's **inbound** shipments of parts from nearly 2,000 suppliers worldwide, and **outbound** shipments of finished goods that total 40,000 pieces of equipment to some 150 countries around the world.[1]

The most recent innovation in supply chain management is the incorporation of suppliers and their workers within the same manufacturing facility. Volkswagen's new automotive assembly plant in Brazil, discussed later in this chapter, provides a good example of this innovation, which is illustrated in Exhibit 11.2D.

FACTORS IMPACTING THE SUPPLY CHAIN

Reduced Number of Suppliers

Companies, as part of their supply chain programs, have significantly reduced the number of vendors they buy from. Managers currently believe in establishing long-term relationships with a few, highly reliable vendors rather than having multiple sources for every purchased item. As seen in Exhibit 11.3, the reduction in the number of suppliers has been significant in recent years, and is even more impressive in light of the fact that most of these companies are now offering a wider variety of products to their customers.

---

[1]Michael Fabey, "Time Is Money: Seamless Logistics Are in Demand," *World Trade*, July 1997, pp. 53–54.

EXHIBIT 11.3

The Trend toward Reducing the Number of Suppliers

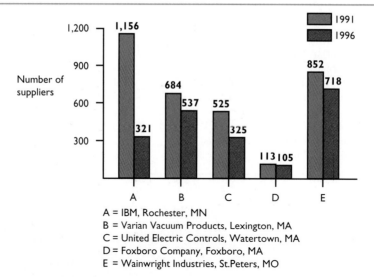

A = IBM, Rochester, MN
B = Varian Vacuum Products, Lexington, MA
C = United Electric Controls, Watertown, MA
D = Foxboro Company, Foxboro, MA
E = Wainwright Industries, St.Peters, MO

Note: IBM, Rochester, and Wainwright Industries are Malcolm Baldrige National Quality Award Winners; Varian Vacuum Products and The Foxboro Company are Massachusetts Quality Award winners; United Electric Controls is a Shingo Prize winner.

Increased Competition

The emergence of a global economy has dramatically increased the number of competitors that offer similar products. As stated earlier in this book, no corner of the world is immune to international competition, and this competition will only increase in intensity in the foreseeable future.

As a result, supply chains will continue to grow in both directions: backwards toward suppliers in other countries and forward toward new customers in these same countries.

Shorter Product Life Cycles

Product life cycles continue to shorten as competition introduces new products at an ever increasing rate in the hope of gaining market share and a competitive advantage. In order to respond quickly to new product introductions, a company needs to have flexible processes that can be easily converted to new product requirements. Flexibility can also be achieved by shifting more responsibility onto suppliers.

Technology

EDI (electronic data interchange)
Direct link between a manufacturer's database and that of the vendor.

Technology continues to have a significant impact on the supply chain. **EDI (electronic data interchange)** provides a direct link between a manufacturer's database and that of its vendors. In addition, the increased use of personal computers allows customers to communicate directly with their vendors' systems. For example, FedEx customers can order a pickup and track the delivery of their packages through their PCs.

The use of technology, in many cases, provides suppliers with a barrier against competitors. A customer will establish an EDI link with only a few vendors. Potential new vendors have to demonstrate significant improvement in price and/or quality to warrant the additional costs of an added EDI link. Similarly, FedEx's customers would be reluctant to change vendors because it would require an investment in time to learn a new computer system with little or no added benefit.

In addition to EDI, a number of other systems have been developed such as quick response (QR) and efficient consumer response (ECR). In all cases these terms refer to the communication throughout a supply or distribution pipeline. This is a paperless communi-

Campbell uses a system they call Continuous Product Replenishment. At the food retailer's warehouse, Campbell product arrives from the plant to replenish inventory at the same steady rate as the consumer takes it off the shelf. CPR is driven by an electronic ordering system managed by Campbell, freeing the retailer from this task. Steady production that meets predetermined inventory levels results in cost efficiencies across the entire supply chain.

cation between customers and vendors. For several years prior to this, there already had been some improvement in communication through the use of open computer systems using UNIX or UNIX-type software, but EDI, QR, and ECR go far beyond that.

quick response (QR) programs
Just-in-time replenishment system using bar-code scanning and EDI.

Quick response (QR) programs have grown rapidly. A survey by Deloitte & Touche showed that 68 percent of retailers have either implemented or plan to implement QR within two years.[2] Quick response is based on bar-code scanning and EDI. Its intent is to create a just-in-time replenishment system between vendors and retailers.

Virtually all medium and large retail stores use *Universal Product Code (UPC)* bar-code scanning. *Point-of-sale (POS)* scanning at the register also uses *price-look-up (PLU),* as reported by 90 percent of the respondents.

efficient consumer response (ECR)
Strategy for bringing distributors, suppliers, and grocers together using bar-code scanning and EDI.

Efficient consumer response (ECR) is a variation of QR and EDI adopted by the supermarket industry as a business strategy where distributors, suppliers, and grocers work closely together to bring products to consumers. They can use bar-code scanning and EDI. Savings come from reduced supply chain costs and reduced inventory.

A study by Kurt Salmon Associates estimated a potential savings of more than $30 billion.[3] In the dry grocery segment this could cut supply-chain inventory from 104 days to 61 days. Another study by McKinsey estimated that dry grocery consumer prices could be reduced an average of 10.8 percent through industrywide adoption of ECR.[4]

Without ECR, manufacturers push products on the markets by offering low prices on large quantities: A few times a year the manufacturer offers the grocer a low price on a large quantity of product. This is forward buying. The manufacturer then works with the supermarket to offer coupons and incentives to entice customers to buy the product during a promotion. Products not sold during the promotion are then stored in inventory to carry that supermarket until the next manufacturer's promotional deal.

[2] "Quick Response Grows," *Chain Store Age Executive,* May 1993, pp. 158–59.

[3] James Aaron Cooke, "The $30 Billion Promise," *Traffic Management,* December 1993, pp. 57–61.

[4] David B. Jenkins, "Jenkins Leads EDI Effort," *Chain Store Age Executive,* March 1993, p. 147.

ECR focuses on the customers to drive the system, not the manufacturers' deals. Customers pull goods through the store and through the pipeline by their purchases. This permits less inventory throughout the system.

Cooke cites a study that estimated that distributors purchase 80 percent of their merchandise during manufacturers' sales or "deals." They may buy four times per year and fill up their warehouses. Until the industry frees itself from this addiction to deal buying, all the great replenishment techniques will be worthless.[5] Most experts predict that the grocery industry will implement ECR philosophy by the year 2000. All companies are preparing for it.

Wal-Mart's Satellite Network, first installed in 1987 in Bentonville, Arkansas, provides another good example of how technology has imparted the structure of the supply chain. This network supports data, voice, and video and allows real-time sales and inventory information.

Wal-Mart's EDI, shown in the photo, installed in 1990, issues electronic purchase orders and receives electronic invoices from virtually all of Wal-Mart's vendors.

Wal-Mart's Retail Link, installed in 1991, allows vendors to directly access in real-time *point-of-sale (POS)* data. This allows vendors to create better forecasts and better inventory management. The POS data come directly from store cash registers so they reflect activity in real time. E-mail capability is also included for corresponding within the supply system concerning scheduling, payments, and so on. Retail Link also includes the spreadsheet Microsoft Excel for Windows, so that spreadsheet data can be accessed throughout the system.

Using Retail Link and point-of-sale data, arrangements have been made with some large suppliers to make their own decisions about Wal-Mart's purchases from them. They directly access point-of-sale data and create their own purchase orders. Wal-Mart is attempting to implement EDI internationally, but little progress in this area has been made so far.[6]

Shared or Reduced Risk

The cost of developing new products is increasing. With product life cycles becoming shorter, the risk associated with these new products also increases. To reduce their own financial exposure, many companies are requesting that vendors take on an increasing percentage of this risk. Volkswagen's new automotive plant in Brazil epitomizes this sharing of risk with vendors. (See OM in Practice.)

REQUIREMENTS FOR A SUCCESSFUL SUPPLY CHAIN

Several elements are mandatory for the successful implementation of a supply chain management program. These elements often overlap and are often dependent on each other.

---

[5]Cooke, "$30 Billion," pp. 57–61.

[6]"Going beyond EDI: Wal-Mart Cited for Vendor Links," *Chain Store Age Executive,* March 1993, pp. 150–51.

Operations Management in Practice

VOLKSWAGEN BUILDS A NEW KIND OF ASSEMBLY PLANT IN BRAZIL

In November 1996, Volkswagen began operations at its new truck and bus assembly plant in Resende, Brazil. Unlike any other automotive assembly plant in the world, this facility has suppliers' personnel working side by side with VW's workers. This latest advancement in supply chain management is the concept of Jose Ignacio Lopez de Arriortua, who is in charge of purchasing for VW. As a result, only 200 out of a total workforce of 1,000 are VW employees. The remaining workers are employed by the major subcontractors like MWM-Cummins, which produces the engines and transmissions, and Rockwell, which produces the suspension systems.

With this revolutionary approach to automotive assembly, VW hopes to increase both productivity and quality. At the same time, VW is sharing the risk of this new venture with its major suppliers, who have to shoulder a large percentage of the fixed operating costs of the plant. In exchange for this risk, these subcontractors hope to develop and maintain a long and profitable relationship with VW.

Sources: Edvaldo Pereira Lima, "VW's Revolutionary Idea," *Industry Week*, March 17, 1997 and Diana J. Schemo, "Is VW's New Plant Lean, or Just Mean?" *The New York Times*, November 19, 1996.

VW's Carmaking Co-op

Like Tom Sawyer and his fence-painting project, José Ignacio López de Arriortua designed Volkswagen's new truck plant in Resende, Brazil, around work done for Volkswagen's benefit by others. Major suppliers are assigned space in the plant and supply their own workers to add components to trucks rolling down the assembly line. Volkswagen's employees, a minority in the plant, supervise the work and inspect finished trucks; only when they pass are the suppliers paid.

Source: *The New York Times*, November 19, 1996.

Trust

A primary ingredient in the establishment of a successful relationship between vendor and customer is the element of trust. Without trust, none of the other factors is possible. Trust allows vendors to participate and contribute in the new product development cycle.

Long-Term Relationships

With suppliers taking on a strategic role in a company, it is necessary to develop long-term relationships that permit the sharing of a strategic vision. The term often used in establishing

Motorola teaches their supply partners its own TQM techniques, even requiring them to take courses in cycle time reduction, customer satisfaction, etc. at Motorola University. Motorola teams tour supplier plants every two years grading them on how they stack up on quality and timeliness.

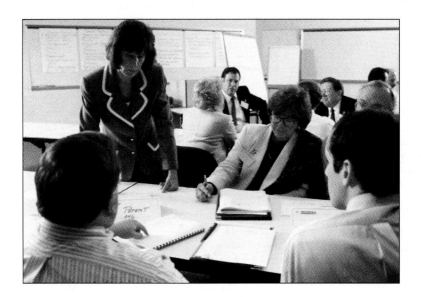

these long-term relationships is *evergreen contracts,* implying they are automatically renewed as long as the vendors perform as agreed.

Information Sharing

Successful supply chain management requires the sharing of information between vendors and customers. This information can include everything from new product design specifications to capacity planning and scheduling, and even access to a customer's entire database.

Individual Strengths of Organizations

If a firm enters into a long-term relationship with a vendor, then it is in that firm's best interest that the vendor remain in business for a long period of time. Thus a good customer will work with a vendor to insure that it is profitable and that it remains financially strong.

The selection of proper vendors is also important. Thus, in addition to financial strengths, each vendor should have some unique operational or engineering strengths with respect to the products it makes and delivers. This permits the firm to incorporate these strengths into its own products, which then provides an added advantage in the marketplace.

The Role of Logistics in the Supply Chain

The continued emphasis on globalization with respect to both suppliers and customers has caused the supply chain to become longer in terms of time and distance. As a consequence, the logistics associated with both the delivery of raw material and components to the company and the delivery of finished goods to its customers have taken on added importance. However, the lengthening of the supply chain runs counter to the firm's need for flexibility to provide customers with a wide variety of products that can be delivered quickly.

Companies have therefore adopted various strategies to compensate for the longer supply chain. For example, companies are locating distribution centers closer to customer markets so they can better serve these markets.

Partnering

Another approach to addressing the issue of a growing supply chain involves the establishment of a strategic alliance or partnership with a firm that specializes in transportation

Operations Management in Practice

TRUCKS KEEP INVENTORIES ROLLING PAST WAREHOUSES TO PRODUCTION LINES

It seems warehouses have grown wheels.

Called "rolling inventories," trucks have become the place of choice for just-in-time stockpiles. Eighteen-wheelers pull up to factory loading docks to deliver parts that go almost immediately onto production lines, bypassing the warehouses.

"Companies now precisely plan their need of inventory so that [intermediate] warehouses aren't needed," says Don Schneider, president of trucking concern Schneider National Inc. and a member of the Chicago Federal Reserve Bank.

To be sure, just-in-time inventory methods aren't new. But as more companies come around to this approach, trucks and railcars have begun to function as warehouses for many producers—adding yet another anomaly to the economic recovery.

The construction of warehouse square footage tumbled nearly 18 percent in 1992 and 9 percent in 1993, even as the economy gained momentum and space in stores and shopping centers grew 6 percent and 12 percent, respectively.

For trucking companies, the trend means new business, but also more demanding customers. Many trucking companies say that in recent years, they've come under increasing pressure to deliver parts within a small window of time. "There are sometimes less than 10-minute lag times," says Larry Mulkey, president of Ryder Dedicated Logistics Inc., a Miami unit of transportation-services company Ryder Systems Inc.

Such use of trucks enables businesses to cut space costs, freeing up capital for investments such as equipment or new employees. "The back room decreases in size because you don't need it to store stockpiles and that means you have more floor space for selling," Mr. Mulkey says.

But a heavy reliance on trucks to keep inventories low isn't without its risks. The General Motors Corp., Toyota Motor Co. joint venture in Fremont, California, once had to shut down its production line because a just-in-time delivery truck broke down on the highway.

Ken Simonson, chief economist of the American Trucking Associations, says trucking for just-in-time orders generally works better in uncongested regions of the country.

But trucking companies have come a long way in eliminating delivery glitches. Mr. Schneider of Schneider National boasts that not one load was late because of the icy, wintry weather that hit much of the nation recently.

Technology enables trucking companies and their clients to track a load's progress from minute to minute. If a problem comes up, another truck can be dispatched immediately to pick up the load. Trucks also have become more reliable mechanically.

Source: Lucinda Harper, "Trucks Keep Inventories Rolling Past Warehouses to Production Lines," *The Wall Street Journal*, February 7, 1994, p. A7A. Reprinted by permission of *The Wall Street Journal* © 1994 Dow Jones & Co., Inc. All rights reserved worldwide.

or logistics. For example, L.L. Bean, a well-known mail order firm specializing in outdoor equipment and clothes, has established such a partnership with FedEx. As a result, FedEx employees, who are physically located on a full-time basis at the L.L. Bean distribution facility in Freeport, Maine, handle all of the outbound shipments to L.L. Bean's customers (including the shipment of some packages by UPS).

An alternative approach to using a logistics partner is for a firm to store finished goods at the logistics partner's hub or distribution center. Establishing an inventory at this point in the distribution channel will significantly reduce the delivery time of critical products. As an illustration, some companies that produce medical products for implants may maintain a supply of their products at FedEx's hub in Memphis, Tennessee. Requests for these products can, in many cases, be delivered the same day or, at most, the next morning, to any location in the United States. The Limited, a chain of high-fashion boutiques, similarly maintains an inventory of high-usage items at FedEx's distribution center in Memphis. Such an arrangement allows retail operations to restock the following day with items that have sold out. (See OM in Practice on Trucks Keep Inventories Rolling Past Warehouses for another role for a logistics partner.)

In-Transit Inventory Costs

The stretching of the supply chain to all corners of the globe has caused managers to take a closer look at the various costs associated with the delivery of products. These costs are often

EXHIBIT 11.4

The Trade-Off between Transportation Costs and the Cost of Capital with Respect to the Shipment of Products

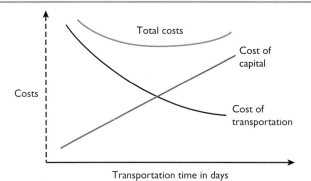

in-transit inventory costs
Combination of transportation costs and carrying costs associated with delivery of products.

referred to as **in-transit inventory costs** and are usually associated with delivery of raw material and components that are in-bound to the plant. The reason for this is that most products are sold FOB at the vendor's plant. (FOB stands for freight-on-board which is the point at which ownership and title to the goods are transferred from the supplier to the customer.)

In deciding which is the most economical mode of transportation to use, a manager needs to take into consideration two cost elements. These are the actual costs of transportation and the in-transit inventory carrying costs of product while in transit. These carrying costs consist primarily of the cost of the capital tied up when items are purchased at the vendor's plant, but are not available for use until they arrive at the firm's plant. (For a more detailed definition of the cost of capital, see Chapter 14.) Typically, the slower the mode of transportation, the lower the transportation costs, the longer the shipment time, and thus the higher the carrying cost. The trade-off between these two costs is shown in Exhibit 11.4.

The total annual costs associated with transporting products from a vendor's plant are:

Total costs = Transportation costs + In-transit inventory carrying costs + Purchase costs

$$TC = DM + (X/365)iDC + DC$$

where

$D =$ Annual demand
$M =$ Transportation cost per unit
$X =$ Transportation time in days
$i =$ Annual cost of capital
$C =$ Unit cost per item

Example

A company located in Hartford, Connecticut, has agreed to purchase an item from a manufacturer in Vancouver, British Columbia, Canada. The purchasing agent in Hartford has identified two alternative methods for shipping the item: truck or cargo ship. If the item is shipped by truck it will take 14 days at a cost of $3 per unit to cross the continent and clear customs. A cargo ship will take 45 days through the Panama Canal, but the transportation cost will only be $1.50 per unit. The company expects to buy 2,000 units per year at a cost of $150 per unit. The in-transit carrying cost of inventory is estimated to be 20 percent per annum. Which mode of transportation should the purchasing agent select?

Solution

A summary of the relevant costs for each mode of transportation are as follows:

	Mode 1 (truck)	Mode 2 (ship)
Number of days in transit (X):	14	45
Transportation cost per unit (M):	$3.00	$1.50

Additional data:

In-transit carrying cost (i):	20% per annum
Annual demand (D):	2,000 units
Unit cost (C):	$150.00

$$TC_1 = DM_1 \qquad + (X_1/365)iDC$$
$$TC_1 = (2,000)(3.00) + (14/365)(0.20)(2,000)(150)$$
$$TC_1 = 6,000 \qquad + 2,301.37$$
$$TC_1 = \$8,301.37$$

$$TC_2 = DM_2 \qquad + (X_2/365)iDC$$
$$TC_2 = (2,000)(1.50) + (45/365)(0.20)(2,000)(150)$$
$$TC_2 = 3,000 \qquad + 7,397.26$$
$$TC_2 = \$10,397.26$$

Based on this analysis, the more economical mode of transportation is by truck, even though the actual transportation cost per unit is twice that of sending the items by ship. Note that when evaluating alternative modes of transportation from the same vendor, the purchase cost remains the same and, for simplicity, is not included in the analysis.

DISINTERMEDIATION

disintermediation
Trend to reduce many of the steps in the supply chain.

Disintermediation is a term coined by futurist Stan Davis.[7] It refers to the growing trend of companies and organizations to try to get closer to both suppliers and customers by eliminating many of the intermediate steps that currently exist in the supply chain.

For example, Wal-Mart, as part of its strategy, built large regional distribution warehouses to store items for restocking its retail operations. As a result, significant capital was tied up in both facilities and inventory. Subsequently, Wal-Mart developed the concept of *cross-docking.* By properly scheduling the arrival of vendor trucks at the receiving dock, Wal-Mart causes items to be unloaded from these trucks and immediately carried across to trucks on the shipping dock that are out-bound for its retail operations. With the introduction of cross-docking, Wal-Mart was able to increase the number of its retail outlets without increasing the number or size of its distribution facilities.

The next step in Wal-Mart's disintermediation process, as we saw earlier in this chapter, was to allow vendors direct, online access to their retail sales data through a satellite network. With this system, vendors decide how much to ship to Wal-Mart, and in many cases, these products are shipped directly to retail operations, thereby totally bypassing distribution centers.

Another example of disintermediation is in the airline industry. Here airlines are increasing their efforts to work directly with customers rather than through travel agents in order to save commission fees. This is being accomplished through airline websites which feature online ticketing instructions and through the increasing use of electronic ticketing.

When disintermediation does take place, there needs to be close coordination and planning among the different firms in the supply chain that are affected.

JIT II®

JIT II®, developed by the Bose Corp. in 1987, is a good example of disintermediation and is now being adopted by a growing number of companies. (The Bose Corp., as stated in the first chapter, produces high-end stereo equipment.) The objective of JIT II® is for the vendor and customer to work much closer together, thereby eliminating many of the intermediate

---

[7]Stanley Davis, *Future Perfect* (Reading, MA: Addison-Wesley, 1987).

steps that now exist. To accomplish this, a vendor employee is provided with physical office space within the purchasing function of the customer. This approach eliminates the need for a buyer for the customer and a salesperson for the vendor.

This vendor representative has full access to the customer's database and can therefore translate the customer's purchase orders directly into orders for his or her company. This individual also participates in the customer's new product design process, offering suggestions for improving products performance and/or reducing costs. The two elements for successfully implementing JIT II® are (*a*) the physical presence of the vendor's representative inside the customer's manufacturing facility and, at the same time, (*b*) the ability to provide the direct data linkage between the customer's planning function and the vendor's manufacturing facility.

CONCLUSION

In today's highly competitive environment, companies are depending more on their suppliers. The reasons for doing so include: (*a*) increased emphasis on core competencies, (*b*) increased need for flexibility, and (*c*) a desire to share risk associated with new product development. As a consequence, the role of the supplier has shifted from being purely transactional, based on low cost, to being a partner that participates in strategic decisions of the firm. This dramatic shift in the role of the supplier has caused companies to establish long-term relationships with a smaller number of suppliers than was previously the case.

Increased competition has also forced companies to look to the four corners of the globe for suppliers that can meet their needs. As a result, the logistics and associated costs of transporting goods over great distances has become a major factor in vendor selection.

However, while the use of international vendors has caused the supply chain to become longer in many cases, there is a trend toward disintermediation, which eliminates many of the intermediate stages in the overall supply chain.

KEY TERMS

disintermediation   p. 393
EDI (electronic data interchange)   p. 386
efficient customer response (ECR)   p. 387
inbound   p. 385

in-transit inventory costs   p. 392
outbound   p. 385
quick response (QR) programs   p. 387
supply chain   p. 382

REVIEW AND DISCUSSION QUESTIONS

1. What are the advantages and disadvantages to a firm having a small number of suppliers?
2. Supply chain management as presented in this chapter pertains primarily to goods. What would be the different steps or elements in a supply chain for a service? Give an example.
3. How has technology accelerated the trend toward disintermediation?
4. What are the main differences between having a vendor's employees working in your manufacturing operation and you hiring your own employees to do the same work?
5. Identify all of the steps in the supply chain for a hamburger that you buy at McDonald's. How might this supply chain differ for a McDonald's located in a developing country?

 INTERNET UPDATE

Conduct a search on the Internet to identify the various types of software programs that are being used by companies to facilitate the management of their supply chains. Describe at least two of these programs in detail. Suggested key words to assist you in your search are SUPPLY, CHAIN, and SOFTWARE.

PROBLEMS

1. An automobile company in Ohio currently purchases 100,000 tires a year from a manufacturer located 50 miles from its assembly plant. The price per tire is $40. Because of the close proximity of the two plants, the vendor delivers these tires free of charge. The purchasing agent has recently been approached by a tire manufacturer in Asia who has agreed to provide these tires for $35 each. Through inquiries, the purchasing agent has determined that it will cost an additional $4.50 per tire to ship the tires from Asia to the plant in Ohio. In addition, it will take approximately six weeks for a shipment to arrive. Currently the cost of capital for the automobile company is 20 percent per year. Which vendor should the purchasing agent buy tires from?

2. A computer company in the greater Boston area currently buys electronic modules at a price of $26 per unit from a vendor located in Tijuana, Mexico. The firm's buyer is currently evaluating two alternative modes for transporting these modules. The first way is overland on a trailer truck. The cost with this method is $2.50 per module and takes approximately two weeks. The second way is to ship the modules air freight, which takes only two days to deliver at a cost of $3 per unit. Currently the computer maker is buying 25,000 modules per year. The cost of capital for the firm is estimated at 18 percent per year. Which mode of transportation do you recommend?

3. As the purchasing agent for a small company located in central France, Laurence Garreau has recently sent out a request for proposal for a small motor used in a subassembly that her firm manufactures for the automobile industry. The annual requirement for this motor is 25,000 units, and she has estimated the cost of in-transit inventory to be 25 percent per year.

    The first quotation she receives is from a company in Southeast Asia. The unit price per motor from this firm is 45 FF (French francs). In addition, the transportation cost per unit is 4 FF. The transit time from Southeast Asia, using an ocean freighter, is estimated to be 50 days in total. The second quotation she receives is from a company in Mexico that is very anxious to do business in Europe. The unit price per motor from this company is 43 FF, and the transportation cost per unit is 6,5 FF, but it will only take 10 days in total to deliver the motors because the company will be using air freight. (Note: In Europe, a comma is used instead of a decimal point to indicate less than a whole unit.)

    a. Evaluate each of these two proposals to determine which is the most economical alternative. What is your recommendation? (Be specific and show all of your calculations.)

    b. What factors, in addition to cost, need to be taken into consideration in arriving at a final decision as to which supplier to use?

SELECTED BIBLIOGRAPHY

Bowersox, Donald J., and David J. Closs. *Logistical Management: The Integrated Supply Chain Process.* New York: McGraw-Hill, 1996.

Cooke, James A. "The $30 Billion." *Traffic Management,* December 1993, pp. 57–61.

Coyle, J. J.; E. J. Bardi; and C. John Langley Jr. *The Management of Business Logistics.* 6th ed. Minneapolis/St. Paul, MN: West, 1996.

Davis, Stanley M. *Future Perfect.* Reading, MA: Addison-Wesley, 1987.

Dixon, Lance E. *JIT II*®. Bose Corporation.

Fabey, Michael. "Time Is Money: Seamless Logistics Are in Demand." *World Trade,* July 1997, pp. 53–54.

"Going Beyond EDI: Wal-Mart Cited for Vendor Links." *Chain Store Age Executive,* March 1993, pp. 150–51.

Jenkins, David B. "Jenkins Leads EDI Effort." *Chain Store Age Executive,* March 1993, p. 147.

Leenders, Michiel R., and Harold E. Fearon. *Purchasing and Supply Management.* 11th ed. Burr Ridge, IL: Irwin/McGraw-Hill, 1997.

Lima, Edvaldo Pereira. "VW's Revolutionary Idea." *Industry Week,* March 17, 1997.

Reitman, Valerie. *The Wall Street Journal,* May 8, 1997, p. A1.

Schemo, Diana J. "Is VW's New Plant Lean, or Just Mean?" *The New York Times,* November 19, 1996.

JUST-IN-TIME SYSTEMS

Chapter Objectives

- Introduce the underlying concepts of just-in-time (JIT) and the Japanese approach to improving productivity.

- Identify the differences between Japanese companies and U.S. firms with respect to implementing JIT, and explore why these differences exist.

- Identify the various elements that need to be included to successfully implement JIT within an organization.

- Illustrate how many JIT concepts have been implemented in services.

The 100 Yen Sushi House is no ordinary sushi restaurant. It is the ultimate showcase of Japanese productivity. As we entered the shop, there was a chorus of *"iratsai,"* a welcome from everyone working in the shop—cooks, waitresses, the owner, and the owner's children. The house features an ellipsoid-shaped serving area in the middle of the room, where three or four cooks were busily preparing sushi. Perhaps 30 stools surrounded the serving area. We took seats at the counters and were promptly served with a cup of "misoshiru," which is a bean paste soup, a pair of chopsticks, a cup of green tea, a tiny plate to make our own sauce, and a small china piece to hold the chopsticks. So far, the service was average for any sushi house. Then, I noticed something special. There was a conveyor belt going around the ellipsoid service area, like a toy train track. On it I saw a train of plates of

sushi. You can find any kind of sushi that you can think of—from the cheapest seaweed or octopus kind to the expensive raw salmon or shrimp dishes. The price is uniform, however, 100 yen per plate. On closer examination, while my eyes were racing to keep up with the speed of the traveling plates, I found that a cheap seaweed plate had four pieces, while the more expensive raw salmon dish had only two pieces.

I saw a man with eight plates all stacked up neatly. As he got up to leave, the cashier looked over and said, "800 yen, please." The cashier had no cash register, since she could simply count the number of plates and then multiply by 100 yen. As the customer was leaving, once again we heard a chorus of *"Arigato Gosaimas"* (thank you), from all the workers.

The owner's daily operation is based on a careful analysis of information. The owner has a complete summary of demand information about different types of sushi plates, and thus he knows exactly how many of each type of sushi plates he should prepare and when. Furthermore, the whole operation is based on the repetitive manufacturing principle with appropriate just-in-time and quality control systems. For example, the store has a very limited refrigerator capacity (we could see several whole fish or octopus in the glassed chambers right in front of our counter). Thus, the store uses the just-in-time inventory control system. Instead of increasing the refrigeration capacity by purchasing new refrigeration systems, the company has an agreement with the fish vendor to deliver fresh fish several times a day so that materials arrive just in time to be used for sushi making. Therefore, the inventory cost is minimum.

In the just-in-time operation system, the safety stock principle is turned upside down. In other words, the safety stock is deliberately removed gradually, to uncover problems and their possible solutions. The available floor space is for workers and their necessary equipment but not for holding inventory. In the 100 Yen Sushi House, workers and their equipment are positioned so close that sushi making is passed on hand to hand rather than as independent operations. The absence of walls of inventory allows the owner and workers to be involved in the total operation, from greeting the customer to serving what is ordered. Their tasks are tightly interrelated and everyone rushes to a problem spot to prevent the cascading effect of the problem throughout the work process.

The 100 Yen Sushi House is a labor-intensive operation, which is based mostly on simplicity and common sense rather than high technology, contrary to American perceptions. I was very impressed. As I finished my fifth plate, I saw the same octopus sushi plate going around for about the thirtieth time. Perhaps I had discovered the pitfall of the system. So I asked the owner how he takes care of the sanitary problems when a sushi plate goes around all day long, until an unfortunate customer eats it and perhaps gets food poisoning. He bowed with an apologetic smile and said, "Well, sir, we never let our sushi plates go unsold longer than about 30 minutes." Then he scratched his head and said, "Whenever one of our employees takes a break, he or she can take off unsold plates of sushi and either eat them or throw them away. We are very serious about our sushi quality." As we laughed, he laughed, along with a 90-degree bow.   ∎

Source: Sang M. Lee, "Japanese Management and the 100 Yen Sushi House," *Operations Management Review* 1, no. 2 (Winter 1983), pp. 45–48.

JIT Logic

JIT (just-in-time)
A coordinated approach that continuously reduces inventories while also improving quality.

JIT (just-in-time) is an integrated set of activities designed to achieve high-volume production using minimal inventories of raw materials, work in process, and finished goods. Parts arrive at the next workstation "just in time" and are completed and move through the operation quickly. Just-in-time is also based on the logic that nothing will be produced until it is needed. Exhibit 12.1 illustrates the process. Need is created by the product being pulled toward the user. When an item is sold, in theory, the market pulls a replacement from the last position in the system—final assembly in this case. This triggers an order to the factory production line where a worker then pulls another unit from an upstream station in the flow to replace the unit taken. This upstream station then pulls from the next station further upstream and so on back to the release of raw materials. To enable this pull process to work smoothly, JIT demands high levels of quality at each stage of the process, strong vendor relations, and a fairly predictable demand for the end product.

JIT can be viewed colloquially as "big JIT" and "little JIT." Big JIT (often termed lean production[1]) is the philosophy of operations management that seeks to eliminate waste in all aspects of a firm's production activities: human relations, supplier relations, technology, and the management of materials and inventories. Little JIT focuses more narrowly on scheduling goods inventories and providing service resources where and when needed. For example, companies such as Manpower Temporary Services and Pizza Hut essentially use

[1]Paul H. Zipkin, "Does Manufacturing Need a JIT Revolution?" *Harvard Business Review* (January–February 1991), p. 41.

EXHIBIT 12.1

Pull System

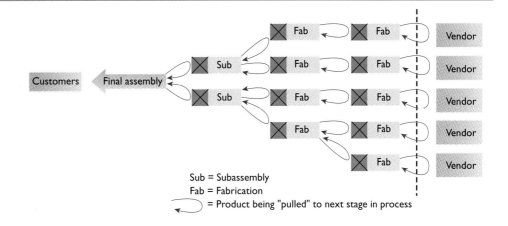

Sub = Subassembly
Fab = Fabrication

= Product being "pulled" to next stage in process

pull signals to fill orders for replacement workers or Sicilian pizzas, respectively. However, they do not necessarily integrate operations around other aspects of the JIT philosophy.

THE JAPANESE APPROACH TO PRODUCTIVITY[2]

To fully appreciate the elements of Big JIT, it is useful to review the history and philosophy of its application in Japan. The ability of Japanese manufacturers to compete in high-quality, low-cost production which was widely publicized in the 1970s and early 1980s (see Exhibits 12.2 and 12.3) still holds despite their current economic problems. Indeed, the Japanese retain the market dominance in televisions, VCRs, cameras, watches, motorcycles, and shipbuilding that they established over 20 years ago—in large part due to JIT.

Many people believe these accomplishments are attributable to cultural differences. They envision the Japanese dedicating their lives to their companies and working long hours for substandard wages, which would be unthinkable in America. The evidence, however, is contrary to these distorted notions. Consider the following: In 1977, a Japanese company named Matsushita purchased a television plant in Chicago from a U.S. company. In the purchase contract, Matsushita agreed that all the hourly personnel would be retrained. Two years later, they still had essentially the same 1,000 hourly employees and had managed to reduce the indirect staff by 50 percent (see Exhibit 12.4). Yet, during that period, daily production had doubled. The quality, as measured by the number of defects per 100 TV sets built, improved 40-fold. Outside quality indicators also improved. Where the U.S. company (Motorola) had spent an average amount of $16 million a year on warranty costs, Matsushita's expenditures were $2 million. (That's for twice as many TV sets, so it's really a 16-to-1 ratio.) These are big differences—differences achieved here in the United States with American workers. The issue is, how do the Japanese do this and what can we learn from them?

As a starting point, it's important to understand that the Japanese, as a nation, have had one fundamental economic goal since 1945: full employment through industrialization. The strategy employed to achieve this goal called for obtaining market dominance in very select product areas. They very carefully chose those industries in which they believed they could become dominant and concentrated on them, rather than diluting their efforts over a broader spectrum.

---

[2]Adapted from Kenneth A. Wantuck, "The Japanese Approach to Productivity," Southfield, MI: Bendix Corporation, 1983.

EXHIBIT 12.2

1977 Hertz Repair Study

Model	Repairs per 100 Vehicles
Ford	326
Chevrolet	425
Pinto	306
Toyota	55

This study, undertaken by Hertz, was the first widely publicized evidence of the Japanese quality superiority in automobiles.

EXHIBIT 12.3

Comparative U.S. and Japanese Inventory Turnover Rates for 15 Industries

* Inventory turnover of Japanese firms in this industry is 191% of that of U.S. firms.
Source: Booz, Allen & Hamilton Survey of 1,500 Companies, 1981.

EXHIBIT 12.4

Quasar Plant Productivity

	Under Motorola	Under Matsushita*
Direct labor employees	1,000	1,000†
Indirect employees	600	300
Total employees	1,600	1,300
Daily production	1,000	2,000
Defect rate per 100 TV sets	160	4
Annual warranty cost ($ millions)	$16	$2

* 2 years later.
† Same people.

The tactics of the Japanese were threefold: (*a*) They imported their technology. (The entire Japanese semiconductor industry was built around a $25,000 purchase from Texas Instruments for the rights to the basic semiconductor process.) Instead of reinventing the wheel, they avoided major R&D expenditures and the associated risks, then negotiated license agreements to make successful, workable new products. (*b*) They concentrated their ingenuity on the factory to achieve high productivity and low unit cost. The best engineering talent available was directed to the shop floor, instead of the product design department. (*c*) Finally, they embarked on a drive to improve product quality and reliability to the highest possible levels, to give their customers product reliability that competitors were not able to supply.

The implementation of these tactics by the Japanese was governed by two fundamental concepts (most of us agree with these concepts in principle, but the difference is the degree to which the Japanese practice them):

eliminate waste
Eliminate everything not essential to production, including safety stocks, waiting times, and extra labor.

1. They are firm believers that in every way, shape, and form you must **eliminate waste.**

2. They have a great respect for people.

Elimination of Waste

When the Japanese talk about waste, the definition given by Fujio Cho, from the Toyota Motor Company, probably states it as well as anyone. He calls it "anything other than the *minimum* amount of equipment, materials, parts, and workers (working time) which are *absolutely essential* to production." That means no surplus, no safety stock. That means nothing is banked for future use. If you can't use it now you don't make it now because that is considered waste. There are seven basic elements under this concept:

1. Focused factory networks.
2. Group technology.
3. *Jidoka*—quality at the source.
4. Just-in-time production.
5. Uniform plant loading.
6. Kanban production control system.
7. Minimized setup times.

focused factory networks
Groups of small plants, each highly specialized in products they manufacture.

Focused Factory Networks   The first element is **focused factory networks.** Instead of building a large manufacturing plant that does everything (i.e., a highly vertically integrated facility), the Japanese build small plants that are highly specialized. There are several reasons for doing this. First, it's very difficult to manage a large installation; the bigger it gets the more bureaucratic it gets. The Japanese style of management does not lend itself to this kind of environment.

Second, when a plant is specifically designed for one purpose it can be constructed and operated more economically than its universal counterpart. It's comparable to buying a special machine tool to do a very specific job instead of trying to adapt a general purpose tool. Fewer than 750 plants in Japan have as many as 1,000 or more employees. The bulk of them, some 60,000 plants, have between 30 and 1,000 workers and over 180,000 have fewer than 30 employees. When we talk about the Japanese approach to productivity and the impressive things they're doing, we're talking primarily about the middle group, in which most of their model manufacturing plants are located.

Two illustrative examples have been cited by the Ford Motor Company: The Escort automobile needed a transaxle, which was going to require a $300 million expansion at the Ford plant in Batavia, Ohio. Ford asked the Japanese for an equivalent quotation and Tokyo–Kogyo offered to construct a brand-new plant with the same rate of output at a competitive unit price for $100 million, a one-third ratio. A second example relates to Ford's Valencia engine plant, which produces two engines per employee per day, and requires 900,000 square feet of floor space. An almost identical engine is produced by the Toyota Motor Company in Japan, where they make nine engines per employee per day in a plant that has only 300,000 square feet of space. The issue is not only productivity per person but also a much lower capital investment to achieve this manufacturing capability.

group technology
Clustering dissimilar machines and operations in one area of the plant to manufacture one family of products.

Group Technology   Inside the plant the Japanese employ a technique called **group technology.** Group technology is nothing new to America; it was invented here, like so many of the techniques the Japanese successfully employ, but only relatively recently has been practiced widely in the United States. A simplified diagram of the technique is shown in Exhibit 12.5. The lower portion shows the way we operate our plants today. Most companies process a job and send it from department to department because that's the way our plants are organized (sheetmetal department, grinding department, etc.). Each machine in those departments is usually staffed by a worker who specializes in that function. Getting a job through a shop can be a long and complicated process because there's a lot of waiting time and moving time involved (usually between 90 percent and 95 percent of the total processing time).

EXHIBIT 12.5

Group Technology versus Departmental Specialty

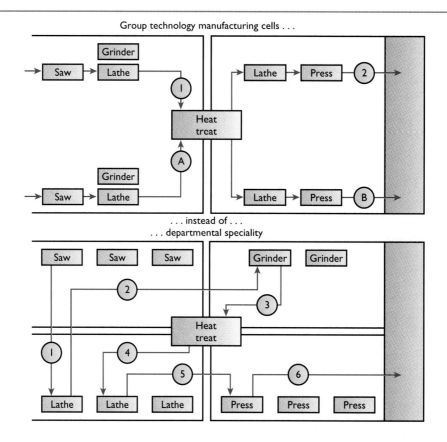

The Japanese, on the other hand, consider all the operations required to make a part and try to group those machines together. The upper part of Exhibit 12.5 shows clusters of dissimilar machines designed to be work centers for given parts or families of parts. One operator runs all three machines shown in the upper-left corner, increasing the utility of the individual operator and eliminating the move and queue time between operations in a given cluster. Thus, not only does productivity go up but the work-in-process (WIP) inventory also comes down dramatically.

To achieve this, people have to be flexible; to be flexible, people must identify with their companies, have a high degree of job security, and undergo continuous training.

Jidoka—Quality at the Source

Jidoka

Japanese concept focusing on controlling the quality of a product at its source.

When management demonstrates a high degree of confidence in people, it is possible to implement a quality concept that the Japanese call **Jidoka.** The word means "Stop everything when something goes wrong." It can be thought of as controlling quality at the source. (In the photo, air bag crash sensors are being inspected by workers at the TRW plant in

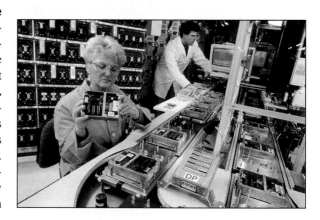

Marshall, Illinois.) Instead of using inspectors to find the problems that somebody else may have created, the worker in a Japanese factory becomes his or her own inspector. This concept was developed by Taiichi Ohno, who was vice president of manufacturing for Toyota Motor Company in the early 1950s.

Ohno was convinced that one of the big problems faced by Toyota was bringing quality levels up to the necessary standards that would permit Toyota to penetrate the world automotive market. He felt that there was too much looking over each other's shoulders; he wanted every individual to be personally responsible for the quality of the product or component that he or she produced.

MANAGEMENT
ENGINEERING

Ohno determined that the best thing to do was to give each person only one part to work on at a time so that under no circumstances would he or she be able to bury or hide problems by working on other parts. Jidoka push buttons were installed on the assembly lines. If anything went wrong—if a worker found a defective part, if he or she could not keep up with production, if production was going too fast according to the pace that was set for the day, or if he or she found a safety hazard—that worker was obligated to push the button. When the button was pushed, a light flashed, a bell rang, and the entire assembly line came to a grinding halt. People descended on the spot where the light was flashing. It was something like a volunteer fire department: People came from the industrial engineering department, from management, from everywhere to respond to that particular alarm, and they fixed the problem on the spot. Meanwhile, the workers polished their machines, swept the floor, or did whatever else they could to keep busy, but the line didn't move until the problem was fixed.

Jidoka also encompasses automated inspection, sometimes called *autonomation*. Just like automation and robotics, the Japanese believe that wherever possible inspection should be done by a machine, because it's faster and more accurate. However, the inspection step is a part of the production process. It therefore does not involve a separate location or person to perform it, and automatically shuts off a machine when a problem arises. This prevents the mass production of defective parts.

Line shutdowns in Japan are encouraged to protect quality and because management has confidence in the individual worker. No one likes to see a line stopped, but Ohno suggests that a day without a single Jidoka drill can mean people aren't being careful enough.

Just-in-Time Production   The Japanese system is based on a fundamental concept called just-in-time production. It requires the production of precisely the necessary units in the necessary quantities at the necessary time, with the objective of achieving plus or minus *zero* performance to schedule. It means that producing one extra piece is just as bad as being one piece short. In fact, anything over the minimum amount necessary is viewed as waste, since effort and material expended for something not needed now cannot be utilized now. (Later requirements are handled later.) That's another unique idea for American managers, since a measure of good performance in the United States has always been to meet or exceed the schedule. It is a most difficult concept for American manufacturing management to accept because it is contrary to current practice in many firms, which is to stock extra material just in case something goes wrong. Exhibit 12.6 highlights what just-in-time is, what it does, what it requires, and what it assumes.

The just-in-time concept applies primarily to a repetitive manufacturing process. It does not necessarily require large volumes, but is restricted to those operations that produce the same parts over and over again. Ideally, the finished product would be repetitive in nature. However, as a Westinghouse team learned during a visit to Mitsubishi Inazawa, a Japanese elevator manufacturer, the repetitive segments of the business may only appear several levels down in the product structure. Even so, applying just-in-time concepts to a portion of the business produced significant improvements for them.

EXHIBIT 12.6

Just-In-Time

What It Is	What It Does
• Management philosophy • "Pull" system through the plant	• Attacks waste (time, inventory, scrap) • Exposes problems and bottlenecks • Achieves streamlined production
What It Requires	**What It Assumes**
• Employee participation • Industrial engineering/basics • Continuing improvement • Total quality control • Small lot sizes	• Stable environment

Source: Adapted from Chris Gopal (of Price Waterhouse), "Notes on JIT."

EXHIBIT 12.7

Inventory Hides Problems

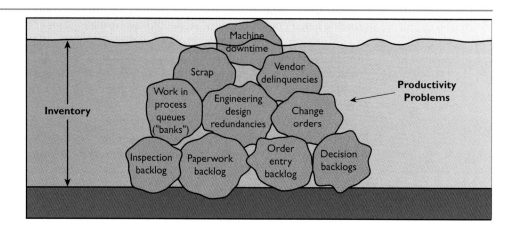

Under just-in-time, the ideal lot size is *one piece*. The Japanese view the manufacturing process as a giant network of interconnected work centers, where the perfect arrangement would be to have each worker complete his or her task on a part and pass it directly to the next worker just as that person was ready for another piece. The idea is to drive all queues toward zero in order to:

• Minimize inventory investment.
• Shorten production lead times.
• React faster to demand changes.
• Uncover any quality problems.

Exhibit 12.7 is an illustration that the Japanese use to depict the last idea. They look on the water level in a pond as inventory and the rocks as problems that might occur in a shop. A lot of water in the pond hides the problems. Management assumes everything is fine. Invariably, the water level drops at the worst possible time, such as during an economic downturn. Management must then address the problems without the necessary resources to solve them. The Japanese say it is better to force the water level down on purpose (especially in good times), expose the problems, and fix them now, before they cause trouble.

The zeal with which the Japanese work to reduce inventories is incredible. To begin with, inventory is viewed as a negative, not as an asset. According to Toyota, "The value of inventory is disavowed." Auto air conditioner manufacturer Nippondenso's attitude is even more severe: inventory is "the root of all evil." Almost universally, the Japanese see inventory as a deterrent to product quality. Finally, since the shop floor is programmed to have very little inventory, the slightest aberration in the process that results in extra parts is readily visible and serves as a red flag to which an immediate response is required.

Because it is impossible to have every worker in a complex manufacturing process adjacent to one another, and since the network also includes outside suppliers, the Japanese recognize that the system must allow for some transit time between centers. However, transfer quantities are kept as small as possible. Typical internal lot sizes are one tenth of a day's production, vendors deliver their products several times a day to their customers, and constant pressure is exerted to reduce the number of lots in the system.

Just-in-time production makes no allowances for contingencies. Every piece is expected to be correct when received. Every machine is expected to be available when needed to produce parts. Every delivery commitment is expected to be honored at the precise time it is scheduled. Consequently, the Japanese place heavy emphasis on quality, preventive maintenance, and mutual trust among all participants in the manufacturing enterprise. The process is gospel and everyone conscientiously adheres to it.

Uniform Plant Loading To properly incorporate the just-in time production concept, it is necessary that production flow as smoothly as possible in the shop. The starting point is what the Japanese call *uniform plant loading*. Its objective is to dampen the reaction waves that normally occur in response to schedule variations. For example, when a significant change is made in final assembly, it creates changes in the requirements in the feeder operations, which are usually amplified because of lot sizing rules, setups, queues, and waiting time. By the time the impact of the change is felt at the start of the supply chain, a 10 percent change at assembly could easily translate into a 100 percent change at the beginning of the operation.

The Japanese say that the only way to eliminate that problem is to make the perturbations at the end as small as possible so that we only get ripples going through the shop, not shock waves. Japanese companies accomplish this by setting up a firm monthly production plan during which the output rate is frozen. Most U.S. manufacturers have been trying to achieve that for years, without success, because they've tried to freeze a specific, sequential configuration. The Japanese circumvent this issue by planning to build the same mix of products every day, even if the total quantities are small. For example if they're only building a hundred pieces a month, they'll build five each day. Because they expect to build some quantity of everything that's on the schedule daily, they always have a total mix that is available to respond to variations in demand.

Going even further, they'll take those five units and intermix them on the assembly line. An example of how Toyota would do this is shown in Exhibit 12.8. Let us assume that three kinds of vehicles are being made in an assembly plant: sedans, hardtops, and station wagons.

EXHIBIT 12.8

Toyota Example of Mixed-Model Production Cycle in a Japanese Assembly Plant

Model	Monthly Quantity	Daily Quantity	Cycle Time (minutes)
Sedan	5,000	250	2
Hardtop	2,500	125	4
Wagon	2,500	125	4

Sequence: Sedan, hardtop, sedan, wagon, sedan, hardtop, sedan, wagon, etc.

The monthly rates shown are then reduced to daily quantities (presuming a 20-day month) of 250, 125, and 125, respectively. From this, the Japanese compute the necessary cycle times. *Cycle time* in Japan is the period of time between two identical units coming off the production line. The Japanese use this figure to adjust their resources to produce precisely the quantity that's needed—no more, no less.

The Japanese do not concern themselves with achieving the rated speeds of their equipment. In American shops, a given machine is rated at 1,000 pieces per hour so if we need 5,000 pieces we run it five hours to obtain this month's requirement. The Japanese produce only the needed quantity each day, as required. To them, cycle time is the driver that defines how they are to assemble their resources to meet this month's production. If the rate for next month changes, the resources are reconfigured.

Kanban Production Control System   The Kanban approach calls for a control system that is simple and self-regulating and provides good management visibility. The majority of factories in Japan don't use Kanban. Kanban is a Toyota Motor Company system, not a generic Japanese one. However, many companies in both the United States and Japan use pull systems with other types of signaling devices. The shop floor/vendor release and control system is called *Kanban* (kahn-bahn), from the Japanese word meaning *card*. It is a paperless system, using dedicated containers and recycling traveling requisitions/cards, which is quite different from our old, manual shop-packet systems. This is referred to as a **Kanban pull system,** because the authority to produce or supply comes from downstream operations. While work centers and vendors plan their work based on schedules, they execute based on Kanbans, which are completely manual.

There are two types of Kanban cards. The production Kanban authorizes the manufacturing of a container of material. The withdrawal Kanban authorizes the withdrawal and movement of that container. The number of pieces in a container never varies for a given part number.

When production rates change, containers are added to or deleted from the system, according to a simple formula. The idea of safety stock is included in the basic calculation but is limited to 10 percent of a single day's demand. This gives the theoretical number of Kanban/containers required. In practice, efforts are made to reduce the number in circulation to keep inventories to a minimum.

The flow of Kanban cards between two work centers is shown in Exhibit 12.9. The machining center shown is making two parts, A and B, which are stored in standard containers next to the work center. When the assembly line starts to use Part A from a full container, a worker takes the withdrawal Kanban from the container and travels to the machining center storage area. He or she finds a container of Part A, removes the production Kanban, and replaces it with the withdrawal Kanban card, which authorizes him or her to move the container. The freed production Kanban is then placed in a rack by the machining center as a work authorization for another lot of material. Parts are manufactured in the order in which cards are placed on the rack (the Japanese call this the Kanban hanging),

Kanban pull system
Manual, self-regulating system for controlling the flow of material. Workers produce product only when the Kanban ahead of them is empty, thereby creating a "pull" system through the factory.

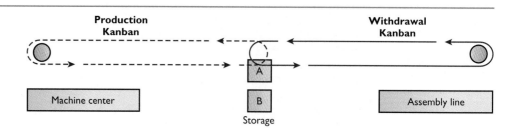

EXHIBIT 12.9

Flow of Two Kanbans

Production Kanban

Withdrawal Kanban

Machine center

Storage

Assembly line

which makes the set of cards in the rack a dispatch list. Many firms use withdrawal cards only. Under the simplest form of one-card system, the worker at the assembly line (or more likely a material handler) walks to the machine center with an empty container and a withdrawal Kanban. He or she would then place the empty container at a designated spot, attach the withdrawal card to a filled container, and carry it back to the assembly line. The worker at the machining center would know that a refill is required. This type of system is appropriate where the same part is made by the same people every day.

If it turns out that the demand for Part A is greater than planned and less than planned for Part B, the system self-regulates to these changes because there can be no more parts built than called for by the Kanban cards in circulation. Mix changes of 10 to 20 percent can easily be accommodated because the shifts are gradual and the increments are small. The ripple effect upstream is similarly dampened.

The same approach is used to authorize vendor shipments. When both the customer and the vendor are using the Kanban system, the withdrawal Kanban serves as the vendor release/shipping document while the production Kanban at the vendor's plant regulates production there.

The whole system hinges on everyone doing exactly what is authorized and following procedures explicitly. In fact, the Japanese use no production coordinators on the shop floor, relying solely on supervisors to ensure compliance. Cooperative worker attitudes are essential to its success.

Results can be impressive. Jidosha Kiki, a Bendix braking components affiliate in Japan, installed the Kanban/just-in-time system in 1977 with the help of its customer, Toyota. Within two years they had doubled productivity, tripled inventory turnover, and substantially reduced overtime and space requirements. Jidosha Kiki stated that this was a slow and difficult learning process for its employees, even considering the Japanese culture, because all the old rules of thumb had to be tossed out the window and deep-rooted ideas had to be changed.

Minimized Setup Times   The Japanese approach to productivity demands that production be run in small lots. This is impossible to do if machine setups take hours to accomplish. In fact, many companies in the United States use the economic order quantity (EOQ) formula to determine what quantity to make in order to absorb a long and costly setup time.

The Japanese have the same formula, but they've turned it around. Instead of accepting setup times as fixed amounts, they fixed the lot sizes (very small) and then went to work to reduce setup time.

That is a crucial factor in the Japanese approach. Their success in this area has received widespread acclaim. Many Americans have been to Japan and witnessed a team of press operators change the dies on an 800-ton press in 10 minutes. Compare their data with those of U.S. firms, as shown in Exhibit 12.10. The Japanese aim for single-digit setup times (i.e., less than 10 minutes) for every machine in their factories. They've addressed not only big things, like presses, but small molding machines and standard machines tools as well.

EXHIBIT 12.10

Minimizing Setup Time—Hood and Fender Press Comparison (800-ton press)

	Toyota	USA	Sweden	Germany
Setup time	10 minutes	6 hours	4 hours	4 hours
Setups/day	3	1	—	½
Lot size	1 day*	10 days	1 month	

*For low-demand items (less than 1,000 month), as large as seven days.

Successful setup time reduction is easily achieved when approached from a methods engineering perspective. The Japanese separate setup time into two segments: *internal*—that part that must be done while a machine is stopped, and *external*—that part that can be done while the machine is operating. Simple things, such as the staging of replacement dies in anticipation of a change, fall into the external category, which, on the average, represents half of the usual setup time.

Another 50 percent reduction can usually be achieved by the application of time and motion studies and practice. (It is not unusual for a Japanese setup team to spend a full Saturday practicing changeovers.) Time-saving devices like hinged bolts, roller platforms, and folding brackets for temporary die staging are commonly seen, all of which are low-cost items.

Only then is it necessary to spend larger sums, to reduce the last 15 percent or so, on things such as automatic positioning of dies, rolling bolsters, and duplicate tool holders. The result is that 90 percent or *more* of the setup times can be eliminated if we have a desire to do so.

Referring again to the Jidosha Kiki Corporation (JKC), Exhibit 12.11 shows the remarkable progress the company made in just four years. These data relate to all the machines in the factory. It's interesting to note that while we are quite impressed that two thirds of their equipment can be changed over in less than 2 minutes, the company is embarrassed that 10 percent still takes more than 10 minutes!

The savings in setup time are used to increase the number of lots produced, with a corollary reduction in lot sizes. This makes the use of just-in-time production principles feasible, which in turn makes the Kanban control system practical. All the pieces fit together.

Respect for People

respect for people
Principal of Japanese management where mutual respect is shown between management and workers.

The second guiding principle for the Japanese, along with elimination of waste, is **respect for people.** This principle, also, has seven basic elements:

1. Lifetime employment.
2. Company unions.
3. Attitude toward workers.
4. Automation/robotics.
5. Bottom-round management.
6. Subcontractor networks.
7. Quality circles.

EXHIBIT 12.11
Setup Reduction Results at JKC

Setup Time	Percent Reduction		
	1976	1977	1980
>60 minutes	30%	0%	0%
30–60 minutes	19	0	0
20–30 minutes	26	10	3
10–20 minutes	20	12	7
5–10 minutes	5	20	12
100 second–5 minutes	0	17	16
<100 seconds	0	41	62

Lifetime Employment   Much has been written about the Japanese concept of lifetime employment. When Japanese workers are hired for permanent positions with a major industrial firm, they have jobs with that company for life (or until retirement age) provided they work diligently. If economic conditions deteriorate, the company maintains the payroll almost to the point of going out of business. We should understand, though, that these kinds of benefits apply only to permanent workers, who constitute about one third of the workforce in Japan. What's important is that the concept is pervasive. When people can identify with the company as the place they're going to spend their working life, not just an interim place to get a paycheck, then they have a tendency to be more flexible and to want to do all they can do to help achieve the company's goals.

Company Unions   When General Douglas MacArthur introduced the union concept to Japan during the post-World War II reconstruction period, he undoubtedly had in mind trade unions, but the Japanese didn't think that way. Japanese workers at Toyota were concerned about Toyota. They really didn't identify with the other automobile manufacturing employees in the rest of the country. They identified not with the kind of work they were doing but rather with the company for which they were working. So Toyota formed a union that included everybody who worked for Toyota, no matter what their skills were. The objective of both the union and management was to make the company as healthy as possible so there would be benefits accruing to the people in a secure and shared method. The resulting relationship was cooperative, not adversarial.

The Japanese system of compensation reinforces these goals because it is based on company performance bonuses. Everybody in a Japanese company, from the lowest employee to the highest, gets a bonus twice a year. In good times the bonus is high (up to 50 percent of their salaries), while in bad times there may be no bonus. As a result, the employees have an attitude that says, "If the company does well, I do well," which is important from the standpoint of soliciting the workers' help to improve productivity.

Attitude toward Workers   The attitude of management toward the workers is also critical. The Japanese do not look at people as human machines. As a matter of fact, they believe that if a machine can do a job, then a person *shouldn't* do it because it's below his or her dignity. A corollary concept says that if workers are really important as people, you must also believe that they can do much more than you are now giving them the opportunity to do.

The Japanese say, "What workers are doing today is only tapping their capability. We must give them an opportunity to do more." Thus, a third and most significant attitude requires that the management system provides every worker with an opportunity to display his or her maximum capabilities. These concepts are practiced, not just discussed, and the Japanese spend more for employee training and education—at all levels—than any other industrial nation.

Automation/Robotics   When people feel secure, identify with the company, and believe that they are being given an opportunity to fully display their talents, the introduction of automation and robotics is not considered as a staff-cutting move. The Japanese feel that this is a way to eliminate dull jobs so people can do more important things, and they have been making major capital investments in these areas. Interestingly enough, Japan has invested one-third or 33 percent of its gross national product in capital improvements over the last 20 years, compared to about 19 percent for the United States during the same period.

In automation, the Japanese have invested first in low-cost enhancements to existing or standard equipment, using some clever approaches. In the capital area they have been concentrating on programmable robots. A recent survey showed that Japan had approximately five times the number of programmable robots (some of them quite simple) as the United States. It is interesting to note that most of those robots were built in the United States. Again, we shipped our technology to Japan where it was used to build products to compete with us. Today, Japan is building its own robots at a rapid pace and has become both the leading robot producer and robot user in the world.

Because the Japanese honestly believe that robots free people for more important tasks, there is little worker resistance to the robotics implementation. In fact, workers go out of their way to figure out how to eliminate their jobs, if they find them dull, because they know the company will find something better and more interesting for them to do.

Bottom-Round Management This mutual reliance between workers and management is a manifestation of the management style the Japanese call **bottom-round management.** It's also been identified as *consensus management* or *committee management*. It is an innate part of the Japanese culture because they have grown up with the concept that the importance of the group supercedes that of the individual. Consider that in Japan more than 124 million people are crowded on a tiny island group about the size of California, 80 percent of which is mountainous. In those circumstances, its citizens must have considerable respect for their neighbors, or social survival would be impossible. This cultural concept is ideal in a manufacturing environment because the process requires that people work together in a group to make a product. The individual cannot function independently, without concern for others, because he or she would only get out of synchronization with the rest of the group and disrupt the process.

Bottom-round management is a slow decision-making process. In attempting to arrive at a true consensus, not a compromise, the Japanese involve all potentially interested parties, talk over a problem at great length, often interrupt the process, seek out more information, and retalk the problem until everyone finally agrees. While we have often criticized the slowness of this method, the Japanese have an interesting response.

They say, "You Americans will make an instant decision and then you'll take a very long time to implement it. The decision is made so quickly, without consulting many of the people it's going to affect, that as you try to implement it you begin to encounter all sorts of unforeseen obstacles. Now, in our system, we take a long time to make a decision, but it only takes a short time to implement it because by the time we've finally reached a conclusion, everybody involved has had their say."

A key to bottom-round management is that decisions are made at the lowest possible level. In essence, the employees recognize a problem, work out a potential solution with their peers, and make recommendations to the next level of management. They, in turn, do the same thing and make the next recommendation up the line. And so it goes, with everyone participating in the process. As a result, top management teams in Japanese companies make very few day-to-day operating decisions, their time being almost totally devoted to strategic planning. Note, though, that the use of bottom-round management makes it extremely difficult to manage a large, complex manufacturing organization. That's another reason why the Japanese build focused factories.

Subcontractor Networks The specialized nature of Japanese factories has fostered the development of an enormous subcontractor network; most subcontractors have fewer than 30 employees. More than 90 percent of all Japanese companies are part of the supplier network, which is many layers deep, because there is so little vertical integration in Japanese factories.

There are two kinds of suppliers: specialists in a narrow field who serve multiple customers (very much like U.S. suppliers), and captives, who usually make a small variety of

bottom-round management
Mutual reliance between management and workers focusing on reaching consensus or agreement.

MANAGEMENT

parts for a single customer. The second kind is more prevalent in Japan. Of course, this idea of sole-sourcing suppliers is diametrically opposite to the U.S. multisource concept. Sole-sourcing arrangements work in Japan because the relationships are based on a tremendous amount of mutual trust. They seek long-term partnerships between customer and supplier. Americans who do business with Japanese companies know that the very first stages of negotiation involve an elaborate ceremony of getting to know one another to determine whether there is a potential long-term relationship in the picture. Japanese businesspeople are rarely interested in a one-time buy, so it's a different way of doing business for Americans.

Suppliers in Japan consider themselves part of their customers' families. Very often key suppliers are invited to company functions such as picnics or parties. In return, suppliers deliver high-quality parts many times per day, often directly to the customer's assembly line, bypassing receiving and inspection. A typical scenario would have the supplier's truck arriving at a precise time of day, the driver unloading the truck, transporting the parts into the factory and delivering them to the assembly line at a given station, depositing the parts, picking up the empty containers, loading them into the truck, and leaving, without any interference. No receiving, no incoming inspection, no paperwork, no delays. It's an almost paper-free system, all built on mutual trust.

Trust is a two-way street. Because so many of the suppliers are small and undercapitalized. Japanese customers advance money to finance them, if necessary. Customer process engineers and quality personnel help vendors improve their manufacturing systems to meet the rigid quality and delivery standards imposed. Efforts are also made to help vendors reduce their production process costs to help ensure their profitability. When there is an economic downturn, however, the customers will perform more of the work in-house instead of buying from vendors. They do this to protect their own work forces. Vendors are small and do not have the permanent, lifetime employment guarantees that the major companies do. However, this is known in advance and suppliers consider this an acceptable risk.

Quality Circles   Another interesting technique, with which many Americans are already familiar, is **quality circles.** The Japanese call them *small group improvement activities (SGIA)*. A quality circle is a group of volunteer employees who meet once a week on a scheduled basis to discuss their function and the problems they're encountering, to try to devise solutions to those problems, and to propose those solutions to their management. The group may be led by a supervisor or a production worker. It usually includes people from a given discipline or a given production area, like Assembly Line A or the machining department. It can also be multidisciplinary, consisting, for instance, of all the material handlers who deliver materials to a department and the industrial engineers who work in that department. It does have to be led, though, by someone who is trained as a group leader. The trainers are facilitators, and each one may coordinate the activities of a number of quality circles. Westinghouse Electric Corporation, for example, has 275 quality circles and about 25 facilitators.

The quality circle really works because it's an open forum. It takes some skill to prevent it from becoming a gripe session, but that's where the trained group leaders keep the members on target. Interestingly enough, only about one third of the proposals generated turn out to be quality related. More than half are productivity oriented. It's really amazing how many good ideas these motivated employees can contribute toward the profitability and the improved productivity of their companies. Quality circles are actually a manifestation of the consensus, bottom-round management approach but are limited to these small groups.

quality circles
Groups of workers who meet to discuss their common area of interest and problems they are encountering.

JIT in the United States

JIT evolved in Japan in great part due to the unique characteristics of that country. Japan is a very small country in area. Distances between most of the major cities are, therefore, relatively short. In addition, a large proportion of its geographic area is mountainous. Consequently, most of Japan's population lives in a relatively small area, with space at a premium. In addition, the Japanese tend to have a strong paternalistic, family-oriented culture that extends to the relationship between large and small companies.

Consequently, the vast majority of Japanese suppliers to the major companies are usually located within a 25-mile radius of the major firms' manufacturing facilities. In addition, most of the sales of these small firms tend to be to a single large customer, thereby making these small companies highly dependent.

In contrast, the United States has a very large geographic area. Suppliers are, therefore, often located thousands of miles away from production facilities. (As companies continue to extend their supply chains globally, their suppliers will become even more remotely located.) In addition, the paternalistic relationship between large companies and small does not exist to the same extent that it does in Japan. Finally, most U.S. firms have a much wider customer base, with any one customer representing only a small percentage of its sales. For these and various other reasons, JIT is practiced differently in the United States than it is in Japan.

"JIT in the United States often stands for *J*umbo-*I*nventory-*T*ransfer," said Peter Frasso, vice president and general manager of Varian Vacuum Products in Lexington, Massachusetts, at the April 1996, Annual Meeting of the Operations Management Association in Boston, Massachusetts. In other words, there are many large companies in the United States that, instead of working with suppliers to synchronize operations, will often try to force suppliers to maintain large stocks of inventory rather than keep these inventories at their own facilities. Thus, while the large firms practice JIT within their own facilities, their suppliers deliver raw material and components from buffer inventories that are frequently located nearby. With this approach, transferring the inventory from the manufacturer to the supplier improves the performance of the large firm at the expense of the smaller supplier, which absorbs all of the risks and costs associated with these inventories. The large distances that often exist between suppliers and customers in the United States also precludes the ability to provide products in small lot sizes at short time intervals (that is, several times a day, as is often the case in Japan).

Nevertheless, other aspects or elements of JIT, such as: (*a*) working with suppliers in a partnership relationship rather than an adversarial one, (*b*) reducing setup times and thus lot sizes, (*c*) encouraging worker participation, and (*d*) reducing inventories and waste, are being adopted by the better companies, with recognizable benefits. A survey of U.S. manufacturers indicated that 86 percent of the respondents acknowledged some benefits from implementing JIT.[3]

Because of these differences, many U.S. companies have adopted an MRP system (as discussed later in Chapter 15) in working with their suppliers. The MRP system provides the suppliers with a forecast of the raw material and component requirements. Typically these requirements are *frozen* for the immediate future, but can change the further out the requirements are. For example, the orders placed with a supplier might be fixed for the next six weeks, but the requirements may change beyond this six-week window. This approach allows suppliers to schedule work efficiently within their own facilities. As illustrated in

---

[3]Richard E. White, "An Empirical Assessment of JIT in U.S. Manufacturers," *Production and Inventory Management Journal* 34, no. 2 (1993), pp. 38–42.

Operations Management in Practice

JIT Is Integral to Saturn's Success

When General Motors announced the Saturn project, its goal was very clear: to recapture the small car market from the Japanese. To accomplish this, GM incorporated many new and innovative concepts in designing Saturn's manufacturing facility in Spring Hill, Tennessee. For example, a much higher percentage of the components are produced on-site instead of at a remote facility and transported to Spring Hill, which is the norm at other automobile assembly plants. Thus the facility includes a foundry to cast crankshafts and engine blocks, as well as huge injection molding machines to make the various plastic components.

Linking these processes together is a just-in-time (JIT) system that is the "tightest" JIT system in the auto business, according to Alec Bedricky, Saturn's VP of purchasing. There are very few buffer inventories separating the vehicle assembly line from the component manufacturing processes. As an illustration, there are usually less than 140 power-trains between the engine plant and the assembly line, representing less than two hours of production.

Suppliers deliver their products to the plant 24 hours a day, and deliveries must be made within a five-minute window to be considered on time. If a late delivery causes a delay in production, the supplier can be fined $500 per minute. The scheduling of both dock times and truck routes are managed by Ryder, Saturn's logistics partner from an office located inside the assemble plant.

Parts are off-loaded and delivered directly to the point of use on the assembly line. There is no receiving area and no incoming inspection of material. Production parts are delivered daily, with larger items like radiators and front-end modules delivered more frequently. For example, seats from the seating supplier are delivered in proper assembly line sequence every 30 minutes.

Source: Adapted from Ernest Rata, "Saturn: Rising Star," *Purchasing,* September 9, 1993, pp. 44–47.

the above OM in Practice, Saturn provides a good example of a growing number of U.S. firms that are successfully implementing many of the concepts of JIT.

IMPLEMENTING JIT PRODUCTION

In this section, our objective is to explain how to accomplish JIT production. To structure our discussion we follow the steps given in Exhibit 12.12, expanding on some of the ideas presented in the Wantuck paper and explaining certain features that were not previously discussed. In going through these steps, we should remember that we are still talking about *repetitive* production systems—those that make the same basic product over and over again. Also keep in mind that we are talking about features of a *total system,* which means that actions taken regarding any one of these features have some impact on other features of the system. Finally, note that different companies use different terms to describe their JIT systems. IBM uses *continuous flow manufacture,* Hewlett-Packard Company uses *stockless production* at one plant and *repetitive manufacturing system* at another, while many other companies use *lean production.* Bob Anastasi, vice-president of manufacturing for CTI Cryogenics, a leading producer of high-technology vacuum pumps located in Mansfield, Massachusetts, refers to it as *synchronized material flow.*

JIT Layouts/Design Flow Process

JIT requires that the plant layout be designed to ensure balanced workflow with a minimum of work in process. This means that we must conceive of each workstation as an integral

EXHIBIT 12.12

How to Accomplish
Just-in-Time Production

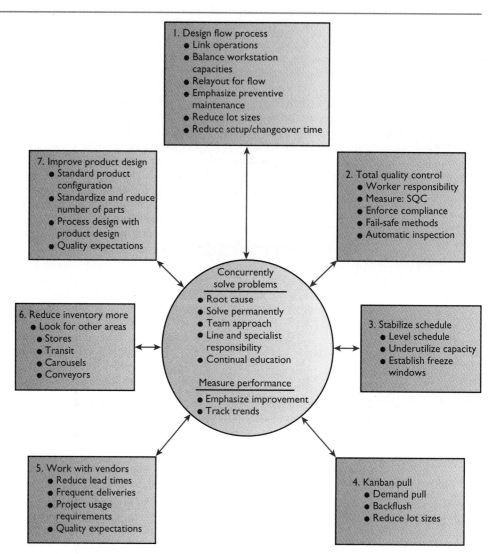

1. Design flow process
   • Link operations
   • Balance workstation capacities
   • Relayout for flow
   • Emphasize preventive maintenance
   • Reduce lot sizes
   • Reduce setup/changeover time

7. Improve product design
   • Standard product configuration
   • Standardize and reduce number of parts
   • Process design with product design
   • Quality expectations

2. Total quality control
   • Worker responsibility
   • Measure: SQC
   • Enforce compliance
   • Fail-safe methods
   • Automatic inspection

Concurrently solve problems
   • Root cause
   • Solve permanently
   • Team approach
   • Line and specialist responsibility
   • Continual education

Measure performance
   • Emphasize improvement
   • Track trends

6. Reduce inventory more
   • Look for other areas
   • Stores
   • Transit
   • Carousels
   • Conveyors

3. Stabilize schedule
   • Level schedule
   • Underutilize capacity
   • Establish freeze windows

5. Work with vendors
   • Reduce lead times
   • Frequent deliveries
   • Project usage requirements
   • Quality expectations

4. Kanban pull
   • Demand pull
   • Backflush
   • Reduce lot sizes

This diagram is modeled after the one used by Hewlett-Packard's Boise plant to accomplish its JIT program.

part of the overall production line, whether or not a physical line actually exists. Capacity balancing is done using the same logic as for an assembly line, and operations are linked through a pull system (described later). This also means that the system designer must have a vision of how all aspects of the internal and external logistics system are related to the layout. Consequently, the concepts of supply chain management are integrally linked to JIT.

Preventive maintenance is emphasized to ensure that a continuous workflow is not interrupted by machine downtime or as a result of poor quality from malfunctioning equipment. Much of this maintenance is carried out by the operators because they are responsible for the quality of products coming off the machines, and also because of their sensitivity to the idiosyncrasies of the machines as a result of working on them day in and day out. Finally, the fact that the JIT philosophy favors many simple machines rather than a few complex ones enables the operators to handle routine maintenance activities.

Reduction in setup/changeover time and lot sizes are interrelated and are key to achieving a smooth flow (and JIT success in general). Exhibit 12.13 illustrates the fundamental

EXHIBIT 12.13

The Impact of JIT on Lot Size

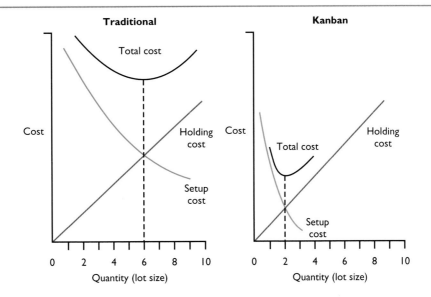

relationship between lot size and setup cost. Under the traditional approach, setup cost is treated as a constant and the optimal order quantity is shown as six. Under the Kanban approach of JIT, setup cost is treated as a variable and the optimal order quantity, in this case, is reduced to two. This type of reduction can be achieved by employing setup time-saving procedures such as those described earlier in the chapter. *The ultimate goal of JIT from an inventory standpoint is to achieve an economic lot size of one.*

Even though we have already described the various types of layouts in Chapter 7, we will briefly describe a line flow operation and a job-shop layout to show how JIT can be applied.

Most people think of high volume assembly lines when they think of JIT. This is because most of the literature and discussions on this topic has been about line layouts. However, job-shop environments, where functions are grouped together, offer perhaps the greatest benefits for JIT application.

In assembly or fabrication lines, the focus is on product flow. Volumes may be high enough or tasks simple enough or costs low enough so that the required resources (people, machines, materials, etc.) can be arranged close together in a simple flow.

The majority of manufacturing plants are process oriented, being organized by function (similar machines are grouped together, paint departments, heat treating, etc.). Many service facilities are also organized by function or process: hospitals, universities, department stores, and so forth. The main reason for this organization is because these machines or processes serve a variety of needs, not one of which is large enough to justify a machine of its own. In this environment, the product or person requiring service must move longer distances.

JIT in a Line Flow or Product Layout   Exhibit 12.14 shows a pull system in a simple line flow. In theory, no one does any work until the product has been pulled from the end of the line. This item could have been sold or used somewhere else. To fill this void created by the pulled item, a replenishment unit is pulled from upstream. In theory, supposing, in Exhibit 12.14, an item of finished goods is pulled from the finished goods inventory (F). The inventory clerk then goes to processing (E) and takes replacement product to fill the void. Because operator E has an operating policy of keeping a specific number of completed units at the workstation, the operator goes upstream to process D to get replacement units which

EXHIBIT 12.14

JIT in a Line Flow Layout

Raw materials for operation A   Market

will then be processed. This pattern continues up to worker A who pulls material from raw material inventory or from whatever process precedes this line. In practice, however, a schedule would be created for the completion of items based on the demand, rather than using inventory clerk F to initiate the chain of events. Operating rules are straightforward: Always keep products which have been completed at your workstation. If someone takes your completed work away, go upstream and get some more to work on. Completed work stays on the "completed" side of the machine. For clarity, we haven't shown it in the exhibit, but materials and parts may also be supplied from side lines feeding each workstation as the product progresses.

JIT in a Functional or Process (Job Shop) Layout   To justify considering JIT as a valid way to produce goods, the basic requirement is that there is a continual need for the product. This doesn't mean that the product has to be produced continuously in every phase of its creation. Product can be produced intermittently in batches throughout the majority of the sequence except for the final processing or final assembly, which is continuous. Consider a firm that produces several products in constant demand. To simplify it a bit further, assume that the demands are relatively constant throughout the entire year. Let's say that management decides to try to match the production rate with the demand rate, letting demand control production by only producing when goods are pulled from the system—that is, just-in-time.

Some of the products require a final assembly—that is, several parts and components produced in various parts of the firm are assembled together and then sold. Other parts require some types of finish machining at a work center and then are sold. In both cases, work on the products is continuous. If there is a demand pull—finished goods are pulled from the system—these steps are truly just-in-time.

The rest of the system preceding this final stage area may not be just-in-time. Consider the machine centers, paint shops, foundries, heat treating areas, and the countless other locations that these parts and components go through before they reach the final stages. Can we operate these locations in the same Kanban and container logic as we normally use for just-in-time? Yes, we can and we should. (See Exhibit 12.15.)

Parts and components produced in different work centers are used in a variety of final products; therefore, these work centers should have completed containers of the entire variety of output that is designated for just-in-time production. Supposing a work center produces 10 different parts used by several products which are produced just-in-time. This work center must maintain containers of completed output of all 10 parts at the work center to be picked up by those users who need them. If a large part of the facility is organized this way, it would be convenient to have a materials handling vehicle make periodic rounds throughout the facility, such as hourly. This vehicle and operator would stop at the just-in-time assembly stations and machine centers and pick up empty containers (and their production move cards if cards are used). These would be dropped off at the corresponding upstream work centers and full containers picked up. By using periodic material handling routes, the system operates in a just-in-time mode with its production Kanbans and withdrawal or move Kanbans.

EXHIBIT 12.15

JIT in a Job-Shop Layout Showing the Materials Handling Vehicle Route Connecting Machine Centers and Line Operations

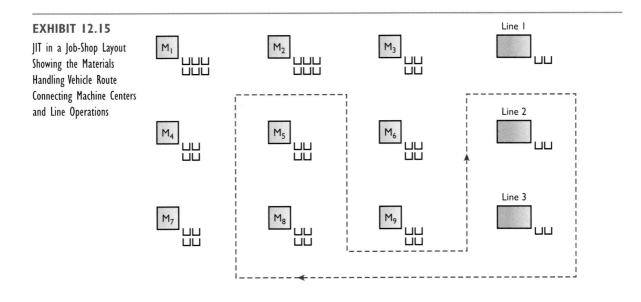

EXHIBIT 12.16

Relationship between JIT and Quality

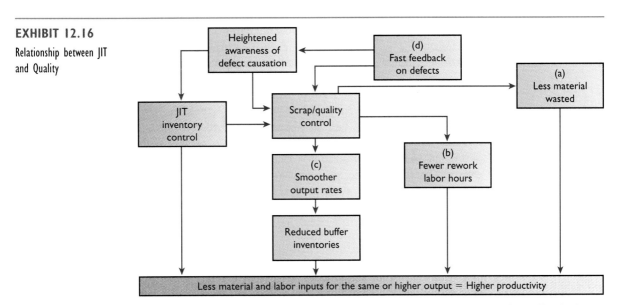

Source: Richard J. Schonberger, "Some Observations on the Advantages and Implementation Issues of Just-in-Time Production Systems," *Journal of Operations Management* 3, no. 1 (November 1982), p. 5.

Total Quality Control

JIT and total quality control have become linked in the minds of many managers—and for good reason. As stated in Chapter 5, total quality control refers to "building in" quality and *not* "inspecting it in." It also refers to all plant personnel taking responsibility for maintaining quality, not just "leaving it to the quality control department." When employees assume this responsibility, JIT is permitted to work at its optimal level, since only good products are pulled through the system. What results is having your cake and eating it too—high quality and high productivity. Exhibit 12.16 illustrates this subtle relationship.

Statistical quality control uses simple control methods (control charts, primarily) to monitor *all* aspects of a production system. If all aspects of a production process (raw materials, machine variability, etc.) are in control, one can assume that the product coming out of that process is good. When items are produced in small lots, such as in the Kanban system, the inspection may be reduced to just two items—the first and the last. If they are perfect, assume that those produced in between are perfect as well.

Stabilize Schedule   Efficient repetitive manufacture requires a level schedule over a fairly long time horizon. This is sometimes referred to as production linearity. (The actual length depends on many factors, but primarily two: (*a*) whether the firm makes to order or makes to stock and (*b*) the range of product options it offers.) As Robert Hall notes,

> A level schedule is one that requires material to be pulled into final assembly in a pattern uniform enough to allow the various elements of production to respond to pull signals. It does not necessarily mean that the usage of every part on an assembly line is identical hour by hour for days on end; it does mean that a given production system equipped with flexible setups and a fixed amount of material in the pipelines can respond.[4]

The term *freeze window* refers to that period of time during which the schedule can't be changed.

Underutilization of capacity is probably the most controversial feature of JIT. Underutilized (or excess) capacity is really the cost incurred by eliminating inventories as a buffer in the system. In traditional manufacturing, safety stocks and early deliveries are used as a hedge against shortfalls in production resulting from such things as poor quality, machine failures, and unanticipated bottlenecks. Under JIT, excess labor and machine capacity provide that hedge in lieu of inventory. However, managers are now recognizing that excess capacity in the form of labor and equipment is generally far less expensive than carrying excess inventory. Moreover, excess labor can be put to work on other activities during those slow periods when it is not needed for direct production. Further, the low idle-time cost incurred by the relatively inexpensive machines favored by JIT producers makes machine utilization a secondary issue for many firms. Finally, much of the excess capacity is by design—workers are expected to have time at the end of their shifts to meet with their work groups, clean up their workstations, and ponder potential improvements.

Kanban Pull

Most people view JIT as a pull system, where the material is drawn or sent for by the users of the material as needed. Production Kanbans are just one of many devices to signal the need for more parts. Note that the signal sent is for a standard lot size conveyed in a standardized container, not just for a "bunch of parts."

Some typical Kanban-type signals used to initiate production are:

"Hey Joe, make me another widget."

A flashing light over a work center, indicating the need for more parts.

A signal marker hanging on a post by the using workstations. (See Exhibit 12.17.)

A pull system typically starts with the master production schedule specifying the final assembly schedule. By referring to the final assembly schedule, material schedulers and supervisors can see the days during the month when each part will be needed. They determine when to schedule supplier deliveries or internal parts manufacture by offsetting lead times

[4]Robert H. Hall, *Zero Inventories* (Homewood, IL: Dow Jones-Irwin, 1983), p. 64.

EXHIBIT 12.17

Diagram of Outbound Stockpoint with Warning Signal Marker

Signal marker hanging on post for part C584 shows that production should start for that part. The post is located so that workers in normal locations can easily see it.

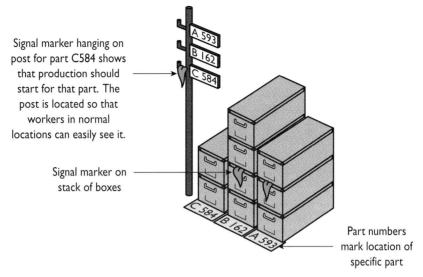

Signal marker on stack of boxes

Part numbers mark location of specific part

Source: Robert Hall, *Zero Inventories* (Homewood, IL: Dow Jones-Irwin, 1983), p. 51.

from final assembly dates. Basically, then, the final assembly schedule exerts the initial pull on the system, with Kanbans controlling the flow.

How many Kanban cards should be used? There can be a two-card system, a one-card system, or no cards at all. We list the rules for the two-card and one-card systems which Hall has described so well.[5]

Rules for the two-card system are simple but strict:

One card, whether a [withdrawal or] move card or a production card, represents only one standard container for one type of part, and exactly the same number of that part that goes into each.

As soon as parts start to be taken from a standard container at its point of use, the move card is detached from the container. It is returned to the supplying operation as authorization to bring another standard container of the same part.

Containers filled with parts should await pick up at clearly designated locations next to the supplying operations. When a full container is taken, the production card is detached and left at the supply point. The move card is attached to the full container and taken to the point of use.

The production card left behind is authorization to the supply operation to make another standard container of the same part and leave it with the production card attached at the same outboard location, ready for pick up.

This system of material control replaces exactly what has been consumed and no more. The two-card system is actually one of the more complex ways of controlling this. Between two operations within sight of each other, no cards are needed at all—only a strict restriction on the inventory between. This can be done by marking a space between operations called a *Kanban square*. If any of the squares are empty, workers fill them up, but leave no extras.

A one-card system uses only the move card. Space restrictions or visible limits sufficiently restrict the quantity of each part in its location specified for pick up. If the move cards are permanently attached to the containers, the returning empty containers serve as signals to be filled up.

---

[5]Robert W. Hall, *Attaining Manufacturing Excellence* (Homewood, IL: Dow Jones-Irwin, 1987), pp. 91–94.

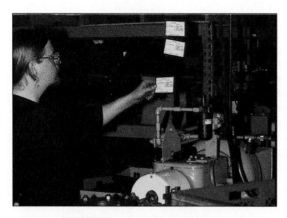

At Bernard Welding Equipment when part bins are emptied, a Kanban card is detached from the container, transferred to the appropriate work cell, and placed on a post to indicate the bin needs to be refilled. The card contains the part number, routing quantity, and bin number.

In a system where operations are within sight of each other, no cards are needed. Workers mark a square between operations. An empty Kanban square on this factory floor visually signals the need to be filled by a disk drive unit.

Replenishment signals can be sent electronically back to the supplying operation to save time. However, care needs to be observed since a large amount of the value of the Kanban system is its simplicity.

Backflush is a term used to designate how component parts are accounted for in a pull system. Rather than keeping track of each individual part on a daily basis by job, JIT systems typically explode the bills of materials periodically, such as once a month, and calculate how many of each part must have gone into the final product(s). This eliminates a major shop-floor data collection activity, thereby further simplifying the production management jobs. Bar-code technology allows Hewlett-Packard's Medical Products Group in Andover, Massachusetts, to backflush on a continuous, ongoing basis. For example, when a printed circuit board is completed with all of its components in place, that board's bar code is scanned into the system. As a result of the scanning, all of the board's components are removed from inventory while, at the same time, the completed board is placed into inventory.

Reducing lot sizes in a pull system means removing interstage inventory. This is accomplished in a variety of ways: (*a*) by better balance of operations so that only two Kanban containers are used between two workstations rather than three, (*b*) by moving workstations closer together to cut transit time, (*c*) by automating processes that have high variability, and of course (*d*) by just-in-time deliveries.

Work with Vendors

All the items in this category, as shown in Exhibit 12.12, except "project usage requirements," have been discussed earlier. *Project usage requirements* means that the vendors are given a long-run picture of the demands that will be placed on their production and distribution systems. This permits them to develop level production schedules. In many U.S. companies this is accomplished with MRP.

Continuous Inventory Reduction

Material transit systems, carousels, and conveyors are places where inventory is held, and thus are targets for inventory reduction efforts. Often there is heated debate when it comes to doing away with them. One reason is that such inventory locations are frequently the focus or the result of a previous inventory improvements effort that has shown good results compared to the system used before that. The people involved in such an effort are unlikely to rush to support the elimination of something that has been working.

Improve Product Design

Standard product configurations and fewer, standardized parts are important elements in good product designs for JIT. When the objective is to establish a simple routine process, anything that reduces variability in the end item or the materials that go into it is worth careful consideration.

Integrating process design with product design refers to the early involvement activities among product designers, process designers, and manufacturing personnel. Besides improving the producibility of the product, such interaction facilitates the processing of engineering changes orders (ECOs). ECOs can be extremely disruptive to the production process. They alter the specifications of the product, which in turn may call for new materials, new methods, and even new schedules. To minimize such disruptions, many JIT producers introduce their ECOs in batches, properly sequenced with the production schedule, rather than one by one, as is common in traditional manufacturing in the United States. While batching sounds obvious and simple, it requires a great deal of coordination and a willingness to delay what may be significant changes in a product design in exchange for maintaining production stability.

Concurrently Solve Problems and Measure Performance

A JIT application is not an overnight, turnkey installation. Rather, it is an evolutionary system that is continually seeking ways of improving production. Improvement comes through looking at problems as challenges rather than threats—problems that can be solved with common sense and detailed, rigorous analysis.

The techniques for problem solving are primarily continuous improvement methods. Effective problem solving means that the problem is solved permanently. Because JIT requires a team effort, problems are treated in a team context. Staff personnel are expected to be seen frequently on the shop floor, and in some companies are expected to arrive a half hour before production workers to ensure that everything is in order, thereby avoiding problems.

Continual education is absolutely essential if the system is to avoid stagnation. While JIT may cost little in the way of hardware, it requires the need for a substantial investment in training people at all levels of the organization to better understand what the system demands and how they fit into it.

Many performance measures emphasize the number of processes and practices changed to improve materials flow and reduce labor content, and the degree to which they do so. If the processes physically improve over time, lower costs follow. According to Hall, a department head in a Japanese JIT system is likely to be evaluated on the following factors:

1. Improvement trends, including number of improvement projects undertaken, trends in costs, and productivity. Productivity is measured as:

$$p = \frac{\text{Measurement of department output}}{\text{Total employees (direct + indirect)}}$$

2. Quality trends, including reduction in defect rates, improvement in process capability, and improvement in quality procedures.
3. Running to a level schedule and providing parts when others need them.
4. Trends in departmental inventory levels (e.g., speed of flow).

5. Staying within budget for expenses.

6. Developing workforce skills, versatility, participation in changes, and morale.[6]

SOME TECHNICAL ISSUES ABOUT KANBAN

Kanban as a Fixed-Order Quantity/Reorder-Point Inventory System

Kanban and the simple fixed-order quantity/reorder point system are both reactive systems. These two systems are designed to replenish inventory, not in anticipation of future orders, but as soon as the inventory is depleted. Also, both assume continuous review, predetermined reorder points, and fixed replenishment quantities. The inventory behavior under the two systems is identical with the one exception that Kanban displays a lumpy usage pattern. The reason for this is that, unlike the fixed-order quantity system where parts are withdrawn one at a time, Kanban withdraws a fixed number of them in standard-sized containers. Such standardized containers, in turn, define the lot size, so each time one is withdrawn, a reorder point is reached.

In light of the basic similarity of the two systems, why has Kanban performed so well, while the fixed-order quantity system has generally failed? The answer is that Japanese management has been able to structure a manufacturing environment conducive to Kanban operation. The major contribution of Japanese management (relative to inventory control) lies in demand management and lead-time management, two features that are implicit in our discussion of JIT.

JIT and Cost Accounting

  ACCOUNTING

Cost accounting systems have focused on direct labor since the Industrial Revolution. However, under JIT (and computer-integrated management) overhead costs are dominant, often 20 times as high as direct labor. Moreover, with permanent employment, workers maintain their own equipment and consequently the distinction between direct and indirect labor has become blurred for cost-allocation purposes. Hewlett-Packard has recognized this and has eliminated the cost category of direct labor, now using simply "labor" instead.

It appears at this time that the primary difference between traditional and JIT cost accounting is the application of overhead on the basis of product time in the system (cycle time) rather than direct labor or machine hours.[7]

COMPANY EXPERIENCES WITH JIT

Exhibit 12.18 summarizes the experiences of five major U.S. companies that have installed JIT (and TQC, total quality control). As can be seen, the impact on these companies' performance measures is overwhelmingly positive. Similar results have been reported in European and British firms. One study of 80 plants in Europe, for example, listed the following benefits from JIT:

1. Average reduction in inventory of about 50 percent.

2. Reduction in throughput time of 50 to 70 percent.

3. Reduction in setup times of as much as 50 percent without major investment in plant and equipment.

---

[6]Ibid., pp. 254–55.

[7]Mohan V. Tatikonda, "Just-in-Time and Modern Manufacturing Environments: Implications for Cost Accounting," *Production and Inventory Management Journal* 28, no. 1 (1988) pp. 1–5.

EXHIBIT 12.18

Summary of JIT/TQC Activities for Five U.S. Companies (® = reduced to)

Company Name (Division)	Product Category	Production Characteristics	Implementation Issues			Results			
			Why Started	How Implemented	Labor Productivity Improvement	Setup Time (Improvement)	Inventory Reductions	Quality Improvements	
Deere & Company	Heavy machinery Farm equipment Lawn-care equipment	Repetitive manufacturing	Survival Foreign competition	Visit to Japan Task force in plant Education Pilot projects Workflow analysis	Subassembly: 19–35% Welding: 7–38% Manufacturing Cost: 10–20% Materials handling: 40%	Presses: 38–80% Drills: 24–33% Shears: 45% Grinders: 44% Average: 45%	Raw steel: 40% Purchased parts: 7% Crane shafts: 30 days® 3 days Average: 31%	Implemented process control charting in 40% of operations	
Black & Decker (Consumer Power Tools)	Electrical products	Repetitive manufacturing Floor space 385,000 sq. ft. Employees: 1,010	Large expenses in inventory carry-ing costs (high interest rates)	Education Balanced flow Rewrote work procedures Started to produce in weekly quantity	Assembly: 24 operators® 6 operators Support: 7® 5	Punch press: 1 hr. ® 1 min. Drastic in many areas	Turns: from 16 to 30	Reduced complaints in packaging 98% 100% customer service level	
Omark Industries	Forestry equipment and sporting goods	Mostly repetitive 18 plants	Corporate task force found JIT/TQC/employee involvement as reason for success	Steering committee Plant study team Presentation by corporate staff Pilot projects	Plant A: 30% Plant B: 30% Plant C: 20%	A: 165® 5 min. B: 43® 17 min. C: 360® 17 min. D: 45® 6 min.	Product A: 92% Product B: 29% Product C: 50%	Product A scrap and rework: 20% Product E cus-tomer service cost: 50%	
Hewlett-Packard (Computer Systems)	Computer and test systems	Forming/assem-bly/testing Many options	Questioned why overseas sup-pliers produced quality products	TQC first Employee training/ involvement Leveled schedule Process simplification	Standard hours: ® 87 hrs. 39 hrs.	Not available	PC Assembly inventory: $675,000 (100)® $190,000 (28)	Solder defects: 5000 PPM® 100 Scrap: $80,000/ mo.® $5,000	
FMC	Industrial equipment Defense Automotive Electrical	Multiple divisions with variety of products 50 manufacturing and mining operations	Survival Absence of patent protection Keen cost competition	Seminars Pilot project Pilot plants Setup time Inventory target Positive reinforcement	Direct labor productivity: 13% (Automotive service equipment division)	Defense equip-ment group: 60%–75% Automotive/ electrical: 80%	Turns: from 1.9 to 4.0 (automotive service equipment division)	Customer service from 88% to 98% Cost of quality: 3.5%® 2.1% (auto. svc. eq. div.)	

423

Source: Adapted from Kiyoshi Suzaki; "Comparative Study of JIT/TQC Activities in Japanese and Western Companies," First World Congress of Production and Inventory Control, Vienna, Austria, 1985, pp. 63–66.

4. Increase in productivity of between 20 and 50 percent.

5. Payback time for investment in JIT averaged less than nine months.[8]

Additional success stories abound in the production control journals. This is not to say that the implementation of JIT is trouble free, however.

JIT IN SERVICES

Service organizations and service operations within manufacturing firms present interesting opportunities for the application of JIT concepts. Despite the many differences between service and manufacturing, both share the most basic attributes of production, because they employ processes that add value to the basic inputs with the objective of creating an end product or service.

JIT focuses on processes, not products and, therefore, it can be applied to any group of processes, from manufacturing to services. The JIT goal is approached by testing each step in the production process to determine if it adds value to the product or service. If these steps do not add value, then the process is a candidate for reengineering. In this way, the production of processes gradually and continually improves.

Both manufacturing and services can be improved with JIT because both are systems of production processes and because JIT is essentially a process-oriented waste-elimination philosophy. The themes for JIT process improvement should therefore apply equally in a service environment.

Application of JIT to Services[9]

Duclos, Siha, and Lummus have suggested the following framework for classifying the ways in which JIT concepts have been applied to service organizations:

- Synchronization and balance of information and workflow.
- Total visibility of all components and processes.
- Continuous improvement of the process.
- Holistic approach to the elimination of waste.
- Flexibility in the use of resources.
- Respect for people.

Synchronization and Balance of Information and Workflow   Because services are intangible, it is important that there be synchronization between demand and capacity. In other words, capacity must be available when the customer demands it. From a workflow balance perspective, Feather and Cross report that the application of JIT techniques identified existing bottlenecks and eliminated unnecessary inventory buffers in the processing of contracts.[10] As as result, throughput time was reduced 60 percent and the backlog in the number of contracts to be processed was reduced 80 percent.

---

[8]Amrik Sohal and Keith Howard, "Trends in Materials Management." *International Journal of Production Distribution and Materials Management* 17, no. 5 (1987), pp. 3–11.

[9]Adapted from L. K. Duclos, S. M. Siha, and R. R. Lummus, "JIT in Services: A Review of Current Practices and Future Directions for Research," *International Journal of Service Industry Management* 6, no. 5 (1995), pp. 36–52.

[10]J. J. Feather, and K. F. Cross, "Workflow Analysis: Just-In-Time Techniques Simplify Administrative Process in Paperwork Operations," *Industrial Engineering* 20 (1988), pp. 32–40.

Total Visibility of All Components and Processes   A major element of JIT is that all operations required to complete a good or a service should be as widely visible as possible to all involved in the process. Inasmuch as customers are usually an integral part of the service delivery process, they will often define value by what they can observe. As an example, many full service restaurants now have open kitchens where the customers can actually see the food being prepared. The Commander's Palace in New Orleans, Louisiana, takes this one step further—customers actually have to walk through the kitchen to get to some of the dining rooms.

Continuous Improvement of the Process   Another critical element in successfully implementing JIT is the recognition of the need for continuous improvement. Service operations provide significant opportunities for achieving these incremental improvements. For example, using JIT techniques, a finance company was able to improve its credit evaluation process and reduce the processing time for a loan from twelve days to four.[11]

Holistic Approach to the Elimination of Waste   To be successful, JIT concepts must be adopted at all levels and in all functional areas within an organization. In addition, as discussed in the previous chapter, the application of JIT concepts should be expanded to include suppliers. In this respect, JIT concepts in this area have been applied successfully in the health care industry. Using JIT concepts and working closely with suppliers, hospital systems have reduced inventories at central stockrooms, with the ultimate goal of eliminating them altogether.

Flexibility in the Use of Resources   Although the successful implementation of JIT requires that the level of units produced remains constant over a given period of time, the mix of those units can vary significantly. This requires a very flexible process that can accommodate a wide variety of products. Many services are highly customized, from the preparation of the food you order at a restaurant to the preparation of your tax return. Thus, a flexible process is necessary for these customized services. Wal-Mart provides a good example of process flexibility with its automated replenishment system which can ship smaller quantities of goods to each store at frequent intervals. With this more flexible system, Wal-Mart has been able to lower the average levels of inventory at each retail store without decreasing the level of customer service that was previously provided.[12,13,14]

Respect for People   Customers' direct involvement with the service delivery process most often requires them to interact directly with employees. Within services, research has shown that the way in which management treats employees highly correlates with the way in which employees treat customers.[15] Thus management must show respect for its employees if it wants them to similarly respect the needs of its customers.

[11]J. Y. Lee, "JIT Works for Services Too," *CMA Magazine* 6 (1990) pp. 20–23.

[12]M. Ballou, "Wal-Mart Picks Progress Tools for Greater Flexibility," *Computerworld* 28, no. 9 (1994), p. 81.

[13]R. Halverson, "Logistical Supremacy Secures the Base—But Will It Translate Abroad?" *Discount Store News* 33, no. 23 (1994), pp. 107–8.

[14]G. Stalk, Jr., "Competing on Capabilities: The New Rules of Corporate Strategy," *Harvard Business Review* 70, no. 2, pp. 57–69.

[15]B. Schneider, and D. E. Bowen, *Winning the Service Game* (Cambridge, MA: Harvard Business School Press, 1995).

CONCLUSION

We have listed many of the potential benefits of just-in-time systems. In our concluding remarks, however, we need to caution that JIT applications are not universal. There are specific requirements for successful implementation and we need to be careful not to be caught up in the excitement and promises.

In 1983, Hewlett-Packard created a videotape on JIT at its Boulder, Colorado, plant. It was an excellent video and fun to watch. Its purpose was to convince viewers that a JIT pull system would produce significant benefits for most manufacturing plants. Although instructors still use this video in their classrooms, many of us caution against the message conveyed.

The video does not carry through a numerical analysis of the performance times, number of defects, work in process, and so on. This can lead to the wrong conclusions—that is, that the JIT pull system was responsible for improved conditions.

In a journal article, Jerry Bowman presented the data.[16] After analyzing the data he commented that the most significant benefits did not result from the pull system but from reducing lot sizes. The HP video showed that the best performance occurred when items were processed using a pull system in lots of one unit. Bowman commented, "If you manufacture in lot sizes of one in a 'flow' environment, you probably couldn't tell whether you were pushing or pulling nor would it matter." Consequently, students have difficulties in distinguishing between an American automobile assembly line and a Japanese automobile assembly line.

JIT is becoming a principal manufacturing management concept and undoubtedly will continue to be so into the next millenium. But again, we caution you to be careful in its use.

 Some of the concepts of JIT have been successfully introduced into service operations. Many of the characteristics that exist in JIT systems already are present in services, and, as a consequence, the benefits of implementing JIT in services have been readily apparent.

KEY TERMS

bottom-round management   p. 410
eliminate waste   p. 400
focused factory networks   p. 401
group technology   p. 401
Jidoka   p. 402

JIT (just-in-time)   p. 398
Kanban pull system   p. 406
quality circles   p. 411
respect for people   p. 408

REVIEW AND DISCUSSION QUESTIONS

1. Stopping waste is one of the most important parts of JIT. Identify some of the sources of waste and discuss how they may be eliminated.
2. Discuss JIT in a job-shop layout and in a line-flow layout.
3. Why is it important for JIT to have a stable schedule?
4. Are there any aspects of the Japanese approach that you could apply to your own current school activities? Explain.

---

[16]D. Jerry Bowman, "If You Don't Understand JIT, How Can You Implement It?" *Industrial Engineering* (February 1991), pp. 38–39.

5. Which objections might a marketing manager have against uniform plant loading?

6. What are the implications for cost accounting of JIT production?

7. Which questions would you want to ask the president of Toyota about his operations management?

8. Explain how cards are used in a Kanban system.

9. In which ways, if any, are the following systems analogous to Kanban: returning empty bottles to the supermarket and picking up filled ones; running a hot dog stand at lunchtime; withdrawing money from a checking account; collecting eggs at a chicken ranch?

10. How does the old saying, "There's no such thing as a free lunch," pertain to the Japanese elimination of inventory?

11. Explain the relationship between quality and productivity under the JIT philosophy.

12. What are the differences between implementing JIT in a manufacturing facility and implementing it in a service operation?

13. Identify some of the ways JIT can be applied to a service operation.

CASE: **XYZ PRODUCTS COMPANY**

XYZ Products Company is a supplier of gizmos for a large computer manufacturer located a few miles away. The company produces three different models of gizmos in production runs ranging from 100 to 300 units.

The production flow of Models X and Y is shown in Case Exhibit 1. Model Z requires milling as its first step, but otherwise follows the same flow pattern as X and Y. Skids can hold up to 20 gizmos at a time. Approximate processing times per unit by operation number and equipment setup times are shown in the following table:

Operation Number and Name		Operation Times (minutes)	Setup Times (minutes)
—	Milling for Z	20	60
1	Lathe	50	30
2	Mod. 14 drill	15	5
3	Mod. 14 drill	40	5
4	Assembly step 1	50	
	Assembly step 2	45	
	Assembly step 3	50	
5	Inspection	30	
6	Paint	30	20
7	Oven	50	
8	Packing	5	

The demand for gizmos from the computer company ranges between 125 and 175 per month, equally divided among X, Y, and Z. Subassembly builds up inventory early in the month to make certain that a buffer stock is always available. Raw materials and purchased parts for subassemblies each constitute 40 percent of the manufacturing cost of a gizmo. Both categories of parts are multiple sourced from about 80 vendors and are delivered at random times. (Gizmos have 40 different part numbers.)

Some other information: Scrap rates are about 10 percent each operation, inventory turns twice yearly, employees are paid on day rate, employee turnover is 25 percent per year, and net profit from operations is steady at five percent per year. Maintenance is performed as needed.

The manager of XYZ has been contemplating installing a new system to help control inventories and to "keep the skids filled." (It is his view that two days of work in front of a workstation motivates the worker to produce at top speed.) He is also planning to add three inspectors to clean up the quality problem. Further, he is thinking about setting up a rework line to speed up repairs. While he is pleased with the high utilization of most of his equipment and labor, he is concerned about the idle time of his milling machine. Finally, he has asked his industrial engineering department to look into high-rise shelving to store parts coming off Machine 4.

QUESTIONS

1. Which of the changes being considered by the manager of XYZ contradict the JIT philosophy?

2. Make recommendations for JIT improvements in such areas as scheduling, layout, Kanban, task groupings, and inventory. Use quantitative data as much as possible; state necessary assumptions.

3. Sketch the operation of a pull system for XYZ's current system.

4. Outline a plan for the introduction of JIT at XYZ.

CASE EXHIBIT I

Gizmo Production Flow

SELECTED BIBLIOGRAPHY

Ballou, M. "Wal-Mart Picks Progress Tools for Greater Flexibility." *Computerworld* 28, no. 9 (1994), p. 81.

Bowman, D. Jerry. "If You Don't Understand JIT, How Can You Implement It?" *Industrial Engineering,* February 1991, pp. 38–39.

Duclos, L. K.; S. M. Siha; and R. R. Lummus. "JIT in Services: A Review of Current Practices and Future Directions for Research." *International Journal of Service Industry Management* 6, no. 5 (1995), pp. 36–52.

Feather, J. J., and K. F. Cross. "Workflow Analysis, Just-in-Time Techniques Simplify Administrative Process in Paperwork Operations." *Industrial Engineering* 20 (1988), pp. 32–40.

Fucini, Joseph J., and Suzy Fucini. *Working for the Japanese.* New York: Free Press, 1990.

Garvin, David A. "Quality on the Line." *Harvard Business Review* 61, no. 5 (September–October 1983), pp. 65–75.

Hall Robert. *Zero Inventories.* Homewood, IL: Dow Jones-Irwin, 1983.

_____. *Attaining Manufacturing Excellence.* Homewood, IL: Dow Jones-Irwin, 1987.

Halverson, R. "Logistical Supremacy Secures the Base—But Will It Translate Abroad?" *Discount Store News* 33, no. 23 (1994), pp. 107–8.

Inman, R. Anthony, and Satish Mehra. "The Transferability of Just-in-Time Concepts to American Small Business," *Interfaces* 20, no. 2 (March–April 1990), pp. 30–37.

Klein, Janice. "A Re-examination of Autonomy in Light of New Manufacturing Practices." *Human Relations* 43 (1990).

Lee, J. Y. "JIT Works for Services Too." *CMA Magazine* 6 (1990), pp. 20–23.

Lee, Sang M. "Japanese Management and the 100 Yen Sushi House." *Operations Management Review* 1, no. 2 (Winter 1983), pp. 45–48.

Ohno, Taiichi. *Toyota Production System: Beyond Large-Scale Production.* Cambridge, MA: Productivity Press, 1988.

Ohno, Taiichi, and Setsuo Mito. *Just-in-Time for Today and Tomorrow.* Cambridge, MA: Productivity Press, 1988.

Rata, Ernest. "Saturn: Rising Star," *Purchasing* (September 9, 1993), pp. 44–47.

Schneider, B., and D. E. Bowen. *Winning the Service Game.* Cambridge, MA: Harvard Business School Press, 1995.

Schonberger, Richard J. *Japanese Productivity Techniques.* New York: Free Press, 1982.

_____. *World Class Manufacturing: The Lessons of Simplicity Applied.* New York: Free Press, 1986.

_____. *Building a Chain of Customers: Linking Business Functions to Create a World-Class Company.* New York: Free Press, 1989.

Sewell, G. "Management Information Systems for JIT Production." *Omega* 18, no. 5 (1990), pp. 481–503.

Shingo, Shigeo. *A Study of the Toyota Production System from an Industrial Engineering Viewpoint.* Cambridge, MA: Productivity Press, 1989.

Sohal, Amrik, and Keith Howard. "Trends in Materials Management." *International Journal of Production Distribution and Materials Management* 17, no. 5 (1987), pp. 3–41.

Stalk, G., Jr. "Competing on Capabilities: The New Rules of Corporate, Strategy." *Harvard Business Review* 70, no. 2, pp. 57–69.

Suzaki, Kiyoshi. *The New Manufacturing Challenge: Techniques for Continuous Improvement.* New York: Free Press, 1987.

Tatikonda, Mohan V. "Just-in-Time and Modern Manufacturing Environments: Implications for Cost Accounting." *Production and Inventory Management Journal* 28, no. 1 (1988), pp. 1–5.

Wantuck, Kenneth A. "The Japanese Approach to Productivity." Southfield, MI: Bendix Corporation, 1983.

White, Richard E. "An Empirical Assessment of JIT in U.S. Manufacturers." *Production and Inventory Management Journal* 34, no. 2 (1993), pp. 38–42.

Zipkin, Paul H. "Does Manufacturing Need a JIT Revolution?" *Harvard Business Review,* January–February 1991, pp. 40–50.

AGGREGATE PLANNING

Chapter Objectives

- Demonstrate how aggregate planning links long-range strategic planning and short-range scheduling.

- Present alternate strategies for matching supply and demand: adjusting supply (an operations function) or adjusting demand (a marketing function).

- Introduce strategies for developing aggregate plans and ways to identify their strengths and weaknesses.

- Define marginal costs and total costs as they pertain to aggregate planning.

- Introduce the concept of yield management as a tool for matching supply and demand in service operations.

Each year, Janet Cramer, the plant manager at Polaroid's Integral Film Assembly Operation in Waltham, Massachusetts, struggles to identify the most efficient way to meet the forecasted sales for film. Janet's plant is the only film assembly operation in the United States. (There is only one other Polaroid film assembly operation in the world, located in The Netherlands.)

Historically, annual sales of Polaroid film has followed a cyclic pattern, with the maximum sales per month taking

place just before Christmas time when retail operations stock their shelves in anticipation of holiday sales. There is also another peak, although somewhat smaller, in late spring and early summer, when customers purchase film for graduations, weddings, and summer vacations.

Four different types of film are assembled at the Waltham plant. The assembly of film into the cartridges for the Polaroid cameras is a highly capital intensive process with very high fixed costs and relatively low variable costs. As a result, Polaroid's operation in Waltham, which includes approximately 470 hourly employees, runs on three shifts, 24 hours a day, five days a week. In addition, the workforce primarily consists of highly skilled individuals who would be difficult to replace.

Even within this highly constrained environment, Janet has several alternatives available to her for scheduling production. The first alternative is to work overtime on Saturdays at a premium pay of 50 percent for all shifts. With this approach, inventory will be carried at an estimated cost of 20 to 25 percent per annum until the peak demand month is reached. The second alternative is to work both Saturdays and Sundays in the months just prior to the peak in order to minimize inventory carrying costs. Working on Sunday pays a premium of double time. However, with this approach there is the concern that worker fatigue (from working seven days a week) will have a negative impact on quality and productivity and, even, on employee morale.

The issues confronting Janet Cramer in selecting an aggregate planning alternative for her operation are typical of those that operations managers face when demand for their products is cyclic. There is often no one right answer, but rather a compromise that takes into consideration all of the various factors that can affect quality, productivity, cost, and employee morale. ∎

Source: Special thanks to Janet Cramer and Laurie Mullane, Polaroid Corp.

The first step in translating long-range strategic plans down to the operational level is the development of an aggregate plan. In essence, aggregate planning is an intermediate- or medium-range planning tool that is used to develop gross requirements, primarily for labor and materials, for the next 12 months. Aggregate planning thus takes a fairly broad view, addressing gross product requirements in total rather than specific products, and determining the number of workers needed in total rather than the number needed in specific skills areas.

In manufacturing, the goal of aggregate planning is to match the demand for the firm's products with its capacity or ability to supply those products, and to do so at minimum cost. The aggregate planning process identifies alternative methods to match supply and demand from the operations management perspective. In services, because the customer interacts directly with the service delivery process, alternative approaches to matching supply and demand are more limited. Thus, for certain types of services, a concept known as *yield management* has been developed which simultaneously manages both supply and demand for a service.

MARKETING

In both manufacturing and services, the marketing function also plays a key role in this matching process through the use of marketing tools such as pricing, advertising, and promotion. Both the marketing and operations management functions need to work together to develop an aggregate plan that is both effective and efficient.

In this chapter we present several quantitative techniques for developing aggregate plans that are applicable to both manufacturing and service organizations.

OVERVIEW OF OPERATIONAL PLANNING ACTIVITIES

Every organization must plan its activities at a variety of levels and operate these as a system. Exhibit 13.1 presents an overall view of planning and shows how aggregate production planning relates to other activities of a manufacturing firm. The time dimension is shown as long, medium, and short range.

planning activities:
long-range planning
Focuses on strategic issues relating to capacity, process selection, and plant location.

Long-range planning is generally done once a year, focusing on a time horizon that is usually greater than a year. The length of the time horizon will vary from industry to industry. For those industries that require many years to plan and construct plants and facilities, and to install specific processes (e.g., refineries), the time horizon may be 5 to 10 or more years. For other industries where the ability to expand capacity is shorter (e.g., clothing manufacturing and many service industries), the time horizon may be two to five years or less.

medium-range planning
Focuses on tactical issues pertaining to aggregate workforce and material requirements for the coming year.

Medium-range planning usually covers the period from 6 to 18 months in the future, with time increments or "buckets" that are monthly and/or quarterly. (The near-term time increments are often monthly, whereas those at the end of the time horizon tend to be quarterly, as these are usually less accurate.) Medium-range planning is typically reviewed and updated quarterly.

short-range planning
Addresses day-to-day issues of scheduling workers on specific jobs at assigned work stations.

Short-range planning covers the period from one day to six months, with the time increment usually being weekly. As with long-range planning, the length of the time horizon for medium- and short-range planning will vary from industry to industry.

Long-Range Planning

Long-range planning begins with a statement of organizational objectives and goals for the next 2 to 10 years. *Corporate strategic planning* articulates how these objectives and goals are to be achieved in light of the company's capabilities and its economic and political environment as projected by its *business forecasting*. Elements of the strategic plan include

EXHIBIT 13.1

Overview of Manufacturing
Planning Activities

product-line delineation, quality and pricing levels, and market penetration goals. *Product and market planning* translates these into individual market and product-line objectives, and includes a long-range production plan (basically a forecast of items to be manufactured for two years or more into the future). *Financial planning* analyzes the financial feasibility of these objectives relative to capital requirements and return on investment goals. *Resource planning* identifies the facilities, equipment, and personnel needed to accomplish the long-range production plan, and thus is frequently referred to as *long-run capacity planning*.

Medium-Range Planning

Aggregate Production Planning   As noted in Exhibit 13.1, this activity provides the primary link between the long-range strategic plans and the intermediate- or medium-range planning activities. Aggregate planning specifies monthly or quarterly output requirements by major product groups either in labor hours required or in units of production for up to

Kawasaki Motors USA produces utility vehicles, motorcycles, all-terrain vehicles, and Jet Ski watercraft at its plant in Lincoln, Nebraska.

While the corporate plan would specify how many units in each product line, the aggregate plan would determine how to meet this requirement with available resources.

aggregate production planning
Process for determining most cost effective way to match supply and demand over next 12–18 months.

18 months into the future. Its main inputs are the product and market plans and the resource plan. **Aggregate production planning** seeks to find that combination of monthly or quarterly workforce levels and inventory levels that minimizes total production-related costs over the planning period while meeting the forecasted demand for product.

Item Forecasting   This provides an estimate of specific products (and replacement parts), which, when integrated with the aggregate production plan, becomes the output requirement for the master production schedule (MPS). The process of monitoring and integrating this information is termed *demand management.*

master production schedule
Weekly schedule of specific end product requirements for the next several quarters.

Master Production Scheduling (MPS)   The MPS generates for the manufacturer the amounts and dates of specific end products. The **master production schedule** is usually fixed or "frozen" over the short run (six to eight weeks). Beyond six to eight weeks, various changes can be made, with essentially complete revisions possible after six months. As shown in Exhibit 13.1, the MPS depends on the product and market plans and resource plans outlined in the aggregate production plan.

rough-cut capacity planning
Determination that adequate production capacity and warehousing are available to meet demand.

Rough-Cut Capacity Planning   This reviews the MPS to make sure that no obvious capacity constraints would require changing the schedule. **Rough-cut capacity planning** includes verifying that sufficient production and warehouse facilities, equipment, and labor are available and that key vendors have allocated adequate capacity to provide materials when needed.

Short-Range Planning

Materials Planning   Also known as *material requirements planning (MRP),* which is discussed in Chapter 15, this system takes the end product requirements from the MPS and breaks them down into their subassemblies and component parts. The materials plan specifies when production and purchase orders must be placed for each part and subassembly to complete the products on schedule.

Capacity Requirements Planning   Capacity requirements planning (CRP) should really be referred to as capacity requirements *scheduling,* because it provides a detailed schedule of when each operation is to run on each work center and how long it will take to process. The information it uses comes from planned (i.e., forecasted) and open (i.e., existing) orders that are generated by the materials plan. The CRP itself helps to validate the rough-cut capacity plan.

Final Assembly Scheduling   This activity identifies the various operations required to put the product in its final form. It is here that customized or final features of the product are scheduled. For example, a printer manufacturer would typically specify from various options a control panel configuration at this scheduling stage.

Input/Output Planning and Control   This refers to a variety of reports and procedures focusing on scheduled demands and capacity constraints derived from the materials plan.

Production Activity Control   Production activity control (PAC) is a relatively new term that is used to describe scheduling and shop-floor control activities. PAC involves the scheduling and controlling of day-to-day activities on the shop floor. At this point, the master production schedule is translated into the immediate priorities of daily work schedules.

Purchase Planning and Control   This activity deals with the acquisition and control of purchased items, again as specified by the materials plan. Input/output planning and control are necessary to make sure that purchasing not only is obtaining materials in time to meet the schedule, but is also aware of those orders that, for various reasons, call for rescheduling the delivery of purchased materials.

In summary, all the planning approaches attempt to balance capacity required with capacity available, and then schedule and control production in light of changes in the capacity balance. A good planning system is complete without being overwhelming, and has the confidence of its users up and down the organization structure.

AGGREGATE PRODUCTION PLANNING

Again, aggregate production planning is concerned with setting production rates by product group or other broad categories for the intermediate term (6 to 18 months). Note again from our first exhibit that the aggregate plan precedes the master schedule. *The main purpose of the aggregate plan is to specify that combination of production rate, workforce level, and inventory on hand that both minimizes costs (efficiency) and satisfies the forecasted demand (effectiveness).* **Production rate** refers to the quantity of product completed per unit of time (such as VCRs per hour or automobiles per day). **Workforce level** is the number of workers needed for production. **Inventory on hand** represents the unsold units of product that are carried over from the previous period.

The process of aggregate planning varies from company to company. In some firms, it is a formalized report containing both planning objectives and the planning premises on which it is based. In other companies, particularly smaller ones, it may be much more informal in the form of verbal communications.

The process by which the plan itself is derived also varies. One common approach is to develop it from the corporate annual plan, as was shown in Exhibit 13.1. A typical corporate plan contains a section on manufacturing that specifies how many units in each major product line need to be produced over the next 12 months to meet the sales forecast. The planner takes this information and attempts to determine how best to meet these requirements with available resources. Alternatively, some organizations combine output requirements into

production rate
Capacity of output per unit of time (such as units per day or units per week).

workforce level
Number of workers required to provide a specified level of production.

inventory on hand
Amount of inventory carried over from one time period to the next.

EXHIBIT 13.2

Required Inputs to the Production Planning System

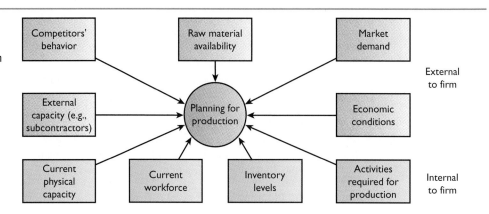

equivalent units and use this as the basis for aggregate planning. For example, a division of General Motors may be asked to produce a certain number of cars of all types at a particular facility. The production planner would then take the average labor hours required for all models as a basis for the overall aggregate plan. Refinements to this plan, specifically model types to be produced, would be reflected in shorter-term production plans. Another approach is to develop the aggregate plan by simulating various master production schedules and calculating corresponding capacity requirements to see if adequate labor and equipment exist at each work center. If capacity is inadequate, additional requirements for overtime, subcontracting, extra workers, and so forth are specified for each product line and combined into a rough-cut plan. This plan is then modified by trial-and-error or mathematical methods to derive a final and, one hopes, lower-cost plan.

Production Planning Environment

Exhibit 13.2 illustrates the internal and external factors that constitute the production planning environment. In general, the external environment is outside the production planner's direct control. In some firms, demand for the product can be managed, but even so, the production planner must live with the sales projections and orders promised by the marketing function. This leaves the internal factors as the variables that can be manipulated in deriving a production plan.

The internal factors themselves differ in their degree of control. Current physical capacity (plant and equipment) is virtually fixed in the short run and, therefore, cannot be increased; union agreements often constrain what can be done in changing the workforce; and top management may set limits on the amount of money that can be tied up in inventories. Still, there is always some flexibility in managing these factors, and production planners can implement one or a combination of the **production planning strategies** discussed here.

Production Planning Strategies

There are essentially three production planning strategies. These strategies involve tradeoffs among workforce size, work hours, inventory, and order backlogs.

1. *Chase strategy.*[1] Match the production rate to exactly meet the order rate by hiring and laying off employees as the order rate varies. The success of this strategy depends on

production planning strategies:

pure strategy Either a chase strategy when production exactly matches demand or a level strategy when production remains constant over a specified number of time periods.

mixed strategy Combination of chase and level strategies to match supply and demand.

---

[1]No relation to one of the authors of this text.

EXHIBIT 13.3

Examples of Pure Chase
and Pure Level Strategies

A. Pure Chase Strategy

B. Pure Level Strategy

having a pool of easily trained applicants to draw on as order volumes increase. There are obvious motivational impacts. When order backlogs are low, employees may feel compelled to slow down out of fear of being laid off as soon as existing orders are completed.

2. *Stable workforce—variable work hours.* Vary the output by varying the number of hours worked through flexible work schedules or overtime. By varying the number of work hours, production quantities can be matched, within limits, to existing orders. This strategy provides workforce continuity and avoids many of the emotional and tangible costs of hiring and firing personnel that are associated with the chase strategy.

3. *Level strategy.* Maintain a stable workforce working at a constant output rate. Shortages and surpluses are absorbed by fluctuating inventory levels, order backlogs, and lost sales. Employees benefit from stable work hours, but inventory costs are increased. Another concern is the possibility of inventoried products becoming obsolete.

When just one of these variables is used to absorb demand fluctuations, it is termed a **pure strategy;** one or more used in combination is a **mixed strategy.** As you might suspect, mixed strategies are more widely applied in industry.

Exhibit 13.3A illustrates a pure chase strategy. Here production is in lockstep with demand. In other words, the number of units required in each time interval is the number of units that production will make. Exhibit 13.3B, on the other hand, demonstrates a pure level strategy. Here production is held constant, regardless of what the demand is. The difference between demand and production is accounted for in a "buffer" inventory of finished goods. When demand exceeds production, the difference is taken out of finished goods inventory ($-I$); when demand is less than production, the difference is placed back into inventory ($+I$). (It is assumed that when demand exceeds production in the initial cycle, as shown in Exhibit 13.3B, that there is sufficient inventory on hand at the beginning of the aggregate planning period to supply the required number of units.)

 Certain industries, due to their inherent operating characteristics, often favor one type of strategy over the other. For example, services tend to follow a chase strategy because the customer is involved in the service delivery process. (If your restaurant is too crowded on a Saturday night, customers will not wait until Monday morning when you have more than enough capacity available to serve them!) Process-oriented facilities, on the other hand, such as breweries and refineries, tend to follow a level strategy because the high fixed costs associated with them require that they operate at a high level of capacity utilization.

Specialty outsourcing companies are being increasingly used to satisfy the needs of companies. Here Norrell Services in Memphis, Tennessee, provides training to temporary workers in high-speed packing techniques. These workers will eventually work for Nike.

Subcontracting   In addition to these strategies, managers may also choose to subcontract some portion of production. This strategy is similar to the chase strategy, but hiring and laying off is translated into subcontracting and not subcontracting. Some level of subcontracting can be desirable to accommodate demand fluctuations. However, unless the relationship with the supplier is particularly strong, a manufacturer can lose some control over schedule and quality. For this reason, extensive subcontracting may be viewed as a high-risk strategy.

Relevant Costs

There are four costs relevant to aggregate production planning. These are:

1. *Basic production costs.* These are the fixed and variable costs incurred in producing a given product type in a given time period. Included are material costs, direct and indirect labor costs, and regular as well as overtime compensation.

2. *Costs associated with changes in the production rate.* Typical costs in this category are those involved in hiring, training, and laying off personnel. Additional one-time costs might also be associated with adding another shift.

3. *Inventory holding costs.* A major component is the cost of capital tied up in inventory. Other components include storage, insurance, taxes, spoilage, and obsolescence.

4. *Backlogging costs.* Usually these costs are very difficult to measure and include costs of expediting, loss of customer goodwill, and loss of sales revenues resulting from cancelled orders because the product is not available.

Budgets   To receive funding, operations managers are generally required to submit annual, and sometimes quarterly, budget requests. Aggregate planning activities are key to the success of the budgeting process. Recall that the goal of aggregate planning is to meet forecasted product demand while minimizing the total production-related costs over the planning horizon by determining the optimal combination of workforce levels and inventory levels. Thus, aggregate planning provides justification for the requested budget amount.

Accurate medium-range planning increases both the likelihood of receiving the requested budget and operating within the limits of the budget.

In the next section, we provide examples of medium-range planning in both a manufacturing and a service setting. These examples illustrate the trade-offs associated with different production planning strategies.

AGGREGATE PLANNING TECHNIQUES

Companies still use simple trial-and-error charting and graphic methods to develop their aggregate plans. Computer spreadsheets and graphics packages are now available to facilitate the process. A trial-and-error approach involves costing out various production planning alternatives and selecting the one with the lowest cost. In addition to the trial-and-error method, there are more sophisticated approaches, including linear programming, the Linear Decision Rule, and various heuristic methods. Of these, only linear programming has seen broad application.

A Trial-and-Error Example: The C&A Company

A firm with pronounced seasonal variation normally plans production with a 12-month time horizon in order to capture the extremes in demand during the busiest and slowest months. However, it is possible to illustrate the general concepts involved in aggregate planning with a shorter time horizon. Suppose we wish to set up a production plan for the C&A Company for the next six months. We are given the information shown in Exhibit 13.4.

EXHIBIT 13.4

Forecasted Demand and Workdays for the C&A Company

	Jan.	Feb.	Mar.	Apr.	May	June	Total
Demand forecast (units)	2,200	1,500	1,100	900	1,100	1,600	8,400
Working days (per month)	22	19	21	21	22	20	125
Costs							
Material cost	$100/unit						
Inventory holding cost	$1.50/unit-month						
Stockout cost	$5/unit/month						
Subcontracting cost	$125/unit						
Hiring and training cost	$200/worker						
Layoff cost	$250/worker						
Labor required per unit	5 hours						
Labor cost (first 8 hours each day)	$4/hour						
Overtime cost (time and a half)	$6/hour						
Inventory							
Beginning inventory	400 units						
Workforce							
Number of workers currently employed	30						

Before we solve this problem, we need to first recognize the differences between full costs and marginal or incremental costs. Full costs are all of the actual, out-of-pocket costs associated with a particular aggregate plan. Included in full costs are the costs of material, labor, and other direct, variable costs. Full costs are often used for developing a projected labor and material budget that will support an aggregate plan.

Marginal or incremental costs are only those unique costs that are different for a particular aggregate plan. Here we assume that the total number of products forecasted over the time horizon need to be built, regardless of the alternative selected. The incremental costs are, therefore, only those costs that are above and beyond those required to build the product by its most economical means (which is usually on the first shift in-house). Included in marginal costs are hiring and firing costs, inventory carrying costs, and overtime and/or second- and third-shift premium costs. To demonstrate the difference, we will use both the full-cost and marginal-cost methods to solve the aggregate planning problem for the C&A Company. You will note that both methods result in selecting the same alternative plan, based on lowest cost. The different alternatives are also ranked in the same order with both methods of costing. The advantage in using the marginal-cost approach is that we do not have to include a lot of numerical figures that have no impact on the final decision.

To properly develop and evaluate an aggregate plan, we need to first divide it into two stages. The first stage is the development of a feasible plan that provides the required number of products under the conditions stated. After this aggregate plan has been developed, the next step is to determine the costs associated with the plan. This is the approach we have taken with the C&A Company. Each alternative aggregate plan is accompanied by both its full and marginal costs.

Many of the costs included in an aggregate plan are presented in a form that is typically not found in the accounting records of a firm. For example, there is usually no cost of carrying inventory. Instead, the individual component costs associated with carrying inventory are listed in separate categories (e.g., the cost of storage is rent, insurance, taxes, etc.; the cost of obsolescence is reflected in higher material and labor costs, etc.).

The first step in evaluating alternative production plans is to convert the demand forecast into production requirements. This is accomplished by subtracting out the amount of inventory on hand at the beginning of the forecast period. In the C&A example, the beginning inventory on hand is 400 units.

Now we are ready to formulate and evaluate alternative aggregate or production plans for the C&A Company. Although one could develop a large number of alternative aggregate plans, we have identified four plans that we will evaluate with the objective of selecting that one with the lowest costs.

Plan 1. Produce to exact monthly production requirements using a regular eight-hour day by varying workforce size (pure chase strategy).

Plan 2. Produce to meet expected average demand over the next six months by maintaining a constant workforce. This constant number of workers is calculated by *averaging* the demand forecast over the horizon. Take the total production requirements for all six months and determine how many workers would be needed if each month's requirements were the same [(8,400 − 400) units × 5 hours per unit ÷ (125 days × 8 hours per day) = 40 workers]. Inventory is allowed to accumulate, and shortages, when they occur, are filled from next month's production by back ordering (pure level strategy).

Plan 3. Produce to meet the minimum expected demand (April) using a constant workforce on regular time. Subcontract to meet additional output requirements. The number of workers is calculated by identifying the minimum monthly production requirement and determining how many workers would be needed for that month [(900 units × 6 months × 5 hours per unit) ÷ (125 days × 8 hours per day) = 27 workers] and subcontracting any

EXHIBIT 13.5

First Alternative: Pure Chase Strategy

	Jan.	Feb.	March	April	May	June	Total
Demand forecast	2,200	1,500	1,100	900	1,100	1,600	8,400
Initial inventory	400						
Production requirements	1,800	1,500	1,100	900	1,100	1,600	8,000
Aggregate plan							
Workers required	51	49	33	27	31	50	
Workers hired	21	0	0	0	4	19	
Workers fired	0	2	16	6	0	0	
Units produced	1,800	1,500	1,100	900	1,100	1,600	8,000
Costs—full							
Regular production	36,000	30,000	22,000	18,000	22,000	32,000	160,000
Material costs	180,000	150,000	110,000	90,000	110,000	160,000	800,000
Hiring costs	4,200	0	0	0	800	3,800	8,800
Firing costs	0	500	4,000	1,500	0	0	6,000
Total full costs	220,200	180,500	136,000	109,500	132,800	195,800	974,800
Costs—incremental							
Hiring costs	4,200	0	0	0	800	3,800	8,800
Firing costs	0	500	4,000	1,500	0	0	6,000
Total incremental costs	4,200	500	4,000	1,500	800	3,800	14,800

EXHIBIT 13.6

Second Alternative: Pure Level Strategy

	Jan.	Feb.	March	April	May	June	Total
Demand forecast	2,200	1,500	1,100	900	1,100	1,600	8,400
Initial inventory	400						
Production requirements	1,800	1,500	1,100	900	1,100	1,600	8,000
Aggregate plan							
Workers required	40	40	40	40	40	40	
Workers hired	10	0	0	0	0	0	
Workers fired	0	0	0	0	0	0	
Units produced	1,408	1,216	1,344	1,344	1,408	1,280	8,000
Monthly inventory	(392)	(284)	244	444	308	(320)	
Cumulative inventory	(392)	(676)	(432)	12	320	0	
Costs—full							
Regular production	28,160	24,320	26,880	26,880	28,160	25,600	160,000
Material costs	140,800	121,600	134,400	134,400	140,800	128,000	800,000
Hiring costs	2,000	0	0	0	0	0	2,000
Firing costs	0	0	0	0	0	0	0
Inventory carrying costs	0	0	0	18	480	0	498
Stockout costs	1,960	3,380	2,160	0	0	0	7,500
Total full costs	172,920	149,300	163,440	161,298	169,440	153,600	969,998
Costs—incremental							
Hiring costs	2,000	0	0	0	0	0	2,000
Firing costs	0	0	0	0	0	0	0
Inventory carrying costs	0	0	0	18	480	0	498
Stockout costs	1,960	3,380	2,160	0	0	0	7,500
Total incremental costs	3,960	3,380	2,160	18	480	0	9,998

EXHIBIT 13.7

Third Alternative: Minimum Workforce with Subcontracting Strategy

	Jan.	Feb.	March	April	May	June	Total
Demand forecast	2,200	1,500	1,100	900	1,100	1,600	8,400
Initial inventory	400						
Production requirements	1,800	1,500	1,100	900	1,100	1,600	8,000
Aggregate plan							
Workers required	27	27	27	27	27	27	
Workers hired	0	0	0	0	0	0	
Workers fired	3	0	0	0	0	0	
Units produced	950	821	907	907	950	864	5,399
Monthly inventory	0	0	0	7	0	0	
Units subcontracted	850	679	193	0	143	736	2,601
Costs—full							
Regular production	19,000	16,420	18,140	18,140	19,000	17,280	107,980
Material costs	95,000	82,100	90,700	90,700	95,000	86,400	539,900
Hiring costs	0	0	0	0	0	0	0
Firing costs	750	0	0	0	0	0	750
Inventory carrying costs	0	0	0	11	0	0	11
Subcontracting costs	106,250	84,875	24,125	0	17,875	92,000	325,125
Total full costs	221,000	183,395	132,965	108,851	131,875	195,680	973,766
Costs—incremental							
Hiring costs	0	0	0	0	0	0	0
Firing costs	750	0	0	0	0	0	750
Inventory carrying costs	0	0	0	11	0	0	11
Subcontracting costs	4,250	3,395	965	0	715	3,680	13,005
Total incremental costs	5,000	3,395	965	11	715	3,680	13,766

monthly difference between requirements and production (minimum workforce with subcontracting strategy).

Plan 4. Produce to meet expected demand for all but the first two months using a constant workforce on regular time. Use overtime to meet additional output requirements (constant workforce with overtime strategy).

The number of workers needed in this alternative is determined as follows:

$$1,100 + 900 + 1,100 + 1,600 = 4,700 \text{ units (March–June)}$$

$$4,700 \text{ units} \times 5 \text{ labor hours per unit} = 23,500 \text{ worker-hours}$$

$$23,500 \text{ worker-hours/8 hours per day} = 2,938 \text{ worker-days}$$

$$2,938 \text{ worker-days/84 days (March–June)} \cong 35 \text{ workers}$$

Having identified each of the four alternatives, the next step is to develop an aggregate plan for each alternative, showing all of the detailed calculations. These are presented in Exhibits 13.5, 13.6, 13.7, and 13.8. Once the details of each production plan have been developed, we can then determine the costs associated with each plan. These costs (both full

EXHIBIT 13.8

Constant Workforce with Overtime Strategy

	Jan.	Feb.	March	April	May	June	Total
Demand forecast	2,200	1,500	1,100	900	1,100	1,600	8,400
Initial inventory	400						
Production requirements	1,800	1,500	1,100	900	1,100	1,600	8,000
Aggregate plan							
Workers required	35	35	35	35	35	35	
Workers hired	5	0	0	0	0	0	
Workers fired	0	0	0	0	0	0	
Units produced—regular	1,232	1,064	1,176	1,176	1,232	1,120	7,000
Units produced—overtime	568	436					1,004
Monthly inventory	0	0	76	276	132	(480)	
Cumulative inventory	0	0	76	352	484	4	
Costs—full							
Regular production	24,640	21,280	23,520	23,520	24,640	22,400	140,000
Overtime production	17,040	13,080	0	0	0	0	30,120
Material costs	180,000	150,000	117,600	117,600	123,200	112,000	800,400
Hiring costs	1,000	0	0	0	0	0	1,000
Firing costs	0	0	0	0	0	0	0
Inventory carrying costs	0	0	114	528	726	6	1,374
Total full costs	222,680	184,360	141,234	141,648	148,566	134,406	972,894
Costs—incremental							
Overtime production	5,680	4,360	0	0	0	0	10,040
Hiring costs	1,000	0	0	0	0	0	1,000
Firing costs	0	0	0	0	0	0	0
Inventory carrying costs			114	528	726	6	1,374
Total incremental costs	6,680	4,360	114	528	726	6	12,414

EXHIBIT 13.9

Summary of Costs for Alternative Aggregate Plans

Alternative	Full Costs	Marginal Costs
Pure chase	$974,800	$14,800
Pure level	$969,998	$ 9,998
Minimum workforce with subcontracting	$973,766	$13,766
Constant workforce with overtime	$972,894	$12,414

costs and marginal costs) are also included in their respective exhibits. A summary of these costs is presented in Exhibit 13.9, showing that the pure level strategy is the lowest cost alternative.

Example

Matt Koslow is the operations manager for the New England Shirt Company. In this capacity he is required to develop an aggregate plan for the next six months with the goal of meeting demand during this period and minimizing costs at the same time. As a first step in developing this plan he obtained from the marketing department the following forecast for shirts:

January	February	March	April	May	June
2,400	1,200	2,800	3,600	3,200	3,600

Matt has estimated the following production data:

Inventory carrying cost	$1.50 per shirt per month
Stockout cost	$3.00 per shirt per month
Hiring cost	$200 per employee
Firing cost	$300 per employee
Labor per shirt	2 hours
Hourly wage	$8.00 per hour
Beginning employment level	30 employees
Beginning inventory level	0 shirts
Hours per employee per day	8 hours
Work days per month	20 days

Using marginal costs, develop both a chase strategy and a level strategy to determine which is the more economical.

Solution   a. See the spreadsheet for marginal cost of chase strategy.

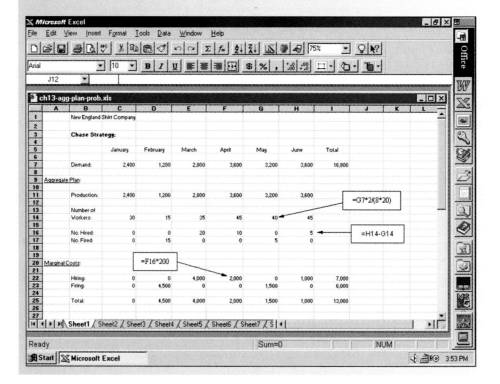

b. See the spreadsheet for marginal cost of level strategy.

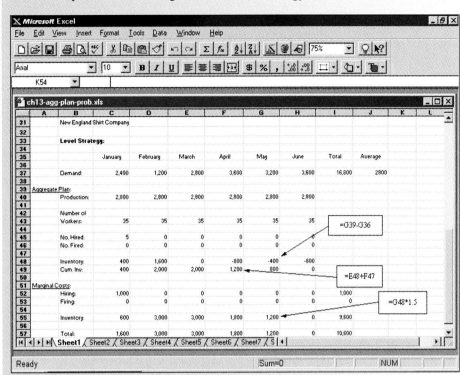

In summary, the costs of each of the strategies are:

Chase strategy $13,000

Level strategy $10,600

Therefore, Matt should elect to go with the level strategy.

Aggregate Planning Applied to Services: Tucson Parks and Recreation Department

Charting and graphic techniques are also very useful for aggregate planning in service applications. The following example shows how a city's parks and recreation department could use the alternatives of full-time employees, part-time employees, and subcontracting to meet its commitment to provide service to the city.

The Tucson Parks and Recreation Department is responsible for developing and maintaining open space, all public recreational programs, adult sports leagues, golf courses, tennis courts, pools, and so forth. There are 336 full-time-equivalent employees (FTEs). Of these, 216 are full-time permanent personnel who provide the administration and year-round maintenance to all areas. The remaining 120 year-long FTE positions are part time, with about 75 percent of them being used during the summer and the remaining 25 percent being used in the fall, winter, and spring seasons. The 75 percent (or 90 FTE positions) show up as approximately 800 part-time summer jobs: lifeguards, baseball umpires, and instructors in summer programs for children. The 800 part-time jobs are derived from 90 FTEs because many of these positions last only for a month or two while the FTEs are a year long.

Currently, the parks and recreation work that is subcontracted amounts to less than $100,000. This is for the golf and tennis pros and for grounds maintenance at the libraries and veterans cemetery.

Because of the nature of city employment, the probable bad public image, and civil service rules, the option to hire and fire full-time help daily and/or weekly to meet seasonal demand is pretty much out of the question. However, temporary part-time help is authorized and traditional. Also, it is virtually impossible to have regular (full-time) staff for all of the summer jobs. During the summer months, the approximately 800 part-time employees are staffing many programs that occur simultaneously, prohibiting level scheduling over a normal 40-hour week. Also, a wider variety of skills is required than can be expected from full-time employees (e.g., umpires; coaches; lifeguards; teachers of ceramics, guitar, karate, belly dancing, and yoga).

Under these conditions, the following three options are open to the department in its aggregate planning.

1. The present method, which is to maintain a medium-level full-time staff and schedule work during off seasons (such as rebuilding baseball fields during the winter months) and to use part-time help during peak demands.
2. Maintain a lower level of staff over the year and subcontract all additional work presently done by full-time staff (still using part-time help).
3. Maintain an administrative staff only and subcontract all work, including part-time help. (This would entail contracts to landscaping firms, pool-maintenance companies, and to newly created private firms to employ and supply part-time help.)

The common unit of measure of work across all areas is full-time equivalent jobs or employees (referred to as FTEs). For example, assume in the same week that 30 lifeguards worked 20 hours each, 40 instructors worked 15 hours each, and 35 baseball umpires worked 10 hours each. This is equivalent to $(30 \times 20) + (40 \times 15) + (35 + 10) = 1,550 \div 40 = 38.75$ FTE positions for that week. Although a considerable amount of workload can be shifted to the off season, most of the work must be done when required.

Full-time employees consist of three groups: (a) the skeleton group of key department personnel coordinating with the city, setting policy, determining budgets, measuring performance, and so forth; (b) the administrative group of supervisory and office personnel who are responsible for or whose jobs are directly linked to the direct-labor workers; and (c) the direct-labor workforce of 116 full-time positions. These workers physically maintain the department's areas of responsibility, such as cleaning up, mowing golf greens and ballfields, trimming trees, and watering grass.

Cost information needed to determine the best alternative strategy is

Full-Time Direct-Labor Employees

Average wage rate	$8.90 per hour
Fringe benefits	17% of wage rate
Administrative costs	20% of wage rate

Part-Time Employees

Average wage rate	$8.06 per hour
Fringe benefits	11% of wage rate
Administrative costs	25% of wage rate
Subcontracting all full-time jobs	$3.2 million
Subcontracting all part-time jobs	$3.7 million

June and July are the peak demand seasons in Tucson. Exhibit 13.10 shows the high seasonal requirements for June and July personnel. The part-time help reaches 575

EXHIBIT 13.10

Actual Demand Requirement for Full-Time Direct Employees and Full-Time Equivalent (FTE) Part-Time Employees

	Jan.	Feb.	March	April	May	June	July	Aug.	Sept.	Oct.	Nov.	Dec.	Total
Days	22	20	21	22	21	20	21	21	21	23	18	22	252
Full-time employees	66	28	130	90	195	290	325	92	45	32	29	60	
Full-time days*	1,452	560	2,730	1,980	4,095	5,800	6,825	1,932	945	736	522	1,320	28,897
Full-time-equivalent part-time employees	41	75	72	68	72	302	576	72	0	68	84	27	
FTE days	902	1,500	1,512	1,496	1,512	6,040	12,096	1,512	0	1,564	1,512	594	30,240

Note: Some workweeks are staggered to include weekdays, but this does not affect the number of workdays per employee.

*Full-time days are derived by multiplying the number of days in each month by the number of workers.

EXHIBIT 13.11

Three Possible Plans for the Parks and Recreation Department

Alternative 1: Maintain 116 full-time regular direct workers. Schedule work during off seasons to level workload throughout the year. Continue to use 120 full-time-equivalent (FTE) part-time employees to meet high demand periods.

Costs	Days per Year (Exhibit 13.9)	Hours (employees × days × 8 hours)	Wages (full-time, $8.90; part-time, $8.06)	Fringe Benefits (full-time, 17%; part-time, 11%)	Administrative Cost (full-time, 20%; part-time, 25%)
116 full-time regular employees	252	233,856	$2,081,318	$353,824	$416,264
120 part-time employees	252	241,920	1,949,875	214,486	487,469
Total cost = $2,751,619			$4,031,193	$568,310	$903,733

Alternative 2: Maintain 50 full-time regular direct workers and the present 120 FTE part-time employees. Subcontract jobs releasing 66 full-time regular employees. Subcontract cost, $2,200,000.

Costs	Days per Year (Exhibit 13.9)	Hours (employees × days × 8 hours)	Wages (full-time, $8.90; part-time, $8.06)	Fringe Benefits (full-time, 17%; part-time, 11%)	Administrative Cost (full-time, 20%; part-time, 25%)	Subcontract Cost
50 full-time employees	252	100,800	$ 897,120	$152,510	$179,424	$2,200,000
120 FTE part-time employees subcontracting cost	252	241,920	1,949,875	214,486	487,469	
Total cost = $3,040,443			$2,846,995	$366,996	$666,893	$2,200,000

Alternative 3: Subcontract all jobs previously performed by 116 full-time regular employees. Subcontract cost $3,200,000. Subcontract all jobs previously performed by 120 full-time-equivalent part-time employees. Subcontract cost $3,700,000.

Cost	Subcontract Cost
0 Full-time employees	
0 Part-time employees	
Subcontract full-time jobs	$3,200,000
Subcontract part-time jobs	3,700,000
Total cost	$6,900,000

EXHIBIT 13.12

Comparison of Costs for All
Three Alternatives

	Alternative 1: 116 Full-Time Direct Labor Employees, 120 FTE Part-Time Employees	Alternative 2: 50 Full-Time Direct Labor Employees, 120 FTE Part-Time Employees, Subcontracting	Alternative 3: Subcontracting Jobs Formerly Performed by 116 Direct Labor Full-Time Employees and 120 FTE Part-Time Employees
Wages	$4,031,193	$2,846,995	—
Fringe benefits	568,310	366,996	—
Administrative costs	903,733	666,893	—
Subcontracting, full-time jobs		2,200,000	$3,200,000
Subcontracting, part-time jobs			3,700,000
Total	$5,503,236	$6,080,884	$6,900,000

fulltime-equivalent positions (although in actual numbers, this is approximately 800 different employees). After a low fall and winter staffing level, the demand shown as "full-time direct" reaches 130 in March when grounds are reseeded and fertilized and then increases to a high of 325 in July. The present method levels this uneven demand over the year to an average of 116 full-time year-round employees by early scheduling of work. As previously mentioned, no attempt is made to hire and lay off full-time workers to meet this uneven demand.

Exhibit 13.11 shows the cost calculations for all three alternatives. Exhibit 13.12 compares the total costs for each alternative. From this analysis, it appears that the department is already using the lowest-cost alternative (Alternative 1).

YIELD MANAGEMENT

Aggregate planning in services is very different from that in manufacturing. This is due, in large part, to the fact that the capacity of service operations is often viewed as highly perishable because it cannot be saved or inventoried for future use. For example, the empty seats in a restaurant on Monday morning cannot be saved for use on Saturday night when it is very busy. Thus services do not have the luxury to choose between chase and level strategies, as do manufacturing firms, but rather must always use the chase strategy. In other words, capacity must be available when the customer wants it.

However, even within this constraint, the service manager has considerable latitude in planning. For those services that have high fixed costs and low variable costs, it is important to maximize capacity utilization even if it means reducing prices to attract additional customers during slow periods of demand. This method, known as **yield management** or *revenue management*, attempts to simultaneously integrate demand management (by changing prices) and supply management (by controlling availability). The goal of yield management is to sell all available capacity, even at discount prices but, at the same time, not turn away a full paying customer because the capacity had been previously sold to a bargain hunter. Examples of industries that apply yield management concepts include airlines that offer discounts for advanced reservations, and car rental agencies and hotels that offer discounts on weekends. (See OM in Practice on National Car Rental.) The concept of yield management is introduced in this chapter; the detailed mathematical theory behind yield management is explained in the next chapter. It is also mentioned in the forecasting chapter.

yield management
Concept used in certain
service operations that
attempts to match supply
and demand.

YIELD MANAGEMENT AT NATIONAL CAR RENTAL

Faced with possible liquidation in 1993 by General Motors, its parent company, National Car Rental was under significant pressure to produce both a substantial and sustainable profit. To accomplish this, management decided to adopt a comprehensive revenue management system. Instead of a constant car rental price all the time, the revenue management system demonstrated that a variable pricing policy which would fluctuate with demand would result in significantly higher profits.

The revenue management system was implemented in two phases. The first phase was introduced in July, 1993, with the goal of showing immediate profits, which it did. The second phase focused on developing a state-of-the-art revenue management system for the car rental industry. This phase was successfully implemented in July 1994.

As a result of this revenue management system, profits were significantly increased, and General Motors was able to sell National Car Rental in 1995 for an amount in excess of $1 billion.

Sources: Ernest Johnson, "1994 Trophy Award: National Car Rental Systems, Inc." *Scorecard: The Revenue Management Quarterly,* First Quarter, 1995. M. K. Geraghty and Ernest Johnson, "Revenue Management Saves National Car Rental," *Interfaces* 27, no. 1 (January–February 1997), pp. 107–27.

After yield management has been applied to a service operation, the service manager would then determine the aggregate workforce requirements in a manner similar to that described previously for a manufacturing company.

In order to take maximum advantage of yield management, a service should have the following characteristics: (*a*) the ability to segment its markets, (*b*) high-fixed and low-variable costs, (*c*) product perishability, and (*d*) the ability to presell capacity.[2]

Market Segmentation

A major issue in the successful implementation of yield management is the ability of the firm to segment its markets. Proper segmentation will prevent all of the firm's customers from taking advantage of price reductions when they are offered to fill available capacity.

Market segmentation can be done in several ways. The first is to impose significant restrictions on customers who use the lower prices. For example, airlines require customers to stay over a Saturday night or to purchase their tickets from 7 to 30 days in advance to qualify for lower airfares. These very same conditions, however, prevent the business traveler, who usually travels midweek on short notice, from taking advantage of the lower fares.

Another method of segmentation is to limit lower prices to specific days of the week or times of the day. Movie theaters offer reduced ticket prices for matinees, which senior citizens can take advantage of during weekdays. Similarly, downtown hotels typically offer discounts on weekends when business travelers are home, as an incentive for tourists.

High-Fixed and Low-Variable Costs

High-fixed and low-variable costs allow a firm to offer significant discounts while still being able to cover variable costs. When a service firm has this type of cost profile, profits are directly related to sales. In other words, the more sales generated, the more profits made.

For example, if the variable cost associated with having a hotel room cleaned is estimated at $25 (which would include the labor to clean the room and the replacement of any material that was consumed, such as soap and shampoo, as well as fresh sheets and towels),

---

[2]Sheryl E. Kimes, "Yield-Management: A Tool for Capacity-Constrained Service Firms," *Journal of Operations Management* 8, no. 4 (October 1989).

then any price that the hotel could get for the room above the $25 variable cost would be financially beneficial (as opposed to leaving the room empty for the night).

Product Perishability

The underlying reason that yield management can be applied to many types of services is the perishability of service capacity. In other words, service capacity cannot be saved for future use. (Wouldn't it be great if the airlines could save all of their empty seats during the year for use during the Thanksgiving and Christmas periods!) Given that capacity in a service operation is perishable, the service manager should try and maximize capacity utilization whenever possible, even if it means offering large discounts to attract customers—provided that the discounted prices exceed the variable cost.

Presold Capacity

A final requirement for the successful implementation of yield management is that the lower-priced capacity can be sold in advance. This limits the availability of capacity to the higher priced market segments. As an illustration, hotels usually work with conference planners several years in advance of a conference, offering a given number of rooms at the lowest room rates. Travel groups usually plan tours within a year before they need them and therefore also receive a discount. Finally, the last-minute customer, or "walk-in," will pay top dollar or the "rack-rate" for a hotel room.

CONCLUSION

Aggregate planning provides the link between the corporate strategic and capacity plans and workforce size, inventory quantity, and production levels. It does not involve detailed planning. It is also useful to point out some practical considerations in aggregate planning.

First, demand variations are a fact of life, so the planning system must include sufficient flexibility to cope with such variations. Flexibility can be achieved by developing alternative sources of supply, cross-training workers to handle a wide variety of orders, and engaging in more frequent replanning during high-demand periods.

Second, decision rules for production planning should be adhered to once they have been selected. However, they should be carefully analyzed prior to implementation by such checks as using simulation of historical data to see what really would have happened if these rules had been in operation in the past.

 Services typically require a chase strategy due to the customer's direct involvement with the service delivery system. However, services, under certain conditions, can successfully apply the concept of yield management, which simultaneously adjusts customer demand and the operation's capacity with the goal of maximizing the firm's profit.

KEY TERMS

REVIEW AND DISCUSSION QUESTIONS

1. What are the basic controllable variables of a production planning problem? What are the four major costs?
2. Distinguish between pure and mixed strategies in production planning.
3. Compare the best plans in the C&A Company and the Tucson Parks and Recreation Department. What do they have in common?
4. How does forecast accuracy relate, in general, to the practical application of the aggregate planning models discussed in the chapter?
5. In which way does the time horizon chosen for an aggregate plan determine whether or not it is the best plan for the firm?
6. Under what conditions is the concept of yield management must appropriate for service operations?

SOLVED PROBLEM

Problem

Jason Enterprises (JE) is producing video telephones for the home market. Quality is not quite as good as it could be at this point, but the selling price is low and Jason has the opportunity to study market response while spending more time in additional R&D work.

At this stage, however, JE needs to develop an aggregate production plan for the six months from January through June. As you can guess, you have been commissioned to create the plan. The following information is available to help you:

	Jan.	Feb.	March	April	May	June
Demand data						
Beginning inventory	200					
Forecast demand	500	600	650	800	900	800
Cost data						
Holding cost			$10/unit/month			
Stockout cost			$20/unit/month			
Subcontracting cost/unit			$100			
Hiring cost/worker			$50			
Layoff cost/worker			$100			
Labor cost/hour—straight time			$12.50			
Labor cost/hour—overtime			$18.75			
Production data						
Labor hours/unit			4			
Workdays/month			22			
Current workforce			10			

What is the cost of each of the following production strategies?

a. Chase strategy; vary workforce (assuming a starting workforce of 10).

b. Constant workforce; vary inventory and stockout only (assuming a starting workforce of 10).

c. Level workforce of 10; vary overtime only; inventory carryover permitted.

d. Level workforce of 10; vary overtime only; inventory carryover not permitted.

Solution

a. Plan 1: Chase strategy; vary workforce (assume 10 in workforce to start).

Month	(1) Production Requirement	(2) Production Hours Required (1) × 4	(3) Hours/Month per Worker 22 × 8	(4) Workers Required (2) ÷ (3)	(5) Workers Hired	(6) Workers Fired
January	300	1,200	176	7	0	3
February	600	2,400	176	14	7	0
March	650	2,600	176	15	1	0
April	800	3,200	176	18	3	0
May	900	3,600	176	20	2	0
June	800	3,200	176	18	0	2

Month	(7) Hiring Cost (5) × $50	(8) Layoff Cost (6) × $100	(9) Straight-Time Cost (2) × $12.50
January	0	$300	$ 15,000
February	350	0	30,000
March	50	0	32,500
April	150	0	40,000
May	100	0	45,000
June	0	200	40,000
	$650	$500	$202,500

Total cost for plan:

Hiring cost	$	650
Layoff cost		500
Straight-time cost		202,500
Total		$203,650

b. Plan 2: Constant workforce; vary inventory and stockout only.

Month	(1) Cumulative Production Requirement	(2) Production Hours Available 22 × 8 × 10	(3) Units Produced (2) ÷ 4	(4) Cumulative Production
January	300	1,760	440	440
February	900	1,760	440	880
March	1,550	1,760	440	1,320
April	2,350	1,760	440	1,760
May	3,250	1,760	440	2,200
June	4,050	1,760	440	2,640

Month	(5) Units Short (1) − (4)	(6) Shortage Cost (5) × $20	(7) Units in Excess (4) − (1)	(8) Inventory Cost (7) × $10	(9) Straight-Time Cost (2) × $12.50
January	$ 0	0	140	1,400	$ 22,000
February	20	400	0	0	22,000
March	230	4,600	0	0	22,000
April	590	11,800	0	0	22,000
May	1,050	21,000	0	0	22,000
June	1,410	28,200	0	0	22,000
		$66,000		$1,400	$132,000

Total cost for plan:

Shortage cost	$ 66,000	
Inventory cost	1,400	
Straight-time cost	132,000	
Total	$199,400	

c. Plan 3: Level workforce of 10; vary overtime only; inventory carryover permitted.

Month	(1) Production Requirement	(2) Standard Time Hours Available 22 × 8 × 10	(3) Standard Time Units Produced (2) ÷ 4	(4) Overtime Required in Units (1) − (3)
January	300	1,760	440	0
February	460*	1,760	440	20
March	650	1,760	440	210
April	800	1,760	440	360
May	900	1,760	440	460
June	800	1,760	440	360
				1,410

*600 − 140 units of beginning inventory in February.

Month	(5) Overtime Required in Hours (4) × 4	(6) Overtime Cost (5) × $18.75	(7) Straight- Time Cost (2) × $12.50	(8) Excess Inventory Costs (3) − (1) × $10
January	0	$ 0	$ 22,000	$1,400
February	80	1,500	22,000	
March	840	15,750	22,000	
April	1,440	27,000	22,000	
May	1,840	34,500	22,000	
June	1,440	27,000	22,000	
		$105,750	$132,000	$1,400

Total cost for plan:

Straight-time cost	$132,000	
Overtime cost	105,750	
Inventory cost	1,400	
Total	$239,150	

d. Plan 4: Constant workforce of 10; vary overtime only; inventory carryover not permitted.

Month	(1) Production Requirement	(2) Standard-Time Hours Available 22 × 8 × 10	(3) Standard-Time Units Produced Min. [(2) ÷ 4; (1)]	(4) Overtime Required in Units (1) − (3)
January	300	1,760	300	0
February	600	1,760	440	160
March	650	1,760	440	210
April	800	1,760	440	360
May	900	1,760	440	460
June	800	1,760	440	360

Month	(5) Overtime Required in Hours (4) × 4	(6) Overtime Cost (5) × $18.75	(7) Standard-Time Cost (2) × $12.50	(8) Excess Inventory Costs (3) − (1) × $10
January	0	$0	$22,000	$1,400
February	640	12,000	22,000	
March	840	15,750	22,000	
April	1,440	27,000	22,000	
May	1,840	34,500	22,000	
June	1,440	27,000	22,000	
		$116,250	$132,000	$1,400

Total cost for plan:

Straight-time cost	$132,000
Overtime cost	116,250
Excess inventory cost	1,400
	$249,650

PROBLEMS

1. Develop a production plan and calculate the annual cost for a firm whose unit demand forecast is fall, 10,000; winter, 8,000; spring, 7,000; summer, 12,000. Inventory at the beginning of fall is 500 units. At the beginning of fall you currently have 30 workers, but you plan to hire temporary workers at the beginning of summer and lay them off at the end of summer. In addition, you have negotiated with the union an option to use the regular workforce on overtime during winter or spring if overtime is necessary to prevent stockouts at the end of those quarters. Overtime is *not* available during the fall. Relevant costs are: hiring, $100 for each temp; layoff, $200 for each regular worker laid off; inventory holding, $5 per unit per quarter; back order, $10 per unit; straight time, $5 per hour; overtime, $8 per hour. Assume that worker productivity is two hours per unit, with eight hours per day and 60 days per season.

2. Develop an aggregate production plan for a four-month period: February through May. For February and March, you should produce to exactly meet the demand forecast. For April and May, you should use overtime and inventory with a stable workforce. However, government constraints put a maximum of 5,000 hours of overtime labor per month in April and May (zero overtime in February and March). If demand exceeds supply, then back orders occur. There are 100 workers on January 31. You are given the following unit demand forecast: February, 80,000; March, 64,000; April, 100,000; May, 40,000. Worker productivity is four units per hour. Assume eight hours per day, 20 days per month and zero inventory on February 1. Costs are: hiring, $50 per new worker; layoff, $70 per worker laid off; inventory holding, $10 per unit per month; straight-time labor, $10 per hour; overtime, $15 per hour; backorder, $20 per unit. Find the total cost of this plan.

3. Develop an aggregate production plan for the next year. The unit demand forecast is spring, 20,000; summer, 10,000; fall, 15,000; winter, 18,000. At the beginning of spring you have 70 workers and 1,000 units in inventory. The union contract specifies that you may lay off workers only once a year, at the beginning of summer. Also, you may hire new workers only at the end of summer to begin regular work in the fall. The number of workers laid off at the beginning of summer and the number hired at the end of summer should result in planned production levels for summer and fall that equal the demand forecasts for summer and fall respectively. If demand exceeds supply, use overtime in spring only, which means that back orders could occur in winter. You are given these costs: hiring, $100 per new worker; layoff,

$200 per worker laid off; holding, $20 per unit per quarter; back-order costs, $8 per unit; straight-time labor, $10 per hour; overtime, $15 per hour. Worker productivity is two hours per unit. Assume eight hours per day and 50 days per quarter. Find the total cost.

4. DAT, Inc. needs to develop an aggregate plan for its product line. Relevant data are:

Production time	I hour per unit
Average labor cost	$10 per hour
Work-week	5 days, 8 hours each day
Days per month	Assume 20 work days per month
Beginning inventory	500 units
Safety stock	One-half of monthly forecast
Shortage cost	$20 per unit per month
Inventory carrying cost	$5 per unit per month

The forecast for January to December 1998 is:

Jan.	Feb.	March	April	May	June	July	Aug.	Sept.	Oct.	Nov.	Dec.
2,500	3,000	4,000	3,500	3,500	3,000	3,000	4,000	4,000	4,000	3,000	3,000

Management prefers to keep a constant workforce and production level, absorbing variations in demand through inventory excesses and shortages. Demand that is not met is carried over to the following month.

Develop an aggregate plan that will meet the demand and other conditions of the problem. Do not try to find the optimum; just find a good solution and state the procedure you might use to test for a better solution. Make any necessary assumptions.

5. Shoney Video Concepts produces a line of CD players to be linked to personal computers for video games. CDs have much faster access time than do tape. With such a computer/CD link, the game becomes a very realistic experience. In a simple driving game where the joystick steers the vehicle, for example, rather than seeing computer graphics on the screen, the player is actually viewing a segment of a CD shot from a real moving vehicle. Depending on the action of the player (hitting a guard rail, for example) the disc moves virtually instantaneously to that segment and the player becomes part of an actual accident of real vehicles (staged, of course).

Shoney is trying to determine a production plan for the next 12 months. The main criterion for this plan is that the employment level is to be held constant over the period. Shoney is continuing in its R&D efforts to develop new applications and prefers not to cause any adverse feeling with the local workforce. For the same reasons, all employees should put in full work weeks, even if this is not the lowest-cost alternative. The number of CD players forecast for the next 12 months is:

Month	Forecast Demand	Month	Forecast Demand
January	600	July	200
February	800	August	200
March	900	September	300
April	600	October	700
May	400	November	800
June	300	December	900

Manufacturing cost is $200 per player, equally divided between materials and labor. Inventory storage costs are $5 per CD player per month. A shortage results in lost sales and is estimated to cost an overall $20 per unit short. (Shortages are not carried forward since the sales are lost.)

The inventory on hand at the beginning of the planning period is 200 units. Ten labor hours are required per CD player. The workday is eight hours.

Develop an aggregate production schedule for the year using a constant workforce. For simplicity, assume 22 working days each month except July, when the plant closes down for three weeks' vacation (leaving seven working days). Make any assumptions you need.

6. The Bentley Chemical Company (BCC) is vitally concerned about generating a production schedule for their products for the coming fiscal year (July–June). The operations manager at BCC, Mr. Perspa Cassidy, has been charged with generating an aggregate plan for this time period so that BCC can meet their demand with the minimum utilization of resources.

Mr. Cassidy first aggregates the various products which BCC sells into a single "aggregate" production unit and forecasts the demand for the following four quarters:

Quarter	Quarter #1 Jul/Aug/Sept	Quarter #2 Oct/Nov/Dec	Quarter #3 Jan/Feb/Mar	Quarter #4 Apr/May/June
Demand forecast	10,000	9,800	9,400	10,200

On March 1 (prior to quarter #1) there were 1,200 units in BCC's inventory and the forecast demand for the fourth quarter of the previous year is 9,900 units. Mr. Cassidy knows that to keep one unit in inventory for one month costs $5; further, BCC uses average inventory when computing inventory costs. The workforce on March 1 consisted of 40 employees, each of whom produces exactly four (4) units in an 8-hour day. For the coming four quarters, Mr. Cassidy has determined the number of productive days for each quarter to be as follows:

Quarter	Quarter #1 Jul/Aug/Sept	Quarter #2 Oct/Nov/Dec	Quarter #3 Jan/Feb/Mar	Quarter #4 Apr/May/June
Number of productive days	56	60	61	63

Each of the regular employees is paid at the rate of $53 per day; however, overtime is available at the rate of $80 per day. BCC has a very strict quality control policy and does not allow any subcontracting. In addition, BCC wishes to maintain their reputation with their customers and has adopted a policy that *all* demand must be met on time.

Mr. Cassidy recognizes that meeting all demand can be difficult. He is faced with two limitations: (1) he is using aggregate units, and (2) he has only his forecasts as a basis for his aggregate plan. However, he believes that his forecasts are quite good and decides to use his figures objectively (i.e., he decides not to keep any safety stock).

The workforce can be increased or decreased at the discretion of Mr. Cassidy, but no more than a 25 percent increase or decrease (using integer values) is allowed in any given quarter due to union regulations. Mr. Cassidy knows that should he wish to hire and/or fire, that the total increase/decrease in the workforce (when using whole people) cannot exceed the 25 percent mark. Fortunately, BCC is located in an area where there is no shortage of skilled labor.

To hire a new individual and train him/her requires exactly one quarter and costs $1,200. All new employees always start on the first day of a given quarter. Hence, they cannot be considered part of the productive labor force until after their first quarter. To fire an individual costs $1,000, and when an individual is fired, he remains part of the productive workforce until the end of the quarter in which he was fired.

Mr. Cassidy believes that he has all the data he needs; hence, he starts to determine the aggregate capacity plan. He selects a strategy of trying to maintain a relatively stable workforce, while letting the inventory levels fluctuate.

a. Perform the initial calculations Mr. Cassidy would need prior to completing the grid that follows.

b. Develop an aggregate plan for Mr. Cassidy by filling in the grid.

c. What is the total cost of Mr. Cassidy's plan?

(1) Qtr.	(2) Demand	(3) Prod. Hours Req. (2) × 2	(4) Prod. Days per Qtr.	(5) Prod. Hrs. per Qtr. per Worker (4) × 8	(6) No. of Empls.	(7) Total Prod. Hrs. Avail. per Qtr. (5) × (6)	(8) Straight-Time Cost (4) × (6) × $53	(9) No. of Units Short	(10) Short Cost	(11) No. of OT Units Req.	(12) No. of OT Days Req. (11)/4
NOW	9,900	19,800	63	504	40	20,160	$133,560	0	$0	0	0
1	10,000		56						0		
2	9,800		60						0		
3	9,400		61						0		
4	10,200		63						0		

(13) Overtime Cost (12) × $80	(14) No. of Unit Sub.	(15) Sub. Cost.	(16) No. of Empls. Hired	(17) Hiring Cost (16) × $1200	(18) No. of Empls. Fired	(19) Firing Cost (18) × $1000	(20) Begin. Inv.	(21) End. Inv.	(22) Ave. Inv. (20) + (21) / 2	(23) Inv. Cost (22) × $15
$0	0	$0	0	$0	0	$ 0	1,200	1,380	1,290	$19,350
								1,380		

CASE: XYZ BROKERAGE FIRM

Consider the national operations group of the XYZ brokerage firm. The group, housed in an office building located in the Wall Street area, handles the transactions generated by registered representatives in more than 100 branch offices throughout the United States. As with all firms in the brokerage industry, XYZ's transactions must be settled within five trading days. This five-day period allows operations managers to smooth out the daily volume fluctuations.

Fundamental shifts in the stock market's volume and mix can occur overnight, so the operations manager must be prepared to handle extremely wide swings in volume. For example, on the strength of an international peace rumor, the number of transactions or XYZ rose from 5,600 one day to 12,200 the next.

Managers of XYZ, not unlike their counterparts in other firms, have trouble predicting volume. In fact, a ran-

dom number generator can predict volume a month or even a week into the future almost as well as the managers can.

How do the operations managers in XYZ manage capacity when there are such wide swings? The answer differs according to the tasks and constraints facing each manager. Here's what two managers in the same firm might say:

Manager A: The capacity in our operation is currently 12,000 transactions per day. Of course, what we should gear up for is always a problem. For example, our volume this year ranged from 4,000 to 15,000 transactions per day. It's a good thing we have a turnover rate, because in periods of low volume it helps us reduce our personnel without the morale problems caused by layoffs. [The labor turnover rate in this department is over 100 percent per year.]

Manager B: For any valid budgeting procedure, one needs to estimate volume within 15 percent. Correlations between actual and expected volume in the brokerage industry have been so poor that I question the value of budgeting at all. I maintain our capacity at a level of 17,000 transactions per day.

Why the big difference in capacity management in the same firm? Manager A is in charge of the cashiering operation—the handling of certificates, checks, and cash. The personnel in cashiering are messengers, clerks, and supervisors. The equipment—file cabinets, vaults, calculators—is uncomplicated.

Manager B, however, is in charge of handling orders, an information-processing function. The personnel are data-entry clerks, EDP specialists, and systems analysts. The equipment is complex—computers, LANs, file servers, and communication devices that link national operations with the branches. The employees under B's control had performed their tasks manually until decreased volume and a standardization of the information needs made it worthwhile to install computers.

Because the lead times required to increase the capacity of the information-processing operations are long, however, and the incremental cost of the capacity to handle the last 5,000 transactions is low (only some extra peripheral equipment is needed), Manager B maintains the capacity to handle 17,000 transactions per day. He holds to this level even though the average number of daily transactions for any month has never been higher than 11,000 and the number of transactions for any one day has never been higher than 16,000.

Because a great deal of uncertainty about the future status of the stock certificate exists, the situation is completely different in cashiering. Attempts to automate the cashiering function to the degree reached by the order-processing group have been thwarted because the high risk of selecting a system not compatible with the future format of the stock certificate.

In other words, Manager A is tied to the chase demand strategy, and his counterpart, Manager B in the adjacent office, is locked into the level capacity strategy. However, each desires to incorporate more of the other's strategy into his own. A is developing a computerized system to handle the information-processing requirements of cashiering; B is searching for some variable costs in the order-processing operation that can be deleted in periods of low volume.

QUESTIONS

1. What appear to be the primary differences between these two departments?

2. Do these differences eliminate certain strategy choices for either manager?

3. Which factors cause the current strategy to be desirable for each manager?

4. What are the mixed or subcontracting possibilities?

5. What are the problems associated with low standardization?

Source: *Management of Service Operations*, 1/E, by Sasser/Olsen/Wykoff, © 1978. Reprinted by permission of Prentice Hall, Inc., Upper Saddle River, NJ.

CASE: LA BUENA COMPAÑÍA DE ESPAÑA, S.A.

La Buena Compañía de España, S.A., (LBC) located just outside of Barcelona, Spain, produces kitchen tables that it sells throughout Western Europe. Sales have been increasing steadily over the past several years, due in large part to the free trade among Western European countries that has resulted from the formation of the European Union (EU).

Jordi Garolera, the operations manager at LBC, is currently developing an aggregate plan for the next six months. In order for him to be able to evaluate alternative plans, Jordi has collected the following information:

Production Data

20 work days per month.

7.5 hours per work day.

2.5 labor-hours per table (average).

On-hand inventory: 300 tables.

Current workforce: 25 workers.

Cost Data

Hourly wages: 800 pesetas (ptas.) per hour.

Hiring costs: 20.000 ptas. per employee.*

---

*In Europe, decimals are separated from whole numbers by a comma, whereas, thousands and millions are separated by periods which is just the reverse of the practice in the United States. Thus US$5,000.00 in the United States would be written as US$5.000,00 in Europe.

Firing costs: 70.000 ptas. per employee.

Material cost per table: 10.000 ptas.

Overtime costs: 50 percent premium.

Inventory carrying costs: 200 ptas. per unit per month.

Stockout costs: 1.000 ptas. per unit per month.

Jordi has just returned from a meeting with the marketing manager who provided him with a sales forecast for the next six months of 12.960 tables, which is broken down as follows by month:

Month	Jan.	Feb.	Mar.	Apr.	May	June
Forecast (Tables)	1.740	1.740	2.460	3.240	2.220	1.860

QUESTIONS

1. Using Excel or a similar spreadsheet, compare the costs of a pure chase strategy and a pure level strategy. Which type of strategy would you recommend?

2. As another alternative, Jordi was considering using a level workforce of 30 employees and working overtime to eliminate any stockouts. Evaluate this alternative and compare it to the pure strategies.

3. What alternative aggregate plans could you suggest to Jordi? What are the relative strengths and weaknesses of these plan(s)?

Source: © 1997 by Mark M. Davis.

SELECTED BIBLIOGRAPHY

Fisk, J. C., and J. P. Seagle. "Integration of Aggregate Planning with Resource Requirements Planning." *Production and Inventory Management,* Third Quarter 1978, p. 87.

Geraghty, M. K., and Ernest Johnson. "Revenue Management Saves National Car Rental." *Interfaces* 27, no. 1 (January–February 1997), pp. 107–27.

Johnson, Ernest. "1994 Trophy Award: National Car Rental Systems, Inc." *Scorecard: The Revenue Management Quarterly,* First Quarter, 1995.

Kimes, Sheryl E. "Yield-Management: A Tool for Capacity-Constrained Service Firms." *Journal of Operations Management* 8, no. 4 (October 1989).

McLeavy, D., and S. Narasimhan. *Production Planning and Inventory Control.* Boston: Allyn & Bacon, 1985.

Plossl, G. W. *Production and Inventory Control: Principles and Techniques.* 2nd ed. Englewood Cliffs, NJ: Prentice Hall, 1985.

Sasser, W. E.; R. P. Olsen; and D. D. Wyckoff. *Management of Service Operations.* Boston: Allyn & Bacon, 1978.

Silver, E. A., and R. Peterson. *Decision Systems for Inventory Management and Production Planning.* 2nd ed. New York: John Wiley & Sons, 1985.

Vollmann, T. E.; W. L. Berry; and D.C. Whybark. *Manufacturing Planning and Control Systems.* 3rd ed. Homewood, IL: Richard D. Irwin, 1992.

INVENTORY SYSTEMS FOR INDEPENDENT DEMAND

Chapter Outline

Chapter Objectives

- Introduce the different types of inventories that can exist in an organization and provide a rationale for why companies maintain inventories.

- Identify the various costs associated with carrying and maintaining inventories.

- Define the classical inventory models and the conditions necessary for them to be applicable.

- Show how the economic order quantity is calculated for each of the different inventory models.

- Introduce the single-period inventory model and the concept of yield management with respect to service operations.

- Present some of the current inventory management trends and issues that exist in companies today.

The senior executives of Alpha Numerics were having their annual retreat to review accomplishments of the past year and to discuss major policy issues for the coming year.* As was the norm, the retreat was held at a small hotel in the mountains of eastern Pennsylvania, well removed from the company's actual manufacturing facility.

"Something's got to go, Fenton. You, me or this inventory—and it's not going to be me."

The first day's meeting had gone well, but in the early evening, after dinner, the subject of inventory control and the number of shortages that had occurred over the past year came up for discussion. The vice president of engineering suggested that, as a solution to the shortage problem, purchasing should order all of the projected material requirements at the beginning of the year.

The vice president of manufacturing was so taken back by this suggestion that, to the amazement of the others in the room, he leaped onto the conference table and shouted out, "Inventory is evil!" He turned to the president and said, "If we were to follow this suggestion, Mr. President, do you have an extra 25,000 square feet of warehouse space where we can store the material?" The president shook his head no. "And do you, Mr. Vice President of Finance, have an extra $5 million dollars to buy all this material?" The VP of finance similarly shook his head.

"And are you, Mr. Vice President of Marketing, going to provide me with a perfect forecast of the products we expect to sell for the next year?" The VP of marketing said, "No, of course not. That would be impossible." And turning to the VP of engineering who had made the initial proposal, he said, "And you'll keep the same designs in the coming year without making any changes, won't you?" The VP of engineering said, "That would be very unrealistic." All of the individuals in the room then looked up to the VP of manufacturing still standing on the conference table and said, "We see what you mean. Inventory is indeed evil!" ■

---

*This meeting of senior corporate executives actually took place, although the name of the firm has been disguised.

**Inventory.
The longer it sits, the harder it is to move.**

Despite what your balance sheet might tell you, inventory is no longer an asset. Today, big inventories can slow business and even bring it to a screeching halt. But you can keep your profits moving in the right direction by boosting productivity in your supply chain.

GE Information Services can help you shorten cycle times, improve inventory turns and eliminate out-of-stock occurrences. We'll show you how to link suppliers, manufacturers and distributors electronically so that your purchase orders and invoices are easily sent and tracked, auditing is greatly simplified and customer buying trends are instantly identified through point-of-sale data. For one large retailer, that meant reducing stock replenishment cycles from 3 days to 3 hours. Another one of our clients now gets spare parts to overseas distributors up to 10 days sooner.

You'd be surprised how much smoother your business will run after a tune-up by GE Information Services.
Productivity. It's All We Do.℠

GE Information Services

For more information, please call 1-800-560-GEIS, or write GE Information Services, MC07F2, 401 N. Washington St., Rockville, MD 20850. Find us on the Internet at http://www.geis.com.

In the past, inventory was perceived as an asset to an organization inasmuch as it appeared as an asset in its financial reports. This view, as shown in the opening vignette, is no longer the accepted norm. With product life cycles becoming increasingly shorter, product obsolescence also becomes more likely. In addition, we now recognize that inventories, particularly work-in-process inventories, tend to conceal problems. Maintaining inventories can also be very expensive. The average annual cost of maintaining inventories across all manufacturing firms is estimated to be 30 to 35 percent of its value, and could even be higher for some products. For these and other reasons, inventory is now seen to be a liability, something to be reduced or eliminated to the greatest extent possible as also shown by this GE advertisement that explains their ability to set up electronic links with suppliers, manufacturers, and distributors to avoid costly inventory.

As a result, probably no topic in operations today is more often discussed or perceived to be more important than inventory. The name of the game is to reduce inventory quantities on hand at all levels: in raw materials and purchased parts through direct delivery by the vendor (often directly to the production line); in work in process by techniques such as just-in-time production or scheduling with small batch sizes; and finally, in finished goods through a better matching of output to market requirements, and shipments to those markets as soon as possible. The growing effort to reduce all inventory is inspired by new measurements and performance evaluation based not on the percentage of resource utilization, but rather on inventory turns and product quality.

There are also changing views concerning the teaching of classical inventory models. On one side, some claim that economic order quantity (EOQ) models are invalid in actual application; others defend their use. While one must be careful when using them, there do exist situations where EOQ models can be successfully applied. More important, from a learning perspective, these models provide a basic framework for understanding the difficult issues involved in inventory management. Just-in-time manufacturing (JIT), for example, is based on the classical production-consumption model.

In this chapter, we present fixed-order and fixed-time period models. Also included are special purpose models, such as the quantity discount model, as well as the ABC technique for classifying items in inventory. We also present the single-period model which addresses highly perishable products as well as inventory issues in services through a discussion of yield management. In addition, we discuss the questions of inventory accuracy and show simple applications of the models in the real-world environment.

DEFINITION OF INVENTORY

Inventory is defined as the stock of any item or resource used in an organization. An *inventory system* is the set of policies and controls that monitors levels of inventory and determines (*a*) what levels should be maintained, (*b*) when stock should be replenished, and (*c*) how large orders should be.

types of inventory: raw material
Vendor-supplied items that have not had any labor added.

finished goods
Completed products still in the possession of the firm.

work-in-process (WIP)
Items that have been partially processed but are still incomplete.

In its complete scope, inventory can include inputs such as human, financial, energy, equipment, and physical items such as **raw materials;** outputs such as parts, components, and **finished goods;** and interim stages of the process, such as partially finished goods or **work-in-process (WIP).** The choice of which items to include in inventory depends on the organization. A manufacturing operation can have an inventory of personnel, machines, and working capital, as well as raw materials and finished goods. An airline can have an inventory of seats; a modern drugstore, an inventory of medicines, batteries, and toys; and an engineering firm, an inventory of engineering talent.

By convention, manufacturing inventory generally refers to materials that contribute to or become part of a firm's product output. In services, inventory generally refers to the tangible goods to be sold and the supplies necessary to administer the service. Customers waiting in line at a service operation can also be viewed as inventory similar to parts waiting to be processed in a factory.

The basic purpose of inventory analysis in manufacturing and stockkeeping services is to specify (*a*) when items should be ordered and (*b*) how large the order should be. Recent trends have modified the simple questions of "when" and "how many." As we saw in an earlier chapter on supply chain management, many firms are tending to enter into longer-term relationships with vendors to supply their needs for perhaps the entire year. This changes the "when" and "how many to order" to "when" and "how many to deliver."

PURPOSES OF INVENTORY

Organizations maintain inventories for several reasons. These include:

1. *To protect against uncertainty.* For purposes of inventory management, we examine uncertainty in three areas. First, there is uncertainty with respect to raw materials, which necessitates raw material inventory. Here, uncertainty pertains both to the lead time that can vary due to unexpected delays and to the amount of raw material received.

Uncertainty also occurs in the transformation process. Here work-in-process (WIP) inventories absorb the variability that exists between the stages of the process, thereby providing independence between operations and improving efficiency.

Finally, uncertainty exists with respect to the demand for a firm's finished products. If the demand for a product were to be known precisely, then it could be possible to produce products so that demand would be exactly met. However, more frequently demand is not totally known, and a safety stock of finished goods inventory is therefore maintained to absorb these variations.

2. *To support a strategic plan.* As we learned in the previous chapter on aggregate planning, when a firm adopts a level strategy an inventory of finished goods is required to buffer the cyclic demand for product from the level output generated by the transformation process. Under these circumstances, when demand exceeds production, the difference is withdrawn from inventory; when demand is less than production, the difference is placed back into inventory.

3. *To take advantage of economies of scale.* Each time we place an order or do a setup to perform an operation, we incur a fixed cost, regardless of the quantity involved. Thus, the larger the quantity ordered or produced, the lower the average total cost per unit. However, as we shall shortly see, there are trade-offs to be considered in determining the proper lot size.

In addition, companies often offer discounts for larger-quantity orders, as an incentive to customers to buy more than they normally would. This results in accumulations of items that otherwise would not exist. Firms offer quantity discounts for several reasons, including the need to reduce excessive stockpiles and to generate positive cash flow. In addition, there are economies of scale with respect to transportation costs, especially when products are shipped in either full trailer loads or full car loads.

Establishing the correct quantity to order from vendors or the size of the lots submitted to the firm's production facilities involves a search for the minimum total cost resulting from the combined effects of four individual costs elements: holding costs, setup or ordering costs, shortage costs, and purchase costs. These are defined below.

INVENTORY COSTS

ACCOUNTING
FINANCE

In making any decision with respect to inventories, the following costs should be taken into consideration:

1. *Holding or carrying costs.* This broad category is usually subdivided into three segments: storage costs, capital costs, and obsolescence/shrinkage costs. Storage costs include the cost of the storage facility in the form of rent or depreciation, insurance, taxes, utilities, security, and facility personnel.

Capital costs can vary, depending on the firm's financial situation. For example, if the firm has an excess of cash, then the capital cost is the interest lost by putting the money into inventory instead of short-term notes. If the firm has an alternative project to invest in, then the capital cost is the opportunity cost of the anticipated return of that project. If the firm has to borrow funds to maintain an inventory, then the capital cost is the interest paid on those funds.

Obsolescence costs recognize that products tend to depreciate in value over time. This is especially true in high-technology industries where newer and better (and often cheaper) products are constantly being introduced. In this category, we also include spoilage costs associated with products that have a short shelf life, like perishable food products and some types of prescription drugs. Shrinkage costs account for pilferage and breakage.

2. *Setup or ordering costs.* These are fixed costs usually associated with the production of a lot internally or the placing of an order externally with a vendor. In other words, these costs are independent of the amount of units that are requested. Setup costs are related to the amount of time needed to adjust the equipment to perform a specific task. This would include the alignment of special tooling like jigs and fixtures. Order costs pertain to the costs involved in placing an order with a vendor. These may include telephone charges, a delivery fee, expediting costs, and the time required to process a purchase order.

3. *Shortage (or stockout) costs.* When the stock of an item is depleted, and a customer orders that product, then a stockout cost is incurred. This is usually the sum of the lost profit and any "ill-will" generated. There is a trade-off between carrying stock to satisfy demand and the costs resulting from stockout. This balance is sometimes difficult to obtain, since it may not be possible to estimate accurately lost profits, the effects of lost customers, or late penalties.

4. *Purchase costs.* These are the actual costs of the material purchased. Purchase costs tend to remain constant unless quantity discounts (which are discussed later in this chapter) are offered.

INDEPENDENT VERSUS DEPENDENT DEMAND

types of demand: independent demand
Pertains to the requirements for end products.

Briefly, the distinction between **independent** and **dependent demand** is this: With independent demand, the demands for various items are unrelated to each other and therefore needed quantities of each must be determined separately or independently. With dependent demand (which is addressed in detail in the next chapter), the need for any one item is a direct result of the need for some other item, usually a higher-level item of which it is a component or subassembly.

types of demand:
  dependent demand
  Requirements for
  components and
  subassemblies that are
  directly dependent on
  the demand for the
  end products in which
  they are used.

In concept, dependent demand is a relatively straightforward computational problem. Needed quantities of a dependent-demand item are simply computed, based on the number needed in each higher-level item where it is used. For example, if an automobile company plans on producing 500 automobiles per day, then obviously it will need 2,000 wheels and tires (plus spares). The number of wheels and tires needed is *dependent* on the production level for automobiles and not derived separately. The demand for automobiles, on the other hand, is *independent*—it comes from many sources external to the automobile firm and is not a part of other products and so is unrelated to the demand for other products.

To determine the quantities of independent items that must be produced, firms usually turn to their sales and market research departments. They use a variety of techniques, including customer surveys, forecasting techniques, and economic and sociological trends. Because independent demand is uncertain, extra units must be carried in inventory.

TYPES OF INVENTORY SYSTEMS

An inventory system provides the organizational structure and the operating policies for maintaining and controlling goods to be stocked. The system is responsible for ordering and receipt of goods: timing the order placement and keeping track of what has been ordered, how much, and from whom. The system must also follow up to provide answers to such questions as: Has the vendor received the order? Has it been shipped? Are the dates correct? Are the procedures established for reordering or returning undesirable merchandise?

Fixed-Order Quantity and Fixed-Time Period Systems

types of inventory
systems:
  fixed-order quantity
  System where the
  order quantity remains
  constant but the time
  between orders varies.

  fixed-time period
  System where the time
  period between orders
  remains constant but
  the order quantity
  varies.

There are two general types of inventory systems: **fixed-order quantity** (also called the Q-system) and **fixed-time period** (also referred to as the P-system).

The basic distinction between the two is that fixed-order quantity models are "event triggered" and fixed-time period models are "time triggered." That is, a fixed-order quantity model initiates an order when the event of reaching a specified reorder level occurs. This event may take place at any time, depending on the demand for the items being considered. In contrast, the fixed-time period model is limited to placing orders at the end of a predetermined time period; only the passage of time triggers the model.

To use the fixed-order quantity model, which places an order when the remaining inventory drops to a predetermined order point, R, the inventory remaining must be continually monitored. Thus, the fixed-order quantity model is a *perpetual* inventory system, which requires that every time a withdrawal from or an addition to inventory is made, records must be updated to ensure that the reorder point has or has not been reached. For the fixed-time period model, inventory is counted only at the end of the review period. No counting takes place in the interim (although some firms have created variations of systems that combine features of both). Some additional differences that tend to influence the choice of systems are:

- The fixed-time period model typically has a larger average inventory since it must also protect against stockout during the review period, T; the fixed-quantity model has no review period.
- The fixed-time period model is preferred when several different items are purchased from the same vendor, and there is potential economies of scale savings from ordering all these items at the same time.
- The fixed-order quantity model favors more expensive items because average inventory is lower.

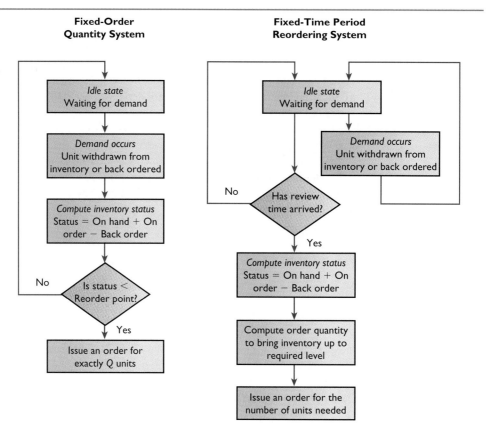

- The fixed-order quantity model is more appropriate for important items such as critical repair parts because there is closer monitoring and therefore quicker response to a potential stockout.
- The fixed-order quantity model requires more time and resources to maintain because every addition or withdrawal is recorded.

Exhibit 14.1 depicts what occurs when each of the two models is put into use and becomes an operating system. As we can see, the fixed-order quantity system focuses on order quantities and reorder points. Procedurally, each time a unit is taken out of stock, the withdrawal is recorded and the amount remaining in inventory is immediately compared to the reorder point. If it has dropped to this point or below, an order for Q items is placed. If it has not, the system remains in an idle state until the next withdrawal.

In the fixed-time period system, a decision to place an order is made after the stock has been counted or reviewed. Whether an order is actually placed depends on the inventory status at that time.

BASIC INVENTORY MODELS

Basic Fixed-Order Quantity Model

The simplest models in this category occur when all aspects of the situation are known with certainty. If the annual demand for a product is 1,000 units, it is precisely 1,000—not 1,000

EXHIBIT 14.2

Basic Fixed-Order Quantity Model

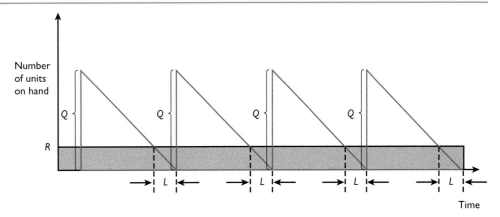

plus or minus 10 percent. In addition, the setup costs and holding costs are known and constant. Although the assumption of complete certainty is rarely valid, it provides a good starting point for our coverage of inventory models.

Fixed-order quantity models attempt to determine both the specific point, R, at which an order will be placed and the size of that order, Q. The order (or reorder) point, R, is always a specified number of units actually in inventory. The solution to a fixed-order quantity model may stipulate something like this: When the number of units of inventory on hand drops to 36, place an order for 57 more units.

Exhibit 14.2 and the discussion about deriving the optimal order quantity are based on the following assumptions of the model:

- Demand for the product is known, constant, and uniform throughout the period.
- Lead time (L), which is the time from ordering to receipt, is constant.
- Price per unit of product is constant (no quantity discounts).
- Ordering or setup costs are constant.
- All demands for the product will be satisfied (no back orders are allowed).
- There is no interaction with other products.

The "sawtooth effect" relating Q and R in Exhibit 14.2 shows that when inventory drops to point R, a reorder is placed. This order is received at the end of the lead time period L, which, as stated above, remains constant.

In constructing any inventory model, the first step is to develop a functional relationship between the variables of interest and the measure of effectiveness. In this case, since we are concerned with cost, the following equation would pertain:

$$\begin{array}{c} \text{Total} \\ \text{annual cost} \end{array} = \begin{array}{c} \text{Annual} \\ \text{purchase cost} \end{array} + \begin{array}{c} \text{Annual} \\ \text{ordering cost} \end{array} + \begin{array}{c} \text{Annual} \\ \text{holding cost} \end{array}$$

or

$$TC = DC + \frac{D}{Q}S + \frac{Q}{2}H \qquad (14.1)$$

where

TC = Total annual cost

D = Annual demand in units

C = Cost per unit

Q = Quantity to be ordered (the optimum amount is termed the **economic order quantity—EOQ**)

S = Setup or ordering cost

H = Annual holding cost per unit

(Often, holding cost is defined as an annual percentage of the cost of the item. In these instances, $H = iC$ where i is the annual percentage carrying cost.)

On the right side of the equation, DC is the annual purchase cost for the units, $(D/Q)S$ is the annual ordering cost (the actual number of orders placed, D/Q, times the cost of each order, S), and $(Q/2)H$ is the annual holding cost (the average inventory, $Q/2$, times the cost per unit for holding and storage, H). These cost relationships are shown graphically in Exhibit 14.3.

The next step is to find that order quantity, Q, for which total cost is a minimum. In Exhibit 14.3, the total cost is minimum at the point where the slope of the total cost curve is zero. Using calculus, the appropriate procedure involves taking the first derivative of total cost with respect to Q and setting this equal to zero. For the basic model considered here, the calculations to obtain the economic order quantity (EOQ) would be as follows:

$$TC = DC + \frac{D}{Q}S + \frac{Q}{2}H$$

$$\text{First derivative} = \frac{dTC}{dQ} = 0 + \left(\frac{-DS}{Q^2}\right) + \frac{H}{2} = 0$$

Solving for Q gives us the economic order quantity, or EOQ,

$$EOQ = \sqrt{\frac{2DS}{H}} \tag{14.2}$$

Because this simple model assumes both constant demand and lead time, no safety stock is necessary, and the reorder point, R, is simply

$$R = \bar{d}L \tag{14.3}$$

EXHIBIT 14.3

Annual Product Costs, Based on Size of the Order

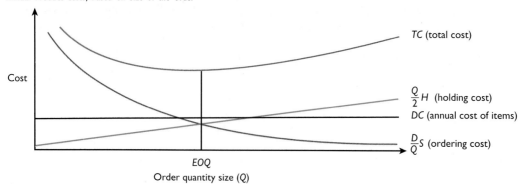

where

R = Reorder point

$\bar{d}$ = Average demand per time period [constant]

L = Number of time periods between placing an order and its delivery [constant]

Example

Find the economic order quantity and the reorder point, given the following data:

Annual demand (D) = 1,000 units

Ordering cost (S) = \$5 per order

Holding cost (H) = \$1.25 per unit per year

Cost per unit (C) = \$12.50

Lead time (L) = 5 days

Average daily demand ($\bar{d}$) = 1,000/365

What quantity should be ordered, and when?

Solution

The optimal order quantity is

$$\text{EOQ} = \sqrt{\frac{2DS}{H}} = \sqrt{\frac{2(1,000)5}{1.25}} = \sqrt{8,000} = 89.4 \text{ units}$$

The reorder point is

$$R = \bar{d}L = \frac{1,000}{365}(5) = 13.7 \text{ units}$$

Rounding to the nearest unit, the inventory policy is as follows: When the number of units in inventory drops to 14, place an order for 89 more units.

The total annual cost will be

$$TC = DC + \frac{D}{Q}S + \frac{Q}{2}H$$

$$= 1,000(12.50) + \frac{1,000}{89}(5) + \frac{89}{2}(1.25)$$

$$= \$12,611.81$$

Note that in this example, the annual purchase cost of the units was not required to determine the order quantity and the reorder point. Also note that in Exhibit 14.3, the total cost curve is relatively flat around the EOQ, which is the norm, indicating that only minor increases in total cost will occur on either side of the EOQ. Thus, in the above example, we might in actuality order 90 units about once a month for the sake of simplicity and convenience without fear of incurring excessive costs.

Fixed-Order Quantity Model with Usage

fixed-order quantity model with usage
Considers a supplier that will provide an order quantity over a period of time rather than all at once.

The basic fixed-order model assumes that the quantity ordered would be received in one lot, but frequently this is not the case. In many situations, production of an inventory item and usage of that item take place simultaneously (referred to as a **fixed-order quantity model with usage**). This is particularly true where one part of a production system acts as a supplier to another part. For example, while aluminum extrusions are being made to fill an order for aluminum windows, the extrusions are cut and assembled before the entire extrusion order is completed. Also, companies are beginning to enter into longer-term arrangements with vendors. Under such contracts, a single order or *blanket* contract may cover product or material needs over a six-month or one-year period with the vendor making deliveries weekly or sometimes even more frequently. Often with blanket contracts, the amount to be delivered each time period will be determined at a future date. This model differs from our previous discussion of process and transfer batch sizes since this model has a continual usage rate d. If we let d denote a constant demand rate for some item going into production and p the production rate of that process that uses the item, we may develop the following total cost equation. (Obviously, the production rate must exceed the demand or usage rate; otherwise Q would be infinite, resulting in continual production):

$$TC = DC + (D/Q)S + (Q/2)H$$

However, with this model, as seen in Exhibit 14.4, Q is not the maximum inventory on hand, because we are consuming the product as it is being delivered over time. Thus, the above equation is rewritten as follows:

$$TC = DC + (D/Q)S + (I_{max}/2)H \qquad (14.4)$$

and

$$I_{max} = (p - d)\,(Q/p) \qquad (14.5)$$

where $(p - d)$ is the amount of inventory that accumulates each time period, and (Q/p) is the number of time periods required to fill the order.

$$TC = DC + \frac{D}{Q}S + \frac{(p - d)QH}{2p}$$

Again differentiating with respect to Q and setting the equation equal to zero, we obtain

$$\text{EOQ} = \sqrt{\frac{2DS}{H} \cdot \frac{p}{(p - d)}} \qquad (14.6)$$

This model is shown in Exhibit 14.4. We can see that the maximum number of units on hand is always less than the order quantity, Q. Note in Equation 14.6, that as p be-

---

EXHIBIT 14.4

Fixed-Order Quantity Model with Usage during Production Time

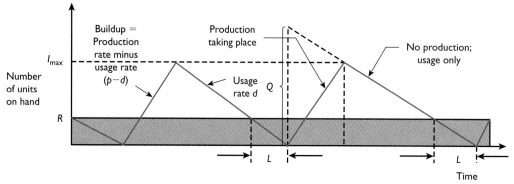

comes very large, the right-hand term $(p/(p-d))$ approaches one and we have our original EOQ formula.

Example

Product X is a standard item in a firm's inventory. Final assembly of the product is performed on an assembly line that is in operation every day. One of the components of product X (call it component X_1) is produced in another department. This department, when it produces X_1 does so at the rate of 100 units per day. The assembly line uses component X_1, at the rate of 40 units per day.

Given the following data, when is the optimal production lot size of component X_1? What is the reorder point?

$$\text{Daily usage rate } (d) = 40 \text{ units per day}$$
$$\text{Annual demand } (D) = 10,000 \ (40 \text{ units per day} \times 250 \text{ working days})$$
$$\text{Daily production } (p) = 100 \text{ units per day}$$
$$\text{Cost of production setup } (S) = \$50$$
$$\text{Annual holding cost } (H) = \$0.50 \text{ per unit per year}$$
$$\text{Cost of component } X_1 \ (C) = \$7 \text{ each}$$
$$\text{Lead time } (L) = 7 \text{ days}$$

Solution

The optimal order quantity and the reorder point for component X_1 are calculated as follows:

$$EOQ = \sqrt{\frac{2DS}{H} \cdot \frac{p}{p-d}} = \sqrt{\frac{2(10,000)50}{0.50} \cdot \frac{100}{100-40}} = 1,826 \text{ units}$$

$$R = dL = 40(7) = 280 \text{ units}$$

This states that an order for 1,826 units of component X_1 should be placed when the stock drops to 280 units

At 100 units per day, this run would take 18.26 days to complete, and provide a 45.65-day supply for the assembly line (1,826/40). Theoretically, the department would be occupied with other work for the 27.39 days when component X_1 is not being produced.

Fixed-Time Period Model

In a fixed-time period system, inventory is counted at fixed intervals, such as every week or every month. Counting inventory and placing orders on a periodic basis is desirable in such situations as when vendors make routine visits to customers and take orders for their complete line of products, or when buyers want to combine orders to save on transportation costs. Other firms operate on a fixed-time period to facilitate planning their inventory count; for example, Distributor X calls every two weeks and employees therefore know that all of Distributor X's products must be counted at that time.

The time interval can be chosen as is convenient, or if only one item is involved it can be estimated by using the EOQ formula. Once the EOQ for the item is calculated, we can determine how many times a year we should place the order, from which we can then determine the period or interval between orders. For example, if the annual demand is 1,200 units and the EOQ is 100 units, then we know that we will place 12 orders throughout the year, and that there is a one-month interval between orders.

EXHIBIT 14.5

Fixed-Time Period Inventory Model

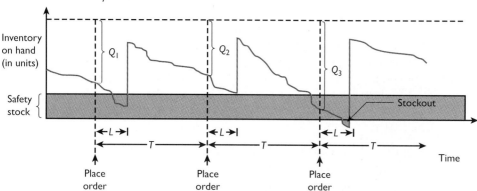

With a fixed-time period model, there is usually a ceiling or "par" inventory that is established for each item. As seen in Exhibit 14.5, the difference between the par value and the quantity on hand when the count is taken is the amount ordered, which will vary from period to period, depending on the actual usage (e.g., Q_1, Q_2, and Q_3, in Exhibit 14.5). Thus, in this model the time interval between orders remains fixed, but the quantity ordered varies, as compared to the fixed-order quantity model where just the reverse is true: the order quantity remains fixed, but the time interval varies.

Quantity-Discount Model

quantity-discount model
Addresses price discounts associated with minimum order quantities.

The **quantity-discount model** takes into consideration the fact that the purchase cost of an item can vary with the order size. This is a discrete or step change rather than a per-unit change. For example, a wheel for a toy car may cost $0.20 each for 1 to 99 wheels, $0.16 each for quantities between 100 to 999 wheels, and $0.13 each for quantities over 1,000 wheels. In each instance, the quantity relates to the size of the order placed. To determine the optimal quantity to order with this model, we first calculate the EOQ for each unit cost. If the resulting EOQs are all feasible, that is, the EOQs fall within their respective quantity ranges, then we select the EOQ that is associated with the lowest unit cost. However, as is more often the case, some of the EOQ's may not be feasible (i.e., the quantity does not fall within the feasible unit cost range). In these situations, we have to calculate the total cost for each unit cost at the EOQ or EOQs where it is feasible. Where it is not feasible, we calculate the total cost at the minimum quantity where the respective unit cost is first applicable. These total costs are then compared and the quantity or EOQ associated with the lowest total cost is the order quantity that is selected.

Procedurally, the largest order quantity (lowest unit price) is solved first; if the resulting Q is valid or feasible, that is the answer. If not, the next largest order quantity (second lowest price) is derived. If that is feasible, the cost of this Q is compared to the cost of using the order quantity at the price break above, and the lowest cost determines the optimal Q.

Example

Consider the following case, where

$D = 10,000$ units (annual demand)

$S = \$20$ to place each order

$i =$ 20 percent of cost (annual carrying costs, storage, interest, obsolescence, etc.)
$C =$ Cost per unit:

Order Size (units)	Cost per Unit
0–499	$C_1 = \$5.00$
500–999	$C_2 = 4.50$
1,000 and over	$C_3 = 3.90$

What quantity should be ordered?

Solution

The appropriate equations from the basic fixed-quantity model are

$$TC = DC + \frac{D}{Q}S + \frac{Q}{2}iC$$

and

$$Q = \sqrt{\frac{2DS}{iC}}$$

Solving for the economic order size at each price, we obtain the following:

Range	Unit Cost	EOQ	Feasible
0–499	$5.00	633	No
500–999	4.50	666	Yes
Over 1,000	3.90	716	No

These results are shown in Exhibit 14.6, which depicts the relationship between the total cost and the order quantity for each of the unit costs. Using the procedure described above, we now calculate the total cost for 666 units at $4.50 per unit and 1,000 units at $3.90 per unit. These calculations are shown in Exhibit 14.7. Comparing these two total costs, the economic order quantity is 1,000 units.

EXHIBIT 14.6

Total Cost Curves for a Quantity-Discount Model

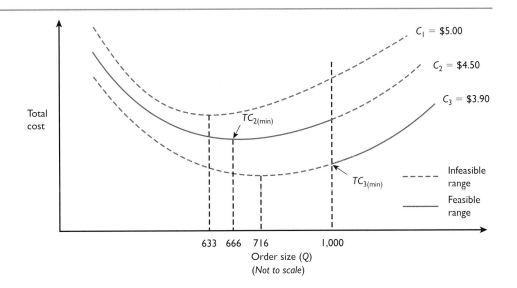

Order size (Q)
(Not to scale)

EXHIBIT 14.7

Total Cost Calculations in a Quantity-Discount Model

	Q = 666 where C = \$4.50	Price Break 1,000
Holding cost $\left(\frac{Q}{2}iC\right)$	$\frac{666}{2}(0.20)4.50$ = \$299.70	$\frac{1,000}{2}(0.20)3.90$ = \$390
Ordering cost $\left(\frac{D}{Q}s\right)$	$\frac{10,000(20)}{666}$ = \$300	$\frac{10,000(20)}{1,000}$ = \$200
Holding and ordering cost	\$600	\$590
Purchase cost (DC)	10,000(4.50)	10,000(3.90)
Total cost	$TC_{2(min)} = \$45,600$	$TC_{3(min)} = \$39,590$

One practical consideration in quantity-discount problems is that the cost reduction from volume purchases frequently makes it seemingly economical to order amounts larger than the EOQ. Thus, when applying the model we must be particularly careful to obtain a valid estimate of product obsolescence and warehousing costs.

Inventories and Service Levels

All of the inventory models presented thus far have assumed that the demand for an item is both constant and known. However, in most real world environments, the demand for an item is not constant, but will vary from period to period (e.g., from day to day, from week to week). Consequently, in these situations it is necessary to build in a safety stock that takes into consideration this variation in demand. This safety stock is in addition to the average demand that is forecasted during the lead time.

The amount of safety stock that a firm should have for any given item is dependent on three factors: (a) the variation in demand, (b) the variability in the lead time required to replenish the item, and (c) the desired level of service that the company wants to provide its customers. Here, service level refers to the probability that all orders placed during the lead time will be filled from inventory and that customers will not have to wait because of a stockout. Thus a 95 percent service level can be interpreted as a 95 percent probability that all orders placed during the lead time will be filled from on-hand inventory.

The larger the variation in demand, the larger the safety stock that is required. Similarly, the longer the lead time, the larger the safety stock that is required. A higher service level simply translates into more safety stock. The impact of these three factors on the amount of safety stock that is required is shown in Exhibit 14.8.

ECONOMIC ORDER QUANTITY MODELS IN RELATION TO THE REAL WORLD

Recently, criticizing classical inventory models seems fashionable to some members of industry and consulting groups. Proportionately, there is much less open criticism from academia. In a manufacturing environment, the major weaknesses associated with the classical EOQ models focus on the numbers. These numbers are the values of setup costs, holding

EXHIBIT 14.8

The Impact of Variation, Lead Time, and Service Level on the Amount of Safety Stock (SS) Required.

A. Differences in Variation in Demand and Longer Lead Time with a Constant Service Level

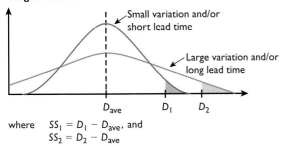

where $SS_1 = D_1 - D_{ave}$, and
$SS_2 = D_2 - D_{ave}$

B. Increase in Service Level with a Constant Variation in Demand and a Constant Lead Time

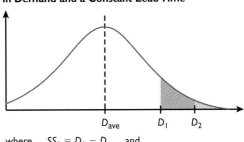

where $SS_1 = D_1 - D_{ave}$, and
$SS_2 = D_2 - D_{ave}$

where the service level for D_2 is greater than the service level for D_1.

EXHIBIT 14.9

Effect of Reduced Setup Cost on Order Size and Total Cost

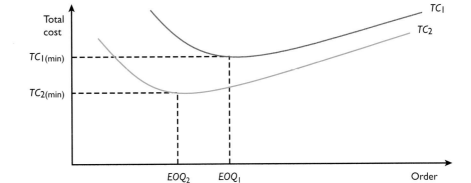

costs, and demands used in the equations. These costs are often very difficult to measure and, therefore, are error prone. Also, demand is rarely constant but instead is usually a fluctuating number.

Elliott Weiss states the problem nicely by explaining that many users of the equations focus on optimizing a set of numbers which often are taken as a given fact.[1] Rather, he states, we should be managing lot sizing and inventory control. The current moves toward reduced inventory costs and quantities, such as just-in-time systems, stress the importance in reducing lot sizes. The means to reducing lot sizes is to reduce setup time and cost. When smaller lots are run, holding cost is reduced. The point is to understand the logic and know where to apply it. The effect on order size resulting from reducing setup costs is shown in Exhibit 14.9. When the setup cost is reduced, the total cost curve shifts from TC_1 to TC_2. Correspondingly, the EOQ is reduced from EOQ_1 to EOQ_2 and the minimum total cost is reduced from TC_{1min} to TC_{2min}.

[1]Elliot N. Weiss, "Lot Sizing Is Dead: Long Live Lot Sizing," *Production and Inventory Management Journal,* First Quarter 1990, pp. 76–78.

PERISHABLE INVENTORY

While all inventories are subject to obsolescence, there are some products that are considered highly perishable in that they are only viable for a very short time period. After that period has elapsed, their value decreases significantly, and the reduced value is often only their salvage or scrap value. Examples of such products include newspapers and Christmas trees. In each case, the value of the product drops dramatically from one time period to the next. (In the case of newspapers, the time period is a day; in the case of Christmas trees, it is the month or so before Christmas.) The determination of the proper or "optimum" inventory level to establish for this group of products is often referred to as the **single-period inventory model.**

Single-Period Inventory Model

Certain characteristics are associated with products that fall into the single-period inventory model. These include: (*a*) the product is only viable for sale during a single time period, (*b*) the demand for the product is highly variable, but follows a known probability distribution, and (*c*) the scrap value of the product or the value of the product after the time period has elapsed is less than the initial cost of the product.

The goal in determining the proper level of inventory for these products is to balance the gross profit generated by the sale of each unit with the cost incurred for each unit that is unsold after the time period has elapsed. Since the demand in these problems follows a probability distribution, we want to pick that level of inventory that maximizes our expected profit. When the probability distribution is discrete, we can solve the problem using an expected value matrix.

Example

Dick Moore sells Christmas trees, which he grows on his farm in upstate New York. Because bad weather and heavy snow is common in the month of December, Dick has always harvested the trees he intends to sell in a given year by December 1. Dick has been selling trees for many years, and has kept detailed records of sales in previous years. From this data, he has determined that probability of selling various quantities of trees in a given year is as follows:

Demand (trees)	Probability
500	0.15
550	0.20
600	0.25
650	0.30
700	0.10

For the coming year, Dick will sell his trees for an average price of $25 each. His cost to grow and cut each tree is estimated to be $10. Any unsold trees at the end of the season can be sold for kindling wood at a price of $5 apiece. What is the optimal number of trees that Dick should harvest?

Solution

Using the above information, we develop the following payoff table to determine the net profit that will be generated for every combination of trees that are cut and customer demand (Note: profit, as defined here, takes into account the opportunity cost associated with lost sales, which is not the strict definition by accounting standards):

Probability	0.15	0.20	0.25	0.30	0.10	
Customer Demand	500	550	600	650	700	
Number of Trees Cut						**Expected Profit**
500	7,500	6,750	6,000	5,250	4,500	$6,000
550	7,250	8,250	7,500	6,750	6,000	7,238
600	7,000	8,000	9,000	8,250	7,500	8,125
650	6,750	7,750	8,750	9,750	9,000	8,575
700	6,500	7,500	8,500	9,500	10,500	8,500

The values in the payoff table can be divided into three groups. In the first group, the number of trees cut exactly equals demand. The profit generated when this happens is

$$\text{Profit} = D(SP - C)$$

where

D = Demand

SP = Selling price per tree

C = Cost per tree

Thus if we have a demand for 550 trees and we cut 550 trees then the profit generated is:

$$\text{Profit} = 550(25 - 10) = 550(15) = \$8,250$$

The second group consists of those combinations where demand exceeds the number of trees cut. Here we have to take into consideration the opportunity cost associated with the lost revenues resulting from unsatisfied demand. The profit generated in these cases is as follows:

$$\text{Profit} = Q(SP - C) - (D - Q)(SP - C)$$

where

Q = Number of trees cut down

If we have a demand for 650 trees and we have only harvested 500 trees then the resulting profit is:

$$\text{Profit} = 500(25 - 10) - (650 - 500)(25 - 10)$$
$$= 500(15) - 150(15)$$
$$= 7,500 - 2,250 = \$5,250$$

The third case is when the quantity of trees we have harvested exceeds the demand. Here we have to sell off the excessive inventory at a loss. The net profit calculated is therefore as follows:

$$\text{Profit} = D(SP - C) - (Q - D)(C - SV)$$

where

SV = scrap value

If we have harvested 700 trees and demand is only for 550 trees then the profit generated is:

$$\begin{aligned} \text{Profit} &= 550(25 - 10) - (770 - 550)(10 - 5) \\ &= 550(15) - (150)(5) \\ &= 8{,}250 - 750 = \$7{,}500 \end{aligned}$$

After we have determined all of the values in the payoff table, we next have to calculate the expected profit associated with each of the quantities of trees that we decide to harvest. This is calculated by multiplying the probability of each demand occurring by the profit generated by that demand. For example, if we decide to harvest 600 trees, then the expected profit from this decision is:

$$\begin{aligned} \text{Expected profit } (600) &= (0.15)(7{,}000) + (0.20)(8{,}000) \\ &\quad + (0.25)(9{,}000) + (0.30)(8{,}250) + (0.10)(7{,}500) \\ \text{EP}(600) &= 1{,}050 + 1{,}600 + 2{,}250 + 2{,}475 + 750 \\ \text{EP}(600) &= \$8{,}125 \end{aligned}$$

Finally, we select that quantity of trees to harvest which yields the maximum expected profit. In this case, Dick Moore should harvest 650 trees because the expected profit from that decision is $8,575, as shown in the table above.

INVENTORY MANAGEMENT IN SERVICES

 In service operations, the "product" sold is considered highly perishable. As discussed in the previous chapter, hotel rooms that are unoccupied for one night cannot be saved for another night. Similarly, airline seats on a plane that are not used on a given date cannot be saved for use at a future time.

Yield Management or Revenue Management

Because the product sold in service operations is so perishable, the approach to managing the sale of the product is similar to that for the single-period inventory problem.

As discussed in Chapter 13, many services have a cost structure that consists of high-fixed and low-variable costs. Examples of such services, as mentioned earlier, include airlines, hotels, and car rental companies. For these types of services, profits are directly related to sales because variable costs, as a percentage of sales, are very low. Consequently, the goal for these firms is to maximize sales or revenues by maximizing capacity utilization, even if it means selling some of the available capacity at reduced prices—as long as these prices are greater than the variable cost. For example, if the variable cost to clean and restock a hotel room with towels, soap, shampoo, and so forth is $25, then any room rate greater than $25 will contribute to profit. Thus it would be better to let a hotel guest have the room for $50 for a night than to let the room remain empty, even if the regular or "rack" rate is $135 per night.

The challenge for managers in these types of service firms is to determine what percentage of available capacity to allocate to different prices. On the one hand, substantial amounts of capacity can usually be sold in advance at rates that are significantly discounted. For example, airlines usually require a 21-day in advance purchase for their super-saver fares, which offer the lowest prices; similarly, organizations holding conferences usually reserve hotel rooms years in advance of their meeting, again at substantially reduced rates.

Operations Management in Practice

THE APPLICATION OF YIELD MANAGEMENT AT AMERICAN AIRLINES

Yield management is widely used today in the airline industry to maximize revenues and profits. American Airlines was one of the first companies to use yield management to (a) establish prices, (b) determine for a given flight what percentage of capacity it should allocate to each price, and (c) determine the restrictions necessary to segment the markets. Listed below is a sampling of the different prices for a round-trip flight between Boston, Massachusetts and London, England.

Fare	Season	Day of Week	Advanced Purchase (days)	Other Restrictions
$324	Low	MW	90	5 day min.; 45 max.
$374	Low	WE	90	5 day min.; 45 max.
$472	Low	MW	21	7 day min.; 21 max.
$523	Low	WE	21	7 day min.; 21 max.
$454	Shoulder	MW	90	5 day min.; 45 max.
$504	Shoulder	WE	90	5 day min.; 45 max.
$575	Shoulder	MW	21	7 day min.; 21 max.
$620	Shoulder	WE	21	7 day min.; 21 max.
$599	High	MW	90	5 day min.; 45 max.
$649	High	WE	90	5 day min.; 45 max.
$740	High	MW	21	7 day min.; 21 max.
$801	High	MW	21	7 day min.; 21 max.
$2,364				Unrestricted coach
$5,260		MW		Business class
$8,552		WE		First class

Definitions:

Low season:	November 1–December 17
	January 6–March 15
Shoulder season:	September 30–October 31
	March 16–June 15
High season:	December 18–January 5
	June 16–September 29
Midweek (MW):	Monday–Thursday
Weekend (WE):	Friday–Sunday

Source: Based on telephone conversations on August 8, 1997, with "Joyce" and "Linda," reservation agents with American Airlines.

At the same time, however, the service manager does not want to turn away a last-minute customer who usually pays the full rate because the capacity had been previously sold at a discounted rate. When this happens, opportunity costs are incurred. The methodology for determining the percentage of capacity to allocate to each market segment or price is referred to as yield management or revenue management. By using yield management, the service manager is simultaneously managing both the supply and demand for the firm's capacity. Demand is controlled by the different price structures: lower prices increase demand; higher prices decrease demand. Supply is controlled by limiting the capacity available at each of the different price structures.

As an illustration of how a service firm will use pricing to manage demand, the accompanying OM in Practice provides a sampling of the different airfares that American Airlines offers between Boston, Massachusetts, and London, England, and the restrictions associated with each airfare. It is important to note that while the level of service is significantly different for first class and business class passengers, the passengers receive the exact same level of service for all other fares. (There are also 7-day advanced purchase prices beginning at $619 round trip and 14-day advanced purchase prices beginning at $544 round trip. The 7-day requires a Saturday night stay over with a 6-month maximum stay and the 14-day has a minimum stay of 7 days with a maximum of 60 days. In addition, there are frequently special fares from time to time when demand is lower than forecast.)

As discussed in detail in the previous chapter, a service should have certain characteristics in order to take full advantage of yield management.

Example

Jacob and Evan Raser own a small hotel with 65 rooms in western Massachusetts. During the summer, there are many cultural activities going on in this region, including the Boston Symphony Orchestra at Tanglewood. The maximum room rate they charge during this time is $150 per night. However, while the hotel is usually sold out on weekends, it is never sold out during the week. From historical data, the two brothers have developed the following probability table with respect to the number of rooms occupied during a weeknight (i.e., Sunday through Thursday nights):

Number of Rooms Occupied	Probability
45	0.15
50	0.30
55	0.20
60	0.35

The variable cost to clean an occupied room is estimated to be $25. The two brothers have recently been approached by a group representing retired people, who are on limited incomes. The group is doing a special promotion for their spring newsletter and want to include a hotel that would offer reduced room rates during the week if the retirees made reservations at least one month in advance. The group assures Jacob and Evan that if the rate was $95 per night, they could sell all the rooms available on a weekday night. How many rooms should Jacob and Evan allocate to this lower rate for weeknights?

Solution

As with the Christmas tree problem, we construct the following payoff table:

Probability	0.15	0.30	0.20	0.35	
Customer Demand	45	50	55	60	
Number of Rooms Available at $150					Expected Profit
45	7,025	6,750	6,475	6,200	$6,543.75
50	6,325	7,300	7,025	6,750	6,906.25
55	5,625	6,600	7,575	7,300	6,893.75
60	4,925	5,900	6,875	7,850	6,640.00

Similarly, as with the Christmas tree problem, the values in the payoff table can be divided into three groups. In the first group, the number of rooms that are reserved for full rate (i.e., $150/night) exactly equals demand. The profit generated when this happens is:

$$\text{Profit} = D(SP - C) + (N - D)(DP - C)$$

where

$D =$ Demand

$SP =$ Standard room rate per night

$DP =$ Discounted room rate per night

$C =$ Variable cost to clean a room per night

$N =$ Total number of rooms in the hotel

Thus if we have a demand for 50 rooms and we allocate 50 rooms for the standard rate then the profit generated is:

$$\text{Profit} = 50(150 - 25) + (65 - 50)(95 - 25)$$
$$= 6,250 + 1,050 = \$7,300$$

The second group consists of those combinations where demand for the standard room rate exceeds the number of rooms allocated for this rate. Here we have to take into consideration the opportunity cost associated with the lost revenues resulting from unsatisfied demand at the standard rate, because the rooms were sold to the retirees at the discounted rate. Thus the opportunity cost is the difference between the standard rate and the discounted rate. The profit generated in these cases is as follows:

$$\text{Profit} = Q(SP - C) + (N - Q)(DP - C) - (D - Q)(SP - DP)$$

where

$Q =$ Number of rooms allocated for the standard rate

If we have a demand for 60 rooms per night at the standard rate and we have only allocated 50 rooms then the resulting profit is:

$$\text{Profit} = 50(150 - 25) + (65 - 50)(95 - 25) - (60 - 50)(150 - 95)$$
$$= 6,250 + 1,050 - 550 = \$6,750$$

The third case is when the number of rooms we have allocated for the standard rate exceeds the demand. Here we have to take into account the opportunity cost of not selling the rooms earlier to the retirees. The net profit calculated is therefore as follows:

$$\text{Profit} = D(SP - C) + (N - Q)(DP - C) - (Q - D)(DP - C)$$

If we have reserved 60 rooms per night for the standard room rate and demand is only for 50 rooms then the profit generated is:

$$\text{Profit} = 50(150 - 25) + (65 - 60)(95 - 25) - (60 - 50)(95 - 25)$$
$$= 6,250 + 350 - 700 = \$5,900$$

After we have determined all of the values in the payoff table, we next have to calculate the expected profit that is associated with the number of rooms that we have reserved for the standard rate. This is calculated by multiplying the probability associated with each level of demand by the profit generated by that demand. For example, if we decide to allocate 55 rooms for the standard rate, then the expected profit from this decision is:

$$\text{Expected profit }(55) = (0.15)(5,625) + (0.30)(6,600) + (0.20)(7,575)$$
$$+ (0.35)(7,300)$$
$$\text{EP}(55) = 843.75 + 1,980 + 1,515 + 2,555$$
$$= \$6,893.75$$

Finally, we select that amount of rooms to allocate for the standard rate that yields the maximum expected profit. In this case, Jacob and Evan should allocate 50 rooms a night during the week for the standard rate and provide the retiree group with 15 rooms a night because this decision provides the maximum expected profit of $6,906.25, as shown in the table above. Below is the Excel spreadsheet solution.

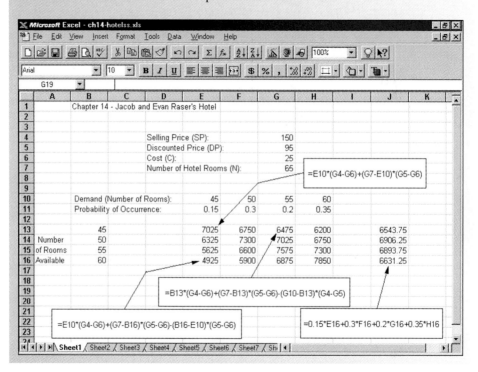

ADDITIONAL ISSUES IN INVENTORY MANAGEMENT

Determining Realistic Costs

Most inventory models give optimal solutions so long as the conditions of the system meet the constraints and/or assumptions of the model. While this is easy to state, it is difficult to implement. Obtaining actual order, setup, carrying, and shortage costs is often difficult—sometimes impossible. Part of the problem occurs because accounting data are usually averages, whereas to determine the proper lot sizes we need the marginal costs. Exhibit 14.10 compares the assumed smoothly ascending cost to the more realistic actual cost. For example, a buyer is a salaried person. The marginal cost for the buyer's labor to place additional orders up to a full workload is zero. When another buyer is hired, it is a step function. (In theory, the marginal cost of the order that caused hiring the new buyer is the cost for the additional buyer.)

EXHIBIT 14.10

Cost to Place Orders versus
the Number of Orders
Placed: Linear Assumption
and Normal Reality

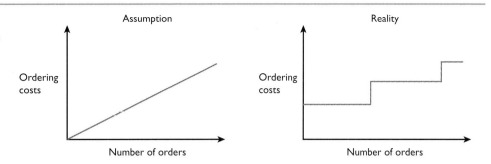

The same problem occurs in determining carrying costs. Warehouse costs, for example, may be close to zero if empty storage areas are available. Also, most companies can only estimate actual carrying costs, since they include obsolescence (a guess, at best), cost of capital (depends on internal money available, alternate investment opportunities, and sources of new capital), and insurance costs (which may range from zero if current insurance premiums cover more than the assets on hand, to the cost of a new policy). It is therefore important that we take these circumstances into consideration when applying the inventory models presented in this chapter.

ABC Inventory Planning

All inventory systems are plagued by two major problems: maintaining adequate control over each inventory item and ensuring that accurate records of stock on hand are kept. In this section, we present **ABC analysis**—an inventory system offering a control technique and inventory cycle counting that can improve record accuracy.

ABC analysis
Method for grouping inventory items by dollar volume to identify those items to be monitored closely.

Maintaining inventory through counting, placing orders, receiving stock, and so on takes personnel time and costs money. When there are limits on these resources, as is most often the case, the logical move is to try to use the available resources to control inventory in the best way. In other words, focus on the most important items in inventory.

In the 18th century, Villefredo Pareto, in a study of the distribution of wealth in Milan, found that 20 percent of the people controlled 80 percent of the wealth. This logic of the few having the greatest importance and the many having little importance has been broadened to include many situations and is termed the *Pareto Principle*. This is true in our everyday lives, where most of the decisions we make are relatively unimportant but a few shape our future, and is certainly true in inventory systems, where a few items account for the bulk of our investment. (As noted earlier in Chapter 5, Pareto analysis is also used in quality management to identify the most frequent types of errors.)

Any inventory system must specify when an order is to be placed for an item and how many units to order. In most situations involving inventory control, there are so many items involved that it is not practical to model and give thorough treatment to each and every item. To get around this problem, the ABC classification scheme divides inventory items into three groupings: high dollar volume (A), moderate dollar volume (B), and low dollar volume (C). Dollar volume is a measure of importance, an item low in cost but high in volume can be more important than a high-cost item with low volume.

If the annual usage of items in inventory is listed according to dollar volume, generally the list shows that a small number of items account for a large dollar volume and that a large number of items account for a small dollar volume. Exhibit 14.11 illustrates this relationship.

EXHIBIT 14.11

Annual Usage of Inventory by Value

Item Number	Annual Dollar Usage	Percent of Total Value
22	$95,000	40.7%
68	75,000	32.1
27	25,000	10.7
03	15,000	6.4
82	13,000	5.6
54	7,500	3.2
36	1,500	0.6
19	800	0.4
23	425	0.2
41	225	0.1
	$233,450	100.0%

EXHIBIT 14.12

ABC Grouping of Inventory Items

Classification	Item Number	Annual Dollar Usage	Percent of Total Value	Percent of Total Items
A	22, 68	$170,000	72.8%	20%
B	27, 03, 82	53,000	22.7	30
C	54, 36, 19, 23, 41	10,450	4.5	50
		$233,450	100.0%	100%

The ABC approach divides this list into three groupings by value: A items constitute roughly the top 15 percent of the items, B items the next 35 percent, and C items the last 50 percent. From observation, it appears that the list in Exhibit 14.11 may be meaningfully grouped with A including 20 percent (2 of the 10), B including 30 percent, and C including 50 percent. These points show clear delineations between sections. The result of this segmentation is shown in Exhibit 14.12. In this example, 20 percent of the items account for 72.8 percent of the value of the inventory.

Segmentation may not always occur so neatly. The objective, though is to try to separate the important from the unimportant. Where the lines actually break depends on the particular inventory under question and on how much personnel time is available (with more time a firm could define larger A or B categories).

The purpose of classifying items into groups is to establish the appropriate degree of control for each item. On a periodic basis, for example, Class A items may be more clearly controlled with weekly ordering, B items may be ordered biweekly, and C items may be ordered monthly or bimonthly. Note that the unit cost of items is not related to their classification. An A item may have a high dollar volume through a combination of either low cost and high usage or high cost and low usage. Similarly, C items may have a low dollar volume either because of low demand or low cost. In an automobile service station, for example, gasoline would be an A item with daily tabulation, tires, batteries, oil, grease, and transmission fluid may be B items and ordered every two to four weeks; and C items would consist of valve stems, windshield wiper blades, radiator caps, hoses, fan belts, oil and gas additives, car wax, and so forth. C items may be ordered every two or three months or even be allowed to run out before reordering since the penalty for stockout is not serious.

Sometimes, an item may be critical to a system if its absence creates a sizable loss. In this case, regardless of the item's classification, sufficiently large stocks should be kept on hand to prevent runout. One way to ensure closer control is to designate this item as an A or a B item, forcing it into the category even if its dollar volume does not warrant such inclusion.

Inventory Accuracy

Inventory records usually differ from the actual physical count and inventory accuracy refers to how well the two agree. The question is, how much error is acceptable? If the record shows a balance of 683 of Part X and an actual count shows 652, is this within reason? Suppose the actual count shows 750, an excess of 67 over the record; is this any better?

Every production system must have agreement, within some specified range, between what the record says is in inventory and what actually is in inventory. There are many reasons records and inventory may not agree. For example, having an open stockroom area allows items to be removed for both legitimate and unauthorized purposes. The legitimate removal may have been done in a hurry and simply not recorded. Sometimes parts are misplaced, turning up months later. Parts are often stored in several locations, but records may be lost or the location recorded incorrectly. Sometimes stock replenishment orders are recorded as received, when in fact they never were. Occasionally, a group of parts are recorded as having been removed from inventory, but the customer order is canceled and the parts are replaced in inventory without canceling the record. To keep the production system flowing smoothly without parts shortages and efficiently without excess balances, it is important that inventory records are accurate.

How can a firm keep accurate, up-to-date records? The first general rule is to keep the storeroom locked. If only storeroom personnel have access, and one of their measures of performance when it comes time for personnel evaluation and merit increases is record accuracy, there is a strong motivation to comply. Every location of inventory storage, whether in a locked storeroom or on the production floor, should have a recordkeeping mechanism.

McKesson, a leading distributor of pharmaceuticals, uses technology to make sure inventory is accurately managed. The machine on the man's arm combines a scanner, computer, and two-way radio to keep track of inventory and speed order delivery.

Operations Management in Practice

COMPANIES ARE REDUCING INVENTORIES RELATIVE TO SALES

The following graph shows a comparison of the ratio of annual sales to average inventory between 1991 and 1996 for several companies. While this ratio varies significantly from company to company due to their respective operating and product characteristics, the important point here is that all have increased this ratio in recent years. In other words, all of these firms have been able to increase their sales without having to increase their inventories proportionately. For many companies, these relative reductions in inventories have occurred even while the variety of products they sell has increased.

A = IBM, Rochester, MN
B = General Scanning, Bedford, MA
C = Foxboro Corp., Foxboro, MA
D = Varian Vacuum Products, Lexington, MA
E = Wainwright Industries, St. Peters, MO

Note: IBM, Rochester and Wainwright Industries are Malcolm Baldrige National Quality Award winners. Foxboro Corp., and Varian Vacuum Products are Massachusetts Quality Award winners.

CURRENT TRENDS IN INVENTORY MANAGEMENT

Managers in leading edge companies are realizing that inventory really isn't an asset, but rather a liability. Consequently, the average amount of inventory that these firms have on hand relative to their annual sales has been going down in recent years, as shown in the graph in the OM in Practice on Companies Are Reducing Inventories Relative to Sales.

Firms have been able to reduce their inventories for several reasons. First, companies have focused their efforts on reducing setup or order costs. The lower these costs, the smaller the economic order quantities. In addition, companies are working much closer now with their vendors. Through these relationships, product throughput times and thus lead times have been reduced significantly, again reducing the need to carry inventory.

CONCLUSION

This chapter introduces the two main categories of inventory demand: independent (referring to the external demand for a firm's end product) and dependent (usually referring to the demand within the firm for items created because of the demand for more complex items of which they are a part). Most industries have items in both categories. In manufacturing, for example, independent demand is common for finished products, service and repair parts, and operating supplies; and dependent demand is common for those parts and materials needed to produce the end product. In wholesale and retail sales of consumer goods, most demand is independent—each item is an end item, with the wholesaler or retailer doing no further assembly or fabrication.

Independent demand, is based on statistics. In addition to deterministic models where demand is constant and known, we also discuss uncertainty in demand and the influence of service levels on safety stock.

We also introduce the single-period inventory model for those instances where a product is highly perishable. We then extend this model to discuss yield management which provides service operations with a methodology to maximize their revenues.

To provide both an efficient and effective way to control inventory, the ABC method was introduced. The importance of inventory accuracy was also noted, and cycle counting was described.

In this chapter we also pointed out that inventory reduction requires a knowledge of the operating system. It is not simply a case of selecting an inventory model off the shelf and plugging in some numbers. In the first place, the model might not even be appropriate. In the second place, the numbers might not be relevant. It is vital to understand that this is also not a trade-off or compromise. Very often determining order quantities is referred to as a trade-off problem; that is, trading off holding costs for setup costs. Note that companies really want to reduce both.

The simple fact is that firms typically have very large investments in inventory, and the cost to carry this inventory runs from 30 to 35 percent and more of the inventory's worth annually. Therefore, a major goal of most firms today is to reduce inventory; they expect this to also lead to improved quality and performance, and to greatly reduce cost.

KEY FORMULAS

Q model
Total annual cost for an order quantity Q, an annual demand D, a per unit cost C, setup cost S, and an annual per unit holding cost H.

$$TC = DC + \frac{D}{Q}S + \frac{Q}{2}H \qquad (14.1)$$

Q model
Optimum or economic order quantity.

$$\text{EOQ} = \sqrt{\frac{2DS}{H}} \qquad (14.2)$$

Q model
Reorder point is based upon an average demand of $\bar{d}$ units per time period (e.g., days, weeks) and lead time L (stated in the same units of time as the demand).

$$R = \bar{d}L \qquad (14.3)$$

Q model with usage
Total annual cost for an order quantity Q, an annual demand D, with a maximum inventory on hand of I_{max}, a per unit cost C, setup cost S, and an annual per unit holding cost H.

$$TC = DC + (D/Q)S + (I_{max}/2)H \qquad (14.4)$$

Q model with usage
Maximum inventory on hand for an order quantity Q, production rate of p units per time period and usage rate of d units per time period.

$$I_{max} = (p - d)(Q/p) \qquad (14.5)$$

Q model with usage

Optimum or economic order quantity when items are produced at a rate of p units per time period and are used at a rate of d units per time period.

$$\text{EOQ} = \sqrt{\frac{2DS}{H} \cdot \frac{p}{(p-d)}} \qquad (14.6)$$

KEY TERMS

ABC analysis   p. 483
economic order quantity (EOQ)   p. 468
fixed-order quantity model with usage   p. 469
quantity-discount model   p. 472
single-period inventory model   p. 476
types of demand   p. 464
   independent demand   p. 464
   dependent demand   p. 465

types of inventory   p. 463
   finished goods   p. 463
   raw material   p. 463
   work-in-process (WIP)   p. 463
types of inventory systems   p. 465
   fixed-order quantity model   p. 465
   fixed-time period model   p. 465

REVIEW AND DISCUSSION QUESTIONS

1. Distinguish between dependent and independent demand in a McDonald's, in an integrated manufacturer of personal copiers, and in a pharmaceutical supply house.

2. Distinguish between work-in-process inventory, safety-stock inventory, and seasonal inventory.

3. Discuss the nature of the costs that affect inventory size.

4. Under which conditions would a plant manager elect to use a fixed-order quantity model as opposed to a fixed-time period model? What are the disadvantages of using a fixed-time period ordering system?

5. There is a current trend to reduce inventories. How is this being accomplished and what is the impact of lower inventories to the firm, its suppliers, and its customers?

6. Discuss the general procedure for determining the order quantity when quantity discounts are involved. Would there be any differences in the procedure if holding costs were a fixed percentage of item cost rather than a constant amount?

7. What two basic questions must be answered by an inventory-control decision rule?

8. Discuss the assumptions that are inherent in production setup cost, ordering cost, and carrying costs. How valid are they?

9. "The nice thing about inventory models is that you can pull one off the shelf and apply it so long as your cost estimates are accurate." Comment.

10. Which type of inventory system would you use in the following situations?

    a. Supplying your kitchen with fresh food.

    b. Obtaining a daily newspaper.

    c. Buying gasoline for your car.

11. Why is it desirable to classify items into groups, as the ABC classification scheme does?

12. In addition to airlines, hotels, and car rental firms, what other types of services would be appropriate for yield management?

13. Call up a hotel and ask about their room rates for weekdays, weekends, high season, and low season. Explain the logic for these prices.

SOLVED PROBLEMS

Problem 1

Items purchased from a vendor cost $20 each, and the forecast for next year's demand is 1,000 units. If it costs $5 every time an order is placed for more units and the carrying cost is $4 per unit per year, what quantity should be ordered each time?

a. What is the total ordering cost for a year?

b. What is the total carrying cost for a year?

Solution

The quantity to be ordered each time is:

$$\text{EOQ} = \sqrt{\frac{2DS}{H}} = \sqrt{\frac{2(1,000)5}{4}} = 50 \text{ units}$$

a. The total ordering cost for a year is:

$$\frac{D}{Q}S = \frac{1,000}{50}(\$5) = \$100$$

b. The carrying cost for a year is:

$$\frac{Q}{2}H = \frac{50}{2}(\$4) = \$100$$

Problem 2

A department store sells (among other things) sports shirts for casual wear. Mr. Koste is in charge of the men's department, and knows that the annual demand for one of these shirts is fairly constant at 250 shirts per year. These shirts are obtained only from the manufacturer, who charges a delivery fee of $65, regardless of the number of shirts delivered with that order. In addition, in-house costs associated with each order total $6.

The manufacturer charges $16.25 per shirt, but is willing to lower the price by 3 percent per shirt if the department store will order at least 2 gross (288) each time. Of course, this means that some shirts must be kept in inventory, and the holding costs have been estimated at 8.5 percent per year.

Should Mr. Koste recommend that the department store accept the offer of the quantity discount?

Solution

$$D = 250$$
$$S = 65 + 6 = \$71$$
$$H = iC$$
$$i = 0.085$$
$$C = \$16.25$$
$$Q = \sqrt{\frac{2DS}{iC}} = \sqrt{\frac{(2)(250)(71)}{(0.085)(16.25)}} \approx 160$$

As $160 < 288$, compute:

$$TC(160) = (16.25)(250) + \left(\frac{250}{160}\right)(71) + \left(\frac{160}{2}\right)(0.085)(16.25)$$

$$= \$4,283.94$$

and

$$TC(288) = [(0.97)(16.25)(250)] + \left(\frac{250}{288}\right)(71) + \left(\frac{288}{2}\right)(0.085)[(0.97)(16.25)]$$

$$= \$4{,}195.19$$

Since the total cost at 288 is lower than that at 160, accept the discount.

Problem 3

Elkin Shoes, Inc. (ESI) is a manufacturing firm that produces a variety of shoes and boots. They have recently started operation of a factory in the USA, and have opened a factory outlet store adjacent to the factory. The production manager at the factory is trying to ascertain the optimal number of sheepskin boots to produce with each production run. After careful analysis, he believes that the following data are correct:

Annual demand for the boots: 12,000 pairs

Days/year the outlet store is open: 240

Daily production capacity of the factory: 200 pairs

Setup cost incurred to start boot production: $800

Annual storage cost per pair of boots: $60

What should the production manager recommend as the optimal production lot size?

Solution

D = Annual demand = 12,000

d = Daily demand = 12,000/240 = 50

p = Daily production = 200

S = Setup cost = $800

H = Holding cost = $60

$$Q = \sqrt{\frac{2DS}{H} \cdot \left(\frac{p}{p-d}\right)} = \sqrt{\frac{(2)(12000)(800)}{60} \cdot \left(\frac{200}{200-50}\right)} \approx 653$$

PROBLEMS

1. Annual demand for an item is 2,500 units. The cost to place an order is $5, and holding cost is 20 percent per annum of the cost of the item. Items have the following cost schedule:

1 to 99	$10.00 each
100 to 199	$ 9.80 each
200 and over	$ 9.60 each

   What is the economic order quantity (EOQ)?

2. Demand for an item is 1,000 units per year. Each order placed costs $10; the annual cost to carry items in inventory is $2 each.

   a. In what quantities should the item be ordered?

   b. Suppose a $100 discount on each order is given if orders are placed in quantities of 500 or more. Should orders be placed in quantities of 500, or should you stick to the decision you made in *a*?

3. Item X is a standard item stocked in a company's inventory of component parts. Each year, the firm, on a random basis, uses about 2,000 of Item X, which costs $25 each. Annual storage

costs, which include insurance and cost of capital, amount to $5 per unit of average inventory. Every time an order is placed, it costs $10.

a. Whenever Item X is ordered, what should the order size be?

b. What is the annual cost for ordering Item X?

c. What is the annual cost for storing Item X?

4. A particular raw material is available to a company at three different prices, depending on the size of the orders, as follows:

Less than 100 pounds	$20 per pound
100 pounds to 999 pounds	$19 per pound
1,000 pounds and more	$18 per pound

The cost to place an order is $40. Annual demand is 3,000 units. Holding (or carrying) cost is 25 percent per annum.

What is the economic order quantity to buy each time?

5. In the past, Taylor Industries has used a fixed-time inventory system that involved taking a complete inventory count of all items each month. However, increasing labor costs are forcing Taylor Industries to examine alternate ways to reduce the amount of labor involved in inventory stockrooms without increasing other costs, such as shortage costs.

The following table is a random sample of 20 of Taylor's items.

Item Number	Annual Usage	Item Number	Annual Usage
1	$ 1,500	11	$13,000
2	12,000	12	600
3	2,200	13	42,000
4	50,000	14	9,900
5	9,600	15	1,200
6	750	16	10,200
7	2,000	17	4,000
8	11,000	18	61,000
9	800	19	3,500
10	15,000	20	2,900

a. What would you recommend Taylor do to cut back its labor cost? (Illustrate using an ABC plan.)

b. Item 15 is critical to continued operations. How would you recommend it be classified?

6. Magnetron, Inc., manufactures microwave ovens for the commercial market. Currently, Magnetron is producing part 2104 in its fabrication shop for use in the adjacent unit assembly area. Next year's requirement for part 2104 is estimated at 20,000 units. Part 2104 is valued at $50 per unit, and the combined storage and handling cost is $8 per unit per year. The cost of preparing the order and making the production setup is $200. The plant operates 250 days per year. The assembly area operates every working day, completing 80 units, and the fabrication shop produces 160 units per day when it is producing part 2104.

a. Compute the economic order quantity.

b. How many orders will be placed each year?

c. If part 2104 could be purchased from another firm with the same costs as described, what would the order quantity be? (The order is received all at once.)

d. If the average lead time to order from another firm is 10 working days and a safety stock level is set at 500 units, what is the reorder point?

7. Garrett Corporation, a turbine manufacturer, operates its plants on an 18-hour day, 300 days a year. Titanium blades can be produced on its turbine blade machine number 1 (TBM1) at a rate of 500 per hour, and the average usage rate is 5,000 per day. The blades cost $15 apiece, and carrying costs are $0.10 per day per blade because of insurance, interest on investments, and space allocation. TBM1 costs $250 to set up for each run. Lead time requires production to begin after stock drops to 500 blades. What is the optimal production run for TBM1?

8. Alpha Products, Inc., is having a problem trying to control inventory. There is insufficient time to devote to all its items equally. Following is a sample of some items stocked, along with the annual usage of each item expressed in dollar volume.

Item	Annual Dollar	Item	Annual Dollar
a	$ 7,000	k	$80,000
b	1,000	l	400
c	14,000	m	1,100
d	2,000	n	30,000
e	24,000	o	1,900
f	68,000	p	800
g	17,000	q	90,000
h	900	r	12,000
i	1,700	s	3,000
j	2,300	t	32,000

Can you suggest a system for allocating inventory control time? Specify where each item from the list would be placed.

9. CU, Incorporated, (CUI) produces copper contacts that it uses in switches and relays, CUI needs to determine the order quantity Q to meet the annual demand at the lowest cost.

The price of copper depends on the quantity ordered. Following are the price-break data and other relevant data for the problem:

Price of copper	$0.82 per pound up to 2,499 pounds
	$0.81 per pound for orders between 2,500 and 4,999 pounds
	$0.80 per pound for orders greater than 5,000 pounds
Annual demand	50,000 pounds per year
Holding cost	20 percent per year
Ordering cost	$30

Which quantity should be ordered?

10. DAT, Inc., produces digital audiotapes to be used in the consumer audio division. DAT doesn't have sufficient personnel in its inventory supply section to closely control each item stocked, so you have been asked to determine an ABC classification. The following shows a sample from the inventory records:

Item	Average Monthly Demand	Price per Unit
1	700	$6.00
2	200	4.00
3	2,000	12.00
4	1,100	20.00
5	4,000	21.00
6	100	10.00
7	3,000	2.00
8	2,500	1.00
9	500	10.00
10	1,000	2.00

Develop an ABC classification for these 10 items.

11. Mike Coggins, owner of Bagel Maker bakery, is trying to decide how many bagels he should make each morning. He currently sells fresh bagels for $5.25 per dozen. Any bagels that are left over at the end of the day are sold the next day as "yesterday's bagels" for $3.00 per dozen. Mike estimates that the material and labor to make a dozen bagels is $3.75. To help him decide how many bagels to make each morning he has collected the following information based on historical data:

	Dozens of Bagels Sold						
	12	14	16	18	20	22	24
	Probability						
Weekdays (Monday–Friday)	.15	.25	.25	.20	.15	.00	.00
Weekends (Saturday–Sunday)	.05	.15	.15	.25	.20	.15	.05

a. How many dozens of bagels should Mike make weekday mornings?

b. How many dozens of bagels should Mike make on weekend mornings?

12. Sonia Groves owns a parking lot in downtown Boston with 100 spaces. She can offer an "early bird" special for $12.00 a day and she knows she can attract as many customers who work in downtown Boston as she is willing to allocate parking spaces at this low daily rate. The hourly rate that she charges is $6.00 and the average customer stays for about 3½ hours. Sonia has collected the following data on how many parking spaces a day she has had occupied at the hourly rate:

Parking spaces	65	70	75	80	85
Probability	.15	.20	.25	.30	.10

If we assume that only one hourly customer per day occupies a given parking space, how many spaces should Sonia allocate for the early bird special in order to maximize her profits?

SELECTED BIBLIOGRAPHY

Anderson, Edward J. "Testing Feasibility in a Lot Scheduling Problem." *Operations Research,* November–December 1990, pp. 1079–89.

Bernhard, Paul. "The Carrying Cost Paradox: How Do You Manage It?" *Industrial Engineering,* November 1989, pp. 40–46.

Davis, Samuel G. "Scheduling Economic Lot Size Production Runs." *Management Science,* August 1990, pp. 985–99.

Fitzsimmons, James, and Mona Fitzsimmons. *Service Management: Operations, Strategy, and Information Technology.* New York: McGraw-Hill, 1998.

Fogarty, Donald W.; John H. Blackstone; and Thomas R. Hoffmann. *Production and Inventory Management.* 2nd ed. Cincinnati, OH: South-Western Publishing, 1991.

Freeland, James R.; John P. Leschke; and Elliott N. Weiss. "Guidelines for Setup Reduction Programs to Achieve Zero Inventory." *Journal of Operations Management,* January 1990, pp. 75–80.

Harris, Ford Whitman. "How Many Parts to Make at Once." *Operations Research,* November–December 1990, pp. 947–51.

Kimes, Sheryl E., "Yield-Management: A Tool for Capacity-Constrained Service Firms." *Journal of Operations Management* 8, no. 4 (1989).

Tersine, Richard J. *Principles of Inventory and Materials Management.* 3rd ed. New York: North-Holland, 1988.

Vollmann, T. E.; W. L. Berry; and D. C. Whybark. *Manufacturing Planning and Control Systems.* 3rd ed. Homewood, IL: Richard D. Irwin, 1992.

Weiss, Elliott N. "Lot Sizing Is Dead: Long Live Lot Sizing." *Production and Inventory Management Journal,* First Quarter 1990, pp. 76–78.

Young, Jan B. *Modern Inventory Operations: Methods for Accuracy and Productivity.* New York: Van Nostrand Reinhold, 1991.

INVENTORY SYSTEMS FOR DEPENDENT DEMAND

Chapter Objectives

- Define the various elements that comprise a materials requirements planning (MRP) system.

- Introduce the fundamental concepts and calculations that drive an MRP system.

- Identify some of the more common problems that confront managers when installing an MRP system.

- Describe how MRP-related systems are used in service operations.

- Introduce some of the more recent manufacturing-oriented systems that have been developed.

FMC Corp. is a $3.75 billion global producer of food machinery, chemicals, and defense equipment. Already skilled at producing high-quality, low-cost products, the company now wants to take advantage of emerging, worldwide markets while being its customers' best supplier.

To do that, FMC plans to supply the sales force with up-to-date information about the markets, the company's product lines, and product availability across their

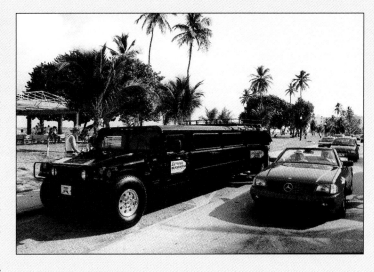

plants. This will allow the sales force to access current information from 112 plants in 20 countries.

In addition, sales representatives will be given tools to analyze available inventory, capacity, cost, and currency considerations in order to achieve the most favorable economics in delivering products to customers. But first, FMC needs to get the right information from the company's multiple ManMan MRP II systems from The Ask Cos. Currently, FMC is working with Ask to develop the capabilities to support its goals.

Customer service is the primary focus at Dow Corning Corp. The company has launched 30 cross-functional teams across five of its eight divisions. These teams are working to change Dow's operational processes, work flows, and the way people perform to increase customer satisfaction and reduce resource consumption.

Of utmost importance is shortening the time-to-market of new products and placing operational activities, such as order entry, into the hands of customers. Key to these plans is an EDI system for the entire supply chain. Dow also plans to replace its 20-year-old, in-house–developed MRP II system with an advanced system that can balance its production resources across all of its divisions. ■

Source: Alice Greene, "Two Ready for the Next Generation," *Computerworld,* June 8, 1992, p. 77.

All of the inventory models presented in the previous chapter operate under an inherent assumption: Demand is independent and constant. However, there are often times when this assumption is not valid. This is particularly true when we are dealing with subassemblies and component parts, the demand for which is often variable and highly dependent on the demand for the final or end product in which they are used. For example, the demand for automobile tires is dependent on the demand for the autos themselves. Once the demand for the autos has been established, the demand for the tires is easily calculated.

Consequently, the classical inventory models previously presented are not appropriate under these circumstances. To address these types of inventory issues, we use a concept known as **materials requirements planning,** or **MRP.**

materials requirements planning (MRP) Determines the number of subassemblies, components, and raw materials required and their build dates to complete a given number of end products by a specific date.

Today, MRP systems, in part or in whole, are used in manufacturing firms both large and small. Exhibit 15.1 shows the percentage of companies within various industries in the United States that have installed MRP II-type systems. The reason is that MRP is a logical and readily understandable approach to the problem of determining the number of parts, components, and materials needed to produce each end item. MRP also provides the time schedule specifying when each of these materials, parts, and components should be ordered or produced.

The original MRP planned only materials. However, as computer power and speed increased over the past 20 or so years and applications expanded, so did the breadth of MRP. Soon it considered resources as well as materials; now MRP also stands for *manufacturing resource planning (MRP II),* which will be discussed later in this chapter.

The main purpose of this chapter is to present an overview of MRP and its underlying logic, and to demonstrate its use through several illustrations. We also discuss samples of existing MRP programs currently in use in industry. Finally, we show that just-in-time (JIT) systems and MRP are not necessarily competing ways for production but can work effectively together.

EXHIBIT 15.1

Percentage of Companies in 11 Industries with Installed MRP II Systems

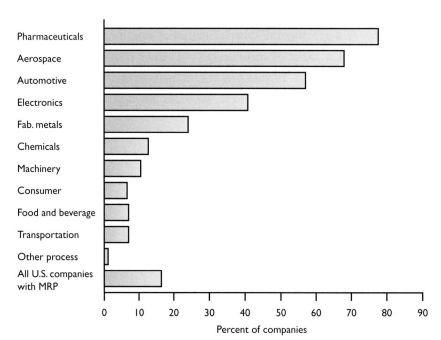

Source: David A. Turbide, *MRP +: The Adaptation, Enhancement, and Application of MRP II* (New York: Industrial Press, 1993), p. 11.

Master Production Schedule

master production schedule (MPS)
Production plan that specifies how many of, and when to build, each end item.

The aggregate production plan, as presented in Chapter 13, specifies product groups. It does not specify exact items. The next level down in the planning process after the development of the aggregate plan is the master production schedule. The **master production schedule (MPS)** is the time-phased plan specifying how many and when the firm plans to build each specific end item. For example, the aggregate plan for a furniture company may specify the total volume of mattresses it plans to produce over the next month or next quarter. The MPS goes to the next step down and identifies the exact size of the mattresses and their models. All the mattresses sold by the company would be specified by the MPS. The MPS also states period by period (which is usually weekly) how many and when each of these mattress types is needed.

Still further down the disaggregation process is the MRP program, which calculates and schedules all of the raw materials, parts, and supplies needed to make each of the different mattresses specified in the MPS.

Time Fences

The question of flexibility within an MPS depends on several factors including: production lead time, the commitment of parts and components to a specific end item, the relationship between the customer and vendor, the amount of excess capacity, and the reluctance or willingness of management to make changes.

Exhibit 15.2 shows an example of a master production schedule time fence. Management defines *time fences* as periods of time, with each period having some specified level of opportunity for the customer to make changes. (The customer may be the firm's own marketing department, which may be considering product promotions, broadening variety, etc.) Note in the exhibit that for the next eight weeks the MPS for this particular firm is frozen. Each firm has its own time fences and operating rules. Under these rules, *frozen* could be defined as anything from absolutely no changes in one firm to only the most minor of changes in another. *Moderately firm* may allow changes in specific products within a product group, so long as parts are available. *Flexible* may allow almost any variations in products, with the provision that capacity remains about the same and that there are no long lead time items involved.

The purpose of time fences is to maintain a reasonably controlled flow through the production system. Unless some operating rules are established and adhered to, the system could be chaotic and filled with overdue orders and constant expediting.

EXHIBIT 15.2

Master Production Schedule Time Fences

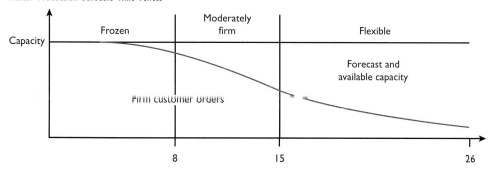

Material Requirements Planning (MRP) Systems

Using an MPS that is derived from an aggregate plan, *a material requirements planning (MRP)* system can then create schedules identifying the specific parts and materials necessary to produce the end items required, the exact numbers of each that are needed, and the dates when orders for these materials should be released and be received or completed within the production cycle. Today's MRP systems use a computer program to carry out these operations. Most firms have used computerized inventory systems for years, but they were independent of the scheduling system; MRP links these two elements together.

Material requirements planning is not new in concept. Logic dictates that the Romans probably used it in their construction projects, the Venetians in their shipbuilding, and the Chinese in building the Great Wall. Building contractors have always been forced into planning for material to be delivered when needed and not before, because of space limitations. What is new is the larger scale and the more rapid changes that can be made through the use of computers. Now firms that produce many products involving thousands of parts and materials can take advantage of MRP.

Purposes, Objectives, and Philosophy of MRP

The main purposes of an MRP system are to control inventory levels, assign operating priorities to items, and plan capacity to load the production system. These may be briefly expanded as follows:

Inventory

Order the right part.

Order the right quantity.

Order at the right time.

Priorities

Order with the right due date.

Keep the due date valid.

The MRP system at Allen-Bradley, a manufacturer of circuit boards, receives an order and schedules appropriate production. Board panels are automatically routed to the required process, such as this robotic cell that inserts nonstandard components.

Capacity

Plan for a complete load.

Plan an accurate load.

Plan for an adequate time to view future load.

The *theme* of MRP is "getting the right materials to the right place at the right time."

The *objectives* of inventory management under an MRP system are to improve customer service, minimize inventory investment, and maximize production operating efficiency.

The *philosophy* of material requirements planning is that materials should be expedited (hurried) when their lack would delay the overall production schedule and de-expedited (delayed) when the schedule falls behind and postpones their need. Traditionally, and perhaps still typically, when an order is behind schedule, significant effort is spent trying to get it back on schedule. However, the opposite is not always true; when an order, for whatever reason, has its completion date delayed, the appropriate adjustments are not made in the schedule. This results in a one-sided effort—late orders are expedited, but early orders are not de-expedited or delayed. Aside from perhaps using scarce capacity, it is preferable not to have raw materials and work in process before they are actually needed, because inventories tie up capital, clutter up stockrooms, delay the introduction of design changes, and prevent the cancellation or delay of existing orders.

Benefits of an MRP System

Manufacturing companies with more than $10 million in annual sales are most likely to have some form of a computerized MRP system. A computerized system is necessary because of the sheer volume of materials, supplies, and components that are part of expanding product lines, and the speed that firms need to react to constant changes in the system. When firms switched from existing manual or computerized systems to an MRP system, they realized many benefits, including:

- More competitive pricing.
- Lower selling price.
- Lower inventory levels.
- Improved customer service.
- Faster response to market demands.
- Increased flexibility to change the master schedule.
- Reduced setup and tear-down costs.
- Reduced idle time.

In addition, the MRP system:

- Gives advanced notice so managers can see the planned schedule before the orders are actually released.
- Tells when to de-expedite as well as expedite.
- Delays or cancels orders.
- Changes order quantities.
- Advances or delays order due dates.
- Aids capacity planning.

In converting to an MRP system, many firms claimed as much as 40 percent reductions in inventory investment.

EXHIBIT 15.3

Industry Applications and
Expected Benefits

Industry Type	Examples	Expected Benefits
Assemble-to-stock	Combines multiple component parts into a finished product, which is then stocked in inventory to satisfy customer demand. Examples: watches, tools, appliances.	High
Fabricate-to-stock	Items are manufactured by machine rather than assembled from parts. These are standard stock items carried in anticipation of customer demand. Examples: piston rings, electrical switches.	Low
Assemble-to-order	A final assembly is made from standard options which the customer chooses: Examples: trucks, generators, motors.	High
Fabricate-to-order	Items manufactured by machine to customer order. These are generally industrial orders. Examples: bearings, gears, fasteners.	Low
Manufacture-to-order	Items fabricated or assembled completely to customer specification. Examples: turbine generators, heavy machine tools.	High
Process	Industries, such as foundries, rubber and plastics, specialty paper, chemicals, paint, drug, food processors.	Medium

Where MRP Can Be Used

MRP is being used in a variety of industries with a job-shop environment (meaning that a number of products are made in batches using the same production equipment). The list in Exhibit 15.3 includes process industries, but note that the processes mentioned are confined to job runs that alternate output products and do not include continuous processes such as petroleum or steel.

As you can see in the exhibit, MRP is most valuable to companies involved in assembly operations and least valuable to those in fabrication. Another factor that affects the degree of benefit gained from an MRP system is the number of levels in the product. The greater the number of levels, the greater the benefit of MRP.

One more point to note: MRP typically does not work well in companies that produce a low number of units annually. This is especially true for companies producing complex expensive products requiring advanced research and design. Under such circumstances, experience has shown that lead times tend to be too long and too uncertain, and the product configuration too complex for MRP to handle. These types of companies need the control features that network scheduling techniques offer, and thus would be better off using project scheduling methods (covered previously in Chapter 10).

MRP System Structure

The MRP portion most closely interacts with the MPS schedule, the bill of materials file, the inventory records file, and the output reports. Exhibit 15.4 shows a portion of Exhibit 13.1 in Chapter 13 with several additions. Note that capacity is not addressed here, nor are there any feedback loops to higher levels. We discuss these elements later in this chapter under MRP II and capacity requirements planning.

Each facet of Exhibit 15.4 is subsequently explained in more detail, but essentially the MRP system works as follows: Forecasted sales and firm orders for products are used to create an MPS, which states the number of items to be produced during specific time periods. A bill of materials file identifies the specific materials used to make each item and the

EXHIBIT 15.4

Overall View of the Inputs to a Standard Material Requirements Planning Program and the Reports Generated by the Program

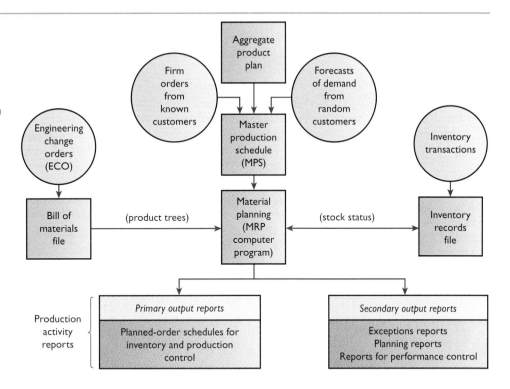

correct quantities of each. The inventory records file contains data such as the number of units on hand and on order. These three sources—(*a*) the MPS, (*b*) the bill of materials file, and (*c*) the inventory records file—become the data sources for the MRP program, which essentially expands or "explodes" the MPS into a detailed order scheduling plan for the entire production sequence.

Demand for Products

As stated above, product demand for end items is primarily derived from two sources: The first is known customers who have placed specific orders, such as those generated by sales personnel, or from interdependent transactions. These orders usually carry promised delivery dates. There is no forecasting involved in these orders—we simply add them up. The second source is forecasted demand. These are the normal independent-demand orders; the forecasting models presented in Chapter 6 can be used to predict the quantities. The demand from the known customers and the forecast demand are combined to become the input for developing the MPS.

Demand for Spare Parts and Supplies   In addition to the demand for end products, customers also order specific parts and components as spare parts to provide for service and repair. These demands for items less complex than the end product are not usually part of the MPS; instead, they are fed directly into the MRP program at their appropriate levels. That is, they are added in as a gross requirement for that part or component.

Bill of Materials File

The **bill of materials (BOM)** file contains the complete product description, listing not only the materials, parts, and components but also the sequences in which the product is created. This BOM file is one of the three main inputs into the MRP program (the other two are the MPS and the inventory records file).

bill of materials (BOM)
A list of subassemblies, components, and raw materials, and their respective quantities, required to produce specific end items.

The BOM file is often called the *product structure* or *product tree file* because it shows how a product is put together. It contains the information necessary to identify each item and the quantity used per unit of the item in which it is used. To illustrate this, consider the product tree for Product A, as shown in Exhibit 15.5. Product A consists of two units of Part B and three units of Part C. Part B consists of one unit of Part D and four units of Part E. Part C consists of two units of Part F, five units of Part G, and four units of Part H. In the past, BOM files have often listed subassemblies and parts as indented files. This clearly identifies each item and the manner in which it is assembled because each indentation signifies the components of the item. A comparison of the indented files in Exhibit 15.6 with the item structure in Exhibit 15.5 shows the ease of relating the two displays. From a computer standpoint, however, storing items in indented parts lists is very inefficient. To compute the amount of each item needed at the lower levels, each item would need to be expanded ("exploded") and summed. A more efficient procedure is to store parts data in a single-level explosion. That is, each item and component is listed showing only its parent and the number of units needed per unit of its parent. This avoids duplication because it includes each assembly only once. Exhibit 15.6 shows a comparison between the single-level list and the indented list for Product A.

A data element (called a *pointer* or *locator*) is also contained in each file to identify the parent of each part and allow a retracing upward through the process.

Low-Level Coding   If all identical parts occur at the same level for each end product, the total number of parts and materials needed for a product can be easily computed. However, consider Product L shown in Exhibit 15.7a. Notice that Item N in Product B, for example, occurs both as an input to L and as an input to M. Item N therefore needs to be lowered to

EXHIBIT 15.5

Product Structure Tree for Product A

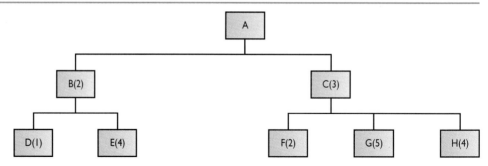

EXHIBIT 15.6

Subassemblies and Parts List in an Indented Format and in a Single-Level List

Subassemblies and Indented Parts List			Single-Level Subassemblies and Parts List	
A			A	
	B(2)			B(2)
		D(1)		C(3)
		E(4)	B	
	C(3)			D(1)
		F(2)		E(4)
		G(5)	C	
		H(4)		F(2)
				G(5)
				H(4)

level 2 (Exhibit 15.7b) to bring all the Ns down to their lowest common level. This is referred to as *low-level coding*. When all identical items are placed at the same level, it becomes a simple matter for the computer to scan across each level and summarize the number of units of each item required.

Inventory Records File

inventory records file
Computerized record-keeping system for the inventory status of all subassemblies, components, and raw materials.

The **inventory records file** in a computerized system can be quite lengthy. Each item in inventory is carried as a separate file, and the range of details carried about an item is almost limitless. Although Exhibit 15.8 is from an earlier version of MRP, it shows the variety of information contained in the inventory records files. The MRP program accesses the *status* segment of the file according to specific time periods (called *time buckets* in MRP slang). These files are accessed as needed during the program run.

The MRP program performs its analysis from the top of the product structure downward, exploding requirements level by level. There are times, however, when it is desirable to identify the parent item that caused the material requirement. The MRP program allows the creation of a *peg record* file either separately or as part of the inventory record file.

EXHIBIT 15.7

Product L Hierarchy in (a) Expanded to the Lowest Level of Each Item in (b)

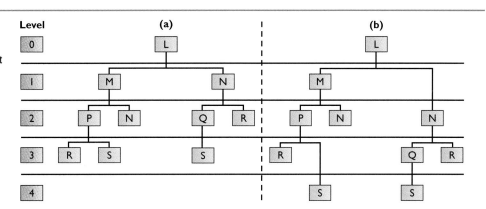

EXHIBIT 15.8

The Inventory Status Record for an Item in Inventory

Item master data segment	Part No.	Description		Lead time	Std. cost	Safety stock
	Order quantity		Setup	Cycle	Last year's usage	Class
	Scrap allowance		Cutting data	Pointers	Etc.	

Inventory status segment	Allocated	Control balance	Period 1 2 3 4 5 6 7 8	Totals
	Gross requirements			
	Scheduled receipts			
	On hand			
	Planned-order releases			

Subsidiary data segment	Order details	
	Pending action	
	Counters	
	Keeping track	

Pegging requirements allows us to retrace a material requirement upward in the product structure through each level, identifying each parent item that created the demand.

Inventory Transactions File   The inventory status file is kept up to date by posting inventory transactions as they occur. These changes are a result of stock receipts and disbursements, scrap and obsolescence losses, wrong parts, canceled orders, and so forth.

MRP Computer Program

The MRP program operates on the inventory file, the MPS, and the BOM file. It works in this way: A list of end items needed by time periods (or time "buckets") is specified by the MPS. A description of the materials and parts needed to make each item is specified in the BOM file. The number of units of each item and material currently on hand and on order are contained in the inventory file. The MRP program "works" on the inventory file (which is segmented into time periods), while continually referring to the BOM file to compute the quantities of each item needed. The number of units of each item required is then corrected for on-hand amounts, and the net requirement is "offset" (set back in time) to allow for the lead time needed to obtain the material and/or to make the items.

If the MRP program being used does not consider capacity constraints, the master scheduler must manually perform some capacity balancing. Through an iterative process, the master scheduler feeds a tentative MPS into the MRP program (along with other items requiring the same resources) and the output is examined for production feasibility. The MPS is then adjusted to try to correct any imbalances, and the program is executed again. This process is repeated until the output is acceptable. Although it would seem to be a simple matter to have the computer simulate some schedules that consider resource limitations, in reality it is a very large and very time-consuming problem for the computer.

To further complicate the problem today, there is often not one MPS but a number of them. Firms will frequently divide the scheduling work among the schedulers by assigning one master scheduler for each major product line. The result of this is competition in that each master scheduler must compete for limited resources for his or her own product line. As a group, however, they are trying to balance resource usage and due dates for the production system as a whole.

Output Reports

Because the MRP program has access to the BOM file, the MPS, and the inventory records file, outputs or reports can take on an almost unlimited range of format and content. These reports are usually classified as *primary* and *secondary* output reports. (With the expansion of MRP into MRP II, many additional reports are available.)

Primary Reports   Primary reports are the main or normal reports used for inventory and production control. These reports include:

1. *Planned orders* to be released at a future time.
2. *Order release notices* to execute the planned orders.
3. *Changes in due dates* of open orders due to rescheduling.
4. *Cancellations or suspensions* of open orders due to cancellation or suspension of orders on the MPS.
5. *Inventory status data.*

Secondary Reports   Additional reports, which are optional in an MRP program, fall into the following main categories:

1. *Planning reports* to be used, for example, in forecasting inventory and specifying requirements over some future time horizon.

2. *Performance reports* for purposes of pointing out inactive items and determining the agreement between actual and programmed item lead times and between actual and programmed quantity usage and costs.

3. *Exceptions reports* that point out serious discrepancies, such as errors, out-of-range situations, late or overdue orders, excessive scrap, or nonexistent parts.

A SIMPLE MRP EXAMPLE

To demonstrate how the various elements of an MRP system are integrated, we present a simple problem explaining how quantities are calculated, lead times are offset, and order releases and receipts are established.

Bill of Materials (Product Structure Tree) File

Suppose that we want to produce Product T, which consists of two parts U, three parts V, and one part Y. Part U, in turn, is made of one part W and two parts X. Part V is made of two parts W and two parts Y. Exhibit 15.9 shows the product structure tree for Product T.

Inventory Records File

Next, we need to consider the time needed to obtain these items, that is, either to produce the parts internally or to obtain them from an outside vendor. Assume that the lead time to make each of the parts and their respective on-hand inventories and scheduled receipts are as follows:

Part	Lead Time (weeks)	On-Hand Inventory	Scheduled Receipts*
T	1	25	—
U	2	5	5
V	2	15	—
W	3	30	—
X	2	20	—
Y	1	10	—

*Subassemblies or parts that have been previously ordered but are not scheduled for delivery until a future date (week three for subassembly U in this example).

Running the MRP Program

If we know when Product T is required, we can create a time schedule chart specifying when all the material necessary to build T must be ordered and received to meet this requirement. Exhibit 15.10 shows which items are needed and when. We have thus created a

---

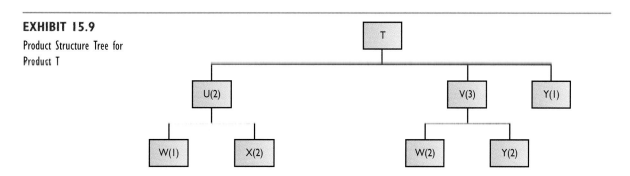

EXHIBIT 15.10

Materials Requirements Plan for Completing 100 units of Product T in Period 8.

Part No. T	1	2	3	4	5	6	7	8	9
Gross requirements								100	
Scheduled receipts									
On-hand inventory: 25								25	
Net requirements								75	
Planned order releases							75		

Part No. U	1	2	3	4	5	6	7	8	9
Gross requirements							150		
Scheduled receipts			5				5		
On-hand inventory: 5							5		
Net requirements							140		
Planned order releases					140				

Part No. V	1	2	3	4	5	6	7	8	9
Gross requirements							225		
Scheduled receipts									
On-hand inventory: 15							15		
Net requirements							210		
Planned order releases					210				

Part No. W	1	2	3	4	5	6	7	8	9
Gross requirements					560				
Scheduled receipts									
On-hand inventory: 30					30				
Net requirements					530				
Planned order releases		530							

Part No. X	1	2	3	4	5	6	7	8	9
Gross requirements					280				
Scheduled receipts									
On-hand inventory: 20					20				
Net requirements					260				
Planned order releases				260					

Part No. Y	1	2	3	4	5	6	7	8	9
Gross requirements					420		75		
Scheduled receipts									
On-hand inventory: 10					10				
Net requirements					410		75		
Planned order releases				410		75			

material requirements plan based on the demand for Product T and the knowledge of how T is made, current inventories on hand, and the time needed to obtain each part.

From this simple illustration, it should be obvious that manually developing a material requirements plan for thousands or even hundreds of items would be impractical—a great deal of computation is needed, and a tremendous amount of data must be available about the inventory status (number of units on hand, on order, and so forth) and about the product structure (how the product is made and how many units of each material are required). A computer is an integral part of every MRP system. However, our emphasis in this chapter is on understanding the general structure of the system and on the supporting computer files that are required because the underlying logic of the program is essentially the same as that for our simple example.

Generally, the MPS, which is the primary driver of the MRP system, deals with end items. If the end item is quite large and/or quite expensive, the MPS may, however, schedule major subassemblies or components instead.

MARKETING
FINANCE
MANAGEMENT
ENGINEERING

All production systems have limited capacity and limited resources. This presents a challenge for the master scheduler. Exhibit 15.11 shows the environment in which the master scheduler works. While the aggregate plan provides the general range of operation, the master scheduler must massage the aggregate plan into an MPS that specifies exactly what is to be produced. These decisions are made while responding to pressures from various functional areas.

To determine an acceptable schedule that is feasible for the shop, trial master production schedules are run through the MRP program in an iterative process. The resulting planned order releases (the detailed production schedules) are reviewed to ensure that resources are available and the completion times are reasonable. What may appear to be a feasible MPS may, in fact, require excessive resources when the resource requirements for the materials, parts, and components for the lower levels are determined. If this occurs (which is the usual case), the MPS is then adjusted to reflect these limitations and the MRP program is run again. To ensure good master scheduling, the master schedul*er* (i.e., the human being) must:

MARKETING
SALES

- Include all demands from product sales, warehouse replenishment, spares, and interplant requirements.
- Never lose sight of the aggregate plan.

EXHIBIT 15.11

The Environment of the Master Scheduler

Management impact on master production scheduler

| Sales and distribution |
| Customer service ship as soon as possible |

| Financial |
| Inventory financing minimum possible |

Master scheduler

| Management |
| Return on investment minimum staff minimum inventory maximum productivity customer service |

| Engineering |
| Engineer to order never enough time |

| Manufacturing |
| Productivity level and fixed schedules |

Source: Romeyn C. Everdell and Woodrow W. Chamberlain, "Master Scheduling in a Multi-Plant Environment," *Proceedings of the American Production and Inventory Control Society* (1980), p. 421.

EXHIBIT 15.12

The Aggregate Plan and the Master Production Schedule for Mattresses

Aggregate production plan for mattresses

Month	1	2
Mattress production	900	950

Master production schedule for mattress models

	1	2	3	4	5	6	7	8
Model 327	200			400		200	100	
Model 538		100	100		150		100	
Model 749			100			200		200

- Be involved with customer order promising.
- Be visible to all levels of management.
- Objectively trade off manufacturing, marketing, and engineering conflicts.
- Identify and communicate all problems.

The upper portion of Exhibit 15.12 shows an aggregate plan for the total number of mattresses planned per month for a furniture manufacturer, without regard to mattress type. The lower portion of the exhibit shows an MPS specifying the exact type of mattress and the quantity planned for production by week. The next level down (not shown) would be the MRP program that develops detailed schedules showing when cotton batting, springs, and hardwood are needed to make the mattresses.

CAPACITY REQUIREMENTS PLANNING (CRP)

In the previous sections of this chapter that focused on the MPS and running the MRP program, we mentioned that production capacity is usually some finite amount and obviously has limits. We also cited the interaction between the scheduler and rerunning the MRP program to obtain feasible schedules in light of this limited capacity. In this section we explicitly point out how capacity is computed and what the usual procedure is for addressing capacity constraints.

Computing Work Center Load

Each work center is generally a functionally defined center where jobs routed to it require the same type of work, on the same type of equipment. From the work center view, if there is adequate capacity, the problem is one of priorities: which job to do first. If there is insufficient capacity, however, the problem must be resolved by the master scheduler.

Exhibit 15.13 shows a work center that has various jobs assigned to it. Note that the capacity per week was computed at the bottom of the exhibit at 161.5 hours. The jobs scheduled for the three weeks result in two weeks with under capacity, and one week requiring over capacity.

Exhibit 15.13 uses the terms *utilization* and *efficiency*. Both of these terms have been defined and used in a variety of ways, some conflicting. In this exhibit, utilization refers to the actual time that the machines are used. *Efficiency* refers to how well the machine is performing while it is being used. Efficiency is usually defined as a comparison of actual performance to a defined standard output or an engineering design rate. For instance, a

EXHIBIT 15.13

Workload for Work Center A

Week	Job No.	Units	Setup Time	Run Time per Unit	Total Job Time	Total for Week
10	145	100	3.5	0.23	26.5	
	167	160	2.4	0.26	44.0	
	158	70	1.2	0.13	10.3	
	193	300	6.0	0.17	57.0	137.8
11	132	80	5.0	0.36	33.8	
	126	150	3.0	0.22	36.0	
	180	180	2.5	0.30	56.5	
	178	120	4.0	0.50	64.0	190.3
12	147	90	3.0	0.18	19.2	
	156	200	3.5	0.14	31.5	
	198	250	1.5	0.16	41.5	
	172	100	2.0	0.12	14.0	
	139	120	2.2	0.17	22.6	128.8

Computing Work Center Capacity

The available capacity in standard hours is 161.5 hours per five-day week, calculated as: (2 machines) (2 shifts) (10 hours/shift) (85% machine utilization) (95% efficiency).

EXHIBIT 15.14

Scheduled Workload for Work Center A

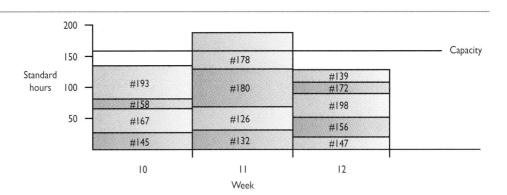

machine used for six hours of an eight-hour shift was utilized ¾ or 75 percent. If the standard output for that machine is established at 200 parts per hour and an average of 250 parts per hour were actually produced, then the efficiency of that machine is 125 percent. Note that in these definitions efficiency can be more than 100 percent, but utilization can never exceed 100 percent.

Exhibit 15.14 shows a loading representation of Work Center A for the three weeks. The scheduled work exceeds capacity for Week 11. There are several options available:

1. Work overtime.
2. Select an alternate work center that could perform the task.
3. Subcontract to an outside shop.
4. Try to schedule part of the work of Week 11 earlier into Week 10, and delay part of the work into Week 12.
5. Renegotiate the due date and reschedule.

An MRP program with a capacity requirements planning module allows rescheduling to try to level capacity. Two techniques used are backward scheduling and forward scheduling—the fourth option on the preceding list. The objective of the master scheduler is to try to level out the load in Exhibit 15.14 so that the requirements for the work center remain within the available capacity.

MANUFACTURING RESOURCE PLANNING (MRP II)

Earlier in this chapter, our discussion of MRP focused only on the *material* requirements that resulted from an explosion of the master schedule. We did not include the needs of all the other types of resources, such as staffing, facilities, and tools. In addition, while we discussed *capacity requirements planning,* we did this somewhat externally to the MRP system. In this section we discuss the logic of more advanced versions of MRP that include a wider range of resources and outputs.

MRP II

An expansion of the materials requirements planning program to include other portions of the production system was natural and to be expected. One of the first to be included was the purchasing function. At the same time, there was a more detailed inclusion of the production system itself—on the shop floor, in dispatching, and in the detailed scheduling control. MRP had already included work center capacity limitations, so it was obvious the name *material requirements planning* no longer adequately described the expanded system. Someone (probably MRP pioneer Ollie Wight) introduced the name **manufacturing resource planning (MRP II)** to reflect the idea that more and more of the firm was becoming involved in the program. To quote Wight,

> The fundamental manufacturing equation is:
>   What are we going to make?
>   What does it take to make it?
>   What do we have?
>   What do we have to get?[1]

manufacturing resource planning (MRP II)
Advanced MRP system which takes into consideration the equipment capacities and other resources that are associated with a manufacturing facility.

MARKETING
FINANCE
ENGINEERING

The initial intent for MRP II was to plan and monitor all the resources of a manufacturing firm—manufacturing, marketing, finance, and engineering—through a closed-loop system generating financial figures. The second important intent of the MRP II concept was that it stimulate the manufacturing system. It is generally conceived now as being a total, companywide system that allows everyone (buyers, marketing staff, production, accounting) to work with the same game plan, use the same numbers, and is capable of simulation to plan and test alternative strategies. (See the OM in Practice on Furniture Manufacturer Uses MRP II to Cut Delivery Time.)

Cost of an MRP II System

Several software companies regularly advertise MRP systems in manufacturing-oriented journals, as well as on the Internet. Prices range from as low as $500 to as high as $300,000 because MRP II systems can vary widely in the types of modules and capabilities that are included.

Costs for the computer hardware also have a wide range. An MRP program for a very small company can be run on a microcomputer with hard disk drives. However, most

---

[1]Oliver Wight, *The Executive's Guide to Successful MRP II* (Williston, VT: Oliver Wight Limited Publications, 1982), pp. 6, 17.

Operations Management in Practice

FURNITURE MANUFACTURER USES MRP II TO CUT DELIVERY TIME

In 1988, Harpers, Inc., an office furniture manufacturer located in California, was experiencing sustained growth in sales, but profits continued to fall. To reverse the downward trend in profits, management determined that it would have to reduce manufacturing costs by 15 percent, reduce product delivery times from six weeks (which was the industry standard) to three weeks, and reduce the new product time-to-market from three years to six months.

At the same time, Harpers recognized the need to focus its efforts on one segment of the office furniture market which was "custom furniture solutions." To accomplish all of this, Harper needed a flexible manufacturing system that would allow customers to change the features of any furniture configuration.

The heart of its manufacturing system was centered around an MRP II system that would "integrate our engineering, marketing, manufacturing, and accounting efforts, and simultaneously engineer and deliver those custom products," said Joe Wisniewski, executive vice president and general manager at Harpers.

The system was installed and running by 1990, and by the end of 1991, 20 percent of the company's furniture was shipping within two weeks, with the remaining orders shipping in four weeks.

Source: Adapted from Robert M. Knight, "Furniture Maker Uses MRP II to Cut Lead Time," *Computerworld*, June 8, 1992, p. 80.

MRP II systems are run on minicomputers or mainframes because of the very large data storage requirements and the number of program modules involved. Lease costs may range from $30,000 to $500,000 per year; however, technology is changing rapidly, with a consequent drop in cost. In terms of additional personnel needed, the experiences of many companies indicate that the overall net change in personnel is close to zero. Companies simply switch people from existing areas into MRP system roles.

The typical MRP II system takes about 18 months to install. However, this can vary widely depending on the size of the application, the condition of the existing databases and how much they may have to be revised, the quality of the bills of materials, routing sheets and inventory records, and the amount of personnel training required. Another factor is whether the firm has already been using an MRP system and is switching to an MRP II system. The entire range of time can vary from as little as several months to as much as three years.

Payback for an MRP installation can be quite short. When larger companies first installed MRP systems some years ago, they realized an average annual return on investment of about 300 percent.[2]

When we think of MRP II, we tend to think of large computer programs with applications confined to business giants. In fact, however, MRP II is also economically feasible for manufacturing companies with annual sales of less than $1 million. In addition, much of the current software is user-friendly and easy to operate.

Prices and quality of software vary widely and not necessarily in a direct relationship. Customer support is another very important factor. This is a buyer beware market, and care should be taken in selecting a program because it is a long-term commitment.

MRP IN SERVICES

 In general, MRP systems have not made significant inroads in service operations. This is due, in part, to the belief that MRP is strictly a manufacturing tool. However, modified versions of MRP are used in service operations where an actual product is manufactured as part of the service delivery process. Examples of these quasi-manufacturing services, as

---

[2]Ibid., pp. 34–35.

stated in an earlier chapter, include restaurants and bakeries where food is prepared on-site. In these types of service operations, the inventory management system usually consists of one or more point-of-sale (POS) terminals (or cash registers) that are connected to a central computer. This computer can be located either on-site at the retail operation or at a remote regional or headquarters location.

The POS terminals are designed for *single item pricing,* where the cashier simply pushes a single key on the terminal that represents a specific item on the menu. The computer system then automatically posts the price of that item. At the same time, within the central computer system, is the bill-of-materials (or recipe) for the item that has just been sold. All of the ingredients that go into that item are subtracted out from the inventory records file. The computer inventory files are then compared against the actual physical inventories on a periodic basis. Typically these systems have reorder points built into them which will automatically signal when a specific item is running low.

Some of these service operations also use this modified MRP system to order raw ingredients to meet future sales, in a manner similar to that of an MRP system in a manufacturing environment. First, a forecast of end items to be sold is generated (for example, hamburgers). The forecasted demand for these items is then "exploded" against the bills of materials (or recipes) for the end items to determine the gross requirements. Finally these requirements are compared to on-hand inventories to determine the actual amounts of raw ingredients to be ordered and the delivery dates for when they are needed.

MISCELLANEOUS MRP ISSUES

Problems in Installing and Using MRP Systems

MRP is very well developed technically, and implementation of an MRP system should be pretty straightforward. Yet there are many problems with existing MRP systems and many "failures" in trying to install them. Why do such problems and outright failures occur with a "proven" system?

The answer partially lies with organizational and behavioral factors. Three major causes of failure have been identified: (*a*) the lack of top management commitment, (*b*) the failure to recognize that MRP is only a software tool and that it needs to be used correctly, and (*c*) the ability to properly integrate MRP and JIT.

Part of the blame for the lack of top management's commitment may be MRP's image. It sounds like a manufacturing system rather than a business plan. However, an MRP system is used to plan resources and develop schedules. And a well-functioning schedule effectively uses the firm's assets with the result of increased profits. MRP should be presented to top management as a planning tool with specific reference to profit results. Intensive executive education is needed, emphasizing the importance of MRP as a closed-loop, integrated, strategic planning tool.

The second cause of the problem concerns the MRP advocates that overdid themselves in selling the concept. MRP was presented and perceived as a complete, stand-alone system to run a firm, rather than part of the total system. The third issue is how MRP can be made to function with JIT. JIT and MRP can live together, but there are few rules as to how they should be integrated. The total system consists of the functional areas of engineering, marketing, personnel, and manufacturing, as well as techniques and concepts such as quality circles, CAD/CAM, and robotics. MRP needs to be *part* of the total system, not the total system by itself.

In many meetings that we have attended, both professional and industrial, we have heard similar installation and operational problems. These problems distill down to the fact that the MRP system essentially runs the firm; its main objective is simply to meet the schedule. As a result, people become subservient to the MRP system. Even such simple decisions as determining a lot size cannot be made outside the system.

As it stands now, MRP is a very formal system that requires strict adherence to its rules in order to function properly. Often supervisors and workers develop an informal system for getting the job done. Their argument is that this informal system arises because the existing formal system is too rigid or inadequate to deal with real inventory scheduling problems. However, when these rules are not adhered to within the formal system, incorrect data is often reported and, as a consequence, worker confidence in the formal system begins to deteriorate. In any event, it appears that employees at all levels must change—from the company president to the lower-level employees. Even though MRP currently does work in many installations, its good features and its shortcomings should be thoroughly understood.

Other problems encountered in using MRP include:

1. *The fallacy of static lead time.* MRP software programs treat lead time as a fixed number, while in reality lead time changes for a variety of reasons, such as normal variation in processing time, waiting for parts, delays in processing due to expedited jobs, breakdown or normal maintenance of machines, and so on.

2. *The misdefinition of lead time.* Manufacturing lead time consists of:
   a. Make-ready time—to write order, enter, prepare job packet, release order, and issue material.
   b. Queue time—time at the operation center waiting for operations to begin.
   c. Setup time—to prepare equipment for operations.
   d. Run time—to perform operations (produce product).
   e. Wait time—time waiting after operation ends.
   f. Move time—to physically move between operations.

3. *Lead time versus fabrication/production quantity.* MRP software, because it considers lead time fixed, does not account for the fact that run time (part of the lead time) varies depending on the quantity of units to be produced.

4. *Bills of materials.* MRP software programs use the bills of materials as a bottoms-up product structure representing the ways firms manufacture products. For many firms, however, especially those producing on an assembly line, products may be produced in a very different sequence than the engineering bills of materials.

5. *Material revision control.* Many MRP programs do not easily allow changes to be made to part numbers or in the way the product is produced.

6. *Lead time versus routing.* Since many MRP programs use the bills of materials structure to schedule the shop floor, poor schedules may result. For example, there may be several routing steps at the same bill of materials level, which require more time than allowed.

7. *Fallacy of infinite capacity planning.* Few MRP programs can recognize a shop overload and reschedule.

8. *The real story of rough-cut planning.* While rough-cut capacity planning was taught as the solution to overloaded work centers, in reality rough-cut capacity planning lies somewhere between the difficult and the impossible. In effect, master schedulers are expected to perform MRP and CRP explosions in their heads. Technically, the only way to really do rough-cut capacity planning is to run the MRP and CRP (capacity requirement plan) each time a change is made in the master schedule. The required computer time makes this impossible.

9. *Capacity planning versus MRP logic.* Because MRP and CRP are not run together when changes are made in the MPS, such changes often create "floating bottlenecks." Bottlenecks appear and disappear, depending on the master production schedule.

10. *MRP logic—a user confuser.* MRP logic differs from system to system. The user should test how the system reacts to, say, accelerating, decelerating, or canceling an order.[3]

Criticisms of the MRP Concept

In addition to the problems previously mentioned with respect to installing and using an MRP system, there are other criticisms as well. Many critics state that MRP schedules are either impossible or are only true on the day that they were created. Too many changes take place in the system for MRP to be able to adjust to all of them.

Accuracy Requirements   Because MRP uses detailed files to schedule, MRP cannot tolerate inaccuracies. In fact, for many years since MRP was introduced, companies have been rated and grouped by class based on the accuracy of their records. Class A companies, for example, have more than 99-percent accuracy. MRP's failures in its scheduling performance had been blamed on inaccurate records. Now we recognize that inaccuracy was not completely to blame; the MRP scheduling technique was also at fault.

MIS **Top Management Commitment**   This is not so much a criticism of MRP, but of top management. As in the case of many programs, MRP needs to be endorsed and continually supported by top management. An MRP system is doomed to failure if management believes its responsibilities end with authorizing purchase of the program and turning over responsibility for running the computer system to the MIS group. Continuous reinforcement and encouragement are needed; everyone must be convinced that the system is worth its time and expense. It also means spending money on training, and perhaps changing the internal measurement and reward system. If this is not done, shop-floor personnel ignore MRP schedules and use their own priorities in doing job selection and in determining process batch sizes.

 MRP as a Database   Although MRP has been criticized for its questioned accuracy in providing workable schedules, MRP has been highly complimented for its detailed database. MRP's database extends throughout the entire facility and is linked through numerous modules. Even if a firm decides to discontinue using MRP to schedule its facilities, it would more than likely continue to maintain MRP files for their informational value.

Safety Stock

Ordinarily, adding a safety stock to required quantities is not advised in an MRP system that is based on derived demand. There is some feeling, however, that when the availability of parts could suffer from a long and inflexible lead time or is subject to strikes or cancellation, a safety stock offers some protection against production delays. A safety stock is sometimes intentionally created by planning for excess. One of the main arguments against using safety stock is that the MRP system considers it a fixed quantity, and the safety stock is never actually used.

Lot Sizing in MRP Systems

The determination of lot sizes in an MRP system is a complicated and difficult problem. Lot sizes are the part quantities issued in the planned order receipt and planned order

[3]Adapted from Gus Berger, "Ten Ways MRP Can Defeat You," *Conference Proceedings, American Production and Inventory Control Society* (1987), pp. 240–43.

release sections of an MRP schedule. For parts produced in house, lot sizes are the production quantities or batch sizes. For purchased parts, these are the quantities ordered from the supplier. Lot sizes generally meet part requirements for one or more periods.

Most lot-sizing techniques deal with how to balance the setup or order costs and holding costs associated with meeting the net requirements generated by the MRP planning process. Many MRP systems have options for computing lot sizes based on some of the more commonly used techniques. It should be obvious, though, that the use of lot-sizing techniques increases the complexity in generating MRP schedules. When fully exploded, the numbers of parts scheduled can be enormous.

We present four lot-sizing techniques using a common example. The lot-sizing techniques presented are lot-for-lot (L4L), economic order quantity (EOQ), least total cost (LTC), and least unit cost (LUC).

Consider the following MRP lot-sizing problem; the net requirements are shown for eight scheduling periods:

Cost per item	$10.00
Order or setup cost	$47.00
Inventory carry cost/period	0.5%

Period net requirements:

1	2	3	4	5	6	7	8
50	60	70	60	95	75	60	55

Lot-for-Lot   Lot-for-lot (L4L) is the most common technique; it:

- Sets planned orders to exactly match the net requirements.
- Produces exactly what is needed each period with none carried over into future periods.
- Minimizes carrying cost.
- Does not take into account setup costs or capacity limitations.

Many times producing enough product to last several periods and incurring holding costs may be cheaper than producing in every period and incurring repeated setup costs. In the case of parts produced in house, the setup cost represents time that resources are not operating but getting ready to produce. This is lost capacity. Not only are setup costs higher, but requiring setups in every period a part is needed also reduces the time available to produce other products.

Exhibit 15.15 shows the lot-for-lot calculations. In each period the lot size exactly matches the net requirements. A setup cost is charged for each period. The lot-for-lot

EXHIBIT 15.15

Lot-for-Lot Run Size for an MRP Schedule

Period	Net Requirements	Production Quantity	Ending Inventory	Holding Cost	Setup Cost	Total Cost
1	50	50	0	$0.00	$47.00	$ 47.00
2	60	60	0	0.00	47.00	94.00
3	70	70	0	0.00	47.00	141.00
4	60	60	0	0.00	47.00	188.00
5	95	95	0	0.00	47.00	235.00
6	75	75	0	0.00	47.00	282.00
7	60	60	0	0.00	47.00	329.00
8	55	55	0	0.00	47.00	376.00

EXHIBIT 15.16

Economic Order Quantity
Run Size for an MRP
Schedule

Period	Net Requirements	Production Quantity	Ending Inventory	Holding Cost	Setup Cost	Total Cost
1	50	351	301	$15.05	$47.00	$ 62.05
2	60	0	241	12.05	0.00	74.10
3	70	0	171	8.55	0.00	82.65
4	60	0	111	5.55	0.00	88.20
5	95	0	16	0.80	0.00	89.00
6	75	351	292	14.60	47.00	150.60
7	60	0	232	11.60	0.00	162.20
8	55	0	177	8.85	0.00	171.05

EOQ assumptions:	
Total requirements	525
Average requirements	65.6
Annual holding cost per unit	$2.60
Annual demand	3,412.5
EOQ	351.25

technique, while minimizing holding costs, orders far too often because it places an order every time a net requirement occurs.

Economic Order Quantity   In Chapter 14 we discussed the EOQ model that explicitly balances setup and holding costs. An inherent assumption in the EOQ model is that there is either fairly constant demand or that safety stock must be kept to accommodate any variability in demand. The EOQ model uses an estimate of total annual demand, the setup or order cost, and the annual holding cost. EOQ was not designed for a system with discrete time periods such as MRP. The lot-sizing techniques used for MRP assume that part requirements are satisfied at the start of the period. Holding costs are then charged only to the ending inventory for the period, not to the average inventory used in the EOQ model. EOQ assumes that parts are used on a continuous basis during the period. The lot sizes generated by EOQ do not always cover the entire number of periods. For example, the EOQ might provide the requirements for 4.6 periods.

Exhibit 15.16 shows the EOQ lot size calculated for this part. Several assumptions are made to determine the EOQ. EOQ requires an estimate of both annual demand and annual holding cost. Since the holding cost per period is $0.05 and the MRP schedule is weekly, the annual holding cost per unit is $2.60 ($0.05 $\times$ 52 weeks). Annual demand is computed by multiplying the average weekly demand for the eight periods by 52 weeks (525/8 $\times$ 52 = 3,412.5). The resulting EOQ is 351 units. The EOQ lot size in Period 1 is enough to meet requirements for Periods 1 through 5 and a portion of Period 6. Then, in Period 6 another EOQ lot is planned to meet the requirements for Periods 6 through 8. Notice that the EOQ plan leaves some inventory at the end of Period 8 to carry forward into Period 9.

Least Total Cost   The least total cost method (LTC) is a dynamic lot-sizing technique that calculates the order quantity by comparing the order cost and the holding costs for various lot sizes and then selects the lot in which these are most nearly equal.

Exhibit 15.17 shows the least total cost lot size results. The procedure to compute least total cost lot sizes is to compare order costs and holding costs for various numbers of periods. For example, costs are compared for producing in Period 1 to cover the requirements for Period 1; producing in Period 1 for Periods 1 and 2; producing in Period 1 to cover

EXHIBIT 15.17

Least Total Cost Run Size for an MRP Schedule

Period	Net Requirements	Production Quantity	Ending Inventory	Holding Cost	Setup Cost	Total Cost
1	50	335	285	$14.25	$47.00	$ 61.25
2	60	0	225	11.25	0.00	72.50
3	70	0	155	7.75	0.00	80.25
4	60	0	95	4.75	0.00	85.00
5	95	0	0	0.00	0.00	85.00
6	75	190	115	5.75	47.00	137.75
7	60	0	55	2.75	0.00	140.50
8	55	0	0	0.00	0.00	140.50

Periods	Quantity Ordered	Carrying Cost	Order Cost	Total Cost	
1	50	$ 0.00	$47.00	$ 47.00	
1–2	110	3.00	47.00	50.00	
1–3	180	10.00	47.00	57.00	
1–4	240	19.00	47.00	66.00	
1–5	335	38.00	47.00	85.00	←Least total cost
1–6	410	56.75	47.00	103.75	
1–7	470	74.75	47.00	121.75	
1–8	525	94.00	47.00	141.00	
6	75	0.00	47.00	47.00	
6–7	135	3.00	47.00	50.00	
6–8	190	8.50	47.00	55.50	←Least total cost

Periods 1, 2, and 3, and so on. The correct selection is that lot size where the ordering costs and holding costs are approximately equal. In Exhibit 15.17 that lot size is 335, because the difference between a $38 carrying cost and a $47 ordering cost is closer than $56.25 and $47. This lot size covers requirements for Periods 1 through 5. Unlike EOQ, the lot size covers only whole numbers of periods.

Based on the Period 1 decision to place an order to cover 5 periods, we are now located in Period 6, and our problem is to determine how many periods into the future we can provide for from here. Exhibit 15.17 shows that holding and order costs are closest in the quantity that covers requirements for Periods 6 through 8. Notice that the holding and order costs here are far apart. This is because our example extends only to Period 8. If the planning horizon were longer, that lot size planned for Period 6 would likely cover more periods into the future beyond Period 8. This brings up one of the limitations of both LTC and LUC (discussed below). Both techniques are influenced by the length of the planning horizon.

Least Unit Cost   The least unit cost method (LUC) is a dynamic lot-sizing technique that adds ordering and inventory carrying cost for each trial lot size and divides by the number of units in each lot size, picking the lot size with the lowest unit cost. In the example in Exhibit 15.18, the lot size of 410 covers Periods 1 through 6. The lot size planned for Period 7 covers through the end of the planning horizon.

Which Lot Size To Choose   Using the lot-for-lot method, the total cost for the eight periods is $376; the EOQ total cost is $171.05; the least total cost method is $140.50; and the least unit cost is $209. The lowest cost was obtained using the least total cost method of $140.50. If there were more than eight periods, the method with the lowest cost could be different.

EXHIBIT 15.18

Least Unit Cost Run Size for an MRP Schedule

Period	Net Requirements	Production Quantity	Ending Inventory	Holding Cost	Setup Cost	Total Cost
1	50	410	360	$18.00	$47.00	$ 65.00
2	60	0	300	15.00	0.00	80.00
3	70	0	230	11.50	0.00	91.50
4	60	0	170	8.50	0.00	100.00
5	95	0	75	3.75	0.00	103.75
6	75	115	115	5.75	47.00	156.50
7	60	0	55	2.75	0.00	159.25
8	55	55	55	2.75	47.00	209.00

Periods	Quantity Ordered	Carrying Cost	Order Cost	Total Cost	Unit Cost
1	50	$ 0.00	$47.00	$ 47.00	$0.9400
1–2	110	3.00	47.00	50.00	0.4545
1–3	180	10.00	47.00	57.00	0.3167
1–4	240	19.00	47.00	66.00	0.2750
1–5	335	38.00	47.00	85.00	0.2537
1–6	410	56.75	47.00	103.75	0.2530 ←Least unit cost
1–7	470	74.75	47.00	121.75	0.2590
1–8	525	94.00	47.00	141.00	0.2686
7	60	0.00	47.00	47.00	0.7833
7–8	115	2.75	47.00	49.75	0.4326 ←Least unit cost

The advantage of the least unit cost method is that it provides a more complete analysis, taking into account ordering or setup costs that might change as the order size increases. If the ordering or setup costs remain constant, the lowest total cost method is more attractive because it is simpler and easier to compute; yet it would be just as accurate under that restriction.

INSTALLING AN MRP SYSTEM

The average time for a company to effectively install an MRP system seems to range from 18 to 24 months—not for the software, but because so much other preparation and training must take place. At the risk of being redundant, we repeat some cautions about installing an MRP system.

Preparation Steps

Bills of Materials The BOM lists all of the materials required to create a product in a hierarchical form, which is usually the way in which a product is produced. The BOM is an extremely important element in an MRP system and, as a consequence, inaccuracies here cannot be tolerated. Without an MRP or some such computer system, BOM accuracy is not critical and firms can live with some errors. A first step prior to installing an MRP system is to review the BOM for all products to ensure that they are correct.

Routing Sheets and Processing Times Similar to the BOM, many firms previously did not need to be specific about which machine or process should be used, since adjustments could always be made manually on the shop floor. The same goes for processing; with the usual longer times in the shop (as opposed to MRP installations) there are opportunities to make up discrepancies (in spite of the fact that the data for accounting purposes would be in error).

Inventory Stock   Most firms have errors in their inventory records. Oftentimes it is because no one wants to take the time necessary to count and verify records and physical stock. Another reason is that often inventory stock is old or obsolete; bringing records up to date may mean that much inventory carried on company books as assets may have to be declared scrap. Few managers are willing to bite the bullet and do this. Reducing inventory directly impacts the bottom line and quickly catches the attention of top management. However, installing an MRP system means that errors must be removed and the inventory carried must be of usable quality.

Procedures   In addition to the actual records previously mentioned, procedures and/or new software must be installed to keep these records up to date. Examples are adding stock to inventory when received from vendors and making appropriate changes when issuing stock to production. Also, ways of handling changes to the bills of materials, routing, or processing times need to be decided.

 Training   Everyone—from top management through to the purchasing staff, supervisors, and the workers on the shop floor—must be trained in the effective use of an MRP system—how to read its reports, which leeways are allowable in quantity or schedule variations, and what results can be expected. People, by nature, are reluctant to change. Throughout MRP's history of more than two decades, we have blamed people whenever poor performance occurred in their MRP system (lack of understanding, lack of top management support, lack of adequate discipline, etc.). While this is now recognized as a problem caused in large part by the MRP itself (noted elsewhere in this chapter), nevertheless without support of all the individuals involved, MRP would be doomed to failure.

ADVANCED MRP-TYPE SYSTEMS

 For more than two decades, MRP systems were the first choice for firms that focused at the plant production level. MRP took as its input the product demands, inventory levels and resource availability, and produced production schedules as well as inventory ordering quantities. During this time the world was changing, with new global competition, multiplant international sites, wide global product demand, international subcontracting, and varying political environments and currency markets. Existing MRP software programs in their standard form could not handle these widened applications.

In today's environment, MRP users want instant access to information on customers' needs, which plants can meet these needs, and companywide inventory levels and available capacity throughout the supply chain.

What has been the response to these needs? There are more than 300 vendors for MRP systems. While most of these were involved with MRP systems from years ago and are still selling and maintaining their existing systems, many others are changing their systems to accommodate the new requirements; other firms are at the state-of-the-art in developing new advanced systems based on MRP logic. In an expected response, many existing firms are modifying their current software programs while others are making major changes in the basic logic and databases.

Various names have been given to this new generation of MRP. The Gartner Group called the new MRP *Enterprise Resource Planning (ERP)*. To fully operate in an enterprise sense, there needs to be distributed applications for planning, scheduling, costing, and so on to the multiple layers of the organization: work centers, sites, divisions, corporate. Multiple languages and currencies are also being included for global applications.

Advanced MRP systems (also called next-generation MRP II) will (or now) include[4]

Client/server architecture.

Relational database with SQL.

Graphic user interface.

Multiple database support.

Front-end systems for decision support.

Automated EDI.

Interoperability with multiple platforms.

Standard application programming interfaces.

Electronic data interchange (EDI) needs to be included for better communication with both customers and suppliers.

Distributed MRP Processing versus Centralized Processing

Many companies want to retain their mainframes and centralized processing systems. To do this and be able to give users throughout the firm reliable real-time information, relational databases are being implemented. Oracle Corp., for example, has a widely used relational database system and fourth-generation language that is being incorporated to enhance existing MRP systems. Sequent Computer Systems is using Oracle's manufacturing software on its computer and is expanding into other areas as the need arises, such as JIT (just-in-time manufacturing) and TQI (total quality through incremental improvements).

Existing MRP systems are limited in access and quite self-contained.

A *centralized process operation* controls such features as engineering, production scheduling, forecasting, order processing, purchasing, and materials planning for multiple plants at one central location. A *decentralized processing operation* distributes these responsibilities among the plants for autonomous operation. A *distributed processing operation* uses a combination of centralized and decentralized controls to allocate resources where they are logically needed and where they can be executed most efficiently.[5]

In distributed MRP processing, remote stations can access data, manipulate it, do local processing, and feed it back into the system. High-performance workstations such as Hewlett-Packard and Sun Microsystems are based on Unix, allowing fairly open communications and exchange. Mainframes, minicomputers, and microcomputers are a mixture that will become common in a truly distributed environment. Other open communication systems include IBM's OS/2 and Hewlett-Packard's MPE/iX.

Focus is on the total organization, but local computation and control are allowed. Local managers get quicker feedback on their performance and can therefore improve themselves by doing their own analysis.

There are two opposing views about centralization versus decentralization. One argument is that shifting to global manufacturing will encourage more decentralized MRP to allow more local control. The counterargument is that global manufacturing will cause centralization since more decision making will take place concerning multiple markets, customers, sources, and so on. Both can be satisfied perhaps by using an OSI (open systems

---

[4]Alice Greene, "MRP II: Out with the Old," *Computerworld,* June 8, 1992, p. 74.

[5]Richard Costello, "Available: Real-Time EDI, Multiplant Functions, More," *Computerworld,* June 8, 1992, p. 79.

interconnect) providing for a fully distributed system. OSI uses a common data architecture that permits both decentralization and data sharing.[6]

SAP America, Inc.'s R/3

SAP America, Inc., has come out with its R/3 MRP software package for open systems. It is a client/server application. The software includes a full variety of manufacturing and financial applications (such as financial and fixed asset accounting), materials management, sales and distribution, human resources, production planning, quality assurance, and plant maintenance. R/3 runs on UNIX, HP MPE/IX, and IBM OS/2.

Many companies are justifiably reluctant to install drastically new systems. They know that being first in new software applications has more disadvantages than advantages. Previously unknown system bugs and errors in logic creep in and can create havoc during the installation and startup phases. Rather than adopting the R/3 package, many firms are installing SAP's earlier R/2 instead. SAP's R/2 system is used by more than 4,000 customers as of 1997. Many of these will switch over to R/3 as needs arise. OS/2-based R/3 software improves the graphic user interface.

Use of R/3 is more widespread in Europe, since SAP AG is a German firm. Companies are responding in different ways. Eastman Chemical, a $3.9-billion company, is installing R/2 and just a very small part of R/3 to see how it runs. However, $40-billion Chevron is using R/3 on a corporatewide basis.

ManMan/X

ManMan/X is a Unix-based software from Ask Computer Systems, Inc. It is based on the Enterprise Resource Planning logic and uses the fourth-generation language (4GL). ManMan/X also supports Hewlett-Packard's MPR/iX, Oracle Corp.'s database, and Informix Inc.'s database.

ManMan/X provides stronger planning and forecasting features (including simulation and net change) than most other MRP systems. ManMan/X will exchange information with other systems. It also includes languages and currency features for global operation.

COMMS
(Customer-Oriented Manufacturing Management System)

Vendors are taking many different approaches to develop new MRP-type advanced programs. A new model of an advanced integrated MRP-type system is being created by Advanced Manufacturing Research, Inc. (AMR), a Boston-based consulting firm. AMR's model is called COMMS (Customer-Oriented Manufacturing Management System). COMMS has added in real-time interaction with the manufacturing plants throughout the supply chain. Currently in development, this model is shown in Exhibit 15.19. It places the customer in the center with the objective of giving customers what they want, when, how, where, and at the price they want. This is a distributed-type system.

 The firms that AMR represents believe that we are entering an era of "customerized" manufacturing where the customer can specify anything and the manufacturer must be able to respond quickly to remain competitive. Note that Exhibit 15.19 shows AMR's COMMS model uniting the departments of the chain around the customer. In practice, when a customer's order is taken, the salesperson can give all the necessary information to the customer: any engineering changes, the schedule, price, and so on. This is possible because the salesperson has direct access to all the databases and schedules.

---

[6]William F. McSpadden, "OSI, Distributed MRP II and You," *Industrial Engineering,* February 1992, pp. 38–39.

EXHIBIT 15.19

A Customer-Oriented Manufacturing Management System (COMMS)

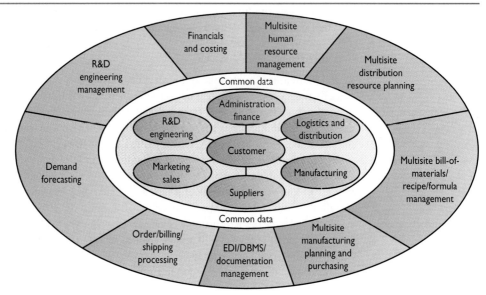

Source: Chris Staiti, "Customers Drive New Manufacturing Software." *Datamation*, November 15, 1993, p. 72. Reprinted with permission. © 1993 by Cahners Publishing Co.

EDI (Electronic Data Interchange)

Roughly 80 percent of MRP packages have an EDI module that allows manufacturers to import and export documents. The new addition to EDI is that it is beginning to be *real-time* interchange rather than batch processing. It is valuable for multiplant MRP. EDI vendors include American Software, IBM, Andersen Consulting, and Symix Computer Systems.

About 85 percent of MRP II packages include an interface with at least one CAD (computer-aided design) system. The CAD integration solutions such as those by Cincom and Micro-MRP are two of the most popular.

Transition to Advanced MRP-Type Systems

How do firms change from existing MRP systems to the advanced ones? That depends on the new system they want. Some systems are easier to use than others, such as Cincom's Control Manufacturing, which uses existing data and transaction processing methods. Others (such as Datalogix and Dunn and Bradstreet software) are more difficult in requiring re-implementation. Still other firms are waiting by the sidelines until more clear paths and possible results are visible. Most larger firms eventually will have to update and expand their MRP system to remain competitive.

CONCLUSION

Since the 1970s, MRP has grown from its purpose of determining simple time schedules, to its present advanced types that tie together all major functions of an organization. During its growth and its application, MRP's disadvantages as a scheduling mechanism have been well recognized. This is largely because MRP tries to do too much in light of the dynamic, often jumpy environment in which it is trying to operate.

MRP is recognized, however, for its excellent databases and linkages within the firm. MRP also does a good job in helping to produce master schedules. Many firms in repetitive manufacturing are installing JIT systems to link with the MRP system. JIT takes the master production schedule as its pulling force but does not use MRP's generated schedule. Results indicate that this is working very well.

Many newer MRP-type software programs have been developed since the early 1990s. Several others are currently in the development stage. These allow more open exchange of data than the earlier systems, embrace a larger part of the firm's operation (such as multiple sites, global customers, languages, and currency rates), and operate in real time.

MRP's service applications have not fared as well, although it is making inroads in various forms in quasi-manufacturing service operations such as restaurants and bakeries. The MRP approach would appear to be valuable in producing services since service scheduling consists of identifying the final service and then tracing back to the resources needed, such as equipment, space, and personnel. Consider, for example, a hospital operating room planning an open-heart surgery. The master schedule can establish a time for the surgery (or surgeries, if several are scheduled). The BOM could specify all required equipment and personnel—MDs, nurses, anesthesiologist, operating room, heart/lung machine, defibrillator, and so forth. The inventory status file would show the availability of the resources and commit them to the project. The MRP program could then produce a schedule showing when various parts of the operation are to be started, expected completion times, required materials, and so forth. Checking this schedule would allow "capacity planning" in answering such questions as "Are all the materials and personnel available?" and "Does the system produce a feasible schedule?"

We still believe that MRP systems will eventually find their way into a greater variety of service applications. One reason for the delay is that even service managers who are aware of it believe that MRP is just a manufacturing tool. Also, service managers tend to be people-oriented and skeptical of tools from outside their industry.

KEY TERMS

bill of materials (BOM)   p. 501
inventory records file   p. 503
manufacturing resource planning
   (MRP II)   p. 510

master production schedule (MPS)   p. 497
materials requirements planning
   (MRP)   p. 496

REVIEW AND DISCUSSION QUESTIONS

1. Because MRP appears so reasonable, discuss reasons why it did not become popular until recently.

2. Discuss the meaning of MRP terms such as *planned order releases* and *scheduled order receipts.*

3. Most practitioners currently update MRP weekly or biweekly. Would it be more valuable if it were updated daily? Discuss.

4. What is the role of safety stock in an MRP system?

5. Contrast the significance of the term *lead time* in the traditional EOQ context and in an MRP system.

6. Discuss the importance of the MPS in an MRP system.

7. MRP systems are difficult to install. Identify the various problems that can occur with the system requirements (ignore behavioral problems).

8. "MRP just prepares shopping lists—it doesn't do the shopping or cook the dinner." Comment.

9. What are the sources of demand in an MRP system? Are these dependent or independent, and how are they used as inputs to the system?

10. State the types of data that would be carried in the bill of materials file and the inventory record file.

11. How does MRP II differ from MRP?

12. Why isn't MRP more widespread in services?

SOLVED PROBLEMS

Problem 1

Product X is made of two units of Y and three of Z. Y is made of one unit of A and two units of B. Z is made of two units of A and four units of C.

Lead time for X is one week; Y, two weeks; Z, three weeks; A, two weeks; B, one week; and C, three weeks.

a. Draw the product structure tree.

b. If 100 units of X are needed in week 10, develop a planning schedule showing when each item should be ordered and in what quantity.

Solution

a.

b.

		3	4	5	6	7	8	9	10
X	LT = 1							100	100
Y	LT = 2					200		200	
Z	LT = 3				300			300	
A	LT = 2		600		600	200			
				200					
B	LT = 1				400	400			
C	LT = 3	1200			1200				

Problem 2

Product M is made of two units of N and three of P. N is made of two units of R and four units of S. R is made of one unit of S and three units of T. P is made of two units of T and four units of U.

a. Show the product structure tree.

b. If 100 Ms are required, how many units of each component are needed?

c. Show both a single-level bill of material and an indented bill of material.

Solution

a.

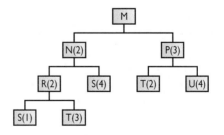

b.
$$M = 100 \qquad S = 800 + 400 = 1{,}200$$
$$N = 200 \qquad T = 600 + 1{,}200 = 1{,}800$$
$$P = 300 \qquad U = 1{,}200$$
$$R = 400$$

c. Single-level BOM

```
M | N
  |   P
N |
  |   R
  |   S
R |
  |   S
  |   T
P |
  |   T
  |   U
```

Indented BOM

```
M |
  | N |
  |   | R |
  |   |   | S
  |   |   | T
  |   | S |
  | P |
  |   | T |
  |   | U |
```

PROBLEMS

1. In the following MRP planning schedule for Item J, indicate the correct net requirements, planned order receipts, and planned order releases to meet the gross requirements. Lead time is one week.

Item J	Week Number					
	0	1	2	3	4	5
Gross requirements			75		50	70
On hand 40						
Net requirements						
Planned order receipt						
Planned order releases						

2. Assume that Product Z is made of two units of A and four units of B. A is made of three units of C and four of D. D is made of two units of E.

   The lead time for purchase or fabrication of each unit to final assembly: Z takes two weeks, A, B, C, and D take one week each, and E takes three weeks.

   Fifty units are required in Period 10. (Assume that there is currently no inventory on hand of any of these items.)

   a. Draw a product structure tree.

   b. Develop an MRP planning schedule showing gross and net requirements, order release and order receipt dates.

   Note: For Problems 3 through 6, to simplify data handling to include the receipt of orders that have actually been placed in previous periods, the six-level scheme shown below can be used. (There are a number of different techniques used in practice, but the important issue is to keep track of what is on hand, what is expected to arrive, what is needed, and what size orders should be placed.) One way to calculate the numbers is as follows:

	Week								
Gross requirements									
Scheduled receipts									
On hand from prior period									
Net requirements									
Planned order receipt									
Planned order release									

3. One unit of A is made of three units of B, one unit of C, and two units of D. B is composed of two units of E and one unit of D. C is made of one unit of B and two units of E. E is made of one unit of F.

   Items B, C, E, and F have one-week lead times; A and D have lead times of two weeks. Assume that lot-for-lot (L4L) lot sizing is used for items A, B, and F; lots of size 50, 50, and 200 are used for items C, D, and E, respectively. Items C, E, and F have on-hand (beginning) inventories of 10, 50, and 150, respectively; all other items have zero beginning inventory. We are scheduled to receive 10 units of A in Week 5, 50 units of E in Week 4, and also 50 units of F in Week 4. There are no other scheduled receipts. If 30 units of A are required in Week 8, use the low-level-coded product structure tree to find the necessary planned order releases for all components.

4. One unit of A is made of two units of B, three units of C, and two units of D. B is composed of one unit of E and two units of F. C is made of two units of F and one unit of D. E is made of two units of D. Items A, C, D, and F have one-week lead times; B and E have lead times of two weeks. Lot-for-lot (L4L) lot sizing is used for Items A, B, C, and D; lots of size 50 and 180 are used for items E and F, respectively. Item C has an on-hand (beginning) inventory of 15; D has an on-hand inventory of 50; all other items have zero beginning inventory. We are scheduled to receive 20 units of Item E in week 4; there are no other scheduled receipts.

   Construct simple and low-level-coded product structure trees and indented and summarized bills of materials.

   If 20 units of A are required in Week 8, use the low-level-coded products structure tree to find the necessary planned order released for all components. (See note prior to Problem 3.)

5. One unit of A is made of one unit of B and one unit of C. B is made of four units of C and one unit of E and F. C is made of two units of D and one unit of E. E is made of three units of F. Item C has a lead time of one week; Items A, B, E, and F have two-week lead times; and Item D has a lead time of three weeks. Lot-for-lot (L4L) lot sizing is used for Items A, D, and E; lots of size 50, 100, and 50 are used for Items B, C, and F, respectively. Items A, C, D, and E have on-hand (beginning) inventories of 20, 50, 100, and 10, respectively; all other items have zero beginning inventory. We are scheduled to receive 10 units of A in week 5, 100 units of C in Week 6, and 100 units of D in Week 4; there are no other scheduled receipts. If 50 units of A are required in Week 10, use the low-level-coded product structure tree to find the necessary planned order releases for all components. (See note prior to Problem 3.)

6. One unit of A is made of two units of B and one unit of C. B is made of three units of D and one unit of F. C is composed of three units of B, one unit of D, and four units of E. D is made of one unit of E. Item C has a lead time of one week; Items A, B, E, and F have two-week lead times; and Item D has a lead time of 3 weeks. Lot-for-lot (L4L) lot sizing is used for Items C, E, and F; lots of size 20, 40, and 160 are used for items A, B, and D, respectively. Items A, B, D, and E have on-hand (beginning) inventories of 5, 10, 100, and 100, respectively; all other items have zero beginning inventories. We are scheduled to receive 10 units of A in Week 3, 20 units of B in Week 7, 60 units of E in week 2, and 40 units of F in Week 5; there are no other scheduled receipts. If 20 units of A are required in Week 10, use the low-level-coded product structure tree to find the necessary planned order releases for all components. (See note prior to Problem 3.)

7. The MRP gross requirements for Item A is shown here for the next 10 weeks. Lead time for A is three weeks and setup cost is $10 per setup. There is a carrying cost of $0.01 per unit per week. Beginning inventory is 90 units.

	Week									
	1	2	3	4	5	6	7	8	9	10
Gross requirements	30	50	10	20	70	80	20	60	200	50

Use either the least total cost or the least unit cost lot-sizing method to determine when and for what quantity the first order should be released.

8. (This problem is intended as a very simple exercise to go from the aggregate plan to the master schedule to the MRP.) Gigamemory Storage Devices, Inc. produces CD ROMs (Read Only Memory) and WORMs (Write Once Read Many) for the computer market. Aggregate demand for the WORMs for the next two quarters are 2,100 units and 2,700 units. Assume that the demand is distributed evenly for each month of the quarter.

   There are two models of the WORM: an internal model, and an external model. The drive assemblies in both are the same but the electronics and housing are different. Demand is higher for the external model and currently is 70 percent of the aggregate demand.

   The bill of materials and the lead times follow. One drive assembly and one electronic and housing unit go into each WORM.

   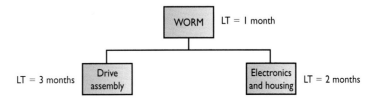

   The MRP system is run monthly. Currently, 200 external WORMs are in stock and 100 internal WORMs. Also in stock are 250 drive assemblies, 50 internal electronic and housing units, and 125 external electronic and housing units.

   Problem: Show the aggregate plan, the master production schedule, and the full MRP with the gross and net requirements and planned order releases.

9. Product A is an end item and is made from two units of B and four of C. B is made of three units of D and two of E. C is made of two units of F and two of E.

   A has a lead time of one week. B, C, and E have lead times of two weeks, and D and F have lead times of three weeks. Currently, there are no units of inventory on hand.

   a. Draw the product structure tree.

   b. If 100 units of A are required in week 10, develop the MRP planning schedule, specifying when items are to be ordered and received.

10. Product A consists of two units of subassembly B, three units of C, and one unit of D. B is composed of four units of E and three units of F. C is made of two units of H and three units of D. H is made of five units of E and two units of G.

    a. Construct a simple product structure tree.

    b. Construct a product structure tree using low-level coding.

    c. Construct an indented bill of materials.

    d. To product 100 units of A, determine the numbers of units of B, C, D, E, F, G, and H required.

11. The MRP gross requirements for Item X are shown here for the next 10 weeks. Lead time for A is two weeks, and setup cost is $9 per setup. There is a carrying cost of $0.02 per unit per week. Beginning inventory is 70 units.

	Week									
	1	2	3	4	5	6	7	8	9	10
Gross requirements	20	10	15	45	10	30	100	20	40	150

   Use either the least total cost or the least unit cost lot-sizing method to determine when and for what quantity the first order should be released.

12. Audio Products, Inc., produces two AM/FM cassette players for automobiles. Both radio/cassette units are identical, but the mounting hardware and finish trim differ. The standard model fits intermediate- and full-size cars, and the sports model fits small sports cars.

Audio Products handles its production in the following way. The chassis (radio/cassette unit) is assembled in Mexico and has a manufacturing lead time of two weeks. The mounting hardware is purchased from a sheet steel company and has a three-week lead time. The finish trim is purchased from a Taiwan electronics company with offices in Los Angeles as prepackaged units consisting of knobs and various trim pieces. Trim packages have a two-week lead time. Final assembly time may be disregarded, since adding the trim package and mounting are performed by the customer.

Audio Products supplies wholesalers and retailers, who place specific orders for both models up to eight weeks in advance. These orders, together with enough additional units to satisfy the small number of individual sales, are summarized in the following demand schedule:

Week

	1	2	3	4	5	6	7	8
Standard model				300				400
Sports model					200			100

There are currently 50 radio/cassette units on hand but no trim packages or mounting hardware.

Prepare a material requirements plan to meet the demand schedule exactly. Specify the gross and net requirements, on-hand amounts, and the planned order release and receipt periods for the cassette/radio chassis, the standard trim and sports car model trim, and the standard mounting hardware and the sports car mounting hardware.

13. Brown and Brown Electronics manufactures a line of digital audiotape players. While there are differences among the various products, there are a number of common parts within each player. The product structure, showing the number of each item required, lead times, and the current inventory on hand for the parts and components, follows:

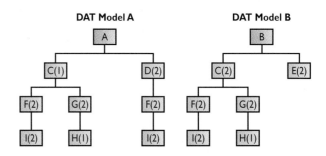

	Number Currently in Stock	Lead Time (weeks)
DAT Model A	30	1
DAT Model B	50	2
Subassembly C	75	1
Subassembly D	80	2
Subassembly E	100	1
Part F	150	1
Part G	40	1
Raw material H	200	2
Raw material I	300	2

Brown and Brown created a forecast that it plans to use as its master production schedule, producing exactly to schedule. Part of the MPS shows a demand for 700 units of Model A and 1,200 units of Model B in Week 10.

Develop an MRP schedule to meet that demand.

CASE: NICHOLS COMPANY

This particular December day seemed bleak to Joe Williams, president of Nichols Company (NCO). He sat in his office watching the dying embers of his fireplace, hoping to clear his mind. Suddenly there came a tapping by someone gently rapping, rapping at his office door. "Another headache," he muttered, "tapping at my office door. Only that and nothing more."*

The intruder was Barney Thompson, director of marketing. "A major account has just canceled a large purchase of A units because we are back ordered on tubing. This can't continue. My sales force is out beating the bushes for customers and our production manager can't provide the product."

For the past several months, operations at NCO have been unsteady. Inventory levels have been too high, while at the same time there have been stockouts. This resulted in many late deliveries, complaints, and cancellations. To compound the problem, overtime was excessive.

HISTORY

Nichols Company was started by Joe Williams and Peter Schaap, both with MBAs from the University of Arizona. Much has happened since Williams and Schaap formed the company. Schaap has left the company and is working in real estate development in Queensland, Australia. Under the direction of Williams, NCO has diversified to include a number of other products.

NCO currently has 355 full-time employees directly involved in manufacturing its three primary products, A, B, and C. Final assembly takes place in a converted warehouse adjacent to NCO's main plant.

THE MEETING

Williams called a meeting the next day to get input into the problems facing NCO and to lay the groundwork for some solutions. Attending the meeting, besides himself and Barney Thompson, were Phil Bright of production and inventory control, Trevor Hansen of purchasing, and Steve Clark of accounting.

The meeting lasted all morning. Participation was vocal and intense.

Bright said, "The forecasts that marketing sends us are always way off. We are constantly having to expedite one product or another to meet current demand. This runs up our overtime."

Thompson said, "Production tries to run too lean. We need a larger inventory of finished goods. If I had the merchandise, my salespeople could sell 20 percent more product."

Clark said, "No way! Our inventory is already uncomfortably high. We can't afford the holding costs, not to mention how fast technology changes around here causing even more inventory, much of it obsolete."

Bright said, "The only way I can meet our stringent cost requirements is to buy in volume."

At the end of the meeting, Williams had lots of input but no specific plan. What do you think he should do?

Use Case Exhibits 1–4 showing relevant data to answer the specific questions at the end of the case.

QUESTIONS

Use Excel (or another spreadsheet if you prefer) to solve the Nichols Company case.

Simplifying assumption: To get the program started, some time is needed at the beginning because MRP backloads the system. For simplicity, assume that the forecasts (and therefore demands) are zero for Periods 1 through 3. Also assume that the starting inventory specified in Case Exhibit 3 is available from Week 1. For the master production schedule, use only the end Items A, B, and C.

To modify production quantities, adjust only Products A, B, and C. Do not adjust the quantities of D, E, F, G, H, and I. These should be linked so that changes in A, B, and C automatically adjust them.

1. Disregarding machine-center limitations, develop an MRP schedule and also capacity profiles for the four machine centers.
2. Work center capacities and costs follow. Repeat Question 1 creating a *feasible* schedule (within the capacities of the machine centers) and compute the relevant costs. Do this by adjusting the MPS only. Try to minimize the total cost of operation for the 27 weeks.

	Capacity	Cost
Work center 1	6,000 hours available	$20 per hour
Work center 2	4,500 hours available	$25 per hour
Work center 3	2,400 hours available	$35 per hour
Work center 4	1,200 hours available	$65 per hour

Inventory carrying cost

End items A, B, and C	$2.00 per unit
Components D, E, F, G, and H	$1.50 per unit
Raw material I	$1.00 per unit

Back-order cost

End items A, B, and C	$20 per unit
Components D, E, F, G, and H	$14 per unit
Raw material I	$ 8 per unit

3. Suppose end items had to be ordered in multiples of 100 units, components in multiples of 500 units, and raw materials in multiples of 1,000 units. How would this change your schedule?

*With apologies to E.A.P.

CASE EXHIBIT 1
Bills of Materials for Products A, B, and C

Product A	Product B	Product C
.A	.B	.C
.D(4)	.F(2)	.G(2)
.I(3)	.G(3)	.I(2)
.E(1)	.I(2)	.H(1)
.F(4)		

CASE EXHIBIT 2
Work Center Routings for Products and Components

Item	Work Center Number	Standard Time (hours per unit)
Product A	1	0.20
	4	0.10
Product B	2	0.30
	4	0.08
Product C	3	0.10
	4	0.05
Component D	1	0.15
	4	0.10
Component E	2	0.15
	4	0.05
Component F	2	0.15
	3	0.20
Component G	1	0.30
	2	0.10
Component H	1	0.05
	3	0.10

CASE EXHIBIT 3
Inventory Levels and Lead Times for Each Item on the Bill of Material at the Beginning of Week 1

Product/Component	On Hand (units)	Lead Time (weeks)
Product A	100	1
Product B	200	1
Product C	175	1
Component D	200	1
Component E	195	1
Component F	120	1
Component G	200	1
Component H	200	1
I (raw material)	300	1

CASE EXHIBIT 4

Forecasted Demand for Weeks 4–27

Week	Product A	Product B	Product C
1			
2			
3			
4	1,500	2,200	1,200
5	1,700	2,100	1,400
6	1,150	1,900	1,000
7	1,100	1,800	1,500
8	1,000	1,800	1,400
9	1,100	1,600	1,100
10	1,400	1,600	1,800
11	1,400	1,700	1,700
12	1,700	1,700	1,300
13	1,700	1,700	1,700
14	1,800	1,700	1,700
15	1,900	1,900	1,500
16	2,200	2,300	2,300
17	2,000	2,300	2,300
18	1,700	2,100	2,000
19	1,600	1,900	1,700
20	1,400	1,800	1,800
21	1,100	1,800	2,200
22	1,000	1,900	1,900
23	1,400	1,700	2,400
24	1,400	1,700	2,400
25	1,500	1,700	2,600
26	1,600	1,800	2,400
27	1,500	1,900	2,500

Selected Bibliography

Biggs, Joseph R., and Ellen J. Long. "Gaining the Competitive Edge with MRP/MRP II." *Management Accounting,* May 1988, pp. 27–32.

Costello, Richard. "Available: Real-Time EDI, Multiplant Functions, More." *Computerworld,* June 8, 1992, p. 79.

Flapper, S. D. P.; G. J. Miltenburg; and J. Wijngaard. "Embedding JIT into MRP." *International Journal of Production Research* 29, no. 2 (1991), pp. 329–41.

Goodrich, Thomas. "JIT & MRP Can Work Together." *Automation,* April 1989, pp. 46–47.

Greene, Alice. "MRPII: Out with the Old." *Computerworld,* June 8, 1992, p. 74.

Greene, Alice. "Two Ready for the Next Generation." *Computerworld,* June 8, 1992, p. 77.

Knight, Robert M. "Furniture Maker Uses MRP II to Cut Lead Time." *Computerworld,* June 8, 1992, p. 80.

McSpadden, William, F. "OSI, Distributed MRPII and You." *Industrial Engineering*, February 1992, pp. 38–39.

Orlicky, Joseph. *Materials Requirements Planning.* New York: McGraw-Hill, 1975. (This is the classic book on MRP.)

Production and Inventory Management Journal and *APICS: The Performance Advantage.* Practitioner journals with numerous articles on MRP and MRP II. Many of these cite the difficulties and experiences of practitioners.

Sipper, Daniel, and Robert Bulfin. *Production Planning, Control and Integration.* New York: McGraw-Hill, 1997.

Staiti, Chris. "Customers Drive New Manufacturing Software." *Datamation,* November 15, 1993, p. 72.

Turbide, David A. *MRP+: The Adaptation, Enhancement and Application of MRP II.* New York: Industrial Press, 1993, p. 11.

Vollmann, Thomas E.; William L. Berry; and D. Clay Whybark. *Manufacturing Planning and Control Systems.* 4th ed. Burr Ridge, IL: Irwin, 1997.

SCHEDULING

Chapter Objectives

- Provide insight into the nature of scheduling and control of intermittent production systems.

- Emphasize the prevalence of job shop environments, notably in the service sector.

- Stress the interaction and dependence of job shop planning and technology.

- Present examples showing the importance of worker scheduling in service sector job shops.

- Identify the major elements of scheduling workers in a service organization.

- Illustrate how technology can facilitate the scheduling of workers.

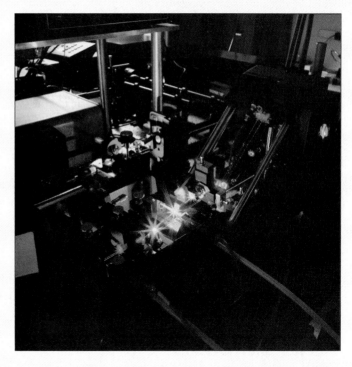

Many service and production operations need large volumes of standardized manufactured goods; the U.S. Space Program, however, often needs one-of-a-kind items designed for specific aerospace missions. The Teledyne Brown Engineering (TBE) Fabrication and Assembly Plant in Alabama is one firm that helps meet such demand.

The TBE plant layout includes precision equipment that allows their engineers to design and build specific items based on a set of blueprints. Using these blueprints, a planner determines what steps are needed to produce the final product and how these steps should be scheduled. Final products are often flight hardware and launch support equipment for some of TBE's major customers: NASA and the U.S. Air Force.

Because of the unique nature of the products made by TBE and the impact of changing technology, TBE cannot standardize their operations. Thus the required steps and the scheduling of these steps are unique for each product. This make-to-order approach requires a versatile plant layout and equipment that can perform multiple operations in an efficient manner.　■

Source: Condensed from James B. Dilworth, "Tour of a Job Shop: Teledyne Brown Engineering Fabrication and Assembly Plant I," *Operations Management: Design, Planning and Control for Manufacturing and Services* (New York: McGraw-Hill, Inc., 1992).

Different industries provide different levels of standardization of the goods and services they produce. In the education industry, for example, there are some graduate schools that require students to follow a "lock-step" curriculum with minimal student choice—thus every student receives basically the same education and the same degree. In contrast, the medical care provided in the health care industry is usually customized, based upon an individual patient's symptoms and the severity of the illness. These differences in standardization result in a wide spectrum of processes ranging from intermittent-type processes (such as job shops) to continuous flow operations (such as assembly lines). (Project-type processes are unique in that there is typically only one single product that is produced; this is addressed in Chapter 10 on project management.)

Intermittent flow operations have both the flexibility and capacity to accommodate multiple products that require different operations in different sequences. The manager or dispatcher may try to group work stations or equipment based on either function or process, but scheduling made-to-order products can often be extremely difficult.

Continuous flow operations, on the other hand, are quite inflexible to changes in products and the sequencing of operations. The scheduling of jobs is, therefore, fixed and thus relatively simple.

THE JOB SHOP DEFINED

job shop
Organization whose layout is process-oriented (vs. product-oriented) and that produces items in batches.

A **job shop** is a functional organization whose departments or work centers are organized around particular processes that consist of specific types of equipment and/or operations, such as drilling and assembly in a factory, scanning and printing in a computer laboratory, or specialized examination rooms in a hospital's emergency room. The good produced or

EXHIBIT 16.1

Major Attributes of a Job Shop

Characteristic	In the Job Shop
Mission	Sells capacity and skills
Item flow	Few or no dominant paths
Bottlenecks	Shift frequently
Equipment selection	General-purpose, flexible
Run length	Short
Setup cost	Low
Labor content	High
Scope of direct jobs	Broad
Controller of work pace	Worker, foreman, dispatcher
Raw material inventory	Low
In-process inventory	High
Finished-goods inventory	Low or none
Suppliers	Frequent use of multiple suppliers
Worker information required for jobs	New instructions needed for each job; specialized training sometimes required.
Scheduling	Uncertain, changes are frequent; job components need to be completed at approximately the same time
Challenges	Estimating requirements, scheduling, fast response to bottlenecks
Response to reduced demand	Lay off workers in affected departments

Source: Adapted from Robert H. Hayes, and Steven C. Wheelwright, *Restoring our Competitive Edge: Competing Through Manufacturing* (New York: Wiley Publishers, 1984), pp. 180–82.

the service provided is based upon an individual order for a specific customer. Exhibit 16.1 identifies some of the major attributes of a job shop.

SCHEDULING IN A JOB SHOP

A schedule is a timetable for performing activities, using resources, or allocating facilities. The purpose of operations scheduling in a job shop is to disaggregate the master production schedule (MPS) into time-phased weekly, daily, and/or hourly activities—in other words, to specify in precise terms the planned workload on the production process in the very short run. Operations control entails monitoring job-order progress and, where necessary, expediting orders and/or adjusting system capacity to make sure that the MPS is met.

In designing a scheduling and control system, provision must be made for efficient performance of the following functions:

1. Allocating orders, equipment, and personnel to work centers or other specified locations. Essentially, this is short-run capacity planning.
2. Determining the *sequence* of order performance; that is, establishing job priorities.
3. Initiating performance of the scheduled work. This is commonly termed the **dispatching of orders.**

dispatching of orders
Releasing of orders to the factory floor.

4. Shop-floor control (or production activity control), which involves:
    a. Reviewing the status and controlling the progress of orders as they are being worked on.
    b. **Expediting** late and critical orders.[1]

expediting
Checking the progress of specific orders to ensure completion in a timely manner.

5. Revising the schedule to reflect recent changes in order status.
6. Assuring that quality control standards are being met.

A simple job shop-scheduling process is shown in Exhibit 16.2. At the start of the day, the job dispatcher (in this case, a production control person assigned to this department) selects and sequences the available jobs to be run at individual workstations. The dispatcher's decisions would be based on the operations and routing requirements of each job, status of existing jobs on the machines, the queue of work before each machine, job priorities, material availability, anticipated job orders to be released later in the day, and worker and machine capabilities. To help organize the schedule, the dispatcher would draw on shop-floor information from the previous day and external information provided by central production control, process engineering, and so on. The dispatcher would also confer with the foreman or supervisor of the department about the feasibility of the schedule, especially with respect to workforce considerations and identifying potential bottlenecks. Visual schedule boards, as shown in the photo of the Bernard Welding Company, are efficient ways to communicate the priority and status of work.

---

[1]Despite the fact that expediting is frowned on by production control specialists, it is nevertheless a reality of life. In fact, a very typical entry-level job in production control is that of expediter or "stock-chaser." In some companies a good expediter—one who can negotiate a critical job through the system or who can scrounge up materials nobody thought were available—is a prized possession.

EXHIBIT 16.2

Typical Scheduling Process

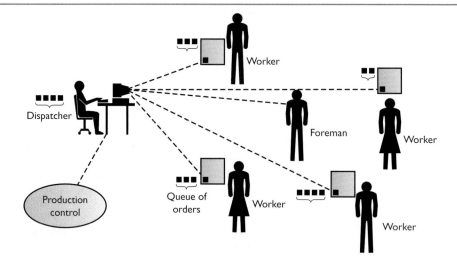

What makes scheduling this job so difficult? Consider the following factors:

- This good/service may never have been done before, so the estimates of the expected length of time for completion of the various components may be quite different from the actual time.

- The sequence of operations is extremely flexible and, with a cross-trained workforce, the number of possible sequences can be huge. Trying to assess the expected results of different sequences with a goal of finding the best sequence is usually very difficult.

- For different operations, the determination of the "best" sequence may vary—for one case it may be the minimization of waste, for another it may be the minimization of idle facilities, for a third it may be the maximization of throughput, and so on. Thus, even with extensive research into the job shop scheduling problem, it is hard to find quantitative or mechanical algorithms that are always appropriate for all situations.

ELEMENTS OF THE JOB SHOP SCHEDULING PROBLEM

 Job shops exist everywhere and, as a result, examples are plentiful. The emergency room at a hospital may be organized by function: the examination rooms are separate from the x-ray room, which is separate from the waiting room. Depending on the needs of the patient, different jobs are performed at different physical locations within the ER, and in some cases, at locations other than the ER. A riding academy not only boards and exercises the horses, but also provides lessons at different levels to different groups. A ski resort may similarly provide different levels of instruction for different students. The kitchen of a restaurant is also a job shop—different orders come in at different times and the different meals may be prepared by different people.

But all these examples share some common elements:

- The "jobs"—whether they are riding students at an academy or orders for dinner at a restaurant—arrive at the job shop in some pattern.

- The ability of the job shop to complete these "jobs" in a given amount of time is dependent upon the capacity or "machinery" in the shop. For example, the number of students who may take riding lessons is limited by the number of horses present at the riding academy; the number of students who enroll in a given class may be limited by the number of seats available in the classroom.

- The ability of the job shop to complete these "jobs" is also dependent on the ratio of skilled workers to "machines." A riding academy may have lots of horses, but the number of riding students is also limited by the availability of skilled instructors. The number of meals that can be prepared in a timely fashion at a restaurant can be limited by the number of chefs working that evening (in addition to the number of ovens, stoves, and other cooking equipment).

- The **flow pattern** of jobs through the shop varies from job to job. At a restaurant, one order might be for a sandwich and salad while another might be for a full seven-course dinner. Consequently, the number and sequence of steps required to fill these two orders is dramatically different.

- Different jobs are often assigned different priorities. Some jobs are marked "rush" or "urgent" and may be from a preferred customer. Medical personnel at the ER in the hospital assign these priorities by performing triage so that the most serious patients are seen first.

- The criteria used to evaluate a given schedule differ from job shop to job shop. A restaurant may try to minimize the wasted food or the idle personnel; Teledyne, in the opening vignette of this chapter, may wish to maximize the reliability of the parts produced.

Job Arrival Patterns   Jobs often arrive in a pattern that follows a known statistical distribution (for example, the Poisson distribution is relatively common), or they may arrive in batches (also called "lot" or "bulk" arrivals), or they may arrive such that the time between arrivals is constant. Further, jobs may come with different priorities.

The "Machinery" in the Shop   The scheduling problem is also dependent on the number and variety of the equipment or "machines" in the shop. Further, as these "machines" become smarter and are more capable of multitasking, the task of scheduling becomes more complicated.

The Ratio of Skilled Workers to Machines   Job shops can be classified as either **machine-limited** or **labor-limited,** depending on whether the workers outnumber the machines or vice versa. In addition, jobs may be classified as *labor-intensive* or *machine-intensive,* depending on how much of the job may be performed using automated processes.

The Flow Pattern of Jobs through the Shop   Exhibit 16.3 shows the various possible flows of jobs through a job shop. In some job shops, all jobs follow the same pattern; in others, the pattern is purely random. Most job shops fall somewhere in between these two extremes. Because of the apparent lack of organization, the flow of material through a job shop is often described as a *jumbled flow.*

Priority Rules for Allocating Jobs to Machines

The process of determining which job is started first on some machine or work center is known as sequencing or priority sequencing. **Priority rules** are the rules used to obtain a job sequence. These can be very simple, requiring only that jobs be sequenced according to one piece of data, such as processing time, due date, or order of arrival. Other rules, though equally simple, may require several pieces of information, typically to derive an index number such as in the *least slack rule* and the *critical ratio rule* (both defined later). Still others, such as Johnson's rule (also discussed later), apply to job scheduling on a sequence of machines and require a computational procedure to specify the order of performance. Ten of the more common priority rules are:

1. *FCFS—first come, first-served.* Orders are run in the order they arrive in the department.

flow pattern
Routes that materials follow through a factory to make a product.

machine-limited systems
Operations where the capacity of the facility is determined by number of machines.

labor-limited systems
Operations where the capacity of the facility is determined by number of workers.

priority rules
Criteria for determining the sequence or priority of jobs through a facility.

EXHIBIT 16.3

Material Flows through a Job Shop

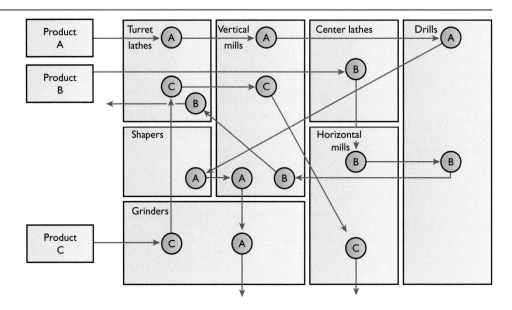

2. *SPT—shortest processing time.* Run the job with the shortest completion time first, next shortest second, etc. This is identical to SOT—shortest operating time.

3. *Due date—earliest due date first.* Run the job with the earliest due date first. DDate—when referring to the entire job; OPNDD—when referring to the next operation.

4. *Start date—due date minus normal lead time.* Run the job with the earliest start date first.

5. *STR—slack time remaining.* This is calculated as the difference between the time remaining before the due date minus the processing time remaining. Orders with the shortest STR are run first.

6. *STR/OP—Slack time remaining per operation.* Orders with shortest STR/OP are run first, calculated as follows:

$$\text{STR/OP} = \frac{\text{Time remaining before due date} - \text{Remaining processing time}}{\text{Number of remaining operations}}$$

7. *CR—critical ratio.* This is calculated as the difference between the due date and the current date divided by the work remaining. Orders with the smallest CR are run first.

8. *QR—queue ratio.* This is calculated as the slack time remaining in the schedule divided by the planned remaining queue time. Orders with the smallest QR are run first.

9. *LCFS—last-come, first-served.* This rule occurs frequently by default. As orders arrive they are placed on the top of the stack and the operator usually picks up the order on top to run first.

10. *Random order—whim.* The supervisors or the operators usually select whichever job they feel like running.[2]

---

[2]This list is modified from Donald W. Fogarty, John H. Blackstone, Jr., and Thomas R. Hoffmann, *Production and Inventory Management* (Cincinnati: South-Western Publishing, 1991), pp. 452–53.

Schedule Evaluation Criteria

The following standard measures of schedule performance are used to evaluate priority rules:

1. Meeting due dates of customers or downstream operations.
2. Minimizing flow time (or throughput time) which is the time a job spends in the shop.
3. Minimizing work in process.
4. Minimizing idle time of machines and workers.

PRIORITY RULES AND TECHNIQUES

Scheduling *n* Jobs on One Machine

Let us compare some of these 10 priority rules in a static scheduling situation involving four jobs on one machine. (In scheduling terminology, this class of problems is referred to as an "*n* job—one-machine problem," or simply *n*/1.) The theoretical difficulty of this type of problem increases as more machines are considered; therefore, the only restriction on *n* is that it be a specified, finite integer.

Consider the following example: Ioannis Kyriakides is the supervisor of Legal Copy-Express, which provides copy services for L.A. law firms in the downtown Los Angeles area. Five customers submitted their orders at the beginning of the week. Specific scheduling data on these orders are as follows:

Job (in order of arrival)	Processing Time (days)	Due Date (days hence)
A	3	5
B	4	6
C	2	7
D	6	9
E	1	2

All orders require the use of the only color copy machine available. Kyriakides must therefore decide on the processing sequence for the five orders. The evaluation criterion is to minimize flow time. Suppose that Kyriakides decides to use the FCFS rule in an attempt to make Legal Copy-Express appear fair to its customers. The FCFS rule results in the following flow times:

			FCFS Schedule				
Job	Processing Time (days)	Due Date (days)	Start		Job Time		Finish
A	3	5	0	+	3	=	3
B	4	6	3	+	4	=	7
C	2	7	7	+	2	=	9
D	6	9	9	+	6	=	15
E	1	2	15	+	1	=	16

Total flow time $= 3 + 7 + 9 + 15 + 16 = 50$ days

Mean flow time $= \frac{50}{5} = 10$ days

Comparing the due date of each job with its flow time, we observe that only Job A will be on time. Jobs B, C, D, and E will be late by 1, 2, 6, and 14 days, respectively. On the average, a job will be late by $(0 + 1 + 2 + 6 + 14)/5 = 4.6$ days.

Let's now consider the SPT rule. Here Kyriakides gives the highest priority to the order that has the shortest processing time. The resulting flow times are:

SPT Schedule

Job	Processing Time (days)	Due Date (days)	Flow Time (days)
E	1	2	0 + 1 = 1
C	2	7	1 + 2 = 3
A	3	5	3 + 3 = 6
B	4	6	6 + 4 = 10
D	6	9	10 + 6 = 16

Total flow time = $1 + 3 + 6 + 10 + 16 = 36$ days
Mean flow time = $\frac{36}{5} = 7.2$ days

SPT results in lower average flow time. In addition, Jobs E and C will be ready before the due date, and Job A is late by only one day. On the average a job will be late by $(0 + 0 + 1 + 4 + 7)/5 = 2.4$ days.

If Kyriakides decides to use the DDate rule, the resulting schedule is:

DDATE Schedule

Job	Processing Time (days)	Due Date (days)	Flow Time (days)
E	1	2	0 + 1 = 1
A	3	5	1 + 3 = 4
B	4	6	4 + 4 = 8
C	2	7	8 + 2 = 10
D	6	9	10 + 6 = 16

Total completion time = $1 + 4 + 8 + 10 + 16 = 39$ days
Mean flow time = 7.8 days

In this case Jobs B, C, and D will be late. On the average, a job will be late by $(0 + 0 + 2 + 3 + 7)/5 = 2.4$ days.

In a similar manner, the flow times of the LCFS, random, and STR rules are as follows:

LCFS Schedule

Job	Processing Time (days)	Due Date (days)	Flow Time (days)
E	1	2	0 + 1 = 1
D	6	9	1 + 6 = 7
C	2	7	7 + 2 = 9
B	4	6	9 + 4 = 13
A	3	5	13 + 3 = 16

Total flow time = 46 days
Mean flow time = 9.2 days
Average lateness = 4.0 days

Random Schedule

Job	Processing Time (days)	Due Date (days)	Flow Time (days)
D	6	9	0 + 6 = 6
C	2	7	6 + 2 = 8
A	3	5	8 + 3 = 11
E	1	2	11 + 1 = 12
B	4	6	12 + 4 = 16

Total flow time　= 53 days

Mean flow time　= 10.6 days

Average lateness = 5.4 days

STR Schedule

Job	Processing Time (days)	Due Date (days)	Flow Time (days)
E	1	2	0 + 1 = 1
A	3	5	1 + 3 = 4
B	4	6	4 + 4 = 8
D	6	9	8 + 6 = 14
C	2	7	14 + 2 = 16

Total flow time　= 43 days

Mean flow time　= 8.6 days

Average lateness = 3.2 days

These results are summarized below:

Scheduling Rule	Total Completion Time (days)	Average Completion Time (days)	Average Lateness (days)
FCFS	50	10.0	4.6
SPT	36	7.2	2.4
DDate	39	7.8	2.4
LCFS	46	9.2	4.0
Random	53	10.6	5.4
STR	43	8.6	3.2

For this example, the SPT is better than the rest of the scheduling rules, but is this always the case? The answer is yes. It can be shown mathematically that the SPT rule yields an optimum solution for the $n/1$ case with respect to the SPT and for other evaluation criteria such as mean waiting time and mean completion time. In fact, so powerful is this simple rule that it has been termed "the most important concept in the entire subject of sequencing."[3] However, it is important to note that the SPT rule totally ignores the due dates of jobs. As a consequence, jobs with longer processing times can often be late.

[3]R. W. Conway, William L. Maxwell, and Louis W. Miller, *Theory of Scheduling* (Reading, MA: Addison-Wesley Publishing, 1967), p. 26. A classic book on the subject.

Scheduling *n* Jobs on Two Machines

The next step up in complexity of job shop types is the $n/2$ case, where two or more jobs must be processed on two machines in a common sequence. As in the $n/1$ case, there is an approach that leads to an optimal solution according to certain criteria. The objective of this approach, termed *Johnson's rule* or *method* (after its developer), is to minimize the flow time, from the beginning of the first job until the completion of the last. Johnson's rule consists of the following steps:

1. List the operation time for each job on both machines.
2. Select the job with the shortest operation time.
3. If the shortest time is for the first machine, do that job first; if the shortest time is for the second machine, do that job last.
4. Repeat Steps 2 and 3 for each remaining job until the schedule is complete.

Example

We can illustrate the application of Johnson's rule by scheduling four jobs through two machines:

***Step 1:* List operation times.**

Job	Operation Time on Machine 1	Operation Time on Machine 2
A	3	2
B	6	8
C	5	6
D	7	4

Solution

***Steps 2 and 3:* Select shortest operation time and assign.**
Job A is shortest on Machine 2 and is assigned first and performed last. (Job A is now no longer available to be scheduled.)

***Step 4:* Repeat Steps 2 and 3 until completion of schedule.**
Select the shortest operation time among the remaining jobs. Job D is second shortest on Machine 2, thus it is performed second to last (remember Job A is last). Now, Jobs A and D are not available anymore for scheduling. Job C is the shortest on Machine 1 among the remaining jobs. Job C is performed first. Now, only Job B is left with the shortest operation time on Machine 1. Thus, according to Step 3, it is performed first among the remaining, or second overall (Job C was already scheduled first).

In summary, the solution sequence is C → B → D → A, and the flow time is 25 days, which is a minimum. Also minimized are total idle time and mean idle time. The final schedule appears in Exhibit 16.4.

EXHIBIT 16.4

Optimal Schedule of Jobs Using Johnson's Rule

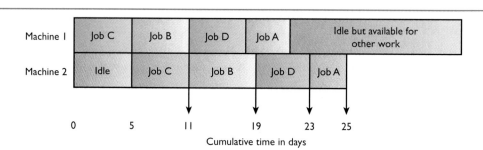

These steps result in scheduling the jobs having the shortest time in the beginning and ending of the schedule. As a result, the amount of concurrent operating time for the two machines is maximized, thus minimizing the total operating time required to complete the jobs.

Johnson's rule has been extended to yield an optimal solution for the $n/3$ case. When flow shop scheduling problems larger than $n/3$ arise (and they generally do), analytical solution procedures leading to optimality are not available. The reason for this is that even though the jobs may arrive in static fashion at the first machine, the scheduling problem becomes dynamic, and a series of waiting lines start to form in front of machines downstream.

Scheduling *n* Jobs on *m* Machines—Complex Job Shops

Complex job shops are characterized by multiple machine centers processing a variety of different jobs arriving at the machine centers in an intermittent fashion throughout the day. If there are n jobs to be processed on m machines and all jobs are processed on all machines, then there are $(n!)^m$ alternative schedules for this job set. Because of the large number of schedules that exist for even small job shops, simulation is the only practical way to determine the relative merits of different priority rules in such situations. As in the n job on one machine case, the 10 priority rules (and more) have been compared relative to their performance on the evaluation criteria previously mentioned.

By way of example, John Kanet and Jack Hayya focused their efforts on due date-oriented priority rules to see which one was best. Their simulation of a complex job shop revealed that total job competition rules of "DDATE, STR, and CR were outperformed by their 'operation' counterparts OPNDD, STR/OP, and OPCR" for all seven of the performance criteria used.[4]

Which priority rule should be used? We believe that the needs of most manufacturers are reasonably satisfied by a relatively simple priority scheme that embodies the following principles:

1. It should be dynamic, that is, computed frequently during the course of a job to reflect changing conditions.
2. It should be based in one way or another on slack time (the difference between the work remaining to be done on a job and the time remaining to do it in). This embodies the due-date features suggested by Kanet and Hayya.

OPT Scheduling Concepts

OPT
A proprietary software package for scheduling production.

OPT is a software system which contains a proprietary algorithm for production scheduling. From OPT (optimized production technology) has evolved the managerial concept of theory of constraints (TOC). OPT/TOC is a production planning and control (PPC) method that attempts to optimize scheduling by maximizing the utilization of the bottlenecks in the process.

Traditional production planning and control is considered today to be no more than a production tool. Integrated PPC is a concept that marries an underlying philosophy of planning with a set of tools to implement that philosophy to optimize the process.

There are three major approaches to integrated PPC: push systems, pull systems, and bottleneck systems. The forerunner to the push systems is a tool developed by Joseph Orlicky at IBM in 1974—material requirements planning (MRP). In the late 1960s, Taichi Ohno at

---

[4]John K. Kanet and Jack C. Hayya, "Priority Dispatching with Operation Due Dates in a Job Shop," *Journal of Operations Management* 2, no. 3 (May 1982), p. 170.

Toyota developed the *kanban* system, the first of the pull systems. Eli Goldratt's OPT, developed in the late 1970s, is considered the genesis of bottleneck systems.[5]

In the bottleneck system approach, the process under consideration is viewed in terms of goods or services in movement, analogous to a river flowing. The good or service produced by the process is the "water" flowing and the bottlenecks are the "blockages" in the stream bed that slow the water. If we think of these blockages as "dams," then OPT/TOC acts to ensure a sufficient quantity of "water" immediately upstream of each "dam" to allow a constant "water" flow over each "dam." In other words, there is always a sufficient quantity of goods or service just before the bottleneck to ensure that the bottleneck is always operating at maximum capacity.

In OPT there is a distinction between bottlenecks and capacity constrained resources. A bottleneck applies to the case in which a stage or a number of stages in a system cannot process the good or service quickly enough to prevent backlogs (both in terms of work-in-progress and demand). A capacity constrained resource (CCR) is a good or service necessary for the creation of the final product that is exhausted before the final product is delivered. To illustrate the difference between a bottleneck and a capacity constrained resource, let's consider a retail laundry that specializes in cleaning shirts.

Claude's Cleaners is noted for their quality and inexpensive service, so much so that there is always a line of customers waiting for the sole clerk, Clark, to process each transaction. Unfortunately, they are not noted for speedy service; it usually takes a week just to get a shirt cleaned and pressed. Claude's has three presses, but they are used only three or four days each week because the starch for the shirts usually runs out. (In an effort to minimize costs, Claude's uses the just-in-time concept for materials management and it takes three days for the starch to be delivered after an order is placed.)

In this service process, Clark is a bottleneck. The starch is a capacity constrained resource (CCR)—as its inventory is increased, the flow through the process component (the presses) is increased. The inventory of starch *acts* like a temporary bottleneck. The effects of CCRs typically can be reduced in the short-term by relatively simple adjustments. Improvements to bottlenecks, on the other hand, are usually expensive and time consuming.

To optimize the flow through a bottleneck in the system, the bottleneck must operate continuously and at full capacity. A planning/control/communication mechanism, known as Drum-Buffer-Rope, is used to accomplish this objective. Since the bottleneck is the slowest component of the process, it sets the pace or tempo for the system—much like a drum beat sets the pace for a marching band. With the output of the process limited to the output of the bottleneck, decreases in output at the bottleneck cannot be recovered. Therefore, an inventory of goods or services, or "buffer inventory," is necessary before the bottleneck so it will always be operating at maximum capacity. To assure that the buffer is maintained at an optimal level (that is, just enough to keep the bottleneck operating), the rate at which the bottleneck is processing (the drum beat) must be communicated to the source of the goods or services that the bottleneck is processing. Since this communication is in one direction—from the bottleneck to the source of the goods or services (input)—and it pulls the input to the buffer, it is referred to as the "rope."

Returning to Claude's Cleaners, Clark is the bottleneck or drum. The buffer would be the inventory of cleaned clothing waiting for the customer. What is the rope? Is there a rope?

The quantity of goods or services sent to the buffer is called the *transfer batch*. Because the purpose of the transfer batch is to maintain the buffer at its optimal level, the quantity will be dependent on the processing rate of the bottleneck. The quantity of goods or services

---

[5]Daniel Sipper and Robert L. Buflin, Jr., *Production: Planning, Control, and Integration* (Burr Ridge, IL: McGraw-Hill, 1998), p. 531.

produced by the bottleneck's input source at one time is referred to as the *process batch*. In bottleneck systems it is critical to recognize that to optimize the entire system transfer batches and process batches may not be of the same quantity.

At Claude's Cleaners, Bettie and Bert box the shirts after they have been pressed. If we consider Bettie and Bert together as a single input source for Clark, then the process batch size from boxing to the pick-up area is two. But, since Clark can only process one transaction at a time, the transfer batch quantity is one.

With the fundamental components of a bottleneck system defined, we can now turn our attention to optimally scheduling such a system. There are five basic steps to scheduling a bottleneck system:

- Determine the bottleneck and CCRs.
- Optimize the CCRs.
- Schedule the bottleneck to its maximum.
- Schedule the process located before the bottleneck.
- Schedule the process located after the bottleneck.

There are nine basic rules that Eli Goldratt has presented for scheduling with OPT.

1. Balance the flow not the capacity.
2. Utilization of a nonbottleneck is determined by a constraint in the system (a bottleneck).
3. Utilization and activation of an input is not the same.
4. Any loss in output at a bottleneck translates into a loss for the entire system.
5. Gains at nonbottlenecks do not translate into gains at the bottleneck or for the entire system.
6. Bottlenecks determine the throughput and inventory levels.
7. For optimization, transfer batches may not equal process batches.
8. The size of the process batches through the system should not be fixed.
9. Schedules should be established after evaluating all constraints simultaneously.

It is not uncommon to find that once a bottleneck has been scheduled that another bottleneck will appear in the process. To optimize a system it may be necessary to repeat the scheduling procedure a number of times.

OPT was developed by Dr. Eli Goldratt in Israel with three partners. It was introduced into the United States in 1979 with the creation of Creative Output, Inc. Over the next seven years as the software was evolving, the OPT management philosophy and rules were developed. With a major dispute between the partners and the essential bankruptcy of Creative Output, Inc., the rights to the OPT software were sold to Scheduling Technologies Group (STG) of the United Kingdom. A number of software packages to schedule bottleneck systems are available, among them are OPT21, OPIS, MICRO-BOSS, MOOPI, and PRIORITY.

OPT's basic advantage is that, by focusing on a single bottleneck resource, the problem is sufficiently simplified that it can be solved well and with intuitive support to the user. However, OPT has a number of disadvantages: "it cannot accommodate multiple and shifting bottlenecks; user interface is not strong; reactive correction to the schedule requires full rerunning; it is proprietary, so not only is the software rigid, but also simple judgmental modifications of schedules are difficult."[6]

---

[6]Morton and Pentico, *Heuristic Scheduling Systems* (New York: John Wiley & Sons, 1993), p. 28.

CONTROL IN THE JOB SHOP

shop-floor control
Set of procedures for maintaining and communicating the status of orders and work centers.

Scheduling job priorities is just one aspect of **shop-floor control** (now often referred to as *production activity control*). The *American Production and Inventory Control Society (APICS) Dictionary* defines a *shop-floor control system* as:

> A system for utilizing data from the shop floor as well as data processing files to maintain and communicate status information on shop orders and work centers.

The major functions of shop-floor control are:

1. Assigning priority to each shop order.
2. Maintaining work-in-process (WIP) quantity information.
3. Conveying shop-order status information to the office.
4. Providing actual output data for capacity control purposes.
5. Providing quantity by location by shop order for WIP inventory and accounting purposes.
6. Providing measures of efficiency, utilization, and productivity of labor and machines.

Exhibit 16.5 illustrates more of the details related to shop-floor control.

Tools of Shop-Floor Control

There are a variety of written forms that can help the supervisor maintain control in the job shop; these are easily generated by the appropriate software and updated frequently through a normal interaction of supervisor and software.

- The *dispatch list* (usually generated on a daily basis) tells the shop foreman what jobs need to be accomplished that day, what priority each has, and how long each will take. Exhibit 16.6A below presents an example of a dispatch list.
- *Exception reports* provide the supervisor with the information needed to handle special cases and problems. An example of this is the anticipated delay report shown in Exhibit 16.6B. Typically made out once or twice a week, these reports are reviewed to determine if any of the delays are serious enough to warrant revision of the master production schedule.
- *The input/output control report,* or simply the I/O report, is used by the supervisor to monitor the relationship between the workload and the capacity of each workstation. If these relationships are significantly out of balance, then the supervisor can identify where adjustments are needed. An example of such a report is shown in Exhibit 16.6C.
- *Status reports* give the supervisor summaries on the performance of the operation, and usually include the number and percentage of jobs completed on time, the lateness of jobs not yet completed, the volume of output, and so forth. Two examples of status reports are the scrap report and the rework report.

input/output control
Assuring the amount of work accepted does not exceed the capacity of the facility.

Input/output control is a major feature of a control system. The major precept of I/O control is that the total workload accepted (the input) should never exceed the capacity to perform jobs (the output). When the input exceeds the output, then backlogs occur. This has several negative consequences: Jobs are completed late, making customers unhappy, and subsequent or related jobs incur a delay before they can be started. This delay also results in unsatisfied customers. Moreover, when jobs pile up at a work center, congestion occurs, processing becomes inefficient, and the flow of work to downstream work centers

EXHIBIT 16.5

Shop-Floor Control

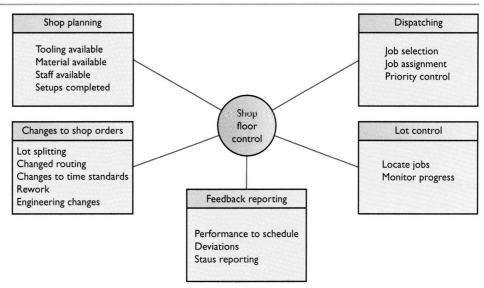

Source: "Shop Floor Control—Closing the Loop," *Inventory Management Newsletter* (Stone Mountain, GA: Center for Inventory Management), August 1982.

EXHIBIT 16.6

Some Basic Tools of Shop-Floor Control

A. Dispatch List
Work center 1501 — Day 205

Start date	Job #	Description	Run time
201	15131	Shaft	11.4
203	15143	Stud	20.6
205	15145	Spindle	4.3
205	15712	Spindle	8.6
207	15340	Metering rod	6.5
208	15312	Shaft	4.6

B. Anticipated Delay Report
Dept. 24 April 8

Part #	Sched. date	New date	Cause of delay	Action
17125	4/10	4/15	Fixture broke	Toolroom will return on 4/15
13044	4/11	5/1	Out for plating — plater on strike	New lot started
17653	4/11	4/14	New part-holes don't align	Engineering laying out new jig

C. Input/Output Control Report (B)
Work center 0162

Week ending	505	512	519	526
Planned input	210	210	210	210
Actual input	110	150	140	130
Cumulative deviation	−100	−160	−230	−310
Planned output	210	210	210	210
Actual output	140	120	160	120
Cumulative deviation	−70	−160	−210	−300

Note: All figures are in standard hours.

becomes sporadic. An analogy of this phenomenon to the flow of water is shown below in Exhibit 16.7.

Gantt chart
Planning tool that plots activities on a time chart.

A simple but effective control device is the **Gantt chart.** It is used to help plan and track jobs, again, using software. A Gantt chart is a type of bar chart that plots tasks to be done against time. It also helps show relationships between jobs. Exhibit 16.8 shows a small Gantt chart for a job shop attempting to complete three jobs (A, B, and C). This chart indicates that Job A is behind schedule by about 4 hours, Job B is ahead of schedule, and Job C has been completed, but only after a delayed start for equipment maintenance. The Gantt chart shows how much ahead or behind schedule we are by comparing where we are now

EXHIBIT 16.7

Shop Capacity Control Load Flow

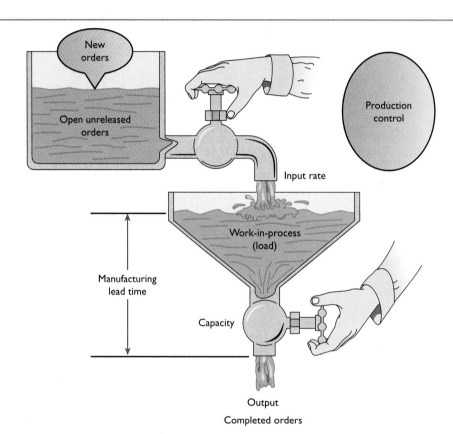

Source: American Production and Inventory Control Society. "Training Aid—Shop Floor Control," undated.

EXHIBIT 16.8   Gantt Chart

Source: Professor Bob Parsons, Management Science Department, Northeastern University, Boston, MA. Used with permission.

to where we planned to be. Other useful controls devices include the PERT and CPM networks discussed in Chapter 10.

Shop-floor control systems in most modern plants are now computerized, with job status information entered directly into a computer as the job enters and leaves a work center. Some plants have gone heavily into bar coding and optical scanners to speed up the reporting process and to cut down on data-entry errors.[7] As you might guess, the key problems in shop-floor control arc data inaccuracy and lack of timeliness. When these occur, the information fed back to the overall planning system is wrong and incorrect production decisions are made. Typical results are excess inventory and/or stockout problems, missed due dates, and inaccuracies in job costing.

Of course, maintaining data integrity requires that a sound data-gathering system be in place; but more important, it requires adherence to the system by everybody interacting with it. Most firms recognize this, but maintaining what is variously referred to as *shop discipline, data integrity,* or *data responsibility* is not always easy. And despite periodic drives to publicize the importance of careful shop-floor reporting by creating data-integrity task forces, inaccuracies can still creep into the system in many ways: A line worker drops a part under the workbench and pulls a replacement from stock without recording either transaction. An inventory clerk makes an error in a cycle count. A manufacturing engineer fails to note a change in the routing of a part. A department supervisor decides to work jobs in a different order than specified in the dispatch list.

SCHEDULING WORKERS IN SERVICE OPERATIONS

 ### Why Scheduling Is Important in Services

As discussed previously, one of the main distinctions between manufacturing and service operations is the customer's direct interaction with the service delivery process. Because of this interaction, the determination of the proper number of workers to schedule at any particular time is critical to the success of every service operation. On one hand, scheduling too few workers results in unnecessarily long customer waiting times. On the other hand, scheduling too many workers results in overstaffing and the incurrence of unnecessarily high labor costs, which negatively affect profits. The service manager, consequently, needs to schedule workers in a way that effectively satisfies customer demand while minimizing unnecessary labor costs.

The cost of labor in most services is a major cost component, often running 35 percent of sales and higher. For some services, in fact, virtually all of the direct costs can be considered as labor (examples of these types of services include consulting, legal work, home care nursing and hair salons). Thus a small but unnecessary increase in labor can have a very significant impact on a firm's profits.

 ### The Sequence for Scheduling Service Workers

Work schedules in service operations are usually developed on a weekly basis for several reasons. First, there are state and federal laws that specify the maximum number of hours and/or days an employee can work in a given week after which overtime premiums must

---

[7]Some companies also use "smartshelves"—inventory bins with weight sensors beneath each shelf. When an item is removed from inventory, a signal is sent to a central computer that notes the time, date, quantity, and location of the transaction.

be paid. Second, the distinction between full-time and part-time workers is often made on the basis of the number of hours worked in a calendar week. Full-time versus part-time status often determines the benefits paid by the employer, and may be related to union contracts that specify the minimum number of hours workers in each category may work. Finally, many workers, especially hourly workers, are paid on a weekly basis that is often mandated by local or state laws.

The sequence for developing a schedule for service workers can be divided into the following four major elements, as illustrated in Exhibit 16.9: (*a*) forecasting customer demand, (*b*) converting customer demand into worker requirements, and (*c*) converting worker requirements into daily work schedules, and converting daily work schedules into weekly work schedules.

Forecasting Demand   Since the delivery of most services takes place in the presence of the customer, the customer's arrival directly correlates with the demand level for the service operation. For example, the customer must be present at a restaurant to partake in the meal being served; the patient must be present in the hospital to receive treatment. In addition to the customer's presence at the point of service, the potential for high variability in the pattern of customer demand makes it extremely important for service managers to efficiently schedule workers. The first step, therefore, in developing a schedule that will permit the service operation to meet customer demand is to accurately forecast that demand.

There are several patterns of demand that need to be considered: variation in demand within days (or even hours), variation across days of the week, and seasonal variations. Because demand is often highly variable throughout a day, forecasting within-day variation is usually done in either hour or half-hour increments. Today, with the use of computers and more sophisticated point-of-sale (POS) equipment, the ability to record customer demand in even shorter time increments is possible (for example, 15-minute time intervals).

To develop a forecast we need to collect historical data about customer demand. The actual number of customers expecting service in a given time interval (that is, half-hour or hour) is the preferred data. Fortunately, there is a wide range of POS equipment available

EXHIBIT 16.9

The Required Steps in a Worker Schedule

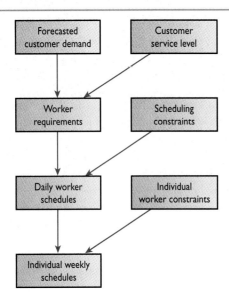

that can capture this type of data, and, in many cases, even download it onto a computer for subsequent analysis.

Converting Customer Demand into Worker Requirements   Worker requirements in service operations can be divided into two major categories: front-of-the-house and back-of-the-house. Front-of-the-house workers are defined as those who have direct contact with the customer. Examples would include a teller at a bank, a cashier at a discount department store, or the check-in personnel at an airline counter. Back-of-the-house workers are those workers who do not interact directly with the customers. Examples here would include a cook in a restaurant and a baggage handler for an airline. (The scheduling of back-of-the-house workers is usually very similar to scheduling workers in a manufacturing environment.)

A necessary element in the conversion of customer demand into front-of-the-house worker requirements is the establishment of a customer-service level. For example, many restaurants offer express lunches within a specified time period. Another example of a specified level of service is at Putnam Investments in Andover, Massachusetts, where Leslie Power states that Putnam's established service level at its call centers is that "93 percent of all the calls should be answered in 20 seconds or less."[8]

Knowing the average number of customers who require service in a given period of time and the average length of time it takes to provide service to each customer, a manager can determine how many workers to schedule for that time period in order to provide the desired level of service. Queuing theory, which was presented earlier in the text, is a mathematically organized approach for establishing the relationship among the three following variables: (*a*) customer demand (for example, customers per hour); (*b*) available capacity, expressed in the number of workers on duty and the average time to service a customer; and (*c*) average customer waiting time.

To facilitate this process of converting customer demand into a specified number of workers, a service organization will often develop a labor requirements table. This table tells the manager how many workers are needed for different levels of demand. For some companies, these tables will also indicate where these workers should be assigned. With this type of table, the service manager only has to look up the forecasted demand in a given time period to determine how many workers to schedule and where they should be assigned. An example of a labor requirements table for a fast food restaurant is shown in Exhibit 16.10.

Converting Worker Requirements into Daily Work Schedules   The next step in the scheduling process is the conversion of worker requirements for each time interval into a daily work or shift schedule. The basic goal here is to schedule a sufficient number of workers in a given time period to meet the expected demand at the target service level. However, there are usually additional factors that also need to be included, such as: (*a*) the minimum length of a shift that might be prescribed by a union contract (for example, when workers are called into UPS, they are guaranteed by their union contract a minimum of three hours work), (*b*) the maximum shift length permitted by state or local labor laws, and (*c*) the company's policies about rest and meal breaks. These factors can significantly affect how efficiently the organization can meet the target service level. These minimum shift constraints often result in a worker schedule where the total number of labor hours needed to meet the minimum shift requirement(s) is greater than the actual number of labor hours required to satisfy customer demand.

---

[8]Conversation with Leslie Power of Putnam Investments on July 20, 1998.

EXHIBIT 16.10

An Example of a Labor Requirements Table for a Fast Food Operation

	Total No. of Workers	Specific Worker Assignments						Sales ($)/Hour Volume Guidelines
		Grill	**Windows**	**Drive-Thru**	**Bin**	**Fry**	**Floaters***	
Minimum staffing level	4	1	1	1	—	—	1	$120
	5	1	1	1	—	—	2	150
	6	2	1	1	—	—	2	180
	7	2	2	1	—	—	2	210
	8	2	2	2	1	—	1	240
	9	2	2	2	1	—	2	275
	10	3	3	2	1	—	1	310
	11	3	3	2	1	1	1	345
	12	3	3	3	1	1	1	385
	13	4	3	3	1	1	1	425
	14	4	3	3	1	1	2	475
	15	4	4	3	1	1	2	525
	16	5	4	3	1	1	2	585
Full staffing level	17	5	5	3	1	1	2	645

*Floaters help out; they patrol the lot, lobby, and restrooms, restock, and cover on breaks.

Source: Adapted from "McDonald's," Harvard Business School Case No. 681–044, 1980.

In developing these schedules, many organizations use part-time rather than full-time workers to effectively meet customer-service goals while simultaneously controlling costs. Since part-time workers are typically paid less and may also be entitled to fewer (or even no) fringe benefits, the average hourly cost of the part-time worker is lower than that of the full-time worker. Part-time workers can be used to meet demand at peak periods (such as meal times in restaurants) or during periods when full-time workers would prefer not to work (such as weekends in hospitals).

Converting Daily Work Schedules into Weekly Work Schedules   The conversion of daily work schedules into weekly work schedules is more complicated than simply repeating the daily schedule procedure. In developing weekly schedules, managers need to take into consideration workers' days off for illness, holidays, and vacations. They also need to factor in the additional cost of paying workers to work on holidays if services are offered on those days. Workforce scheduling in a hospital, for example, can be particularly challenging on major holidays. In addition, these weekly schedules need to be assigned to specific individuals. Therefore, inputs into this module include individual worker constraints such as days off, hours available for work, and so forth.

The Use of Technology in Scheduling

As in most facets of business, information technology has had a significant impact on the ability of the manager to schedule workers. Early computer programs for scheduling workers were often cumbersome to use and also very limited in their applications. However, the advent of faster and more powerful computers coupled with newer software programs has resulted in worker scheduling programs that are both significantly more user friendly and, at the same time, more flexible in their applications.

The use of these automated scheduling programs has several advantages. First, it significantly reduces the amount of time a manager has to devote to developing a weekly work schedule. Previously, when manually scheduling workers, it was not uncommon for a manager in a complex service environment to devote one entire eight-hour day every

EXHIBIT 16.13

General Problems in
Nurse Scheduling

Problem	Possible Solution
Accuracy of patient load forecast	Forecast frequently and rebudget monthly. Closely monitor seasonal demands, communicable diseases, and current occupancy
Forecasting nurse availability	Develop work standards for nurses for each level of possible demand (requires systematic data collection and analysis)
Complexity and time to rebudget	Use available computer programs
Flexibility in scheduling	Use variable staffing: Set regular staff levels slightly above minimum and absorb variation with broadskilled float nurses, part-time nurses, and overtime

Though most hospitals still use trial-and-error methods in schedule development, management scientists have applied optimizing techniques to the problem with some success. For example, a linear programming model has been developed that assumes a known, short-run (three to four days) demand for nursing care and develops a staffing pattern that:[10]

1. Specifies the number of nurses of each skill class to be assigned among the wards and nursing shifts.
2. Satisfies total nursing personnel capacity constraints.
3. Allows for limited substitution of tasks among nurses.
4. Minimizes the cost of a nursing care shortage for the scheduling period.

A major problem confronting health care managers today is the changing mix of patient needs and how it affects nurse staffing requirements. With the growing trend toward more outpatient treatment, patients who are hospitalized today are typically very ill, and thus require, on average, more individual attention. Under these conditions, the demands for nursing skills can actually increase, even though the number of patients in a designated area has remained unchanged.

Because of these increased patient needs, many hospitals are adapting a worker skill mix that incorporates lower-skilled technical support personnel to assist in the delivery of patient care, with the goal of reducing their overall labor costs. This additional parameter of different worker skills has to be taken into consideration when determining personnel staffing requirements.

Scheduling Consecutive Days Off   A practical problem encountered in many service organizations is setting schedules so that employees can have two consecutive days off even though the operation is open seven days a week. The importance of the problem stems from the fact that the Fair Labor Standards Act requires that overtime be paid for any hours worked (by hourly workers) in excess of 40 hours per week. Obviously, if two consecutive days off can't be scheduled each week for each employee, the likelihood of unnecessary overtime is quite high. In addition, most people probably prefer two consecutive days off per week. The following heuristic procedure was modified from that developed by James Browne and Rajen Tibrewala to deal with this problem.[11]

---

[10]D. Warner and J. Prawda, "A Mathematical Programming Model for Scheduling Nursing Personnel in a Hospital," *Management Science* 19, no. 4 (December 1972), pp. 411–22.

[11]James J. Browne and Rajen K. Tibrewala, "Manpower Scheduling," *Industrial Engineering* 7, no. 8 (August 1975), pp. 22–23.

Objective. Find the schedule that minimizes the number of five-day workers with two consecutive days off, subject to the demands of the daily staffing schedule and assuming that the workers have no preference for which days they get off.

Procedure. Starting with the total number of workers required for each day of the week, create a schedule by adding one worker at a time. This is a two-step procedure:

Step 1   Circle the lowest pair of consecutive days off. The lowest pair is the one where the highest number in the pair is equal to or lower than the highest number in any other pair. This ensures that the days with the highest requirements are covered by staff. (Monday and Sunday may be chosen even though they are at opposite ends of the array of days.) In case of ties choose the days-off pair with the lowest requirement on an adjacent day. This day may be before or after the pair. If a tie still remains, choose the first of the available tied pairs. (Do not bother using further tie-breaking rules, such as second lowest adjacent days.)

Step 2   Subtract 1 from each of the remaining five days (i.e., the days not circled). This indicates that one less worker is required on these days, since the first worker has just been assigned to them.

Step 3   The two steps are repeated for the second worker, the third worker, and so forth, until no more workers are required to satisfy the schedule.

Example

	M	Tu	W	Th	F	S	Su
Requirement	4	3	4	2	3	1	2
Worker 1	4	3	4	2	3	1	2
Worker 2	3	2	3	1	2	1	2
Worker 3	2	1	2	0	2	1	1
Worker 4	1	0	1	0	1	1	1
Worker 5	0	0	1	0	0	0	0

Solution

This solution consists of five workers covering 19 worker days, although slightly different assignments may be equally satisfactory.

The schedule: Worker 1 is assigned S–Su off; Worker 2, F–S off; Worker 3, S–Su off; Worker 4, Tu–W off; and Worker 5 works only on Wednesday, since there are no further requirements for the other days.

CONCLUSION

Job shops are prevalent throughout both the manufacturing and service sectors (see the banking and nursing examples above). Job shop scheduling has now become computer dependent and is inseparable from total manufacturing planning and control systems. In fact, the scheduling of the job shop is an integral part of this larger system.

Worker scheduling is especially important in service operations where labor is often a significant cost component. Here, too much labor negatively influences profits, but insufficient labor has a negative impact on customer service and hence, adversely affects future sales.

Like all aspects of operations management, job shops are affected by larger trends in the global economy. Jobs shops are becoming more specialized, and the training required of the workforce is becoming increasingly sophisticated. Furthermore, the use of automated processes and technologically advanced approaches to jobs will continue to increase. The information linkages between the job shop and the rest of the firm will be accessed more frequently by all involved parties. Costs (notably energy) will continue to rise, as will competitive pressures. The customer base will be better educated, more international in scope, and more socially aware, putting greater responsibility on the job shop to be socially responsible. Natural resources will become less available, and government regulation of the use of such resources may continue to rise. In short, job shop scheduling will remain a necessary part of the operation of the firm and, for the foreseeable future, will remain a difficult task.

KEY TERMS

dispatching of orders p. 535	labor-limited systems p. 537
expediting p. 535	machine-limited systems p. 537
flow pattern p. 537	OPT p. 543
Gantt chart p. 548	priority rules p. 537
job shop p. 534	shop-flow control p. 546
input/output control p. 546	

REVIEW AND DISCUSSION QUESTIONS

1. Identify the characteristics of a job shop. Why are they so prevalent, especially in the service sector?

2. What practical considerations are deterrents to using the SPT rule?

3. What priority rule do you use in scheduling your study time for midterm examinations? If you have five exams to study for, how many alternative schedules exist?

4. Why is it difficult to schedule workers in a service environment?

5. In the United States, there are certain assumptions made about the customer-service priority rules used in banks, restaurants, and retail stores. If you have the opportunity, ask an international student what rules are used in his or her country. To what factors might you attribute the differences, if any?

6. What job characteristics would lead you to schedule jobs according to "longest processing time first"?

7. In what way is the scheduling problem in the home office of a bank different from that of a branch?

8. Identify an example of a job shop where you are the scheduler/dispatcher. It might be your kitchen, your computer workstation, or something else. What priority rules would you use for this job shop, and why?

9. List some of the problems that a job shop scheduler faces when trying to estimate the personnel and machinery needed for a made-to-order job that has never been done before.

10. Assume you are the desk clerk at an upscale hotel and that you handle all registrations. You are dealing with your customers on a first-come, first-served basis when a professional football team arrives. They are playing a team from your city and will be staying at your hotel. How will you handle their registrations?

11. In many job shops, the percentage of work done by automated processes is increasing. For example, in a copy center the copy machines now collate and staple automatically. In hospitals, more and more diagnoses are made by machines with remote sensors. Discuss how the capacity of machines to "do more" impacts the role of the job shop scheduler.

12. Examples of two-dimensional Gantt charts were presented in the chapter; could a Gantt chart have three dimensions? Provide several examples.

13. What are some of the goods and services produced by a bottleneck system that you use? What characteristics do they have in common?

14. How does a bottleneck system affect the customer, the company, and the employees who work within the system?

15. In a service environment, can customer co-production be utilized to lessen the effects of a bottleneck? How?

SOLVED PROBLEM

Problem 1

Joe's Auto Seat Cover and Paint Shop is bidding on a contract to do all the custom work for Smiling Ed's used car dealership. One of the main requirements in obtaining this contract is rapid delivery time, since Ed—for reasons we shall not go into here—wants the cars facelifted and back on his lot in a hurry. Ed has said that if Joe can refit and repaint five cars that Ed has just received (from an unnamed source) in 24 hours or less, the contract will be his. Following is the time (in hours) required in the refitting shop and the paint shop for each of the five cars. Assuming that cars go through the refitting operations before they are repainted, can Joe meet the time requirements and get the contract?

Car	Refitting Time (hours)	Repairing Time (hours)
A	6	3
B	0	4
C	5	2
D	8	6
E	2	1

Solution

This problem can be viewed as a two-machine flow shop and can be easily solved using "Johnson's rule."

	Original Data		Johnson's Rule	
Car	Refitting Time (hours)	Repainting Time (hours)	Order of Selection	Position in Sequence
A	6	3	4th	3rd
B	0	4	1st	1st
C	5	2	3rd	4th
D	8	6	5th	2nd
E	2	1	2nd	5th

Graph of Johnson solution (not to scale):

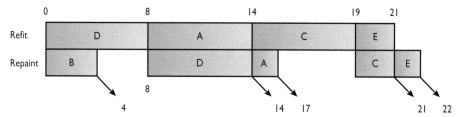

The total time for the five cars is 22 hours.

PROBLEMS

1. Joe has three cars that must be overhauled by his ace mechanic, Jim. Given the following data about the cars, use the STR/OP priority rule (least slack remaining per operation) to determine Jim's scheduling priority for each.

Car	Customer Pick-Up Time (hours hence)	Remaining Overhaul Time (hours)	Remaining Operations
A	10	4	Painting
B	17	5	Wheel alignment, painting
C	15	1	Chrome plating, painting, seat repair

2. There are seven jobs that must be processed in two operations: A and B. All seven jobs must go through A and B in that sequence—A first, then B.

   a. Determine the optimal order in which the jobs should be sequenced through the process using these times:

Job	Process A Time	Process B Time
1	9	6
2	8	5
3	7	7
4	6	3
5	1	2
6	2	6
7	4	7

   b. Draw a graph similar to the solved problems showing the sequence of jobs.

   c. What is the total completion time for all seven jobs?

3. The following list of jobs in a critical department includes estimates of their required times:

Job	Required Time (days)	Days to Delivery Promise	Slack
A	8	12	4
B	3	9	6
C	7	8	1
D	1	11	10
E	10	−10	—
F	6	10	4
G	5	−8	—
H	4	6	2

   a. Use the shortest operation time rule to schedule these jobs:

      What is the schedule?   What is the mean flow time?

   b. The boss doesn't like the schedule in (a). Jobs E and G must be done first, for obvious reasons (they are already late). Reschedule and do the best you can while scheduling Jobs E and G first and second, respectively.

      What is the new schedule?   What is the new mean flow time?

4. A manufacturing facility has five jobs to be scheduled into production. The following table gives the processing times plus the necessary wait times and other necessary delays for each of the jobs. Assume that today is April 3 and the jobs are due on the dates shown:

Job	Days of Actual Processing Time Required	Days of Necessary Delay Time	Total Time Required	Date Job Due
1	2	12	14	April 30
2	5	8	13	April 21
3	9	15	24	April 28
4	7	9	16	April 29
5	4	22	28	April 27

   Determine two schedules, stating the order in which the jobs are to be done. Use the critical ratio priority rule for one. You may use any other rule for the second schedule as long as you state what it is.

5. An accounting firm, Debits R Us, would like to keep its auditing staff to a maximum of four people yet satisfy the staffing needs and the policy of two days off per week. Given the following requirements, is this possible? What should the schedule be?

   Requirements (Monday through Sunday): 4, 3, 3, 2, 2, 4, 4.

6. Jobs A, B, C, D, and E must go through Processes I and II in that sequence (i.e., Process I first, then Process II).

   Use Johnson's rule to determine the optimal sequence to schedule the jobs to minimize the total required time.

Job	Required Processing Time on A	Required Processing Time on B
A	4	5
B	16	14
C	8	7
D	12	11
E	3	9

7. Joe was able to land a job as production scheduler in a brand-new custom refinishing auto service shop located near the border. This system is capable of handling 10 cars per day. The sequence now is customizing first, followed by repainting.

Car	Customizing Time (hours)	Painting (hours)	Car	Customizing Time (hours)	Painting (hours)
1	3.0	1.2	6	2.1	0.8
2	2.0	0.9	7	3.2	1.4
3	2.5	1.3	8	0.6	1.8
4	0.7	0.5	9	1.1	1.5
5	1.6	1.7	10	1.8	0.7

In what sequence should Joe schedule the cars?

SELECTED BIBLIOGRAPHY

Abernathy, W.; N. Baloff; and J. Hershey. "The Nurse Staffing Problem: Issues and Prospects." *Sloan Management Review* 13, no. 1 (Fall 1971), pp. 87–109.

Baker, K. R. "The Effects of Input Control in a Simple Scheduling Model." *Journal of Operations Management* 4, no. 2 (February 1984), pp. 99–112.

Berry, W. L.; R. Penlesky; and T. E. Vollmann. "Critical Ratio Scheduling: Dynamic Due-Date Procedures under Demand Uncertainty." *IIE Transactions* 16, no. 1 (March 1984), pp. 81–89.

Bolander, S. F.; R. C. Heard; S. M. Seward; and S. G. Taylor. *Manufacturing Planning and Control in the Process Industries.* Falls Church, VA: APICS, 1981.

Browne, James J., and Rajen K. Tibrewala. "Manpower Scheduling." *Industrial Engineering* 7, no. 8 (August 1975), pp. 22–23.

Buffa, Elwood S., and Jeffrey G. Miller. *Production-Inventory Systems: Planning and Control.* 3rd ed. Homewood, IL: Richard D. Irwin, 1979.

Conway, Richard W.; William L. Maxwell; and Louis W. Miller. *Theory of Scheduling.* Reading, MA: Addison-Wesley Publishing, 1967.

Dilworth, James B. *Operations Management: Design, Planning and Control for Manufacturing and Services.* New York: McGraw-Hill, Inc., 1992.

Fogarty, Donald W.; John H. Blackstone, Jr.; and Thomas R. Hoffmann. *Production and Inventory Management.* Cincinnati: South-Western Publishing, 1991.

Gershkoff, I. "Optimizing Flight Crew Schedules." *Interfaces* 19, no. 4 (July–August 1989), pp. 29–43.

Hall, R. W. *Driving the Productivity Machine.* Falls Church, VA: APICS, 1981.

Johnson, S. M. "Optimal Two Stage and Three Stage Production Schedules with Setup Times Included." *Naval Logistics Quarterly* 1, no. 1 (March 1954), pp. 61–68.

Kaner, John K., and Jack C. Hayya. "Priority Dispatching with Operation Due Dates in a Job Shop." *Journal of Operations Management* 2, no. 3 (May 1982), p. 170.

Moody, P. E. *Strategic Manufacturing: Dynamic New Directions for the 1990s.* Homewood, IL: Richard D. Irwin, 1990.

Morton, and Pentico. *Heuristic Scheduling Systems.* New York: John Wiley and Sons, 1993, p. 28.

Plossl, George W. *Production and Inventory Control: Applications.* Atlanta, GA: George W. Plossl Educational Services, 1983.

Richter, H. "Thirty Years of Airline Operations Research." *Interfaces* 19, no. 4 (July–August 1989), pp. 3–9.

Sandman, W. E. with J. P. Hayes. *How to Win Productivity in Manufacturing.* Dresher, PA: Yellow Brook of Pennsylvania, 1980.

Sipper, Daniel, and Robert L. Buflin, Jr. *Production: Planning, Control, and Integration.* Burr Ridge, IL: McGraw-Hill, 1998, p. 531.

Vollman, Thomas E.; William L. Berry; and D. Clay Whybark. *Manufacturing Planning and Control.* 4th ed. Homewood, IL: Irwin, 1997.

Warner, D., and J. Prawda. "A Mathematical Programming Model for Scheduling Nursing Personnel in a Hospital." *Management Science* 19, no. 4 (December 1972), pp. 411–22.

$\mathcal{A}\quad p\quad p\quad e\quad n\quad d\quad i\quad x\quad e\quad \delta$

Appendix A

INTEREST TABLES FOR FINANCIAL ANALYSIS

TABLE I

Compound Sum of $1

Year	1%	2%	3%	4%	5%	6%	7%
1	1.010	1.020	1.030	1.040	1.050	1.060	1.070
2	1.020	1.040	1.061	1.082	1.102	1.124	1.145
3	1.030	1.061	1.093	1.125	1.158	1.191	1.225
4	1.041	1.082	1.126	1.170	1.216	1.262	1.311
5	1.051	1.104	1.159	1.217	1.276	1.338	1.403
6	1.062	1.126	1.194	1.265	1.340	1.419	1.501
7	1.072	1.149	1.230	1.316	1.407	1.504	1.606
8	1.083	1.172	1.267	1.369	1.477	1.594	1.718
9	1.094	1.195	1.305	1.423	1.551	1.689	1.838
10	1.105	1.219	1.344	1.480	1.629	1.791	1.967
11	1.116	1.243	1.384	1.539	1.710	1.898	2.105
12	1.127	1.268	1.426	1.601	1.796	2.012	2.252
13	1.138	1.294	1.469	1.665	1.886	2.133	2.410
14	1.149	1.319	1.513	1.732	1.980	2.261	2.579
15	1.161	1.346	1.558	1.801	2.079	2.397	2.759
16	1.173	1.373	1.605	1.873	2.183	2.540	2.952
17	1.184	1.400	1.653	1.948	2.292	2.693	3.159
18	1.196	1.428	1.702	2.026	2.407	2.854	3.380
19	1.208	1.457	1.754	2.107	2.527	3.026	3.617
20	1.220	1.486	1.806	2.191	2.653	3.207	3.870
25	1.282	1.641	2.094	2.666	3.386	4.292	5.427
30	1.348	1.811	2.427	3.243	4.322	5.743	7.612

Year	8%	9%	10%	12%	14%	15%	16%
1	1.080	1.090	1.100	1.120	1.140	1.150	1.160
2	1.166	1.188	1.210	1.254	1.300	1.322	1.346
3	1.260	1.295	1.331	1.405	1.482	1.521	1.561
4	1.360	1.412	1.464	1.574	1.689	1.749	1.811
5	1.469	1.539	1.611	1.762	1.925	2.011	2.100
6	1.587	1.677	1.772	1.974	2.195	2.313	2.436
7	1.714	1.828	1.949	2.211	2.502	2.660	2.826
8	1.851	1.993	2.144	2.476	2.853	3.059	3.278
9	1.999	2.172	2.358	2.773	3.252	3.518	3.803
10	2.159	2.367	2.594	3.106	3.707	4.046	4.411
11	2.332	2.580	2.853	3.479	4.226	4.652	5.117
12	2.518	2.813	3.138	3.896	4.818	5.350	5.936
13	2.720	3.066	3.452	4.363	5.492	6.153	6.886
14	2.937	3.342	3.797	4.887	6.261	7.076	7.988
15	3.172	3.642	4.177	5.474	7.138	8.137	9.266
16	3.426	3.970	4.595	6.130	8.137	9.358	10.748
17	3.700	4.328	5.054	6.866	9.276	10.761	12.468
18	3.996	4.717	5.560	7.690	10.575	12.375	14.463
19	4.316	5.142	6.116	8.613	12.056	14.232	16.777
20	4.661	5.604	6.728	9.646	13.743	16.367	19.461
25	6.848	8.623	10.835	17.000	26.462	32.919	40.874
30	10.063	13.268	17.449	29.960	50.950	66.212	85.850

TABLE I	Year	18%	20%	24%	28%	32%	36%
(Concluded)	1	1.180	1.200	1.240	1.280	1.320	1.360
	2	1.392	1.440	1.538	1.638	1.742	1.850
	3	1.643	1.728	1.907	2.067	2.300	2.515
	4	1.939	2.074	2.364	2.684	3.036	3.421
	5	2.288	2.488	2.932	3.436	4.007	4.653
	6	2.700	2.986	3.635	4.398	5.290	6.328
	7	3.185	3.583	4.508	5.629	6.983	8.605
	8	3.759	4.300	5.590	7.206	9.217	11.703
	9	4.435	5.160	6.931	9.223	12.166	15.917
	10	5.234	6.192	8.594	11.806	16.060	21.647
	11	6.176	7.430	10.657	15.112	21.199	29.439
	12	7.288	8.916	13.215	19.343	27.983	40.037
	13	8.599	10.699	16.386	24.759	36.937	54.451
	14	10.147	12.839	20.319	31.691	48.757	74.053
	15	11.974	15.407	25.196	40.565	64.359	100.712
	16	14.129	18.488	31.243	51.923	84.954	136.97
	17	16.672	22.186	38.741	66.461	112.14	186.28
	18	19.673	26.623	48.039	85.071	148.02	253.34
	19	23.214	31.948	59.568	108.89	195.39	344.54
	20	27.393	38.338	73.864	139.38	257.92	468.57
	25	62.669	95.396	216.542	478.90	1033.6	2180.1
	30	143.371	237.376	634.820	1645.5	4142.1	10143.

	Year	40%	50%	60%	70%	80%	90%
	1	1.400	1.500	1.600	1.700	1.800	1.900
	2	1.960	2.250	2.560	2.890	3.240	3.610
	3	2.744	3.375	4.096	4.913	5.832	6.859
	4	3.842	5.062	6.544	8.352	10.498	13.032
	5	5.378	7.594	10.486	14.199	18.896	24.761
	6	7.530	11.391	16.777	24.138	34.012	47.046
	7	10.541	17.086	26.844	41.034	61.222	89.387
	8	14.758	25.629	42.950	69.758	110.200	169.836
	9	20.661	38.443	68.720	118.588	198.359	322.688
	10	28.925	57.665	109.951	201.599	357.047	613.107
	11	40.496	86.498	175.922	342.719	642.684	1164.902
	12	56.694	129.746	281.475	582.622	1156.831	2213.314
	13	79.372	194.619	450.360	990.457	2082.295	4205.297
	14	111.120	291.929	720.576	1683.777	3748.131	7990.065
	15	155.568	437.894	1152.921	2862.421	6746.636	15181.122
	16	217.795	656.84	1844.7	4866.1	12144.	28844.0
	17	304.914	985.26	2951.5	8272.4	21859.	54804.0
	18	426.879	1477.9	4722.4	14063.0	39346.	104130.0
	19	597.630	2216.8	7555.8	23907.0	70824.	197840.0
	20	836.683	3325.3	12089.0	40642.0	127480.	375900.0
	25	4499.880	25251.	126760.0	577060.0	2408900.	9307600.0
	30	24201.432	191750.	1329200.0	8193500.0	45517000.	230470000.0

TABLE 2

Sum of an Annuity of $1 for *N* Years

Year	1%	2%	3%	4%	5%	6%
1	1.000	1.000	1.000	1.000	1.000	1.000
2	2.010	2.020	2.030	2.040	2.050	2.060
3	2.030	3.060	3.091	3.122	3.152	3.184
4	4.060	4.122	4.184	4.246	4.310	4.375
5	5.101	5.204	5.309	5.416	5.526	5.637
6	6.152	6.308	6.468	6.633	6.802	6.975
7	7.214	7.434	7.662	7.898	8.142	8.394
8	8.286	8.583	8.892	9.214	9.549	9.897
9	9.369	9.755	10.159	10.583	11.027	11.491
10	10.462	10.950	11.464	12.006	12.578	13.181
11	11.567	12.169	12.808	13.486	14.207	14.972
12	12.683	13.412	14.192	15.026	15.917	16.870
13	13.809	14.680	15.618	16.627	17.713	18.882
14	14.947	15.974	17.086	18.292	19.599	21.051
15	16.097	17.293	18.599	20.024	21.579	23.276
16	17.258	18.639	20.157	21.825	23.657	25.673
17	18.430	20.012	21.762	23.698	25.840	28.213
18	19.615	21.412	23.414	25.645	28.132	30.906
19	20.811	22.841	25.117	27.671	30.539	33.760
20	22.019	24.297	26.870	29.778	33.066	36.786
25	28.243	32.030	36.459	41.646	47.727	54.865
30	34.785	40.568	47.575	56.085	66.439	79.058

Year	7%	8%	9%	10%	12%	14%
1	1.000	1.000	1.000	1.000	1.000	1.000
2	2.070	2.080	2.090	2.100	2.120	2.140
3	3.215	3.246	3.278	3.310	3.374	3.440
4	4.440	4.506	4.573	4.641	4.770	4.921
5	5.751	5.867	5.985	6.105	6.353	6.610
6	7.153	7.336	7.523	7.716	8.115	8.536
7	8.654	8.923	9.200	9.487	10.089	10.730
8	10.260	10.637	11.028	11.436	12.300	13.233
9	11.978	12.488	13.021	13.579	14.776	16.085
10	13.816	14.487	15.193	15.937	17.549	19.337
11	15.784	16.645	17.560	18.531	20.655	23.044
12	17.888	18.977	20.141	21.384	24.133	27.271
13	20.141	21.495	22.953	24.523	28.029	32.089
14	22.550	24.215	26.019	27.975	32.393	37.581
15	25.129	27.152	29.361	31.772	37.280	43.842
16	27.888	30.324	33.003	35.950	42.753	50.980
17	30.840	33.750	36.974	40.545	48.884	59.118
18	33.999	37.450	41.301	45.599	55.750	68.394
19	37.379	41.446	46.018	51.159	63.440	78.969
20	40.995	45.762	51.160	57.275	72.052	91.025
25	63.249	73.106	84.701	93.347	133.334	181.871
30	94.461	113.283	136.308	164.494	241.333	356.787

TABLE 2

(Concluded)

Year	16%	18%	20%	24%	28%	32%
1	1.000	1.000	1.000	1.000	1.000	1.000
2	2.160	2.180	2.200	2.240	2.280	2.320
3	3.506	3.572	3.640	3.778	3.918	4.062
4	5.066	5.215	5.368	5.684	6.016	6.362
5	6.877	7.154	7.442	8.048	8.700	9.398
6	8.977	9.442	9.930	10.980	12.136	13.406
7	11.414	12.142	12.916	14.615	16.534	18.696
8	14.240	15.327	16.499	19.123	22.163	25.678
9	17.518	19.086	20.799	24.712	29.369	34.895
10	21.321	23.521	25.959	31.643	38.592	47.062
11	25.733	28.755	32.150	40.238	50.399	63.122
12	30.850	34.931	39.580	50.985	65.510	84.320
13	36.786	42.219	48.497	64.110	84.853	112.303
14	43.672	50.818	59.196	80.496	109.612	149.240
15	51.660	60.965	72.035	100.815	141.303	197.997
16	60.925	72.939	87.442	126.011	181.87	262.36
17	71.673	87.068	105.931	157.253	233.79	347.31
18	84.141	103.740	128.117	195.994	300.25	459.45
19	98.603	123.414	154.740	244.033	385.32	607.47
20	115.380	146.628	186.688	303.601	494.21	802.86
25	249.214	342.603	471.981	898.092	1706.8	3226.8
30	530.312	790.948	1181.882	2640.916	5873.2	12941.0

Year	36%	40%	50%	60%	70%	80%
1	1.000	1.000	1.000	1.000	1.000	1.000
2	2.360	2.400	2.500	2.600	2.700	2.800
3	4.210	4.360	4.750	5.160	5.590	6.040
4	6.725	7.104	8.125	9.256	10.503	11.872
5	10.146	10.846	13.188	15.810	18.855	22.370
6	14.799	16.324	20.781	26.295	33.054	41.265
7	21.126	23.853	32.172	43.073	57.191	75.278
8	29.732	34.395	49.258	69.916	98.225	136.500
9	41.435	49.153	74.887	112.866	167.983	246.699
10	57.352	69.814	113.330	181.585	286.570	445.058
11	78.998	98.739	170.995	291.536	488.170	802.105
12	108.437	139.235	257.493	467.458	830.888	1444.788
13	148.475	195.929	387.239	748.933	1413.510	2601.619
14	202.926	275.300	581.859	1199.293	2403.968	4683.914
15	276.979	386.420	873.788	1919.869	4087.745	8432.045
16	377.69	541.99	1311.7	3072.8	6950.2	15179.0
17	514.66	759.78	1968.5	4917.5	11816.0	27323.0
18	700.94	1064.7	2953.8	7868.9	20089.0	49182.0
19	954.28	1491.6	4431.7	12591.0	34152.0	88528.0
20	1298.8	2089.2	6648.5	20147.0	58059.0	159350.0
25	6053.0	11247.0	50500.0	211270.0	824370.0	3011100.0
30	28172.0	60501.0	383500.0	2215400.0	11705000.0	56896000.0

TABLE 3

Present Value of $1

Year	1%	2%	3%	4%	5%	6%	7%	8%	9%	10%	12%	14%	15%
1	.990	.980	.971	.962	.952	.943	.935	.926	.917	.909	.893	.877	.870
2	.980	.961	.943	.925	.907	.890	.873	.857	.842	.826	.797	.769	.756
3	.971	.942	.915	.889	.864	.840	.816	.794	.772	.751	.712	.675	.658
4	.961	.924	.889	.855	.823	.792	.763	.735	.708	.683	.636	.592	.572
5	.951	.906	.863	.822	.784	.747	.713	.681	.650	.621	.567	.519	.497
6	.942	.888	.838	.790	.746	.705	.666	.630	.596	.564	.507	.456	.432
7	.933	.871	.813	.760	.711	.665	.623	.583	.547	.513	.452	.400	.376
8	.923	.853	.789	.731	.677	.627	.582	.540	.502	.467	.404	.351	.327
9	.914	.837	.766	.703	.645	.592	.544	.500	.460	.424	.361	.308	.284
10	.905	.820	.744	.676	.614	.558	.508	.463	.422	.386	.322	.270	.247
11	.896	.804	.722	.650	.585	.527	.475	.429	.388	.350	.287	.237	.215
12	.887	.788	.701	.625	.557	.497	.444	.397	.356	.319	.257	.208	.187
13	.879	.773	.681	.601	.530	.469	.415	.368	.326	.290	.229	.182	.163
14	.870	.758	.661	.577	.505	.442	.388	.340	.299	.263	.205	.160	.141
15	.861	.743	.642	.555	.481	.417	.362	.315	.275	.239	.183	.140	.123
16	.853	.728	.623	.534	.458	.394	.339	.292	.252	.218	.163	.123	.107
17	.844	.714	.605	.513	.436	.371	.317	.270	.231	.198	.146	.108	.093
18	.836	.700	.587	.494	.416	.350	.296	.250	.212	.180	.130	.095	.081
19	.828	.686	.570	.475	.396	.331	.276	.232	.194	.164	.116	.083	.070
20	.820	.673	.554	.456	.377	.312	.258	.215	.178	.149	.104	.073	.061
25	.780	.610	.478	.375	.295	.233	.184	.146	.116	.092	.059	.038	.030
30	.742	.552	.412	.308	.231	.174	.131	.099	.075	.057	.033	.020	.015

Year	16%	18%	20%	24%	28%	32%	36%	40%	50%	60%	70%	80%	90%
1	.862	.847	.833	.806	.781	.758	.735	.714	.667	.625	.588	.556	.526
2	.743	.718	.694	.650	.610	.574	.541	.510	.444	.391	.346	.309	.277
3	.641	.609	.579	.524	.477	.435	.398	.364	.296	.244	.204	.171	.146
4	.552	.516	.482	.423	.373	.329	.292	.260	.198	.153	.120	.095	.077
5	.476	.437	.402	.341	.291	.250	.215	.186	.132	.095	.070	.053	.040
6	.410	.370	.335	.275	.227	.189	.158	.133	.088	.060	.041	.029	.021
7	.354	.314	.279	.222	.178	.143	.116	.095	.059	.037	.024	.016	.011
8	.305	.266	.233	.179	.139	.108	.085	.068	.039	.023	.014	.009	.006
9	.263	.226	.194	.144	.108	.082	.063	.048	.026	.015	.008	.005	.003
10	.227	.191	.162	.116	.085	.062	.046	.035	.017	.009	.005	.003	.002
11	.195	.162	.135	.094	.066	.047	.034	.025	.012	.006	.003	.002	.001
12	.168	.137	.112	.076	.052	.036	.025	.018	.008	.004	.002	.001	.001
13	.145	.116	.093	.061	.040	.027	.018	.013	.005	.002	.001	.001	.000
14	.125	.099	.078	.049	.032	.021	.014	.009	.003	.001	.001	.000	.000
15	.108	.084	.065	.040	.025	.016	.010	.006	.002	.001	.000	.000	.000
16	.093	.071	.054	.032	.019	.012	.007	.005	.002	.001	.000	.000	
17	.080	.060	.045	.026	.015	.009	.005	.003	.001	.000	.000		
18	.069	.051	.038	.021	.012	.007	.004	.002	.001	.000	.000		
19	.060	.043	.031	.017	.009	.005	.003	.002	.000	.000			
20	.051	.037	.026	.014	.007	.004	.002	.001	.000	.000			
25	.024	.016	.010	.005	.002	.001	.000	.000					
30	.012	.007	.004	.002	.001	.000	.000						

Year	1%	2%	3%	4%	5%	6%	7%	8%	9%	10%
TABLE 4										
1	0.990	0.980	0.971	0.962	0.952	0.943	0.935	0.926	0.917	0.909
2	1.970	1.942	1.913	1.886	1.859	1.833	1.808	1.783	1.759	1.736
3	2.941	2.884	2.829	2.775	2.723	2.673	2.624	2.577	2.531	2.487
4	3.902	3.808	3.717	3.630	3.546	3.465	3.387	3.312	3.240	3.170
5	4.853	4.713	4.580	4.452	4.329	4.212	4.100	3.993	3.890	3.791
6	5.795	5.601	5.417	5.242	5.076	4.917	4.766	4.623	4.486	4.355
7	6.728	6.472	6.230	6.002	5.786	5.582	5.389	5.206	5.033	4.868
8	7.652	7.325	7.020	6.733	6.463	6.210	6.971	5.747	5.535	5.335
9	8.566	8.162	7.786	7.435	7.108	6.802	6.515	6.247	5.985	5.759
10	9.471	8.983	8.530	8.111	7.722	7.360	7.024	6.710	6.418	6.145
11	10.368	9.787	9.253	8.760	8.306	7.887	7.449	7.139	6.805	6.495
12	11.255	10.575	9.954	9.385	8.863	8.384	7.943	7.536	7.161	6.814
13	12.134	11.348	10.635	9.986	9.394	8.853	8.358	7.904	7.487	7.103
14	13.004	12.106	11.296	10.563	9.899	9.295	8.745	8.244	7.786	7.367
15	13.865	12.849	11.938	11.118	10.380	9.712	9.108	8.559	8.060	7.606
16	14.718	13.578	12.561	11.652	10.838	10.106	9.447	8.851	8.312	7.824
17	15.562	14.292	13.166	12.166	11.274	10.477	9.763	9.122	8.544	8.022
18	16.398	14.992	13.754	12.659	11.690	10.828	10.059	9.372	8.756	8.201
19	17.226	15.678	14.324	13.134	12.085	11.158	10.336	9.604	8.950	8.365
20	18.046	16.351	14.877	13.590	12.462	11.470	10.594	9.818	9.128	8.514
25	22.023	19.523	17.413	15.622	14.094	12.783	11.654	10.675	9.823	9.077
30	25.808	22.397	19.600	17.292	15.373	13.765	12.409	11.258	10.274	9.427

Present Value of an Annuity of $1

Year	12%	14%	16%	18%	20%	24%	28%	32%	36%
1	0.893	0.877	0.862	0.847	0.833	0.806	0.781	0.758	0.735
2	1.690	1.647	1.605	1.566	1.528	1.457	1.392	1.332	1.276
3	2.402	2.322	2.246	2.174	2.106	1.981	1.868	1.766	1.674
4	3.037	2.914	2.798	2.690	2.589	2.404	2.241	2.096	1.966
5	3.605	3.433	3.274	3.127	2.991	2.745	2.532	2.345	2.181
6	4.111	3.889	3.685	3.498	3.326	3.020	2.759	2.534	2.339
7	4.564	4.288	4.039	3.812	3.605	3.242	2.937	2.678	2.455
8	4.968	4.639	4.344	4.078	3.837	3.421	3.076	2.786	2.540
9	5.328	4.946	4.607	4.303	4.031	3.566	3.184	2.868	2.603
10	5.650	5.216	4.833	4.494	4.193	3.682	3.269	2.930	2.650
11	5.988	5.453	5.029	4.656	4.327	3.776	3.335	2.978	2.683
12	6.194	5.660	5.197	4.793	4.439	3.851	3.387	3.013	2.708
13	6.424	5.842	5.342	4.910	4.533	3.912	3.427	3.040	2.727
14	6.628	6.002	5.468	5.008	4.611	3.962	3.459	3.061	2.740
15	6.811	6.142	5.575	5.092	4.675	4.001	3.483	3.076	2.750
16	6.974	6.265	5.669	5.162	4.730	4.033	3.503	3.088	2.758
17	7.120	6.373	5.749	5.222	4.775	4.059	3.518	3.097	2.763
18	7.250	6.467	5.818	5.273	4.812	4.080	3.529	3.104	2.767
19	7.366	6.550	5.877	5.316	4.844	4.097	3.539	3.109	2.770
20	7.469	6.623	5.929	5.353	4.870	4.110	3.546	3.113	2.772
25	7.843	6.873	6.097	5.467	4.948	4.147	3.564	3.122	2.776
30	8.055	7.003	6.177	5.517	4.979	4.160	3.569	3.124	2.778

AREAS OF THE STANDARD NORMAL DISTRIBUTION

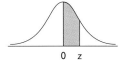

0   z

An entry in the table represents the proportion under the shaded curve which is between z = 0 and a positive value of z. Areas for negative values of z are obtained by symmetry.

z	.00	.01	.02	.03	.04	.05	.06	.07	.08	.09
0.0	.0000	.0040	.0080	.0120	.0160	.0199	.0239	.0279	.0319	.0359
0.1	.0398	.0438	.0478	.0517	.0557	.0596	.0636	.0675	.0714	.0753
0.2	.0793	.0832	.0871	.0910	.0948	.0987	.1026	.1064	.1103	.1141
0.3	.1179	.1217	.1255	.1293	.1331	.1368	.1406	.1443	.1480	.1517
0.4	.1554	.1591	.1628	.1664	.1700	.1736	.1772	.1808	.1844	.1879
0.5	.1915	.1950	.1985	.2019	.2054	.2088	.2123	.2157	.2190	.2224
0.6	.2257	.2291	.2324	.2357	.2389	.2422	.2454	.2486	.2517	.2549
0.7	.2580	.2611	.2642	.2673	.2703	.2734	.2764	.2794	.2823	.2852
0.8	.2881	.2910	.2939	.2967	.2995	.3023	.3051	.3078	.3106	.3133
0.9	.3159	.3186	.3212	.3238	.3264	.3289	.3315	.3340	.3365	.3389
1.0	.3413	.3438	.3461	.3485	.3508	.3531	.3554	.3577	.3599	.3621
1.1	.3643	.3665	.3686	.3708	.3729	.3749	.3770	.3790	.3810	.3830
1.2	.3849	.3869	.3888	.3907	.3925	.3944	.3962	.3980	.3997	.4015
1.3	.4032	.4049	.4066	.4082	.4099	.4115	.4131	.4147	.4162	.4177
1.4	.4192	.4207	.4222	.4236	.4251	.4265	.4279	.4292	.4306	.4319
1.5	.4332	.4345	.4357	.4370	.4382	.4394	.4406	.4418	.4429	.4441
1.6	.4452	.4463	.4474	.4484	.4495	.4505	.4515	.4525	.4535	.4545
1.7	.4554	.4564	.4573	.4582	.4591	.4599	.4608	.4616	.4625	.4633
1.8	.4641	.4649	.4656	.4664	.4671	.4678	.4686	.4693	.4699	.4706
1.9	.4713	.4719	.4726	.4732	.4738	.4744	.4750	.4756	.4761	.4767
2.0	.4772	.4778	.4783	.4788	.4793	.4798	.4803	.4808	.4812	.4817
2.1	.4821	.4826	.4830	.4834	.4838	.4842	.4846	.4850	.4854	.4857
2.2	.4861	.4864	.4868	.4871	.4875	.4878	.4881	.4884	.4887	.4890
2.3	.4893	.4896	.4898	.4901	.4904	.4906	.4909	.4911	.4913	.4916
2.4	.4918	.4920	.4922	.4925	.4927	.4929	.4931	.4932	.4934	.4936
2.5	.4938	.4940	.4941	.4943	.4945	.4946	.4948	.4949	.4951	.4952
2.6	.4953	.4955	.4956	.4957	.4959	.4960	.4961	.4962	.4963	.4964
2.7	.4965	.4966	.4967	.4968	.4969	.4970	.4971	.4972	.4973	.4974
2.8	.4974	.4975	.4976	.4977	.4977	.4978	.4979	.4979	.4980	.4981
2.9	.4981	.4982	.4982	.4983	.4984	.4984	.4985	.4985	.4986	.4986
3.0	.4987	.4987	.4987	.4988	.4988	.4989	.4989	.4989	.4990	.4990

Source: Paul G. Hoel, *Elementary Statistics* (New York: John Wiley & Sons, 1960), p. 240.

AREAS OF THE CUMULATIVE STANDARD NORMAL DISTRIBUTION

TABLE I

Areas Under the
Standardized Normal Curve
from $-\infty$ to $-z$

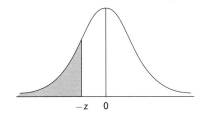

.09	.08	.07	.06	.05	.04	.03	.02	.01	.00	z
.0002	.0003	.0003	.0003	.0003	.0003	.0003	.0003	.0003	.0003	−3.4
.0003	.0004	.0004	.0004	.0004	.0004	.0004	.0005	.0005	.0005	−3.3
.0005	.0005	.0005	.0006	.0006	.0006	.0006	.0006	.0007	.0007	−3.2
.0007	.0007	.0008	.0008	.0008	.0008	.0009	.0009	.0009	.0010	−3.1
.0010	.0010	.0011	.0011	.0011	.0012	.0012	.0013	.0013	.0013	−3.0
.0014	.0014	.0015	.0015	.0016	.0016	.0017	.0018	.0018	.0019	−2.9
.0019	.0020	.0021	.0021	.0022	.0023	.0023	.0024	.0025	.0026	−2.8
.0026	.0027	.0028	.0029	.0030	.0031	.0032	.0033	.0034	.0035	−2.7
.0036	.0037	.0038	.0039	.0040	.0041	.0043	.0044	.0045	.0047	−2.6
.0048	.0049	.0051	.0052	.0054	.0055	.0057	.0059	.0060	.0062	−2.5
.0064	.0066	.0068	.0069	.0071	.0073	.0075	.0078	.0080	.0082	−2.4
.0084	.0087	.0089	.0091	.0094	.0096	.0099	.0102	.0104	.0107	−2.3
.0110	.0113	.0116	.0119	.0122	.0125	.0129	.0132	.0136	.0139	−2.2
.0143	.0146	.0150	.0154	.0158	.0162	.0166	.0170	.0174	.0179	−2.1
.0183	.0188	.0192	.0197	.0202	.0207	.0212	.0217	.0222	.0228	−2.0
.0233	.0239	.0244	.0250	.0256	.0262	.0268	.0274	.0281	.0287	−1.9
.0294	.0301	.0307	.0314	.0322	.0329	.0336	.0344	.0351	.0359	−1.8
.0367	.0375	.0384	.0392	.0401	.0409	.0418	.0427	.0436	.0446	−1.7
.0455	.0465	.0475	.0485	.0495	.0505	.0516	.0526	.0537	.0548	−1.6
.0559	.0571	.0582	.0594	.0606	.0618	.0630	.0643	.0655	.0668	−1.5
.0681	.0694	.0708	.0721	.0735	.0749	.0764	.0778	.0793	.0808	−1.4
.0823	.0838	.0853	.0869	.0885	.0901	.0918	.0934	.0951	.0968	−1.3
.0985	.1003	.1020	.1038	.1056	.1075	.1093	.1112	.1131	.1151	−1.2
.1170	.1190	.1210	.1230	.1251	.1271	.1292	.1314	.1335	.1357	−1.1
.1379	.1401	.1423	.1446	.1469	.1492	.1515	.1539	.1562	.1587	−1.0
.1611	.1635	.1660	.1685	.1711	.1736	.1762	.1788	.1814	.1841	−0.9
.1867	.1894	.1922	.1949	.1977	.2005	.2033	.2061	.2090	.2119	−0.8
.2148	.2177	.2206	.2236	.2266	.2296	.2327	.2358	.2389	.2420	−0.7
.2451	.2483	.2514	.2546	.2578	.2611	.2643	.2676	.2709	.2743	−0.6
.2776	.2810	.2843	.2877	.2912	.2946	.2981	.3015	.3050	.3085	−0.5
.3121	.3156	.3192	.3228	.3264	.3300	.3336	.3372	.3409	.3446	−0.4
.3483	.3520	.3557	.3594	.3632	.3669	.3707	.3745	.3783	.3821	−0.3
.3859	.3897	.3936	.3974	.4013	.4052	.4090	.4129	.4168	.4207	−0.2
.4247	.4286	.4325	.4364	.4404	.4443	.4483	.4522	.4562	.4602	−0.1
.4641	.4681	.4721	.4761	.4801	.4840	.4880	.4920	.4960	.5000	−0.0

TABLE 2

Areas Under the
Standardized Normal Curve
from $-\infty$ to $+z$

z	.00	.01	.02	.03	.04	.05	.06	.07	.08	.09
.0	.5000	.5040	.5080	.5120	.5160	.5199	.5239	.5279	.5319	.5359
.1	.5398	.5438	.5478	.5517	.5557	.5596	.5636	.5675	.5714	.5753
.2	.5793	.5832	.5871	.5910	.5948	.5987	.6026	.6064	.6103	.6141
.3	.6179	.6217	.6255	.6293	.6331	.6368	.6406	.6443	.6480	.6517
.4	.6554	.6591	.6628	.6664	.6700	.6736	.6772	.6808	.6844	.6879
.5	.6915	.6950	.6985	.7019	.7054	.7088	.7123	.7157	.7190	.7224
.6	.7257	.7291	.7324	.7357	.7389	.7422	.7454	.7486	.7517	.7549
.7	.7580	.7611	.7642	.7673	.7703	.7734	.7764	.7794	.7823	.7852
.8	.7881	.7910	.7939	.7967	.7995	.8023	.8051	.8078	.8106	.8133
.9	.8159	.8186	.8212	.8238	.8264	.8289	.8315	.8340	.8365	.8389
1.0	.8413	.8438	.8461	.8485	.8508	.8531	.8554	.8577	.8599	.8621
1.1	.8643	.8665	.8686	.8708	.8729	.8749	.8770	.8790	.8810	.8830
1.2	.8849	.8869	.8888	.8907	.8925	.8944	.8962	.8980	.8997	.9015
1.3	.9032	.9049	.9066	.9082	.9099	.9115	.9131	.9147	.9162	.9177
1.4	.9192	.9207	.9222	.9236	.9251	.9265	.9279	.9292	.9306	.9319
1.5	.9332	.9345	.9357	.9370	.9382	.9394	.9406	.9418	.9429	.9441
1.6	.9452	.9463	.9474	.9484	.9495	.9505	.9515	.9525	.9535	.9545
1.7	.9554	.9564	.9573	.9582	.9591	.9599	.9608	.9616	.9625	.9633
1.8	.9641	.9649	.9656	.9664	.9671	.9678	.9686	.9693	.9699	.9706
1.9	.9713	.9719	.9726	.9732	.9738	.9744	.9750	.9756	.9761	.9767
2.0	.9772	.9778	.9783	.9788	.9793	.9798	.9803	.9808	.9812	.9817
2.1	.9821	.9826	.9830	.9834	.9838	.9842	.9846	.9850	.9854	.9857
2.2	.9861	.9864	.9868	.9871	.9875	.9878	.9881	.9884	.9887	.9890
2.3	.9893	.9896	.9898	.9901	.9904	.9906	.9909	.9911	.9913	.9916
2.4	.9918	.9920	.9922	.9925	.9927	.9929	.9931	.9932	.9934	.9936
2.5	.9938	.9940	.9941	.9943	.9945	.9946	.9948	.9949	.9951	.9952
2.6	.9953	.9955	.9956	.9957	.9959	.9960	.9961	.9962	.9963	.9964
2.7	.9965	.9966	.9967	.9968	.9969	.9970	.9971	.9972	.9973	.9974
2.8	.9974	.9975	.9976	.9977	.9977	.9978	.9979	.9979	.9980	.9981
2.9	.9981	.9982	.9982	.9983	.9984	.9984	.9985	.9985	.9986	.9986
3.0	.9987	.9987	.9987	.9988	.9988	.9989	.9989	.9989	.9990	.9990
3.1	.9990	.9991	.9991	.9991	.9991	.9992	.9992	.9992	.9993	.9993
3.2	.9993	.9993	.9994	.9994	.9994	.9994	.9994	.9995	.9995	.9995
3.3	.9995	.9995	.9995	.9996	.9996	.9996	.9996	.9996	.9996	.9997
3.4	.9997	.9997	.9997	.9997	.9997	.9997	.9997	.9997	.9997	.9998

NEGATIVE EXPONENTIAL DISTRIBUTION: VALUES OF e^{-x}

x	e^{-x} (value)	x	e^{-x} (value)	x	e^{-x} (value)	x	e^{-x} (value)
0.00	1.00000	0.50	0.60653	1.00	0.36788	1.50	0.22313
0.01	0.99005	0.51	.60050	1.01	.36422	1.51	.22091
0.02	.98020	0.52	.59452	1.02	.36060	1.52	.21871
0.03	.97045	0.53	.58860	1.03	.35701	1.53	.21654
0.04	.96079	0.54	.58275	1.04	.35345	1.54	.21438
0.05	.95123	0.55	.57695	1.05	.34994	1.55	.21225
0.06	.94176	0.56	.57121	1.06	.34646	1.56	.21014
0.07	.93239	0.57	.56553	1.07	.34301	1.57	.20805
0.08	.92312	0.58	.55990	1.08	.33960	1.58	.20598
0.09	.91393	0.59	.55433	1.09	.33622	1.59	.20393
0.10	.90484	0.60	.54881	1.10	.33287	1.60	.20190
0.11	.89583	0.61	.54335	1.11	.32956	1.61	.19989
0.12	.88692	0.62	.53794	1.12	.32628	1.62	.19790
0.13	.87809	0.63	.53259	1.13	.32303	1.63	.19593
0.14	.86936	0.64	.52729	1.14	.31982	1.64	.19398
0.15	.86071	0.65	.52205	1.15	.31664	1.65	.19205
0.16	.87514	0.66	.51685	1.16	.31349	1.66	.19014
0.17	.84366	0.67	.51171	1.17	.31037	1.67	.18825
0.18	.83527	0.68	.50662	1.18	.30728	1.68	.18637
0.19	.82696	0.69	.50158	1.19	.30422	1.69	.18452
0.20	.81873	0.70	.49659	1.20	.30119	1.70	.18268
0.21	.81058	0.71	.49164	1.21	.29820	1.71	.18087
0.22	.80252	0.72	.48675	1.22	.29523	1.72	.17907
0.23	.79453	0.73	.48191	1.23	.29229	1.73	.17728
0.24	.78663	0.74	.47711	1.24	.28938	1.74	.17552
0.25	.77880	0.75	.47237	1.25	.28650	1.75	.17377
0.26	.77105	0.76	.46767	1.26	.28365	1.76	.17204
0.27	.76338	0.77	.46301	1.27	.28083	1.77	.17033
0.28	.75578	0.78	.45841	1.28	.27804	1.78	.16864
0.29	.74826	0.79	.45384	1.29	.27527	1.79	.16696
0.30	.74082	0.80	.44933	1.30	.27253	1.80	.16530
0.31	.73345	0.81	.44486	1.31	.26982	1.81	.16365
0.32	.72615	0.82	.44043	1.32	.26714	1.82	.16203
0.33	.71892	0.83	.43605	1.33	.26448	1.83	.16041
0.34	.71177	0.84	.43171	1.34	.26185	1.84	.15882
0.35	.70469	0.85	.42741	1.35	.25924	1.85	.15724
0.36	.69768	0.86	.42316	1.36	.25666	1.86	.15567
0.37	.69073	0.87	.41895	1.37	.25411	1.87	.15412
0.38	.68386	0.88	.41478	1.38	.25158	1.88	.15259
0.39	.67706	0.89	.41066	1.39	.24908	1.89	.15107

x	e^{-x} (value)	x	e^{-x} (value)	x	e^{-x} (value)	x	e^{-x} (value)
0.40	.67032	0.90	.40657	1.40	.24660	1.90	.14957
0.41	.66365	0.91	.40252	1.41	.24414	1.91	.14808
0.42	.65705	0.92	.39852	1.42	.24171	1.92	.14661
0.43	.65051	0.93	.39455	1.43	.23931	1.93	.14515
0.44	.64404	0.94	.39063	1.44	.23693	1.94	.14370
0.45	.63763	0.95	.38674	1.45	.23457	1.95	.14227
0.46	.63128	0.96	.38289	1.46	.23224	1.96	.14086
0.47	.62500	0.97	.37908	1.47	.22993	1.97	.13946
0.48	.61878	0.98	.37531	1.48	.22764	1.98	.13807
0.49	.61263	0.99	.37158	1.49	.22537	1.99	.13670
0.50	.60653	1.00	.36788	1.50	.22313	2.00	.13534

Appendix E

ANSWERS TO SELECTED PROBLEMS

Supplement 3

2. *a.*

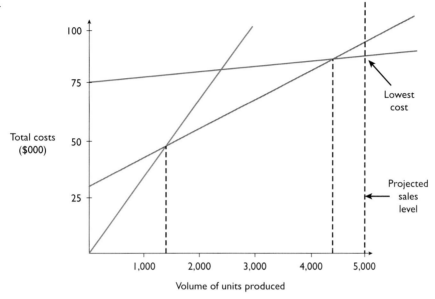

Volume of units produced

b. Break-even between Alternatives 1 and 2:

$$32x = 30,000 + 12x$$
$$20x = 30,000$$
$$x = 1,500 \text{ units}$$

Break-even between Alternatives 2 and 3:

$$30,000 + 12x = 75,000 + 2x$$
$$10x = 45,000$$
$$x = 4,500 \text{ units}$$

c. Based on lowest total costs, The company should choose Alternative 3, which is to invest the $75,000 in fixed costs and use unskilled labor.

7. The straight-line depreciation method yields a 15.9 percent return. The sum-of-the-years' digits yields a 17.1 percent return. Thus, neither method of depreciation will provide the minimum 20 percent return.

Chapter 5

1. *a.* Not inspecting cost = $20/hour. Cost to inspect = $9/hour. Therefore, inspect.
   b. $.18 each.
   c. $.22 per unit.

Supplement 5

1. *a.* $C_{pk} = .889$.
   b. $C_{pk} = 1.11$.
      The process is capable but needs to adjust mean downward to achieve 100 percent perfect quality.

2. *a.* $p = .067$.
      UCL = .194.
      LCL = 0.
   b. Stop the process. There is wide variation and two are out of limits.

Chapter 6

2. *a.* 15.
   b. 14.3.
   c. 13.4.
   d. $Y = a + bX = 10.8 + .77X$.
   e. $Y = 10.8 + .77(7) = 16.2$.

9. MAD = 58.3
   TS = −6
   Model is poor at giving a good forecast.

Chapter 7

1. Output/day: 24B + 24D.
   Process times: 12 min./B and 8 min./D.
   BB/DDD BB BB/DDD repetitively.

2. *a.* 27 seconds.
   b. 7 stations.
   c. 78.3 percent.
   d. Reduce cycle time to 25 seconds and work 8½ minutes overtime.

4. $44,500.

Supplement 8

1. $\bar{t}_s = 4.125$ minutes.
   $\bar{n}_j = 4.05$ cars.
   $\bar{n}_s = 4.95$ cars.

2. *4 spaces:* Stand busy 67.2 percent
   5 spaces: Stand busy 69.6 percent
   6 spaces: Stand busy 71.15 percent
   7 spaces: Stand busy 72.22 percent
   8 spaces: Net loss = $160;
   7 spaces should be leased.

Supplement 9

1. *a.* 1.65 minutes.
   b. 1.90 (minutes rounded).
   c. $56.93.

5. *a.* $NT = .9286$ minute/part.
   b. $ST = 1.0679$ minute/part.
   c. Daily output = 449.50.
      Day's wages = $44.49.

Chapter 10

1. *b.* A–C–D–E–G.
   c. 26 weeks.
   d. 6 weeks (15 − 9).

8. *a.* Critical path is A–C–D–F–G.
   b.

Day	Cost	Activity
First	$1,000	A
Second	1,200	C
Third	1,500	D (or F)
Fourth	1,500	F (or D)
	$5,200	

Chapter 11

1.

Transportation Costs	Carrying Costs
TC = $450,000.00	$80,547.95
= $530,547.95	

   Cost per tire: $5.305479
   Total cost: $40.30548

   Continue buying from current supplier at $40.00 per tire delivered.

Chapter 13

1. Total cost = $413,600.

4. Ending inventory = safety stock.
   Inventory cost includes forecast and safety stock.
   Shortage cost is only based on the forecast.
   Total cost = $413,750.

Chapter 14

1. TC = $24,254.50.
   Q at 200 is the optimum order size.

4. TC = $56,370.
   1,000 at a time.

5. *a.* A (4, 13, 18), B (2,5,8,10,11,14,16), C (remainder).
   b. Classify as A.

Chapter 15

2.
```
              Z
        ┌─────┴─────┐
      A(2)         B(4)
    ┌──┴──┐
  C(3)   D(4)
          │
         E(2)
```

7. Least total cost method: Order 250 units in period one for periods 1–8;
   Least unit cost method: Order 450 units in period one for periods 1–9.

10. *c.* .A
```
    .B(2)
            .E(4)
            .F(3)
        .C(3)
            .D(3)
            .H(2)
                .E(5)
                .G(2)
    .D(1)
```

d. Level 0   100 units of A

Level 1   200 units of B

300 units of C

Level 2   600 units of F

600 units of H

1000 units of D

Level 3   3800 units of E

1200 units of G

Chapter 16

1.

Car	Priority
C	First
A	Tie for second
B	Tie for second

4. Average totals: 10,600; 8,800.

Aggregate runout time = 2.295 weeks.

7. Johnson's method: E, A, B, D, C.

UNIFORMLY DISTRIBUTED RANDOM DIGITS

56970	10799	52098	04184	54967	72938	50834	23777	08392
83125	85077	60490	44369	66130	72936	69848	59973	08144
55503	21383	02464	26141	68779	66388	75242	82690	74099
47019	06683	33203	29603	54553	25971	69573	83854	24715
84828	61152	79526	29554	84580	37859	28504	61980	34997
08021	31331	79227	05748	51276	57143	31926	00915	45821
36458	28285	30424	98420	72925	40729	22337	48293	86847
05752	96045	36847	87729	81679	59126	59437	33225	31280
26768	02513	58454	56958	20575	76746	40878	06846	32828
42613	72456	43030	58085	06766	60227	96414	32671	45587
95457	12176	65482	25596	02678	54592	63607	82096	21913
95276	67524	63564	95958	39750	64379	46059	51666	10433
66954	53574	64776	92345	95110	59448	77249	54044	67942
17457	44151	14113	02462	02798	54977	48340	66738	60184
03704	23322	83214	59337	01695	60666	97410	55064	17427
21538	16997	33210	60337	27976	70661	08250	69509	60264
57178	16730	08310	70348	11317	71623	55510	64750	87759
31048	40058	94953	55866	96283	40620	52087	80817	74533
69799	83300	16498	80733	96422	58078	99643	39847	96884
90595	65017	59231	17772	67831	33317	00520	90401	41700
33570	34761	08039	78784	09977	29398	93896	78227	90110
15340	82760	57477	13898	48431	72936	78160	87240	52710
64079	07733	36512	56186	99098	48850	72527	08486	10951
63491	84886	67118	62063	74958	20946	28147	39338	32109
92003	76568	41034	28260	79708	00770	88643	21188	01850
52360	46658	66511	04172	73085	11795	52594	13287	82531
74622	12142	68355	65635	21828	39539	18988	53609	04001
04157	50070	61343	64315	70836	82857	35335	87900	36194
86003	60070	66241	32836	27573	11479	94114	81641	00496
41208	80187	20351	09630	84668	42486	71303	19512	50277
06433	80674	24520	18222	10610	05794	37515	48619	62866
39298	47829	72648	37414	75755	04717	29899	78817	03509
89884	59651	67533	68123	17730	95862	08034	19473	63971
61512	32155	51906	61662	64430	16688	37275	51262	11569
99653	47635	12506	88535	36553	23757	34209	55803	96275
95913	11085	13772	76638	48423	25018	99041	77529	81360
55804	44004	13122	44115	01601	50541	00147	77685	58788
35334	82410	91601	40617	72876	33967	73830	15405	96554
57729	88646	76487	11622	96297	24160	09903	14047	22917
86648	89317	63677	70119	94739	25875	38829	68377	43918
30574	06039	07967	32422	76791	30725	53711	93385	13421
81307	13114	83580	79974	45929	85113	72268	09858	52104
02410	96385	79067	54939	21410	86980	91772	93307	34116
18969	87444	52233	62319	08598	09066	95288	04794	01534
87863	80514	66860	62297	80198	19347	73234	86265	49096
08397	10538	15438	62311	72844	60203	46412	65943	79232
28520	45247	58729	10854	99058	18260	38765	90038	94209
44285	09452	15867	70418	57012	72122	36634	97283	95943
86299	22510	33571	23309	57040	29285	67870	21913	72958
84842	05748	90894	61658	15001	94005	36308	41161	37341

Photo Credits

p. 413: Courtesy Ryder Integrated.

p. 419 (left): Courtesy Bernard Welding Equipment Company.

p. 419 (right): Courtesy McDonnell-Douglas.

Chapter 13

p. 431: Courtesy of Polaroid.

p. 434 (left): Courtesy Kawasaki Motors Manufacturing Corporation, U.S.A.

p. 434 (right): Courtesy Kawasaki Motors Manufacturing Corporation, U.S.A.

p. 438: Ed Kashi.

Chapter 14

p. 461: Courtesy EAL.

p. 462: ©1995 GE Information Services Inc.

p. 485: Ovak Arslanian.

Chapter 15

p. 495: Photos © De Kerrle/Gamma Liaison.

p. 498: Photo courtesy Allen-Bradley, a Rockwell Interactive Company.

Chapter 16

p. 533: © PhotoDisc.

p. 535: Courtesy Bernard Welding Equipment Company.

p. 549: The Stock Market.

Name Index

Master production schedule (MPS) (*Cont.*)
    relationship to aggregate plan, 507
    time fences, 497
Material requirements planning. *See* MRP
Matsushita, 30, 31, 399
Maytag, 135
Mazda, 124
MBNA, 111
MBNQA. *See* Malcolm Baldrige National Quality
    Award
Mean absolute deviation (MAD), 211, 212–214
Mean squared error (MSE), 219, 220
Medium-range planning, 432, 433–434
Micro-MRP, 522
Micro-niching, 68
Milestones, 351, 354
Miller Brewing Company, 57
Milliken, 113
Mitsubishi Inazawa, 403
Mixed-model line balancing, 262–263
Modularization, of processes, 117
Motion economy, 329
Motorola, 40, 71, 113, 156, 187, 340, 390, 399
Moving average forecasting methods, 198
    simple, 199, 201–203
    weighted, 203–204
MPS. *See* Master production schedule
MRP (material requirements planning), 434,
       496, 498
    advanced systems, 519–522
    applications, 500
    benefits, 412–413, 499
    bill of materials file, 501–503, 518
    capacity requirements planning, 508–510
    criticisms, 514
    example, 505–507
    installing systems, 518–519
    inventory records file, 503–504
    lot sizing, 514–518
    objectives and philosophy, 499
    output reports, 504–505
    problems, 512–514, 519
    purposes, 498–499
    relationship to master production schedule,
       497, 500, 507
    in services, 511–512, 523
    software, 504, 520–522
    system structure, 500–505
MRP II (manufacturing resource planning), 510
    advanced systems, 519–520
    costs of system, 510–511
Mrs. Fields' Cookies, 67
MSE (mean squared error), 219
Multiple regression analysis, 220–221
Multistage processes, 116
MWM-Cummins, 389

N

NAFTA (North American Free Trade Agreement), 22
NASA, 533
Nashua Corp., 142
National Bicycle Industrial Company (NBIC),
    29, 30–31
National Car Rental, 449
National Institute of Standards and Technology
    (NIST), 152–153

National R$_x$ Services, 13
NBC, 134
NBIC. *See* National Bicycle Industrial Company
NC. *See* Numerically controlled (NC) machines
NCR Corp., 71
Net present value (NPV), 92
Neural networks, 221
New United Motor Manufacturing Inc.
    (NUMMI), 326
New York Stock Exchange (NYSE), 292–293
Newly industrialized countries (NICs), 22
NICs. *See* Newly industrialized countries
Nike, 438
Nintendo, 242
Nippondenso, 405
Nissan, 32
NIST (National Institute of Standards and
    Technology), 152–153
Nordstrom, 60, 62
Normal distribution, 177–178, 568–570
Norrell Services, 438
North American Free Trade Agreement
    (NAFTA), 22
Northeast Delta Dental, 152
Northeast Utilities, 316
Northern Telecom, Inc., 8
Norwalk Furniture Corporation, 66, 67
NPV. *See* Net present value
Numerically controlled (NC) machines, 63, 64
NUMMI. *See* New United Motor Manufacturing Inc.
NYSE. *See* New York Stock Exchange

O

Obsolescence, 86
OC. *See* Operating characteristic (OC) curves
OMA. *See* Operations Management Association
Omark Industries, 423
100 Yen Sushi House, 397–398
Operating characteristic (OC) curves, 173–174
Operational planning and control, 6–7, 24
Operations charts, 327
Operations management
    application to services, 8, 17–18
    applications in other functional areas, 4, 5, 9,
       14–15
    corporate perspective, 5–7
    definition, 5
    history of, 15–18
    increased recognition, 8–10
    job opportunities, 14, 15
    new paradigm for, 9–10
    operational perspective, 7–8
Operations Management Association (OMA),
    31, 412
Operations research, 5, 17
Operations strategy, 22, 23, 24
    components, 23
    developing, 24
    emergence of, 10, 23–24
    implementation, 33–34
    integration with corporate strategy, 24, 34–37
    trade-offs, 27–30
Opportunity costs, 78
OPT (optimized production technology), 543–545
Oracle Corp., 520
Order-qualifiers, 30–31